PowerPC System Architecture

MINDSHARE, INC.

TOM SHANLEY

Addison-Wesley Publishing Company

Reading, Massachusetts • Menlo Park, California • New York

Don Mills, Ontario • Wokingham, England • Amsterdam

Bonn • Sydney • Singapore • Tokyo • Madrid • San Juan

Paris • Seoul • Milan • Mexico City • Taipei

Library of Congress Cataloging-in-Publication Data

ISBN: 0-201-40990-9

Sponsoring Editor: Keith Wollman
Project Manager: Eleanor McCarthy
Production Coordinator: Deborah McKenna
Cover design: Barbara T. Atkinson
Set in 10 point Palatino by MindShare, Inc.

1 2 3 4 5 6 7 8 9 -MA- 9998979695
First printing, February 1995

Addison-Wesley books are available for bulk purchases by corporations, institutions, and other organizations. For more information please contact the Corporate, Government, and Special Sales Department at (800) 238-9682.

To Nick and Frances, my Mom and Dad.

Contents

Chapter 6: Applications Instructions

Chapter 7: Address Modes, Branch Prediction

Chapter 8: Real and Virtual Paging Models

Chapter 9: Cache Management Issues

Chapter 10: Misaligned Transfers and Performance

Chapter 11: Shared Resource Acquisition

Chapter 12: Memory Usage Bits (WIMG)

Part Three

The Operating System — Supervisor Privilege Level

Chapter 15: Operating System Registers

Chapter 17: Address Translation Overview

Chapter 18: Virtual Paging

Chapter 22: The Timebase and the Decrementer

Chapter 23: Big vs. Little-Endian

Volume Two

The PowerPC 601 Processor

Part Four

The PowerPC 601 Processor

Chapter 24: PPC 601 Microarchitecture Overview

Chapter 25: 601 User Register and Instruction Set

Chapter 26: 601 OS Register and Instruction Set

Chapter 27: 601 Processor Startup State

Chapter 28: PPC 601 Interrupts

Chapter 29: PPC 601 MMU Operation

Chapter 30: 601 Cache and Memory Unit

Chapter 31: Bus Transaction Causes

Chapter 32: PPC 601 Split-Bus Concept

Chapter 33: PPC 601 Memory Address Phase

Chapter 34: PPC 601 Data Phase

Chapter 36: 601 External Control Transaction

Chapter 37: 601 Relationship with the L2 Cache

Chapter 38: 601 Multiprocessor Support

Chapter 39: Other PPC 601 Bus Signals

Appendices

Figures

Figures

Tables

Foreword

For several years, I have had the pleasure of working with Tom as he delivered courseware to the IBM technical community. It has been my observation that to be a student in one of his architecture classes is to be ignited, charged and educated. By the way, Tom teaches from the book. It is no wonder that the same clarity and depth that he brings to the classroom are evident in all of his books.

In writing the *PowerPC System Architecture* book, he departs from his noted ISA-to-Pentium building block structure to establish a new platform. Tom intends for you to learn this new architecture. Assuming no prior PowerPC knowledge, he begins with the most basic PowerPC concepts and then systematically steps through learning phases that ultimately end with the most advanced PowerPC processor features.

Hardware and software system developers will find *PowerPC System Architecture* to be a powerful reference book. My customers have.

Jim Edwards

Program Manager,
IBM Education

Acknowledgments

To John Swindle for his tireless attention to detail and his marvelous teaching ability. To the editorial staff at Addison-Wesley for their patience. To the folks at Computer Literacy Bookshops for their collective support in the initial launch of this book series. And finally, to the 1200 or so engineers at IBM's PowerPC Personal Systems division who contributed to this book by not being shy with their comments when attending my PowerPC classes.

The MindShare Architecture Series

The MindShare Press series of books on system architecture include *ISA System Architecture, EISA System Architecture, 80486 System Architecture, PCI System Architecture, Pentium Processor System Architecture, PowerPC System Architecture* and *PCMCIA System Architecture.*

Rather than duplicating common information in each book, the series uses the building-block approach. *ISA System Architecture* is the core book upon which the 486, Pentium and EISA books build. PCMCIA and PCI can be implemented in any type of machine. The *PowerPC System Architecture* book is the foundation of a series on PowerPC processors. The figure below illustrates the relationship of the books to each other.

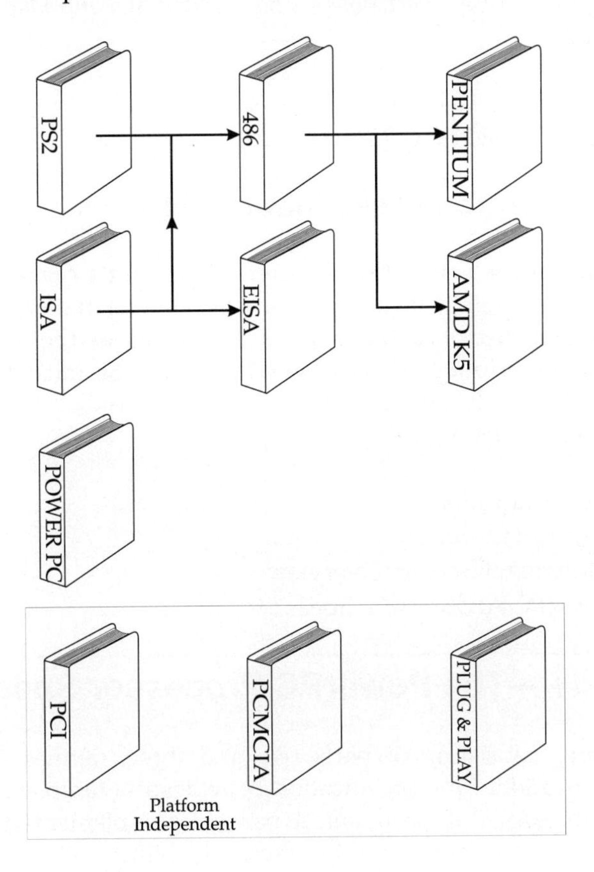

Architecture Series Organization

Use the Glossary!

This is the single, strongest suggestion the author can offer to the reader. A glossary containing over 450 terms is included in appendix A. Use it. The PowerPC processors are a new technology and introduce literally hundreds of new terms and acronyms in both the software and hardware realms. The author has made every attempt to define each term and acronym within the body of the book, but the reader will find the glossary indispensable.

Organization of The Book

PowerPC System Architecture is organized into two volumes preceded by an introductory section entitled *Part One — Background and Introduction*. The two volumes are titled:

- Volume One — *The PowerPC Processor Specification*
- Volume Two — *The PPC 601 Processor*

Part One — Background and Introduction

Part one introduces the concept of the prefetcher, the L1 cache, the L2 cache and demand-mode paging. It provides an overview of the typical PowerPC system design and describes the basic relationships of the subsystems involved. A basic description of the PowerPC processor microarchitecture is presented. The PowerPC software specification is introduced. Part one consists of the following chapters:

- Technology Background
- PowerPC System Overview
- Processor Microarchitecture Overview
- Intro to PowerPC Architecture Spec

Volume One —The PowerPC Processor Specification

The first volume, consisting of parts two and three, defines the PowerPC processor specification. This specification provides the template upon which all PowerPC processors are designed. A particular implementation of a PowerPC processor will provide a subset of these capabilities, all of them, or all of the defined capabilities plus additional capabilities outside the scope of the specification. A complete description of both the 32-and-64-bit PowerPC processor specification is provided.

Part Two — User Privilege Level Facilities

Part two provides a description of the instructions, registers and other facilities available to the applications programmer. Applications programs are run at the user privilege level. The processor is placed into the user privilege level when the Privilege Mode bit, PR, in the Machine State Register, or MSR, is set to one (in other words, MSR[PR] = 1). The chapters that comprise part two are:

- Applications Registers
- Applications Instructions
- Addressing Modes, Branch Prediction
- Real and Virtual Paging Models
- Cache Management Issues
- Misaligned Transfers and Performance
- Shared Resource Acquisition
- Memory Usage Bits (WIMG)
- Access Order
- The Timebase

Part Three — Supervisor Privilege Level Facilities

Part three provides a description of the instructions, registers and other facilities available to the operating system programmer. The operating system is run at the supervisor privilege level. The processor is placed into the supervisor privilege level when the privilege mode bit, PR, in the Machine State Register, or MSR, is set to zero (in other words, MSR[PR] = 0). The chapters that comprise part three are:

- Operating System Registers
- Operating System Instructions
- Address Translation Overview
- Block — Large Memory Region
- Virtual Paging
- I/O and Memory-Mapped I/O
- Interrupts
- The Timebase and the Decrementer
- Big vs. Little-Endian

Volume Two — The PPC 601 Processor

The second volume of this book consists of part four. This part focuses specifically on the PPC 601 processor and describes how it fits within or deviates from the specification. This part also provides a complete description of the PPC 601 processor's external bus structure and operation. It is important to note that the external bus that a PowerPC processor uses to communicate with the rest of the machine is outside the scope of the PowerPC processor specification. As an example, it would be perfectly "legal" to build a PowerPC processor that glues right onto the PCI bus. It would be possible to build a processor with the same bus structure as an Intel Pentium processor.

Part Four — The PowerPC 601 Processor

Part four describes how the PPC 601 processor adheres to or deviates from the PowerPC processor specification (described in parts two and three). The bus structure and protocol are defined. The processor's relationship to the L2 cache is defined. The mechanism utilized to acquire ownership of shared resources is described. A summary of the PPC 601 processor's multiprocessing support mechanisms is provided. The remainder of the processor's interface signals are discussed.

The chapters that comprise part four are:

- PPC 601 Microarchitecture Overview
- 601 User Register and Instruction Set
- 601 OS Register and Instruction Set
- 601 Processor Startup State
- PPC 601 Interrupts
- PPC 601 MMU Operation
- 601 Cache and Memory Unit
- Bus Transaction Causes
- PPC 601 Split-Bus Concept
- PPC 601 Memory Address Phase
- PPC 601 Data Phase
- PPC 601 I/O Transactions
- 601 External Control Transaction
- 601 Relationship with the L2 Cache
- 601 Multiprocessor Support
- Other PPC 601 Bus Signals

Who Should Read This Book

This book is intended for use by hardware and software design and support personnel. Due to the tutorial methods employed to describe each subject, personnel outside of the design field may also find the text useful.

Prerequisite Knowledge

We highly recommend that you have a comfortable knowledge of the general functions performed by a processor, including hardware and software interaction, prior to reading this book. Several MindShare publications provide background that is helpful in understanding the subject matter covered in this book.

Documentation Conventions

This section defines the typographical conventions used throughout this book.

Hex Notation

All hex numbers are followed by an "h." Examples:

9A4Eh
0100h

Binary Notation

All binary numbers are followed by a "b." Examples:

0001 0101b
01b

Decimal Notation

When required for clarity, decimal numbers are followed by a "d." Examples:

256d
128d

Signal Name Representation

Each signal that assumes the logic low state when asserted is followed by a pound sign (#). As an example, a PPC 601 processor asserts the TS# signal (by driving it to the low state) to indicate that it has initiated a memory or an external control transaction.

Signals not followed by a pound sign are asserted when they assume the logic high state. As an example, a PPC 601 processor asserts TT3 (by driving it to the high state) to indicate that it requires the use of the data bus to transfer data with the currently-addressed target.

Bit Field Identification (logical bit or signal groups)

All bit fields are designated as follows:

[X:Y],

where "X" is the most-significant bit and "Y" is the least-significant bit of the field. As an example, the PPC 601 address bus consists of A[0:31], where A0 is the most-significant and A31 the least-significant bit of the address bus.

Processor Register Bit Identification

An individual bit with a register is designated as follows:

MSR[31] or MSR[LE]

where MSR is the register name (in this case, the machine state register), 31 is the bit position within the register, and LE is the name of the bit (in this case, the little-endian bit).

A bit field within a register is designated as follows:

XER[25:31]

where XER is the register name (in this case, the integer exception register) and bits 25 through 31 is the bit field within the register.

We Want Your Feedback

MindShare values your comments and suggestions. You can contact us via mail, phone, fax or internet email.

Phone: (214) 231-2216
Fax: (214) 783-4715
E-mail: mindshar@interserv.com

To request information on public or private seminars, email your request to: mindshar@interserv.com or call our bulletin board at (214) 705-9604.

Bulletin Board

Because we are constantly on the road teaching, we can be difficult to get hold of. To help alleviate problems associated with our migratory habits, we have initiated a bulletin board to supply the following services:

- Download of course abstracts.
- Download of tables of contents of each book in the series.
- Facility to inquire about public architecture seminars.
- Message area to log technical questions.
- Message area to log suggestions for book improvements.
- Facility to view book errata and clarifications.

The bulletin board may be reached 24-hours a day, seven days a week.

BBS phone number: (214) 705-9604

Mailing Address

MindShare, Inc.
2202 Buttercup Drive
Richardson, Texas 75082

Part One

Background and Introduction

Part One introduces the concept of the prefetcher, the L1 cache, the L2 cache and demand-mode paging. It provides an overview of the typical PowerPC system design and describes the basic relationships of the subsystems involved. A basic description of the PowerPC processor microarchitecture is presented. The PowerPC software specification is introduced.

The chapters that comprise Part One are:

- Technology Background
- PowerPC System Overview
- Processor Microarchitecture Overview
- Intro to PowerPC Processor Spec

Chapter 1

This Chapter

This chapter highlights the role of the four tools incorporated into most of today's processors that enhance access to memory:

- The instruction prefetcher
- The L1 cache — The role of the unified and split code/data cache is discussed.
- The L2 cache — The concept of the look-aside and look-through cache is discussed, as well as the write-through and write-back policies in handling memory writes.
- The demand-mode paging mechanism

The Next Chapter

The next chapter presents a basic discussion of a typical PC platform based on the PowerPC processor. It describes the relationship of the processor, main memory and bus masters residing on the PCI or standard expansion bus (ISA, EISA or Micro Channel).

Memory Bottleneck

The task of any microprocessor is to fetch instructions from memory, decode them, and execute them. Since the processor is constantly reaching into memory to fetch the next instruction to be executed, the following factors have a major impact on the performance of the processor:

- The data bus width — in other words, how many instructions can the processor fetch from memory at one time.
- The speed at which memory read transactions can be executed on the bus. As an example, instructions could be fetched from memory more rapidly using a bus capable of running at 33MHz than one only capable of running at 8MHz.

- The amount of time it takes the memory subsystem to recognize that it is being addressed and to then deliver the requested information. In other words, the access time of the memory.

The processor must always perform a memory read transaction on its external bus to fetch the next instruction from memory. Since the processor core is typically capable of running at a much faster rate than the external bus and the external DRAM or ROM memory has a very slow access time, the core stalls whenever it is forced to request something from external memory. In this discussion, the processor core is defined as the integer, floating-point and branch processing units within the microprocessor. The integer and floating-point units must perform load or store operations to read data operands from memory or to store them into memory. The branch processing unit controls the instruction fetch mechanism.

The following sections describe the mechanisms frequently utilized in processor and/or system design to optimize memory access time:

- The instruction prefetcher
- The L1 cache implemented as a unified code/data cache
- The L1 cache implemented as separate code and data caches
- The look-aside L2 cache
- The look-through L2 cache
- Demand-mode paging

Prefetcher

The first attempt that was made to keep the core from suffering starvation was the inclusion of the instruction prefetcher. The prefetcher is a gambler — it assumes that the next instruction the core will request is the one from the next sequential memory location. Since the single most predictable aspect of program execution is that it proceeds through memory in a linear manner most of the time, this assumption made by the prefetcher is usually correct.

When the branch processor instructs the prefetcher to fetch its next instruction from location n, the prefetcher fetches the instruction from memory location n and then proceeds to fetch the instruction from memory location n + 1 without being told. After placing this instruction into an internal buffer called the prefetch queue, the prefetcher fetches the instruction from location n + 2 without being told. In other words, the prefetcher's job is to attempt to keep the prefetch queue full. The integer, floating-point and branch processing units feed off the bottom end of this queue while the prefetcher attempts to keep the other end fed at an equal or greater rate. The prefetch queue is typically not very deep. As an example, the following processors have prefetch queues of the indicated depth:

- PowerPC 601 — 32 bytes
- Intel 286 — 6 bytes
- Intel 386 — 16 bytes
- Intel 486 — 32 bytes
- Intel Pentium — 128 bytes

There is obviously a problem inherent in the fact that the processor core can typically feed off the bottom end of the queue much quicker than the prefetcher can access external memory (due to the typically slow external bus speed and DRAM/ROM access times).

Internal, Level One (L1) Cache

General

Static RAM, or SRAM, has a much faster access time than DRAM or ROM memory. Virtually all of today's advanced processors include a high-speed SRAM cache on board the processor chip itself. When the instruction prefetcher request an instruction from a particular memory address, the cache performs a very fast lookup in its directory to determine if the requested information is already in the cache. Initially (at start-up time), the cache is empty. Any lookups result in a cache miss. This forces the cache to issue a request to the processor's bus interface to perform a memory read on the external bus to read the desired information from memory.

Since the cache knows that the external world (i.e., the bus and memory) is very slow, it fetches a relatively large amount of information from external memory when forced to perform an external memory read. Rather than fetching just the originally requested item, it will make good use of its time on the external bus by fetching not only the requested item, but a relatively large block of information that includes the requested item. This block of information is referred to as a cache block, or line. When it receives the requested block, it immediately forwards the requested item to the requester (e.g., the prefetcher) and stores the block in the cache along with the memory address that it was fetched from. If the prefetcher should request anything from within this memory block from this point forward, the cache lookup will result in a hit and the requested information will be delivered to the prefetcher without the necessity of accessing external memory. Since the cache can typically perform the lookup and the delivery of the requested information in one tick of the processor clock, this results in very fast fulfillment of memory requests.

Unified Code/Data Cache

As indicated earlier, the instruction prefetcher is not the only one that needs to perform memory accesses. From time to time, the integer and floating-point units must perform load operations in order to read a data operand from memory into one of the processor's registers, or store operations to store data operands from the registers into memory.

Many processors (e.g., the Intel 486 and the PowerPC 601) incorporate a unified code/data cache. When the instruction prefetcher issues a request for an instruction fetch from memory, the cache (on a miss) fetches a block of instructions from memory and places them in the cache. If the integer or floating-point unit issues a load request to fetch a data operand from memory, the cache performs a lookup. In the event of a miss, it fetches a block of data from memory and places it into the cache.

In other words, the cache contains a mixture of code and data and services requests from both the instruction prefetcher and the integer and floating-point units.

The down-side of this approach is that the cache typically cannot service simultaneous requests from both the instruction prefetcher and the other units. It will typically stall the prefetcher while it services the other units(s). Another negative is that, as the cache fills up, it may have to cast out instructions to make room for new data being read into the cache.

Split Code and Data Caches

The contention on the unified code/data cache can be avoided by providing two separate L1 caches: one dedicated to servicing requests from the prefetcher while the other is dedicated to servicing requests from the integer and floating-point processors. With this type of architecture, simultaneous requests for information from the prefetcher and the other units can be serviced at the same time. In addition, as new data is requested, it will cause a cast out of old data rather than instructions (from the code cache).

As examples, the following processors have the indicated size and structure:

- Intel 486 processor has a unified 8KB, 4-way set-associative L1 cache.
- Intel Pentium processor has split code and data L1 caches, each 8KB in size and each is 2-way set-associative.
- PowerPC 601 processor has a unified 32KB, 8-way set-associative L1 cache.

For a review of various cache structures (2-way, 4-way, etc.), refer to the MindShare publication entitled *ISA System Architecture*.

External, Level Two (L2) Cache

General

The inclusion of the L1 cache provides some relief for the memory access problem. It doesn't eliminate the problem, however. Whenever there is a miss on the L1 cache, the processor must perform a series of memory read transactions on the bus to access the requested information from DRAM or ROM memory. Due to the typically slow bus speed and the slow access memory, this results in poor performance (and the unit within the processor core that requested the information is stalled until the requested item has been fetched from memory).

The system designer may include another cache outside the processor that intercepts all memory requests and performs a lookup. If the request can be serviced from this L2 cache, the requested information can be fed back to the processor very rapidly. If the SRAM used to implement the L2 cache is fast enough to match the processor's bus speed, the requested information can be fed to the processor using zero wait state transactions, the fastest type of bus transfer. Although the delivery of information to the processor from the L2 cache is accomplished as fast as the bus speed will permit, the request fulfillment is not as fast as the L1 cache, but is substantially faster than an access to DRAM or ROM memory.

There are two variations on the L2 cache: look-aside and look-through.

Look-Aside Cache

Figure 1-1 illustrates the relationship of the look-aside L2 cache to the processor and memory. It sits off to the side of the processor bus and watches for memory accesses initiated by the processor. When it sees one, it performs a lookup to determine if the target information is currently resident in the cache. If it is, it instructs the main memory not to respond and it supplies the requested information to the processor. If the lookup results in a cache miss, the processor's cache block fill request is fulfilled directly from memory, resulting in slow performance. The L2 cache, however, snarfs the cache block from the data bus as the data passes from the memory subsystem back to the processor. It places the block into its cache and stores the source memory address in its directory. If the processor ever requests any information from within this block again, the request is fulfilled from the L2 cache. It may appear that the L2 cache is useless because it only makes copies of blocks that are also placed into the processor's L1 cache. As time goes on, however, the L1 cache may need to overwrite its copy of the block with new information that it is bringing into its cache. Although the block is therefore eliminated in the L1 cache, it remains in the L2 cache and is available to service processor requests for this information.

The L2 cache is always substantially larger than the L1 cache. This means that, at a given instant in time, the L2 cache contains a superset of the information currently resident in the L1 cache.

The advantage of the look-aside L2 cache is that it does not inject any latency into a memory access when the lookup results in a cache miss. In other words, the L2 cache performs its lookup at the same time that the address and transaction type are presented to the memory subsystem.

The disadvantage of the look-aside cache is that every processor bus transaction appears on the system bus, making the system bus less available for other processors (in a multiprocessor environment) or intelligent bus masters.

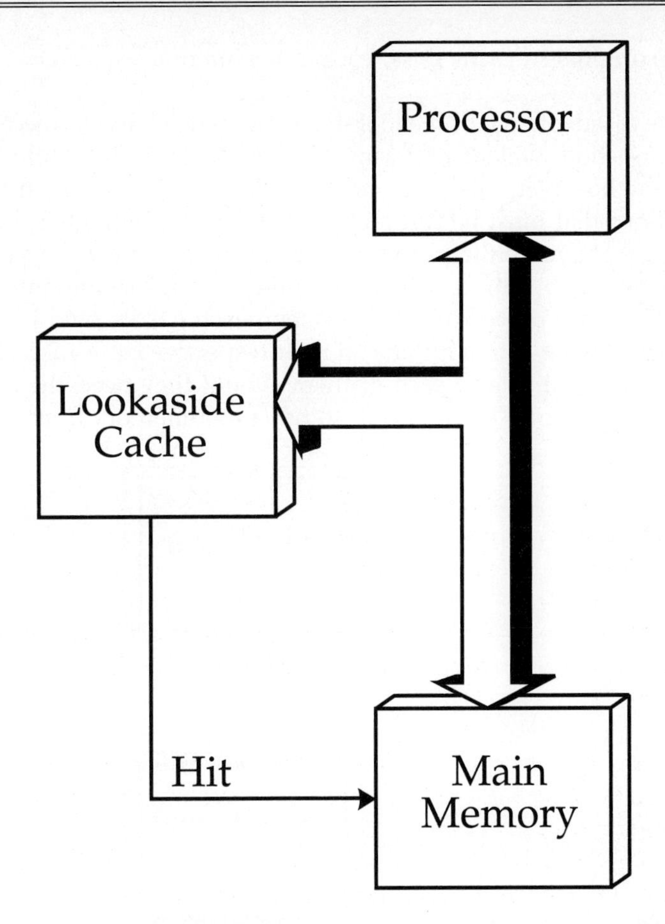

Figure 1-1. The Look-Aside L2 Cache

Look-Through Cache

Figure 1-2 illustrates the relationship of the look-through L2 cache to the processor and memory. Unlike the look-aside cache, the look-through cache sits in between the processor and the system bus. It intercepts and attempts to fulfill all processor memory requests from its cache. If the lookup results in a hit, the cache fulfills the request and the system bus isn't needed at all. This leaves the system bus more available for other processors and/or intelligent bus masters. If the lookup results in a cache miss, the L2 cache uses the system bus to fetch the requested block from memory. It makes a copy of the block in its cache and also passes the block back to the processor. The processor makes a copy in its cache and also passes the originally requested information (that caused the original L1 cache miss) back to the internal requester.

The disadvantage of the look-through cache is that it injects latency in the bus transaction while it performs its cache lookup. In a multiprocessing environment, however, this disadvantage is far out-weighed by the lessening of transactions that must be run on the system bus. The higher the hit rate on the L2 cache, the more the processor is decoupled from the system bus. This makes the system bus more available to other processors and intelligent bus masters. If the other processors in the system each has its own L2 cache and they are experiencing a high hit rate on their respective L1 or L2 caches, the system bus is more available to each of them should they need the bus (on an L2 cache miss or if the processor needs to run a non-memory transaction).

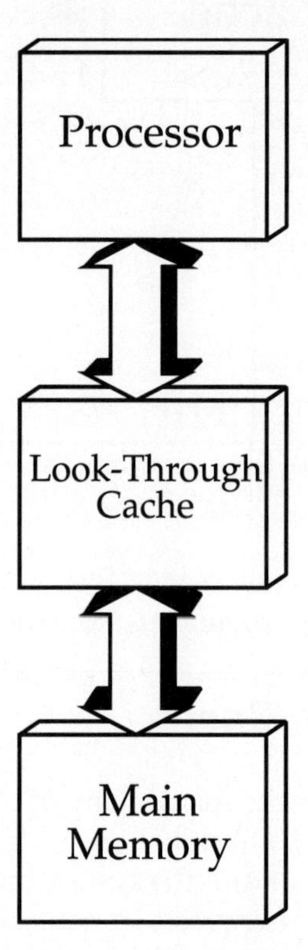

Figure 1-2. The Look-Through L2 Cache

Cache Handling of Memory Writes

General

A cache may be designed to handle memory writes in one of two ways: it may utilize a write-through or a write-back policy. These two methods are also referred to as the store-through and store-in policies. The following two sections define the two policies.

Write-Through Cache

Assume that the processor core must perform a memory write to update one or more bytes in memory. The memory write is submitted to the L1 cache for a lookup. If the target location(s) currently reside in the cache, the data is updated in the cache. In addition, the byte or bytes are also updated in external memory by performing a memory write bus transaction. In other words, the write-through policy always ensures that the data in the cache and memory are in agreement.

If the target location(s) are not in the L1 cache, the processor just performs a memory write to update the byte(s) in memory.

Write-Back Cache

Once again assume that the processor core must perform a memory write to update one or more bytes in memory. The memory write is submitted to the L1 cache for a lookup. If the target location(s) currently reside in the cache, the data is updated in the cache. The byte or bytes are not updated in external memory, however. The cache contains the latest copy of the information and the external memory now contains stale data. The L1 cache marks its copy of the data as modified to reflect the fact that it is different than the data in memory.

If the target location(s) to be updated are not currently in the L1 cache, the processor may be designed to take either of the following actions:

- Perform a memory write to update the byte(s) in memory
- Perform a memory read transaction to read the cache block from memory that contains the byte(s) to be updated. Upon receiving the cache block,

the target byte(s) are updated and the cache block is marked modified. This is commonly referred to as an "allocate-on-write" policy.

MESI Cache Protocol

General

This section provides a brief introduction to the MESI cache protocol. Figure 1-3 illustrates a very basic system comprised of the following parts:

- Two processors with write-back L1 caches
- External bus used to communicate with external devices
- Main memory controller
- Inter-cache communication, or snoop, signals

Assume that processor one is executing a load instruction to load a word from memory into one of the processor's internal registers. The memory read request is submitted to processor one's L1 cache for a lookup. At this time, the cache does not have a copy of the block that contains the requested data. In other words, the lookup selects an invalid entry, resulting in a cache miss.

In response, the processor initiates a memory read transaction on the external bus to read the requested data from main memory. Any bus transaction consists of an address phase and a data phase. During the address phase it drives the following information onto the bus:

- The target memory address
- The transaction type (in this case, a memory read)
- It asserts the snoop command signal to force other processors with caches (the snoopers) to perform a lookup in their caches (a snoop) using the memory address to be read from and report the results back to the initiating processor.

During the data phase, the data is transferred between the processor and memory.

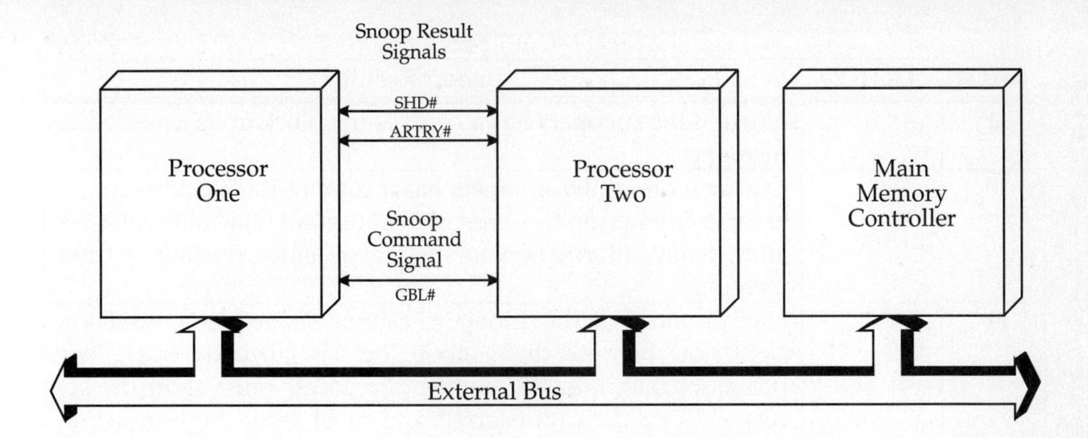

Figure 1-3. Multiple-Cache System

Snoop-Related Signals

If this is a 601 processor, the snoop-related signals are:

- The snoop command signal is GBL#
- The snoop result signals are SHD# (Shared) and ARTRY# (Address Retry)

The 601 snoop results are defined in table 1-1.

Table 1-1. 601 Snoop Result

SHD#	ARTRY#	Snoop Result
1	1	None of the snoopers has a copy of the block to be accessed in memory.
0	1	One or more of the snoopers has a copy of the block the processor is attempting to access in memory but none of them have altered any information in their copy since reading it from memory.
1	0	One or more of the snoopers cannot snoop the transaction right now because their snoop logic is currently busy. The processor that initiated the memory access must abort the access with no data transferred and must retry the transaction again later. This is necessary because one of the busy devices may have a copy of the target block in its cache and may have modified it since reading the block from memory. If this is the case and the processor proceeded with the data transfer, it would be accessing a stale block in memory and wouldn't know it.
0	0	This indication has one of two possible meanings: 1. One of the snoopers has a copy of the target block and has modified it since reading it from memory. 2. One or more of the snoopers has a copy of the target block in its cache and has not modified it since reading it from memory. In addition, one or more of the remaining snoopers cannot snoop the transaction at this time because their snoop logic is currently busy. In either case, the processor that initiated the memory access must abort the access with no data transferred and must retry the transaction again later. This is necessary because one of the busy devices may have a copy of the target block in its cache and may have modified it since reading the block from memory. If this is the case and the processor proceeded with the data transfer, it would be accessing a stale block in memory and wouldn't know it.

Exclusive State

When processor one initiates this memory read, it also asserts the snoop command signal line to force processor two to perform a lookup, or snoop, in its L1 cache and to report the snoop result back to processor one at the end of the address phase. Assume that processor two's L1 cache does not currently contain a copy of the requested data (the lookup selects an invalid cache block entry). Processor two's L1 cache reports back to processor one (using the snoop result signals) that it does not have a copy of the requested cache block. The snoop result is also visible to the main memory controller. The main memory controller supplies the requested block of data to processor one. The data requested by the load instruction is immediately routed to the target register specified by the load when the data comes on board the processor chip. At the conclusion of the memory read, processor one enters the data block in its L1 cache and marks its copy of the block as Exclusive (because the snoop result indicated that no other processor had a copy of the data block). In other words, the cache block is in the E state.

Shared State

Next assume that processor two executes a load instruction from one or more locations within the same cache block. It experiences a miss in its L1 cache and initiates a memory read to fetch the requested block from memory. It asserts the snoop command signal to force processor one to perform a snoop in its L1 cache. Since processor one's L1 cache has a copy of the block (in the E state), it indicates (using the snoop result signals) that it has a copy and that its copy is still a mirror image of the block in main memory (in other words, it has not altered its copy since bringing it into the cache). SHD# is asserted and ARTRY# is not. When processor two completes the memory read, it places its copy of the block into its L1 cache in the Shared, or S, state, indicating that at least one other cache has a copy of the block and that all copies are still the same as memory. In addition, processor one's L1 cache changes the state of its copy from E to S because it is now aware of at least one other cache that has a copy of the block.

Modified State

Next assume that processor one is executing a store instruction to update one or more bytes in memory. It performs a lookup in its L1 cache and has a hit on the shared block from the previous example. There are three possible ways of handling this, but only one is correct:

- Processor one could write the data into the block in its L1 cache and then marks its copy as modified. This is the wrong thing to do. Processor two would not know that a change had occurred to the block and that its copy is stale.

- Processor one could write the data into its L1 copy of the block and mark it modified and then perform a special transaction on the external bus to kill processor two's copy of the block. This is also the wrong thing to do. There is a window of opportunity inherent in this scenario for processor two to access stale data from its copy of the block. In the period of time from the update of processor one's L1 cache until the kill transaction is seen by processor two, processor two's L1 cache contains a stale copy of the block.
- **The third option is the correct one**. Processor one should first broadcast the kill transaction on the external bus to kill any copies of the block in other caches. Only after the kill transaction is successfully completed should processor one accept the write data into its copy of the block and then mark it modified.

By definition then, when a processor marks its copy of a block as modified, it has already killed all other copies of the block in other caches. In other words, a block marked as modified is the only copy of the block. In addition, a modified block has been altered since being copied from memory into the cache and the block in memory is stale.

Backoff or Retry

Read Attempt and Backoff

Next assume that processor two executes a load instruction within the same block and experiences a miss on its L1 cache. As a result, the processor initiates a memory read bus transaction to read the block from memory. It asserts the snoop command signal to force processor one to snoop the access in its L1 cache. Processor one's L1 cache has a hit on a modified block in its cache and indicates this to processor two and to the main memory controller by asserting SHD# and ARTRY#. This causes processor two to backoff, or abort, its read attempt. When processor two detects the snoop result at the end of address phase of the transaction, it aborts its read attempt. The snoop result also causes the memory controller to abort the data transfer.

Snoop Push-Back

After processor one has forced processor two to backoff, it initiates a memory write transaction to deposit the modified cache block into memory. This is referred to as a snoop push-back of a modified block to memory. While it is performing the push-back, processor two requests the use of the bus again to re attempt its memory read, but it cannot begin the transaction until processor one completes the memory write. When the push-back is completed, processor one changes the state of its copy of the block from modified to shared (because the cache block and memory are now the same and it knows that the other processor will immediately read the block from memory into its cache).

Retry

Processor two then acquires ownership of the bus and retries its memory read. It once again instructs processor one to perform a snoop and report the result. This time the snoop result indicates that processor one has an unmodified copy of the block (just SHD# is asserted). This means that processor two is about to read fresh data from memory. Processor two and memory therefore proceed with the memory read and the block is placed in processor two's L1 cache in the shared state (because processor one had indicated that it also has a copy of the cache block).

Snoop Hit On Modified Block During Memory Write

If processor two had attempted a memory write (of less than an entire cache block) instead of a memory read, the same sequence of events would have occurred with the following exception — after processor one had deposited the modified block in memory, it would have invalidated its copy. This is done because processor two will write over a portion of the block in memory when it retries its transaction and processor one's copy will then be stale.

If processor two had attempted a memory write and had indicated that it was going to write the entire cache block into memory, processor one would invalidate its copy of the block without performing a push-back of the modified block to memory. This is done because the modifications to the cache block were made earlier in time than this latest memory write and processor two has indicated that it will overwrite the entire cache block.

Mass Storage — Very Slow Access Device

Most of the information, both instructions and data, that the processor requires resides on mass storage devices. Since mass storage devices are typically mechanical in nature, the access time to read data from or write data to mass storage can be very lengthy.

The amount of storage available on the array of mass storage devices connected to a system is far greater than the amount of physical DRAM memory available in the system. This means that the system can only keep a relatively small amount of the information from mass storage resident in main memory at a given instant in time.

When the end-user indicates that he or she wishes to run a particular program, the operating system could load the entire program file into memory from mass storage. It would not be unusual for the program to consume one meg or more of system DRAM memory. This would be a very wasteful usage of memory, however. As an example, one of today's powerful word processors incorporates literally hundreds of features. During a typical work session, the end-user will only utilize a handful of these features. This basically means that only a small portion of the code and data that comprise the word processing program would actually be accessed during the work session.

In a multitasking operating system environment such as OS/2, the user is permitted to specify more than one program to be run simultaneously. If each of these programs were loaded into memory in their entirety, huge amounts of system DRAM would be consumed unnecessarily. The memory required by the operating system itself must also be factored in. The operating system consists of a myriad of services, many of which may seldom be invoked (executed) during a particular work session. To keep the entire operating system resident in memory would therefore also be wasteful.

Rather than load the entire operating system and each application program into memory, the operating system will usually only bring a relatively small amount of the initial program code into memory. This code will be enough to get the program started. The remaining portion of the program and/or data required by the program will only be read from storage into memory on demand. This results in a much more efficient usage of memory and permits the operating system to run many applications simultaneously (more than would actually fit in memory if loaded in their entirety).

Paging Uses System DRAM As Mass Storage Cache

Virtually all of today's advanced processors include a paging, or memory management unit (MMU). The paging unit considers all information currently in memory and those on mass storage to be organized into 4KB pages of information. When a memory request is made, the paging unit performs a lookup in a special directory, known as the page table, to determine if the target page is currently resident in memory and if so where it was placed when it was read from mass storage. If the page is not currently present in memory, a page fault interrupt occurs and the processor automatically suspends the currently-running program and jumps to the page fault handler program. This program first determines if the currently-running program is permitted access to the page of information (in other words, does the page belong to the program). If access is not permitted, the program will be aborted and the end-user will be informed that it attempted to touch information that did not belong to it.

If the program is permitted access to the page of information, the page fault interrupt handler performs a mass storage read to read the target page into an available 4KB page in DRAM memory. After the page is resident in memory, the handler makes a page table directory entry indicating where the mass storage page was physically placed in memory. The handler then restarts the suspended program which then reattempts the instruction that caused the page fault.

When the target memory address is submitted to the page table for a lookup this time, a match is found. The address of the page in memory is supplied by the page table entry. The lower twelve bits of the target memory address are used as an index into the 4096 byte page in memory. The physical memory address of the target location is then used to perform a lookup in the L1 cache.

Using the paging unit, the processor treats DRAM memory as a cache for pages from mass storage device. On a miss in the page table, the target page is read from mass storage into memory. From that point forward any accesses within that page will result in a hit on the page table and mass storage doesn't have to be accessed. Since DRAM is much faster access than a mechanical device, this can result in a substantial increase in performance. It should also be remembered that the information from DRAM can then be cached in the L1 and/or L2 caches, yielding another substantial increase in performance.

Paging Summary

Refer to figure 1-4. The fastest accesses result when there is a hit on the L1 cache. In the event of an L1 cache miss, a memory transaction is initiated on the processor's bus. If it results in a hit on the L2 cache, the need to access DRAM or ROM is avoided and, in the case of a look-through L2 cache, the system bus remains available for others to use.

The L2 cache contains a superset of the L1 cache and a subset of main memory. If the access results in a miss on the L2 cache, DRAM or ROM must be accessed. Memory contains a superset of the information contained in the L2 and L1 caches, and a subset of the information on the mass storage array.

Mass storage is slower than DRAM. DRAM is slower than L2. L2 is slower than L1.

If the paging unit determines that the requested information is not currently resident in memory, the operating system is instructed to fetch the target page from mass storage and place it into DRAM memory. This access to a mechanical device does result in decreased performance, but any subsequent accesses within the page will not require a mass storage access (because the page is already resident in memory). Once the page has been placed into memory, the L1 and L2 caches can begin to cache information from it, resulting in a further increase in performance.

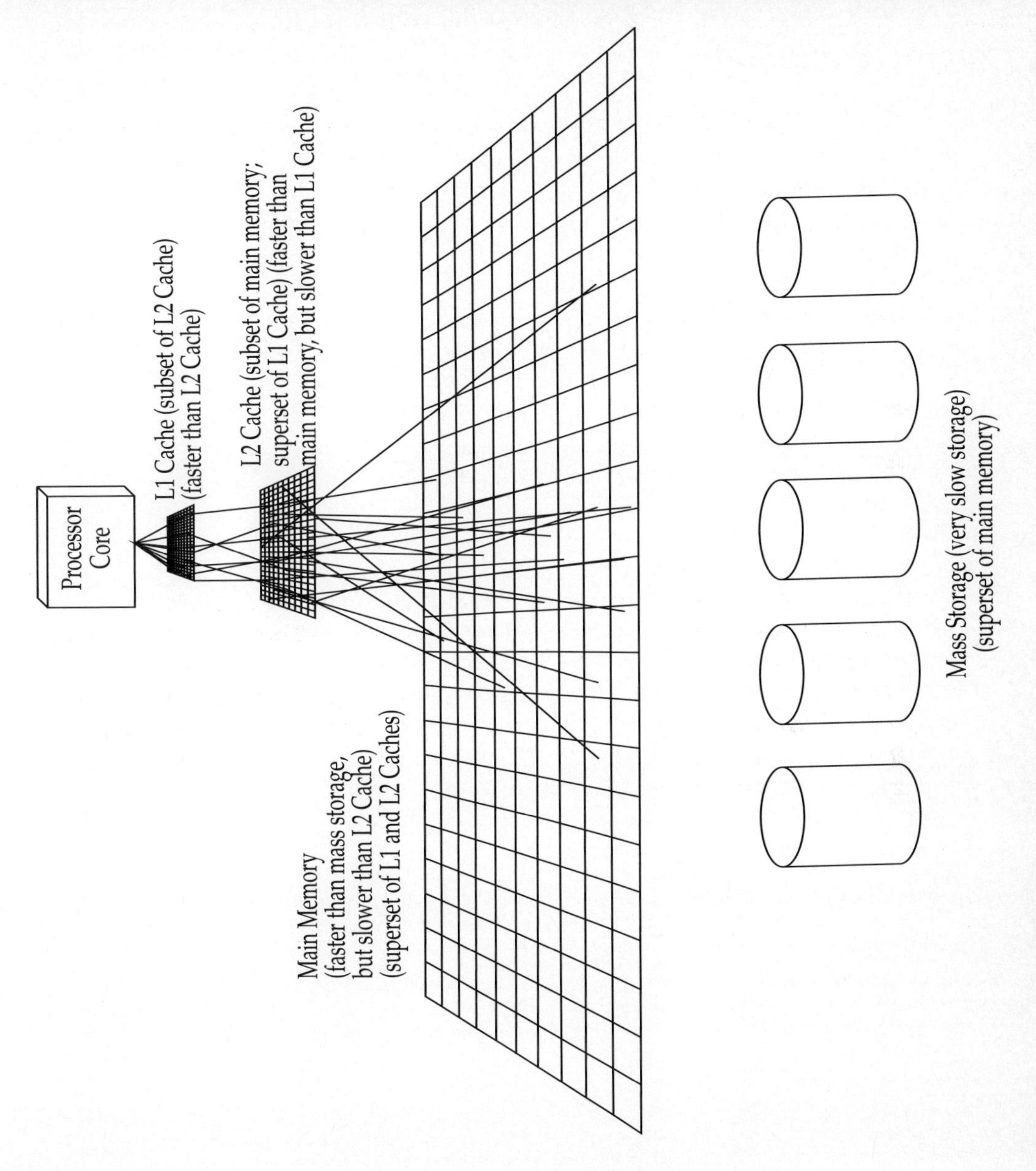

Figure 1-4. The Memory Hierarchy

The author would like to express his thanks to the engineer at IBM Charlotte who suggested this illustration. IBM's rules preclude my using your name, but you know who you are.

Chapter 2

The Previous Chapter

The previous chapter introduced the role of the instruction prefetcher, L1 and look-aside and look-through L2 caches. It provided a basic description of the write-through and write-back policies utilized by caches. The concept of demand mode paging was introduced.

This Chapter

This chapter presents a basic discussion of a typical PC platform based on the PowerPC processor. It describes the relationships of the processor, main memory and bus masters residing on the PCI or standard expansion bus (ISA, EISA or Micro Channel).

The Next Chapter

The next chapter introduces the basic building blocks of a PowerPC processor and describes their relationships to each other.

System Overview

Figures 2-1, 2-2, 2-3 and 2-4 illustrate typical PowerPC system designs. Figure 2-1 represents a system with a single host processor with a look-through L2 cache. Figure 2-2 represents a system with a single host processor with a look-aside L2 cache. The system illustrated in figure 2-3 contains an array of two host processors, each with its own dedicated look-through L2 cache. Figure 2-4 illustrates a system with two host processors that share a look-aside L2 cache. The signals shown in the figures are PPC 601 bus-specific and are explained later in the book. For a detailed description of PCI bus operation, refer to the MindShare publication entitled *PCI System Architecture*.

The host processor (or array of host processors) represents the core of the system. The processor (or processors) resides on the host bus and must utilize the host bus to communicate with memory or I/O devices.

The main memory may reside directly on the host bus (refer to figures 2-2 and 2-4) or may be attached to the host/PCI bridge via a dedicated memory bus (refer to figures 2-1 and 2-3).

The host/PCI bridge typically incorporates the following functions:

- In the case of a single processor system, the host/PCI bridge may incorporate a look-through L2 cache that is associated with the host processor (see figure 2-1). In another single-processor configuration (figure 2-2), main memory and a look-aside cache may reside on the host bus with the processor.
- In the case of a multiprocessor system, each host processor will either have its own local L2 cache (figure 2-3) or they will share a look-aside cache that resides on the host bus(figure 2-4). The host/PCI bridge will typically not incorporate a cache.
- As shown in figures 2-1 and 2-3, the host/PCI bridge may incorporate the DRAM controller for the main memory. It therefore controls access to main memory from both the host and PCI sides of the bridge.
- When the host processor initiates a transaction destined for a device on the other side of the bridge, the bridge must acquire ownership of the PCI bus and then initiate the PCI equivalent of the host bus transaction.
- When a PCI bus master initiates a transaction that must be bridged over to the host bus side, the bridge must translate the transaction into the host bus equivalent.

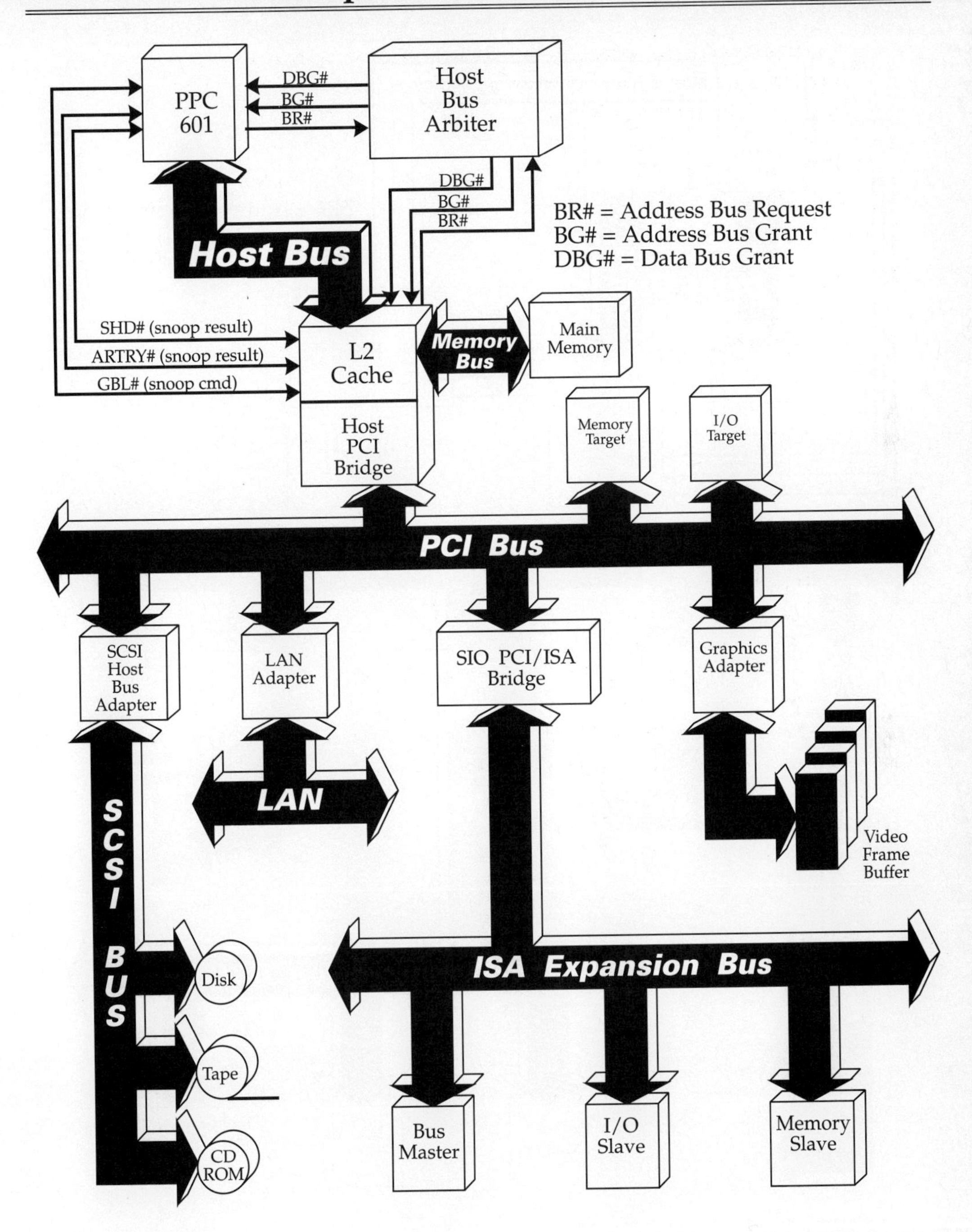

Figure 2-1. Single Host Processor System with Look-Through L2 Cache

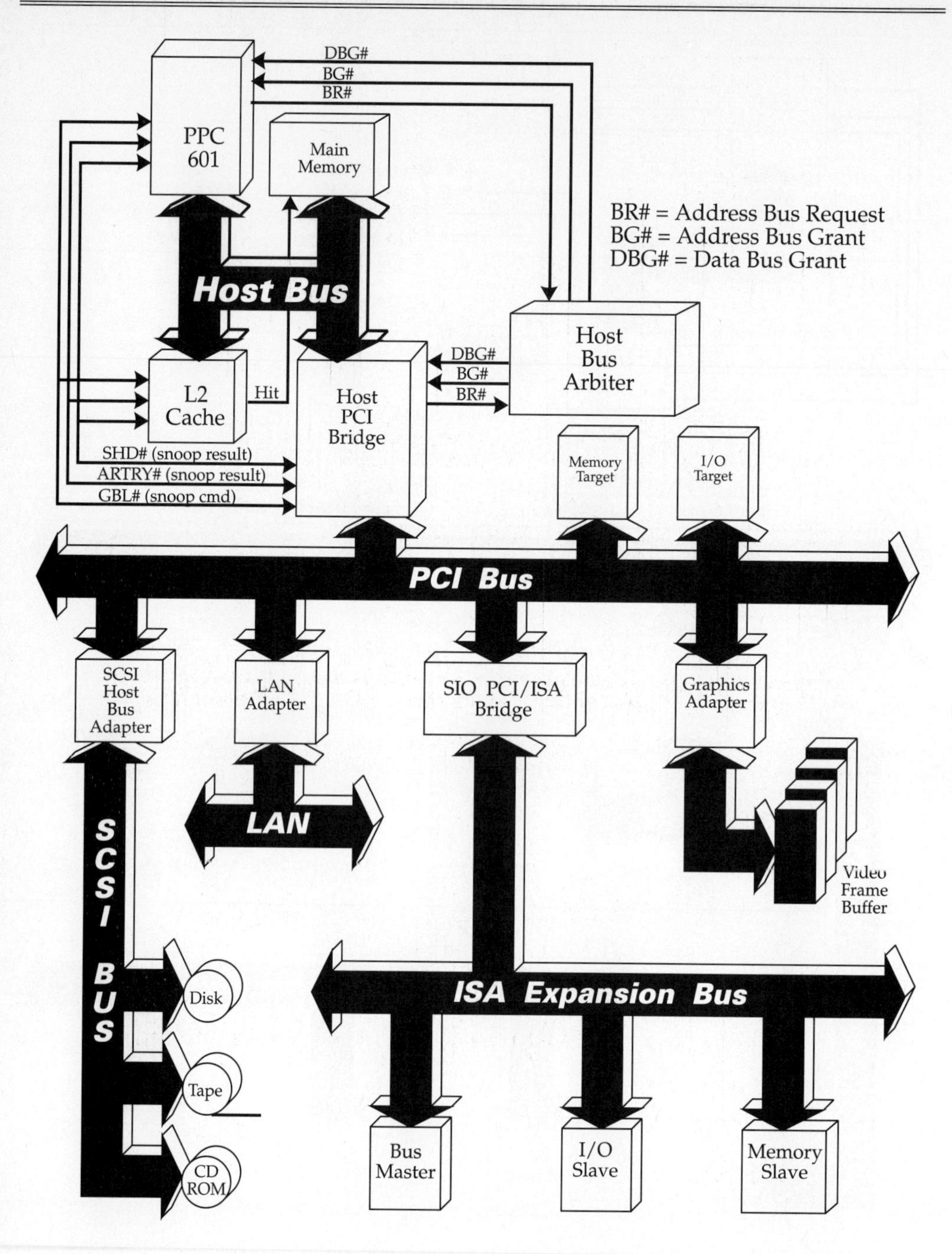

Figure 2-2. Single Host Processor System with Look-Aside L2 Cache

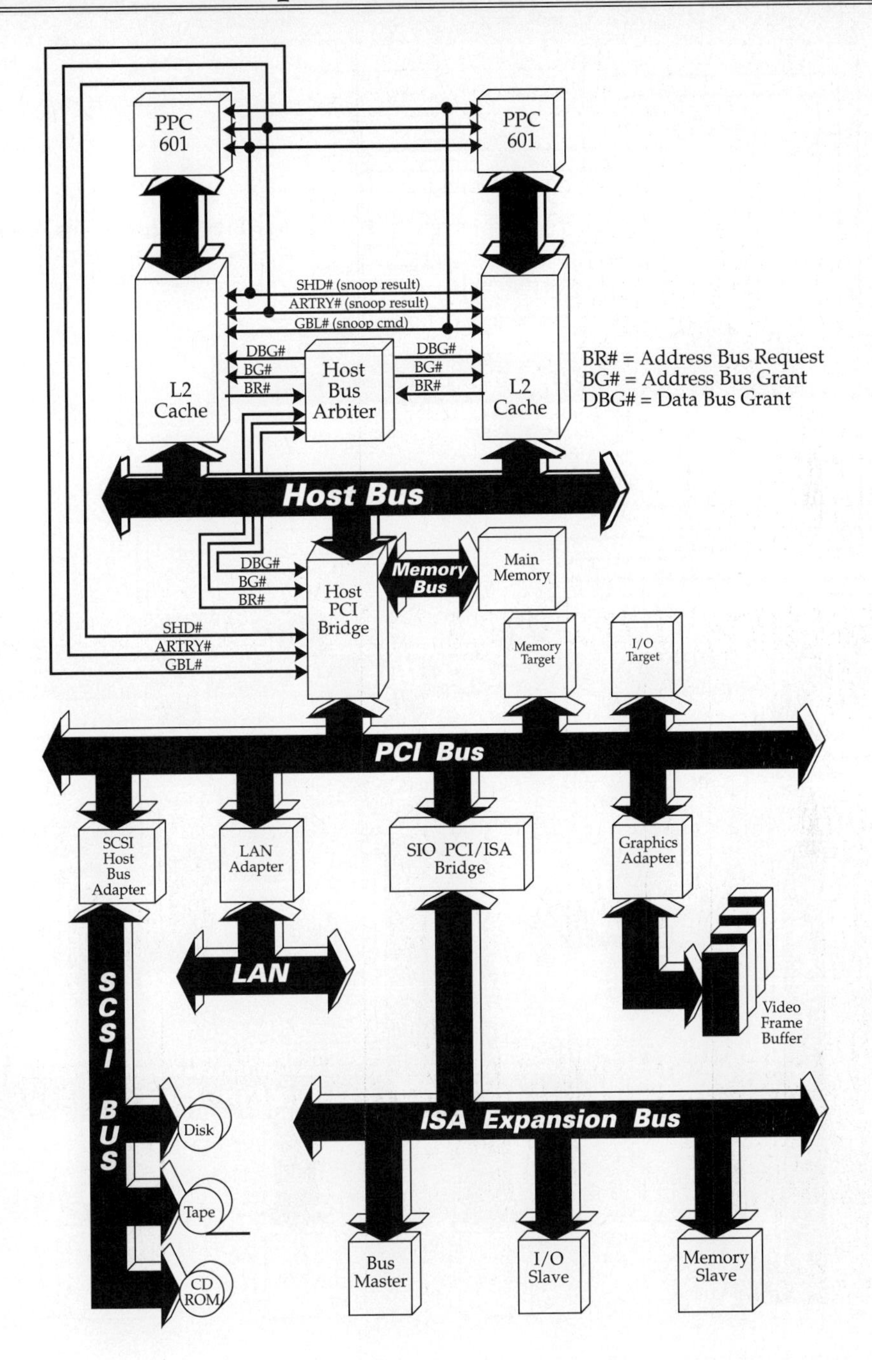

Figure 2-3. Dual Host Processor System with Dedicated Look-Through L2 Caches

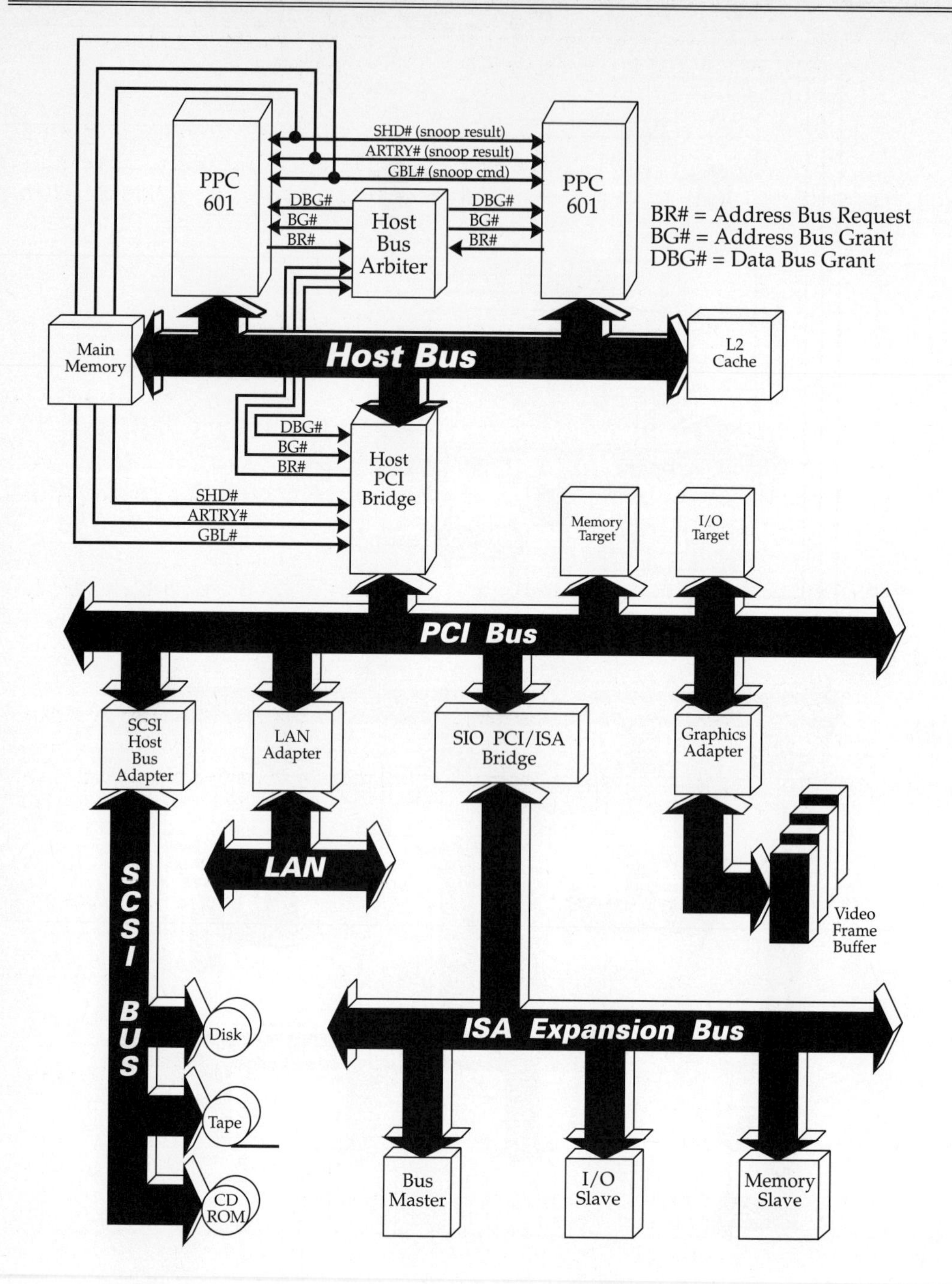

Figure 2-4. Dual Host Processor System with Shared Look-Aside L2 Cache

Intro to Subsystem and Bus Relationships

The following sections provide a very basic introduction to the relationships of host, PCI and standard expansion bus devices to each other. A more detailed discussion of cache-related issues can be found in the following chapters:

- PPC 601 Cache and Memory Unit Operation
- The PPC 601 Processor's Relationship With the L2 Cache
- The PPC 601 Memory Address Phase

Host Processor Transactions

When the host processor initiates a bus transaction, the target device resides on one of the three system buses:

- Host bus — If the target device is on the host bus, the host/PCI bridge does not need to bridge the transaction over to the PCI bus.
- PCI bus — If the target device is on the PCI bus, the transaction must be bridged over to the PCI bus.
- Standard expansion bus — If the target device is on the standard expansion bus(e.g., EISA, ISA or Micro Channel), the transaction must be bridged over to the PCI bus and then bridged over onto the expansion bus.

If the host processor is accessing cacheable memory, the L2 cache may be able to service the transaction. In a typical platform design, the only memory cached from by the host processor and the L2 cache is main memory.

PCI Bus Master Transactions

When a PCI bus master initiates a bus transaction, the target device resides on one of the three system buses:

- Host bus — If the target device is on the host bus, the host/PCI bridge must bridge the transaction over to the host bus.
- PCI bus — If the target device is on the PCI bus, the transaction does not need to be bridged onto the host or standard expansion bus.

- Standard expansion bus — If the target device is on the standard expansion bus (e.g., EISA, ISA or Micro Channel), the transaction must be bridged over to the expansion bus.

If the PCI bus master is accessing main memory, it may be accessing memory information that currently resides in the host processor's L2 and L1 caches. Unless the caches can watch and possibly interfere in the PCI bus master's memory access, the PCI bus master may read data from an area of memory that had previously been copied into a cache and was then modified by the host processor. In this case, the PCI master would read stale data from memory. It's therefore obvious that the caches must snoop the PCI master's memory access in their caches. If it is determined that the master is about to access stale information, the bridge must issue a retry to the PCI master, causing it to abort its memory access and to retry it again at a later time. The cache with the modified copy of the block must then perform a snoop push-back of the modified block into memory. The block in the cache is then marked shared and the PCI bus master is permitted to read from that area of memory.

In another scenario, the PCI master may writing data into an area of memory that had previously been copied into the caches. Unless the caches snoop main memory writes performed by PCI masters, memory would be updated by the write and the cache copy of the data would then be stale. The host processor may subsequently read the stale data from the cache and make bad decisions based on it. This must be prevented. The caches snoop all memory writes performed by PCI masters. In the event of a hit on a cache copy of the data to be updated by the PCI master, the cache will either have to invalidate its copy or latch the new data (snarf it) into the cache to keep its copy current.

Standard Expansion Bus Master Transactions

When a bus master on the standard expansion bus initiates a bus transaction, the target device resides on one of the three system buses:

- **Expansion bus** (e.g., EISA, ISA or Micro Channel) — If the target device is on the expansion bus, the expansion bus/PCI bridge does not need to bridge the transaction over to the PCI bus.
- **PCI bus** — If the target device is on the PCI bus, the transaction must be bridged over to the PCI bus.
- **Host bus** — If the target device is on the host bus, the transaction must be bridged over to the PCI bus and then be bridged over onto the host bus.

If the expansion bus master is accessing main memory, the caches must snoop these transactions. The same issues must be dealt with that applied when a PCI bus master is accessing main memory.

Concurrent Bus Operation

The two bridges permit the three buses to be used concurrently under certain circumstances. This is possible when an expansion bus master is performing a transfer with a target on the expansion bus, a PCI master is performing a transfer with a PCI target and the host processor is performing a transfer with a target that resides on the host bus.

Chapter 3

The Previous Chapter

The previous chapter presented a basic discussion of a typical PC platform based on the PowerPC processor. It described the relationships of the processor, main memory and bus masters residing on the PCI or standard expansion bus (ISA, EISA or Micro Channel).

This Chapter

This chapter provides a basic definition of the PowerPC processor architecture. It introduces the role of the following elements of the processor's architecture:

- System interface
- Cache
- Memory Management Unit (MMU)
- Instruction unit
- Instruction dispatcher
- Integer, or fixed-point, processor
- Floating-point processor
- Branch processor

The Next Chapter

The next chapter introduces the PowerPC software architecture specification. This specification defines the registers, instructions and other facilities accessible by the programmer. The differentiation is made between the software environment and the hardware environment within which the software is executed. The three divisions of the software architecture are introduced: the user instruction set architecture, the virtual environment architecture and the operating environment. 32-bit and 64-bit processor differences are discussed, as well as the basic differences between the Power and PowerPC architectures. The three PowerPC instruction classes are introduced.

Introduction

Figure 3-1 illustrates the basic hardware elements that comprise a PowerPC processor. The processor's instruction unit may or may not be capable of issuing more than one instruction simultaneously (in other words, superscalar capability is optional). The following sections provide a brief description of each element that comprise the processor. It should be noted that a PowerPC processor may incorporate more than one integer and/or floating-point units. As an example, the PPC 604 processor incorporates two integer units.

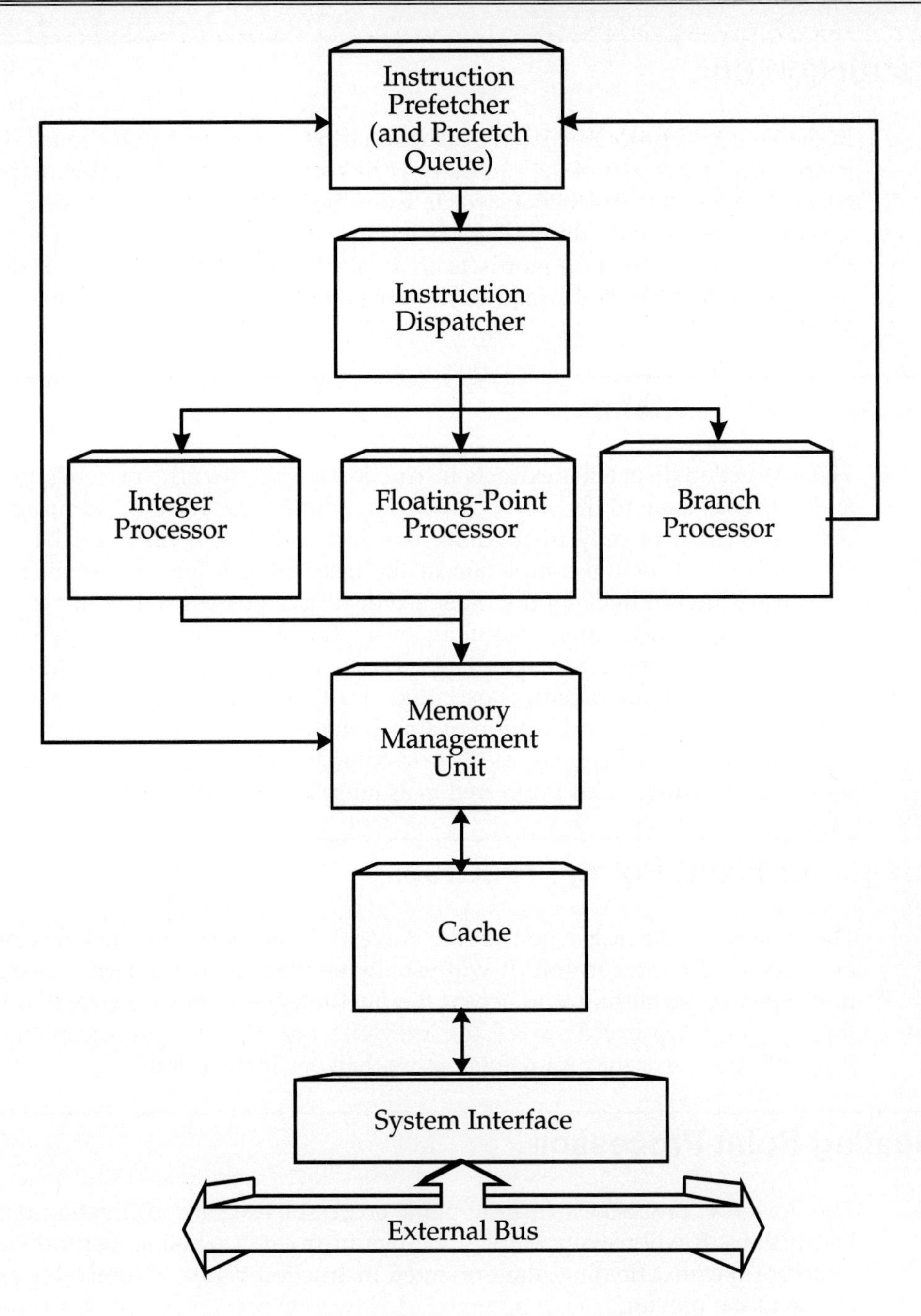

Figure 3-1. Basic Hardware Elements of a PowerPC Processor

Instruction Unit

In the PowerPC processor, each instruction is one word, or 32-bits, long. The instruction unit is part of the processor core. It implements an instruction prefetcher that fetches instruction words from memory. Unless the branch unit specifically commands the prefetcher to alter its normal fetch path, the prefetcher fetches instruction words from sequential words in memory. It does this by sending the next sequential word-aligned memory address to the MMU.

Instruction Dispatcher

The instruction dispatcher extracts instruction words from the prefetch queue and forwards them to the correct processing unit for decode and execution. It may be capable of only dispatching one instruction at a time and be constrained to wait for the completion of the instruction before dispatching the next instruction in line. On the other hand, it may possess the ability to dispatch multiple instructions simultaneously (in other words, a superscalar implementation). It is a rule that the PowerPC processor must appear to operate as if only one instruction is executed at a time (even if it is a superscalar implementation). One implication of this is that interrupts caused by instructions will be reported serially, as if incurred by the attempted execution of one instruction at a time. This is referred to as interrupt ordering.

Integer, or Fixed-Point, Processor

The majority of the instructions in the PowerPC processor's instruction set are executed by the integer unit. It will usually employ its own internal instruction pipeline, permitting it to accept the next integer-oriented instruction before it completes execution of the previous one that it had accepted. A PowerPC processor may implement more than one integer unit.

Floating-Point Processor

The PowerPC processor's floating-point processor executes all floating-point instructions. It will usually employ its own instruction pipeline, permitting it to accept the next floating-point-oriented instruction before it completes execution of the previous one it accepted. A PowerPC processor may implement more than one floating-point unit.

Branch Processor

The branch processor executes all branch instructions. When a conditional branch instruction is received, it is evaluated to determine if the condition specified for the branch has been met. If it has, the branch execution unit instructs the instruction prefetcher to alter its program flow so as to fetch the next instruction from the branch target address (rather than from the next sequential address). In addition, the instructions that follow the branch that have already been prefetched are flushed.

The processor may implement static branch prediction, wherein a hint (a bit embedded in the branch instruction word itself) provided by the compiler at the time the branch instruction was created tells the branch processor to predict the branch as taken or not taken (without waiting for the specified condition to be met).

In a superscalar design, the branch can be extracted from the instruction stream by the branch unit early and evaluated. If the hint bit indicates that the branch will be taken, the branch unit commands the instruction prefetcher to alter the program flow. In the event that the prediction proves correct (when the indicated condition has been resolved by one of the other units), the instruction unit will have already fetched the instructions starting at the branch target address. If the branch is incorrectly predicted, the branch processor must flush all of the new instructions from the instruction pipeline and must resume prefetching at the correct location (the one that follows the branch in memory).

Memory Management Unit (MMU)

If the MMU has been enabled by the operating system, it examines the target memory address supplied by the integer processor, the floating-point processor or the instruction prefetcher in order to determine if the target address maps to a page that is currently present in memory or to a large region of memory space that has been defined as a block by the operating system. A block is a large region of memory (128KB to 256MB in size) with one set of operational rules (cacheability, write-through or write-back, etc.). Do not confuse this type of block with a cache block. The cache block is defined later in this section. Pages and blocks are defined in the chapter entitled "Address Translation Overview."

The MMU receives the address from the instruction unit and attempts to translate it into the corresponding physical memory address by searching the page table. If the processor implements either a code cache or a combined code/data cache and the MMU considers the target area of memory to be cacheable (the method for determining cacheability will be covered in the chapter entitled "Memory Usage Bits WIMG"), the physical memory address is then submitted to the cache for a lookup. If the target area of memory is considered non-cacheable by the MMU or results in a miss in the cache, the physical address is submitted directly to the system interface by the MMU so that it can perform the required bus transaction.

Cache

If the requested code or data is in the cache, the cache supplies the item to the requester. If the prefetcher had requested an instruction word (each instruction is 32-bits, one word, in length), the prefetcher places it in the prefetch queue, which, in turn, feeds instructions to the processing units to be decoded and executed. If the requested data or instruction isn't currently in the cache and the target area of memory is considered cacheable by the MMU, the physical memory address is submitted to the system interface by the cache with a request for the block of information that contains the requested item. The system interface then performs a burst cache block-fill memory read bus transaction to fetch the requested block from external memory. The term cache block refers to the size of the block of information a cache will read from memory whenever it experiences an instruction fetch or a load miss. The cache block size is processor design-dependent.

When the cache block has been read from memory, the requested item is routed directly back to the requester and the block of information is placed in the cache to satisfy possible future requests.

If there is no cache or if the target area of memory is considered non-cacheable by the MMU, the physical memory address is submitted directly to the system interface. The system interface then performs a memory read bus transaction to fetch the requested data or instruction from external memory.

Memory Unit (MU)

A PowerPC processor may incorporate a special buffer that latches memory read and write requests issued by the execution units and the cache, permitting them to unstall. It then issues a series of requests to the system interface to perform the required bus cycles on the external bus. This unit is referred to as the memory unit, or MU. It is not pictured in the illustration.

System Interface

When a request is received from another unit within the processor, the system interface unit performs the required bus transaction(s) to satisfy the request. The manner in which the bus is implemented is outside the scope of the PowerPC architecture specification. As an example, it would be permissible to interface a PowerPC processor directly to the PCI bus.

Chapter 4

The Previous Chapter

The previous chapter provided a basic definition of the PowerPC processor architecture. It introduced the role of the following elements of the processor's architecture:

- System interface
- Cache
- Memory Management Unit, or MMU
- Instruction unit
- Instruction dispatcher
- Integer, or fixed-point, execution unit
- Floating-point execution unit
- Branch execution unit
- Memory Unit

This Chapter

This chapter introduces the PowerPC processor software architecture specification. This specification defines the processor registers, instructions and other facilities accessible by the programmer. The differentiation is made between the software environment and the hardware environment within which the software is executed. The three divisions within the software architecture (as defined by the PowerPC processor specification) are introduced: the user instruction set architecture, the virtual environment architecture and the operating environment. 32-bit and 64-bit processor differences are discussed. The three PowerPC instruction classes are introduced.

The Next Chapter

The next chapter describes the registers that are available to the applications programmer when the processor is operating at the user privilege level (MSR[PR] = 1). The applications-level register set for both 32 and 64-bit versions of the PowerPC processor are described.

User vs. Supervisor Privilege Level

At a given instant in time, the processor is executing either operating system software or an applications program. When the operating system is executing, the processor must make all registers, instructions and other facilities available to the programmer so that the operating system has full control over the machine. When an applications program is executing, however, only a subset of the registers, instructions and facilities should be accessible to the programmer.

The privilege mode bit in the machine state register selects the privilege level the processor is executing in while a program is being executed. When cleared to zero, the processor is operating at the supervisor privilege level and all facilities are available. When set to one, the processor is operating at the user privilege level and a subset of the overall facilities are available to the programmer.

Software vs. Hardware Architecture

There is a great degree of variance regarding the usage of many terms considered standard within the computer industry. This makes it necessary to define a term before using it. The term architecture is one of them. Within the context of PowerPC technical literature, the phrase *PowerPC Architecture* refers to the processor instruction and register sets and the associated processor facilities provided by a processor that are visible to and are accessible by the programmer.

It should be stressed that a wide degree of latitude in processor design is achievable while still remaining within the bounds of the PowerPC software architecture. The exact implementation of the internal cache, memory management unit, etc., may vary greatly while still presenting a front-end to the software that adheres to the specification.

As used in all of MindShare's books, the term *system architecture* refers to the overall system architecture. The system architecture consists of one or more host processors, the processor bus, a local bus (such as PCI or the VL bus) and an expansion bus (such as the ISA, EISA, or the Micro Channel bus). It also includes bus master, memory and I/O target devices.

The remainder of this chapter provides a brief introduction to the PowerPC processor software architecture.

Introduction to PowerPC Software Architecture

General

As stated earlier, the PowerPC architecture defines the instruction set and hardware environment that are available to the operating system and applications programmer. The specification defines the software architecture as being divided into three distinct sections:

- **User instruction set architecture** (available at user privilege level). Defines the instructions that may be successfully executed, the registers that may be read and/or written, and the interrupts that may occur while the processor is executing at the user privilege level.
- **Virtual environment architecture**. Describes memory page/block attributes (coherence, write-through or write-back, and caching permission). Instructs the programmer to program with the assumption that the processor has separate code and data caches. Describes the cache management instructions. Addresses issues related to processors with a unified code/data cache and issues related to a write-through data cache implementation. Describes weak and strong bus transaction order. Describes the reservation mechanism used to implement memory-based semaphores. Dictates that the processor will supply a demand-mode paging mechanism to map logical to physical memory addresses. The operating system supports this function by programming the MMU and setting up page tables in memory to be used for mapping.
- **Operating environment architecture** (available at supervisor privilege level). Defines the instructions that may be successfully executed, the registers that may be read and/or written, and the interrupts that may occur while the processor is executing at the supervisor privilege level.

It's important to note that all of the facilities described in the user architecture are available at the user privilege level. Although the functionality provided by the virtual environment architecture supports user mode programs, the ability to use the instructions and registers associated with the virtual environment are only available when the processor is operating at the supervisor privilege level. The facilities provided within the operating environment architecture are only available when the processor is operating at the supervisor privilege level. ***In this book, the discussion of the software architecture has been divided into two parts: "Part Two — User Privilege Level Facilities"; and "Part Three —Supervisor Privilege Level Facilities."***

A description of PowerPC 601's implementation of the PowerPC software architecture may be found in Part Four — The PowerPC 601 Processor.

Instruction Length and Alignment

All PowerPC processor instructions are 32-bits, or one word, in length. By definition, each instruction resides in memory aligned on an address divisible by four (in other words, on a word-aligned boundary).

Length of Data Operands

The programmer may load, store or manipulate data operands with the following lengths:

- The byte, consisting of eight bits, is the smallest data object that may be loaded from or stored into memory or I/O.
- The halfword consists of two bytes, or 16 bits, of information.
- The word consists of four bytes, or 32 bits, of information.
- The doubleword consists of eight bytes, or 64 bits, of information.

With the exception of floating-point operands (which, by definition, are 64-bits long), the 32-bit PowerPC processor does not provide the programmer with load or store instructions to load or store doublewords from or to memory or I/O.

64 and 32-Bit Processor Implementations

The PowerPC architecture permits both 64 and 32-bit processor implementations. The PPC 601, PPC 603 and PPC 604 are 32-bit implementations of the PowerPC processor, while the PPC 620 is a 64-bit implementation.

Basic Characteristics of 64-Bit Processor Implementations

In the 64-bit implementation, most registers (except for some special purpose registers, or SPRs) are 64 bits wide. In a 64-bit processor, 32 or 64-bit mode may be software selected by the operating system. Most instructions provided in 64-bit mode are also available when the processor is operating in 32-bit mode. The mode selection controls:

- the generation of effective addresses (the terms effective and logical address are interchangeable in this book).
- how status bits are set.
- how the Count Register is tested by conditional branch instructions.

In a 64-bit processor, instructions that place a 64-bit result into the specified target register will do so irrespective of whether the processor is currently operating in 32 or 64-bit mode. Also irrespective of mode, effective address computation uses all 64 bits of the specified registers and produces a 64-bit effective address. However, in 32-bit mode, the upper 32-bits of the computed effective address are ignored when accessing a data operand, and are set to zero when fetching instructions.

Basic Characteristics of 32-Bit Processor Implementations

In the 32-bit implementation, all registers are 32-bits (except floating-point registers which are 64 bits wide), and the processor generates 32 bit effective addresses.

Instruction Classes

General

All instructions may be divided into three classes:

- **Defined**. This class encompasses all instructions defined in the three subdivisions of the PowerPC architecture: the user, virtual and operating environments. These instructions are guaranteed to be supported in all implementations, except as stated in the instruction descriptions. The exceptions are instructions that are only supported in the 64 or 32-bit implementations.
- **Illegal**. For 64-bit implementations, this class includes all instructions that are defined only for 32-bit implementations. As an example, there are no segment registers in a 64-bit processor. Therefore, any attempt to move a value to or from a segment register on a 64-bit processor will result in a program exception. For 32-bit implementations, this class includes all in-

structions that are defined only for 64-bit implementations. As an example, there is no Address Space Register in a 32-bit processor. Therefore, any attempt to move a value to or from the ASR on a 32-bit processor will result in a program exception. An instruction consisting entirely of zeros is guaranteed to be invalid in all current and future PowerPC processor implementations. This rule exist to increase the chances that an attempt to execute code from a zeroed data area or an uninitialized data area will result in an illegal instruction exception.

- **Reserved**. These instructions provide services outside the scope of the PowerPC architecture definition. This would include POWER architecture instructions that have not been included in the PowerPC architecture definition and implementation-specific instructions.

Forms of Defined Instructions

Defined instructions fall into three categories:

- The **preferred form** — Some of the defined instructions have preferred forms that will execute substantially faster than the instruction in any other valid form. These instructions are: load/store multiple, load/store string, and or load/store immediate.
- An **invalid instruction form** — Some of the defined instructions have invalid forms. They are invalid if one or more fields of the instruction are coded incorrectly.
- **Optional instructions** — Some of the instructions within the defined class are optional. They are listed in the PowerPC software documentation.

POWER vs. PowerPC Architecture

The POWER architecture refers to the programming environment available in the IBM RS/6000 product line based on the POWER architecture. ***A discussion of the POWER architecture is outside the scope of this publication***. To a large extent, the PowerPC architecture provides binary compatibility with the POWER architecture. Many of the PowerPC instructions are identical (at the binary level) to the POWER instructions. Some of these instructions that are binary-compatible utilize different mnemonic names. Appendix C lists the major differences between the two architectures. Part Four of this book defines the differences between the PPC 601 implementation and the PowerPC processor specification.

Volume One: The PowerPC Processor Specification

The first volume, consisting of parts two and three, defines the PowerPC processor specification. This specification provides the template upon which all PowerPC processors are designed. A particular implementation of a PowerPC processor provides a subset of these capabilities, all of them, or all of the defined capabilities plus additional capabilities outside the scope of the specification. A complete description of both the 32-and-64-bit PowerPC processor specification is provided.

Volume two focuses on the PPC 601 processor.

Part Two

Applications Programs: User Privilege Level

Parts two and three provide the description of the PowerPC processor specification. All aspects of both 32 and 64-bit processor implementations are covered.

Part two provides a description of the instructions, registers and other facilities available to the applications programmer. Applications programs are executed at the user privilege level. The processor is placed into the user privilege level when the privilege mode bit, PR, in the machine state register, or MSR, is set to one (in other words, MSR[PR] = 1). The chapters that comprise Part two are:

- Applications Registers
- Applications Instructions
- Address Modes, Branch Prediction
- Real and Virtual Paging Models
- Cache Management Issues
- Misaligned Transfers and Performance
- Shared Resource Acquisition
- Memory Usage Bits (WIMG)
- Access Order
- The Timebase

Chapter 5

The Previous Chapter

The previous chapter introduced the PowerPC processor software architecture specification. This specification defines the processor environment visible to and accessible by the programmer. The differentiation was made between the software environment and the hardware environment within which the software is executed. The three divisions of the software architecture were introduced: the user instruction set architecture, the virtual environment architecture and the operating environment. 32-bit and 64-bit processor differences are discussed. The three PowerPC instruction classes were introduced.

This Chapter

This chapter describes the registers that are available to the applications programmer when the processor is operating at the user privilege level (MSR[PR] = 1). The applications-level register set for both 32 and 64-bit versions of the PowerPC processor are described.

The Next Chapter

The next chapter describes the instructions that are available to the applications programmer when the processor is operating at the user privilege level (MSR[PR] = 1).

General

The bits within all PowerPC processor registers are numbered using the big-endian numbering scheme. Bit 0 is the most-significant bit, or msb, and is the left-most bit in the register. Bit 31 (or 63, if it is a 64-bit register) is the least-significant bit, or lsb, and is the right-most bit in the register.

Figure 5-1 illustrates the registers that are available to the applications programmer. The processor is executing an applications program when the privilege mode bit in the machine state register is set to one (i.e., MSR[PR] = 1).

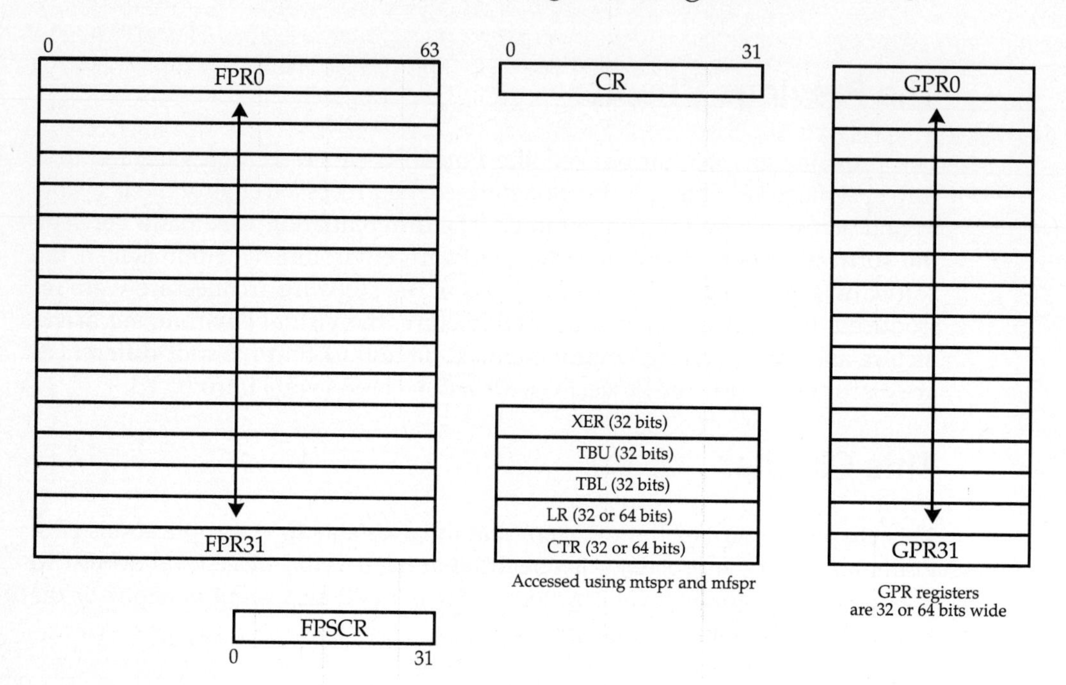

Figure 5-1. The User Mode Register Set

General Purpose Registers (GPRs)

There are 32 General Purpose Registers, **GPR0 – GPR31**. Each of these registers is a 64-bit (in a 64-bit processor) or a 32-bit (in a 32-bit processor) register. The programmer may perform register-to-register, register-to-memory, memory-to-register, register-to-IO, or IO-to-register operations using the integer instruction set.

The GPRs may be used to load, store or manipulate data operands. In addition, the PowerPC processor uses the GPR registers to perform register indirect addressing. This subject is covered in the chapter entitled "Address Modes, Branch Prediction."

Condition Register (CR)

The bits within this 32-bit register reflect the result of certain operations and provides a mechanism for testing bits and branching when the specified condition is met. The CR register is illustrated in figure 5-2. The register contains eight 4-bit fields designated CR0 – CR7. CR0 contains condition flag bits that reflect the result of integer instruction execution. CR1 contains copies of some of the floating-point condition code status bits from the floating-point status and control register, or FPSCR. The CR2 – CR7 fields contain user-definable condition bits.

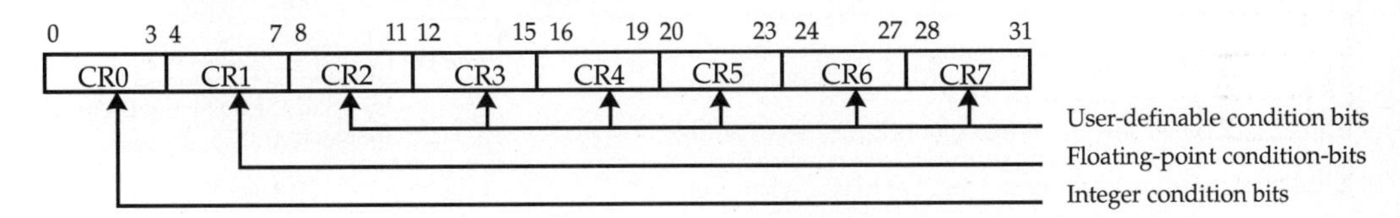

Figure 5-2. The Condition Register (CR)

The CR0 bits reflect the following integer conditions:

- Bit 0 will be set to one if the result was **negative**. It is also referred to as the **LT** (less than) bit.
- Bit 1 will be set to one if the result was **positive**. It is also referred to as the **GT** (greater than) bit.
- Bit 2 will be set to one if the result is **zero**. It is also referred to as the **EQ** (equal) bit.
- Bit 3 reflects the state of the **SO (summary overflow)** bit from the XER register (refer to the next section).

The CR1 bits reflect the following floating-point conditions:

- Bit 4 reflects the state of the **floating-point interrupt** bit, **FX**, from the FPSCR. FX is set to one if any floating-point interrupt occurs (whether or not the corresponding exception type is enabled).
- Bit 5 reflects the state of the **FEX** bit from the FPSCR. FEX is set to one if any enabled **floating-point exception** occurs.
- Bit 6 reflects the state of the **VX** bit from the FPSCR register. VX is set to one if any of the **floating-point invalid operation** exception conditions are detected.
- Bit 7 reflects the state of the OX bit from the FPSCR register. OX is set to one if a floating-point overflow occurs.

Integer Exception Register (XER)

This is a 32-bit register in both 32 and 64-bit PowerPC processors. It is illustrated in figure 5-3. The meaning of each bit or bit field is indicated in the illustration.

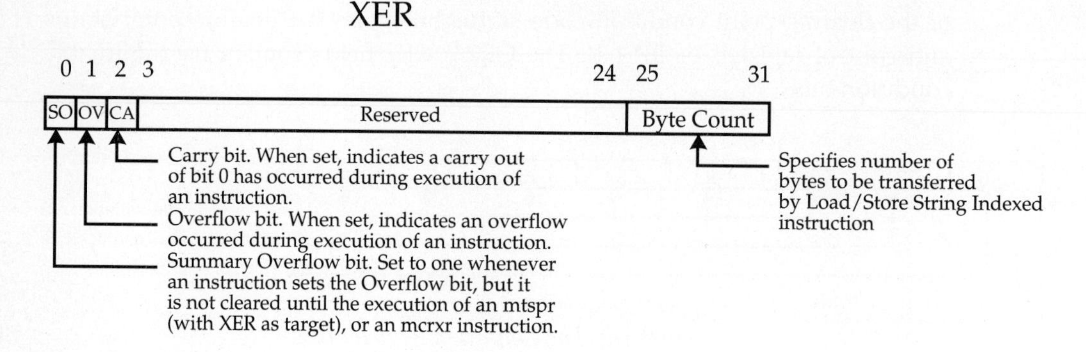

Figure 5-3. The Fixed-Point, or Integer, Exception Register (XER)

Link Register (LR)

The Link register provides the branch target address for branch conditional to link instructions (if the specified condition is met). It can also be used to store the return address for conditional and unconditional branch and link instructions. For more information, refer to the section on branch addressing in the chapter entitled "Address Modes, Branch Prediction."

Using the branch conditional to link instruction with the address of a target routine in LR, the programmer can conditionally call a routine at the same privilege level. When a branch and link instruction is executed, the address of the instruction after the branch instruction is stored in the Link register. The programmer may then use the address in LR as the return address to return to the calling program.

LR is 64 bits wide in a 64-bit implementation and 32 bits wide in a 32-bit implementation. The least-significant two bits are forced to zeros to word-align the addresses (because all instructions are word-aligned in memory). Figure 5-4 illustrates the link register.

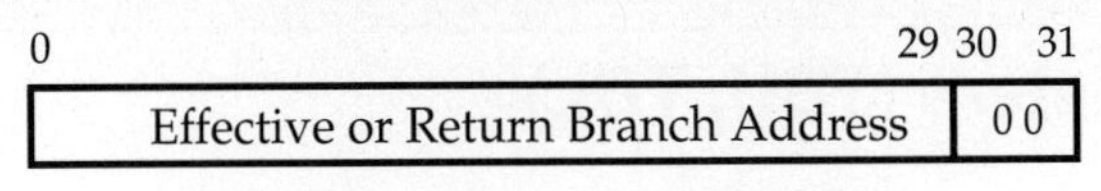

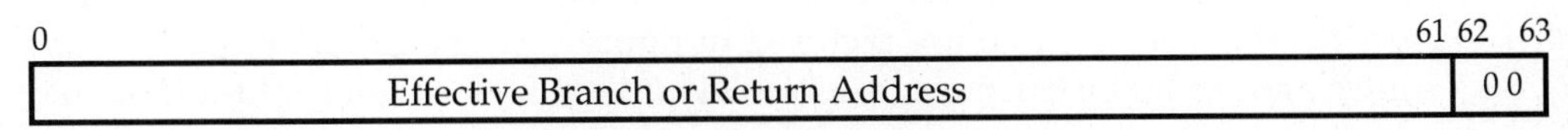

Figure 5-4. The Link Register (LR)

Count Register (CTR)

The CTR register can hold a loop count to be used with appropriately coded branch instructions that may be placed at the end of conditional loops. Each time the conditional branch is executed, it automatically decrements CTR and tests for a count exhausted condition.

CTR can also provide the branch target address for the Branch Conditional To Count Register instruction. As with the link register, it may therefore be used to call a routine at the same privilege level. It is 32 bits wide in 32-bit processors and 64-bits wide in 64-bit processors. Figure 5-5 illustrates the CTR register.

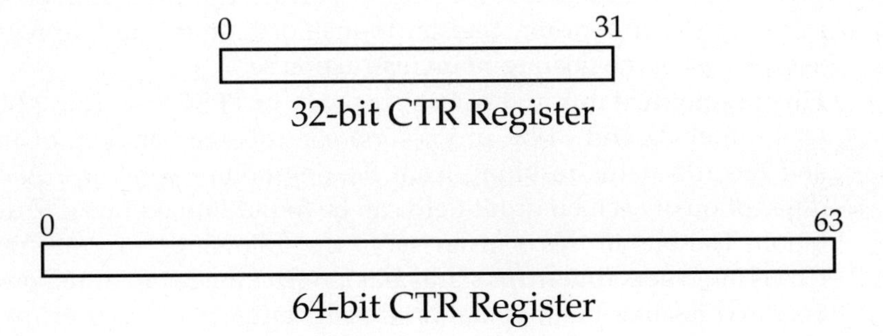

Figure 5-5. The Count Register (CTR)

TimeBase Registers (TBU, TBL)

The timebase is used to track the passage of time. At the user privilege level, applications programs may read from but may not alter the contents of the timebase. Only the operating system may write to the timebase registers. A description of the timebase may be found in the chapter entitled "The Time-Base." In both 32 and 64-bit processors, the timebase is implemented as two 32-bit registers. They are referred to as Timebase Upper, or TBU, and Time-base Lower, or TBL and are pictured in figure 5-6. The programmer uses the mftb and mftbu instructions, respectively, to read the contents of the TBL and TBU registers into GPR registers.

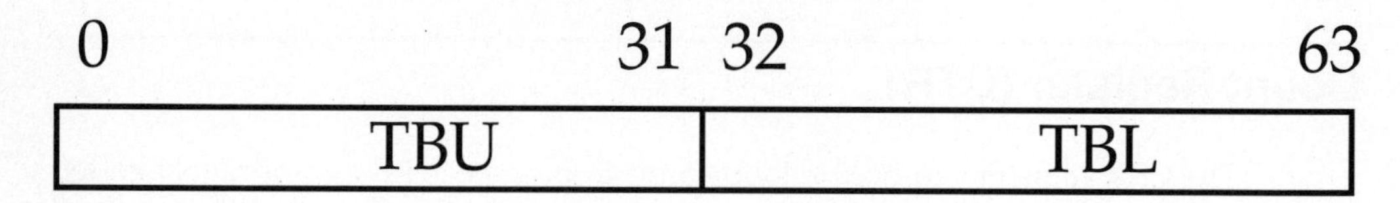

Figure 5-6. The TimeBase Registers

Floating-Point Registers

The registers used by the floating-point unit at the user privilege level are:

- **floating-point registers**, or **FPRs**, each 64-bits wide (in both 32 and 64-bit processors) — designated as FPR0 – FPR31. The programmer may perform register-to-register, register-to-memory, or memory-to-register operations using the floating-point instruction set.
- **Floating-point status and control register,** or **FPSCR** — This 32-bit register (in both 32 and 64-bit processors) controls the handling of interrupts and records status resulting from floating-point operations. A complete description of each bit or bit field can be found in the PowerPC documentation. The bits in this register serve the following purposes: reflect detected interrupts (interrupt status bits); reflect the result of the previously-executed floating-point operation (result status bits; no interrupt encountered); provide a mechanism for selectively enabling or disabling types of interrupts (interrupt enable bits); provide a mechanism for placing the

floating-point unit in IEEE or non-IEEE mode (the NI bit); and for controlling rounding (the RN bits). Figure 5-7 illustrates the FPSCR.

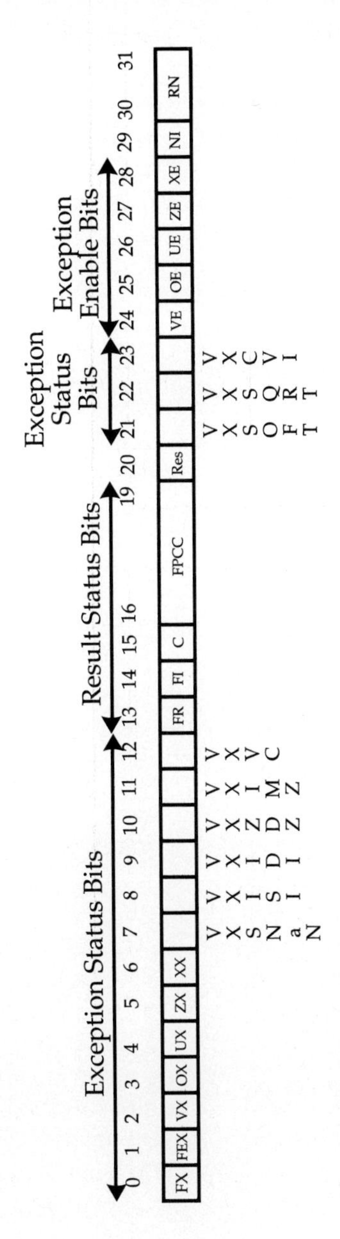

Figure 5-7. Floating-Point Status and Control Register (FPSCR)

Chapter 6

The Previous Chapter

The previous chapter described the registers that are available to the applications programmer when the processor is operating at the user privilege level (MSR[PR] = 1).

This Chapter

A detailed description of each instruction in the PowerPC instruction set may be found in the vendor-supplied PowerPC documentation. This chapter provides a summary of and an introduction to the instructions available to the applications programmer when the processor is operating at the user privilege level (MSR[PR] = 1).

The Next Chapter

The next chapter describes the addressing modes that may be utilized with load, store and branch instructions. It also provides a brief description of the PowerPC branch prediction mechanism.

Branch-Oriented Instructions

The branch-oriented instructions that may be executed by the processor at the user privilege level include the following:

- **Unconditional branch** to the effective address specified by the programmer in the GPR register set, or forward/backward relative to the address from which the branch instruction was fetched.
- **Branch conditional** to the effective address specified by the programmer in the GPR register set, or forward/backward relative to the address from which the branch instruction was fetched.
- **Branch conditional to link register** — If the specified condition is met, the processor branches to the target address specified in the LR.

- **Branch conditional to count register** — If the specified condition is met, the processor branches to the target address specified in the CTR.
- **System call** — The applications programmer uses the sc instruction to invoke the operating system services. The parameters associated with the request are set up in the GPR register set prior to execution of the sc instruction (the layout of the parameters is OS-specific). When executed, the sc instruction causes a system call exception. The SRR0 register is set to the address of the instruction that follows the sc in memory. The SRR1 register records the state of the MSR register control bits at the point of interruption so that the processor can be returned to its original operational state after the exception has been handled by the operating system. The processor then branches to the sc exception handler. At the conclusion of the handler execution, the final instruction executed must be a return from interrupt (rfi) instruction. This causes the MSR state to be restored from SRR1 and execution to resume at the instruction after the sc (saved in SRR0). A detailed discussion of interrupts can be found in the chapter entitled "Interrupts."
- The **trap instruction** — compares the contents of a GPR with either another GPR or an immediate value, and, if the specified conditions are met, invoke the system trap handler. The trap instruction can be used to make conditional calls to operating system services (as opposed to the sc, which is an unconditional call to the OS services).
- **Condition register logical instructions** — permit logical operations (for instance, the XOR function) to be performed on the CR contents.

For a description of branch addressing, refer to the chapter entitled "Address Modes, Branch Prediction."

Integer Memory Access Instructions

The integer instructions that access memory at the user privilege level may be divided into the following categories:

- **Load instructions** — load a single data operand into a register from memory.
- **Store instructions** — store a single data operand from a register into memory.
- **Load/Store instructions with byte reversal** — In a PowerPC system operating in big-endian mode, these instructions have the effect of loading or storing information in little-endian order. In a PowerPC system in little-

endian mode, these instructions have the effect of loading or storing information in big-endian order. The endian-related issues are covered in detail in the chapter entitled "Big vs. Little-Endian."

- **Load/Store multiple instructions** — load or store multiple words between the GPR registers and memory. The effective start address specified by the programmer must be word-aligned. An alignment exception will result if the start address is not word-aligned.
- **Move assist instructions** — Unlike the load/store multiple instructions, these instructions are used to load/store data between the GPR registers and memory without concern for alignment. Although this group of instructions are frequently referred to as the move assist instructions in the vendor documentation, they are actually called load/store string instructions and are used to load or store a string of bytes starting at a byte-aligned address.
- **Storage Synchronization instructions** — used to control the order in which memory accesses are performed on the external bus and are seen by other processors (or devices other than processors that access memory). In short, they are used to perform atomic memory access sequences (e.g., read/modify/writes on memory semaphores). A detailed description of memory semaphores can be found in the chapter entitled "Shared Resource Acquisition."

Non-Memory Integer Instructions

The remainder of the integer instructions do not access memory-based operands. Rather, they use the GPRs as source operands, and place results into GPRs, the XER, and the CR.

This instruction group consists of add, subtract, negate, multiply, divide, compare, logical, rotate, shift, and move to/from system register instructions.

Floating-Point Instructions

Memory Access Floating-Point Instructions

A suite of floating-point load and store instructions are provided by the floating-point processor.

Floating-Point Register-to-Register Move Instructions

These instructions enable data to be copied from one FPR to another. Modifications to the data may be made during the copy.

Floating-Point Arithmetic Instructions

Instructions are provided to facilitate add, subtract, multiply, divide, combined multiply/add and multiply/subtract.

Floating-Point Rounding and Conversion Instructions

The following instructions are provided:

- round to single-precision
- convert floating-point number to integer doubleword
- convert floating-pointer number to integer doubleword with round toward zero
- convert floating-point number to integer word
- convert floating-point number to integer word with round toward zero
- convert from integer doubleword to floating-point integer

Floating-Point Compare Instructions

Two forms of the floating-point compare instruction are supported.

FPSCR Register Access Instructions

These instructions provide the capability to:

- copy the contents of FPSCR to a target FPR
- copy a field within the FPSCR to the specified field within the CR
- copy an immediate value into a field within the FPSCR
- copy a field within the specified FPR to the specified field within the FPSCR
- clear the specified bit within the FPSCR
- set the specified bit within the FPSCR

Cache Management Instructions

The following sections provide a brief description of the cache management instructions. Before proceeding, it is important to define the meaning of the term "cache block" — the block of information that a cache copies from memory and records in the cache. The size of a cache block is cache design-dependent. The term cache block should not be confused with the term block. A block is a large region of memory (128KB to 256MB in size) defined by the operating system. This subject is described in the chapter entitled "Address Translation Overview." The author has made every attempt to always use the term cache block when discussing an item in the cache. The term block is used when discussing a large region of memory.

Brief Definition of WIM Bits

The operating system uses the WIM bits to define if an address range is cacheable, whether a write-through or write-back policy should be used for memory writes, and whether other processors may also access the same area of memory. These are all issues that affect how the processor's L1 cache will operate. When the operating system first reads a page of information from mass storage, it sets up a page table entry to define:

- Where the page originated (virtual segment ID and page number within the virtual segment)
- Where it was placed in memory (the start memory address of the 4KB memory page)
- Whether the area of memory is cacheable (I = 0 indicates cacheable, while I = 1 indicates non-cacheable)
- Whether to use a write-through or write-back policy when handling stores into the memory page (W = 1 indicates write-through, while W = 0 indicates write-back)
- Whether multiple caching processors access the memory page (M = 1 indicates that they do, while M = 0 indicates that this processor is only one that accesses this area of memory). If multiple caches do access the memory area but the operating system doesn't require that they be aware of changes that other processors may be making to their own local copies of the cached data, M could be set to zero.
- Whether to permit read/write, read-only, or no accesses within the memory page (the K and PP bits)

A complete discussion of all of the page attributes can be found in the chapters entitled "Memory Usage Bits (WIMG)," "Address Translation Overview" and "Virtual Paging."

The operating system can also define a large region of memory space as a block, rather than a page, and assign WIM bits to define the operational rules within the block of memory space.

Instruction Cache Block Invalidate (icbi) Instruction

If the target address specified is contained in the code cache, it is invalidated.

If the target cache block is within a page marked as not-readable, the system data storage interrupt handler may be invoked (because the currently-running program should not be trying to invalidate cached code from a page it can't read from).

If the target address is within a page or block with M = 1, this indicates that the page or block may be shared with other processors. The target cache block must therefore also be invalidated in all other system caches (by broadcasting a kill transaction on the bus). Although the processor need not update the page access history bits, if it does, it will be recorded as a load (not a store). In other words, the page's referenced bit will be set, but not its changed bit.

For a discussion of icbi usage regarding self-modifying code, refer to the chapter entitled "Cache Management Issues."

Data Cache Block Store (dcbst) Instruction

Purpose

Execution of the dcbst instruction causes the processor, if it has a copy of the target cache block in the modified state in its data cache, to deposit the modified cache block back into main memory. If the cache block isn't present in this processor's data cache and the address is within a page or block that may be accessed by other processors (M = 1), the processor should perform a bus transaction to instruct any processor with a copy in the modified state to deposit it in memory and mark its copy exclusive. For a discussion of the W, I and M bits, refer to the chapter entitled "Memory Usage Bits (WIMG)."

An example usage of the dcbst instruction can be found in the chapter entitled "Cache Management Issues."

Cache Miss

If the processor executing the dcbst instruction experiences a miss on its data cache, it must assume (if M = 1) that another processor may have a copy of the target cache block in the modified state. In order to force all other processors to perform a cache lookup, this processor must generate a bus transaction with the specified cache block address and instruct all other processors to perform a lookup. Processors with copies of the target cache block in the exclusive or shared state will ignore the transaction. Processors that experience a miss will ignore the transaction. If any processor experiences a hit on a modified cache block, it must perform a burst memory write transaction to deposit the modified cache block in memory. After writing the cache block to memory, that processor will mark its copy of the cache block exclusive. This indicates that it is the only cache with a copy of the cache block and that the cache block is identical to the block in memory.

Hit on Cache Block in Exclusive State

If the processor executing the dcbst instruction experiences a hit on a cache block in the exclusive state in its data cache, no action is necessary (because no other cache has a copy of the block).

Hit on Cache Block in Shared State

If the processor executing the dcbst instruction experiences a hit on a cache block in the shared state in its data cache, no action is necessary (because although one or more other caches have a copy of the block, it none of them have modified it since it was read from memory).

Hit on Cache Block in Modified State

If the processor executing the dcbst instruction experiences a hit on a cache block in the modified state in its data cache, it performs a burst memory write transaction to deposit the modified cache block into memory. After writing the cache block to memory, the processor will mark its copy of the cache block exclusive. This indicates that it is the only cache with a copy of the cache block and that the cache block is identical to the block in memory.

Rules

If the target address is within a page or block marked as not-readable, the system data storage interrupt handler may be invoked (because it doesn't make sense to attempt to test for data cached from a page or block that can't be read from).

Data Cache Block Flush (dcbf) Instruction

The dcbf instruction instructs the cache to perform a lookup on the specified target address.

- If the cache experiences a hit on a modified cache block, the target block is written back to memory and then invalidated in the cache.
- If it hits on a cache block in the exclusive state, the cache block is invalidated.
- If it hits on a cache block in the shared state and M = 1 (other processors access this area of memory), the cache block is invalidated in this processor's cache and the processor broadcasts a flush transaction to force all other processors to take the same action in their L1 caches.
- If it misses the cache, the processor broadcasts a flush transaction to force all other processors to flush the cache block from their L1 caches.

This instruction acts the same as the dcbst instruction with the following addition — the data cache that flushes the modified block to memory then invalidates its copy of the block.

Data Cache Block Set to Zero (dcbz) Instruction

Results

The programmer specifies a cache block start address with the dcbz instruction. If the block is already in the data cache, it is set to zero and marked modified. If the block isn't in the data cache, an entry is created in the data cache and is marked modified.

Specified Area Not Accessed by Other Processors (M = 0)

On a data cache miss, the processor creates a data cache entry containing all zeros and marks the new cache block modified (because it's not the same as memory).

On a hit on a data cache block in the exclusive state, the processor sets the block to all zeros and marks the cache block modified (because it's not the same as memory).

On a hit on a data cache block in the modified state, the processor enters all zeros into the cache block and leaves it in the modified state.

Specified Area Accessed by Other Processors (M = 1)

On a data cache miss, the processor takes the following actions:

- Broadcasts a kill transaction to all other processors instructing them to perform a lookup in their data caches. In the event of a cache hit, the other processors must invalidate, or kill, their copies of the cache block (because this processor is about to change the entire block).
- Creates a data cache entry containing all zeros and marks the new cache block modified (because it's not the same as memory).

On a hit on a data cache block in the exclusive state, the processor sets the block to all zeros and marks the cache block modified (because it's not the same as memory).

On a hit on a data cache block in the shared state, the processor broadcasts a kill transaction, sets its copy of the block to all zeros and marks the cache block modified (because it's not the same as memory).

On a hit on a data cache block in the modified state, the processor enters all zeros into the cache block and leaves it in the modified state.

If Paging Disabled — Possible Problem When Least Expected

Assume that the operating system has disabled paging for data accesses by setting MSR[DR] to zero, and that a dcbz instruction is executed. When paging is disabled and a data access is attempted, the processor acts as if the WIM bits are set to 001b (write-back policy (W = 0), cacheable memory (I = 0), other processors also access the addressed area (M = 1)).

In the event of a cache miss on the specified address, the processor creates a data cache entry containing all zeros and marks the new cache block modified (because it's not the same as memory). This may create a problem at a later time because there may not be any physical memory residing within the address range covered by the cache block. If the data cache needs the room occupied by the newly established cache block, it will have to cast it back to memory. When the processor initiates a burst memory write transaction to deposit the modified cache block in memory, the system may note that the target memory address doesn't exist and generate a machine check to the processor. Assuming that the machine check interrupt is enabled (MSR[ME] = 1), the processor will branch to the machine check interrupt handler. Since the cast out is completely asynchronous to program flow, the operating system programmer will have no idea why the check was taken.

Rules

1. If the target page or block is marked read-only, the system data storage interrupt will be invoked by the processor (because the dcbz is essentially a store operation).
2. If the page or block is marked write-through, one of two actions is taken: the target block in main memory is set to zero; or the system alignment interrupt handler may be invoked. If the alignment handler is invoked (the processor designer may choose to do this because the write-through to memory is essentially a violation of the intent of the dcbz instruction), it should set the target block in memory to zeros.
3. If the page or block is cache-inhibited, one of two actions is taken: the target block in main memory is set to zero; or the system alignment interrupt handler may be invoked (the processor designer may choose to do this because the dcbz instruction assumes that the targeted memory area is cacheable). If the alignment handler is invoked, it should set the target block in memory to zeros.
4. This access is recorded by the page access history bits as a store.

Data Cache Block Touch (dcbt) Instruction

Description

A programmer uses this instruction as a performance hint to the processor. It informs the processor that a subsequent instruction may attempt to read from the location indicated. In response, the processor may schedule a low-priority cache block fill operation to prefetch the data block into the cache. In response to the dcbt instruction, the processor will determine if the memory unit has room in its posted read queue for the cache block fill request. If it doesn't, the request to load the cache block from memory isn't fulfilled. If a queue position exists, the system interface will post the read in the queue, but will mark it discardable if a higher priority request arrives (due to the execution of subsequent instructions) prior to the initiation of the burst memory read transaction to fulfill the dcbt request. If another higher-priority request requires action and no other queue position is available, the system interface will discard the dcbt fill request. If the request is not discarded and the bus becomes available and no other higher-priority queue entries exists, the system interface will read the requested cache block from memory and make the cache entry.

In the event that the dcbt request is fulfilled, the processor will experience good performance if it should attempt to access any data within the new block that has been established in the cache. In the event that the request is discarded and the block is not read into the cache, the processor will experience a cache miss if it should attempt to access any data within the specified cache block. The cache block will then be read from memory as a high-priority operation to fulfill the request.

Example Usage

An example — the programmer may be processing a portion of a data structure in memory (e.g., a customer record) and either know or strongly suspect that a portion of the data structure that resides within a cache block other than the one currently being processed will be accessed soon. The programmer could execute a dcbt instruction to request that the processor schedule a low-priority operation to read the specified cache block into the cache from memory.

Rules

1. If the page is marked inaccessible for reads, no action is taken.
2. If the page or block is marked cache-inhibited, no action is taken.
3. If caching is permitted from the page or block and M = 1 and the block is not currently present in the data cache, the block may be read from memory (if the read request isn't discarded due to queue space constraints and other, higher-priority requests).
4. If caching is permitted from the page or block and M = 0 and the block is not currently present in the data cache, the block may be read from memory (if it isn't discarded due to queue space constraints and other, higher-priority requests) without instructing other processors to snoop the transaction.
5. This access may not be recorded by the page access history bits, but if it is, it will be recorded as a load.

Data Cache Block Touch for Store (dcbtst) Instruction

The dcbtst instruction informs the processor that a subsequent instruction may attempt to write to the location indicated. It operates the same as the dcbt instruction with the following exception. If the processor performs the cache block fill transaction to fetch the target cache block from external memory, it will use a read with intent to modify transaction type (described in part four of this book). This will cause all other caching processors that may have a copy of the target cache block to flush it from their respective caches. When the processor completes the cache block read, it will place the cache block in its cache in the exclusive state. If a subsequent store is performed within the bounds of the cache block, the processor can immediately store into it and then mark it as modified. It will not have to take the extra time to flush copies of the block from other caches before writing into the block.

Chapter 7

The Previous Chapter

The previous chapter provided a summary of and an introduction to the instructions available to the applications programmer when the processor is operating at the user privilege level (MSR[PR] = 1).

This Chapter

This chapter describes the addressing modes that may be utilized with load, store and branch instructions. It also provides a brief description of the PowerPC branch prediction mechanism.

The Next Chapter

The next chapter provides a brief introduction to addressing with the memory management unit disabled (real mode addressing) and enabled (block or page address translation takes place).

Introduction

The effective address, or EA, is the 32 or 64 bit target address calculated by a load or store or by the instruction prefetcher. This section describes the manner in which the effective address is calculated.

If the sum of the start effective address and the target operand size exceeds the maximum permissible effective address (FFFFFFFFh if the processor is operating in 32-bit mode; FFFFFFFFFFFFFFFFh if the processor is operating in 64-bit mode), this results in the operand wrapping around from the end of effective address space to effective address zero. If the processor is operating in little-endian mode, the least-significant three bits of the effective address (A[29:31] in a 32-bit effective address; A[61:63] in a 64-bit effective address) will be modified by the processor (if the data operand size is a word, halfword, or byte) before the effective address is submitted to the MMU for usage in the access. The subject of little vs. big-endian operation is covered in the chapter entitled "Big vs. Little-Endian."

Load/Store Addressing

General

The following forms of addressing are supported for load/stores:

- Indirect with immediate index
- Indirect with index
- Indirect

A load instruction is used to load a byte, halfword, word, or doubleword from memory or I/O into a GPR or FPR register. A store instruction is used to store a byte, halfword, word, or doubleword into memory or I/O. Note that the integer doubleword load and store instructions are only available on 64-bit PowerPC processors (because the 32-bit processor only has 32-bit GPR registers).

The following sections describe the three addressing techniques.

Indirect with Immediate Index

The load indirect with immediate index takes the following form:

```
lwz     rD, n(rA)
```

where rD is the destination register the operand is loaded into, n is the 16-bit signed immediate index, and rA is the base effective address that the index is added to yield the effective address that the operand will be read from (in either a memory or I/O segment). Each instruction in the PowerPC architecture is one word, or 32 bits, in length. Since the immediate index value is encoded in the instruction itself, the maximum value of the index is limited by the width of the index bit field within the instruction (16 bits). The immediate value may be any value from negative 32768 to positive 32767.

Examples of integer loads using indirect addressing with immediate index follow. It should be noted that the lis and li instructions are actually assembled as addis and addi instructions. The forms shown are permitted by the assembler for added readability.

```
lis     r2, x'3000'     #place address 30000100h in GPR 2
ori     r2, r2, x'0100'
lbz     r1, 4(r2)       #load byte from location 30000100h + 4
                        #into lsb of GPR1 & zero its upper 3 bytes
lhz     r1, 4(r2)       #load 2 bytes from location 30000100h + 4
                        #into lsbs of GPR1 and zero upper 2 bytes
lwz     r1, 4(r2)       #load word from loc. 30000100h + 4 in GPR 1
ld      r1, 4(r2)       #load dw from loc. 30000100h + 4 into GPR1
```

Examples of integer stores using indirect addressing with immediate index follow:

```
lis     r2, x'3000'       #load 30000000 into GPR 2
ori     r2, r2, x'0100'   # or 0100h into lower half of GPR 2
li      r1, x'3210'       #load data 3210h into GPR 1
stb     r1, 4(r2)         #store lsb from GPR 1 in loc. 30000100h + 4
sth     r1, 4(r2)         #store 2 lsb's from GPR1 in loc.30000100+4
stw     r1, 4(r2)         #store word from GPR 1 in loc. 30000100h+4
std     r1, 4(r2)         #store dw from GPR1 in loc.30000100h + 4
```

Indirect with Index

The load indirect with index takes the following form:

```
lwz     rD, rA, rB
```

where rD is the destination register the operand is loaded into, and rA and rB are the two GPR registers that, added together, yield the effective address that the operand will be read from (in either a memory or I/O segment). Unlike the immediate index, the index is specified in a GPR register rather than encoded within the instruction itself. This means that the index can range up to 4G in a 32-bit processor, or 2^{64} in a 64-bit processor.

Examples of integer loads using indirect addressing with index follow:

```
lis     r2, x'0200'     #place address 02000100h in GPR 2
ori     r2, r2, x'0100'
li      r3, 4           #load index into GPR 3
lbz     r1, r3, r2      #load byte from location 02000100h + 4
                        #into lsb of GPR1 and zero its upper 3 bytes
lhz     r1, r3, r2      #load 2 bytes from location 02000100h + 4
                        #into lsbs of GPR1 and zero upper 2 bytes
lwz     r1, r3, r2      #load word from loc. 02000100h + 4 in GPR 1
ld      r1, r3, r2      #load dw from location 02000100h + 4 in GPR1
```

Examples of integer stores using indirect addressing with index follow:

```
lis     r2, x'0400'     #load 04000000 into GPR 2
ori     r2, r2, x'0100' #or 0100h into lower half of GPR 2
li      r1, x'3210'     #load data 3210 into GPR 1
li      r3, 4           #load index into GPR 3
stb     r1, r3, r2      #store lsb from GPR 1 in loc. 04000100h + 4
sth     r1, r3, r2      #store 2 lsb's from GPR 1 in loc.04000100 + 4
stw     r1, r3, r2      #store word from GPR 1 in loc. 04000100h + 4
std     r1, r3, r2      #store dw from GPR1 in loc. 04000100h + 4
```

Indirect

The integer load with indirect addressing takes the following form:

```
lwz     rD, 0, rB
```

where rD is the destination register the operand is loaded into, and rB holds the effective address that the operand will be read from (in either a memory or I/O segment).

Examples of integer loads using indirect addressing follow:

```
lis     r2, x'3000'      #place address 30000100h in GPR 2
ori     r2, r2, x'0100'
lbz     r1, 0, r2        #load byte from location 30000100h
                         #into lsb of GPR1 and zero its upper 3 bytes
lhz     r1, 0, r2        #load 2 bytes from location 30000100h
                         #into lsbs of GPR1 and zero upper 2 bytes
lwz     r1, 0, r2        #load word from location 30000100h into GPR 1
ld      r1, 0, r2        #load dw from location 30000100h into GPR1
```

Examples of integer stores using indirect addressing with index follow:

```
lis     r2, x'1234'      #load 12340000 into GPR 2
ori     r2, r2, x'0100'  #or 0100 into lower half of GPR 2
li      r1, x'3210'      #load data 3210 into GPR 1
stb     r1, 0, r2        #store lsb from GPR 1 in loc. 12340100h
sth     r1, 0, r2        #store 2 lsb's from GPR 1 in loc.12340100h
stw     r1, 0, r2        #store word from GPR 1 in loc. 12340100h
std     r1, 0, r2        #store dw from GPR1 into location 12340100h
```

Branch Addressing

General

There are four forms of the branch instruction:

- Branch
- Branch Conditional
- Branch Conditional To Count Register
- Branch Conditional To Link Register

The following sections describe each form of the branch instruction.

Branch (unconditional)

The branch instruction can assume any of the following forms (examples of each follow this bullet list):

- **Branch relative with no return** — The programmer specifies an immediate value indicating the direction and magnitude of the branch relative to the address of the branch instruction itself. The maximum immediate value that can be specified is limited by the width of the signed 24-bit field in the instruction used for this purpose. The 24-bit field is extended to a 26-bit field by adding two zeros to its least-significant end. The return address is not saved in the link register, so the target routine cannot return to the caller. Using this branch addressing form, the programmer may branch backward a maximum of 2^{25} locations or forward 2^{25} - 1 locations.
- **Branch relative with return** — Same as branch relative with no return, except that the return address is placed in the link register. The return address is the address of the instruction that follows the branch. It can then be used by the called routine to return to the caller.
- **Branch absolute with no return** — The programmer specifies an immediate value indicating the absolute address to branch to. The maximum immediate value that can be specified is limited by the width of the signed 24-bit field in the instruction used for this purpose. The 24-bit field is extended to a 26-bit field by adding two zeros to its least-significant end. The specified absolute effective address may be in the range from effective address zero – 2^{26}. The return address is not saved in the link register, so the target routine cannot return to the caller.
- **Branch absolute with return** — Same as branch absolute with no return, except that the return address is placed in the link register. The return address is the address of the instruction that follows the branch. It can then be used by the called routine to return to the caller.

Examples:

```
b       offset #branch relative (+- offset) with no return
ba      target #branch absolute to target with no return
bl      offset #branch relative (+- offset) with return in LR
bla     target #branch absolute to target with return in LR
```

Branch Conditional

The branch conditional instruction can assume any of the following forms (examples of each follow this bullet list):

- **Branch conditional relative with no return** — The programmer specifies an immediate value indicating the direction and magnitude of the branch relative to the address of the branch instruction itself. The maximum immediate value that can be specified is limited by the width of the signed 14-bit field in the instruction used for this purpose. The 14-bit field is extended to a 16-bit field by adding two zeros to its least-significant end. Using this branch addressing form, the programmer may branch backward a maximum of 2^{15} locations or forward 2^{15} locations. The return address is not saved in the link register, so the target routine cannot return to the caller.
- **Branch conditional relative with return** — Same as branch relative with no return, except that the return address is placed in the link register. The return address is the address of the instruction that follows the branch. It can then be used by the called routine to return to the caller.
- **Branch conditional absolute with no return** — The programmer specifies an immediate value indicating the absolute address to branch to. The maximum immediate value that can be specified is limited by the width of the signed 14-bit field in the instruction used for this purpose. The 14-bit field is extended to a 16-bit field by adding two zeros to its least-significant end. The specified absolute effective address may be in the range from effective zero – 2^{16}. The return address is not saved in the link register, so the target routine cannot return to the caller.
- **Branch conditional absolute with return** — Same as branch absolute with no return, except that the return address is placed in the link register. The return address is the address of the instruction that follows the branch. It can then be used by the called routine to return to the caller.

Examples:

```
loop:  xxx
       xxx
       bne    loop    #branch conditional relative, no return

loop:  xxx
       xxx
       bnel   error   #branch conditional relative with return
       bnea   x'0100' #branch conditional absolute, no return
       bnela  x'0100' #branch conditional absolute with return
```

Branch Conditional to Count Register

The branch conditional to count register instruction can have either of the following two forms (examples of each follow this bullet list):

- **Branch conditional to count register without return** — The count register, CTR, contains the branch address. The least-significant two bits are always zero because instructions are one word long and are always word aligned in memory. The return address is not saved in the link register, so the target routine cannot return to the caller.
- **Branch conditional to count register with return** — Same as the branch conditional to count register without return, except the address of the instruction that follows the branch is saved in the link register. It can then be used by the called routine to return to the caller.

Examples:

```
bnectr          #branch conditional to address in CTR, no return
bnectrl         #branch conditional to address in CTR with return
```

Branch Conditional to Link Register

The branch conditional to link register instruction can have either of the following two forms (examples of each follow this bullet list):

- **Branch conditional to link register without return** — The link register, LR, contains the branch address. The least-significant two bits are always zero because instructions are one word long and are always word-aligned in memory. The return address is not saved in the link register, so the target routine cannot return to the caller.
- **Branch conditional to link register with return** — Same as the branch conditional to link register without return, except the address of the instruction that follows the branch is saved in the link register. It can then be used by the called routine to return to the caller.

Examples:

```
bnelr  #branch conditional to LR without return
bnelrl #branch conditional to LR with return
```

Instruction Prefetcher Effective Address Generation

Unless directed otherwise by the branch execution unit, the instruction prefetcher forms the effective address of the next instruction by adding four to the start address of the previous instruction. Instructions are naturally word-aligned on address boundaries divisible by four.

Branch Prediction

Unless told otherwise when the instruction is coded, the assembler clears the branch prediction hint bit in the instruction. This has the following effects:

- A backward relative conditional branch is predicted taken
- A forward relative conditional branch is predicted not taken
- A conditional branch to the address contained in LR or CTR is predicted not taken

If the programmer (or the compiler) knows the most-likely outcome of a conditional branch, a suffix may be appended to the conditional branch to force the assembler to set or clear the hint bit. A "+" suffix indicates that the branch is to be taken, while a "-" suffix indicates it should not be taken. This has the following effects:

- If the branch direction is backwards (branch relative backwards), adding the "+" suffix causes the hint bit to be cleared. This causes the processor to predict the branch taken.
- If the branch direction is backwards (branch relative backwards), adding the "-" suffix causes the hint bit to be set. This causes the processor to predict the branch not taken (fall through).
- If the branch direction is branch relative forward or branch absolute, adding the "+" suffix causes the hint bit to be set. This causes the processor to predict the branch taken.
- If the branch direction is branch relative forward or branch absolute, adding the "-" suffix causes the hint bit to be cleared. This causes the processor to predict the branch not taken (fall through).

It should be noted that the PowerPC processor specification does not preclude the inclusion of dynamic branch prediction capability in a processor. When dynamic branch prediction is implemented (as it is in the PPC 604), the processor maintains a branch target buffer, or BTB, in which execution history is continually updated for each conditional branch instruction. The Pentium and PPC 604 processors both use dynamic branch prediction, while the PPC 601 and 603 processors employ static branch prediction.

Chapter 8

The Previous Chapter

The previous chapter describes the addressing modes that may be utilized with load, store and branch instructions. It also provides a brief description of the PowerPC branch prediction mechanism.

This Chapter

This chapter introduces real mode addressing and virtual memory paging.

The Next Chapter

The next chapter discusses cache management issues related to self-modifying code, the icbi instruction and the dcbz instruction.

MMU Disabled — Real Mode Addressing

When the system is first powered up, the system asserts the reset signal to the processor. This presets default values into the processor's register set, including the machine state register, or MSR. The MSR[IR] and MSR[DR] bits are cleared by reset. This disables the MMU so that it will not translate addresses for instruction fetches or data load/stores. When the power has stabilized, the system removes reset from the processor and the processor begins to fetch and execute instructions from memory.

When the MMU is disabled, any effective address submitted to the MMU for translation is used as is — no address translation takes place. The processor is said to be operating in real address mode — all addresses are considered to be memory addresses and the effective memory address is equal to the physical memory address.

Since the MMU is disabled, it cannot perform page table searches or block address translations. This means that it cannot determine what the WIM bit settings are. When operating in real address mode, the processor therefore uses default WIM bit settings of 001b:

- W = 0 instructs the processor to utilize a write-back policy when handling stores.
- I = 0 indicates that all memory accesses are considered to be cacheable: the processor will perform cache lookups and, in the event of a cache miss, will issue a cache block fill request to the processor's system interface. When the requested cache block has been read from memory, it will be placed in the cache.
- M = 1 instructs the processor to assume that other processors may also access the same area of memory. The processor must therefore instruct all other processors to snoop its memory reads and writes and report back snoop results.

The effective memory address space and the physical memory address space are equal in size. In a 32-bit processor both spaces are 4GB in size, while in a 64-bit processor, both are 2^{64} in size. This is illustrated in figures 8-1 and 8-2. It should be noted that the system more than likely has significantly less than the maximum amount of physical memory installed. In other words, although the processor may be capable of addressing up to 4GB of physical memory, the system probably has significantly less physical memory actually installed. Any attempt to access memory that does not physically exist will more than likely result in a fatal error (a machine check) being signaled by the platform.

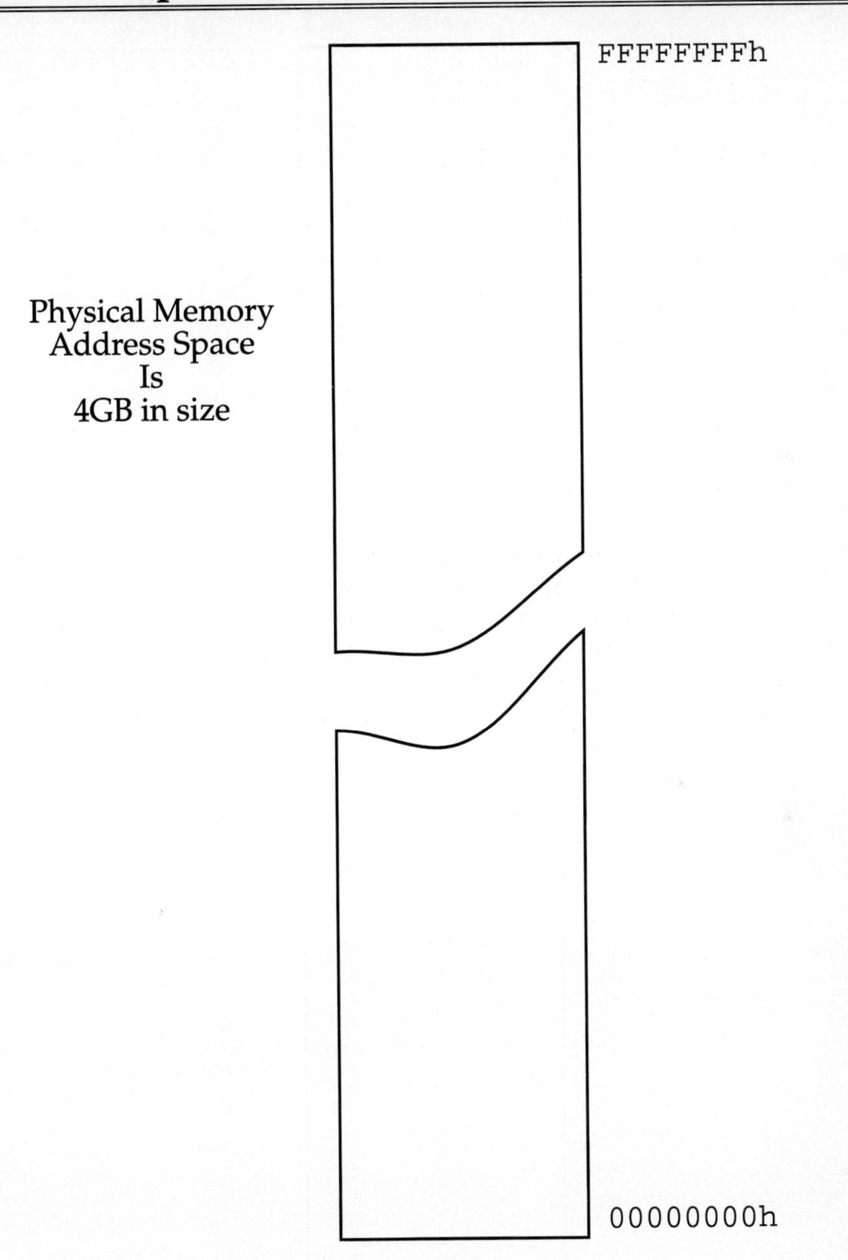

Figure 8-1. Memory Addressable by 32-bit Processor Using Real Mode Addressing

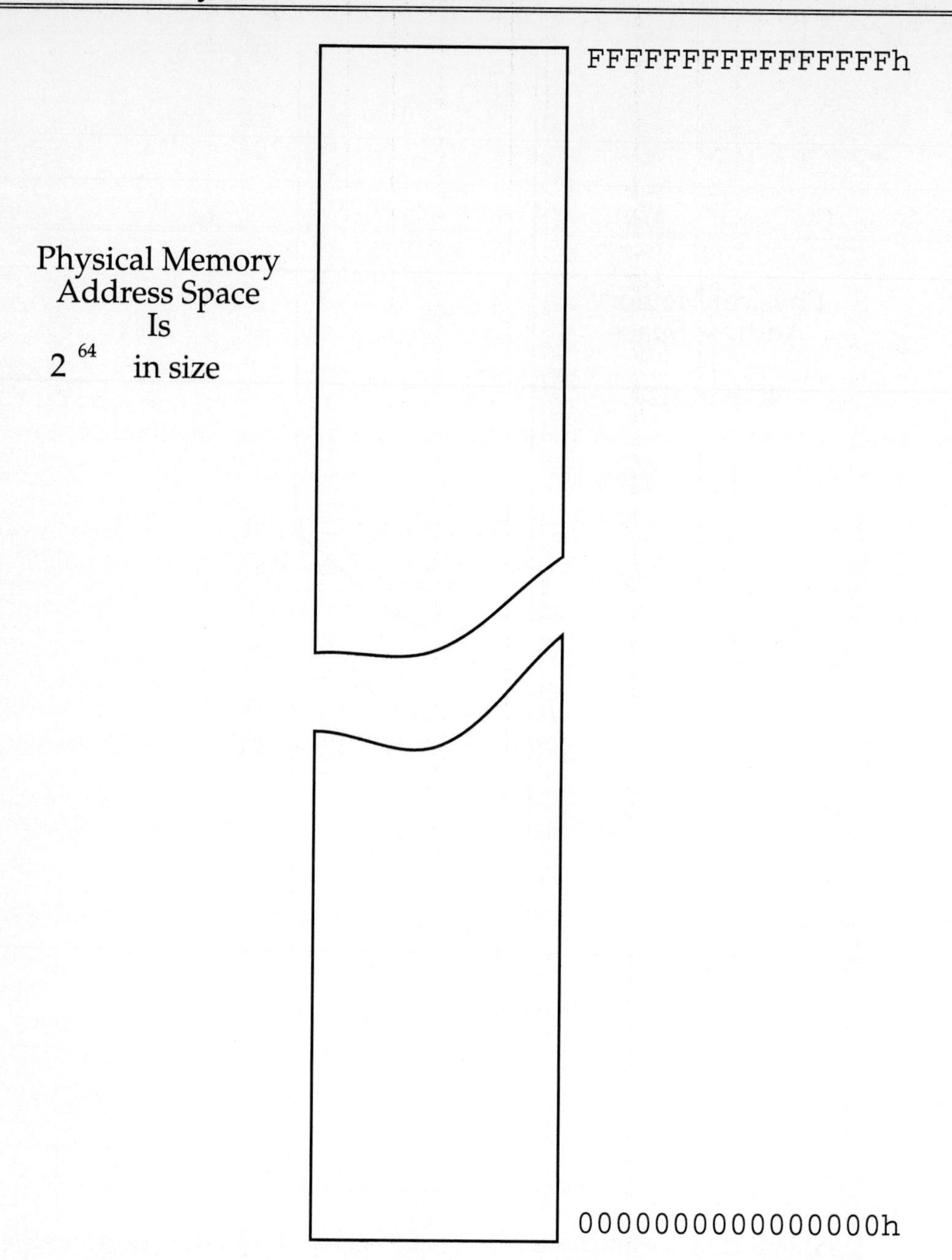

Figure 8-2. Memory Addressable by 64-bit Processor Using Real Mode Addressing

Addressing With MMU Enabled

When the processor is operating at the user privilege level, the applications program generates a 64-bit (with a 64-bit processor operating in 64-bit mode) or 32-bit (in a 32-bit processor or a 64-bit processor operating in 32-bit mode) effective, or logical address. This is submitted to the MMU for translation to the physical memory address before submission to the cache for a lookup. Although the MMU performs address translation for the applications programmer, the registers and tables utilized by the MMU for address translation are not accessible at the user privilege level and are therefore invisible to the applications programmer. These registers and tables may only be accessed by the operating system when the processor is operating at the supervisor privilege level.

The implementation of the paging mechanism is described in the chapters entitled "Address Translation Overview," "Block — Large Memory Region" and "Virtual Paging."

Chapter 9

The Previous Chapter

This chapter introduces real mode addressing and virtual memory paging.

This Chapter

This chapter discusses cache management issues related to self-modifying code, the icbi instruction and the dcbz instruction.

The Next Chapter

The next chapter deals with the negative performance impact introduced when the PowerPC processor is instructed to perform misaligned transfers.

General

The PowerPC architecture doesn't define a specific L1 cache organization, permitting latitude in the design of the PowerPC processor's L1 cache. To ensure that a program will function correctly on all PowerPC processors, however, the programmer should assume that the processor possesses separate code (instruction) and data caches (see figure 9-1).

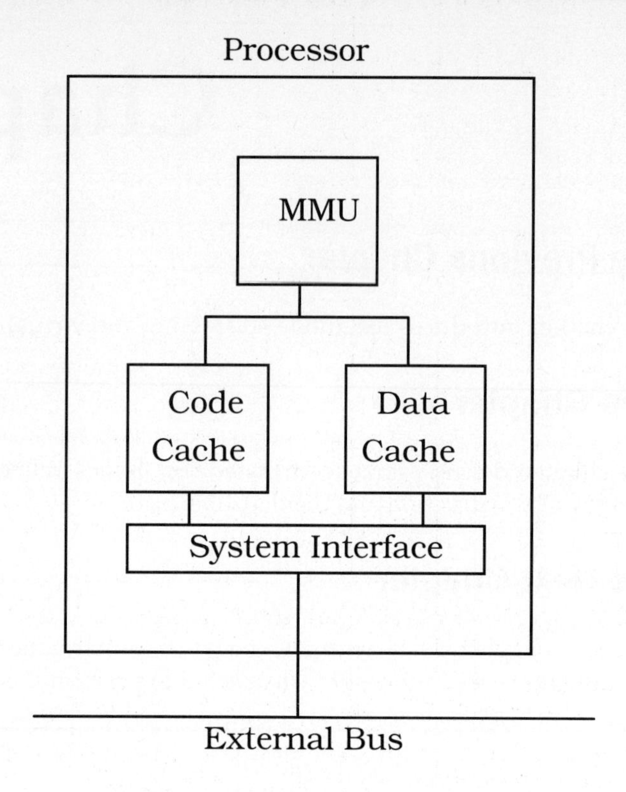

Figure 9-1. Split L1 Code and Data Caches

Self-Modifying Code and the icbi Instruction

A PowerPC processor is not required to update entries in the code cache when stores are performed to the data cache. This being the case, when self-modifying code uses stores to alter code that it has previously read into the data cache (using loads), there is no guarantee that the code cache can observe these alterations. If the target information is currently resident in the instruction cache, it will not reflect the change(s) made by the store(s). When the instruction unit subsequently fetches the code from the code cache, it will be the modified code and the program will not perform according to the programmer's expectations.

It is therefore the programmer's responsibility to ensure that when code modifications are made in the data cache (using stores), the code cache must then be forced to erase unmodified copies of the code that may reside in the code cache. The PowerPC architecture defines a special cache management instruction, icbi (instruction cache block invalidate) that may be used for this purpose. The programmer supplies the effective address as an argument for the icbi instruction. The code cache performs a lookup, and, in the case of a cache hit, the target cache block is erased from the code cache.

isync Instruction Eliminates Stale Code from Pipeline

After code has been modified in the data cache and the stale code has been eliminated from the code cache, the programmer must take into account that the code may have already been prefetched from the code cache and may be in the instruction pipeline. In order to ensure that the stale code is not present in the instruction pipeline, the programmer should execute an isync instruction. This causes the processor to flush all instruction after the isync in the stream to be flushed from the instruction pipeline and prefetch queue.

dcbst Instruction Writes Modified Instruction to Memory

The programmer should also execute a dcbst instruction to force the data cache to write the modified code back to memory. The modified cache block is copied into the MU's posted write buffer. The next time that the instruction prefetcher attempts to access the modified code, it results in a miss on the code cache. The code cache issues a cache block fill read request to the MU. When the MU has a posted memory read and write with the same address, it always performs the memory write transaction on the bus before it performs the memory read. After the write completes, the MU issues a burst read request to the system interface. The processor then performs a burst memory read to read the cache block from memory into the code cache. The altered instruction is routed to the prefetch queue and is dispatched for execution.

If the programmer does not execute the dcbst instruction, the code cache will fetch the stale cache block from memory. The processor does not snoop its own data cache on a miss in its code cache.

Unified Code/Data Cache

A PowerPC processor with a unified code/data cache mixes code and data within one cache. In this type of processor, the icbi instruction need not operate as it would in a processor with separate code and data caches. One option available to the processor designer is to treat it as a no-op. If it isn't treated as a no-op, the processor must follow the following rules:

- The processor will not invalidate a block in the cache that is marked as modified. In the case of code that had been modified in the unified cache via a store instruction, the modified instruction would be erased by this action.
- The processor will not set the changed history bit (in the page table entry). This is because the icbi does not make any change to the copy of the code block in memory. It acts either as a no-op (in the case of a cache miss or a hit on a modified block) or just erases the copy of the block from the code cache (in the case of a hit on a cache block in the exclusive or shared state).
- Although technically the processor should not treat the icbi as a load (in updating the page access history bits by setting the referenced bit to one), it would not violate the architecture to do so.
- If the block addressed by the icbi is within a page or block marked as inaccessible for reads, the system data storage interrupt handler will be invoked. Execution of an icbi within an area of memory where reads are not permitted implies that the programmer is attempting to invalidate code in the cache that never could have been read into the cache.

Considerations for Write-Through Cache

General

Usage of some of the cache management instructions must be modified if the processor's data cache implementation is strictly write-through in nature. These instructions must operate as already defined for a split-cache except as specified in this section. Some of the differences depend on whether the write-through is directly to main memory or to a level two cache.

Write-Through to Main Memory

When executing the dcbz instruction, the processor may invoke the system alignment interrupt handler regardless of the WIM setting. This action is taken because writing the cache block of zeros through to memory violates the intent of the dcbz instruction — to expeditiously set up a block of all zeros in the cache without accessing memory.

When executing the dcbst or the dcbf instructions, no action is necessary. This is true because there is no such thing as a modified block in a write-through cache.

Write-Through to L2 Cache

When executing the dcbz instruction, the processor may invoke the system alignment interrupt handler regardless of the WIM setting. This action is taken because writing the cache block of zeros through to memory violates the intent of the dcbz instruction — to expeditiously set up a block of all zeros in the cache without accessing memory.

If the L2 cache is the interface to main memory for all processors and other mechanisms that access main memory (in other words, it's a look-through cache), that cache can be considered as main memory from the perspective of all processor L1 caches (because it acts as the memory target). Figures 9-2 and 9-3 illustrate the orientation of the lookaside and look through L2 cache, respectively.

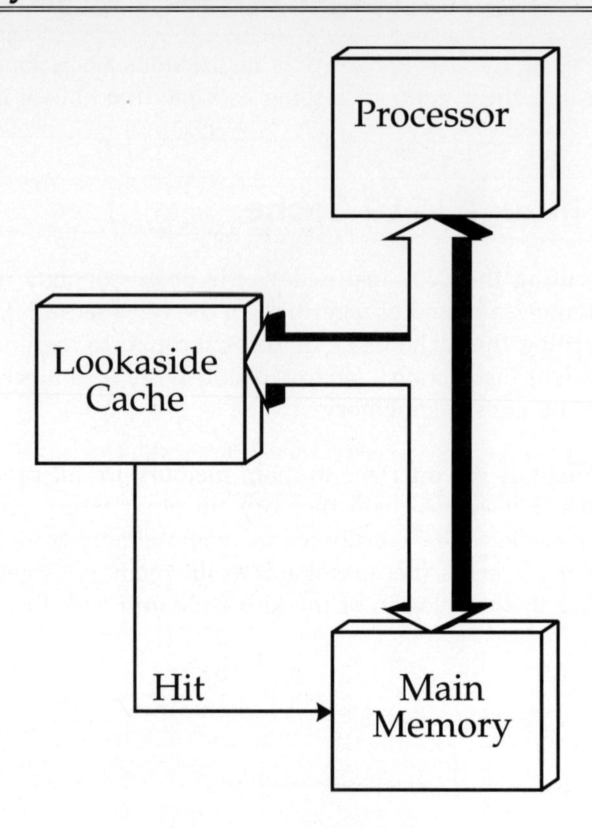

Figure 9-2. The Look-Aside L2 Cache

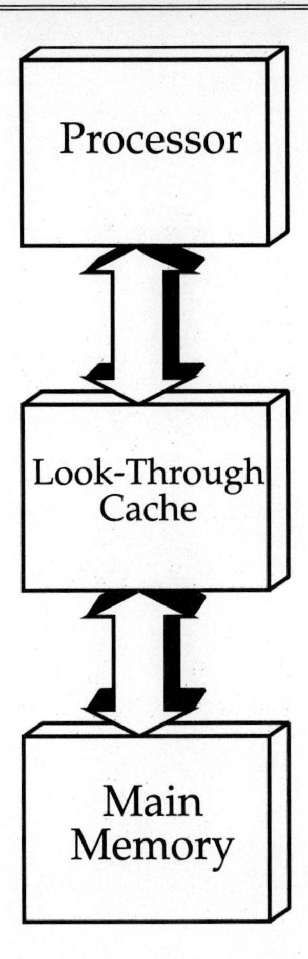

Figure 9-3. The Look-Through L2 Cache

Chapter 10

The Previous Chapter

The previous chapter discusses cache management issues related to self-modifying code, the icbi instruction and the dcbz instruction.

This Chapter

This chapter deals with the negative performance impact introduced when the PowerPC processor is instructed to perform misaligned transfers. It also cautions against the possible side effects that may result if the alignment interrupt handler restarts an instruction that causes multiple accesses.

The Next Chapter

The next chapter describes the PowerPC architecture mechanism (memory semaphores) used to synchronize the accesses of multiple processors to a shared resource (e.g., a data structure in memory).

Transfers Guaranteed to Complete in Single Access

The access of a data item in memory is considered atomic if it can be completed in a single data transfer. In the PowerPC architecture, the following single-register accesses always result in single accesses:

- a byte (8 bit) access, because any single location resides with a word
- a halfword (16 bit) access aligned on a halfword address boundary (address divisible by two), because the entire halfword resides within a single word
- a word (32 bit) access aligned on a word address boundary (address divisible by four)
- a doubleword (64 bit) access aligned on a doubleword address boundary (address divisible by eight)

No other accesses are guaranteed to be atomic. In particular, load/store multiples (versions of the load and store instructions that cause multiple words or strings of bytes to be transferred between the GPR register set and memory or I/O) aren't atomic, nor are floating-point doubleword accesses on a 32-bit implementation (because the doubleword straddles two words).

Misaligned Transfer Performance Impact

General

An aligned access is defined as one where the specified start address of the target operand is a multiple of the operand size. As an example, assume that a load or store must access memory to transfer a word (four bytes) between one of the processor's GPR registers and memory and that the specified start address is divisible by four. This word access is aligned. The same would be true for:

- a doubleword (eight bytes) transfer starting at an address divisible by eight
- a halfword (two bytes) transfer starting at an address divisible by two
- a single-byte transfer starting at any byte address

When the processor performs a transfer and it is aligned, performance (in other words, transfer speed) is optimal. When the processor must access an operand that crosses an address boundary, it can result in decreased efficiency.

Crossing Cache Block Boundary

If a transfer crosses a cache block boundary, the worst-case performance scenario would be a double miss on the cache. The processor would have to perform two cache block burst fill memory read transfers to get the two cache blocks on board the L1 cache. It should be noted that the cache block size for the processor's L1 cache is processor design-dependent. If the application programmer wishes to know the processor's cache block size, the information must be requested from the operating system. The processor version register, or PVR, may only be read from while the processor is operating at the supervisor privilege level (MSR[PR] = 0]). The operating system can check the PVR, determine the processor type, and return the cache block size. The method used to do this is operating system-specific.

Crossing Page Boundary

If a transfer crosses a page boundary (a 4KB address boundary), the worst-case performance scenario would be a double page fault (refer to the chapter entitled "Virtual Paging" for a detailed description of page faults). This would necessitate two 4KB reads from mass storage in order to fetch the two target pages into memory before the data transfer can take place. Since mass storage devices are typically mechanical in nature, the resulting performance hit can be enormous.

Crossing Block Boundary

If the transfer crosses a block boundary (as defined in a BAT register), a page fault may be incurred (because a block boundary is also a page boundary). This could necessitate a mass storage read before the data transfer can take place.

Crossing Segment Boundary

If the transfer crosses a segment boundary (an address divisible by 256MB), a page fault may be incurred (because a segment boundary is also a page boundary). This could necessitate a mass storage read before the data transfer can take place.

Dealing with Instruction Restart

General

If a misaligned memory access crosses a page, memory block, or memory segment boundary and the access rights (as defined by attribute bits in a page table entry or a block definition register) change or the processor experiences a page fault, an interrupt may cause the access to be aborted after part of it has already been performed. In the course of handling the interrupt, the interrupt handler may alter the access rights to permit the access and then restart the instruction again (by executing the rfi instruction at the end of the interrupt handler). This would cause the byte or bytes that have already been read or written to be read or written a second time.

Example Problem

Assuming that the area of memory is occupied by a series of memory-mapped I/O ports and a boundary is crossed, instruction restart would cause the first set of accesses (prior to the interrupt) to be re-executed. This would cause double accesses to the first series of memory-mapped I/O ports and could result in spurious operation of the I/O device.

Rules

In this type of scenario, the following rules apply:

- A single-register instruction that accesses an aligned operand need never be restarted (because it doesn't cross any boundaries).
- A single-register instruction that accesses an unaligned operand may be restarted if the access crosses a page, memory block or memory segment boundary.
- Load/store multiple and move assist instructions (versions of the load and store instructions used to transfer strings of bytes between the GPR register set and memory or I/O) may be restarted if, in the course of the transfer, a page, memory block, or memory segment boundary is crossed.

The programmer should assume that any unaligned access in an ordinary memory segment might be restarted and plan accordingly.

Chapter 11

The Previous Chapter

The previous chapter discussed the negative performance impact introduced when the PowerPC processor is instructed to perform misaligned transfers. It also cautioned against the possible side effects that may result if the alignment interrupt handler restarts an instruction that causes multiple accesses.

This Chapter

This chapter describes the PowerPC architecture mechanism (memory semaphores) used to synchronize the accesses of multiple processors to a shared resource (e.g., a data structure in memory).

The Next Chapter

The next chapter describes the mechanism provided to the PowerPC operating system programmer to specify the caching-related rules within each area of memory (the WIM bits). It also discusses the issue of guarded memory and the G bit.

Special Note

All instances of the following two instructions in this chapter are immediately followed by a large black dot:

1. stwcx•
2. stdcx•

The large black dot represents a period and has been illustrated in this manner to ensure that the reader doesn't confuse it with the period at the end of a sentence. A load or a store instruction followed immediately by a period suffix indicates that the condition register (CR) is updated and the overflow bit (OV) in the CR is enabled.

Protecting Access to Shared Resource

In some circumstances a processor must perform a series of two or more accesses to a particular area of memory (for example, a data structure) with the assurance that no other processor has accessed the same memory until the processor's series of accesses have been completed. In other words, the processor needs to perform an atomic series of accesses within the data structure with the assurance that no other processor has interfered with the data structure in between this processor's individual accesses to it.

The following is an example of a situation that would require this ability to lock out other masters from accessing a particular target. Assume that the host system is running multiple tasks under a multitasking operating system (such as OS/2, Unix, or Windows NT). A bit in a memory location is used to indicate the availability of a shared resource, such as the example data structure in memory. This is referred to as a memory semaphore. When a task needs to access the data structure, it must read from the memory location that protects access to the structure and check the state of the semaphore bit that indicates the structure's availability. If the semaphore bit is a zero, this indicates that the structure is available. The task would then set the bit to a one and write the byte back into the memory location. In this manner, the task has reserved the resource (the data structure) for itself and may then initiate a print job without fear that another task will attempting to access the data structure.

If any other task should check the state of the respective semaphore bit while the first task is performing accesses within the data structure, the state of the semaphore bit will tell it that the data structure is currently unavailable. The second task must therefore periodically check the semaphore that controls access to the data structure to determine when the first task has relinquished ownership. When the first task has its accesses within the data structure, it must read from the memory location, set the semaphore bit back to a zero and write the resulting byte back into the memory location thereby marking the data structure available again.

Semaphore Contention

Assume that task **A** is running on processor **A** and task **B** is running on processor "B." Task **A** must access the shared data structure. The programmer executes a load instruction to read the semaphore from memory to test and possibly update it. Using the bus to communicate with memory, processor **A** initiates and completes a memory read bus cycle. Task **A** checks the state of the semaphore bit and it is zero, indicating that the data structure is currently available. Task **A** sets the bit to a one in processor **A**'s register (to mark the data structure unavailable to other tasks) and then executes a store instruction to placed the updated semaphore back in memory. The store causes processor **A** to requests and use the bus to perform the memory write bus cycle.

At this time, the task running on processor **B** also wants access to the data structure, so it executes a load instruction to read the same semaphore location from memory for testing. As a result, processor **B** requests access to the bus and is granted access before processor **A** (because it has higher priority or is next in line for a bus access). Processor **B** then initiates a memory read bus cycle to read the semaphore from memory. Task **B** determines that the semaphore bit is zero, indicating that the data structure is available. It flips the bit to a one and then performs a store to update the semaphore in memory (the same location that processor **A** will update when it regains access to the bus). When processor **B**'s memory write bus cycle completes, processor **B** surrenders the bus. The bus arbiter then grants the bus to processor "A." Processor **A** then performs the memory write bus cycle to update the same memory location.

Tasks **A** and **B** now each believe that the data structure belongs solely to them and mayhem will result. This situation could be prevented if processor **A** were able to perform the memory read, the bit test and set in the register and the memory write as an atomic, indivisible operation with the assurance that no other master has accessed the same area of memory until the atomic series of accesses has been completed.

PowerPC Architecture Solution

The PowerPC architecture instruction set provides a mechanism that operates in the following manner.

Semaphore Read and Establishing Reservation

The processor performs a read from the target memory semaphore using a special form of the load instruction, the lwarx (load word and reserve indexed) or the ldarx (load doubleword and reserve indexed; only implemented in a 64-bit processor). The contents of the target memory location is loaded into one of the GPR registers.

The processor executing the lwarx or ldarx internally latches the lwarx instruction's target address into a reservation buffer. This indicates the start address of the reserved area. The size of the reserved area is the cache block size (processor implementation-dependent).

The method that the processor uses to communicate the performance of the semaphore read and the establishment of the reservation is processor implementation-dependent. The PPC601 processor uses the following methods to communicate this information to the external environment:

- It asserts its reservation output, RSRV#, indicating that the reservation has been established by the performance of the memory read.
- If the semaphore is in a cacheable area of memory and results in an L1 cache miss, the processor initiates a four beat burst memory read atomic transaction (atomic indicates that a semaphore is being read from memory) to read the cache block containing the semaphore from memory.
- If the semaphore is in a cacheable area of memory and the semaphore is already in the L1 cache, no bus transaction is necessary, but the processor still asserts its RSRV# output.
- If the semaphore is in a non-cacheable area of memory, the processor performs a single-beat memory read atomic transaction.

The actions taken by external logic in recognition of the assertion of RSRV# or the performance of the memory read atomic transaction is platform design-dependent. The following are possibilities:

- External logic will take no action to the semaphore access performed by the processor. This is the worst-case scenario, because it means that the external hardware will not prevent other bus master from using the bus or from accessing the memory semaphore. When dealing with memory semaphores, the programmer must program to this model (i.e., always plan worst-case).
- The bus arbiter will detect RSRV# asserted and will refuse to give the bus to any other bus master until RSRV# is deasserted. In other words, the arbiter responds by establishing a bus lock. This ensures that no other bus master will be permitted to access the semaphore while the processor is performing the read/modify/write operation on the semaphore. Generally speaking, this is a wasteful approach — in an effort to prevent any bus master from storing into a specific cache block in memory, all bus masters will be prevented from using the bus for any reason whatever.

- If the processor performs a read atomic transaction to read the semaphore from memory (non-cacheable or not in cache), the memory target could be designed to lock just the cache block being accessed. The arbiter would also note which bus master has performed the read and established the lock. If any other bus master attempts to access any other cache block in the memory target, it will be permitted to do so. If a bus master other than the one that established the lock attempts to access the locked block, it will be issued a retry. Only the master that established the lock will be permitted to access the locked block. When the master has performed the memory write atomic to update the semaphore, the memory target will unlock the block.

Bit Test and Set Operation

Having established the reservation and fetched the memory-based semaphore into a GPR register for testing, the processor performs a bit test and set operation on a bit or bits within the register to determine if the bit (or bits) is already set. If it isn't, the processor sets the bit in the register.

Another Processor Cancels Reservation

If another processor (or mechanism capable of performing memory writes, such as a DMA controller) was able to acquire the bus and perform a store into any location within the reserved area after the performance of the lwarx but before the updated semaphore is stored back to memory, the processor that established the reservation snoops the store transaction performed by the other processor. If the target address is within the range of the reserved area, the processor deasserts its RSRV# output and internally clears the reservation and its reservation buffer. This could happen if the arbiter or memory target is not designed to prevent another master from accessing the reserved area.

Semaphore Update

Having completed the bit test and set operation, the processor executes a store word conditional, stwcx•, or a store doubleword conditional instruction, stdcx• (only implemented in a 64-bit processor), to update the memory-based semaphore. Before actually performing the store into memory to update the memory-based semaphore, the stwcx• instruction first checks to determine if the reservation is still intact. If it is, the data is stored into memory and the reservation is then cleared. When the PPC601 performs the store caused execution of the stwcx• or stdcx•, it takes the following action:

- If the store is in a cacheable area of memory (I = 0) and results in a store hit on a cache block in the exclusive state, the word or doubleword is updated in the L1 cache and the RSRV# output is deasserted.
- If the store is in a cacheable (I = 0), write-back area of memory (W = 0) with M = 1 and it results in a store hit on a cache block in the shared state, the processor performs a kill transaction to kill copies of the cache block in other system caches. The word or doubleword is then updated in the L1 cache, the state of the cache block is changed from shared to modified and the RSRV# output is deasserted.
- If the store is in a cacheable (I = 0), write-through (W = 1) area of memory and results in a store hit on the L1 cache, the processor performs a single-beat memory write atomic transaction to update the semaphore in memory. It also deasserts RSRV#.
- If the store is in a cacheable (I = 0), write-back area of memory (W = 0) with M = 1 and it results in a store miss on the L1 cache, the processor performs a read-with-intent-to-modify atomic transaction to read the cache block containing the semaphore into the L1 cache and then store into it and mark it modified. It then deasserts RSRV#.
- If the store is in a non-cacheable area of memory (I = 1), the processor performs a single-beat memory write atomic transaction to write the word or doubleword into memory. It then deasserts RSRV#.

When the semaphore update has been successfully completed, the EQ bit in field CR0 of the CR (conditional register) is set, indicating that the data was successfully stored.

When Update Is Unsuccessful

If the reservation was cleared before the processor executed its stwcx• when another processor (or other mechanism, such as a DMA controller) stored into the reserved area, the equal bit (EQ) in CR0 is cleared and the store to memory does not take place (because another entity has already updated the memory-based semaphore). If this is the case, the processor was unsuccessful in acquiring ownership of the data structure (shared resource) and must periodically perform the lwarx, bit test and set, stwcx• sequence until it completes successfully. Only then has the processor acquired ownership of the data structure and may then perform accesses within it.

An Example

Step One — Establish Resource Lock

When the programmer wishes to acquire ownership of a shared resource, a call is made to the lock_req routine (see listing that follows). An instruction-by-instruction description of the routine follows the listing. A listing and explanation of the test_and_set routine follows.

```
lock_req:                              #Lock request entry point
        li      r4,1                   #r4 set to lock value
                                       #add code here to save LR contents
loop:   bl      test_and_set           #Call test and set routine
        bne-    loop                   #If already locked, try again
        isync                          #Stall stream until all
                                       #previous instructions have
                                       #completed without causing an
                                       #interrupt.Also see notes.
                                       #add code to restore return address to LR
        blr                            #Return to caller
```

1. ***li r4, 1*** — GPR 4 with has the immediate value one loaded into it. This is the value that the test_and_set routine will attempt to store into the memory semaphore to mark the resource as locked to other tasks.
2. ***bl test_and_set*** — Branch and link to the test_and_set routine. The processor branches to the test_and_set routine and stores the return address (of the cmpwi instruction) in the link register.
3. ***bne- loop*** — If the equal bit (EQ) in CR0 isn't set to one, branch back to the loop label. On exit from test_and_set, the equal bit is cleared to zero if the semaphore had already been locked by another task (semaphore contained a non-zero value when read by the test_and_set routine). If this is the case, branch back to the loop label and keep trying until test_and_set is successful in acquiring ownership of the resource (it was successful in detecting the semaphore cleared to zero and then setting it to a non-zero value). If the equal bit is set to one on return from test_and_set, resource acquisition has been successful. Go to the next instruction.
4. ***isync*** — Execution of the isync instruction causes the processor to stall until all previous instructions have completed to the point where they will not cause interrupts. isync is primarily intended for situations where an

instruction loads a new value into a segment or BAT register with MMU address translation enabled (MSR[IT] and/or MSR[DT] are set to one) and the target addresses specified in subsequent load or store instructions must be translated. In a superscalar architecture, the instruction that alters the segment or BAT register and subsequent loads or stores can be dispatched and begin execution in parallel. In this case, the isync instruction should be placed in the instruction stream after the segment or BAT register update and before the subsequent instructions. When executed, it causes the processor to stall until all instructions prior to the isync have completed all updates to registers (i.e., segment or BAT register) and flushes all instructions that follow the isync from the prefetch queue as well as from any of the execution units that they may already been dispatched to for execution. The flush is necessary to avoid the possibility that a load or store that follows the isync may use the old segment or BAT register information to perform an address translation. When the isync has completed, the instructions that follow the isync are refetched and are dispatched. **In this case, the isync has been included to stall execution until the *bne- loop* conditional branch has been resolved.**

5. ***blr*** — Branch to return address in link register — in other words, return to calling program (exit from lock_req).

The following is a listing of the test_and_set routine. An instruction-by-instruction description of the test_and_set routine follows the listing.

```
test_and_set:                    #Test_and_set entry point
loop:   lwarx   r5,0,r3          #Read semaphore, set reservation
        cmpwi   r5,0             #Chk for semaphore already locked
        bne-    loop             #Exit loop if already locked (=1)
        stwcx.  r4,0,r3          #Attempt to set lock
        bne-    loop             #If reservation blown, try again
        isync
exit:   blr                      #Return to caller.
                                 #EQ = 1, success
                                 #EQ = 0, failure
```

1. ***loop: lwarx r5, 0, r3*** — On entry to test_and_set, GPR 3 should contain the address of the semaphore to be tested. The load word and reserve instruction reads the semaphore word from the address specified in GPR 3 in places it in GPR 5 for examination. Execution of the lwarx also causes the processor to latch the cache block-aligned address into the internal

reservation register and to set its reservation bit. The PPC 601 processor also asserts its RSRV# output.

2. ***cmpwi r5, 0*** — The integer unit compares the semaphore value loaded into GPR 5 by the previous instruction to the value zero. If GPR 5 contains the value zero, the equal bit CR0 is set to one, indicating that another task has not yet established a lock on the semaphore (by setting it to a non-zero value). If GPR 5 contains a non-zero value, the equal bit in CR0 is cleared, indicating that another task has already established ownership of the lock and the shared resource that it guards access to.
3. ***bne exit*** — If the compare indicated that the semaphore has already been set to a non-zero value by another task (the semaphore loaded into GPR 5 is not zero), branch to the exit label and return to the calling program (the lock_req routine). If the compare indicates that the semaphore is currently set to zero, no other task has established ownership of the semaphore yet. The processor falls through to the instruction that follows this one.
4. ***stwcx. r4, 0, r3*** — The processor attempts to store the non-zero value supplied (in GPR 4) by the caller into the semaphore word in memory. The store will take place only if the reservation is still intact (i.e., no other processor has successfully performed a store into the cache block within which the semaphore resides). The processor will set the equal bit in CR0 to one if the store is successful or will clear it to zero if unsuccessful. Successful performance of the store will clear the processor's reservation. If performed to an area of memory currently reserved by another processor, it will also clear that processor's reservation.
5. ***bne- loop*** — The programmer determines if the processor was able to successfully perform the store and write a non-zero value into the semaphore in memory. If the store was not successful (because some other processor successfully performed a store within the granularity of the reserved cache block), the cleared state of the equal bit in CR0 causes the processor to branch back to the loop label. The programmer spins in this loop until it is successful in setting the semaphore to a non-zero value or until another processor has successfully set the semaphore to a non-zero value.
6. ***exit: blr*** — The processor branches to the instruction pointed to by the link register, returning to the caller. On return to the caller, the equal bit in CR0 will be set to one if test_and_set was successful in setting the semaphore to a non-zero value, thereby establishing a lock on the resource. The equal bit is cleared if another task established the lock first.

Step Two — Access the Resource

Having acquired exclusive ownership of the shared resource, the programmer can perform a series of loads and/or stores to the resource it has gained ownership of.

Step Three — Unlock Resource

When the programmer has completed all accesses to the resource, a call is performed to the unlock_req routine. This routine is listed below and is followed by an instruction-by-instruction explanation.

```
unlock_req:                       #Unlock request entry point
        sync                      #Stall until all updates to
                                  #shared resource (data
                                  #structure) have been
                                  #performed in memory.
        li      r1, 0             #r1 = 0 (used to clear lock)
        stw     r1, 0 (r3)        #Unconditional update of
                                  #memory semaphore to clear
                                  #lock.
        blr                       #return to caller
```

1. ***sync*** — It is generally required that all stores performed to a shared memory data structure be performed on the external bus before the current resource owner gives up ownership of the resource. This ensures that all changes to the data structure are visible to all processors. The sync instruction forces the MU to perform all posted memory writes on the external bus before program execution is permitted to move beyond the sync instruction.
2. ***li r1, 0*** — prepare to clear semaphore lock. The zero value in GPR 1 will subsequently be stored into the semaphore word in memory.
3. ***stw r1, 0 (r3)*** — Clear the semaphore word to zero (on entry to unlock_req, GPR 3 contains the semaphore address).
4. ***blr*** — Perform a branch to link register to return to the caller.

OS Supplies Semaphore Primitives

It should be noted that applications programs typically call semaphore test-and-set primatives supplied by the operating system. They do not access semaphores directly.

Chapter 12

The Previous Chapter

The previous chapter describes the PowerPC architecture mechanism (memory semaphores) used to synchronize the accesses of multiple processors to a shared resource (e.g., a data structure in memory).

This Chapter

This chapter describes the mechanism provided to the PowerPC operating system programmer to specify the caching-related rules within each area of memory (the WIM bits). It also discusses the issue of guarded memory and the G bit.

The Next Chapter

The next chapter discusses the PowerPC processor's ability to post memory reads and writes. As a direct result of this ability, the processor may not perform the posted memory accesses in the same order as that specified by the programmer. Since it is sometimes crucial that the accesses be performed in the specified order, this chapter discusses the three methods that can be used to enforce strict ordering of memory accesses:

- The sync instruction.
- The eieio instruction.
- Performing a read after each write.

Introduction

Whenever a memory access is initiated by the instruction unit or by one of the execution units, the logical, or effective, address is submitted to the MMU for translation to a physical memory address. Either the memory block or page address translation mechanism in the MMU will perform the translation. Along with mapping the logical address to a physical memory address, the

MMU obtains the WIM bits from a block address translation (BAT) register or from a page table entry (PTE). The BAT registers and the PTEs are set up by the operating system. These bits define the operating rules when performing accesses within a memory page or block.

The location of the WIM and the G bits in a page table entry or the block address translation registers can be found in the chapters entitled "Block — Large Memory Region" and "Virtual Paging."

It should be noted that references to the GBL# (Global), SHD# (Shared), BR# (Bus Request) and ARTRY# (Address Retry) bus signals in this chapter's text are processor-specific. The bus architecture is processor implementation-specific and is not part of the PowerPC architecture specification. The exact mechanisms used by a particular PowerPC processor for these functions may vary from processor to processor.

Write-Through (W) Bit

General

The W bit is the write-through bit. The operating system uses the W bit to define how this processor's data cache deals with memory writes (stores) within this page or memory block. W = 0 instructs the cache to use a write-back policy in handling stores, while W = 1 instructs it to use a write-through policy.

Write-Through Policy

When a store miss occurs within a write-through page or block, the processor initiates a memory write transaction on the its external bus and the data is stored in memory.

When a store hit occurs on a cache block within a write-through page or block, the data is updated in the cache and the processor initiates a memory write transaction on the its external bus and the data is also stored in memory.

Write-Back Policy

Store Miss

When WI = 00 (caching enabled and write-back policy), the processor uses an allocate-on-write policy. In other words, if a store misses the cache, the processor initiates a read with intent to modify, or rwitm, transaction. This will read the entire cache block from memory and place it in the cache.

If M = 0, other processors do not access the page or block (or, if they do, it is not required that they be aware of changes that other processors may be making to their own local copies of the cache block) and the read therefore isn't snooped by other caching entities (this processor does not assert GBL# to instruct them to report snoop results). Upon completing the rwitm, the processor stores the data in its cache and immediately permits the store to modify the cache block and marks it as modified. In other words, the cache block goes from the invalid state directly to the modified state.

If M = 1, other processors may also access the target memory page or block. GBL# is asserted by this processor during the rwitm and the read is snooped by other caching entities. If any of them experience a hit on the target cache block in the shared or exclusive state, they will invalidate them. This action is taken because the processor that originated the rwitm has indicated that it intends to immediately modify the cache block upon acquiring it.

If any of the snoopers experience a hit on a modified cache block, a retry is issued to the processor that initiated the rwitm. The snooper then acquires the bus and performs a snoop push back to deposit the modified cache block into memory. Upon conclusion of the push back, the snooper invalidates its copy. The other processor reinitiates the rwitm and the transaction is snooped again, but neither SHD# nor ARTRY# is asserted because the cache block doesn't exists in any other caches. The processor stores the data in its cache and immediately permits the store to modify the cache block and marks it as modified. In other words, the cache block goes from the invalid state directly to the modified state.

Store Hit on Cache Block in Exclusive State

If M = 0 and the target cache block is in the exclusive state, the store is performed into the cache block and the cache block state is changed from exclusive to modified.

If M = 1, the processor doesn't have to invalidate copies of the cache block in other caches (because this cache has an exclusive copy of the cache block). The store is performed into the cache block and the cache block state is changed from exclusive to modified.

Store Hit on Cache Block in Shared State

If M = 0, other processors do not access the target page or block in memory. The processor therefore doesn't have to kill copies of the cache block in other caches before modifying the cache block. This combination really doesn't make sense. If no other processor had accessed this area of memory, then the cache block would be exclusive rather than shared.

If M = 1 and the target cache block is in the shared state, the processor must cause all copies of the target cache block in other caches to be invalidated before the store is performed into the cache block and the cache block state is changed from exclusive to modified. This is accomplished (on the 601 bus) by performing a kill transaction.

Store Hit on Cache Block in Modified State

If the target cache block is in the cache and has already been modified, the store updates the cache block and it remains in the modified state. Since it has already been marked modified, the processor doesn't have to issue a kill transaction (even if M = 1) to clear the cache block out of other caches (because this processor already killed all other copies when it first modified the cache block).

Cache Inhibit (I) Bit

The processor uses the I bit to define whether or not this processor's data cache keeps copies of data read (loaded) from this page or memory block. I = 0 specifies caching enabled, while I = 1 specifies caching inhibited.

Memory Coherency (M) Bit

General

The operating system sets M to zero if the page or memory block isn't accessed by any other processor/caching entity (or, if they do, it is not required that they be aware of changes that other processors may be making to their own local copies of the cache block). Conversely, the operating system will set a page or memory block's M to one if multiple processors/caching entities may access the page or memory block.

Page or Block Local to This Processor (M = 0)

In the case where M = 0, the operating system considers the page or memory block to be local to this processor. When the processor first attempts to read a data item that has not previously been read from the target page or memory block, it experiences an L1 cache read miss. In response, it initiates a burst memory read to copy the cache block from external memory and place it into its cache. During the address phase of this burst read transaction, it deasserts its GBL# output, indicating that the access is to an area of memory that is local to the processor initiating the burst read. The deassertion of GBL# instructs all other processors/caching entities that they shouldn't snoop the transaction (because they don't access this area of memory or, if they do, it is not required that they be aware of changes that other processors may be making to their own local copies of the cache block). GBL# reflects the state of M.

Since no other processor/caching entity has a copy of the cache block being read, none of them will assert SHD# and/or ARTRY#. Sampling SHD# deasserted instructs the processor performing the burst read to store the cache block in its cache in the exclusive state. Any subsequent store that the processor performs to any location within this cache block entry causes the cache block to be updated. If the W bit = 0, the data is not written through to memory and the cache block transitions from the exclusive to the modified state. If the W bit = 1, the data is written through to memory, but GBL# is not asserted (because M = 0), so the memory update is not snooped by any other processor/caching entity.

Page or Block Accessed by Other Processors (M = 1)

General

In the case where M = 1, the operating system is indicating that the page or memory block may be accessed by multiple processors. When the processor first attempts to read a data item that has not previously been read from the target page or memory block, it experiences a cache read miss. In response, it initiates a burst memory read to copy the cache block from external memory and place it into its cache. During the address phase of this burst read transaction, it asserts its GBL# output, indicating that the access is to an area of memory that is accessed by other processors/caching entities. The assertion of GBL# instructs all other processors/caching entities to snoop the transaction (because they may share this area of memory) and to report the snoop results to this processor on SHD# and ARTRY#. GBL# reflects the state of M.

One of the following will result when the other processors/caching entities snoop the transaction.

Snoop Miss

If all of the snoopers are free to snoop right now and none has a copy of the cache block being read, none of them will assert SHD# or ARTRY#. This tells the processor performing the burst read that no one else has a copy of the target cache block, so, when it has completed the burst read operation, it stores the cache block in its cache in the exclusive state.

Snooper(s) Busy — Try Again Later

If any of the snoopers are busy and cannot snoop right now and no other snooper has a copy of the cache block, just ARTRY# will be asserted (by the busy snoopers). This tells the processor that initiated the burst read that it would be dangerous to proceed with the read because the entity (or entities) that can't snoop right now might have a modified copy of the cache block. If it proceeds with the read, therefore, it might fetch stale information from memory. In response to the retry, the processor should wait one clock before retrying the read.

Snoop Hit on Modified Cache Block

If any snooper has a copy of the cache block in the modified state, it asserts ARTRY# and SHD# and BR#. The combination of ARTRY# and SHD# indicates that the snooper has a copy of the cache block in the modified state. It is instructing the processor that initiated the burst read to retry the read one clock later. The snooper also asserted BR# to indicate that it requires access to the bus in order to burst write the modified cache block into memory. This is known as a snoop push back operation. After it completes the burst write, it changes the state of its copy of the cache block from modified to shared (because the master that experienced the retry will subsequently retry the read and place the block into its own cache). When the burst write is performed to deposit the modified cache block into memory, all other entities snoop the transaction (because it asserts GBL#). The cache block just deposited into memory is now a mirror image of memory (so the cache block is no longer modified, just shared). The processor that received the retry then reacquires the bus (from the bus arbiter) and restarts the burst read. The transaction is again snooped by all entities. This time, however, the processor that wrote the cache block to memory only asserts SHD# (because the cache block is no longer marked modified). This instructs the processor performing the burst read to proceed and to store the cache block in its cache in the shared state.

Snoop Hit on Clean Cache Block

If one or more of the snoopers has a copy of the cache block in the exclusive or shared state, it asserts SHD#. The assertion of SHD# informs the processor performing the burst read to store the cache block in the shared state. Assuming that none of the snoopers has a modified copy of the cache block, ARTRY# will not be asserted. If a snooper has a copy in the exclusive state, it changes the state of its copy from exclusive to shared (because, at the conclusion of the burst read, the other processor will also have a copy of the cache block).

M = 1 and Write-Through Page or Block

The cache would accept the data supplied by the store instruction and would also propagate the write data through to the bus as a memory write transaction (because W = 1) with GBL# asserted (because M = 1). The entire cache block isn't written to memory, just the byte or bytes being updated by the store instruction. Other caching entities will snoop the transaction (because GBL# is asserted). In the event of a hit on one or more of their caches on the cache block in the shared state, each will mark its copy invalid. None of them would have copies in the modified state, because there isn't a modified state in a write-through area of memory. None of them would have a copy in the exclusive state because this cache has a copy of the block (so they would be sharing it).

Supported WIM Bit Settings

Table 12-1 defines the acceptable settings of the WIM bits for a page or memory block.

Table 12-1. WIM Bit Settings

W	I	M	Description
0	0	0	Caching is enabled within the page or memory block (I = 0). A write-back policy may be used to handle stores within the page or memory block (W = 0). The cache need not inform other caches external to the processor of changes made to the cache block (M = 0). Other processors do not have to snoop this processor's memory accesses.
0	0	1	Caching is enabled within the page or memory block (I = 0). A write-back policy may be used to handle stores within the page or memory block (W = 0). The processor must inform other caches external to the processor (M = 1) regarding changes made within this page or memory block.
0	1	0	Caching is inhibited within this page or memory block (I = 1). All loads and stores within this page or memory block bypass the cache and access memory (because caching is inhibited). The processor doesn't instruct other caches in the system to snoop its memory accesses within this page or memory block (M = 0). Since caching is inhibited, the setting of the W bit has no effect.
0	1	1	Caching is inhibited within this page or memory block (I = 1). All loads and stores bypass the cache and access memory. The processor instructs other caches in the system to snoop its memory accesses within this page or memory block (M = 1). Since caching is inhibited, the setting of the W bit has no effect.
1	0	0	Caching is enabled within this page or memory block (I = 0). All load and store hits access the cache and all store hits also update memory (W = 1). The processor doesn't instruct other caches in the system to snoop its memory accesses within this page or memory block (M = 0).
1	0	1	Caching is enabled within this page or memory block (I = 0). All load and store hits access the cache and all store hits also update memory (W = 1). The processor instructs other caches in the system to snoop its memory accesses within this page or memory block (M = 1).
1	1	0	**This mode is not supported.**
1	1	1	**This mode is not supported.**

Guarded Storage (G) Bit

Speculative Accesses

A PowerPC processor may be designed to perform speculative memory accesses. In other words, using otherwise idle resources, it may access memory locations before the program flow actually dictates that the access is to be performed. This is done to save time and, therefore, to increase performance. It may take the form of prefetching instructions along the execution path that the processor thinks will be taken. This is very common in today's processor designs. The processor may also utilize otherwise idle resources to execute a load or store instruction that it is speculating would be executed as the processor proceeds along the projected execution path. Certain speculative operations are prohibited by the specification:

- A speculative store may not be performed on the external bus until it is determined that the store instruction will definitely be executed. Remember, multiple instructions are executing simultaneously in a superscalar processor. A branch instruction previous to the store instruction may alter program flow and the store will never execute to completion.
- Speculative loads from guarded memory (see next section) are prohibited with one exception — when it has been determined that a load (or store) will definitely be executed, the processor may load the entire cache block (containing the requested data) from memory into the cache. In a sense, the other memory locations within the cache block are being loaded speculatively.
- Other than a machine check, the processor may not report an error associated with a speculative instruction's execution until it has been determined that the instruction will definitely be executed.

Except as noted earlier, speculative loads from guarded memory are prohibited. Speculative loads from unguarded memory are permitted. If a machine check is encountered when performing a speculative load from unguarded memory, the machine check interrupt may occur even though the instruction that was speculatively-executed would not actually have been executed (due to a program flow misprediction).

Only one side-effect (other than machine check) of speculative execution is permitted — when the result of a speculatively-executed instruction is abandoned (because of a program flow misprediction), the page access history bits in the PTE may have already been updated to reflect the load access.

The processor may perform speculative load or store accesses within guarded memory only under the following circumstances:

- The target location is in the cache. Since it's already in the cache, it's obviously safe to access that region of memory. In this case, the speculative access may be performed from the cache.
- The target memory is enabled for caching (I = 0) and it has been determined that the load or store is on the program path that will be taken (in the absence of any interrupts). In this case, the entire cache block may be loaded into the cache from memory (even though the load or store only deals with a subset of the cache block).
- The target memory is not cacheable (I = 1), it has been determined that the load or store will definitely be executed and no prior instructions can cause an interrupt.

The processor may not prefetch instructions from guarded memory except under the following conditions:

- The target memory location is in the cache. In this case, the target location may be read from the cache.
- Instruction address translation is enabled (MSR[IR] = 1) and an instruction has been previously fetched from the page (the page access history referenced bit has been set).
- It has been determined that the instruction to be prefetched will definitely be executed (if no interrupts occur). If instruction address translation is disabled (MSR[IR] = 0), only the cache block containing the target instruction may be prefetched.

Speculative Access Problem

Memory locations within a guarded area are not well-behaved: there may be holes (memory regions unoccupied by physical memory) or it may contain memory-mapped I/O locations. Unimplemented memory locations would return bad data and would not accept data to be stored. Speculative accesses to memory-mapped I/O ports may cause erratic operation of the affected I/O device(s).

Solution — Mark Misbehaved Areas Guarded

A page or memory block is marked guarded if G = 1 in the referenced page table entry or block address translation register. G is assumed to be one if address translation is disabled (for all memory data and/or instruction accesses, not restricted to just this page or memory block) via the MSR address translation bits (IR and DR).

The processor will not perform speculative accesses within pages or blocks with G set to one. The processor will also not perform speculative accesses when the MMU is disabled (it assumes that G = 1 because it doesn't have access to the block or page address translation logic).

Chapter 13

The Previous Chapter

The previous chapter described the mechanism provided to the PowerPC operating system programmer to specify the caching-related rules within each area of memory (the WIM bits). It also discussed the issue of guarded memory and the G bit.

This Chapter

This chapter discusses the PowerPC processor's ability to post memory reads and writes. As a direct result of this ability, the processor may not perform the posted memory accesses in the same order as that specified by the programmer. Since it is sometimes crucial that the accesses be performed in the specified order, this chapter discusses the three methods that can be used to enforce strict ordering of memory accesses:

- The sync instruction
- The eieio instruction
- Performing a read after each write

The Next Chapter

The next chapter describes the timebase facility provided to applications programmer by the PowerPC processor when operating at the user privilege level.

Time and Order of Memory Accesses

The PowerPC processor doesn't necessarily perform memory accesses in the order specified by the program. As an example, assume that there are load instructions in the instruction stream and that the first experiences a miss in the cache and the second a hit. The second access will be immediately fulfilled from the cache, followed later by fulfillment of the first access from memory.

If the programmer wants to ensure that a sequence of memory accesses occurs in strict order, the sync or the eieio instruction must be used.

When a store instruction is performed to a memory location, it is natural to assume that the memory access has been completed when the processor moves on to the instruction after the store. This is not necessarily the case with the PowerPC processor. The processor typically implements a buffer for posting memory read and write transactions. The buffering unit is referred to as the memory unit, or MU. When a memory store instruction is executed, the target address and the data to be stored is memorized by the MU and the integer unit is permitted to move on to subsequent instructions. As long as the MU has room in its posted write buffer, any additional stores are also memorized. When there are one or more memory accesses posted in the MU, the MU issues a request to the system interface unit to acquire the bus to perform the highest-priority transaction currently resident in the MU. As the bus becomes available, the MU unloads the posted transactions to the bus. The order in which the posted stores are performed is not necessarily that specified by the programmer. For additional information about MU operation, refer to the chapter entitled "601 Cache and Memory Unit."

Sync Instruction — Processor Stalls Until MU Flushed

When a sync instruction is executed, the processor will ensure that all previously-posted memory reads and writes are completed on the bus before program execution proceeds past the sync instruction. It should be noted that usage of the *sync instruction is generally frowned upon* because it stalls the processor core until all of the posted transactions have been successfully performed on the bus. Other methods for enforcing access ordering are discussed after this topic.

As an example, assume that the programmer wishes to gain exclusive ownership of a shared resource such as a memory data structure (for a detailed discussion of acquiring ownership of a shared resource, refer to the chapter entitled "Acquiring Ownership of Shared Resource"). After establishing ownership of the data structure using the associated memory semaphore, the programmer then performs a number of accesses within the data structure. Prior to relinquishing ownership of the data structure, the programmer executes a sync instruction. This forces the processor to stall on the sync instruction until all posted memory reads and writes have been performed on the bus. Upon completion of the sync instruction, the data structure in memory has had all updates made to it. When the last posted memory transaction has been completed on the bus, the sync instruction causes an address-only sync transaction to be performed. If the system has a posted write buffer built into the look-through L2 cache associated with the processor or in the host/PCI bridge, the sync transaction causes this buffer to flush all posted writes to memory now. After the sync instruction has completed, the programmer then relinquishes ownership of the data structure.

It should be noted that the posted reads and writes are not necessarily performed on the bus in the order that they were generated by the instruction stream.

eieio Instruction — Specifying Order of Posted Writes

When an eieio instruction (enforce in-order execution of I/O) is executed, all writes posted prior to the execution of the eieio instruction are marked for performance on the bus before any writes that may be posted subsequent to the execution of the eieio instruction. Although the processor will not necessarily perform these write transactions on the bus immediately, the programmer is assured that they will be performed on the bus before any subsequently posted writes.

As an example, assume that the programmer must write two parameter words and then one command word to a fixed-disk controller and that the controller's ports are implemented as memory-mapped I/O ports. If the programmer executes the three stores in order, the processor will post the writes but not perform them immediately. In addition, when it does acquire the external bus and performs the memory write transactions, it may not perform them in the same order as that specified by the programmer. This might result in improper operation of the disk controller (because it might receive the command word before the parameters and proceed to execute the command using old parameters).

To ensure that the first two stores (to write the parameter words to the disk controller) are performed prior to the store of the command word, the programmer should follow the first two stores with an eieio instruction. This would mark these two stores for performance on the bus prior to any subsequently posted writes. The third store (to the command register) would be executed after the eieio and posted in the write queue. When the processor's system interface performs the three memory write transactions, the first two stores will be performed before the third one.

Other Flush Method Yields Better Performance than Sync

In the example cited in the previous section, the following code sequence was executed to output two parameter words to the disk controller, followed by the output of the command word:

1. Perform two stores to the parameter ports.
2. Execute an eieio instruction to mark these two stores to be performed on the bus before any subsequently posted stores.
3. Perform the store to the command word register.

To force the MU to force the three posted writes to be performed in the specified order on the bus, the programmer only has to follow each write with a read from the same address. The MU always compares the target address for each posted read with the target address of each of the posted writes currently in the MU. If there is a match, the write will be performed on the bus before the read. Performing a read from the same address that was stored to therefore causes the processor to first perform the memory write bus transaction, followed immediately by the memory read from the same address. If the L2 cache implements a posted write buffer, it will post the write. The read that follows causes it to force the posted write to memory. The memory read is then fulfilled. The data returned by the load (read) is not used.

Unlike the sync instruction, this method does not stall the processor core. Rather, the MU post the store and the subsequent load request and permits the integer unit to move on to the next instruction. The result — better performance.

Multiple-Access Instruction Accesses Cannot Be Ordered

Some single instructions cause multiple accesses. Examples would be a misaligned transfer or execution of a load/store multiple or a move assist instruction. There is no guaranteed order to the completion of the individual accesses that comprise the overall data transfer caused by the execution of the instruction. Since it is impossible to embed a sync instruction within a single instruction, there is no way to guarantee the order of the accesses generated by the instruction.

eieio and sync on PPC 601 Processor

On the PPC601 processor, the eieio instruction has the same effect as the sync instruction — both stall the processor until the MU has flushed its buffers and then cause the broadcast of an address-only sync transaction. This means that execution of the eieio instruction on the 601 causes a processor stall resulting in performance degradation. It is therefore highly-recommended that the read after write method be used to order and force memory accesses to memory-mapped I/O ports.

Chapter 14

The Previous Chapter

The previous chapter discussed the PowerPC processor's ability to post memory reads and writes. As a direct result of this ability, the processor may not perform the posted memory accesses in the same order as that specified by the programmer. Since it is sometimes crucial that the accesses be performed in the specified order, this chapter also discussed the three methods that can be used to enforce strict ordering of memory accesses:

- The sync instruction
- The eieio instruction
- Performing a read after each write

This Chapter

This chapter describes the PowerPC architecture timebase facility as it appears when the processor is operating at the user privilege level (MSR[PR] = 1).

This chapter is the final one in part two of the book. Part two describes the facilities available when the processor is operating at the user privilege level.

The Next Chapter

The next chapter describes the registers that become available to the operating system programmer when the processor is operating at the supervisor privilege level (MSR[PR] = 0). The register set for both the 32 and 64-bit versions of the processor are described.

The Time Base

The time base is implemented as one 64-bit register (in a 64-bit processor) (or two 32-bit registers in a 32-bit processor) and is illustrated in figure 14-1. It consists of an upper (TBU) and a lower half (TBL). One is added to the least-significant bit (63) periodically. The frequency at which the counter is incremented is implementation-dependent. When the time base has incremented to FFFFFFFFFFFFFFFFh and is incremented one more time, it wraps around to 0000000000000000h. The wrap-around event is not signaled in any way.

The PowerPC architecture specification does not relate the time base frequency to the frequency of any other system clock (such as the CPU or bus clock). In addition, the time base frequency is not required to remain constant. As an example, the system may slow down the clock to conserve power when the system is in sleep mode. There are certain requirements which must be met so that system software can accurately track time-of-day and to permit the implementation of interval timers. One of the following conditions must be met:

- The system (platform) must provide an implementation-dependent interrupt to indicate when the update frequency has changed. It must also provide a means (a machine-readable port) to allow determination of the current update frequency.
- or, the update frequency must be under the control of the system software.

TBU and TBL are read-only at the user (application) privilege level. The programmer uses the move from time base, or mftb, instruction to read the current value into a GPR for evaluation. In the case of a 32-bit PowerPC processor implementation, the programmer would have to perform two mftb instructions to move the upper and lower halves of the time base into two separate 32-bit GPRs. Suggested software implementations of the time-of-day function are discussed in detail in the specification.

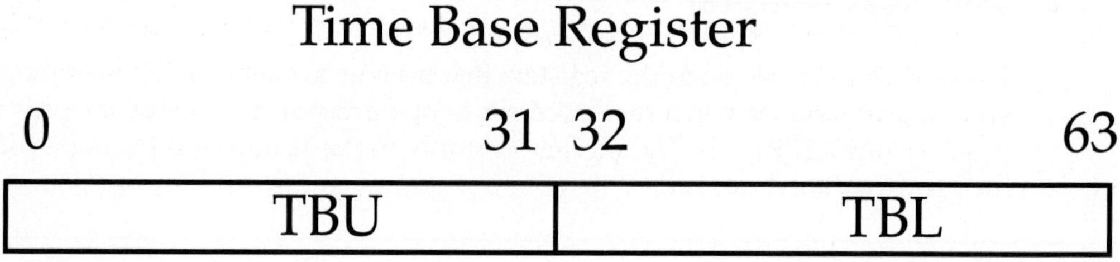

Time Base Register

0 — 31	32 — 63
TBU	TBL

Figure 14-1. The Time Base Register

Part Three

The Operating System – Supervisor Privilege Level

Parts two and three comprise the description of the PowerPC processor specification. All aspects of both 32 and 64-bit processor implementations are covered.

Part three provides a description of the instructions, registers and other facilities available to the operating system programmer. The operating system is executed at the supervisor privilege level. The processor is placed into the supervisor privilege level when the privilege mode bit, PR, in the machine state register, or MSR, is set to zero (in other words, MSR[PR] = 0).

The chapters that comprise part three are:

PowerPC 601 Systems Architecture

- Operating System Registers
- Operating System Instructions
- Address Translation Overview
- Virtual Paging
- Block: Large Memory Region
- I/O and Memory-Mapped I/O
- Interrupts
- The Timebase and the Decrementer
- Big vs. Little-Endian

Chapter 15

The Previous Chapter

The previous chapter described the PowerPC architecture timebase facility as it appears when the processor is operating at the user privilege level (MSR[PR] = 1).

This Chapter

This chapter describes the additional registers that become available to the operating system programmer when the processor is operating at the supervisor privilege level (MSR[PR] = 0). The register set for both the 32 and 64-bit versions of the processor are described.

The Next Chapter

The next chapter describes the additional instructions that become available to the operating system programmer when the processor is operating at the supervisor privilege level (MSR[PR] = 0).

Placing Processor In Supervisor Mode

The processor is placed in supervisor mode by clearing the MSR[PR] bit to zero. This occurs automatically whenever an interrupt occurs. When placed in supervisor mode, the programmer has full access to all registers and full use of the entire instruction set.

32-Bit Processor's OS Register Set

Figure 15-1 illustrates the registers that become accessible when the processor is operating at the supervisor privilege level. The OS programmer can also utilize the registers that are available at the user privilege level.

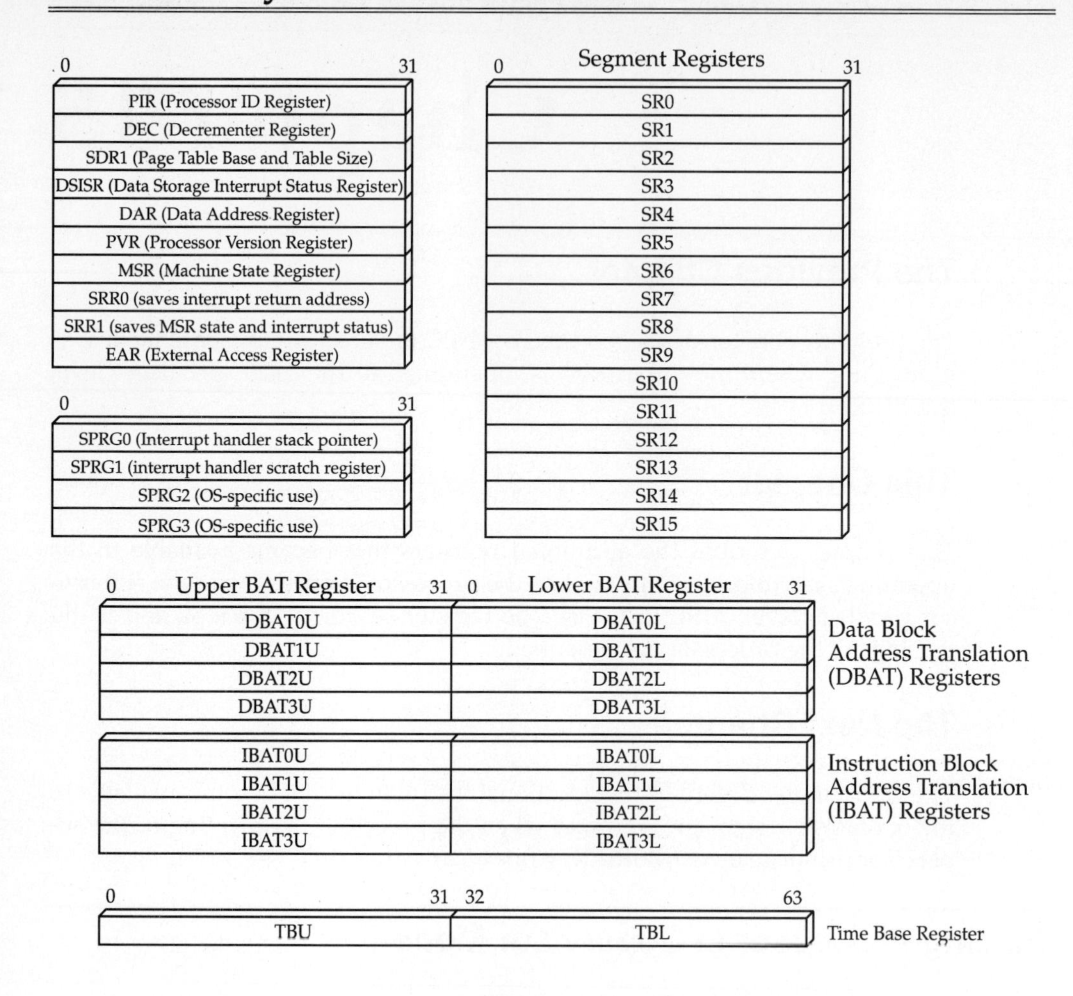

Figure 15-1. 32-bit Processor's OS Register Set

Machine State Register (MSR)

In a 32-bit processor, MSR is a 32-bit register. Figure 15-2 illustrates the 32-bit MSR register. At any given instant in time, the bits within MSR indicate the current operational characteristics of the processor. The MSR can be modified by the following instructions:

- The move to MSR instruction (mtmsr) can be used to set a new set of values into the MSR register.

- When the system call (sc) instruction is executed, it causes a system call interrupt. The processor saves a subset of the MSR bits in SRR1 and then changes the state of a number of the MSR bits to place the processor into the proper operational mode to service the interrupt.
- At the end of any interrupt handler, execution of a return from interrupt (rfi) instruction causes the processor to restore the MSR bits from those in SRR1 and then resume program fetching at the address specified in SRR0.

The programmer may copy the contents of the MSR register into a GPR register using the move from MSR, or mfmsr, instruction.

Power Management, Bit 13 (POW)

Power management is enabled by setting the POW bit, bit 13, to one and disabled by clearing it to zero. In processor implementations that possess electrical power management capability, this bit enables or disables power management. POW is automatically cleared whenever an interrupt is taken (after its original state is saved in SRR1).

Interrupt Endian Mode, Bit 15 (ILE)

When an interrupt is taken, the processor automatically saves the current state of MSR[LE] into SRR1 and then copies MSR[ILE] to MSR[LE]. This automatically places the processor into the desired endian mode for interrupt servicing. ILE = 0 selects big-endian mode, while ILE = 1 selects little-endian mode. For a detailed discussion of endian-related issues, refer to the chapter entitled "Big vs. Little-Endian."

External Interrupt Enable, Bit 16 (EE)

When EE is set to one, the processor will recognize interrupts received from the external interrupt controller and from the internal Decrementer. When cleared to zero, recognition of these interrupts is disabled. When an interrupt is taken, EE is cleared after being saved in SRR1.

Privilege Mode, Bit 17 (PR)

When set to one, the processor is operating at the user privilege level. A subset of the register and instruction sets are available to the applications programmer. When cleared to zero, the processor is operating at the supervisor privilege level. The complete register and instruction sets are available to the operating system programmer. When an interrupt is taken, PR is cleared after being saved in SRR1.

Floating-Point Available, Bit 18 (FP)

When set to one, the processor's floating-point unit is enabled to execute floating-point instructions. When cleared to zero, the processor will generate a floating-point unavailable interrupt whenever a floating-point instruction is received for execution.

Machine Check Enable, Bit 19 (ME)

When set to one, the processor will take the machine check interrupt whenever a machine check condition is detected. If the machine check caused an invalid value to be placed into SRR0 and/or SRR1, the processor clears the MSR[RI] bit to indicate that the interrupt is not recoverable (i.e., execution of an rfi instruction will not permit the processor to resume execution at the point of interruption). When cleared to zero, generation of the machine check interrupt is disabled. If a machine check occurs with ME cleared, the processor enters the checkstop state (i.e., it freezes). When an interrupt occurs, ME is cleared after being saved in SRR1. For more information on machine check and checkstop, refer to the chapter entitled " 601 OS Register and Instruction Set."

Floating-Point Interrupt Mode, Bits 20 and 23 (FE[0:1])

The state of the FE bits defines the type of interrupts the floating-point unit may generate. The following table defines the FE bit settings:

FE0	FE1	Floating-Point Interrupts That Will Be Recognized
0	0	None.
0	1	Imprecise non-recoverable.
1	0	Imprecise recoverable.
1	1	Precise.

When an interrupt occurs, the FE bits are cleared after being saved in SRR1. A detailed discussion of interrupts may be found in the chapter entitled "Interrupts."

Single-Step Trace Enable, Bit 21 (SE)

When set to one, the processor will branch to the trace interrupt handler upon the successful completion of each instruction. When cleared to zero, single-step trace interrupts are disabled. The trace interrupt handler will be part of a debug program. When an interrupt occurs, the SE bit is cleared after being saved in SRR1. A detailed discussion of interrupts may be found in the chapter entitled "Interrupts."

Branch Trace Enable, Bit 22 (BE)

When set to one, the processor will branch to the trace interrupt handler upon the successful completion of each branch instruction (whether or not the branch is taken). When cleared to zero, branch trace interrupts are disabled. The trace interrupt handler will be part of a debug program. When an interrupt occurs, the BE bit is cleared after being saved in SRR1. A detailed discussion of interrupts may be found in the chapter entitled "Interrupts."

Interrupt Prefix, Bit 25 (IP)

When set to one, the processor sets the upper three hex digits of the interrupt handler entry address to FFFh. When cleared to zero, the upper three hex digits of the address are set to 000h. For additional discussion, refer to the chapter entitled "Interrupts."

Instruction Address Relocation, Bit 26 (IR)

When set to one, the MMU will perform address translation for instruction fetches. When cleared to zero, the MMU will not perform address translation for instruction fetches (i.e., real address mode is used). When an interrupt occurs, the IR bit is cleared after being saved in SRR1. This is done because the entry points for the interrupt handlers reside at fixed physical memory addresses. For more information, refer to the chapter entitled "Interrupts."

Data Address Relocation, Bit 27 (DR)

When set to one, the MMU will perform address translation for data loads and stores. When cleared to zero, the MMU will not perform address translation for data accesses (i.e., real address mode is used). When an interrupt occurs, the DR bit is cleared after being saved in SRR1. This is done because the entry points for the interrupt handlers reside at fixed physical memory addresses. For more information, refer to the chapter entitled "Interrupts."

Recoverable Interrupt, Bit 30 (RI)

General

A detailed discussion of interrupts may be found in the chapter entitled "Interrupts." The RI bit in MSR and SRR1[30] are closely associated with each other. At initialization time, the operating system programmer sets RI to one. The first time an interrupt occurs, the processor copies MSR[RI] to SRR1[30] and then clears RI to zero.

On Entry to an Interrupt Handler

On entry to each interrupt handler, the processor automatically copies MSR[RI} to SRR1[30] and then clears RI to zero. On entry to the interrupt handler, the programmer should:

- Check the state of SRR1[30] to determine if the interrupted program is restartable. SRR1[30] = 0 indicates it that it would be unsafe to execute an rfi at the end of this interrupt handler, while SRR1[30] = 1 indicates the interrupted program may be safely resumed by executing an rfi at the conclusion of the interrupt handler.
- Set RI to one when sufficient state has been saved to permit recovery if the interrupt handler is interrupted by a machine check or a system reset.

If the interrupt handler should be interrupted after RI is set to one, SRR1[30] is then set to one when MSR[RI] is copied to SRR1 by the processor (RI is then cleared by the processor). SRR1[30] = 1 indicates to the second-level interrupt handler that the first-level interrupt handler can be restarted successfully when the rfi is executed at the conclusion of the second-level handler.

If the first-level interrupt handler were interrupted before saving state and setting RI to one, a zero would be copied from MSR[RI] to SRR1[30] on entry to the second-level interrupt handler. Upon examining SRR1[30] on entry to the second-level handler, SRR1[30] cleared to zero indicates that the programmer must not execute an rfi at the end of the second-level handler.

On Exit from an Interrupt Handler

Just prior to exiting from an interrupt handler, the programmer should take the following actions:

- Set the RI bit to zero. This must be done because the instructions that follow will reload SRR0 and SRR1 with the values to be used by the processor when it executes the rfi at the end of the interrupt handler. If the processor should be interrupted while in the process of initializing SRR0 and SRR1, execution of the rfi could have disastrous effects.
- Disable external interrupt recognition by clearing MSR[EE] to zero to prevent the instructions that set up SRR0 and SRR1 from being interrupted.
- Set SRR0 and SRR1 for use by the rfi instruction in returning to the interrupted program. SRR1[30] must be set to one.
- Execute the rfi instruction. SRR1[30] will be copied back into MSR[RI], setting it to one. This will ensure that SRR1[30] will be set to one again when the next interrupt occurs.

On Entry to the Machine Check or System Reset Interrupt Handlers

A machine check or system reset interrupt may corrupt the state of SRR0 and/or SRR1 or other processor resource that is necessary to resume execution of the interrupted program. If this is the case, the processor will clear SRR1[30] to zero (rather than just copying the state of MSR[RI] to SRR1[30]). This indicates to the machine check or reset handler that the interrupted program cannot be safely resumed by executing an rfi instruction.

Endian Mode, Bit 31 (LE)

The state of the LE bit defines whether the processor is using big or little-endian storage addressing. When set to one, the processor is in little-endian mode, while LE cleared to zero places it in big-endian mode. The state of LE after reset has been removed is zero, placing the processor in its native big-endian addressing mode. When an interrupt occurs, the processor saves LE in SRR1 and then copies MSR[ILE] into LE, automatically placing the processor in the endian mode preferred by the OS for interrupt handling.

A complete description of endian-related issues can be found in the chapter entitled "Big vs. Little-Endian."

State of MSR after Reset Removed

Table 15-1 indicates the state of MSR after reset has been removed.

Table 15-1. 32-bit MSR State After Reset Removed

Bit	Name	State	Effect
13	POW	0	Full-power mode.
15	ILE	-	Must be initialized by OS.
16	EE	0	External and Decrementer interrupts are disabled.
17	PR	0	Processor is operating at the supervisor privilege level.
18	FP	0	Floating-point unit is disabled.
19	ME	1	Recognition of machine checks is enabled.
20	FE0	0	All floating-point interrupts are disabled. See also bit 23.
21	SE	0	Single-step trace interrupts are disabled.
22	BE	0	Branch trace interrupts are disabled.
23	FE1	0	See bit 20.
25	IP	1	The upper three hex digits of all interrupt handler entry points is FFFh.
26	IR	0	The MMU's ability to perform address translation for instruction fetches is disabled.
27	DR	0	The MMU's ability to perform address translation for load/store data accesses is disabled.
30	RI	0	SRR0 and SRR1 do not contain valid information that will permit execution of an rfi instruction to resume program execution at the point of interruption.
31	LE	0	Processor performs all access addressing using its native big-endian addressing mode.

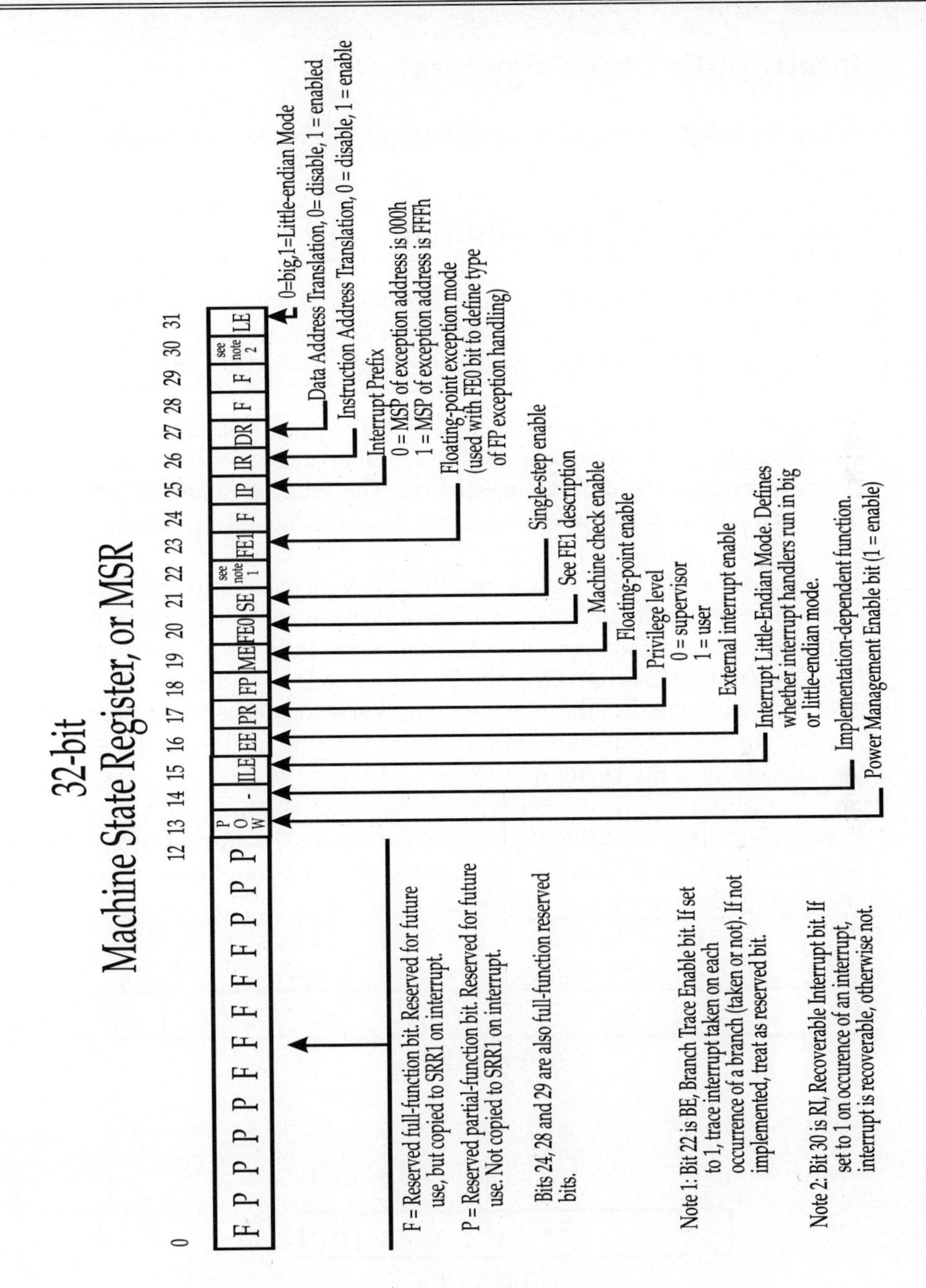

Figure 15-2. 32-bit Machine State Register, or MSR

Interrupt-Related Registers

For a detailed description of interrupts, refer to the chapter entitled, "Interrupts."

Save/Restore Register 0 (SRR0)

In a 32-bit processor, SRR0 is a 32-bit register. When an interrupt occurs, the branch processor automatically copies the address of the currently-executing instruction or that of the next instruction to be executed to SRR0.

The address of the currently-executing instruction (the CIA, or current instruction address) is copied to SRR0 if the interrupt was caused by a failed attempt to execute the current instruction. The interrupt handler can then use SRR0 as a pointer to the instruction that has experienced a problem.

The address of the next instruction (the NIA, or next instruction address) is copied to SRR0 if the interrupt was caused by an event other than a failed instruction execution attempt (such as an external interrupt). After the interrupt handler has finished handling the interrupt and executes an rfi instruction (return from interrupt), the rfi causes the processor to use SRR0 as the address at which to resume execution. Also refer to the next section on the SRR1 register for additional information.

Figure 15-3 illustrates SRR0. Since SRR0 points to the current or next instruction and all instructions are word-aligned, the least-significant two bits, 30:31, are reserved (not used).

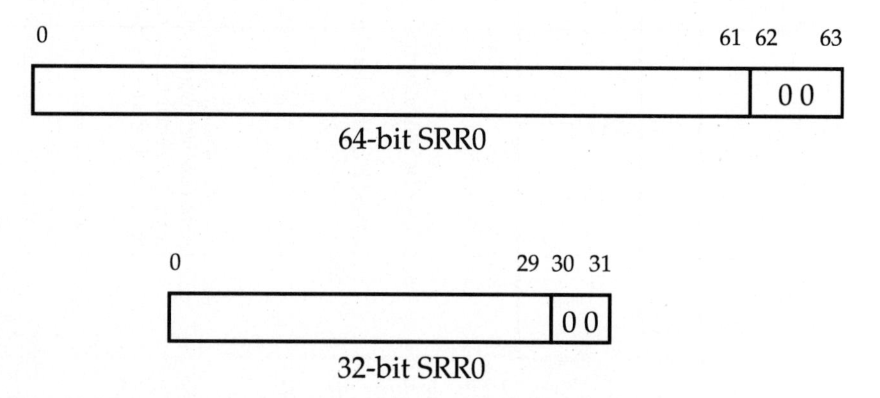

Figure 15-3. Save/Restore Register 0 (SRR0)

Save/Restore Register 1 (SRR1)

In a 32-bit processor, SRR1 is a 32-bit register. When an interrupt occurs, the processor copies machine state information from the MSR to SRR1. In effect, this saves a snapshot of the processor's state at the point of interruption so that it can be restored (by an automatic copyback into MSR from SRR1 caused by execution of the rfi instruction) after the interrupt has been handled by the operating system. In addition to machine state information, the processor saves status information specific to the interrupt into SRR1. For more information on interrupts, refer to the chapter entitled "Interrupts."

Specifically, in a 32-bit implementation, the processor copies the following bit fields from MSR to the identical bit fields in SRR1: 0, 5:9, and 16:31. It also places interrupt-specific status information in bit fields 1:4 and 10:15 of SRR1.

After saving interrupt-specific information and the current state of the processor (bit fields from MSR) into SRR1 and set SRR0 to point to the instruction that caused the interrupt or the next instruction to be executed (after interrupt servicing), the processor changes the state of certain MSR bits and jumps to the interrupt vector address associated with the interrupt being recognized. The MSR bits that are changed place the processor in a new operating mode, or context, to handle the interrupt condition. The bit changes that comprise this context change are:

- The LE bit is set to the same state as the ILE bit. Depending on the state of the ILE bit, the mode to be used during the execution of the interrupt handler is either little or big-endian.
- If servicing a machine check interrupt, the ME bit is cleared. This precludes recognition of another machine check interrupt while in the interrupt handler.
- BE is set to zero, disabling branch trace interrupts recognition while in the interrupt handler.
- DR is set to zero, disabling logical-to-physical data address translation while in the interrupt handler.
- EE is set to zero, disabling external interrupt recognition while in the interrupt handler.
- FE0 and FE1 are set to zero, disabling floating-point interrupts while in the interrupt handler.
- FP is set to zero, disabling the floating-point processor while in the interrupt handler.

- IR is set to zero, disabling logical-to-physical instruction address translation while in the interrupt handler.
- POW is set to zero, disabling power management while in the interrupt handler.
- PR is set to zero, placing the processor at the supervisor privilege level while in the interrupt handler.
- RI is set to one if the interrupt is recoverable, to zero if unrecoverable.
- SE is set to zero, disabling recognition of the single-step trace interrupt while in the interrupt handler.

When the processor executes the rfi instruction at the end of the interrupt handler, the contents of the respective bit fields in SRR1 are copied back to MSR, automatically returning the processor to its pre-interrupt operational context. The contents of SRR0 supplies the address at which to resume program execution. Figure 15-4 illustrates SRR1.

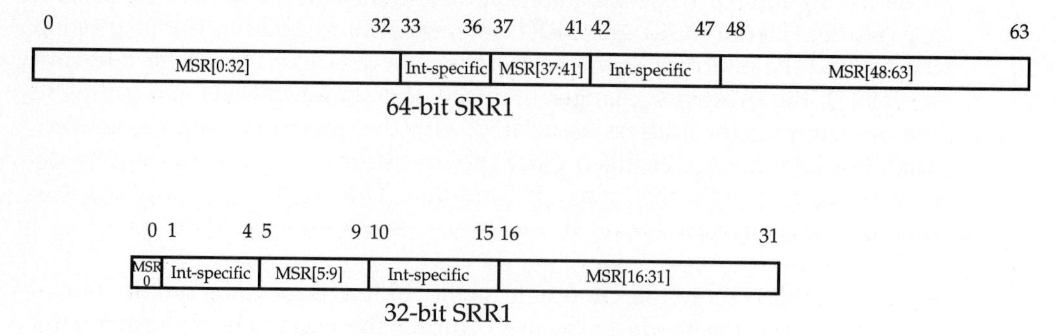

Figure 15-4. Save/Restore Register 1 (SRR1)

Special Purpose Registers G0 – G3

Some of the integer processor's SPRs can only be accessed when the processor is operating at the supervisor privilege level. They are special purpose general registers 0 – 3, SPRG0 – SPRG3. These registers are used as follows:

- **SPRG0** — The operating system may load SPRG0 with the physical, or real, start address of an area of memory (essentially its stack area) to be used by the first-level interrupt handler. Each PowerPC processor in the system should have mutually-exclusive addresses loaded into its respective SPRG0.

- **SPRG1** — When the first-level interrupt handler is entered, the programmer may temporarily save the content of one of the GPRs in this register so that the GPR can be used to perform a series of indirect stored. The start address of the first-level interrupt handler's save, or stack, area may then be copied from SPRG0 to the GPR register. The handler can then use that GPR as the indirect base address pointer to perform saves of additional GPRs (including the one copied to SPRG1) into the handler's unique save, or stack, area.
- **SPRG2** — Available for use by the operating system programmer.
- **SPRG3** — Available for use by the operating system programmer.

Data Address Register (DAR)

When an interrupt occurs that is associated with a failed attempt to perform a memory data access, the effective, or logical address of the data operand is placed into the DAR. This register is associated with the data storage and alignment interrupts. The DAR is 32 bits wide.

Data Storage Interrupt Status Register (DSISR)

When a data storage or an alignment interrupt occurs, the contents of DSISR defines the cause of the interrupt. This is a 32-bit register. Figure 15-5 illustrates its contents after a data storage interrupt, while figure 15-6 illustrates its contents after an alignment interrupt.

Additional information about the data storage and alignment interrupts can be found later in the chapter entitled "Interrupts."

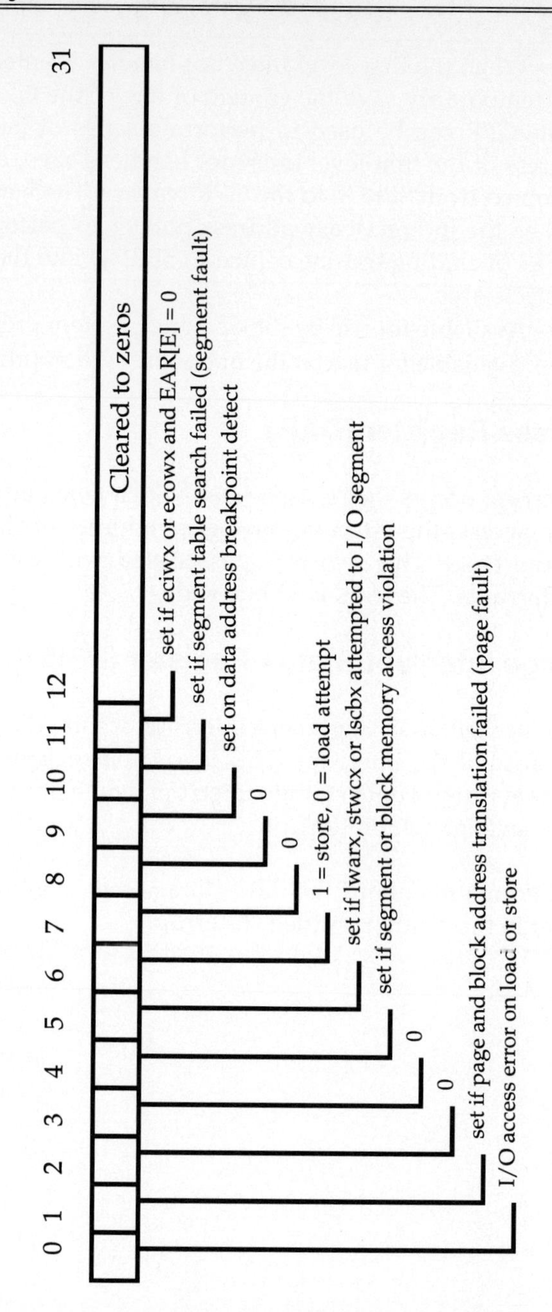

Figure 15-5. Data Storage Interrupt Status Register (DSISR) after Data Storage Interrupt

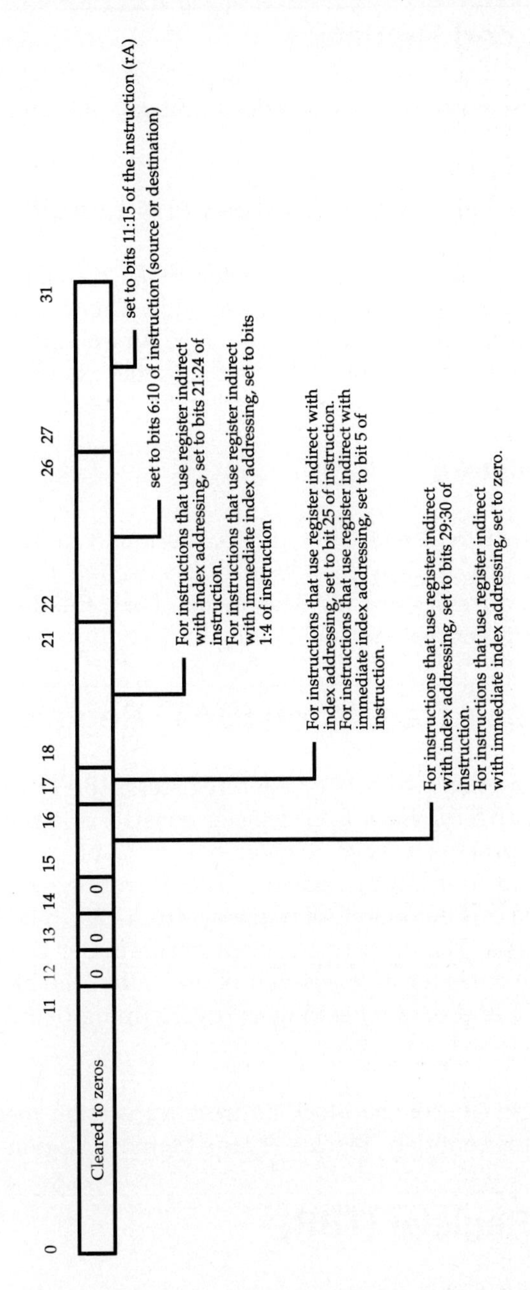

Figure 15-6. Data Storage Interrupt Status Register (DSISR) after Alignment Interrupt

Paging-Related Registers

For a detailed discussion of paging, refer to the chapter entitled "Virtual Paging."

SDR1 — Page Table Base Address and Length

Referred to as the search descriptor register, SDR1 contains the physical base memory address and the length of the page table. The format of the page table size field in SDR1 is slightly different in the 32 and 64-bit SDR1 implementations. For a full description of SDR1, refer to the chapter entitled "Virtual Paging."

Segment Registers

The sixteen segment registers, SR0 – SR15, are found in 32-bit, but not 64-bit processors. They are used by the OS to map effective segment addresses to virtual segment addresses or to I/O segments. For a full description of SDR1, refer to the chapter entitled "Virtual Paging."

Block Address Translation (BAT) Registers

The processor contains two sets of BAT registers, IBATs (instruction BATs) and DBATs (data BATs). Each BAT register consists of an upper and a lower half. In a 32-bit processor, each register half is 32-bit wide. There are four IBAT registers and four DBAT registers. The operating system uses the BAT registers to define certain regions of memory, from 128KB to 256MB in size, as code or data blocks. The operating system programmer can then specify one set of operational rules for accesses that occur within the block. A block may contain both code and data by setting up overlapping definitions in an IBAT and a DBAT.

A complete description of the block address translation mechanism may be found in the chapter entitled "Block — Large Memory Region."

Time Base Register (TBR)

The time base is a 64-bit register consisting of an upper and lower half referred to as TBU and TBL. The time base is pictured in figure 15-7. It can be both read and written at the supervisor privilege level. A description of the time base can be found in the chapter entitled "The Timebase and the Decrementer."

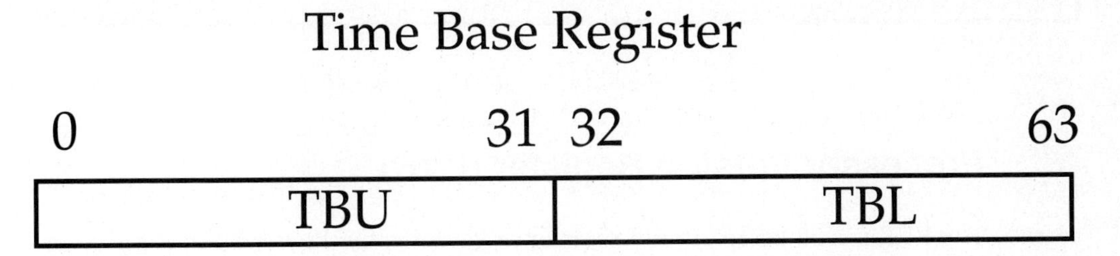

Figure 15-7. Time Base Upper and Lower Registers

Decrementer Register (DEC)

The DEC register decrements at the same rate that the timebase increments. When its count is exhausted, the processor will generate a decrementer interrupt if MSR[EE] is set to one. The operating system programmer initializes the DEC with a time slice value before starting a task. It then permits the task to start (or resume) execution. The DEC will continually decrement in the background while the task is executing. When the task's time slice has been exhausted, the decrementer interrupt returns control back to the operating system. The DEC is a 32-bit register in both 32 and 64-bit processors. It may not be accessed by user mode programs, but may be both read and written at the supervisor privilege level. The mfspr and mtspr instructions are used to access the DEC register, but the programmer may use the friendlier form mfdec and mtdec.

Processor ID Register (PIR)

The PIR is a 32-bit register that can be used by the OS to assign an ID to the processor. Aside from any OS-specific usage of the assigned ID, the processor uses the ID when communicating with I/O devices. This topic is covered in the chapter entitled "PPC 601 I/O Transactions." The PIR is pictured in figure 15-8. The ID may range in value from 0 – Fh.

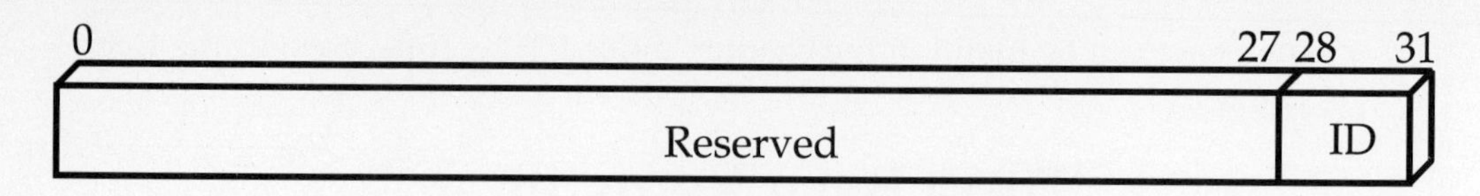

Figure 15-8. Processor ID Register (PIR)

Processor Version Register (PVR)

The PVR is a 32-bit read-only register. It contains the PowerPC processor version, or model, and the revision number. A mfspr instruction is used to transfer its contents to a GPR. The processor must be operating at the supervisor privilege level in order to access this register.

Figure 15-9 illustrates the PVR. The values encoded in the version field are assigned by the PowerPC architecture specification, while the revision number field indicates the engineering change level of that version processor.

Processor Version Register
(PVR)

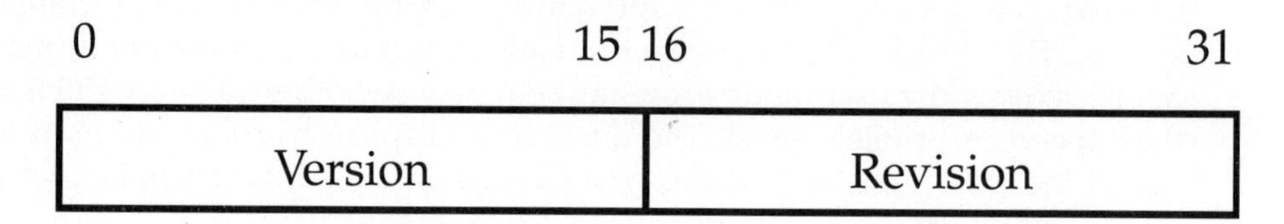

Figure 15-9. Processor Version Register (PVR)

External Access Register (EAR)

The EAR is an optional register that may or may not be implemented in a processor. It is pictured in figure 15-10. The processor cannot successfully execute the optional ecowx or eciwx instructions unless a resource ID has been placed in the EAR and the enable bit set to one. An attempt to execute either instruction with an uninitialized EAR results in a data storage interrupt. For a detailed description of this subject (as implemented on the PPC 601 processor, refer to the chapter entitled "601 External Control Transaction."

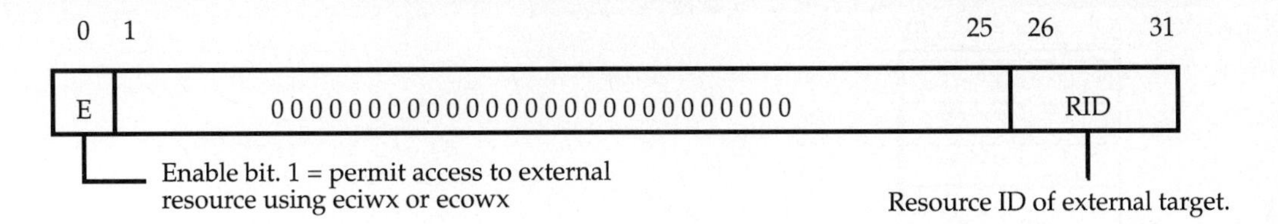

Figure 15-10. External Access Register (EAR)

64-Bit Processor's OS Register Set

Figure 15-11 illustrates the registers that become accessible (in addition to the user mode register set) when a 64-bit processor is operating at the supervisor privilege level. In most cases, the registers serve the same functions as they do in a 32-bit processor (although they may be 64 instead of 32 bits wide). The sections that follow cite any differences between the 64 and 32-bit processor implementations.

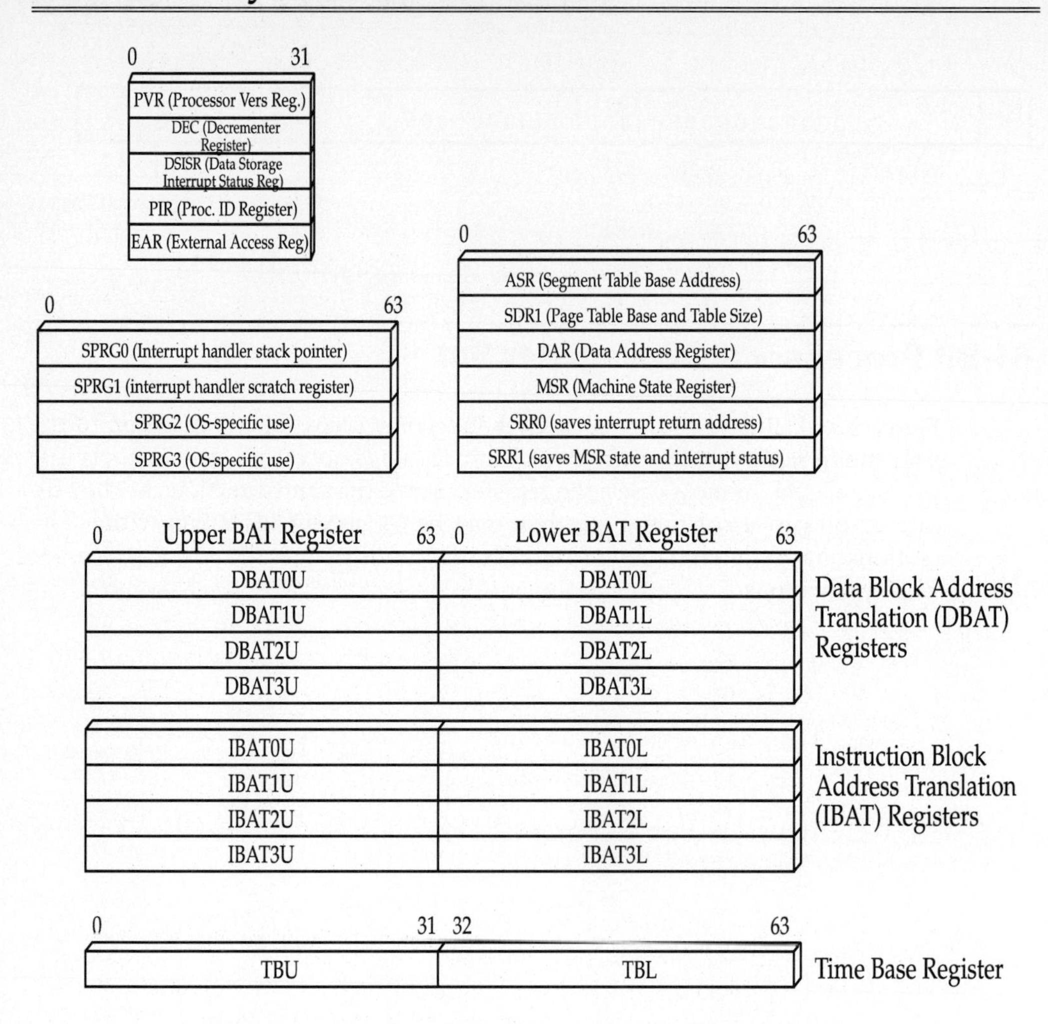

Figure 15-11. 64-bit Processor's OS Register Set

Machine State Register (MSR)

General

In a 64-bit processor, MSR is a 64-bit register. At any given instant in time, the bits within MSR indicate the current operational characteristics of the processor. The 64-bit MSR contains one bit that is not found in the 32-bit processor's MSR register — the sixty-four bit mode bit. Figure 15-12 illustrates the 64-bit

MSR register. Refer to the section in this chapter entitled "32-Bit Processor's OS Register Set" for additional information.

Sixty-Four Bit Mode, Bit 0 (SF)

After reset is removed, the SF bit is set to one, placing the processor in 64-bit mode. When an interrupt occurs, the processor saves the state of the SF bit in SRR1 and then sets SF to one, placing the processor in 64-bit mode to service the interrupt.

In 64-bit mode, the processor forms full 64-bit effective addresses. The current instruction address, or CIA, and next instruction address, or NIA, pointers contain full 64-bit addresses.

When operating in 32-bit mode, the processor follows the following rules:

- Only the lower 32 bits of the computed effective address are used to perform instruction fetches and data loads or stores.
- If the programmer uses a load or store with update, the computed 64-bit effective address is placed in the GPR register specified as the update register.
- Any time a branch with link instruction is executed, the upper 32 bits of the computed effective return address are forced to zero in the LR.
- The upper 32 bits of the address placed into SRR0 and DAR are forced to zero when an interrupt occurs.

When the processor changes from 32 to 64-bit mode, the NIA and CIA address pointers are not affected. The CIA still points to the currently-executing instruction and the NIA points to the next instruction to be executed. However, when the processor changes from 64 to 32-bit mode, the upper 32 bits of the NIA and CIA are set to zero.

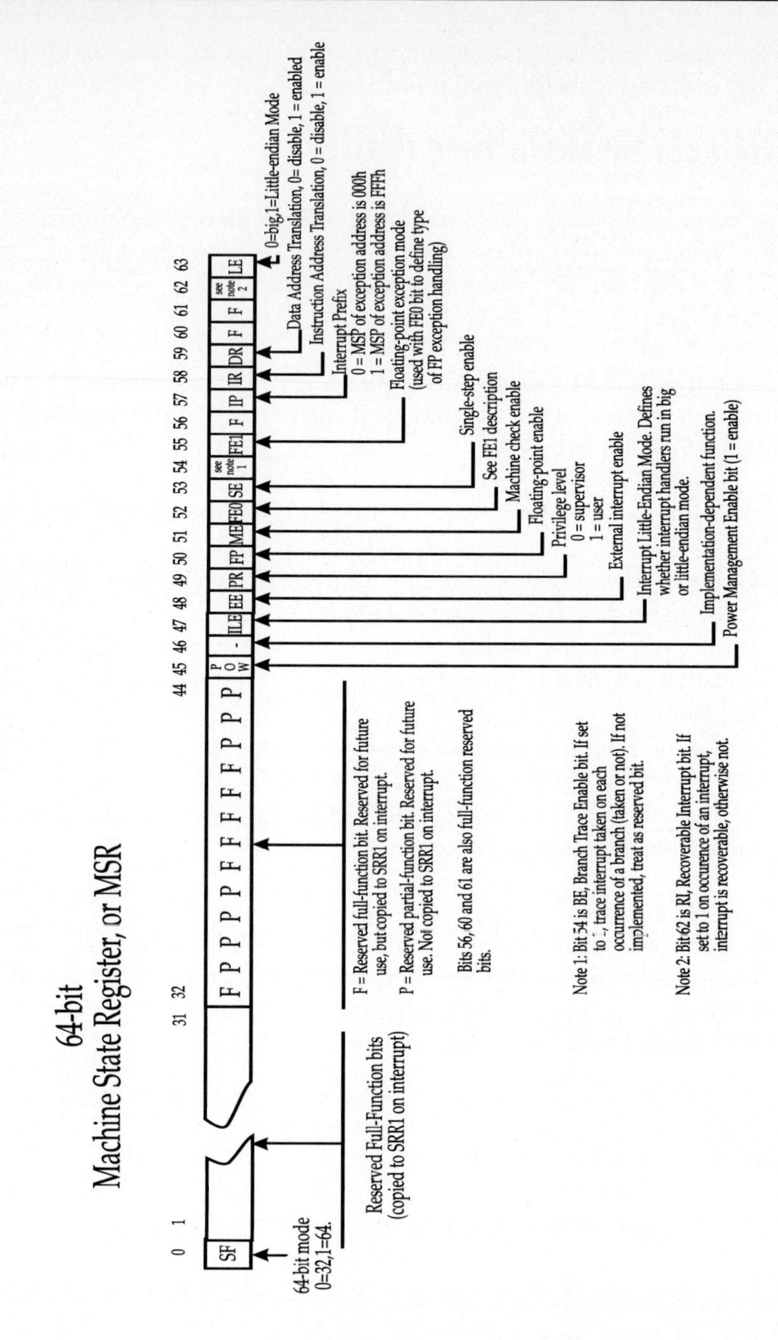

Figure 15-12. 64-bit Machine State Register (MSR)

Interrupt-Related Registers

Save/Restore Register 0 (SRR0)

In a 64-bit processor, SRR0 is a 64-bit register and serves the same purpose as the SRR0 register in the 32-bit processor. Refer to the section in this chapter entitled "32-Bit Processor's OS Register Set" for additional information. Figure 15-3 illustrates SRR0. Since SRR0 points to the current or next instruction and all instructions are word-aligned, the least-significant two bits, 62:63, are reserved (not used).

Save/Restore Register 1 (SRR1)

In a 64-bit processor, SRR1 is a 64-bit register. and serves the same purpose as the SRR1 register in the 32-bit processor. Refer to the section in this chapter entitled "32-Bit Processor's OS Register Set" for additional information. Specifically, in a 64-bit implementation, the processor copies the following bit fields from MSR to the identical bit fields in SRR1: 0:32, 37:41 and 48:63. It also places interrupt-specific status information in bit fields 33:36 and 42:47 of SRR1. The contents of SRR0 supplies the address at which to resume program execution. Figure 15-4 illustrates SRR1.

Special Purpose Registers G0 – G3

Other than the fact that these registers are 64-bits wide, the SPRG registers serve the same purpose as in the 32-bit processor. Refer to the section in this chapter entitled "32-Bit Processor's OS Register Set" for additional information.

Data Address Register (DAR)

Other than the fact that the DAR register is 64-bits wide, it serves the same purpose as in the 32-bit processor. Refer to the section in this chapter entitled "32-Bit Processor's OS Register Set" for additional information.

Data Storage Interrupt Status Register (DSISR)

DSISR is identical in the 32 and 64-bit processors. Refer to the section in this chapter entitled "32-Bit Processor's OS Register Set" for additional information.

Paging-Related Registers

SDR1 — Page Table Base Address and Size

Referred to as the search descriptor register, SDR1 contains the physical base memory address and the length of the page table. The format of the page table size field is slightly different than in the 32-bit processor's SDR1 register and the register is 64 rather than 32 bits wide. For a full description of SDR1, refer to the chapter entitled "Virtual Paging."

Address Space Register (ASR) – Segment Table Base Address

The ASR register does not exist in the 32-bit processor. The OS places the physical memory base address of the segment table in the ASR. For a full description of the ASR, refer to the chapter entitled "Virtual Paging."

Block Address Translation (BAT) Registers

The BAT registers in the 64-bit processor serve the same purpose as they do in a 32-bit processor, but each BAT register half is 64 rather than 32 bits in width. Refer to the section in this chapter entitled "32-Bit Processor's OS Register Set" for additional information. A complete description of the block address translation mechanism may be found in the chapter entitled "Block — Large Memory Region."

Time Base Register (TBR)

The time base is implemented identically in the 32 and 64-bit processor. The time base is pictured in figure 15-7. It can be both read and written at the supervisor privilege level. A complete description of the time base can be found in the chapter entitled "The Timebase and the Decrementer."

Processor ID Register (PIR)

The PIR is implemented identically in the 32 and 64-bit processor. Refer to the section in this chapter entitled "32-Bit Processor's OS Register Set" for additional information. The PIR is pictured in figure 15-8. Refer to the section in this chapter entitled "32-Bit Processor's OS Register Set" for additional information.

Processor Version Register (PVR)

The PVR is a 32-bit read-only register in both the 32 and 64-bit processors. Refer to the section in this chapter entitled "32-Bit Processor's OS Register Set" for additional information. It contains the PowerPC processor version, or model, and the revision number. A mfspr instruction is used to transfer its contents to a GPR. The processor must be operating at the supervisor privilege level in order to access this register.

Figure 15-9 illustrates the PVR. The values encoded in the version field are assigned by the PowerPC architecture specification, while the revision number field indicates the engineering change level of that version processor.

EAR Register

The optional EAR register is implemented in the same manner as it is in a 32-bit processor. Refer to the discussion earlier in this chapter.

Chapter 16

The Previous Chapter

The previous chapter described the additional registers that become available to the operating system programmer when the processor is operating at the supervisor privilege level (MSR[PR] = 0). The register set for both the 32 and 64-bit versions of the processor were described.

This Chapter

This chapter describes the additional instructions that become available to the operating system programmer when the processor is operating at the supervisor privilege level (MSR[PR] = 0).

The Next Chapter

The next chapter provides an overview of the memory management unit's (MMU's) address translation capabilities. It introduces the concept of blocks, segments and pages and provides a basic discussion of block and page address translation.

Interrupt-Related Instructions

System Call Instruction

It should be noted that *the sc, or system call, instruction is not a privileged instruction*. It does, however, cause an interrupt to the OS. Execution of the sc instruction causes a system call interrupt. The processor saves the address of the instruction following the sc instruction in SRR0, saves a subset of the machine state bits from MSR to SRR1, sets/clears the appropriate MSR bits to perform a switch to the supervisor privilege level context, and jumps to the system call interrupt handler.

Trap Instruction

It should be noted that *the trap instruction is not a privileged instruction*. If the condition specified by the programmer as an operand is met, the trap instruction causes the system trap interrupt to be taken. The processor saves the address of the instruction following the trap instruction in SRR0, saves a subset of the machine state bits from MSR to SRR1, sets/clears the appropriate MSR bits to perform a switch to the supervisor privilege level context, and jumps to the program interrupt handler.

Return from Interrupt (rfi) Instruction

RFI is a privileged instruction. At the end of any interrupt handler, the programmer executes an rfi, or return from interrupt, instruction. This copies the saved state bits from SRR1 back to MSR, restoring the state of the processor to its context before recognition of the interrupt. The processor resumes execution at the return address specified in SRR0. SRR0 will contain the address of either:

- the instruction that caused the interrupt, or
- the next instruction to be executed

SPR-Related Privileged Instructions

Many of the processor's registers are implemented as special-purpose registers, or SPRs. The following two privileged instructions may be executed to move values between a specified GPR and an SPR.

- The move to special purpose register instruction (mtspr)
- The move from special purpose register instruction (mfspr)

MSR-Related Privileged Instructions

The following two privileged instructions may be executed to move values between a specified GPR register and the MSR register.

- The move to machine state register instruction (mtmsr)
- The move from machine state register instruction (mfmsr)

Privileged Cache Management Instruction — dcbi

There is only one privileged cache management instruction — dcbi. This is the data cache block invalidate instruction. In response, the processor performs a lookup in its data cache.

- In the event of a cache miss in this processor's data cache, no action is taken in this processor's cache. If M = 1, indicating that other processors/caching entities also access this memory area, the processor will also broadcast a kill transaction to eliminate any possible copies of the target cache block in other caches.
- In the event of a cache hit on a cache block in the exclusive state in this processor's data cache, the cache entry is invalidated. It is not necessary to perform a kill transaction because no other caches have a copy of the target cache block.
- In the event of a cache hit on a cache block in the shared state in this processor's data cache, the cache entry is invalidated. If M = 1, the processor also broadcasts a kill transaction to eliminate any possible copies of the target cache block in other caches.
- In the event of a cache hit on a cache block in the modified state in this processor's data cache, the cache entry is invalidated. It is not necessary to perform a kill transaction because no other caches have a copy of the target cache block.

If the target effective address in within an I/O, or direct-store, segment, the instruction is treated as a no-op.

The dcbi instruction is intended for use in maintaining the page table (at the operating system level). For more information, refer to the chapter entitled " 601 Multiprocessor Support" under the heading "Ensuring Unified View of Page Table."

Paging-Related Privileged Instructions

Segment Register Read/Write Instructions

In a 32-bit processor, the following privileged instructions are provided to permit a value to be moved between the specified GPR and segment registers.

- Move to segment register (mtsr)
- Move from segment register(mfsr)
- Move to segment register indirect (mtsrin)
- Move from segment register indirect (mfsrin)

These instructions are only defined for 32-bit processors and will cause the program interrupt if executed on a 64-bit processor (because the segment registers do not exist in a 64-bit processor.

TLB Management Instructions

The TLB, or translation lookaside buffer, is a high-speed, lookaside cache in the MMU that caches page table entries to improve performance for future accesses within the page. Inclusion of the TLB in a PowerPC is optional. If a 32 or 64-bit processor implements a TLB (translation lookaside buffer) in the MMU, it supports the following privileged instructions. A complete description of the MMU, TLB and usage of these instructions may be found in the chapter entitled "Virtual Paging."

- **TLB invalidate entry (tlbie)** instruction — The tlbie instruction invalidates an entry if there is a match on the effective address provided as an operand. This instruction is only necessary in processors that implement a TLB.
- **TLB invalidate all (tlbia)** instruction — All TLB entries are invalidated. This instruction is only necessary in processors that implement a TLB.
- **TLB synchronize (tlbsync)** instruction — This instruction will not complete until the processor has finished all previously issued tlbie and tlbia instructions and they have been received and completed by all other processors. This ensures that all processors with a TLB are dealing with up-to-date page table information.

SLB Management Instructions

The segment lookaside buffer, or SLB, is a high-speed, lookaside cache in the MMU that caches segment table entries to improve performance for future accesses within the effective segment. Inclusion of the SLB in a PowerPC is optional. 64-bit processors that implement an SLB must support the following privileged instructions. A complete description of the MMU, SLB and usage of these instructions may be found in the chapter entitled "Virtual Paging."

- **SLB invalidate entry (slbie)** instruction — The SLB invalidates an entry if there is a match on the effective address provided as an operand. This instruction is only necessary in 64-bit processors that implement an SLB.
- **SLB invalidate all (slbia)** instruction — All SLB entries are invalidated. This instruction is only necessary in 64-bit processors that implement an SLB.

Chapter 17

The Previous Chapter

The previous chapter described the additional instructions that become available to the operating system programmer when the processor is operating at the supervisor privilege level (MSR[PR] = 0).

This Chapter

This chapter provides an overview of the memory management unit's (MMU's) address translation capabilities. It introduces the concept of blocks, segments and pages and provides a basic discussion of block and page address translation.

The Next Chapter

The next chapter provides a detailed description of virtual paging as implemented in both the 32 and 64-bit versions of the PowerPC processor.

Memory Areas Defined as Blocks or Pages

General

Whenever an access must be performed for the integer, floating-point, or instruction units the effective address is submitted to the memory management unit, or MMU, for translation to a physical memory or I/O address. If effective-to-physical address translation is turned off (MSR[IR] and/or MSR[DR] = 0), then no address translation takes place and the physical memory address to be accessed is the same as the effective address. This is referred to as real address mode.

Refer to figure 17-1. If, on the other hand, address translation is enabled, the MMU first determines if the effective address has been mapped into a memory block by the operating system programmer. If it has, then segmentation (memory and I/O) is ignored and the block address translation, or BAT, logic translates the effective address to a physical memory address within the block. If the effective address has not been mapped into a memory block, the MMU translates the effective address into either a page address or an I/O address. The following sections provide an overview of each process.

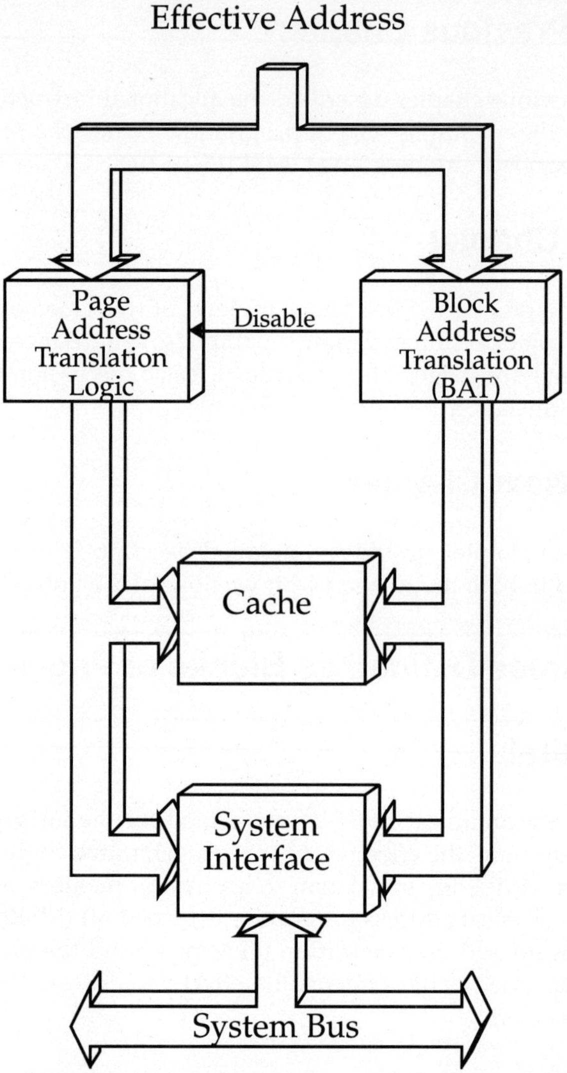

Figure 17-1. MMU Submits Effective Address to Block and Page Address Translation Logic Simultaneously

Block — Large Memory Region With One Set of Operational Rules

Defining an area of memory as a block rather than a page can have distinct advantages. An example would be a large video frame buffer or a large array of floating-point numbers in memory. The operating system programmer would like to define the rules of operation within the memory area encompassed by the buffer. If the buffer were 1MB in size and the operating system programmer were forced to treat it as a contiguous set of 256 pages each 4KB in size, the programmer would have to define 256 page definitions in the page table, each with identical access rules. On the other hand, the operating system programmer could define it as one block with one set of access rules. The benefit to this approach is obvious.

The operating system programmer may define certain large areas of effective address space as memory blocks. The block definition set up by the operating system programmer defines the following characteristics of a block:

- Start effective, or logical, address of the block
- Block size. From 128KB to 256MB in size
- Start physical memory address of the block
- Caching policies within the memory block. This includes the policy for handling memory writes (W bit), cacheability of the memory within the block (I bit), and whether the block of memory is also accessed by other processors in the system (M bit).
- Access rights within the block. The block may be designated as read/writable, read-only or inaccessible to the currently-running program.

Using a special set of BAT registers located in the MMU, the operating system programmer may define up to four instruction blocks and four data blocks in memory. The definition of regions of memory as blocks is covered in the chapter entitled "Block — Large Memory Region."

Effective, or Logical, Segments

General

Assuming that address translation is enabled (MSR[IR] and/or MSR[DR] = 1) and that the effective address hasn't been mapped to a memory block (using a BAT register), the MMU considers the processor's effective address space as being divided into segments of equal size. Each segment is 256MB in size and starts on an address divisible by 256MB. A 32-bit processor generates 32-bit effective addresses, for a total of 4GB of effective address space. As illustrated in figure 17-2, this space is divided into 16 segments by the MMU.

A 64-bit processor generates 64-bit effective addresses, for a total of 2^{64} bytes of effective address space. As illustrated in figure 17-3, this space is divided into 2^{36} segments by the MMU.

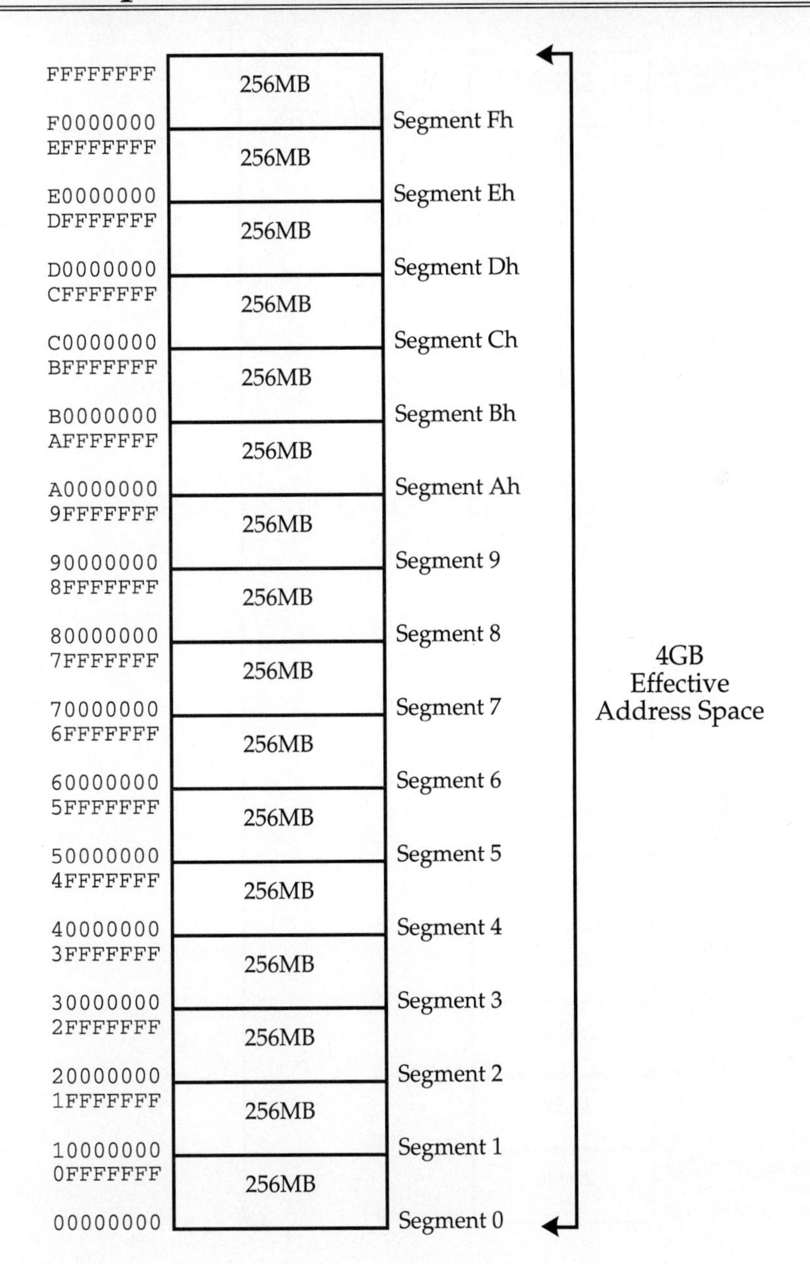

Figure 17-2. 32-bit Processor Has 4GB of Effective Address Space Divided into 16 Segments of 256MB Each

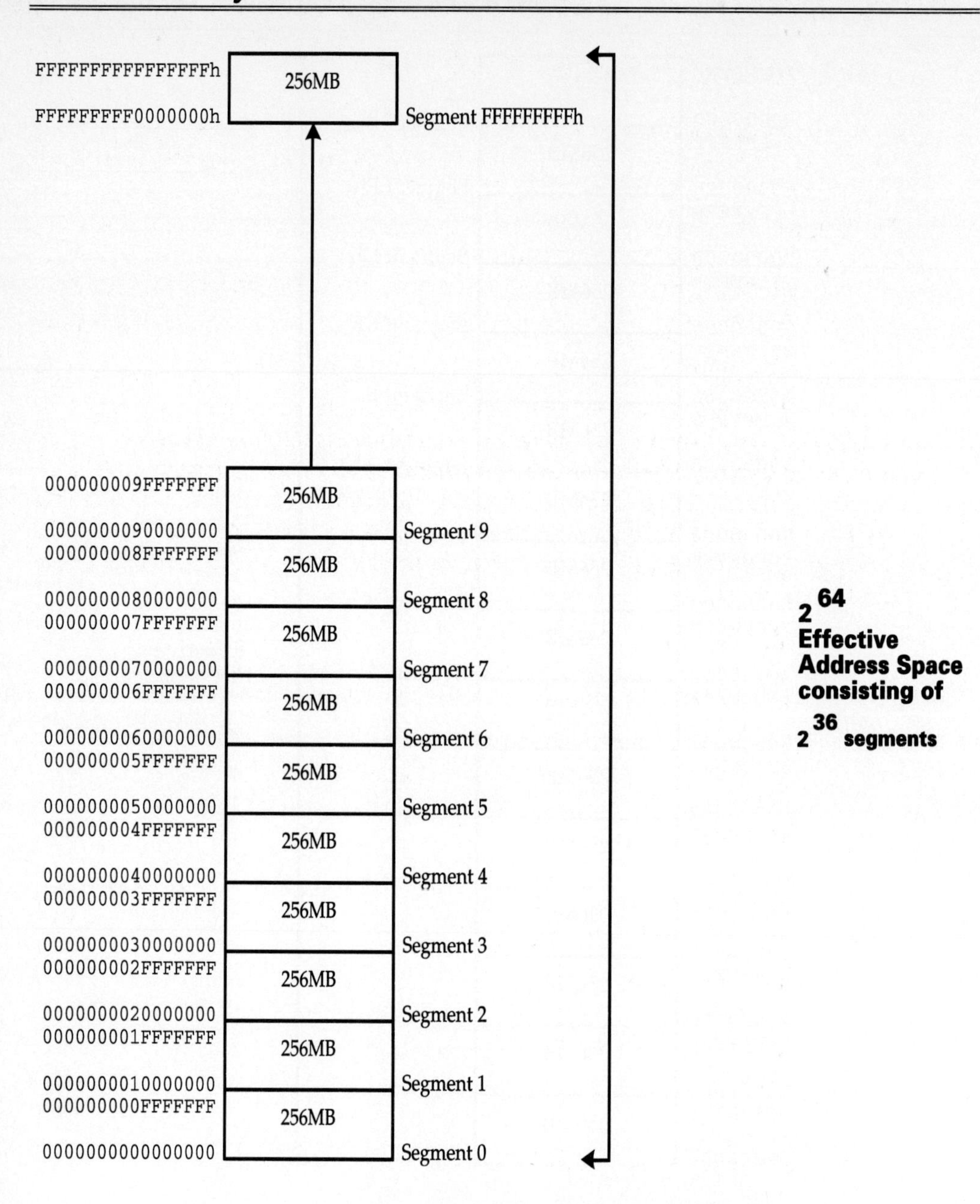

Figure 17-3. 64-bit Processor Has 16EB of Effective Address Space Divided into 2^{36} Segments of 256MB Each

Segment Type — Memory or I/O

The operating system programmer can define each segment as either a memory or an I/O segment. The MMU determines the segment type by testing the state of the segment type, or T, bit. This bit is contained in:

- the segment register in a 32-bit processor.
- a segment table entry, or STE, of the memory-based segment table in a 64-bit processor.

If the T bit is set to zero, the address falls within a memory segment and memory page address translation will take place. If the T bit is set to one, the address falls within an I/O segment. The subject of I/O segments is covered in the chapter entitled "I/O and Memory-Mapped I/O." Figure 17-4 illustrates the use of the 16 segment registers in mapping each of the 16 effective segments to either a virtual memory or an I/O segment. All but one of the segments are defined as memory segments. The other segment is defined as an I/O segment.

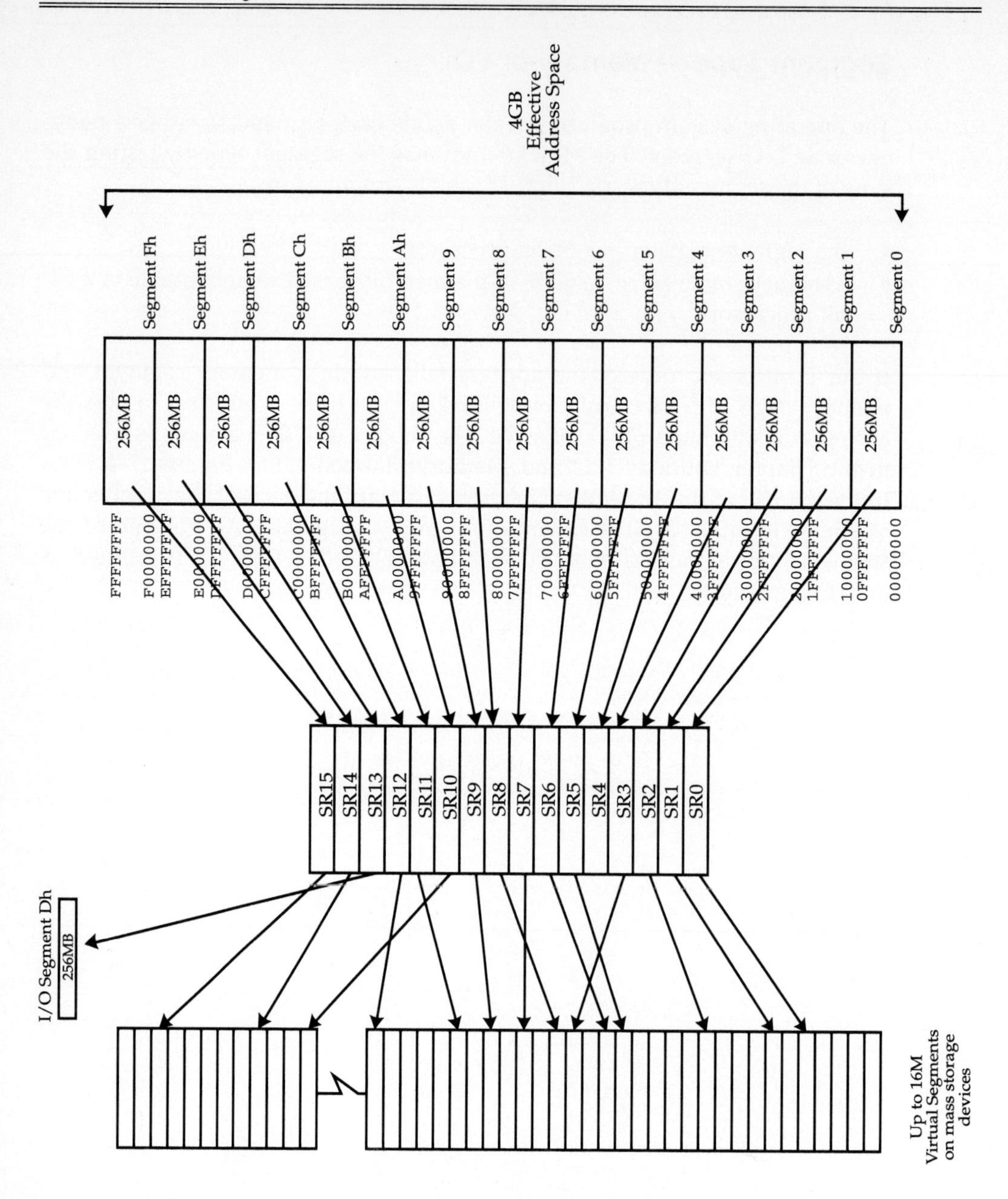

Figure 17-4. Example Effective Segments Mapped to Virtual Memory and I/O Segments

Memory Segment Consists of Pages

Each 256MB memory segment is divided into 64K (2^{16})pages, each of which is 4KB in size. Figure 17-5 illustrates the division of each memory segment into 64K pages, each 4KB in size.

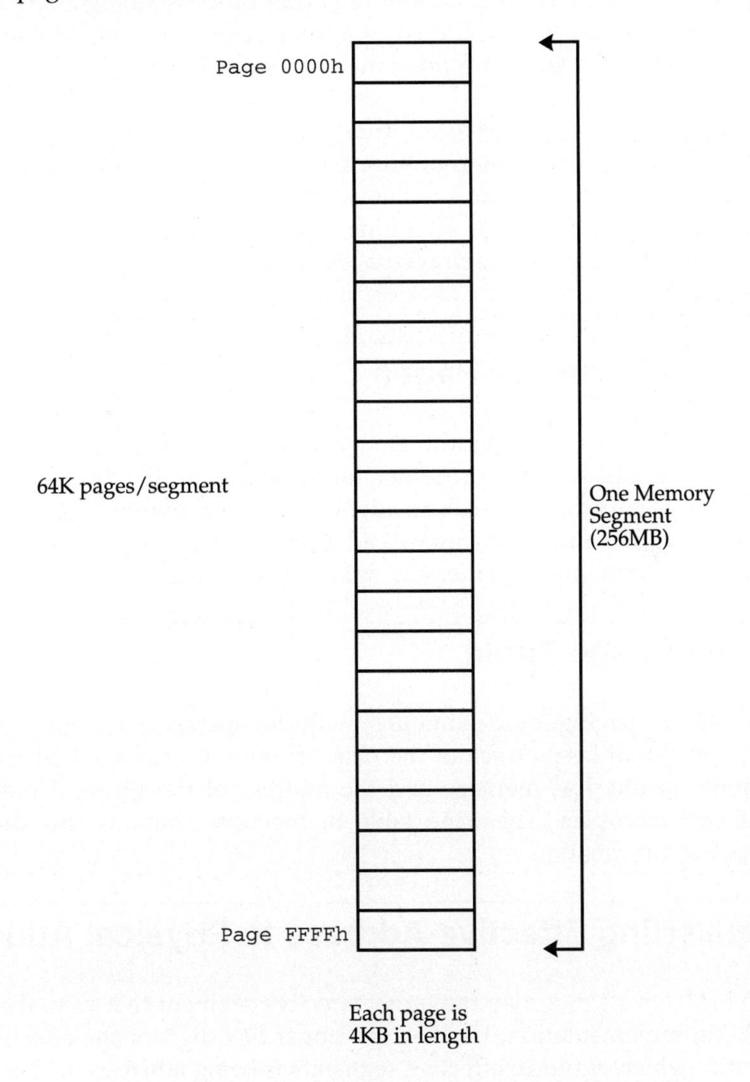

Figure 17-5. Each Memory Segment Divided Into Pages

Virtual Segments and Address Translation

The operating system programmer can view mass storage (i.e., hard drives, CD-ROMs, etc.) as an extension of physical memory. The combined storage supplied by physical memory and the array of mass storage devices attached to the system may be considered as a huge array of storage divided into segments with each segment divided into pages of 4KB each.

As an example, a 1GB drive could be viewed as consisting of four segments, each consisting of 64K pages of information (code and/or data). Each segment of mass storage-based information can be thought of as a virtual segment of information pages and the operating system, with the aid of the MMU, can keep track of what mass storage pages are currently in physical memory and their location.

Physical Memory Pages

The MMU thinks of physical memory as an array of physical pages of available storage. In a 32-bit processor implementation, the MMU considers the 4GB physical memory space to be divided into one million pages (2^{32}/4KB) of storage available to hold pages read from mass storage devices. In a 64-bit implementation, physical memory space consists of 2^{64}/4KB pages of storage.

Role of Page Table

The MMU's paging logic maintains, with the operating system programmer's aid, a map that keeps track of the pages from mass storage that are currently resident in physical memory and the address of the physical memory page that each occupies. The page table in memory contains this directory, or mapping, information.

Converting Effective Address to Physical Address

The MMU must first map the target effective segment to a virtual segment. In a 32-bit implementation, EA[0:3], the upper hex digit of the effective address identify which of the 16 effective segments is being addressed. This bit field is used to select 1-of-16 segment registers in the MMU. The contents of the selected segment register identifies whether the target segment is a memory or an I/O segment. If a memory segment (the register's T bit = 0), the 24-bit virtual segment address contained in the register identifies which virtual segment the effective segment is mapped to. This 24-bit field in a segment register permits the operating system programmer to map an effective segment to any of 16M virtual segments, each of which consists of 64K pages, each 4KB in length. In other words, the MMU can track up to 2^{52} bytes of information, some of which is currently resident in physical memory.

When a load, a store or an instruction access is attempted, the MMU determines whether or not the target page (in a 32-bit implementation, bits EA[4:19] of the effective address) from the selected virtual segment is currently present in physical memory. The MMU consults the page table in memory to determine the presence or absence of the page in physical memory. If the page is present, the MMU must then substitute the physical address of the target page in memory (extracted from the page table entry, or PTE) for the target effective segment and page. The lower 12 bits of the effective address are not translated but are directly used to identify the target location (1-of-4096) within the page.

Overview of Demand-Mode Paging

General

When the system is first started, all pages of code and data are resident on mass storage devices and memory is empty. When the operating system is loaded, it takes over management of these pages. The total number of pages of information, each 4KB in size, contained on the system's mass storage devices usually far exceeds the size of physical RAM memory. The operating system keeps track of the location of each page on mass storage. In addition, it loads pages into memory on demand and keeps track of their location in physical memory using the page table. When a program attempts access to an effective address in memory, the MMU's paging mechanism searches the page table to determine if the page is currently resident in physical memory. If it is, the paging mechanism substitutes the physical page address for the effective page address. In other words, the paging mechanism in the MMU maps accesses within effective pages to physical pages in memory. In the event that the MMU cannot find a match in the page table, a page fault interrupt occurs and the operating system's page fault handler is invoked. The handler determines which of the following conditions is true:

- If the target page is in memory but is not currently mapped in the page table, the handler makes a page table entry, or PTE, and then restarts the instruction that caused the access attempt. This will now result in a page table hit and a successful page address translation.
- If the target page is not currently in memory and the currently-running program is permitted access to it, the handler makes a memory allocation call to find an available 4KB memory block. It then makes a call to the operating system mass storage request handler to read the requested page from mass storage to memory. Finally, the page fault handler makes a page table entry and then restarts the instruction that caused the access attempt. This will now result in a page table hit and a successful page address translation.
- If the currently-running program is not permitted access to the target page, the operating system terminates the program, indicates an access violation to the user, and resumes execution of another program.

Introduction to Page Table Scan

The operating system maintains a table in memory that contains the virtual-to-physical page mapping for all or most of the pages of information currently resident in memory. This table is referred to as the page, or hash, table. The MMU must scan one or more entries in the page table in order to determine if the mapping information is currently present in the table. The page table is structured as follows (refer to figure 17-6):

- The SDR1 register contains the physical start address of the table and its length
- The table consists of a series of page table entry groups, or PTEGs. The number of PTEGs in the table is a function of its size
- Each PTEG consists of eight page table entries, or PTEs

Each PTE contains the following information:

- A valid bit that indicates whether its contents is valid or not
- Virtual segment and page number of the page (i.e., the page's point of origin)
- The page in physical memory that the page resides in
- The caching attributes, shared memory indicator and speculative access permission for the page (WIMG bits)
- The access rights for the page (read/writable, read-only, or inaccessible)

Indexing Into Page Table

The MMU could be designed to walk through every entry in the page table looking for a match on the target virtual segment and page number. This would result is abysmal performance. Rather than use this approach, it makes more sense to select a relatively small portion of the page table to search. If the target virtual segment number were used as an index into the table, the table would consume a huge area of memory (a 32-bit processor has 16M virtual segments while a 64-bit processor has 2^{36}). If the target page number alone were used to index into the page table, the table could be of a reasonable size (64K PTE groups), but any access to the same page in any segment (e.g., 16 million possible segments in a 32-bit processor) would select the same page table entry group, or PTEG, to search. At a given instant in time, only a very small number of instances of that page number from all possible virtual segments could be tracked in the selected PTEG in the table.

Instead, the MMU creates a more unique index by combining the target virtual segment number and the page number. In a 32-bit processor, this is accomplished in the following manner — the 16-bit page number is extended to 19 bits by appending three zero bits to its upper end. The MMU then performs an exclusive-OR between the resulting 19-bit page number and the lower 19 bits of the virtual segment number.

Because the upper five bits of the virtual segment number are not included in the exclusive-OR, 32 segments will yield the same pattern in the lower 19 bits. When any of these are combined with the same page number, then, an identical table index will result.

The page table set up in memory by the operating system programmer may be vary in length from 64K to 32MB. The index must therefore be adjusted to match the actual table length.

Page Table Scan

This approach selects a PTEG to scan for a match on the virtual segment/page number. This is referred to as the primary hash. In examining each page table entry, or PTE, in a PTEG, the MMU looks for a match on the 24-bit virtual segment and also compares the target page number to the page number stored in each PTE.

If a match isn't found in the primary PTEG, the MMU inverts the 19 bit index and selects a secondary PTEG to scan in the same relative position at the opposite end of the table. This is referred to as the secondary hash. It then scans this group looking for a match.

The MMU scans up to two groups of eight page table entries each looking for a match, for a total of 16 comparisons. At a given instant in time, the page table could contain page mappings for 16 of the possible 32 pages that the MMU might scan these 16 entries for.

Rationale for Table Scanning

On the surface, it might appear that scanning up to 16 page table entries for a match before causing a page fault interrupt would adversely affect performance. In reality, however, this should be viewed as going to lengths to avoid page faulting. A page fault causes a serious performance hit (due to the necessity of reading the missing page into memory from a mechanical mass storage device).

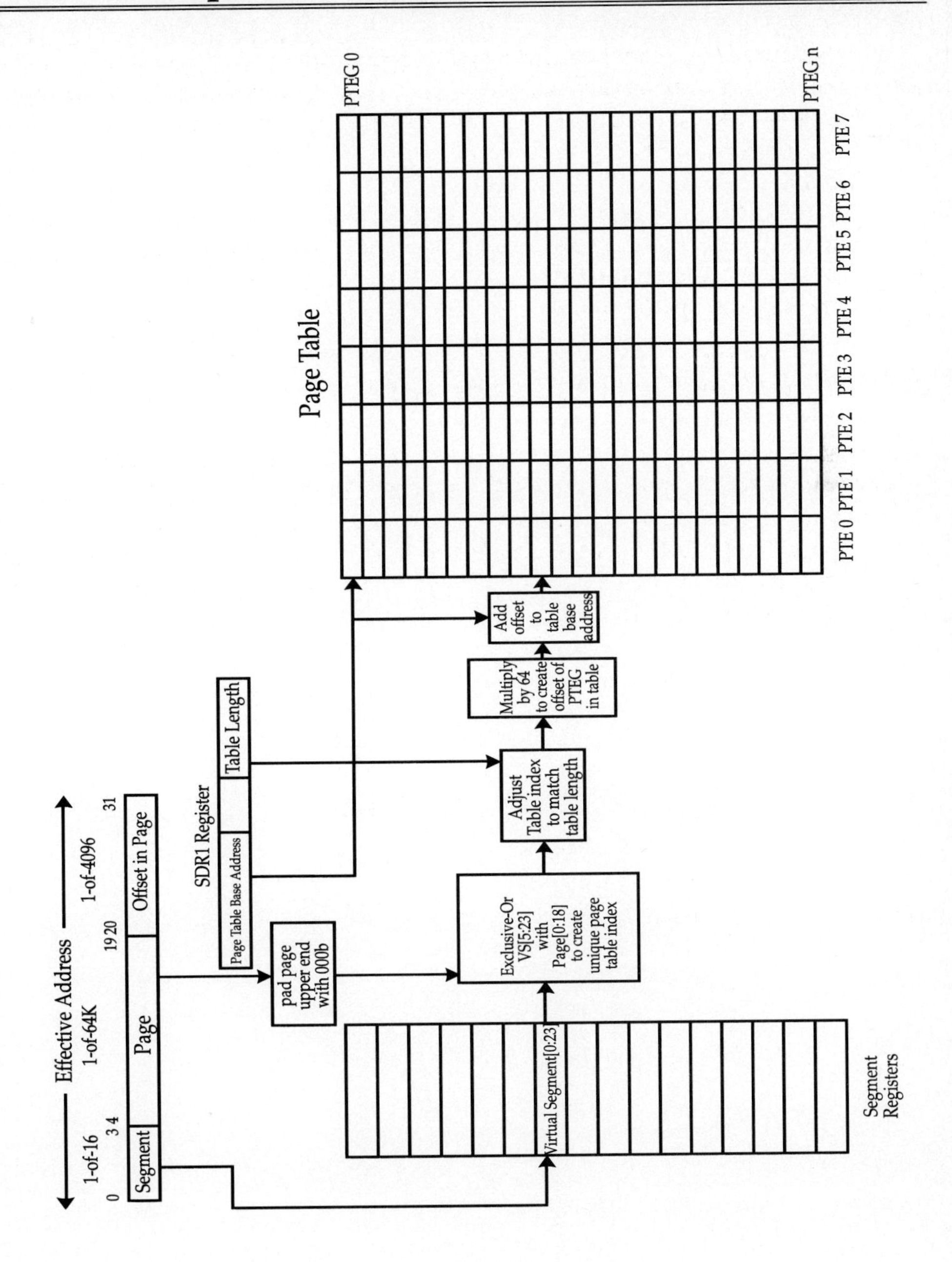

Figure 17-6. Page Table Index Creation

Chapter 18

The Previous Chapter

The previous chapter provided an overview of the memory management unit's (MMU's) address translation capabilities. It introduced the concept of blocks, segments and pages and provided a basic discussion of block and page address translation.

This Chapter

This chapter provides a detailed description of virtual paging as implemented in both the 32 and 64-bit versions of the PowerPC processor.

The Next Chapter

The next chapter provides a detailed description of the MMU's block address translation capabilities.

32-bit PowerPC Processor Paging Implementation

4GB = 16 Segments of Space

The 32-bit PowerPC processor generates 32-bit effective addresses in order to address one of the following:

- an integer data operand to be loaded from or stored into memory
- a floating-point operand to be loaded from or stored into memory
- an instruction to be fetched from memory

Assuming that the target effective address does not map into a region of memory defined as a block by the BAT registers, the effective address is examined by the MMU's paging logic to determine if the target page is currently resident in memory.

As a first step, the MMU determines the target effective segment that is being addressed. Since each segment of space is 256MB in size (refer to the previous chapter), the overall 4GB effective address space is divided into 16 segments. The target effective address lies within one of these 16 segments. The MMU determines the target segment by examining the upper four bits of the effective address, EA[0:3]. This nibble can contain any value from 0d through 15d. Figure 18-1 illustrates the division of the effective address space into segments.

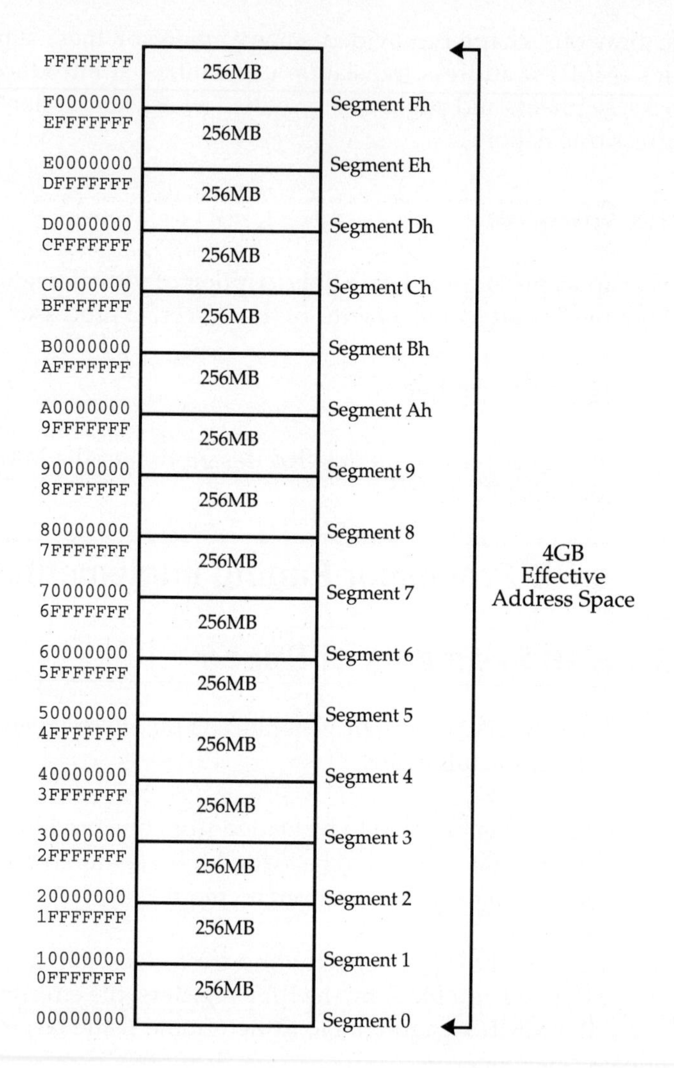

Figure 18-1. Segmentation of 32-bit Processor's 4GB Effective Address Space

Segment Type Determination

The processor uses the target effective segment number as an index into a stack of 16 segment registers, SR0 through SR15. Bit 0 of the selected segment register identifies the segment as a memory or an I/O segment. Known as the segment type, or T, bit, T = 0 indicates that this is a memory segment, while T = 1 indicates that it is an I/O segment.

Assuming that the target address is within a memory segment, figure 18-2 illustrates the segment register's contents.

Memory Segment Format (T = 0)

0 1 2 3 7 8 31

T	Ks	Ku	Reserved	Virtual Segment ID (1-of-16M)

Key bits. When segment access attempted, MSR[PR] selects which key bit to check for access permission. Selected key bit is used with PP bits to verify access permitted. PP bits are supplied by Page Table Entry.

T = 0 for a memory segment.

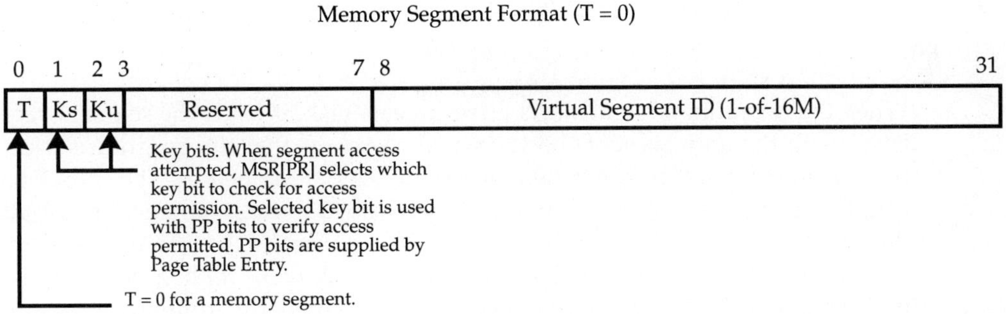

Figure 18-2. Format of a 32-bit Processor's Segment Register When Mapped To a Memory Segment

Discussion of the I/O segment is outside the scope of this chapter. A detailed description of accesses within an I/O segment may be found in the chapter entitled "The PPC 601 I/O Transactions." Figure 18-3 illustrates the format of a segment register's contents if the T bit = 1, indicating that the effective segment is mapped to an I/O segment.

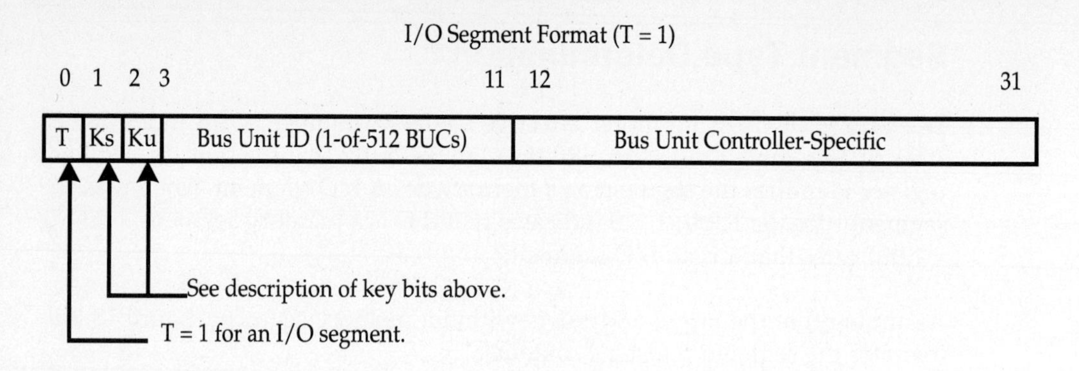

Figure 18-3. Format of 32-Bit Processor's Segment Register if Mapped to an I/O Segment

When the operating system starts or resumes a task, it loads the segment registers with the addresses of the 16 virtual segments that the program's effective address space is permitted access to. As described in the previous chapter, the virtual segments are typically mapped to mass storage. The 24-bit virtual segment ID field in each segment register permits the operating system programmer to map each effective segment to any of 16 million possible virtual segments. The privilege level of the currently running program (contained in MSR[PR]) selects one of the two key bits from the segment register. The key bit will be used in conjunction with the page protection bits (PP bits) from a page table entry to define the program's access rights within the target page. Figure 18-4 illustrates an example of effective to virtual segment mapping via the segment registers. Segment Dh maps to an I/O segment while the other 15 segments map to virtual memory segments.

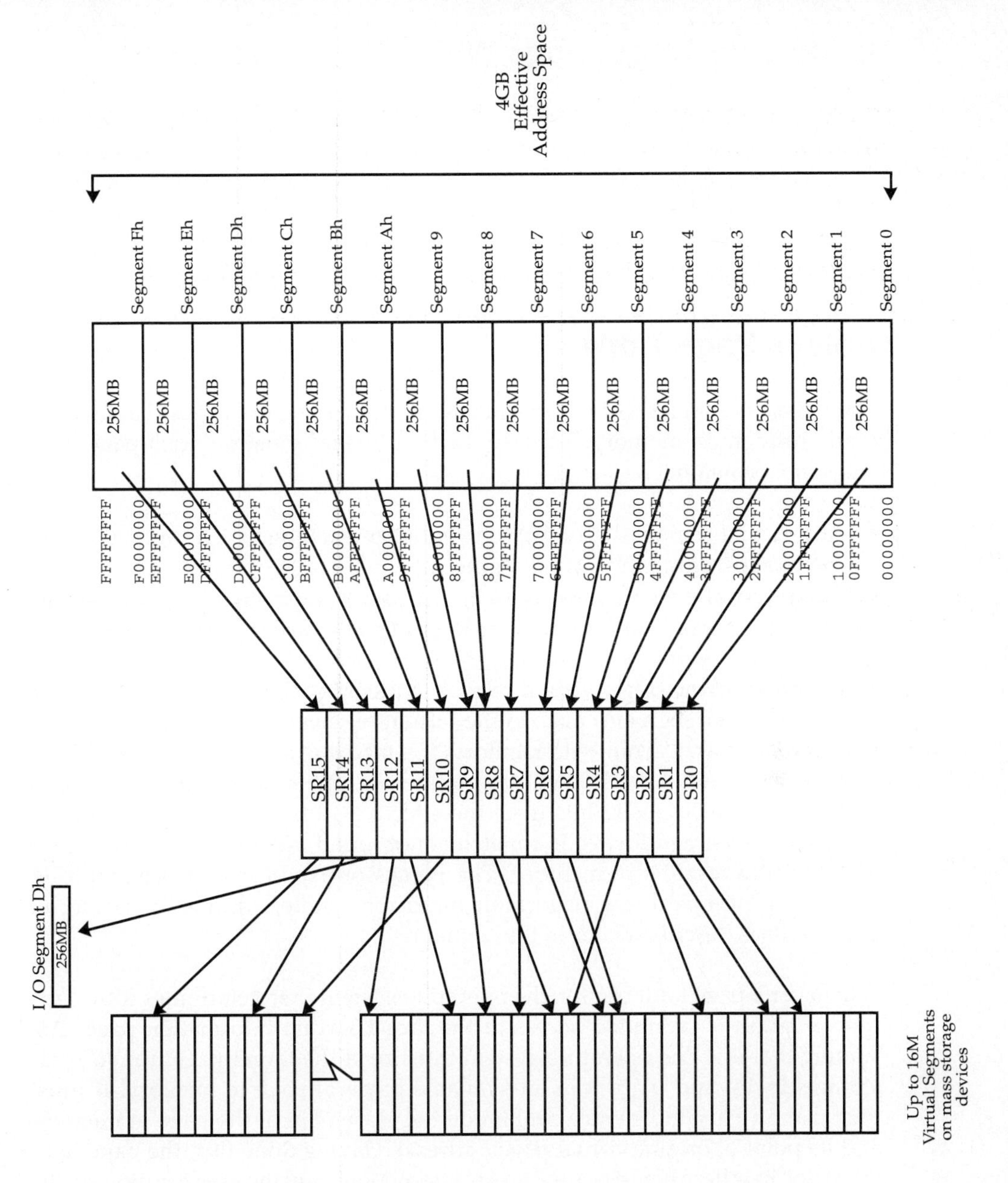

Figure 18-4. Example of Effective to Virtual Segment Mapping.

Identifying Target Page Within Virtual Segment

Each memory segment consists of 64K pages of information. The upper hex digit of the effective address, EA[0:3], identify the target effective segment and its associated segment register. The next four hex digits, or 16 bits, of the effective address, EA[4:19], identify the target page within the virtual segment. The lower three hex digits, or 12 bits, of the effective address, EA[20:31], identify the exact start address of the target operand within the page.

Role of Page Table

The page table consists of a series of entries that define the pages that are currently resident in memory. To keep track of this information, each page table entry must contain:

- the virtual segment (1-of-16M virtual segments) and page number (1-of-64K pages within the virtual segment)
- the physical page in memory (1-of-1M pages) the virtual page was stored in when it was read from mass storage at some earlier point in time

To determine if the target virtual page is in memory, the MMU must compare the target virtual segment/page to the virtual segment/page numbers that the table indicates are currently in memory. If a match is found, the physical page address from the page table entry supplies the upper 20 bits of the physical address and the lower 12 bits from the effective address supply the lower 12 bits of the physical address. If a match is not found, the target virtual page is not currently resident in memory. The processor experiences a page fault interrupt and jumps to the page fault interrupt handler routine. Handling of page faults is described later in this chapter.

Whenever a page fault occurs, the operating system first determines if the current program is permitted access to the target virtual information page. Assuming that it is, the operating system must read the target page from a mass storage device and place it in an available physical page in memory. It must then make a page table entry containing the placement of the page in memory and its point of origin (virtual page address). Having done this, the page fault interrupt handler then executes an rfi instruction, causing re-execution of the load or store or instruction fetch that caused the page fault. Since the page is now present in memory and the mapping information is present in the page table, the page table search will be successful and the target operand can be read or written successfully.

Page Table Location and Length Determination

In order to search the page table for a match, the processor must know the start, or base, address of the page table in physical memory. It must also know the size of the page table in order to the know the bounds of the search. Both the start address and the size of the page table are contained in search descriptor register one, or SDR1. Figure 18-5 illustrates the format of SDR1. The bits set to zero are reserved bits.

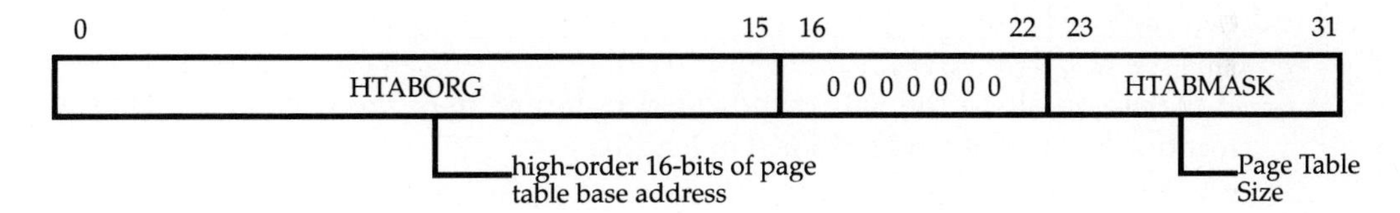

Table Search Descriptor Register, SDR1

Figure 18-5. 32-bit Storage Description Register One (SDR1)

The page table is also referred to as the hash table. The HTABORG field contains the start address, or origin, of the page table. The HTABMASK field contains the size of the page table in memory. The page table must reside on an address boundary that is divisible by its size. As an example, if the page table is 256KB in size (as defined by the contents of the HTABMASK field), it could start at memory address 00000000h, 00040000h, 00080000h, etc. Table 18-1 defines the interpretation of the HTABMASK field.

Table 18-1. HTABMASK Field Definition (32-bit Processor)

Fields Contents	Page Table Size
000000000b	64KB
000000001b	128KB
000000011b	256KB
000000111b	512KB
000001111b	1MB
000011111b	2MB
000111111b	4MB
001111111b	8MB
011111111b	16MB
111111111b	32MB

If SDR1 contained the values indicated in figure 18-6, the page table starts at location 12340000h and is 256KB in length.

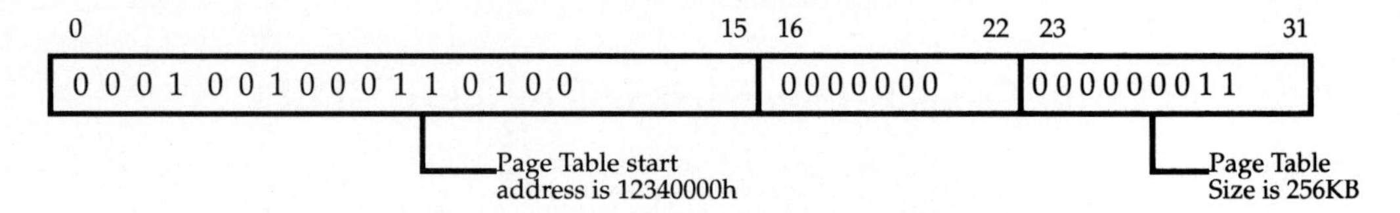

Table Search Descriptor Register, SDR1

Figure 18-6. Sample SDR1 Contents

Organization of Page Table

The page table organization is illustrated in figure 18-7. It consists of page table entry groups, or PTEGs, each containing a group of eight page table entries, or PTEs. Each PTE consists of eight bytes of information. The number of PTEGs that comprise the table depends on the size of the table. As illustrated in table 18-1, the maximum size of the page table is 32MB. A page table this size would consists of 512K PTEGs (512K x 8 PTEs x 8 bytes per PTE = 32MB).

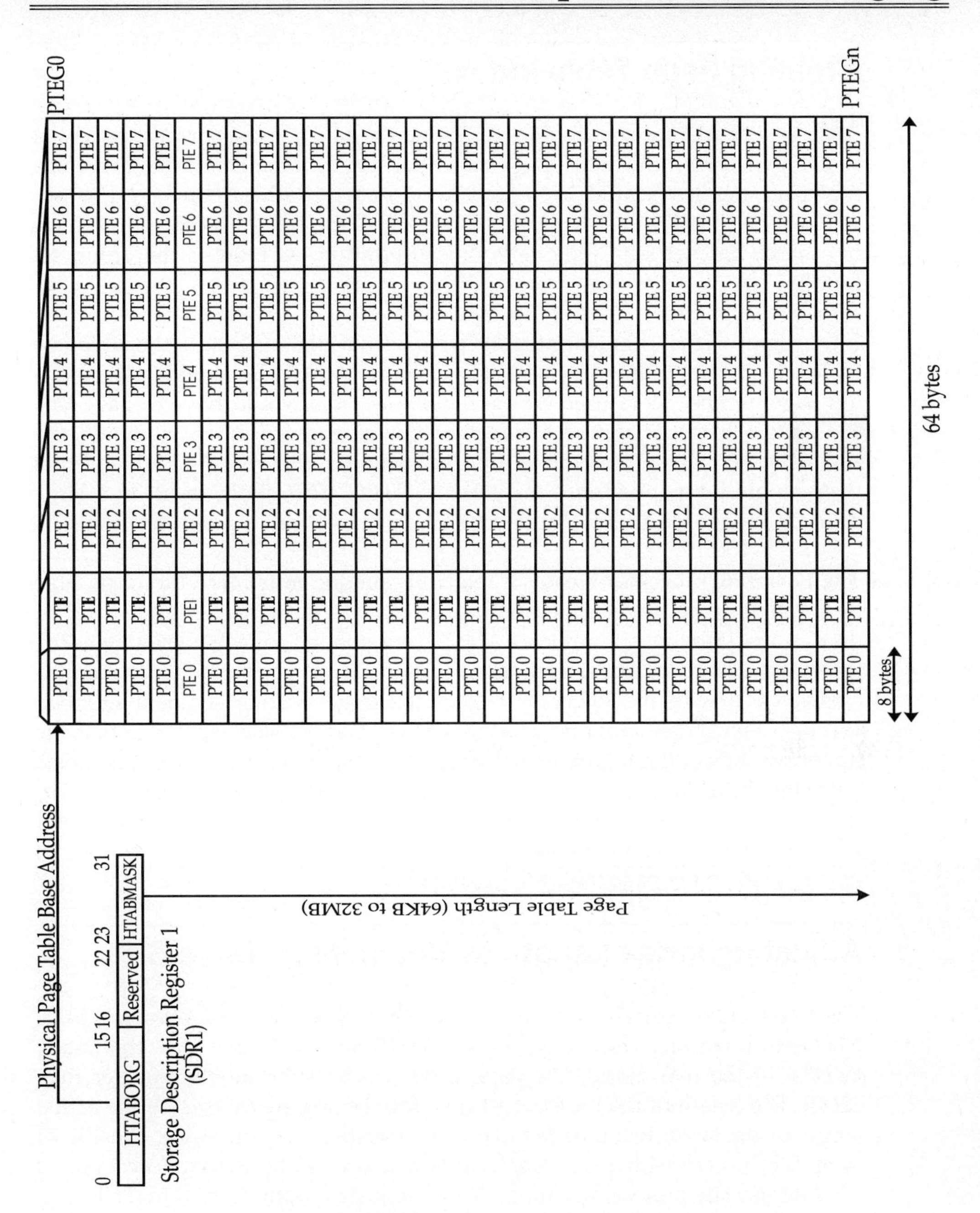

Figure 18-7. The Page Table Structure (32-bit Processor)

Creating Page Table Index

From a performance standpoint, designing the MMU to perform a sequential search throughout the entire page table looking for a match on the target virtual page number would be a terrible approach. Rather than take this approach, the MMU will select a particular PTEG to scan for a match, resulting in a much quicker scan. The next logical question — "How is the group selected?"

If the target virtual segment number were used as the index into the table, the table would have to have 16M PTEGs (an unreasonably large table). If the target page number were used as the index, the table would have to have 64K PTEGs (a reasonable number). However, any given page exists within all 16M segments. At a given moment in time, only eight of these 16M possible virtual pages could be mapped into the selected PTEG. This could result in a large number of page faults and a corresponding degradation in performance.

The PowerPC processor creates a relatively unique index into the page table by combining the target page number with the target virtual segment ID. To do this, the 16-bit page number, EA[4:19], is extended to 19 bits by appending three zero bits to its upper end. The resultant 19-bit page number is then exclusive-OR'd with the lower 19 bits of the target virtual segment number. With a 19-bit index, any one of 512K PTEGs may be selected. Note that the upper five bits of the target virtual segment number are not part of the index. Since this field can assume any of 32 values, the same page in 32 separate virtual segments will select the same PTEG. At a given moment in time, the eight PTEs in the PTEG can have mappings for eight of the 32 pages. The odds of having a hit on the page table are getting better.

Adjusting Index Length to Match Page Table Size

The 19 bit index created in the previous step permits selection of any of 512K PTEGs in the table. Only a page table 32MB in size would have this many PTEGs. In the real world, the page table will be substantially smaller than 32MB. The length of the index must therefore be adjusted to match the actual length of the table. If the page table were 256KB in size, it would consists of 4096 PTEGs, each 64 bytes in length. It only takes a 12 bit field to select one of 4096 items. The index must therefore be adjusted from 19 bits to 12 bits in length. This is accomplished by ANDing the nine bit HTABMASK field with the upper nine bits of the 19 bit index. The HTABMASK field contains

000000011b for a 256KB table, so the AND process would strip the upper seven bits of the index's upper nine bits. This would leave the least-significant two bits plus the lower ten bits of the index — a twelve bit index.

Converting Index Into Offset Within Page Table

Each PTEG is 64 bytes long (8 bytes/PTE x 8 PTEs = 64 bytes). To create the offset (from the table's base address) of the selected PTEG within the table, the index must be multiplied by 64. This is accomplished by left-shifting the index by six bits and filling the lower six bits with zero. The resultant offset is then added to the table base address, forming the physical start address of the selected PTEG in memory.

Primary Scan, or Hash

The physical address produced by the table index process is used to access PTE 0 in the selected PTEG. The MMU checks to determine if the entry should be used to translate the virtual address to a physical page address. This process is described under the heading "Testing the Page Table Entry." If a match is achieved, the 20 bit physical page address from the entry is concatenated with the lower 12 bits of the effective address to form the 32 bit physical address to be accessed. The address translation has been completed.

If it doesn't match, the MMU adds eight to the PTEG start address to point to PTE one of the selected PTEG. The comparison process is repeated for each of the eight entries in the primary PTEG until either a match is found or all of the entries have been scanned. If no match is found, the secondary PTEG is scanned. The secondary PTEG is in the same relative position as this PTEG but at the opposite end of the table. The secondary PTEG may contain entries that would not fit in the primary PTEG. In other words, the secondary PTEG can act as an overflow area for the primary PTEG.

It should be noted that some accesses will select the opposite PTEG first rather than this PTEG. In this case, the other PTEG is the primary for those accesses and this PTEG is the overflow area, or secondary PTEG, for the other PTEG.

Secondary Scan, or Hash

The index into the table is formed in the same manner as described for the primary hash with the following exception — after the lower 19 bits of the virtual segment address and the zero-extended virtual page address are exclusive-OR'd, the discrete index value produced is inverted. After the inversion, the steps utilized to form the primary PTEG index are repeated. This selects a PTEG in the same relative position at the opposite end of the table. The PTEG pointed to by the resultant physical address is then scanned for a match. If no match is found, a page fault interrupt is generated.

Testing Page Table Entry

During the scan of a PTEG, the MMU checks each PTE for the following:

- The PTE must be valid — This is indicated by the V bit being set to one.
- If this is the primary PTEG scan, the hash, or H, bit must be cleared to zero or the PTE will not be included in the scan. If the set to one, this indicates the entry is an overflow entry from the group at the opposite end of the table. If this is the secondary PTEG scan, the H bit must be set to one or the entry will not be included in the scan. During the secondary scan, the target virtual segment/page is only compared to valid entries with the hash bit set to one because these entries are overflows for the primary PTEG.
- The virtual segment address in the PTE must be equal to the virtual segment address, VA[0:23], presented to the page translation logic by the selected segment register.
- The six bit abbreviated page index, or API, in the entry must be equal to the upper six bits of the effective page address, EA[4:9], presented to the page translation logic.

If all of these conditions are met, the table scan terminates and the virtual to physical address translation takes place. Figure 18-8 illustrates the format of the page table entry for a 32-bit PowerPC processor.

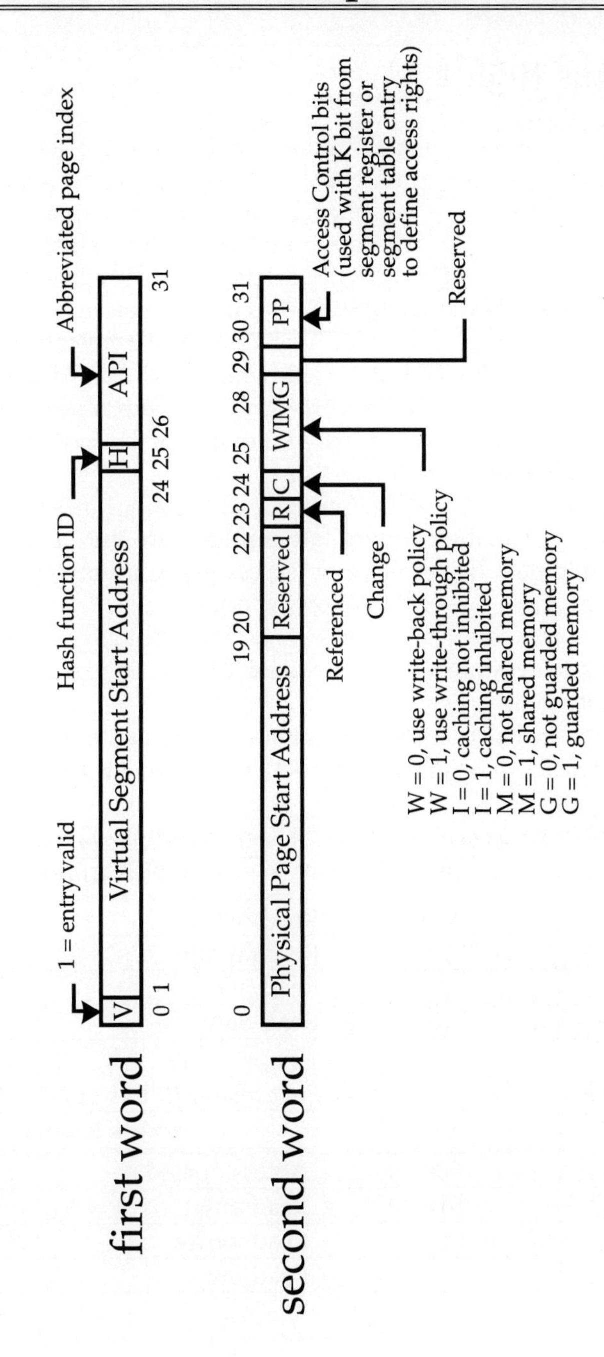

Figure 18-8. PTE Format For a 32-bit Processor

Access Rights

If a match is found on a PTE, the MMU checks the state of the key and page protection bits to determine if the access in progress violates the page access rights. The key bit is supplied by the segment table, while the PP bits are supplied by the PTE. There are two key bits, designated Ks and Ku, in the segment register. The privilege level of the currently running program (indicated by the state of MSR[PR]) is used to select which key bit to use when checking for a page protection violation. If an application program is running (MSR[PR] = 1), the Ku bit is used, while Ks is used if the operating system is running (MSR[PR] = 0). Table 18-2 indicates the access rights within the page if the selected key bit = 0. Table 18-3 indicates the access rights within the page if the selected key bit = 1.

If an access violation occurs (attempted store into a read-only or no access page; attempted load from a no access page; attempted instruction fetch in a no access page), one of the following occurs:

- On a load/store violation, a data storage interrupt is taken and DSISR[4] is set to one
- On an instruction fetch violation, an instruction storage interrupt is taken and SRR1[4] is set to one (SRR1[36] for a 64-bit processor)

Table 18-2. Meaning of Page Protection (PP) Bits In PTE When Key Bit = 0

PP	Access Rights
00b	Read/write.
01b	Read/write.
10b	Read/write.
11b	Read-only.

Table 18-3. Meaning of Page Protection (PP) Bits In PTE When Key Bit = 1

PP	Access Rights
00b	Access denied.
01b	Read-only.
10b	Read/write.
11b	Read-only.

Why Entire Page Address Doesn't Have to Be in PTE

The lower ten bits of the target page address were included in the computation of the table index that selected the PTEG to scan. Only pages with their lower ten bits equal to this value should have entries in this PTEG. Ensuring that this is true is the responsibility of the operating system programmer who builds and maintains the table. This being the case, accesses to any pages with a different value in the lower ten bits will not select this PTEG to scan.

The PTEs in this group need only contain the upper six bits of the page address. This is referred to as the abbreviated page index, or API. In order to have a match on a PTE, the valid bit must be set, the hash bit must be in the appropriate state (0 for primary PTEG scan, 1 for secondary PTEG scan), the virtual segment number stored in the PTE must match the target virtual segment number, and the upper six bits of the target page number must match the six bit abbreviated page index, or API, field in the PTE.

Two Examples of Page Address Translation

Example One

Assumptions

The following conditions are assumed to be true:

- The following instruction has been fetched from memory, decoded and is currently being executed — ***lwz r1, 0, r2***
- **GPR2 contains the value 30001000h**. This is the effective address of the word to be loaded into GPR1
- **Privilege level** of the currently running program is user (MSR[PR] = **1**]
- **SDR1 contains the value 00040003h**. This indicates that the page table is 256KB in size and starts at physical memory location 00040000h. A 256KB page table consists of 4096 PTEGs (256KB/64 bytes per PTEG = 4096 PTEGs).
- **SR3 contains 60123456h**. The T bit is set to 0, indicating that effective segment 3 is a memory segment. The two Key bits are set to 11b and MSR[PR] = 1 selects Ku to be used with the PTE's PP bits to define the access rights within the target page. Effective segment 3 is mapped to virtual segment 123456h.
- None of the DBAT registers have been set up to define regions of memory as blocks

Step-by-Step Explanation of Example One

1. The integer unit submits the effective address in GPR2, 30001000h, to the MMU.
2. The MMU does not compare the target effective address to the DBAT registers (because none of their valid bits are set).
3. The upper digit of the effective address, EA[0:3], contains a 3, selecting segment register 3, or SR3. SR3 contains the value 60123456h.
4. The T bit in SR3 is set to zero, indicating that the access is within a memory segment. The Ku bit (set to 1) is to be used with the PTE's PP bits to define the access rights within the target page. Effective segment 3 is mapped to virtual segment number 123456h.
5. SR3 outputs the virtual segment number, 123456h. The target page within the segment is specified by the next four digits of the effective address, EA[4:19]. This field identifies page 0001h as the target page. The target location within the page is specified by the lower three digits of the effective address, EA[20:31]. This field identifies location 000h as the target location within the page. In other words, the programmer is attempting to load the word that starts at location 000h in page 0001h of virtual segment 123456h. The entire virtual address is therefore 1234560001000h.
6. The 19 bit raw index into the page table is formed by exclusive-OR'ing the 19 bit page number (padded with three upper bits of zero) with the lower 19 bits of the virtual segment address. This is illustrated below:

   010 0011 0100 0101 0110b — lower 19 bits of virtual segment
   000 0000 0000 0000 0001b — 19 bit page number
   010 0011 0100 0101 0111b — 19 bit raw index

7. The length of this index would be correct if the page table were 32MB in size and contained 512K PTEGs. Since the page table is only 256KB in size, however, the page table size field in SDR1 must be used to adjust the index length to 12 bits. This is accomplished by and'ing the nine bit size field with the upper nine bits of the raw index to strip off the upper seven bits of the raw index:

   010 0011 01b — upper 9 bits of raw index
   000 0000 11b — 9 bit page table size field
   000 0000 01b — upper 9 bits of adjusted index

8. The full adjusted page table index is then 000 0000 0100 0101 0111b. The selected PTEG is therefore number 00457h. To calculate the offset of PTEG

00457h in the table, this value is then multiplied by 64 bytes per PTEG by left-shifting it six bits positions and zero-filling the lower six bits. This yields the following 25 bit offset into the page table:

0 0000 0001 0001 0101 1100 0000b

9. The 25 bit offset is then OR'd with the table base address from SDR1 to yield the exact start address of the selected PTEG in physical memory. For this operation, the table start address is padded with zeros to a length of 32 bits, and the offset is right-justified.

```
0000 0000 0000 0100 0000 0000 0000 0000b  table start from SDR1
        0 0000 0001 0001 0101 1100 0000b  25-bit offset
0000 0000 0000 0101 0001 0101 1100 0000b  start address of PTEG 00457h
```

10. The resultant start address of the PTEG selected for the primary scan, PTEG 00457h, is therefore 000515C0h. PTE 0 of this PTEG starts at this address.
11. Assume that PTE 0 through PTE7 of PTEG 00457h contain the values indicated in table 18-4.
12. The V bit in PTE 0 is cleared, so this is not a valid PTE entry. The MMU adds eight to the PTE start address to yield the start address of PTE 1, 000515C8h.
13. In PTE 1, the V bit is set, indicating that this is a valid PTE entry. However, the Hash bit is set to one, indicating that this PTE is an overflow for the sibling PTEG at the opposite end of the table and should be excluded from the primary PTEG scan.
14. The MMU adds eight to the PTE start address to yield the start address of PTE 2, 000515D0h. The V bit is set, indicating that this is a valid PTE entry. The Hash bit is clear, indicating that this PTE should be included in the scan of the primary PTEG. The target virtual segment number, 123456h is compared to the VSID, yielding a match. The upper six bits of the target page number, 000000b, are compared to the API, also yielding a match. The target page is therefore in memory and is stored in page 20000h in physical memory. The MMU appends the lower three digits of the effective address, 000h, to the lower end of the memory page address, yielding a 32-bit physical address of 20000000h. The combination of the Ku bit value (from SR3) and the page protection bit field from PTE 2 is 110b indicates that the page is read/writable, so the load access is permitted. The WIMG bits indicate that the page is cacheable (I = 0), a write-back policy should be used for stores within the page (W = 0), the page is

shared with other processors (M = 1), and speculative accesses are permitted within the page.

Table 18-4. Sample PTEG Number 00457h

PTE Element	PTE 0	PTE 1	PTE 2	PTE 3	PTE 4	PTE 5	PTE 6	PTE 7
V bit	0b	1b	1b	x	x	x	x	x
VSID	-	456789h	123456h	x	x	x	x	x
H bit	-	1b	0b	x	x	x	x	x
API	-	001001b	000000b	x	x	x	x	x
Memory Page	-	19863h	20000h	x	x	x	x	x
R bit	-	1b	0b	x	x	x	x	x
C bit	-	0b	0b	x	x	x	x	x
WIMG bits	-	0010b	0010b	x	x	x	x	x
PP bits	-	10b	10b	x	x	x	x	x

The load is therefore permitted. The data cache is checked for a hit. If the target cache block is valid, the requested data, the contents of memory locations 20000000h through 200000003h, are placed in GPR1. In the event of a cache miss, the cache block containing the target locations is read from external memory, the requested word is routed directly to GPR1, and the cache block read from memory is stored in the cache in either the exclusive or shared state (depending on the snoop results reported during the external memory read).

Example Two

Assumptions for Example Two

With the following exception, assume the same set of assumptions that existed for the first example — PTEG 00457h contains the values indicated in table 18-5.

Table 18-5. Second Example, Contents of PTEG 00457h

PTE Element	PTE 0	PTE 1	PTE 2	PTE 3	PTE 4	PTE 5	PTE 6	PTE 7
V bit	0b	1b	1b	1b	1b	1b	1b	1b
VSID	-	456789h	123456h	590456h	987654h	546531h	100000h	560000h
H bit	-	1b	1b	0b	1b	0b	0b	0b
API	-	001001b	000001b	111000b	101010b	111111b	000000b	000111b
Memory Page	-	19863h	20000h	98765h	99999h	A3A59h	3B7A4h	23000h
R bit	-	1b	0b	1b	1b	1b	1b	1b
C bit	-	0b	0b	1b	0b	1b	1b	0b
WIMG bits	-	0010b	0010b	0010b	0010b	0010b	0010b	0010b
PP bits	-	10b	10b	10b	10b	10b	10b	10b

Step-by-Step Explanation of Example Two

1. PTE 0 is invalid, PTE 1, 2, and 4 are excluded from the primary scan, and PTE 3, 5, 6 and 7 are scanned (because their hash bits are zero, indicating that they are part of the primary group) but do not yield a compare (because the target virtual segment and page numbers do not match those contained in these PTEs.
2. Having failed to find a compare in the primary PTEG, the MMU must select the secondary PTEG to scan. To do this, the MMU inverts the raw index and then processes it in the same manner discussed in the first example. The following steps describe this procedure.
3. The raw index was 010 0011 0100 0101 0111b. Inverted it yields:

   101 1100 1011 1010 1000b

4. The length of this index would be correct if the page table were 32MB in size and contained 512K PTEGs. Since the page table is only 256KB in size, however, the page table size field in SDR1 must be used to adjust the index length to 12 bits. This is accomplished by and'ing the nine bit size field with the upper nine bits of the raw index to strip off the upper seven bits of the raw index:

101 1100 10b	upper 9 bits of raw index
000 0000 11b	9 bit page size field
000 0000 10b	upper 9 bits of adjusted index

5. The full adjusted page table index is then 000 0000 1011 1010 1000b. This is a binarily-weighted field. The selected secondary PTEG is therefore number 00BA8h. To calculate the offset of PTEG 00BA8h in the table, this value is then multiplied by 64 bytes per PTEG by left-shifting it six bits positions and zero-filling the lower six bits. This yields the following 25 bit offset into the page table:

   0 0000 0010 1110 1010 0000 0000b

6. The 25 bit offset is then OR'd with the table base address from SDR1 to yield the exact start address of the selected PTEG in physical memory. For this operation, the table start address is padded with zeros to a length of 32 bits, and the offset is right-justified.

```
0000 0000 0000 0100 0000 0000 0000 0000b  table start from SDR1
          0 0000 0010 1110 1010 0000 0000b  25-bit offset
-----------------------------------------
0000 0000 0000 0110 1110 1010 0000 0000b  start address of PTEG 00BA8h
```

7. The resultant start address of the PTEG selected for the secondary scan, PTEG 00BA8h, is therefore 0006EA00h. PTE 0 of this PTEG starts at this address.
8. Assume that the secondary PTEG, number 00BA8h, contains the values indicated in table 18-6.

Table 18-6. Contents of the Secondary PTEG, Number 00BA8h

PTE Element	PTE 0	PTE 1	PTE 2	PTE 3	PTE 4	PTE 5	PTE 6	PTE 7
V bit	0b	1b	1b	1b	1b	1b	1b	1b
VSID	-	456789h	123456h	590456h	987654h	546531h	100000h	560000h
H bit	-	1b	1b	0b	1b	0b	0b	0b
API	-	001001b	000000b	111000b	101010b	111111b	000000b	000111b
Memory Page	-	19863h	45020h	98765h	99999h	A3A59h	3B7A4h	23000h
R bit	-	1b	0b	1b	1b	1b	1b	1b
C bit	-	0b	0b	1b	0b	1b	1b	0b
WIMG bits	-	0010b	0010b	0010b	0010b	0010b	0010b	0010b
PP bits	-	10b	10b	10b	10b	10b	10b	10b

9. PTE 0 is invalid and PTE 3, 5, 6 and 7 are excluded from the secondary scan (because the Hash bit is set to 0). PTE 1, 2 and 4 are included in the scan.
10. PTE 1 has a mismatch on the VSID and API.
11. PTE 2 has a match on the VSID and the API, so this is a hit. The target page in memory starts at location 45020000h.
12. The target location is formed by OR'ing the three lower digits of the effective address, 000h, with the page start address, 45020000h, yielding location 45020000h as the target physical start address. The contents of locations 45020000h through 45020003h are loaded into GPR1.

TLB — Performance Enhancement Tool

The PowerPC architecture specification states that a processor will usually incorporate a translation lookaside buffer to minimize the performance impact of searching the page table for a match.

When the MMU attempts to read a page table entry from the page table, the target entry may or may not currently be present in the data cache. If it's not in the cache, the processor must access external memory to get the entry. This can take a considerable amount of time if the access must be performed from DRAM memory rather than from an L2 cache. Once the PTE is in the data cache, however, it can be accessed quickly.

The data cache's replacement algorithm may cause the copy of the PTE to be discarded when its place is needed to store a new cache block in. In other words, PTEs may not stay in the data cache for long periods of time. This being the case, the processor designer may choose to incorporate a special purpose high-speed cache to hold nothing but PTEs. The first time that a match is found on a PTE in the page table, the MMU automatically stores the entire PTE in the TLB (translation lookaside) cache. From that point forward, the MMU searches the TLB before searching the page table for an address matching. In the event of a hit on the TLB, the physical page address, the WIMG bits and the page protection bits are supplied by the TLB in a single tick of the processor clock.

The processor designer may design the MMU:

- with no TLB
- with a unified code/data TLB that caches PTEs for both code and data pages
- with separate code and data TLBs

Managing TLB

In the event that the operating system programmer alters or deletes a PTE using a store instruction, the PTE is changed in the data cache and possibly in memory, but the change is not visible to the TLB. Unless the TLB's copy of the PTE is erased, the old PTE copy in the TLB will be used instead of the new one in the data cache. In order to facilitate TLB maintenance, the PowerPC architecture supplies two instructions for this purpose:

- The tlbie, or TLB invalidate entry, instruction is used to erase a single page table entry from the TLB when the entry has been altered or deleted.
- The tlbia, or TLB invalidate all, instruction is used to erase every entry in the TLB when a task switch occurs and a new page table start address is placed in SDR1.

Page Fault Handler's Job

Page Fault Interrupt

If the scan of the primary and secondary PTEGs does not yield a hit, the processor experiences a page fault interrupt. If caused by an attempted load or store, a data storage interrupt is taken and DSISR[1] is set to one to indicate a data page fault occurred. If caused by an attempted instruction fetch, an instruction storage interrupt is taken and SRR1[1] is set to one to indicate that a code page fault occurred.

Is Current Program Permitted to Access Target Page?

The operating system must determine if the current program is permitted access to the target page. This is handled in an operating system-specific fashion and is outside the scope of the PowerPC architecture specification.

Memory Allocation Call

The page interrupt handler makes a memory allocation call to the operating system requesting a free 4KB page of memory to place the page in. If the call is successful, the operating system returns the start physical address of a page in DRAM memory that the page may be read into. If the call is unsuccessful, the page fault handler must choose a page that is currently in memory to overwrite with the requested page. This subject is covered in the section entitled "Unsuccessful Memory Allocation Call — Must Reuse a PTE."

Successful Memory Allocation Call — Page Read Initiated

Mass Storage Read Request by Operating System

The page fault handler issues a call to the operating system to read the target page into the physical page in memory. The operating system is supplied with the following parameters:

- The target virtual segment number and page number.
- The physical start memory address of the page in memory that the page is to be read into.

The operating system uses the virtual address to identify a logical mass storage device and the logical page on the device. This information, along with the physical address of the memory buffer, is passed to the mass storage device driver.

Request Passed to Device Driver

If, as an example, the target device is connected to a SCSI host bus adapter, or HBA, the SCSI device driver builds a command descriptor block, or CDB, in memory containing the target controller and device, the command type (a read) the start logical block (sector) number and the number of blocks (sectors) to read. It then performs a series of I/O writes to the SCSI HBA's register set, passing it the start memory address of the command descriptor block, or CDB, the start address of the memory buffer to place the data in, and the memory address of the location to place the termination status in.

Application Program Put to Sleep

The operating system then puts the task that experienced the page fault to sleep (because it would be wasteful for the processor to hang until the disk read operation has been completed). An entry is made in the operating system's event queue linking a subsequent interrupt from the SCSI HBA to the return address of the page fault handler. The operating system then resumes execution of another task.

Transfer of Page to Memory

The SCSI HBA has bus master capability. It will run a series of memory write transactions on the bus to deposit the requested page into memory. When it has completed the transfer it will deposit the completion status in memory and generate an interrupt to inform the operating system that the operation has been completed and the requested page is in memory.

Page Transfer Completed

The external interrupt is taken by the processor. The external interrupt handler polls the external interrupt controller to request the identity of the highest priority device requesting service. Assuming that it is the SCSI HBA, the SCSI HBA's interrupt handler is invoked. The handler checks the completion status. Assuming there were no errors indicated, a good completion is returned to the device driver which, in turn, returns good completion status back to the operating system. The operating system links the interrupt event to the page fault handler and resumes its execution.

Making Page Table Entry

The handler attempts to locate an unused entry in the primary PTEG. If an unused entry cannot be found, it attempts to find one in the secondary PTEG. Assuming that an unused entry is found, the handler records the address of the source virtual segment/page and that of the target physical page in the PTE. It sets the valid bit to one, sets the hash bit to the appropriate state, and sets the referenced bit and clears the changed bit in the PTE's page history field. It sets the WIMG bits to the appropriate state to indicate caching policy, memory sharing and speculative access rules of operation within the page. It also sets the page protection, or PP, bits to indicate whether the page is read-only, read/writable or inaccessible.

If an unused PTE cannot be found in the primary or secondary PTEG, the operating system programmer must replace one of the current PTEs with the PTE for the new page. The basic procedure followed will be the same as that described under the heading "Unsuccessful Memory Allocation Call — Must Reuse a PTE."

Re-Execution of Instruction

Having made the page table entry, the page fault handler executes a rfi, resuming execution of the program that experienced the page fault at the same instruction. The page table scan now results in a hit and the access (load, store or instruction fetch) completes successfully.

Unsuccessful Memory Allocation Call —Reuse a PTE

General

In the event that the operating system memory allocator cannot find a free 4KB page of physical memory to place the new page in, one of the pages of information currently in memory must be replaced with the newly requested page. The page fault handler may utilize an OS-specific method to track the least-recently used of the 16 PTEs that comprise the PTEs in the primary and secondary PTEGs. Utilizing this information, it identifies the PTE to be replaced.

The page to be replaced may be in one of the following states (as indicated by its page history bits):

- It may not have been referenced at all since being placed in memory (referenced and changed bits both zero).
- It may have been read from but not stored into since being placed in memory (referenced bit set but changed bit clear).
- It may have been stored into since being placed in memory (referenced and changed bits both set).

Replacing Page That Hasn't Been Referenced

If the old page hasn't been referenced at all, the page fault handler will:

1. Delete the PTE and execute a tlbie instruction with the address of the altered PTE to cause the TLB to erase its copy of the old PTE.
2. Place the new page over the old page and alter the PTE to reflect the new source virtual segment page and the operating rules within the page.

Replacing Page That Has Been Referenced but not Updated

If the old page has been read from but not written into, the steps that must be taken by the page fault handler depend on the mechanism that the operating system will use to transfer the new page into memory. The mass storage subsystem that the operating system will access to place the page in memory will either possess bus master capability or not.

The page fault handler will first delete the current page table entry from the page table and, with a tlbie instruction, from the MMU's TLB. This will prevent any accesses within the page during the transfer of the new page into memory.

If the mass storage subsystem doesn't possess bus master capability:

1. The programmer will be responsible for performing an interleaved load/store transaction series to read the new page from the mass storage controller and write it into memory. When it performs the write transactions to write the new page of information into memory, it will instruct all other processors to snoop the write addresses (if the page is accessed by other processors, M will equal 1). This will cause any copies of code or data from the old page that are in other caches to be eradicated. None of the caches will have lines in the modified state (because the page hasn't been modified — the changed page history bit is cleared). At the conclusion of the page write, all vestiges of the old page in other caches will have been eradicated. The series of stores performed by this processor will also cause copies of data from the old page that may have been in this processor's data cache to be automatically updated with data from the new page.
2. If the old page contained any code, the programmer must also execute a program loop with an icbi instruction embedded within it to eradicate all traces of the old page's code from this processor's code cache.

If the mass storage subsystem possesses bus master capability:

The mass storage subsystem itself will perform the series of memory writes necessary to deposit the new page into memory. It will also instruct all caches to snoop these writes and to kill any copies of information that may have been cached from the old page. Since all processors (including the one that instructed the bus master to dump the new page into memory) can detect and snoop the memory writes the bus master performs, all vestiges of code and data in all caches is automatically eliminated.

The page fault handler may then alter the PTE to reflect the new source virtual segment page, its location in memory, and the operating rules within the page (WIMG and PP).

Replacing Page That Has Been Modified

If the old page has been modified (the page history change bit is set), the page fault handler must ensure that the following actions are taken:

1. The page fault handler will first delete the current page table entry from the page table and, with a tlbie instruction, from the MMU's TLB. This will prevent any accesses within the page during the transfer of the old page to mass storage and the new page into memory.
2. Force all processors with modified cache blocks from the old page to write these modifications to the page in memory and then invalidate their copies of the cache blocks.
3. Force all processors with clean copies (in the exclusive or shared state) of cache blocks from the old page to invalidate them.
4. Write the old page in memory back to mass storage.
5. Read the new page into the vacated page in memory.
6. Update the PTE to record the placement of the new page into memory.
7. Restart the load, store or instruction fetch that caused the page fault. It will now complete successfully (without a page fault) because there will be a hit on the page table.

If the mass storage subsystem doesn't possess bus master capability:

1. The page fault handler will first delete the current page table entry from the page table and, with a tlbie instruction, from the MMU's TLB. This will prevent any accesses within the page during the transfer of the old page to mass storage and the new page into memory.
2. The programmer must force this processor to deposit all modified copies of cache blocks from the old page into memory and then invalidate the copies. Clean copies of cache blocks (in the exclusive or shared state) from the old page will just be invalidated. This can be accomplished by utilizing a dcbf instruction in a 4KB spin loop through the 4KB space. This will force the data cache to change copies of cache blocks from the old page that are currently in the exclusive or shared state to the invalid state. A cache block in the modified state will be written back to memory and then marked invalid. This is known as a flush operation. The dcbf instruction forces the processor executing it to broadcast a transaction instructing all other processors to snoop the specified address and flush on a cache hit.

3. If the old page contained any code, the programmer must also execute a spin loop with an icbi instruction embedded within it to eradicate all traces of the old page's code from this processor's code cache.
4. Now that the old page in memory has received all updates from the processors, the old page can be written to mass storage. This would be accomplished by performing a series of interleaved load/store transactions to read the data from memory and write it to the mass storage controller.
5. The new page is then read from mass storage and placed in memory by once again performing a series of interleaved load/store transactions to read the data from the mass storage controller and write it to memory.
6. The programmer updates the PTE to record the placement of the new page into memory.
7. An rfi is executed to restart the load, store or instruction fetch that caused the page fault. It will now complete successfully (without a page fault) because there will be a hit on the page table.

If the mass storage subsystem possesses bus master capability:

1. The page fault handler will first delete the current page table entry from the page table and, with a tlbie instruction, from the MMU's TLB. This will prevent any accesses within the page during the transfer of the old page to mass storage and the new page into memory.
2. The operating system commands the mass storage controller to read the old page from memory and save it on mass storage.
3. To read the old page from memory, the mass storage controller performs a series of memory read (load) transactions and instructs all processors to snoop the read transactions. Each time that the bus master attempts to read a cache block from memory that has been modified by a processor, the processor that experienced the snoop hit on a modified cache block will force the bus master off the bus, deposit the modified cache block into memory, and then permit the bus master to re acquire the bus and read the cache block from memory. In this manner, the snooping processors will ensure that the bus master is reading fresh data from memory. The processors will then mark those cache blocks shared (they think that the bus master is caching the data).
4. Having completed the movement of the old page to mass storage, the bus master is then commanded to write the new page into the vacated page in memory.
5. As the bus master performs the series of memory writes to place the new page into memory, it will instruct all processors to snoop the mem-

ory write transactions it is performing. If any of the snooping processors have copies of cache blocks from the old page in their caches, they will then invalidate those copies (because the bus master is altering that area of memory, rendering the old cache blocks stale).

6. The programmer updates the PTE to record the placement of the new page into memory.
7. An rfi is executed to restart the load, store or instruction fetch that caused the page fault. It will now complete successfully (without a page fault) because there will be a hit on the page table.

For a description of the process used to read a new page into memory when a page fault has occurred, refer to the section entitled "Successful Memory Allocation Call — Page Read Initiated."

64-bit PowerPC Processor Paging Implementation

2^{64} Bytes = 2^{36} Segments of Space

Like the 32-bit processor, the 64-bit processor's effective address space is divided into segments of 256MB each. Whereas the 32-bit processor only had 4GB of effective address space, however, the 64-bit processor (when operating in 64-bit mode — MSR[SF] = 1) has 2^{36} segments of space. It would therefore not be feasible to have 2^{36} segment registers on the processor chip for mapping the effective segment address to a virtual segment address. Instead, this function is performed by a segment table in memory.

Segment Type Determination

The address space register, or ASR, contains the base physical memory address of the segment table, or STAB. The STAB is fixed at 4KB in size and must reside on a 4KB address boundary. It is organized as illustrated in figure 18-9. There are 32 segment table entry groups, or STEGs. Each STEG consists of eight segment table entries, or STEs. Each STE is 16 bytes long and has the format illustrated in figures 18-10 or 18-11, depending on whether it is a memory or an I/O STE.

Each STE contains a Type bit indicating whether it maps an effective segment address to a virtual memory segment or an I/O segment. This discussion focuses on the memory segment (T = 0).

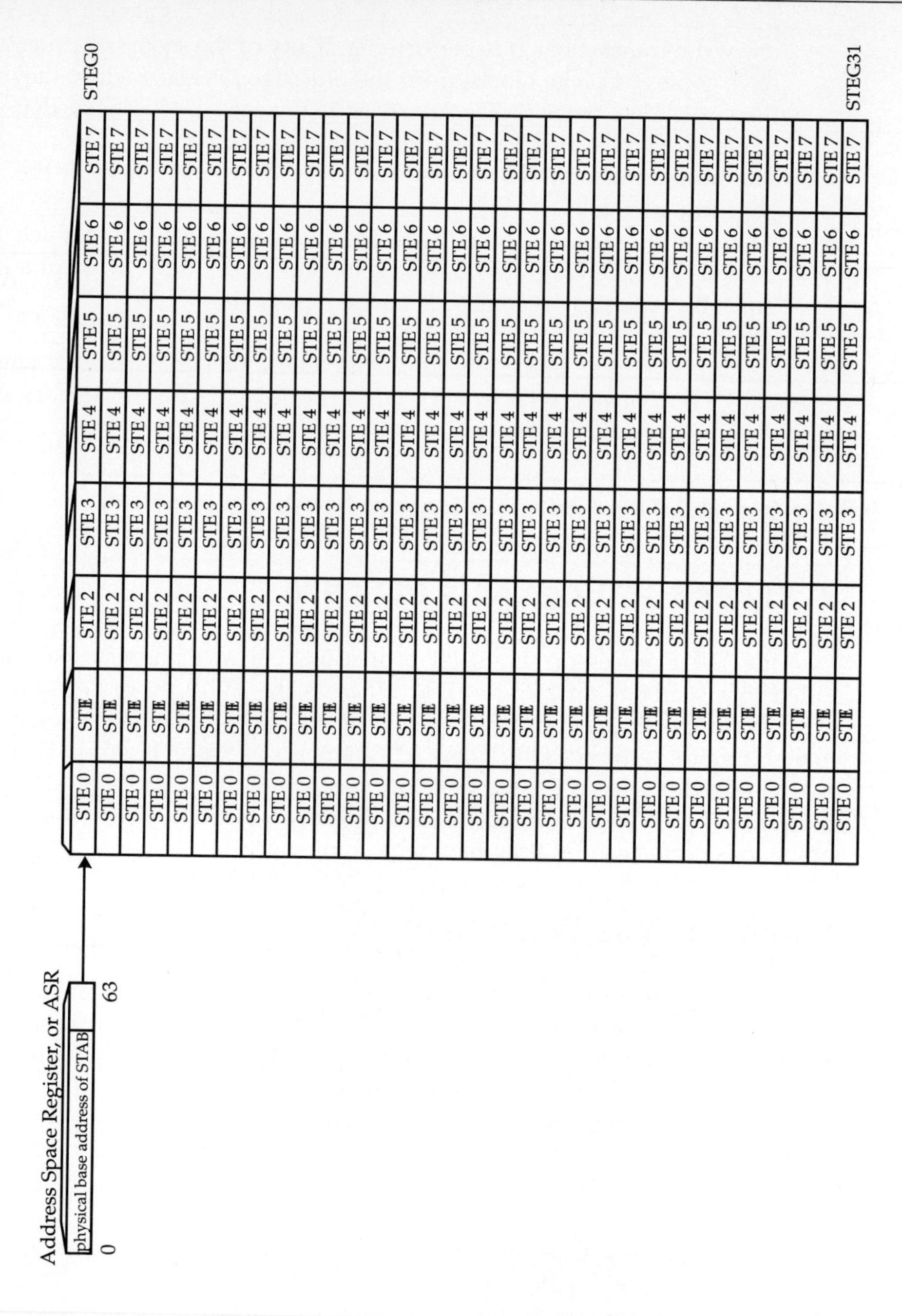

Figure 18-9. The Segment Address Table (STAB)

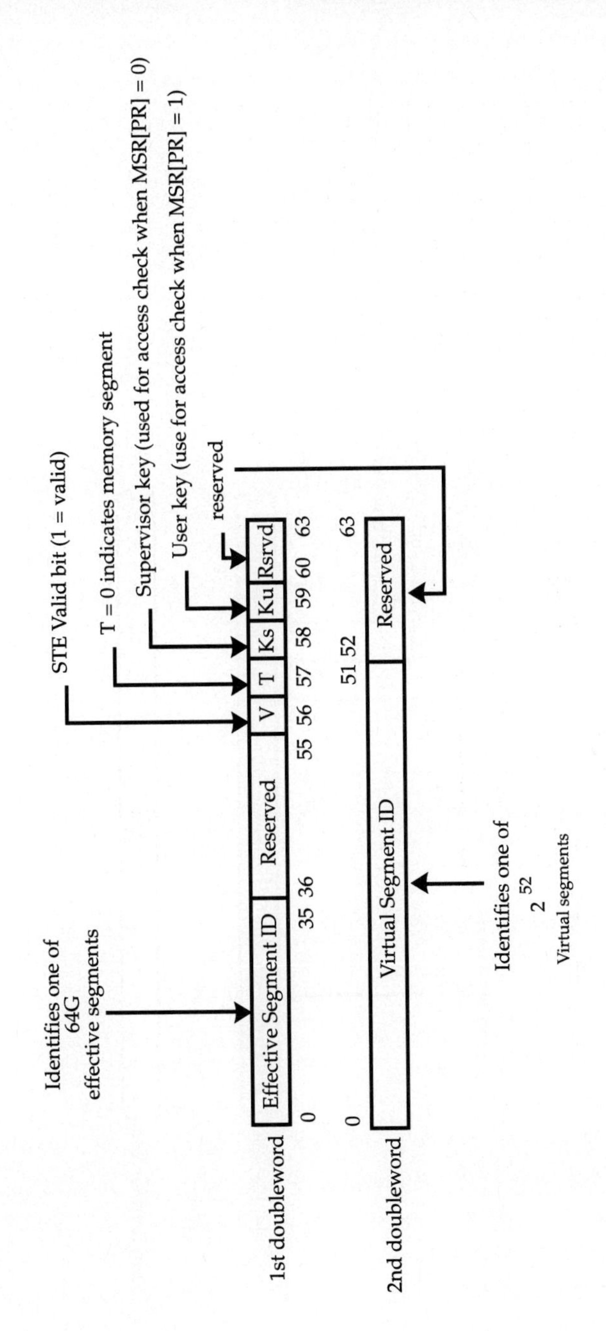

Figure 18-10. Memory Segment Descriptor, 64-bit Processor (STE with T=0)

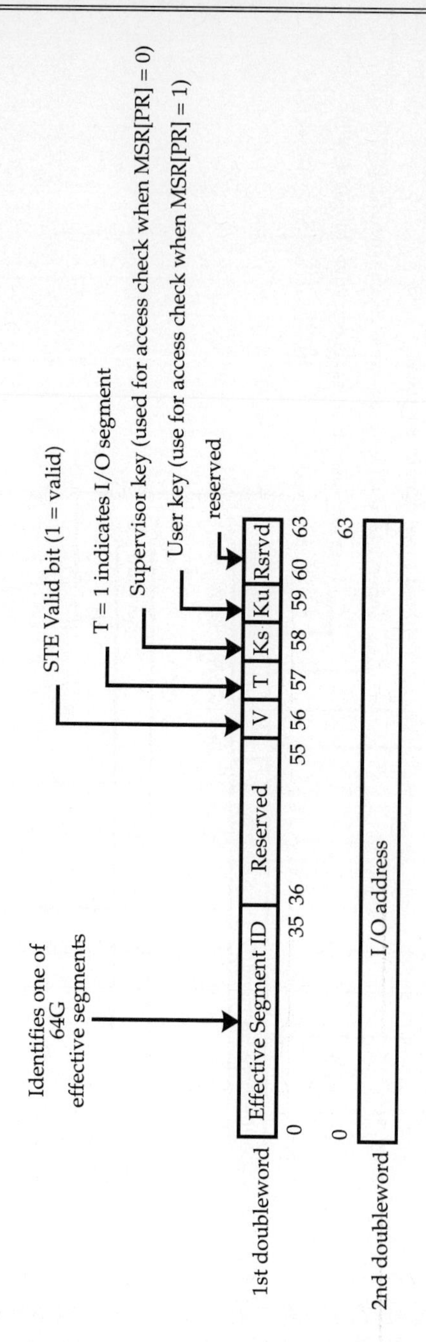

Figure 18-11. I/O Segment Descriptor for 64-bit Processor (STE with T = 1)

Creating STAB Index

The index into the STAB consists of the lower five bits of the effective segment address, EA[31:35]. This selects one of the 32 STEGs to scan during the primary hash, or scan. Because each STEG is 128 bytes in length (8 STEs of 16 bytes each), the index is multiplied by 128 to compute the offset of the primary STE within the STAB. This is accomplished by left-shifting the index seven bits and filling with zeros. This 12 bit offset is then concatenated with the upper 52 bits from the ASR (the 4KB-aligned STAB base address) to form the 64-bit start address of the STEG for the primary scan.

Primary Hash

Starting with STE 0 in the selected STEG, the effective segment ID, or ESID, in each valid entry (V bit = 1) is compared with the effective segment being addressed (identified by EA[0:35]). If the STE isn't valid (V = 0) or there is a mismatch on the effective segment ID, the MMU skips to the next STE in the STEG and checks for a match. If a match is found, the STE supplies the 52 bit virtual segment ID to be used in the page table scan. With a 52 bit virtual segment ID field, the operating system may map the effective segment to any of 2^{52} virtual segments of mass storage.

If a match isn't found in the primary STEG, the secondary hash must be performed.

Secondary Hash

The secondary index is formed by inverting the lower five bits of the effective segment address to select the primary STEG's overflow STEG in the same relative position at the opposite end of the STAB. Because each STEG is 128 bytes in length (8 STEs of 16 bytes each), the index is multiplied by 128 to compute the offset of the secondary STE within the STAB. This is accomplished by left-shifting the index seven bits and filling with zeros. This 12 bit offset is then concatenated with the upper 52 bits from the ASR (the 4KB-aligned STAB base address) to form the 64-bit start address of the STEG for the secondary scan.

Starting with STE 0 in the secondary STEG, the effective segment ID in each valid entry (V bit = 1) is compared with the target effective address. If the STE isn't valid (V = 0) or there is a mismatch on the effective segment ID, the MMU skips to the next STE in the STEG and checks for a match. If a match is found, the STE supplies the 52 bit virtual segment ID to be used in the page table scan.

If a match isn't found in the secondary STEG, a segment fault interrupt occurs. It will take the form of a data storage or an instruction storage interrupt depending on whether the processor was attempting a load/store or an instruction fetch.

Segment Fault Handler

If a segment fault occurs during a load or store attempt, the data storage interrupt is taken. DSISR[10] is set to indicate a search failure in the STAB.

The segment fault handler must determine what virtual segment to map the effective segment to and then create an entry in the primary or secondary STEG to record this mapping. An rfi instruction is then executed, causing the load/store or the instruction fetch to be reattempted. The STAB search is successful on this attempt and the virtual segment ID is supplied by the STE to be used in the page table search.

SLB — Performance Enhancement Tool

The PowerPC architecture specification states that the processor designer will usually (it's not mandatory) include a special high-speed cache in the MMU to store STE entries in for fast access. A hit on this segment lookaside buffer, or SLB, would preclude the necessity of a STAB search, resulting in better performance.
The processor designer may design the MMU in any of the following ways:

- The MMU will not have an SLB
- The MMU will have a unified code/data SLB that contains segment mappings (STEs) for both code and data accesses
- The MMU will have separate code and data SLBs

Managing SLB

Just as with the TLB that is used to cache page table entries, the programmer must erase an entry from the SLB whenever a STAB entry is altered or deleted. Two instructions are provided for this purpose: slbie and slbia. The slbie instruction is used to delete a single STE from the STAB, while the slbia is used to delete all SLB entries when a new STAB is pointed to by the ASR.

Identifying Target Page Within Virtual Segment

Bits EA[0:35] identify the target effective segment, EA[36:51] identify the target page within the segment (1-of-64000 pages), while EA[52:63] identify the start address of the operand within the target page.

EA[0:35] is mapped to a 52 bit virtual segment by the STAB search. EA[36:51] identify the target page within the virtual segment.

Role of Page Table

Page table usage in a 64-bit processor is identical to that described earlier in this chapter for the 32-bit processor.

Page Table Location and Length

Just as with the 32-bit processor, SDR1 contains the start address and length of the page table in memory. Figure 18-12 illustrates the 64-bit processor's SDR1 register. The bits marked as zeros are reserved. The minimum size of the page table is 256KB (vs 64K for a 32-bit processor) and it must reside on a boundary divisible by its size. The maximum size of the table is 64 terabytes (vs 32MB for a 32-bit processor). Table 18-7 defines the table size field in SDR1. The value indicated in the SDR1 HTABMASK field indicates the table size and the number of right-justified bits in the 28 bit size mask should be set to ones when the field is used to adjust the raw index length.

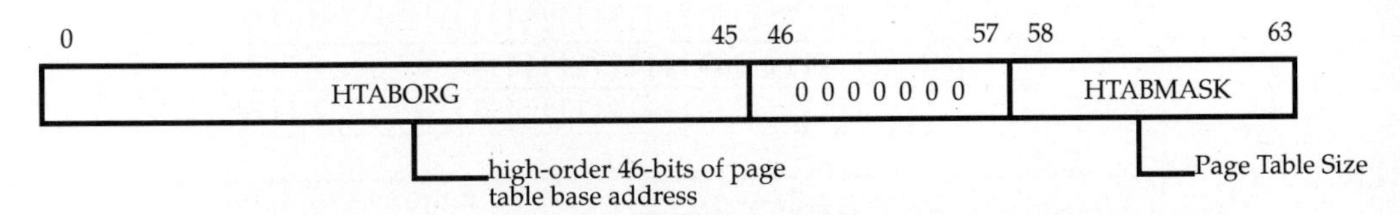

Table Search Descriptor Register, SDR1

Figure 18-12. 64-bit Storage Description Register One (SDR1)

Table 18-7. HTABMASK Field Definition (64-bit Processor)

Field Contents	Mask Decoded From Field	Page Table Size
000000	0000000000000000000000000000	256KB
000001	0000000000000000000000000001	512KB
000010	0000000000000000000000000011	1MB
000011	0000000000000000000000000111	2MB
000100	0000000000000000000000001111	4MB
000101	0000000000000000000000011111	8MB
000110	0000000000000000000000111111	16MB
000111	0000000000000000000001111111	32MB
001000	0000000000000000000011111111	64MB
001001	0000000000000000000111111111	128MB
001010	0000000000000000001111111111	256MB
001011	0000000000000000011111111111	512MB
001100	0000000000000000111111111111	1GB
001101	0000000000000001111111111111	2GB
001110	0000000000000011111111111111	4GB
001111	0000000000000111111111111111	8GB
010000	0000000000001111111111111111	16GB
010001	0000000000011111111111111111	32GB
010010	0000000000111111111111111111	64GB
010011	0000000001111111111111111111	128GB
010100	0000000011111111111111111111	256GB
010101	0000000111111111111111111111	512GB
010110	0000001111111111111111111111	1TB (terabytes)
010111	0000011111111111111111111111	2TB
011000	0000111111111111111111111111	4TB
011001	0001111111111111111111111111	8TB
011010	0011111111111111111111111111	16TB
011011	0111111111111111111111111111	32TB
011100	1111111111111111111111111111	64TB

Organization of Page Table

The 64 bit processor's page table is organized in the same manner as the 32 bit processor's with the following exception — each PTE is 16 bytes long, rather than eight. Each PTEG is therefore 128 bytes long. Figure 18-13 illustrates the structure of the 64-bit processor's page table.

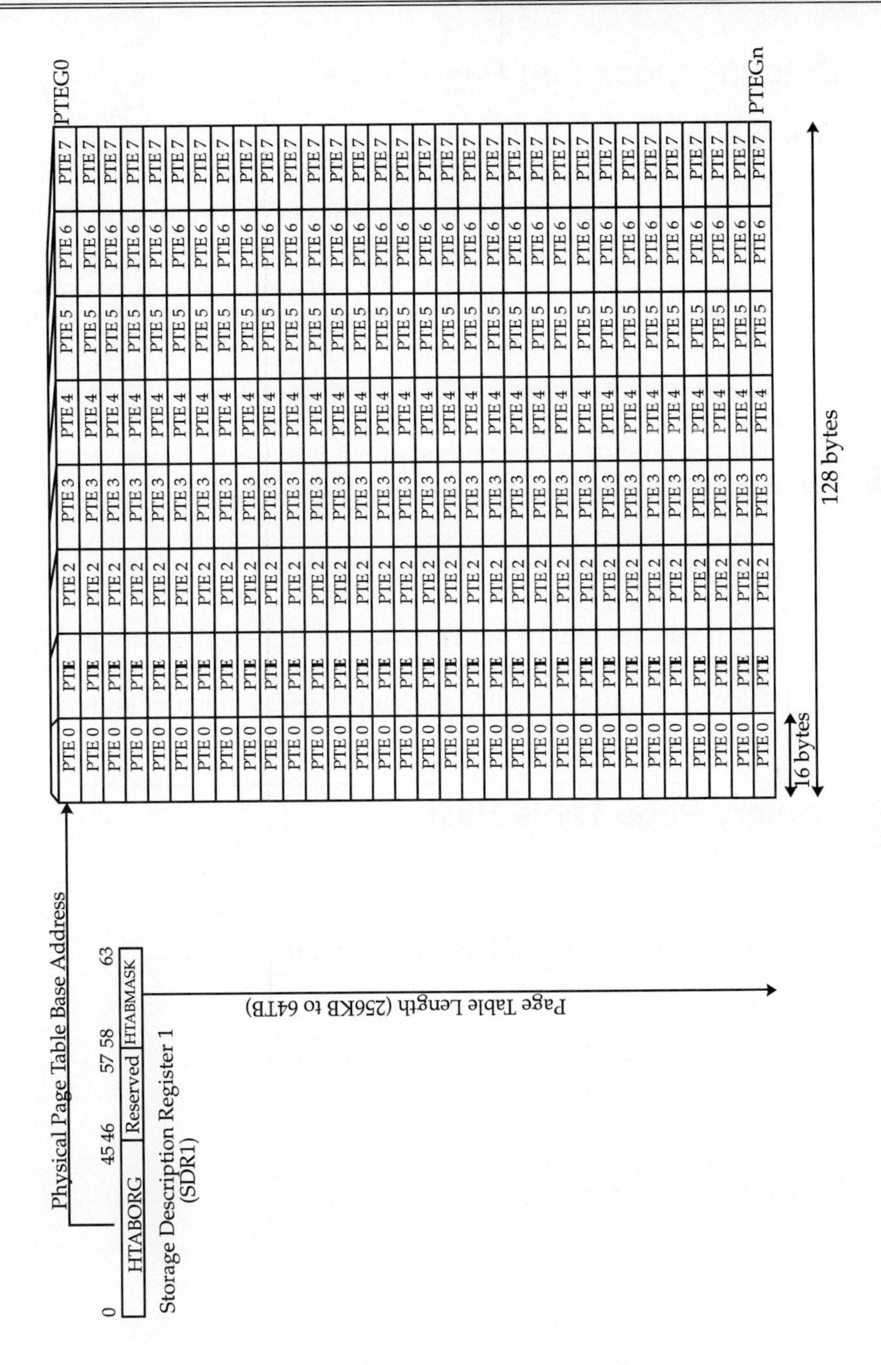

Figure 18-13. Page Table Structure (64-bit Processor)

Creating Index into Page Table

With the following exception, the same procedure is used as that for the 32 bit processor — prior to exclusive-OR'ing the page number and virtual segment number, the 16 bit page number is extended to 39 bits (rather than 19 bits) by padding its upper end with 23 bits of zero.

Adjusting Index Length to Match Page Table Size

With the following exception, the same procedure is used as that for the 32 bit processor — the upper 28 bits of the raw index are AND'd with the decoded 28 bit table size mask to clear the required number of upper raw index bits. This shortens the index to match the actual table length.

Converting Index into Offset within Page Table

The index is then multiplied by 128 bytes per PTEG (vs 64 bytes per PTEG in a 32 bit processor) to create the offset within the page table. The offset is added to the table base address to yield the start physical memory address of PTE 0 in the selected primary PTEG.

Primary Page Table Hash

With the following exception, the scan is the same as that performed in the 32 processor — each PTE is 16 bytes in length (rather than 8 bytes for a 32 bit processor). The PTE format is illustrated in figure 18-14.

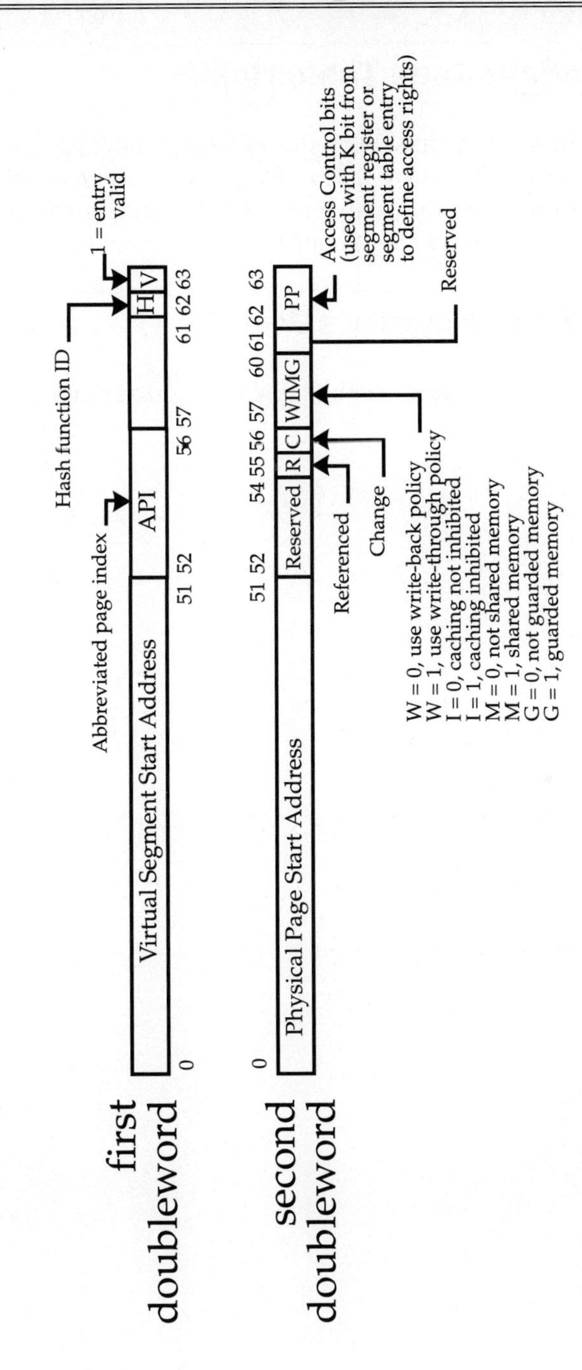

Figure 18-14. The Page Table Entry, or PTE, for 64-bit Processor

Secondary Page Table Hash

If the primary scan fails, the index of the secondary PTEG to scan is formed by inverting the 39-bit raw index. The address of the secondary PTEG is then computed (in the same manner as that for the primary PTEG) and the secondary PTEG is scanned for a match.

Page Fault Handler's Job

The page fault handler has the same function as that for a 32-bit processor.

Chapter 19

The Previous Chapter

The previous chapter provided a detailed description of virtual paging as implemented in both the 32 and 64-bit versions of the PowerPC processor.

This Chapter

This chapter provides a detailed description of the MMU's block address translation capabilities.

The Next Chapter

The next chapter provides an introduction to the implementation of I/O and memory-mapped I/O in the PowerPC environment.

Block Address Translation Overview

The operating system programmer can set up the MMU to define a large areas of memory as a block, rather than as a series of pages. The operating system programmer assigns the block a set of operational rules that govern the performance of accesses within the block. Examples of large memory areas having special needs would be large video frame buffers and areas of memory containing large arrays of floating-point information. The size of a block may be set at any power of two from 128KB to 256MB in size. Blocks must begin on addresses divisible by their size. The largest block size that can be specified is processor implementation-dependent and may be less than 256MB. Unlike pages, the PowerPC processor does not provide a mechanism to "page" blocks or portions of blocks in and out of memory. In other words, the entire block is memory-resident.

The block address translation, or BAT, mechanism, inspects the effective address to determine if is within an effective address range that should be converted to a physical address within a memory block. If it isn't, the BAT mechanism permits the page or I/O translation mechanism (described in the chapter entitled "Virtual Paging") to handle the address translation. Figure 19-1 illustrates the relationship of the BAT and page address translation logic to each other.

If the target effective address does reside within an area designated as a block, the MMU checks the blocks access rights bits to determine if the access is permitted. If it isn't, the MMU generates an interrupt. If permitted, the MMU translates the effective address into a physical address within the block and, if the block is considered cacheable, it submits the physical address to the cache for a lookup. If the block isn't cacheable, the MMU submits the physical address directly to the MU for submission to the system interface.

In addition to the effective-to-physical address mapping information, the BAT translation mechanism permits the operating system programmer to also define:

- The access types permitted within the block. These bits define the privilege level the currently running program must be at in order to permit access within the block. In addition, they define whether the target block is read/writable, read-only or inaccessible.
- The policy to be used by the data cache in handling memory writes within this block (write-through or write-back). The W bit of the WIMG bit field is used for this purpose.
- The cacheability of the information within this block. The I bit of the WIMG bit field is used for this purpose.
- If block is also accessed by other processors/caching entities in the system. The M bit of the WIMG bit field is used for this purpose.
- If the target physical block in memory resides within guarded memory (defined later in this chapter). The G bit of the WIMG bit field is used for this purpose.

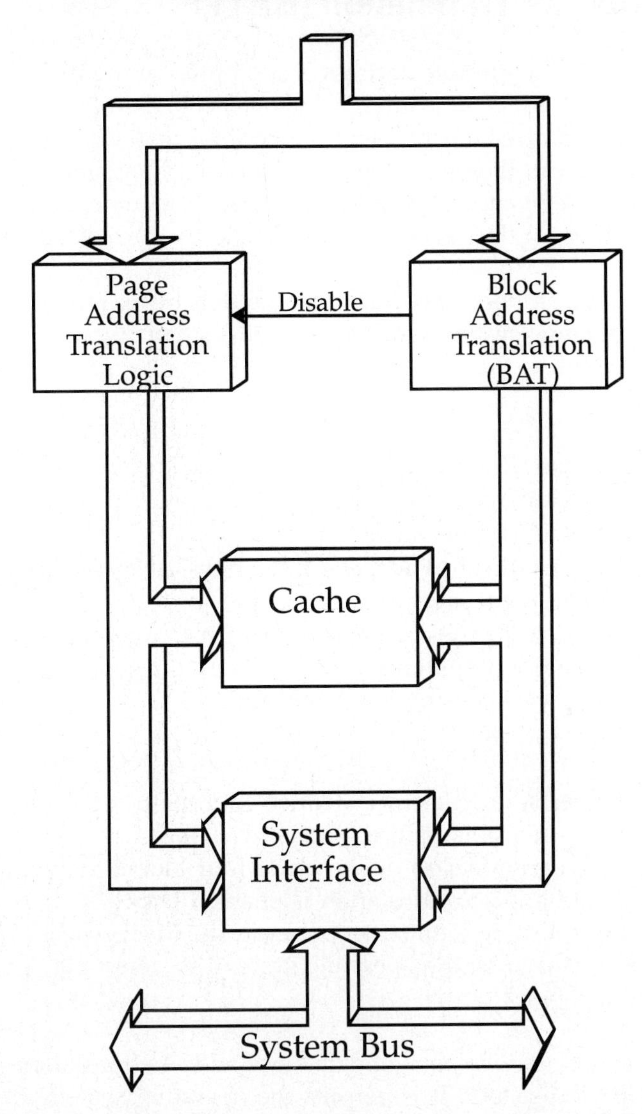

Figure 19-1. Relationship of BAT and Page Translation Logic

Block Address Translation (BAT) Process

Whenever an effective address is submitted to the BAT registers and the paging logic within the MMU, a hit on the BAT registers supersedes the page translation mechanism. Using the BAT mechanism, the operating system programmer can therefore define a block that overlaps with one or more pages within a segment. When this is the case, it is unnecessary to provide page table entries for the pages that are overlaid by the block definition.

To define an effective address range that maps to a physical memory block, the operating system programmer must set up a pair of special-purpose registers known as the upper and lower BAT registers with the following information:

- The **start effective address** of the effective address range to be mapped to a physical memory block
- The length of the block
- The **start physical address** of the physical memory block that the effective address range is mapped to
- Set the BAT register pair's **Valid bit** to one, indicating that it contains a valid block definition
- The access rights within the block
- The WIMG bits

The PowerPC architecture defines four pairs of instruction block address translation registers, referred to as IBAT registers. This permits the operating system programmer to define up to four blocks as instruction blocks. When instruction address translation is enabled (MSR[IR] = 1) and the instruction unit is requesting an instruction fetch, the MMU checks the IBATs (that have been initialized by the operating system) to determine if the effective address maps to a block.

It also defines four pairs of data block address translation registers, referred to as DBAT registers. This permits the operating system programmer to define up to four blocks as data blocks. When data address translation is enabled (MSR[DR] = 1), the MMU checks the DBATs (that have been initialized by the operating system) to determine if the load or store address maps to a block. Figure 19-2 illustrates the BAT registers.

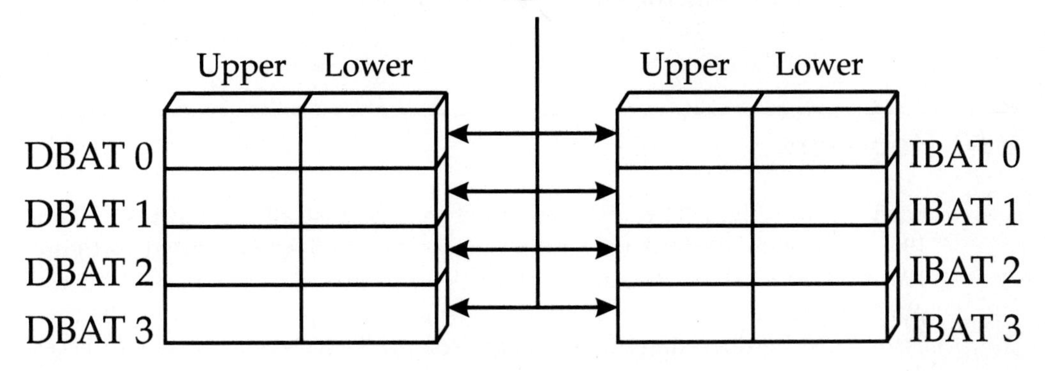

Figure 19-2. The BAT Registers

If the effective address doesn't have a hit on any of the BAT registers, the BAT doesn't perform address translation. In this case, the paging logic is responsible for address translation.

If the effective address hits on one of the DBAT or IBAT register pairs, the BAT first checks the access rights bits in the DBAT or IBAT register pair to verify that the access is permitted. If it isn't, the BAT generates an interrupt to report the violation to the operating system. If the access is permitted, the BAT performs the effective-to-physical address translation in the following manner:

- The start effective address of the block is subtracted from the target effective address to yield the offset of the target location within the block
- The offset is then added to the physical block start address to yield the target physical address to access

This is a general description of the process. The exact process is described later in this section.

If the effective address has a hit on more than one of the DBAT or IBAT register pairs, this is a programming error (because the effective address cannot be mapped to two separate areas of memory). The result will be undefined. It may include an access violation, a machine check or a checkstop condition.

If the same block will be used for both data and instruction accesses, the operating system programmer must set up both an IBAT and a DBAT register pair with the same mapping information. This will not result in a double-hit because the MMU only compares the effective address to the DBATs on a data access and the IBATs on an instruction access. This double-mapping must be done even if the processor has a unified code/data cache.

BAT Registers

Each pair of 32-bit BAT registers is structured as illustrated in figures 19-3 and 19-4. Each pair of 64-bit BAT registers is structured as illustrated in figures 19-5 and 19-6. The BAT register pair is implemented as a pair of special-purpose registers, accessed using the mfspr and mtspr instructions. The processor must be operating at the supervisor privilege level in order to access them.

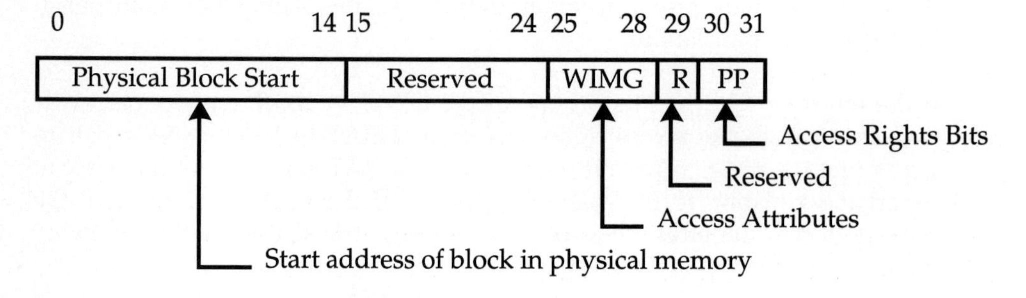

Figure 19-3. 32-bit Lower BAT Register Format

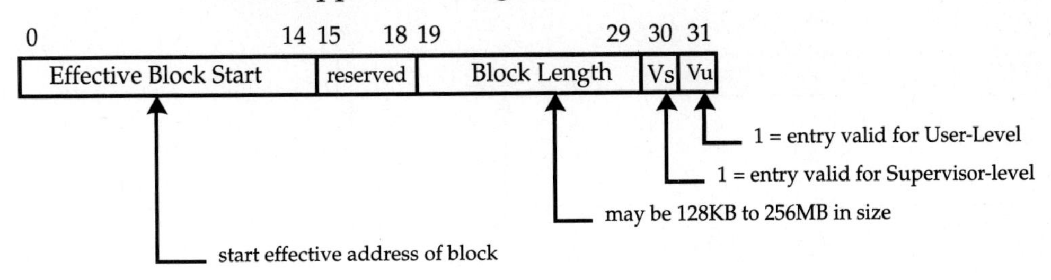

Figure 19-4. 32-bit Upper BAT Register Format

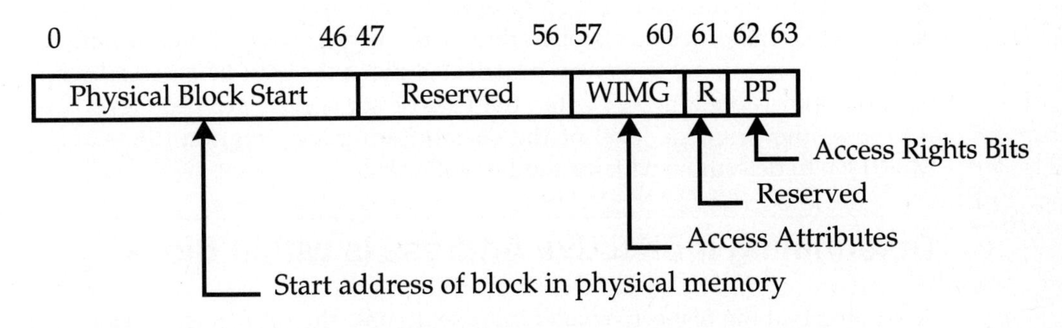

Figure 19-5. 64-bit Lower BAT Register Format

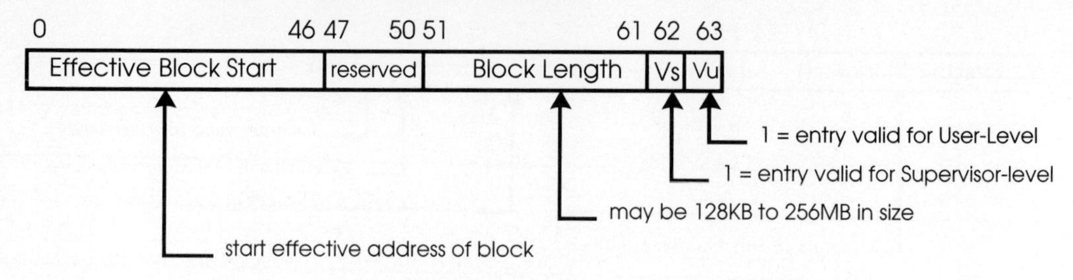

Figure 19-6. 64-bit Upper BAT Register Format

Block Address Translation

Determining if BAT Entry Valid

The two valid bits in the upper BAT are used by the operating system programmer to define whether the BAT entry is valid for use in user mode, supervisor mode, or both. If Vs is set to one, the block is defined for use in supervisor mode, while a zero indicates that this entry does not describe a block that can be accessed while the processor is operating at the supervisor privilege level. If Vu is set to one, the block is defined for use in user mode, while a zero indicates that this entry does not describe a block that can be accessed while the processor is operating at the user privilege level. If both Vs and Vu are set to one, this entry describes a block that can be accessed while the processor is operating at either the user or supervisor privilege level. The BAT uses the privilege level of the currently-running program (the state of MSR[PR]) to determine which valid bit to check.

Determining if Effective Address Is within Block

Assuming that the respective valid bit is set to one, the BAT must determine if the target effective address is within the bounds of the block defined by this entry. In order to do this, the 11-bit Block Length field in the upper BAT is used to create the start effective address of the target block. Table 19-1 defines the valid values that may be programmed into the Block Length field. The BAT inverts the contents of the Block Length field and ANDs it with the following bits in the target effective address:

- bits 36:46 of the target effective address in 64-bit implementation, or
- bits 4:14 of the target effective address in 32-bit implementation

This process strips off the lower bits of the effective address that are part of the offset within the block and leaves just the block start address. The block start address is then compared with the effective block start address in the upper BAT. If it doesn't match, the target effective address is not within the block defined by this BAT register pair. If, on the other hand, they compare, then the target effective address is within the block described by this BAT register pair.

Table 19-1. Block Length Encoding

Block Length	Block Length Field Contents
128KB	00000000000b
256KB	00000000001b
512KB	00000000011b
1MB	00000000111b
2MB	00000001111b
4MB	00000011111b
8MB	00000111111b
16MB	00001111111b
32MB	00011111111b
64MB	00111111111b
128MB	01111111111b
256MB	11111111111b

Access Rights

Assuming that they compare, the MMU determines if the access is permitted by checking the PP bit field in the lower BAT. Table 19-2 defines the access types permitted within the defined block. If the access isn't permitted, an access interrupt is generated.

Table 19-2. Access Types Permitted

PP bit Field	Access Types Permitted
00b	none
01b	read-only
10b	read/write
11b	read-only

Effective-to-Physical Address Translation

If permitted, the physical target address is created in the following manner:

- The physical block start address from the lower BAT register is substituted for the effective block start address
- The one bits that were masked out of the effective address for the comparison are reinstated
- Effective address bits 47:63 (or 15:31 in a 32-bit implementation) are concatenated to the lower end

Access Rules (WIMG)

The resulting physical memory address is used to perform the memory access. This access is subject to the conditions dictated by the state of the WIMG bits in the lower BAT register. For a detailed discussion of the WIMG bits, refer to the chapter entitled "Memory Usage Bits (WIMG)."

Chapter 20

The Previous Chapter

The previous chapter provided a detailed description of the MMU's block address translation capabilities.

This Chapter

This chapter provides an introduction to the implementation of I/O and memory-mapped I/O in the PowerPC environment.

The Next Chapter

The next chapter provides a detailed description of interrupts, or exceptions, as implemented in the PowerPC architecture environment. This includes interrupt handler-related issues and hardware interrupts.

Introduction

I/O targets may be implemented utilizing either of the traditional methods:

- I/O mapped ports
- Memory-mapped ports

The following sections discuss both approaches.

I/O Mapped Ports

I/O Segment

The operating system programmer may map one or more of the effective segments to I/O space. This is accomplished by setting the segment type, or T, bit to a one. Figures 20-1 and 20-2 illustrate the 32-bit processor's segment register and the 64-bit processor's segment table entry, respectively. An I/O segment is also referred to as a direct-store segment.

Accesses within an I/O segment utilize the assumed WIMG bit setting of 0101b: non-cacheable (I = 1), M = 0 and speculative accesses prohibited (G = 1).

In a 32-bit processor, the system interface is supplied with the following information to address the I/O device:

- The key bit selected by the privilege level of the currently-running program is supplied by the segment register
- The 9-bit I/O bus unit controller (BUC) number (1-of-512 BUCs) is supplied by the segment register
- The 16-bit BUC-specific field is supplied from the segment register
- The least-significant hex digit from the segment register supplies the upper digit of the I/O port address, while the lower 28 bits of the effective address, EA[4:31] supplies the lower seven digits of the I/O port address

In a 64-bit processor, the system interface is supplied with the following information to address the I/O device:

- The key bit selected by the privilege level of the currently-running program is supplied by the segment table entry
- 32-bits bits are supplied by the lower 32 bits of the second doubleword of the segment table entry
- The lower 28 bits of the effective address, EA[4:31]

The addressed external I/O controller can use the K bit to determine whether or not to permit the access.

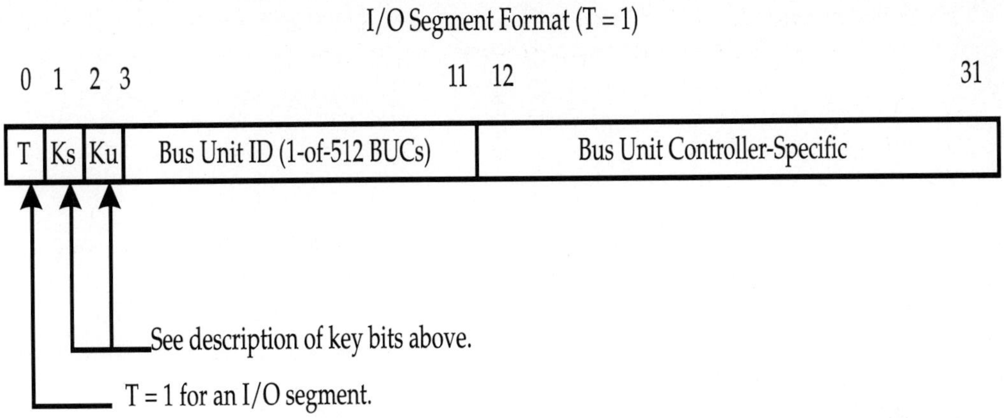

I/O Segment Format (T = 1)

0 1 2 3 11 12 31

T	Ks	Ku	Bus Unit ID (1-of-512 BUCs)	Bus Unit Controller-Specific

See description of key bits above.

T = 1 for an I/O segment.

Figure 20-1. 32-bit Processor's Segment Register

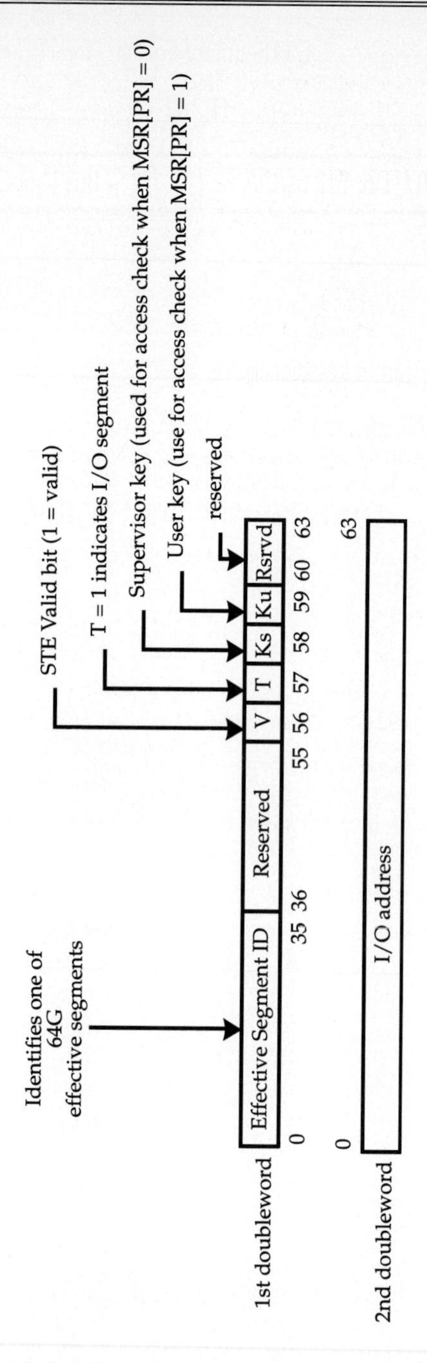

Figure 20-2. 64-bit Processor's Segment Table Entry

I/O Bus Transaction

The nature of the resulting I/O transaction performed on the external bus is processor-bus specific (i.e., the bus protocol is outside the scope of the PowerPC processor specification). A detailed explanation of I/O accesses may be found in the chapter entitled "The PPC 601 I/O Transaction."

Memory-Mapped I/O Ports

I/O Targets can be designed to decode memory rather than I/O bus transactions. Since the programmer desires real-time communication with I/O devices, however, the operating system should set up either a page table entry or a BAT register with the WIMG bits set to 0101b: non-cacheable (I = 1); memory coherency not required (M = 0) and speculative accesses prohibited (G = 1). When caching is inhibited, the W bit has no effect.

All memory reads and writes bypass the cache. The programmer should ensure that either eieio or sync instructions or read after write are utilized to enforce strong ordering of I/O stores (refer to the chapter entitled "Access Order" for additional information).

Chapter 21

The Previous Chapter

The previous chapter provided an introduction to the implementation of I/O and memory-mapped I/O in the PowerPC environment.

This Chapter

This chapter provides a detailed description of interrupts as implemented in the PowerPC architecture environment. This includes interrupt handler-related issues and hardware interrupts. It should be noted that the term exception is synonymous with the term interrupt.

The Next Chapter

The next chapter provides a description of the timebase and decrementer facilities and their operational characteristics when the processor is operating at the supervisor privilege level.

Location of Interrupt Table

When an interrupt occurs, the processor saves the instruction pointer in SRR0 and the machine state and interrupt status information in SRR1. Having done this, the processor then jumps to the interrupt handler entry point associated with the interrupt type currently being serviced. The base address of the interrupt table is selected by the state of the interrupt prefix, or IP, bit in MSR as detailed in the following list:

- In a 32-bit processor with IP = 0, the interrupt vector table base address is 00000000h. With IP = 1, the base address is FFF00000h.
- In a 64-bit processor with IP = 0, the interrupt vector table base address is 0000000000000000h. With IP = 1, the base address is FFFFFFFFFFF00000h.

The processor forms the address to jump to by adding the offset associated with the interrupt type to the base address. At startup time, after reset is removed, IP is set to one, setting the table base address to FFF00000h (32-bit processor) or FFFFFFFFFFF00000h (64-bit processor).

Interrupt Handler Entry Points

The interrupt handler entry point offsets are listed in table 21-1.

Table 21-1. Interrupt Handler Entry Points

Interrupt Type	Entry Point In Interrupt Table
Reserved	00000h
System reset	00100h
Machine check	00200h
Data Storage	00300h
Instruction storage	00400h
External	00500h
Alignment	00600h
Program	00700h
Floating-point unavailable	00800h
Decrementer	00900h
Reserved	00A00h
Reserved	00B00h
System call	00C00h
Trace	00D00h
Floating-point assist	00E00h
Reserved	00E10h – 00FFFh
Reserved (implementation-specific)	01000h – 02FFFh

Use of any reserved interrupt vector locations may cause compatibility problems with future processor implementations.

Examples

The following would be the entry points for the indicated interrupt handlers if MSR[IP] is set to zero:

- Reset interrupt handler entry point is 00000100h for a 32-bit processor and 0000000000000100h for a 64-bit processor.
- System call interrupt handler entry point is 00000C00h for a 32-bit processor and 0000000000000C00h for a 64-bit processor.

The following would be the entry points for the indicated interrupt handlers if MSR[IP] is set to one:

- Reset interrupt handler entry point is FFF00100h for a 32-bit processor and FFFFFFFFFFF00100h for a 64-bit processor.
- System call interrupt handler entry point is FFF00C00h for a 32-bit processor and FFFFFFFFFFF00C00h for a 64-bit processor.

Interrupts Cause a Context Switch

Whenever an internal or external interrupt occurs, the processor takes the actions described in the following paragraphs.

SRR0 = CIA if Instruction-Caused Interrupt

The address of the currently-executing instruction, or CIA, is copied to SRR0 if the interrupt was caused by a failed attempt to execute the current instruction. The interrupt handler can then use SRR0 as a pointer to the instruction that has experienced a problem.

SRR0 = NIA if Not Instruction-Caused Interrupt

The next instruction address, or NIA, is copied to SRR0 if the interrupt was cause by an event other than a failed instruction execution attempt (such as an external interrupt). After the interrupt handler has finished handling the interrupt and executes an rfi instruction (return from interrupt), the rfi causes the processor to use SRR0 as the address at which to resume execution.

SRR1 Used for MSR State Save

When an interrupt occurs, the processor copies machine state information from the MSR to SRR1. In effect, this saves a snapshot of the processor's state at the point of interruption so that it can be restored (by copying it back into MSR from SRR1) after the interrupt has been handled by the operating system. In addition to machine state information, the processor saves status information specific to the interrupt in SRR1.

Specifically, in a 32-bit implementation, the processor copies the following bit fields from MSR to the identical bit fields in SRR1: 0, 5:9, and 16:31. It also places interrupt-specific status information in bit fields 1:4 and 10:15 of SRR1.

In a 64-bit implementation, the processor copies the following bit fields from MSR to the identical bit fields in SRR1: 0:32, 37:41 and 48:63. It also places interrupt-specific status information in bit fields 33:36 and 42:47 of SRR1.

Context Switch

After saving interrupt-specific information and the current state of the processor (bit fields from MSR) into SRR1 and setting SRR0 to point to the instruction that caused the interrupt or the next instruction to be executed (after interrupt servicing), the processor changes the state of certain MSR bits and jumps to the interrupt vector address associated with the interrupt being recognized. The MSR bits that are changed place the processor in a new operating mode, or context, to handle the interrupt condition. The bit changes that comprise this context change are listed in table 21-2.

Table 21-2. Effect of an Interrupt on MSR Bits

MSR Bit	State after interrupt
IP	MSR[IP] is not affected, so the interrupt table is not relocated.
ILE	MSR[ILE] is not affected, so the preferred endian mode for interrupt processing is not disturbed.
LE	MSR[ILE] is copied to MSR[LE] to place the processor in the desired endian mode to service the interrupt. If the processor has been reset, however, LE is cleared (ILE is not copied to it).
ME	MSR[ME] is undisturbed, permitting recognition of machine check interrupts (for more information, see description of the machine check interrupt).
SF	If a 64-bit processor, MSR[SF] is set to one, placing the processor in 64-bit mode to service the interrupt.
BE	MSR[BE] is cleared, disabling branch trace interrupt recognition.
DR	MSR[DR] is cleared, disabling address translation for data accesses.
EE	MSR[EE] is cleared, disabling recognition of external or decrementer interrupts.
FE0 and FE1	MSR[FE0:FE1] are cleared, disabling floating-point interrupts.
FP	MSR[FP] is cleared, disabling floating-point unavailable interrupts.
IR	MSR[IR] is cleared, disabling address translation for instruction fetches.
POW	MSR[POW] is cleared, disabling power management.
PR	MSR[PR] is cleared, placing the processor in the supervisor privilege level.
RI	MSR[RI] is cleared, indicating the interrupt is not recoverable.
SE	MSR[SE] is cleared, disabling recognition of the single-step trace interrupt.

The Stack and the State Save

The operating system initializes SPRG0 with the stack pointer at startup time. Upon entry to an interrupt handler, the programmer takes the following steps:

- Copy one of the GPR registers into SPRG1. This frees up the GPR to be used for a series of indirect stores to the stack in memory.
- Copy the stack pointer from SPRG0 to the GPR register.
- Use the GPR register as an address pointer to save SRR0 and SRR1.
- Set MSR[RI] to one. For more information regarding RI, refer to the section in this chapter entitled "The Recoverable Interrupt Bit."

- Use the GPR register that has been freed up to save any other registers that will be altered while in the interrupt handler.
- Use the GPR register to save the contents of SPRG1.

Return from Interrupt (rfi)

When the processor executes the rfi instruction at the end of the interrupt handler, the contents of the respective bit fields in SRR1 are copied back to MSR, automatically returning the processor to its pre-interrupt operational context. Execution resumes at the location pointed to by SRR0. If the interrupt was caused by a failed attempt to execute an instruction, SRR0 points to the failed instruction. Execution of this instruction will be re attempted. If the interrupt was caused by an event other than a failed instruction, SRR0 points to the instruction that would have been executed if the interrupt event had not occurred. Execution will therefore resume at the next instruction. For more information, also refer to the section in this chapter entitled "The Recoverable Interrupt Bit."

Recoverable Interrupt Bit

General

The RI bit in MSR and SRR1[30] are closely associated with each other. At initialization time, the operating system programmer sets RI to one. Each time an interrupt occurs, the processor copies MSR[RI] to SRR1[30] and then clears RI to zero.

On Entry to Interrupt Handler

On entry to each interrupt handler, the processor automatically copies MSR[RI] to SRR1[30] and then clears RI to zero. On entry to the interrupt handler, the programmer should:

- Check the state of SRR1[30] to determine if the interrupted program is restartable. SRR1[30] = 0 indicates it that it would be unsafe to execute an rfi at the end of this interrupt handler, while SRR1[30] = 1 indicates the interrupted program may be safely resumed by executing an rfi at the conclusion of the interrupt handler.
- Set RI to one when sufficient state information has been saved to permit recovery if the handler is interrupted.

If the interrupt handler should be interrupted after RI is set to one, SRR1[30] is then set to one when MSR[RI] is copied to SRR1 by the processor (RI is then cleared by the processor). SRR1[30] = 1 indicates to the second-level interrupt handler that the first-level interrupt handler can be resumed successfully when the rfi is executed at the conclusion of the second-level handler.

If the first-level interrupt handler were interrupted before saving state and setting RI to one, a zero would be copied from MSR[RI] to SRR1[30] on entry to the second-level interrupt handler. Upon examining SRR1[30] on entry to the second-level handler, SRR1[30] cleared to zero indicates that the programmer must not execute an rfi at the end of the second-level handler.

On Exit from Interrupt Handler

Just prior to exiting from an interrupt handler, the programmer should take the following actions:

- Set the RI bit to zero. This must be done because the instructions that follow will reload SRR0 and SRR1 with the values to be used by the processor when it executes the rfi at the end of the interrupt handler. If the processor should be interrupted while in the process of initializing SRR0 and SRR1, execution of the rfi could have disastrous effects.
- Disable external interrupt recognition by clearing MSR[EE] to zero to prevent the instructions that set up SRR0 and SRR1 from being interrupted.
- Set SRR0 and SRR1 for use by the rfi instruction in returning to the interrupted program. SRR1[30] must be set to one.
- Execute the rfi instruction. SRR1[30] will be copied back into MSR[RI], setting it to one. This will ensure that SRR1[30] will be set to one again when the next interrupt occurs.

On Entry to Machine Check or System Reset Handlers

A machine check or system reset interrupt may corrupt the state of SRR0 and/or SRR1 or other processor resource that is necessary to resume execution of the interrupted program. If this is the case, the processor will clear SRR1[30] to zero (rather than just copying the state of MSR[RI] to SRR1[30]). This indicates to the machine check or reset handler that the interrupted program cannot be safely resumed by executing an rfi instruction.

Interrupts Originated by Instruction Execution

The processor may generate an interrupt during the execution of or at the completion of an instruction. The following sections describe each of the instruction-caused interrupts. Table 21-3 provides a listing of these interrupts and their causes.

Table 21-3. Interrupts Caused by Attempted Execution of Instruction

Interrupt Type	Caused By
Data Storage	Attempt to load/store semaphore in I/O space. Data page fault. Attempted execution of ecowx or eciwx instruction within I/O segment or without the EAR register initialized. Access rights violation on load/store.
Instruction Storage	Code page fault. Attempted instruction fetch from I/O segment. Instruction fetch violates page or block access rights.
Alignment	Refer to section in this chapter entitled "Alignment Interrupt."
Program	Floating-point interrupt. User attempt to execute privileged or an illegal instruction. Trap instruction executed and specified condition(s) met.
Floating-Point Unavailable	Attempt to execute floating-point instruction with the floating-point unit disabled (MSR[FP] = 0).
System Call	Execution of a system call, or sc, instruction.
Trace Interrupt	Implementation of this interrupt optional. Caused by either a single-step or a branch trace interrupt.
Floating-Point Assist	Implementation of this interrupt optional. Caused by attempt to execute relatively infrequent, complex floating-point operation (i.e., computations involving denormalized numbers).

Data Storage Interrupt

The data storage interrupt is generated when the processor attempts to execute an instruction and there is something wrong with the target address or the access violates the page or block access rights (as specified by the selected K bit and the PP bits). Its offset in the interrupt table is 00300h. The cause of the interrupt is indicated in the data storage interrupt status register, or DSISR. The possible causes are:

- Attempt to perform an lwarx, stwcx, ldarx or stdcx within an I/O segment. These instructions are used to load and store memory semaphores and semaphores don't reside in I/O space.
- Attempt to execute an eciwx or ecowx instruction within an I/O segment. The target address specified must map into a memory segment.
- No page table entry found for the target effective address of a load, store, dcbst, dcbf, dcbz or dcbi. In other words, the processor experienced a page fault on a data access attempt. The page fault handler should be invoked.
- The data access attempt violates the page or block access rights indicated by the state of the PP and K bits. in the page table entry or the PP bits in a BAT register.
- Attempt to execute an ecowx or eciwx when the EAR register has not been initialized with the resource ID and the enable bit in the EAR is not set to one.

Table 21-4 defines the state of the DSISR register upon entry to the data storage interrupt handler. The data access register, or DAR, will contain the target address specified by the instruction. The DAR contents on entry to the data storage interrupt handler is defined in table 21-5.

When a data storage interrupt occurs, SRR1 is set as follows:

- If this is a 64-bit processor, SRR1[33:36] and [42:47] are set to zero. If this is a 32-bit processor, SRR1[1:4] and [10:15] are set to zero.
- The other SRR1 bits are copied from the corresponding bits in the MSR register.

A stwcx or an stdcx might cause a data storage interrupt if the store were performed. If the reservation has been lost, however, the store is not performed. In this case, it is processor-dependent whether or not a data storage interrupt would be generated. If a move assist instruction has a byte transfer count of zero specified in XER, a data storage interrupt is not generated.

Table 21-4. DSISR Bits After Data Storage Interrupt

Bit	Description
0	Set to one if target location is mapped to an I/O segment.
1	Set to one if both page and block translation failed (i.e., a page fault).
2:3	Set to zero.
4	Set to one if the access violated the protection attributes for the target block or page.
5	Set to one if the target of an ecowx, eciwx, lwarx, ldarx, stwcx or stdcx is within an I/O segment. Also set to one if the target of an lwarx, ldarx, stwcx or stdcx is within a block or page designated as write-through.
6	0 = load, 1 = store.
7:8	Set to zero.
9	Set if a match was detected on the DABR (data access breakpoint register). See the chapter entitled "601 OS Register and Instruction Set" for more information on debug facilities.
10	In a 64-bit processor, set to one if the segment table scan failed to find a match. In other words, a segment fault occurred.
11	Set to one if ecowx or eciwx attempted with an uninitialized EAR register (EAR[0] = 0).
12:31	Set to zero.

Table 21-5. DAR Contents After Data Storage Interrupt

Circumstance	DAR Contents
Byte, halfword or word access to memory segment.	Set to effective address of byte in first word accessed in page.
Doubleword access to memory segment.	Set to effective address of byte in first doubleword in page.
Byte, halfword or word access to block.	Set to effective address of byte in first word accessed in he block.
Doubleword access to block.	Set to effective address of byte in first doubleword in block.
Any access to I/O segment.	Set to any effective address in range of effective addresses being addressed.

Instruction Storage Interrupt

The instruction storage interrupt occurs when an instruct fetch is attempted under any of the following conditions:

- The effective address cannot be translated by the block or page address translation logic in the MMU. In other words, a page fault has occurred while attempting an instruction fetch.
- The effective address is mapped to an I/O segment by the segment register or an entry in the segment table. Instructions cannot be fetched from I/O space.
- The fetch attempt is within a page or block that denies access to the program.

The instruction storage interrupt vector is 00400h in the interrupt table. The interrupt has the following effects:

- The MSR bits are set as indicated in table 21-2.
- SRR0 contains the effective address of the next instruction to be executed.
- SRR1[33] (64-bit) or SRR1[1] (32-bit) is set to one if the effective address of the fetch could not be translated by the block or page translation logic in the MMU.
- SRR1[34] (64-bit) or SRR1[2] (32-bit) is set to zero.
- SRR1[35] (64-bit) or SRR1[3] (32-bit) is set to one if the effective address of the fetch was mapped to an I/O segment.
- SRR1[36] (64-bit) or SRR1[4] (32-bit) is set to one if the access is not permitted by the block or page access rights.
- SRR1[42] (64-bit) or SRR1[10] (32-bit) is set to one on a 64-bit processor if the segment table search fails to find a match on the virtual effective segment address.
- SRR1[43:47] (64-bit) or SRR1[11:15] (32-bit) are set to zero.
- The remaining SRR1 bits are copied from the corresponding bits in MSR.

Alignment Interrupt

The alignment interrupt is associated with unsuccessful attempts to access memory due to misaligned operands. The offset of the alignment handler's entry point in the interrupt table is 00600h. The alignment interrupt can be caused by the following events:

- Operand of floating-point load or store isn't word-aligned.
- Operand of an integer doubleword load or store isn't word-aligned.
- Operand of lmw, stmw, lwarx, stwcx is not word-aligned or the operand of a ldarx or stdcx is not doubleword-aligned.
- Operand of a floating-point load or store is in an I/O segment.
- Operand of an elementary or string load or store crosses a page or block boundary.
- Operand of a lmw or stmw crosses a segment or block boundary.
- Operand of a dcbz is in a write-through or non-cacheable page.
- Attempt to execute a load/store multiple or a load/store string instruction while the processor is operating in the little-endian storage mode (MSR[LE] = 1).

In the alignment interrupt handler, the programmer may examine DSISR to determine the cause of the interrupt. Table 21-6 defines the DSISR bits related to the alignment interrupt. The bit fields in DSISR are extracted from the instruction that caused the interrupt. The programmer may determine the instruction type from these bits (rather than using SRR0 to fetch the offending instruction). Table 21-7 (much easier to digest that table 21-6) provides the mapping between the DSISR contents and the instruction type. The interrupt handler emulates the instruction and requires the following information:

- Is the instruction a load or a store?
- The length of the operand: halfword, word or doubleword (a byte load or store cannot cause an alignment interrupt).
- Is it a string, multiple or elementary operation?
- Is it an integer or floating-point operation?
- Is the instruction a load or store with update?
- Is byte reversal specified?
- Is the instruction a dcbz?

For additional information regarding the bit settings in DSISR, refer to the PowerPC Architecture manual. The DAR register is set to the effective address of the target location (refer to table 21-5). SRR0 is set to the effective address of the instruction that caused the interrupt. SRR1 is set as follows:

- If this is a 64-bit processor, SRR1[33:36] and [42:47] are set to zero. If this is a 32-bit processor, SRR1[1:4] and [10:15] are set to zero.
- The other SRR1 bits are copied from the corresponding bits in the MSR register.

Table 21-6. State of DSISR Bits After Alignment Interrupt

Bit(s)	Description
0:11	Set to zero.
12:13	On a 64-bit processor, set to bits 30:31 of the instruction (extended opcode field) if it is a DS form instruction; set to zeros if D or X-form instruction. Set to zeros on 32-bit processor.
14	Set to zero.
15:16	Set to the two least-significant bits of the extended opcode field (29:30) if the instruction is of the X-form. Set to zeros if instruction is of the D or DS-form.
17	Set to bit 25 of the instruction's extended opcode if the instruction is of the X-form. Set to the least-significant bit (bit 5) of the instruction's opcode if the instruction is of the D or DS-form.
18:21	Set to bits 21:24 of the instruction's extended opcode if the instruction is of the X-form. Set to bits 1:4 of the instruction's opcode if the instruction is of the D or DS-form.
22:26	Set to bits 6:10 of the instruction. These bits define the integer or the floating-point source or target GPR or FPR register (but they are undefined for a dcbz instruction).
27:31	For an update form instruction, set to bits 11:15 of the instruction (the source or target GPR register). For the load multiple instructions (lmw, lswi and lswx), set to any register number not in the range of registers to be loaded. The content of these bits are undefined for other instructions.

Table 21-7. DSISR-to-Instruction Type Mapping

Hex Value In DSISR[15:21]	Instruction Is
00h	lwarx, lwz
01h	ldarx
02h	stw
04h	lhz
05h	lha
06h	sth
07h	lmw
08h	lfs
09h	lfd
0Ah	stfs
0Bh	stfd
0Dh	ld, ldu, lwa
0Fh	std, stdu
10h	lwzu
12h	stwu
14h	lhzu
15h	lhau
16h	sthu
17h	stmw
18h	lfsu
19h	lfdu
1Ah	stfsu
1Bh	stfdu
20h	ldx
22h	stdx
25h	lwax
28h	lswx
29h	lswi
2Ah	stswx
2Bh	stswi
30h	ldux
32h	stdux
35h	lwaux
42h	stwcx.
43h	stdcx.
48h	lwbrx
4Ah	stwbrx

Table 21 - 7, cont.

4Ch	lhbrx
4Eh	sthbrx
54h	eciwx
56h	ecowx
5Fh	dcbz
60h	lwzx
62h	stwx
64h	lhzx
65h	lhax
66h	sthx
68h	lfsx
69h	lfdx
6Ah	stfsx
6Bh	stfdx
6Fh	stfiwx
70h	lwzux
72h	stwux
74h	lhzux
75h	lhaux
76h	sthux
78h	lfsux
79h	lfdux
7Ah	stfsux
7Bh	stfdux

Program Interrupt

The program interrupt will be taken when any of the following conditions arise:

- Any enabled precise floating-point interrupt occurs.
- Attempt to execute an instruction: with an illegal opcode; or with an invalid opcode/extended opcode combination; or that is optional and is not implemented on this processor (with the exception of optional instructions that are treated as no-ops). It is also permissible to generate a program interrupt when execution of an invalid form instruction is attempted.
- Attempt to execute a privileged instruction while the processor is operating at the user privilege level (MSR[PR] = 1). Some processors may also

generate the program interrupt when an attempt is made to execute a mtspr or mfspr with an invalid SPR field if bit zero of the SPR field is one and the processor is operating at the user privilege level.
- Execution of a trap instruction where the trap condition is met.

The program interrupt has the following effects on registers:

- Except when caused by an imprecise floating-point interrupt, SRR0 is set to the effective address of the instruction that caused the interrupt (i.e., the CIA). If caused by an imprecise floating-point interrupt, SRR0 will point either to the instruction that caused the interrupt or to a subsequent instruction. If it points to a subsequent instruction, that instruction has not yet been executed. The programmer must scan backward in memory to discover the last floating-point instruction in the instruction stream. This is the one that caused the interrupt. For more information regarding the floating-point interrupt, refer to the PowerPC Architecture manual.
- For a 32-bit processor, SRR1[1:4] and [10] are set to zero. If a 64-bit processor, SRR1[33:36] and [42] are set to zero.
- For a 32-bit processor, SRR1[11] is set to one if the program interrupt was caused by a floating-point interrupt. If a 64-bit processor, SRR1[43] is set to one under the same condition.
- For a 32-bit processor, SRR1[12] is set to one if the program interrupt was caused by an illegal instruction type. If a 64-bit processor, SRR1[44] is set to one under the same condition.
- For a 32-bit processor, SRR1[13] is set to one if the program interrupt was caused by an attempt to execute a privileged instruction in user mode. If a 64-bit processor, SRR1[45] is set to one under the same condition.
- For a 32-bit processor, SRR1[14] is set to one if the program interrupt was caused by a trap instruction. If a 64-bit processor, SRR1[46] is set to one under the same condition.
- For a 32-bit processor, SRR1[15] is set to one if SRR0 contains the effective address of the instruction that caused the interrupt; it is set to zero if SRR0 contains the effective address of a subsequent instruction. If a 64-bit processor, SRR1[47] is used for this purpose.
- Other bits in SRR1 are copied from their respective bits in MSR.
- The MSR bits are set as indicated in table 21-2.

The offset of the program interrupt's vector in the interrupt table is 00700h.

Floating-Point Unavailable Interrupt

This interrupt is generated when the processor attempts to execute a floating-point instruction with the floating-point unit disabled (MSR[FP] = 0), or if the processor doesn't include a floating-point unit. The offset of the floating-point unavailable interrupt's vector in the interrupt table is 00800h. This interrupt has the following effect on registers:

- SRR0 is set to the effective address of the instruction that caused the interrupt (i.e., the CIA).
- In a 32-bit processor, SRR1[1:4] and [10:15] are set to zero. In a 64-bit processor, SRR1[33:36] and [42:47] are set to zero.
- The other bits in SRR1 are copied from their respective bits in MSR.
- The MSR bits are set as indicated in table 21-2.

System Call Interrupt

This interrupt is generated when the processor executes a system call, or sc, instruction. The offset of the system call interrupt's vector in the interrupt table is 00C00h. This interrupt has the following effect on registers:

- SRR0 is set to the effective address of the instruction following the system call instruction (i.e., the NIA).
- In a 32-bit processor, SRR1[0:15] are defined. In a 64-bit processor, SRR1[32:47] are defined.
- The other SRR1 bits are copied from their respective bits in MSR.
- The MSR bits are set as indicated in table 21-2.

Trace Interrupt

This interrupt is optional. The offset of the trace interrupt's vector in the interrupt table is 00D00h. It occurs under the following conditions:

- The single-step trace interrupt is enabled (MSR[SE] = 1) and any instruction other than an rfi completes execution successfully.
- The branch trace interrupt is enabled (MSR[BE] = 1) and a branch instruction completes execution successfully.

The trace interrupt has the following effect on registers:

- SRR0 is set to the effective address of the instruction that would have been executed next (i.e., the NIA) if trace interrupts were not enabled.
- If this is a 32-bit processor, SRR1[1:4] and [10:15] are processor-dependent. If this is a 64-bit processor, SRR1[33:36] and [42:47] are processor dependent.
- The other bits in SRR1 are copied from their respective bits in MSR.
- MSR bits are altered as indicated in table 21-2.

Floating-Point Assist Interrupt

This interrupt is optional. If implemented, the offset of its interrupt vector in the interrupt table is 00E00h. It is caused by the attempt to execute relatively infrequent and complex floating-point instructions (i.e., computations involving denormalized numbers). It has the following effect on registers:

- SRR0 is set to the effective address of the instruction that would have been executed next if the interrupt had not occurred (i.e., the NIA).
- If this is a 32-bit processor, SRR1[1:4] and [10:15] are processor-dependent. If this is a 64-bit processor, SRR1[33:36] and [42:47] are processor dependent.
- The other bits in SRR1 are copied from their respective bits in MSR.
- MSR bits are altered as indicated in table 21-2.

Interrupts from Source other than Instruction

Interrupts that originate from a source other than instruction execution are listed in table 21-8.

Table 21-8. Interrupts Not Caused by Instructions

Interrupt Type	Cause
System reset	Assertion of the processor's hard or soft reset input signals by external logic.
Machine check	Assertion of TEA# to the processor when the processor is enabled to recognize machine checks (MSR[ME] = 1).
External	Assertion of the processor's external interrupt input signal by external logic when external interrupt recognition is enabled (MSR[EE] = 1).
Decrementer	Exhaustion of the decrementer register, DEC, when external interrupt recognition is enabled (MSR[EE] = 1).

System Reset Interrupt

This interrupt only occurs if the processor's hard or soft reset input signal is asserted by external logic. The architecture specification does not define what state this will leave the processor in (in other words, it's processor dependent). It does define that the processor will jump to offset 00100h within the interrupt table. The interrupt table base address is specified by the state of the MSR[IP] bit after reset (processor-dependent). If the hard reset has corrupted or altered the processor's state such that it could not reliably resume executing the interrupted program after the interrupt is handled, the processor reset causes MSR[RI] to be cleared.

SRR0 is set to the address of the next instruction that would have been executed if the interrupted had not occurred (i.e., the NIA). SRR1 is set as follows:

- In a 32-bit processor, SRR1[1:4] and [10:15] are cleared to zero. SRR1[30] is cleared if the processor cannot recover from the interrupt, else it's set to one. The remainder of the SRR1 bits are copied from the corresponding bits in MSR.
- In a 64-bit processor, SRR1[33:36] and [42:47] are cleared to zero. SRR1[62] is cleared if the processor cannot recover from the interrupt, else it's set to one. The remainder of the SRR1 bits are copied from the corresponding bits in MSR.

Except as indicated in this section, the MSR bits are set to the states indicated in table 21-2.

Machine Check Interrupt and Checkstop State

A machine check indicates that some type of serious logic failure has occurred. The causes of a machine check are processor-dependent. If a machine check occurs and machine check interrupt handling is disabled (MSR[ME] = 0), the processor enters the checkstop state. When checkstop is entered, the processor cannot execute instructions. The contents of all registers are frozen within two clocks after the checkstop occurs. Generally, the only way to exit the checkstop state is to assert and then deassert the processor's hard reset input signal.

If a machine check condition is detected and the machine check interrupt is enabled (MSR[ME] = 1], the processor takes the following actions:

- The processor makes its best effort to set SRR0 to the effective address of the instruction that was executing or was about to be executed.
- The state of SRR1 is processor-dependent.
- MSR[ME] is cleared, disabling further recognition of machine check conditions.

Except as indicated in this section, the MSR bits are set to the states indicated in table 21-2.

External Interrupt

If the MSR[EE] bit is set to one, recognition of the external interrupt is enabled. It is generated when the processor's external interrupt input signal is asserted by external logic and MSR[EE] = 1.

When the external interrupt occurs, the MSR bits are altered as described in table 21-2. SRR0 is set to the effective address of the instruction that would have been executed next if the external interrupt had not occurred (i.e., the NIA). SRR1 is set as follows:

- If this is a 64-bit processor, SRR1[33:36] and [42:47] are set to zero. If this is a 32-bit processor, SRR1[1:4] and [10:15] are set to zero.
- The other SRR1 bits are copied from the corresponding bits in the MSR register.

The offset of the external interrupt vector in the interrupt table is 00500h. In the external interrupt handler, the programmer must interrogate the external interrupt controller to determine the highest-priority hardware interrupt request currently pending. In a PowerPC machine that incorporates the PCI bus, the interrupt controller typically resides in the PCI-to-expansion bus bridge (e.g., the PCI/ISA bus bridge). The programmer must stimulate the host/PCI bridge to perform a PCI interrupt acknowledge transaction. This is typically accomplished via a memory-mapped I/O port implemented on the host side of the host/PCI bridge. In the external interrupt handler, the programmer performs a load from this port. The processor initiates a single-beat memory read transaction to request the interrupt vector. When the host/PCI bridge detects the read in progress, it asserts AACK# to claim the transaction. The processor then awaits data bus acquisition and TA#, signaling the presence of the interrupt vector on data path 0. The bridge acquires ownership of the PCI bus and initiates the interrupt acknowledge transaction on the PCI bus. When the interrupt controller detects the transaction, it drives the 8-bit interrupt vector associated with the highest-priority pending interrupt request onto data path 0 and asserts TRDY#. When the host/PCI bridge samples TRDY# asserted, it latches the vector and ends the PCI transaction. The bridge then passes the vector back to processor on data path 0 and asserts TA# to indicate its presence on the bus. The processor latches the byte and passes it to the integer execution unit for placement in the specified GPR register. The programmer then uses this byte as an index into the table of start addresses of hardware interrupt service routines. It then jumps to the device-specific interrupt service routine associated with the highest-priority device currently requesting service.

Decrementer Interrupt

This interrupt is generated when the processor exhausts the count in the decrementer register, DEC, and external interrupt recognition is enabled (MSR[EE] = 1). The offset of the decrementer interrupt's vector in the interrupt table is 00900h. This interrupt has the following effect on registers:

- SRR0 is set to the effective address of the instruction that would have been executed next if the interrupt had not occurred (i.e., the NIA).
- In a 32-bit processor, SRR1[1:4] and [10:15] are set to zero. In a 64-bit processor, SRR1[33:36] and [42:47] are set to zero.
- The other bits in SRR1 are copied from their respective bits in MSR.
- The MSR bits are set as indicated in table 21-2.

For more information on the decrementer, refer to the chapter entitled "601 User Register and Instruction Set."

Precise Interrupts

A precise interrupt has the following basic characteristics:

- All instructions that occur earlier in the instruction stream than the interrupt event have completed execution.
- Instructions subsequent to the event that caused the interrupt will not be executed until after the interrupt has been handled.

Imprecise Interrupts

An imprecise interrupt has the following basic characteristics:

- All instructions that occur earlier in the instruction stream than the interrupt event have completed execution.
- Instructions subsequent to the instruction that caused the interrupt may have executed before the interrupt was recognized.

The PowerPC architecture only defines one imprecise interrupt — the imprecise mode floating-point interrupt.

Partially-Executed Instructions

There are two types of instructions that may cause multiple accesses:

- Load/store multiple or load/store string instructions cause multiple words or bytes to be transferred between memory and a set of registers.
- A single load or store, also referred to as an elementary load or store, may also cause multiple accesses if it crosses a word boundary.

Under certain circumstances, an instruction that generates multiple accesses can be interrupted during the course of its execution. If this should occur, some memory locations and/or registers may have already been modified (even though the instruction has not yet completed). This can happen under the following circumstances:

- A load multiple or load string instruction may cause an alignment or data storage interrupt. In this case, one or more target registers may have already been loaded from memory.
- A store multiple or store string instruction may cause an alignment or data storage interrupt. In this case, one or more memory locations may have already been stored into.
- An elementary store of a single data object that crosses a page or block boundary may cause an alignment or data storage interrupt. In this case, one or more bytes in memory prior to the boundary may have already been stored into before the interrupt occurred. If the instruction normally alters CR0 (this would be a stwcx or stdcx), the bits within CR0 are undefined. If the instruction is in the update form, the update register (rA) is not altered.
- A floating-point load that crosses a page or block boundary may cause an alignment or data storage interrupt. In this case, one or more bytes in memory prior to the boundary may have already been read from before the interrupt occurred. The target register of the load may have been altered. If the instruction is in the update form, the update register (rA) is not altered.
- A load or a store within an I/O segment may cause a data storage interrupt. Some of the resulting address/data transactions may not have been initiated on the bus. All initiated transfers are completed before the interrupt and all transfers yet to be initiated are aborted before they begin. The instruction completes before the interrupt is reported.

In each of the cases mentioned above, the number of memory locations and/or registers altered prior to the generation of the interrupt is processor implementation, instruction and boundary-dependent. However, memory protection is not violated.

To ensure the restartability of the instruction, the architecture specifically prohibits partial execution of an elementary integer load that causes an alignment or data storage interrupt. In this case, the target register is not loaded. If the instruction is in the update form, the specified update register is not updated.

Ordered Interrupts — Caused by Instruction Fetch, Decode or Execution

General

In the PowerPC architecture it is permissible for a processor to execute instructions in an order other than that specified by the program. This would be possible in a processor that incorporates superscalar capability. Multiple execution units have access to the instruction prefetch queue. Whenever any of the execution units is ready to accept another instruction, it can extract an instruction (applicable to this execution unit) from one of a number of locations within the prefetch queue. It is not necessarily limited to just the next sequential location in the queue. It can then immediately begin execution of the instruction. If there is a problem with the decode or execution of the instruction, an interrupt condition must be generated.

It is a rule, however, that the program must appear to execute in strict program order (in other words, as if the stream of instructions being fetched from memory are being executed in serial fashion). This rule applies to interrupts that are incurred by each of the execution units, as well. The interrupts must be reported one at a time to the operating system in strict order of occurrence in the program flow.

Before a PowerPC processor recognizes an interrupt caused by a particular instruction, it must first execute all instructions that appear earlier in the instruction stream and handle any interrupts associated with them. In other words, the interrupts associated with each instruction are queued up in the proper program order before being reported, one at a time, to the operating system.

If a single instruction generates multiple interrupts, the processor handles them in order of occurrence. The order in which instruction-caused interrupts are reported is defined in table 21-9. At the instruction fetch pipeline stage, an instruction storage interrupt could occur. If the instruction is fetched successfully, it could experience either an illegal instruction or privilege violation program interrupt during the decode stage. If it passes successfully to the execution stage, the types of interrupts it could experience are instruction type-dependent. The following two sections describe the order in which interrupts would be reported at the execution stage.

Integer Instruction Interrupt Ordering

If it is an integer instruction, it could cause either:

- a program trap or
- a system call or
- either an alignment or data storage interrupt.

When it completes execution, it would cause a trace interrupt (if the single-step trace interrupt is implemented and has been enabled).

Floating-Point Instruction Interrupt Ordering

If it is a floating-point instruction, it could cause a floating-point unavailable interrupt if MSR[FP] = 0. If the floating-point unit is enabled, the instruction could cause one of the following:

- a program interrupt caused by a precise mode floating-point enabled interrupt or
- a floating-point assist interrupt (if implemented) or
- either an alignment or data storage interrupt.

When it completes execution, it would cause a trace interrupt (if the single-step trace interrupt is implemented and has been enabled).

Table 21-9. Instruction-Caused Interrupt Ordering

Pipeline Stage	Integer Instruction can cause the following interrupt(s):	Floating-Point Instruction can cause the following interrupts:
Fetch	Instruction storage interrupt.	Instruction storage interrupt.
Decode	Illegal instruction or Privileged instruction	Illegal instruction or Privileged instruction
Execution	Either program trap or system call or alignment or data storage; then Trace (if implemented and enabled)	Floating-point unavailable or either: precise FPU. program interrupt or floating-point assist or either alignment or data storage; then trace (if implemented and enabled)

Unordered Interrupts: External Source and Asynchronous to Program Flow

The following two interrupt types are not caused by instructions and are considered critical. They bypass all interrupt ordering (ordering described in the previous sections):

- machine check
- system reset

Interrupt Priorities

General

The PowerPC processor uses a fixed-priority scheme to determine which interrupt to service if multiple interrupt conditions exist simultaneously. In order of precedence, highest-to-lowest, the priorities are:

1. System reset. This the highest priority interrupt and it is not maskable. If the processor's hard reset signal input is asserted, the processor will generate this interrupt regardless of any other interrupt conditions that may exist.
2. Machine check. This is the second-highest priority interrupt and it is not maskable. If a machine check condition exist and the system reset interrupt condition doesn't, the processor will generate this interrupt regardless of any other interrupt conditions that may exist.
3. Instruction-dependent. This interrupt condition is described in the next section.
4. Program interrupt due to imprecise floating-point interrupt. It is maskable (using the MSR's FE0 and FE1 bits). This interrupt is generated after all other interrupts associated with the current instruction have been reported and if no higher priority interrupt condition exists when it is to be reported.
5. External. The external interrupt is maskable (using the MSR[EE] bit). This interrupt is generated when:
   - recognition of the external interrupt is enabled (MSR[EE] =1) and
   - the processor's INT input signal is asserted by external logic and
   - after all other interrupts associated with the current instruction have been reported and if no higher priority interrupt condition exists when it is to be reported.
6. Decrementer. This is the lowest priority interrupt. It is maskable (using the MSR[EE] bit]. It is generated when:
   - recognition of the external interrupt is enabled (MSR[EE] =1) and
   - the processor's DEC register count is exhausted and
   - after all other interrupts associated with the current instruction have been reported and if no higher priority interrupt condition exists when it is to be reported.

Instruction-Specific Interrupts

The instruction-specific interrupts described in the following paragraphs will be generated if no higher priority interrupt condition exists (system reset or machine check). These are the interrupts associated with instruction fetch, decode and execution. Assuming a higher priority interrupt does not exist, the next interrupt in order (see earlier discussion of ordering) is generated. Within this category of instruction-specific interrupts, one instruction may generate multiple interrupt conditions. If multiple interrupts are generated by a single instruction, the interrupts will be handled are handled in the order described for each instruction type described in table 21-10.

Table 21-10. Interrupt Priority for Instruction That Generates Multiple Interrupt Conditions

Instruction Type	Priority (higher to lower)
Integer Load and Stores	• Alignment. • Data Storage. • Trace (if implemented and enabled).
Floating-Point Loads and Stores	• Floating-point unavailable. • Alignment. • Data Storage. • Trace (if implemented and enabled).
Other Floating-Point Instruction	• Floating-point unavailable. • Precise mode floating-point program interrupt. • Floating-point assist. • Trace (if implemented and enabled).
rfi and mtmsr	• Program interrupt while attempting to execute a privileged instruction while in user mode. • Precise mode floating-point program interrupt. • Trace (if implemented and enabled).
Other instruction-specific interrupts	• Program interrupt due to a trap condition being met. • System call interrupt due to the execution of an sc instruction. • Program interrupt while attempting to execute a privileged instruction while in user mode. • Program interrupt due to an attempt to execute an illegal instruction.
Instruction Storage interrupt during instruction fetch	This is the lowest priority interrupt within the class of interrupts associated with instruction fetch, decode and execution.

Chapter 22

The Previous Chapter

The previous chapter provided a detailed description of interrupts as implemented in the PowerPC architecture environment. This included interrupt handler-related issues and hardware interrupts.

This Chapter

This chapter provides a description of the timebase and decrementer facilities and their operational characteristics when the processor is operating at the supervisor privilege level. This chapter concludes part three of the book, the discussion of the facilities that become available to the operating system programmer when the processor is operating at the supervisor privilege level.

The Next Chapter

The next chapter begins part four of the book — the discussion of the PPC 601 processor. This chapter provides a discussion of the PPC 601' s microarchitecture and the relationships of the processor's functional units to each other.

Time Base and Decrementer

General

The time base's primary function is to keep track of the time-of-day. It is implemented as continuously-running counter incremented at a processor-dependent frequency.

The decrementer operates at the same frequency as the time base. It's function is to provide an interrupt after a programmer-specified internal of time.

Time Base

In both 32 and 64 bit processors, the time base is implemented as a 64 bit register divided into an upper (TBU) and lower half (TBL). The time base register is illustrated in figure 22-1. At power-up, the time base register is not initialized to a known value and it immediately begins counting. When the counter has incremented to its maximum value, FFFFFFFFFFFFFFFFh, it rolls over to 0000000000000000h and continues counting. The frequency that drives the counter is processor implementation-dependent and it is permissible for it to change during operation. In order for system software to be able to properly track the time of day, it must either:

- be alerted (probably via an interrupt) whenever the frequency is changed by the system. The system must then supply the frequency prior to and after the change. The interrupt handler can then store this information along with a time/date stamp.
- be able to control the time base frequency.

The time base register may be set to a known value by writing to it. The processor must be operating at the supervisor privilege level to do this. The time base register may be read from at either the user or supervisor privilege level. The move to time base upper, or mttbu, instruction is used to write to the upper half of the time base, while the move to time base lower, or mttbl, instruction is used to write to its lower half. In order to preclude the incrementing of the time base upper half by a carry from the lower half while loading the registers, the lower half should be set to zero first. This is illustrated in the following code sequence:

```
lwz    r0,upper(r1)        # r0 = upper time base value
lwz    r1,lower(r1)        # r1 = lower time base value
li     r2,0                # set lower time base to 0 to
mttbl  r2                  # prevent carry to  upper half
mttbu  r0                  # init time base upper half
mttbl  r1                  # init time base lower half
```

Time Base Register

0 31	32 63
Time Base Upper	Time Base Lower

Figure 22-1. The Time Base Upper and Lower Registers

Decrementer

The decrementer, or DEC, register is a 32-bit register driven by the same frequency as the time base. The programmer may read or write the DEC register at the supervisor privilege level using the mfdec and mtdec instructions, but it may only be read at the user level. Whenever the DEC is decremented from 00000000h to FFFFFFFFh, bit 0 changes from a 0 to a 1. If the decrementer interrupt is enabled (MSR[EE] = 1), this will result in the generation of a decrementer interrupt. If the programmer moves a value into the DEC register that changes bit 0 from a 0 to a 1, this will also cause a decrementer interrupt (if MSR[EE] =1). Performing a read from the DEC register does not alter its contents.

Chapter 23

The Previous Chapter

The previous chapter provided a description of the timebase and decrementer facilities and their operational characteristics when the processor is operating at the supervisor privilege level.

This Chapter

This chapter provides a detailed description of the PowerPC processor operation in both its native big-endian storage mode and when operating in little-endian storage mode. This includes a discussion of necessary external hardware support mechanisms. This chapter concludes part three of the book, the discussion of the facilities that become available to the operating system programmer when the processor is operating at the supervisor privilege level.

The Next Chapter

The next chapter begins part four of the book — the discussion of the PPC 601 processor. This chapter provides a discussion of the PPC 601 processor's microarchitecture and the relationships of the processor's functional units to each other.

General

There is a great deal of confusion within the design community regarding the storage method used by the PowerPC when it is operating in little-endian mode. This discussion starts by defining the classic big and little-endian storage methods and then focuses on the PowerPC operation when in little-endian mode.

Intel Little-Endian vs PowerPC Big-Endian Storage

The following illustration shows the same four bytes of data resident in a PowerPC processor's GPR 1 register and in an Intel processor's EAX register. Although the bit numbering within the registers use reversed numbering schemes, in both cases the least-significant byte is the right-most in the register and the most-significant byte is the left-most. In addition, in both cases the left-most bit in each byte is the most-significant bit.

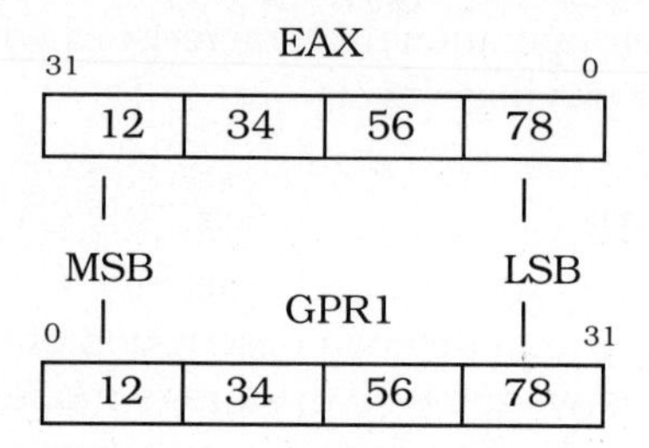

Now assume that the Intel processor's data segment starts at location zero and the following instruction is executed:

```
mov  [0100], EAX
```

Also assume that the PowerPC processor's GPR 2 register contains the address 00000100h, that the processor is in big-endian mode, MMU address translation is turned off, and that the following instruction is executed:

```
stw  r1, 0, r2
```

In both cases, the programmer is directing the processor to store the four bytes contained in the specified register into memory starting at location 0000100h. The data is stored in memory as indicated in table 23-1.

Table 23-1. Example of Big-Endian Storage Method

Memory Address	Intel	PowerPC (in big-endian mode)
00000100h	78h	12h
00000101h	56h	34h
00000102h	34h	56h
00000103h	12h	78h

The Intel processor used the little-endian storage method — the byte from the "little end," or the LSB, of the source register was stored in memory at the start address specified by the programmer. The four bytes are stored in memory in ascending memory addresses starting at the specified address in LSB-to-MSB order.

The PowerPC processor used the "big-endian" storage method — the byte from the "big end," or the MSB, of the source register was stored in memory at the start address specified by the programmer. The four bytes are stored in memory in ascending memory addresses starting at the specified address in MSB-to-LSB order.

Now assume that the PowerPC processor is operating in little-endian mode and the same store instruction is executed. The data from GPR 1 is stored in memory in the order indicated in table 23-2.

Table 23-2. Example of PowerPC Little-Endian Storage Method

Memory Address	Contents
00000100h	not stored into by instruction
00000101h	not stored into by instruction
00000102h	not stored into by instruction
00000103h	not stored into by instruction
00000104h	12h
00000105h	34h
00000106h	56h
00000107h	78h

It appears that the PowerPC storage method is radically different from Intel's method when operating in little-endian mode. The explanation provided in the following section highlights the fact that, when operating in little-endian mode, the PowerPC is placing data in memory in exactly the same manner that the Intel Pentium processor would.

Explanation of Big and Little-Endian Addressing

Refer to figure 23-1 during this discussion. To a great degree, both the PowerPC processors and the Intel Pentium processor interface with main memory in the same manner:

- The processor places an address divisible-by-eight on the address bus. The PowerPC 601 processor uses A[0:28], while the Pentium uses A[31:3]. This identifies a block of eight locations starting at this address (e.g., 00000100h, 00000108h, etc.). In PowerPC terminology, this is referred to as a doubleword, while it is referred to as a quadword in the Intel world.
- Each of the processors has eight data paths that it uses to transfer data between itself and the currently-addressed group of eight locations. They are referred to as paths 0 – 7.
- Each of the processors indicates the data paths that will be used in this transaction. The PowerPC processors indicate the start data path on A[29:31] and the number of data paths (starting with the one indicated by A[29:31]) to be used. This not only tells the memory which data paths to transfer data over, but also the locations that are being addressed during this transaction. The Pentium processor uses its eight byte enable outputs, BE[7:0]#, to indicate the data paths to be used (and, therefore the locations being addressed within the group of eight locations).

Figure 23-1 indicates that the data path connection between the processor and memory is reversed for the two processor types, however.

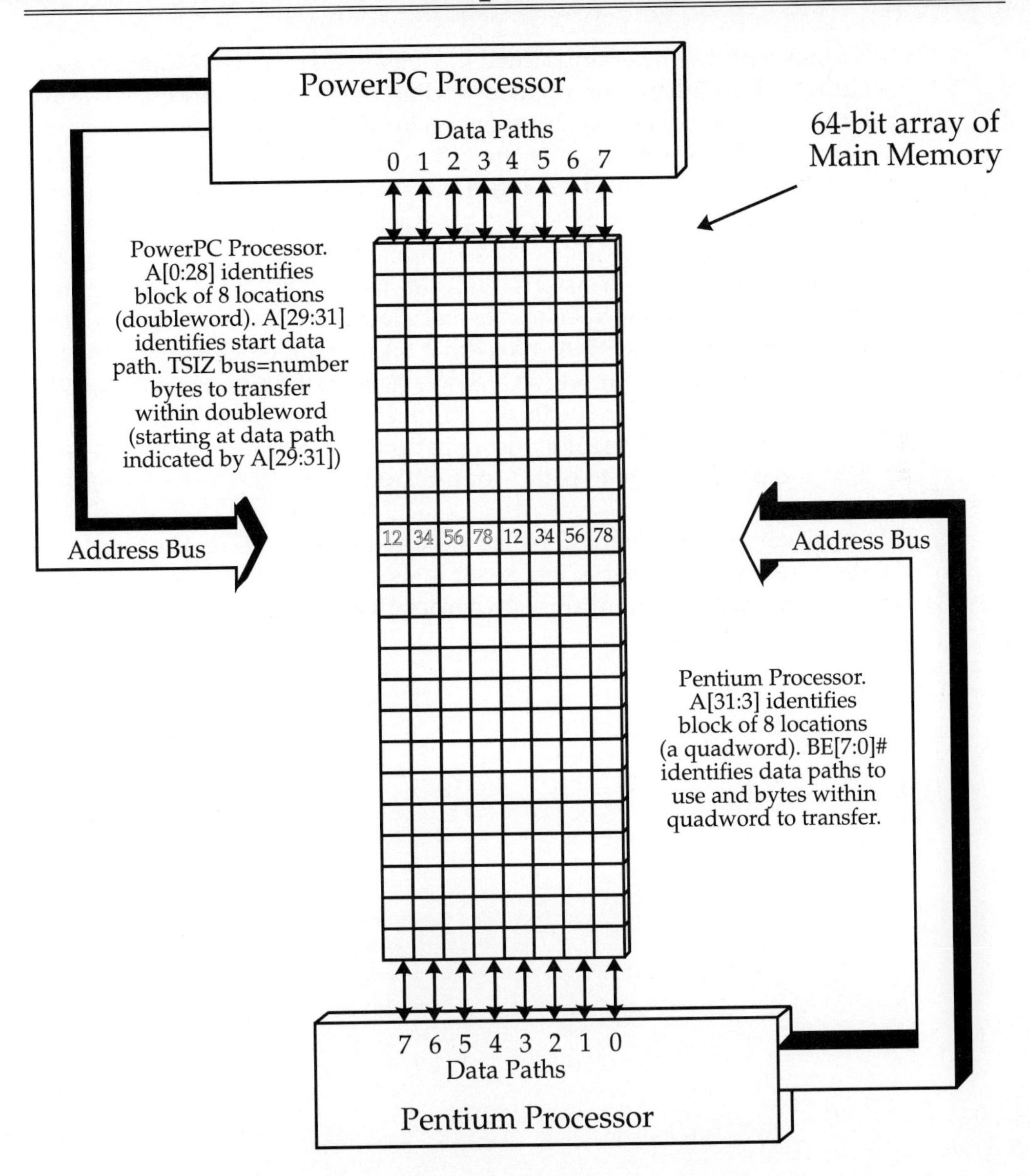
PowerPC Processor
Data Paths
0 1 2 3 4 5 6 7
64-bit array of Main Memory
PowerPC Processor. A[0:28] identifies block of 8 locations (doubleword). A[29:31] identifies start data path. TSIZ bus=number bytes to transfer within doubleword (starting at data path indicated by A[29:31])
Address Bus
12 34 56 78 12 34 56 78
Address Bus
Pentium Processor. A[31:3] identifies block of 8 locations (a quadword). BE[7:0]# identifies data paths to use and bytes within quadword to transfer.
7 6 5 4 3 2 1 0
Data Paths
Pentium Processor

Figure 23-1. Relationship of PowerPC and Pentium Processor to 64-bit Memory Array

Once again consider the example cited in table 23-1. The PowerPC processor is operating in big-endian storage mode, while the Pentium processor always operates in little-endian mode. When performing the four byte store into memory, both processors identify the group of eight locations starting at address 00000100h. The two processors store the four bytes in memory as follows:

- The Pentium processor asserts BE[3:0]#, indicating that it is using data paths [3:0] to write the data into memory locations. It drives 78h onto data path 0, 56h onto path 1, 34h onto path 2, and 12h onto path 3.
- The PowerPC processor sets A[29:31] to 000b, indicating that path 0 is the start data path and places 100b on TSIZ[0:2] indicating that a total of bytes will be transferred to memory using paths 0 - 3. It drives 12h onto path 0, 34h onto path 1, 56h onto path 2, and 78h onto path 3.

This results in the data being stored as indicated in figure 23-2. The four bytes of data stored by the PowerPC processor is shown white-filled, while the four bytes written by the Pentium are shown black-filled.

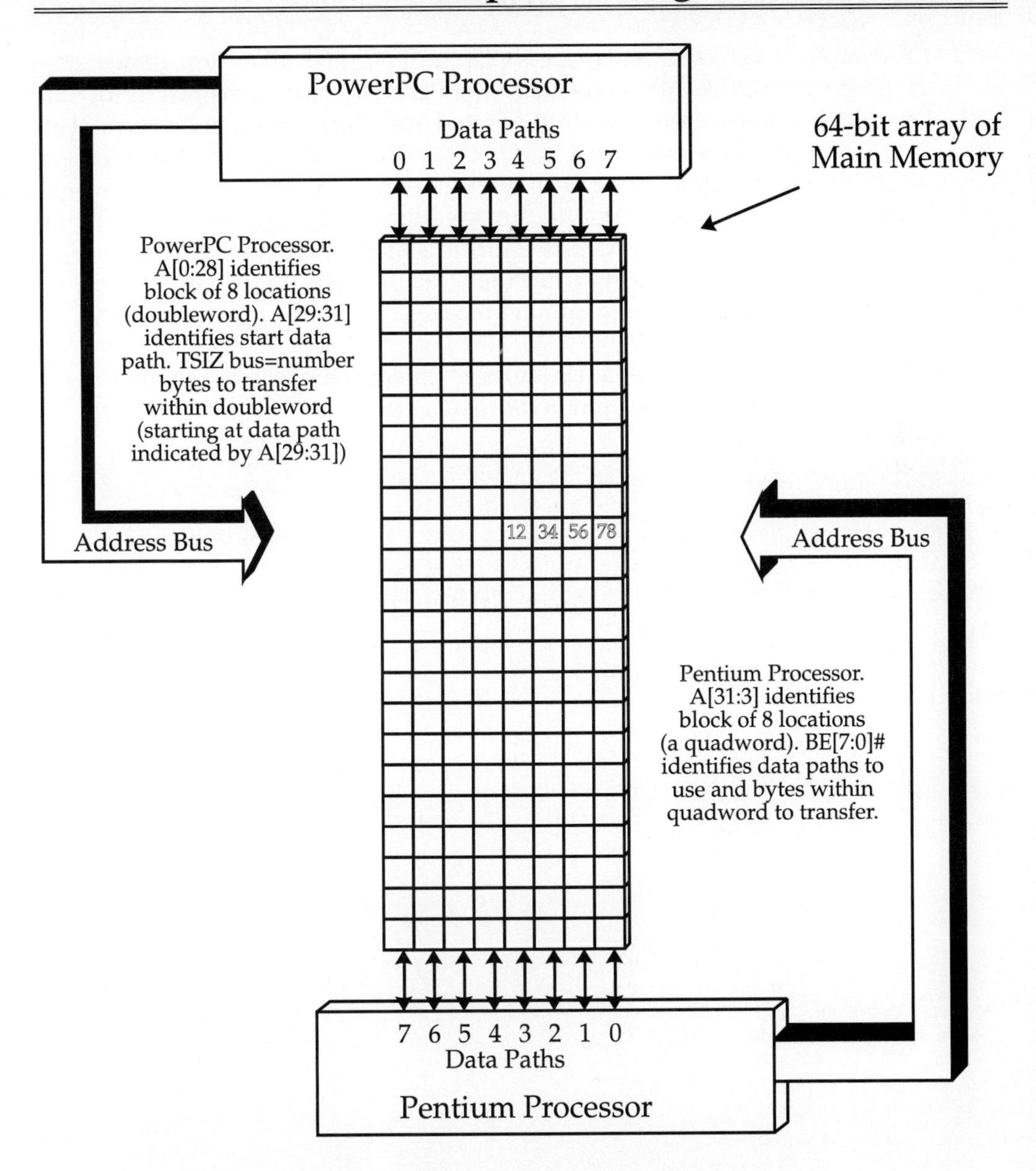
PowerPC Processor
Data Paths
0 1 2 3 4 5 6 7
64-bit array of
Main Memory
PowerPC Processor. A[0:28] identifies block of 8 locations (doubleword). A[29:31] identifies start data path. TSIZ bus=number bytes to transfer within doubleword (starting at data path indicated by A[29:31])
Address Bus
12 34 56 78
Address Bus
Pentium Processor. A[31:3] identifies block of 8 locations (a quadword). BE[7:0]# identifies data paths to use and bytes within quadword to transfer.
7 6 5 4 3 2 1 0
Data Paths
Pentium Processor

Figure 23-2. Example of Two Processors Storing Same Four Bytes into Memory Starting at Location 00000100h.

A compliant PowerPC processor is placed into little-endian storage mode by setting the MSR[LE] bit to one, while the PPC 601 processor is placed into little-endian mode by setting HID0[LE] bit to one. If the same four bytes are then stored into memory starting at location 00000100h, the processor stores them into exactly the same memory locations that the Pentium processor would store them into. The result of the store is illustrated in figure 23-3. From the perspective of the PowerPC processor, it is storing the four bytes into locations 00000104h – 00000107h, while these are locations 00000103h – 00000100h from the perspective of the Pentium processor.

When operating in little-endian storage mode, the PowerPC processor accomplishes this transformation in the manner described in the next section.

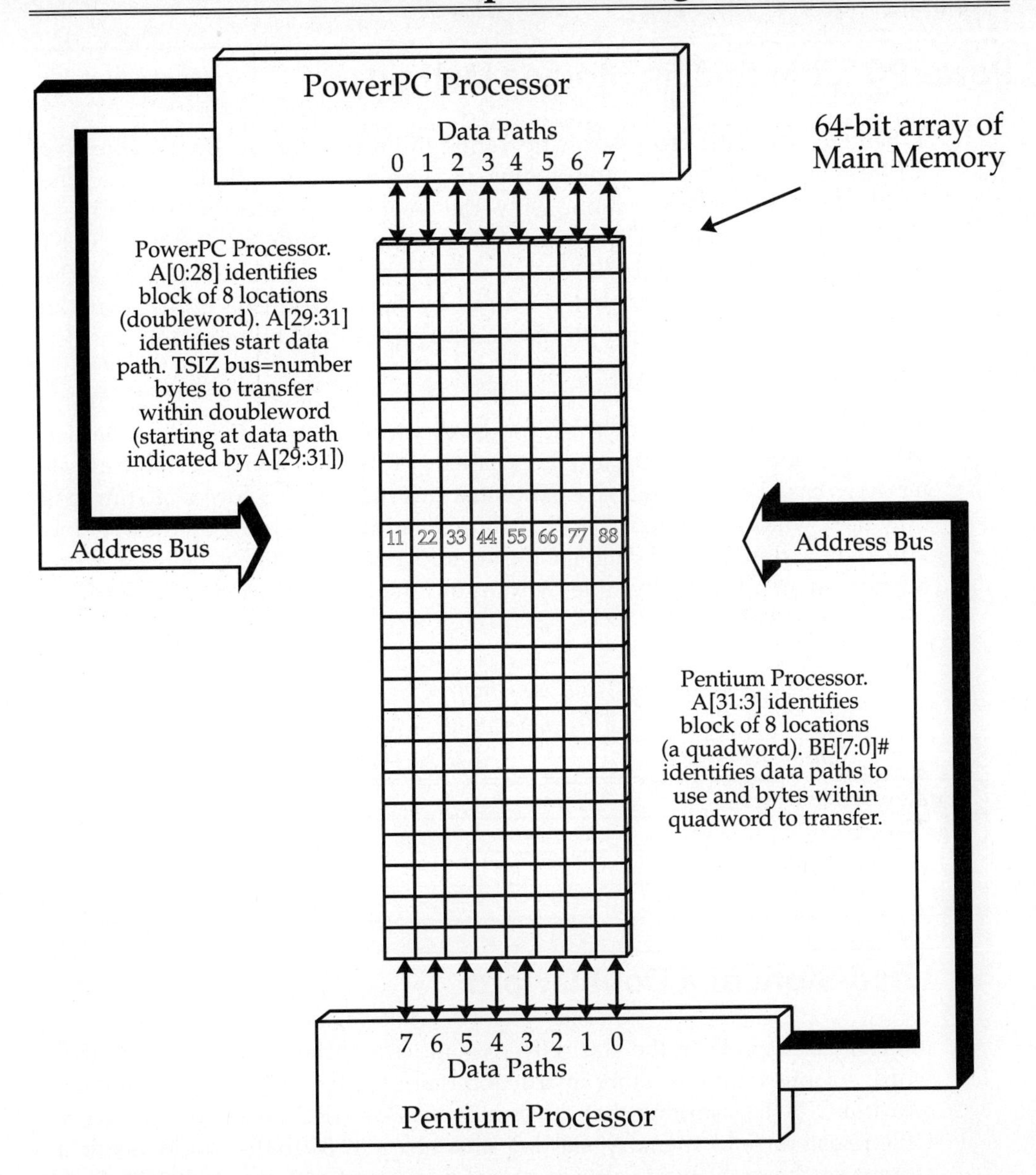
PowerPC Processor
Data Paths
0 1 2 3 4 5 6 7
64-bit array of Main Memory
PowerPC Processor. A[0:28] identifies block of 8 locations (doubleword). A[29:31] identifies start data path. TSIZ bus=number bytes to transfer within doubleword (starting at data path indicated by A[29:31])
Address Bus
11 22 33 44 55 66 77 88
Address Bus
Pentium Processor. A[31:3] identifies block of 8 locations (a quadword). BE[7:0]# identifies data paths to use and bytes within quadword to transfer.
7 6 5 4 3 2 1 0
Data Paths
Pentium Processor

Figure 23-3. PowerPC Processor Operating in Little-Endian Storage Mode Stores 12345678h into Memory Starting at Location 00000100h.

PowerPC Little-Endian Storage Method

When the PowerPC processor is operating in little-endian mode, the effective address specified by the programmer is altered before submitting it to the MMU for address translation. Only the lower three bits of the address, EA[29:31], are affected. The lower twelve bits of the effective address aren't translated by the MMU, but are used directly as the lower twelve bits of the physical memory address that is output by the MMU. This means that the lower three bits of the target physical address produced by the MMU are also affected.

The alteration performed on the lower three address bits is defined by the size of the operand that will be stored or loaded. Table 23-3 defines the address alterations based on operand size. Note that this method of address alteration is only used when the operand is aligned on an address divisible by the operand size (i.e., a doubleword aligned on an address divisible by eight; a word aligned on an address divisible by four; or a halfword aligned on an address divisible by two).

Table 23-3. Address Transformation When Processor Operating in Little-Endian Storage Mode

Operand Size	EA[29:31] Exclusive-ORd with
doubleword (8 bytes)	no change
word (4 bytes)	100b
halfword (2 bytes)	110b
byte	111b

Load/Store of a Doubleword

No change is made to the start effective address if the operand is a doubleword. As an example, a store instruction that specifies storage of the doubleword in GPR 1 (assuming that this is a 64 bit PowerPC processor with 64-bit GPR registers) into memory starting at address 00000100h would result in storage of the eight byte value in memory starting at location 00000100h in big-endian order (even though the processor is operating in little-endian mode). Assume that GPR 1 contains the following value — 1122334455667788h. Table 23-4 illustrates the manner in which the data is stored in memory.

Table 23-4. Storage of Doubleword by PowerPC Processor Operating in Little-Endian Storage Mode

Location	Contents
00000100h	11h
00000101h	22h
00000102h	33h
00000103h	44h
00000104h	55h
00000105h	66h
00000106h	77h
00000107h	88h

Figure 23-4 illustrates the results of the store. The PowerPC processor doesn't have to modify the lower three bits of the address at all if an 8-byte object is being read from or written to memory while the processor is operating in little-endian storage mode. From the perspective of a Pentium processor, 88h is stored in location 00000100h and 11h is stored in location 00000107h.

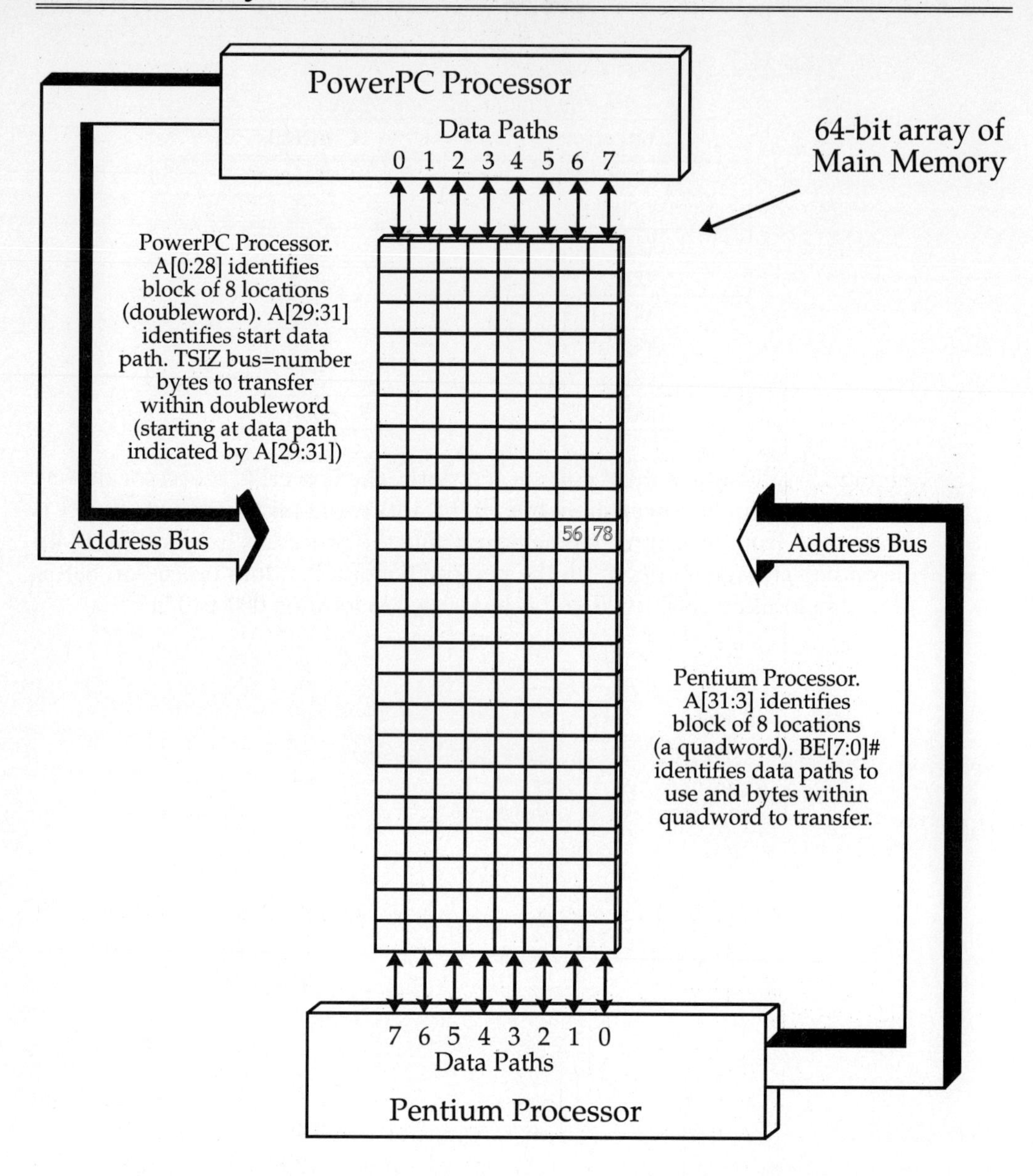
PowerPC Processor
Data Paths
0 1 2 3 4 5 6 7
64-bit array of Main Memory
PowerPC Processor. A[0:28] identifies block of 8 locations (doubleword). A[29:31] identifies start data path. TSIZ bus=number bytes to transfer within doubleword (starting at data path indicated by A[29:31])
Address Bus
56 78
Address Bus
Pentium Processor. A[31:3] identifies block of 8 locations (a quadword). BE[7:0]# identifies data paths to use and bytes within quadword to transfer.
7 6 5 4 3 2 1 0
Data Paths
Pentium Processor

Figure 23-4. Example Doubleword Store into Memory While Processor Operating in Little-Endian Storage Mode.

Load/Store of a Word

Refer to figure 23-3. Assume that GPR 1 currently contains 12345678h, GPR 2 contains 00000100h and the following instruction is executed:

```
stw  r1, 0, r2
```

The least-significant three bits of the effective address specified by the programmer, 00000100h, are exclusive-OR'd with 100b, yielding the address 00000104h. The four bytes in GPR 1 are stored in locations 00000104h – 00000107h in big-endian order. Table 23-5 indicates the result in memory.

Table 23-5. Example Storage of Word in Memory

Location	Contents
00000100h	not stored into
00000101h	not stored into
00000102h	not stored into
00000103h	not stored into
00000104h	12h
00000105h	34h
00000106h	56h
00000107h	78h

Load/Store of a Halfword

Assume that GPR 1 currently contains 12345678h, GPR 2 contains 00000100h and the following instruction is executed:

```
sth  r1, 0, r2
```

The least-significant three bits of the effective address specified by the programmer, 00000100h, are exclusive-OR'd with 110b, yielding the address 00000106h. The two least-significant bytes, 5678h, in GPR 1 are stored in locations 00000106h – 00000107h in big-endian order. Table 23-6 and figure 23-5 indicate the result in memory. From the perspective of the Pentium processor, the two bytes have been stored into locations 00000100h and 00000101h.

Table 23-6. Example Storage of Halfword in Memory

Location	Contents
00000100h	not stored into
00000101h	not stored into
00000102h	not stored into
00000103h	not stored into
00000104h	not stored into
00000105h	not stored into
00000106h	56h
00000107h	78h

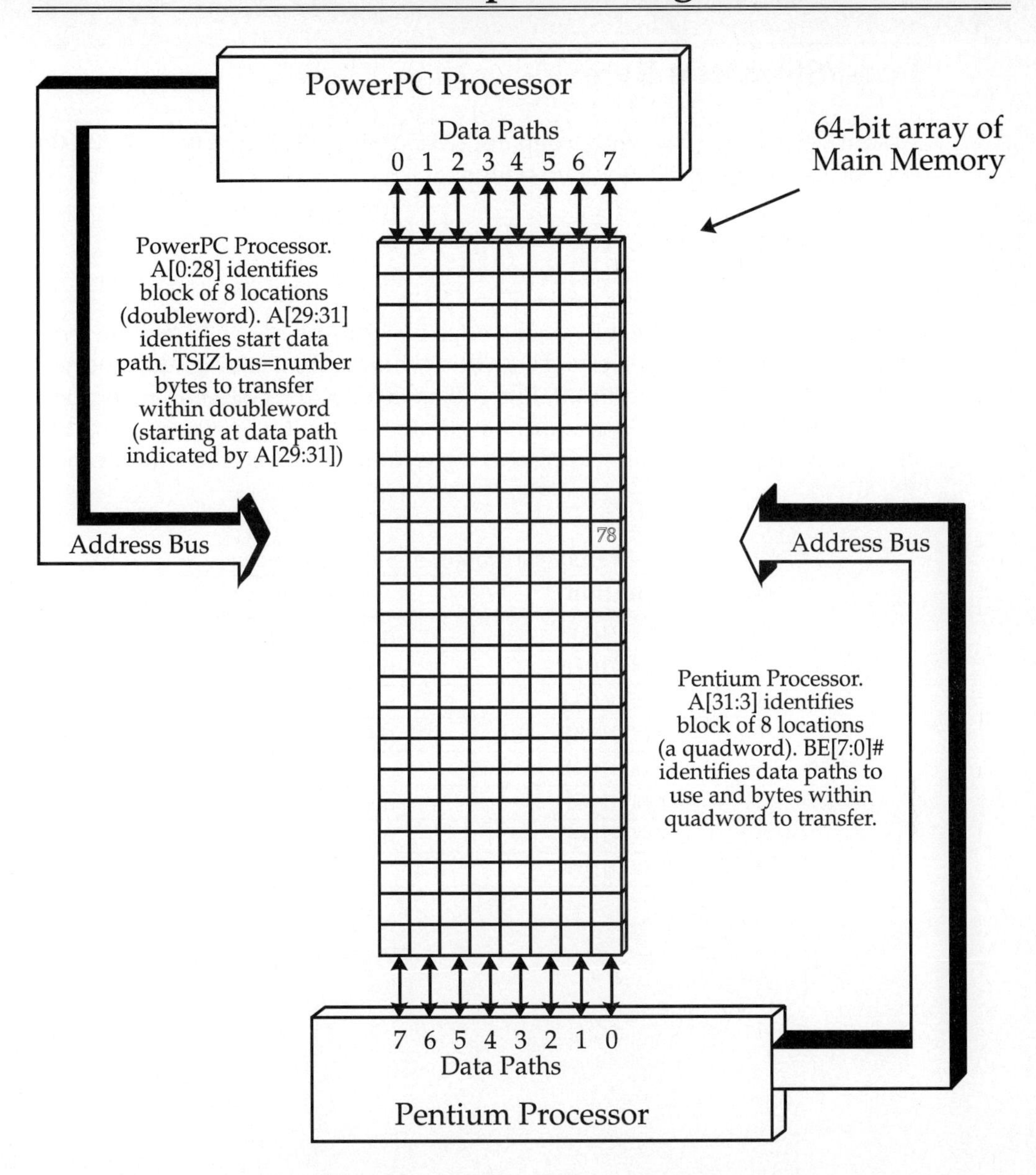
PowerPC Processor
Data Paths
0 1 2 3 4 5 6 7
64-bit array of Main Memory
PowerPC Processor. A[0:28] identifies block of 8 locations (doubleword). A[29:31] identifies start data path. TSIZ bus=number bytes to transfer within doubleword (starting at data path indicated by A[29:31])
Address Bus
78
Address Bus
Pentium Processor. A[31:3] identifies block of 8 locations (a quadword). BE[7:0]# identifies data paths to use and bytes within quadword to transfer.
7 6 5 4 3 2 1 0
Data Paths
Pentium Processor

Figure 23-5. Example Storage of Halfword In Memory

Load/Store of a Byte

Assume that GPR 1 currently contains 12345678h, GPR 2 contains 00000100h and the following instruction is executed:

```
stb  r1, 0, r2
```

The least-significant three bits of the effective address specified by the programmer, 00000100h, are exclusive-OR'd with 111b, yielding the address 00000107h. The least-significant byte, 78h, in GPR 1 is stored in location 00000107h. Table 23-7 and Figure 23-6 indicate the result in memory. From the perspective of the Pentium processor, the byte has been stored into location 00000100h.

Table 23-7. Example Storage of Byte in Memory

Location	Contents
00000100h	not stored into
00000101h	not stored into
00000102h	not stored into
00000103h	not stored into
00000104h	not stored into
00000105h	not stored into
00000106h	not stored into
00000107h	78h

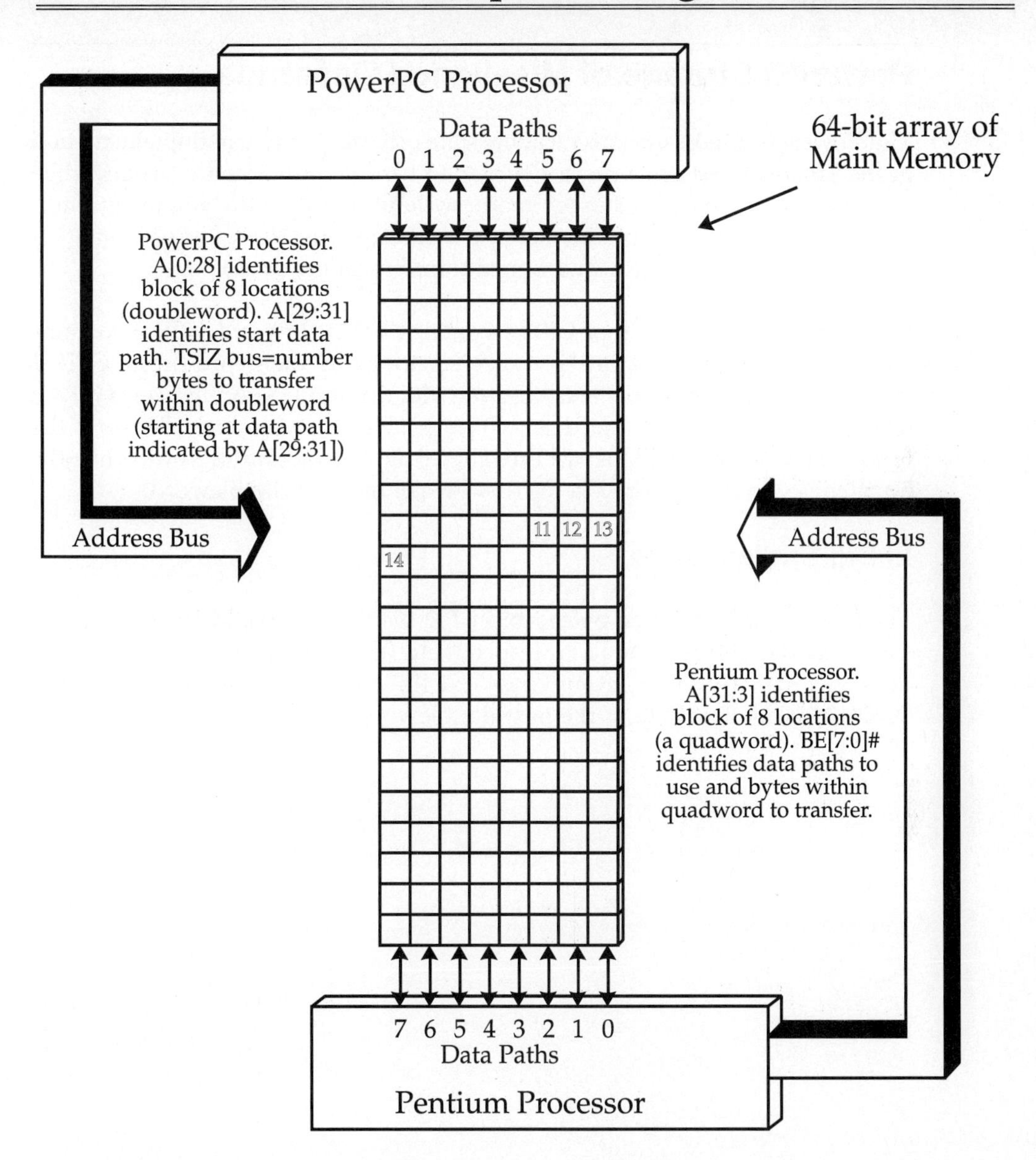
PowerPC Processor
Data Paths
0 1 2 3 4 5 6 7
64-bit array of Main Memory
PowerPC Processor. A[0:28] identifies block of 8 locations (doubleword). A[29:31] identifies start data path. TSIZ bus=number bytes to transfer within doubleword (starting at data path indicated by A[29:31])
Address Bus
11 12 13
14
Address Bus
Pentium Processor. A[31:3] identifies block of 8 locations (a quadword). BE[7:0]# identifies data paths to use and bytes within quadword to transfer.
7 6 5 4 3 2 1 0
Data Paths
Pentium Processor

Figure 23-6. Example Storage of Byte in Memory

PowerPC Storage of Misaligned Operands

The PowerPC processor specification states that a particular implementation of the processor may or may not be able to handle misaligned transfers while operating in little-endian storage mode without invoking the alignment interrupt. The following discussion makes the assumption that an implementation of the processor can handle misaligned transfers (some or all).

As an example, assume that GPR 1 contains 11121314h and GPR 2 contains 00000105h and that a store is executed to store the word from GPR 1 (11121314h) into memory starting at the location specified in GPR 2 (00000105h). This word straddles two doublewords in memory. Three of the bytes would be stored in the last three bytes of the first doubleword, while the fourth byte would be stored in the first byte of the next doubleword.

In Big-Endian Mode

The most-significant three bytes from GPR 1, 111213h, would be stored in locations 00000105h – 00000107h, respectively (the last three bytes in the first doubleword). The LSB from GPR 1, 14h, would be stored in location 00000108h (the first byte of the next doubleword). This is illustrated in figure 23-7.

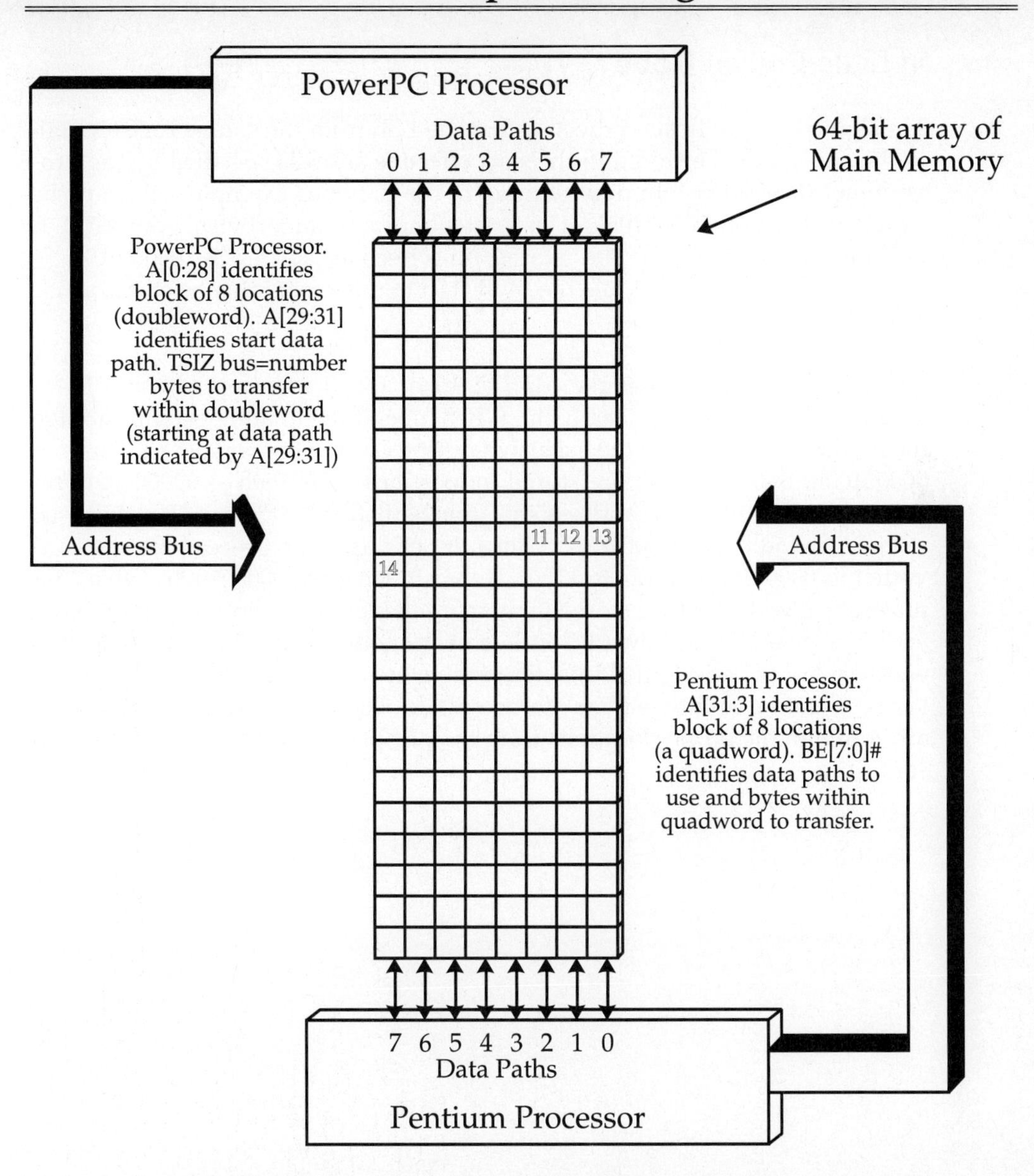
PowerPC Processor
Data Paths
0 1 2 3 4 5 6 7
64-bit array of Main Memory
PowerPC Processor. A[0:28] identifies block of 8 locations (doubleword). A[29:31] identifies start data path. TSIZ bus=number bytes to transfer within doubleword (starting at data path indicated by A[29:31])
Address Bus
11 12 13
14
Address Bus
Pentium Processor. A[31:3] identifies block of 8 locations (a quadword). BE[7:0]# identifies data paths to use and bytes within quadword to transfer.
7 6 5 4 3 2 1 0
Data Paths
Pentium Processor

Figure 23-7. Example Storage of Misaligned Word in Memory With Processor in Big-Endian Storage Mode

In Little-Endian Mode

The PowerPC specification dictates that the LSB from the source register (14h in this case) must be stored in the start effective address specified by the programmer (00000105h). In other words, in the previous example, 14h must be stored in location 00000105h. The least-significant three bytes from GPR 1, 121314h, must therefore be stored in effective addresses 00000107h – 00000105h, respectively, while the MSB (11h in this case) must be stored in effective address 00000108h.

The effective address that the MSB (12h) of the first group of three bytes would be stored in is 00000107h. When operating in little-endian storage mode, the processor uses the exclusive-or process and converts the address to 00000100h. Bytes 121314h are stored in locations 00000100h — 00000102h, respectively. The effective address that the MSB from GPR 1, 11h, would be stored in would be 00000108h. Using the exclusive-or process, this is converted to 0000010Fh and byte 11h is stored in location 0000010Fh. Table 23-8 illustrate how the word is stored in memory in big-endian mode, in Intel little-endian format, and in PowerPC little endian mode. Figure 23-8 illustrates the end-result of the misaligned transfer of the word to memory when the processor is operating in little-endian storage mode. The net result is that the bytes are stored in the proper locations from the perspective of the Pentium processor.

Table 23-8. Example of Misaligned Word Storage

Location	Big-endian	Intel	PPC Little-endian
00000100h	-	-	12h
00000101h	-	-	13h
00000102h	-	-	14h
00000103h	-	-	-
00000104h	-	-	-
00000105h	11h	14h	-
00000106h	12h	13h	-
00000107h	13h	12h	-
00000108h	14h	11h	-
00000109h	-	-	-
0000010Ah	-	-	-
0000010Bh	-	-	-
0000010Ch	-	-	-
0000010Dh	-	-	-
0000010Eh	-	-	-
0000010Fh	-	-	11h

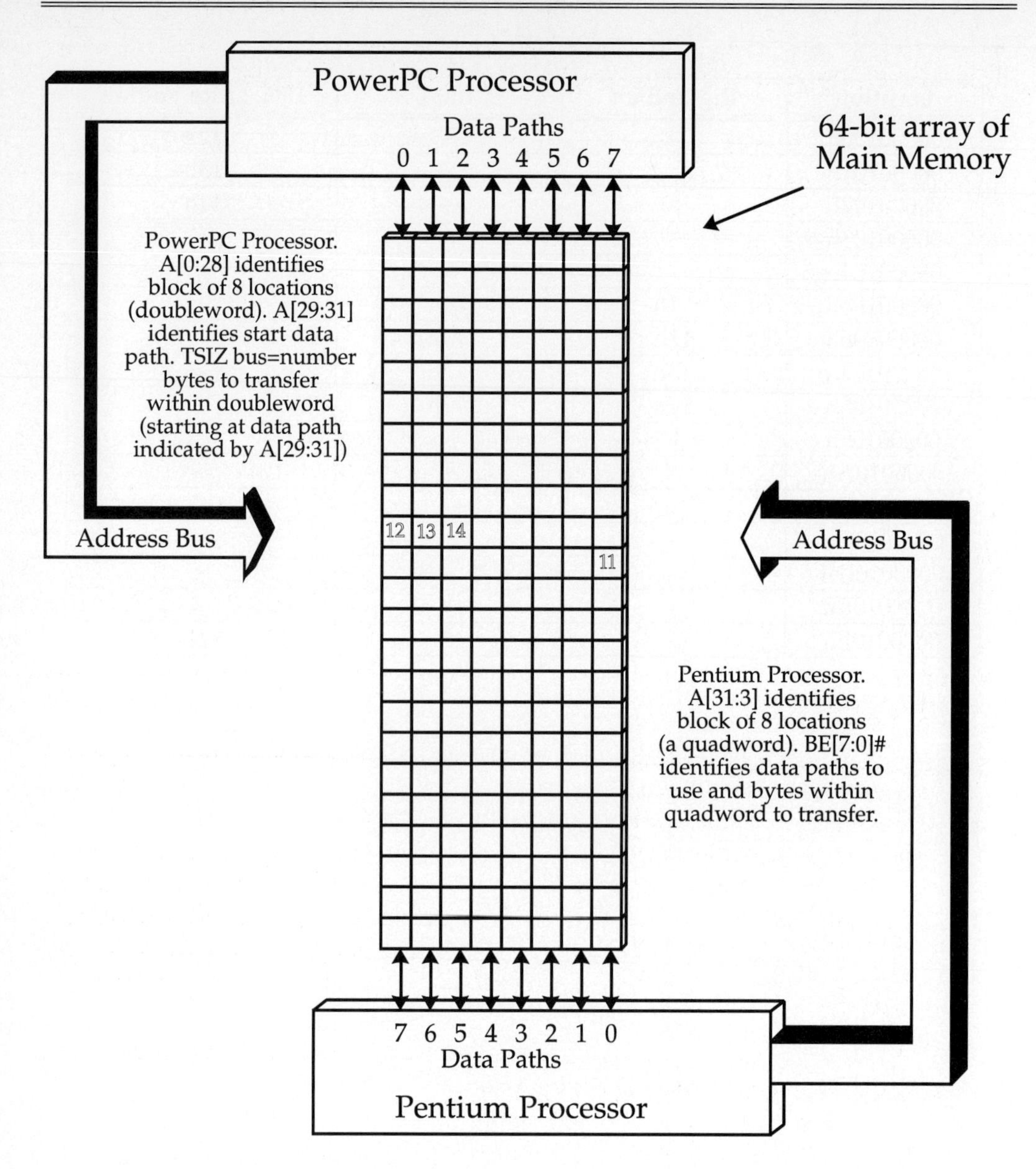
PowerPC Processor
Data Paths
0 1 2 3 4 5 6 7
64-bit array of Main Memory
PowerPC Processor. A[0:28] identifies block of 8 locations (doubleword). A[29:31] identifies start data path. TSIZ bus=number bytes to transfer within doubleword (starting at data path indicated by A[29:31])
Address Bus
12
13
14
11
Address Bus
Pentium Processor. A[31:3] identifies block of 8 locations (a quadword). BE[7:0]# identifies data paths to use and bytes within quadword to transfer.
7 6 5 4 3 2 1 0
Data Paths
Pentium Processor

Figure 23-8. Example of Word Stored in Memory Using Misaligned Transfers

601 Alignment Interrupt and Little-Endian Mode

When the PPC 601 processor is operating in little-endian mode, it automatically invokes the alignment interrupt when any of the following instructions are executed:

- lmw and stmw.
- lscbx
- lswi and stswi
- lswx and stswx

This is done because the transfers are handled as a series of word transfers and the word addresses that would be generated are not those that the programmer naturally expects (because of the adjustment of the lower three bits of the address).

Any attempt to transfer a misaligned operand will result in an alignment interrupt when the PPC 601 is operating in little-endian mode.

Switching Endian Modes

PowerPC Processors in General

The endian mode is selected by setting or clearing the LE bit in the MSR register. After reset, the default of LE is cleared, placing the processor in its native big-endian mode. To select little-endian mode, the programmer must change the state of LE to a one. Since this requires the ability to access the MSR, the selection can only be made by the operating system at the supervisor privilege level.

601 Endian Mode Selection

The PPC 601 processor is non-compliant with the PowerPC processor specification in that the LE bit is located in the HID0 register, rather than the MSR. The PPC 601 requires the execution of the following code sequence in order to change endian modes:

```
sync
sync
sync
set/clear HID0[28] to choose the desired endian mode
sync
sync
sync
```

When executing the indicated code sequence, the following rules must be followed in order to ensure proper processor operation:

- External and decrementer interrupts must be disabled by clearing the MSR[EE] bit.
- The instructions that form the code sequence must not cross a page or block boundary. If the boundary was crossed while attempting to fetch the next instruction in the sequence, an interrupt could be incurred (due to a protection violation or a page fault). This would cause the sequence to be interrupted in mid-sequence.
- If the mode is to be changed dynamically after system initialization, address translation must be turned off (by clearing MSR[IT] and MSR[DT]) and any writes posted in the Memory Unit (MU) must be flushed to memory by executing a sync or an eieio instruction.

Selection of Interrupt Handler Endian Mode

The PPC 601 processor is also non-compliant with the processor specification in that it does not implement the ILE bit in the MSR. ILE, or interrupt little-endian, is copied to the LE bit whenever an interrupt is taken. This automatically places the processor in the desired endian mode to be used during execution of the interrupt handlers. The PPC 601 processor remains in its current endian mode when an interrupt is taken. If the programmer desires that the handler run in the opposite endian mode, the code sequence described earlier must be executed.

Problems Related to Endian Storage Mode

The little-endian storage mode implemented in the PowerPC processors is intended to transfer data to/from main memory in a manner that permits interchange of information (through memory) between a PowerPC processor and little-endian processors (or bus masters). The following sections describe the various scenarios that must be dealt with.

Passing Data to Bus Masters through Memory

Example — SCSI Host Bus Adapter (HBA)

A device driver issues a transfer request to a SCSI HBA in the following manner:

- The driver creates a data structure, referred to as the command descriptor block, or CDB, in main memory that includes the target SCSI controller, logical unit (LUN), request type and parameters associated with the request (e.g., start record number and number of records to be transferred to/from main memory).
- On a block read request, the driver makes a memory allocation call to the operating system to request the start physical DRAM address of a buffer to place the data in. On a write request, the applications program passes the device driver the start physical memory address of the data buffer in main DRAM memory.
- The driver makes a memory allocation call to the operating system requesting the physical start physical address of a small buffer in DRAM that the completion status will be deposited in at the termination of the requested transfer.
- The driver then performs a series of writes to the I/O ports or memory-mapped I/O ports in the SCSI HBA to tell it the start address of the CDB, the data buffer and the completion status buffer.

When the SCSI HBA is ready to process the request, it arbitrates for ownership of the PCI bus (most PowerPC PC platforms will implement the PCI bus) and then initiates a memory read transaction to read the CDB from main memory. Virtually all SCSI host bus arbiters designed to work in the PC environment expect the CDB to be stored in main memory in little-endian format. If the processor built the CDB in memory while operating in big-endian storage mode, the SCSI HBA, addressing memory using little-endian addressing would read a scrambled CDB from memory. Obviously, this would result in spurious operation of the SCSI HBA.

Processor Operating in Big-Endian Storage Mode

If the processor is operating in big-endian storage mode when it writes the CDB into main memory, the CDB is not being written into memory in the order expected by the SCSI HBA. The system designer can fix the problem in one of two ways:

- Include address translation and data bus steering logic between the processor and main memory that, when enabled, converts the address placed on the bus by the processor to the correct little-endian address. In addition, since the processor is driving the data onto the incorrect data lanes, the steering logic must copy the data to the correct data paths. Before the processor starts writing the CDB data into memory, the translation/steering logic must be enabled.
- The processor is storing the data into memory in big-endian storage format. When the SCSI HBA begins the memory read to read the CDB from main memory, it utilizes little-endian memory addressing and data path usage. The programmer must instruct the bridge to automatically convert the SCSI access to perform a big-endian transfer with main memory.

As an example, if the processor writes the word 11223344h to memory starting at address 00000100h, the address on the bus would be 00000100h and the four data bytes would be driven out on data paths 0 – 3. This is illustrated in figure 23-9. The MSB from the source GPR, 11h, is driven onto data path 0 and the LSB, 44h, onto data path 3. Assuming that the first methodology is used, the address translation logic (when enabled) applies the exclusive-or to A[29:31], converting the address to 00000104h. The steering logic must steer the data as follows:

- MSB, 11h, on path 0 to path 4.
- 22h on path 1 to path 5.
- 33h on path 2 to path 6.
- LSB, 44h, on path 3 to path 7.

The address and data path usage after address translation/data bus steering is illustrated in figure 23-9.

It should be noted that the data written into memory by the processor only requires manipulation if the processor writes it into memory a byte, halfword, or word at a time. This would occur if the CDB is in a page or block designated as non-cacheable or cacheable with a write-through policy for memory writes.

If the processor writes the CDB into memory as a series of doublewords, the data is written into memory correctly from the little-endian perspective and no address translation/data steering is necessary. The processor would utilize eight-byte (doubleword) writes if it is a 64-bit PowerPC processor using std instructions in a page or block designated as non-cacheable or cacheable write-through.

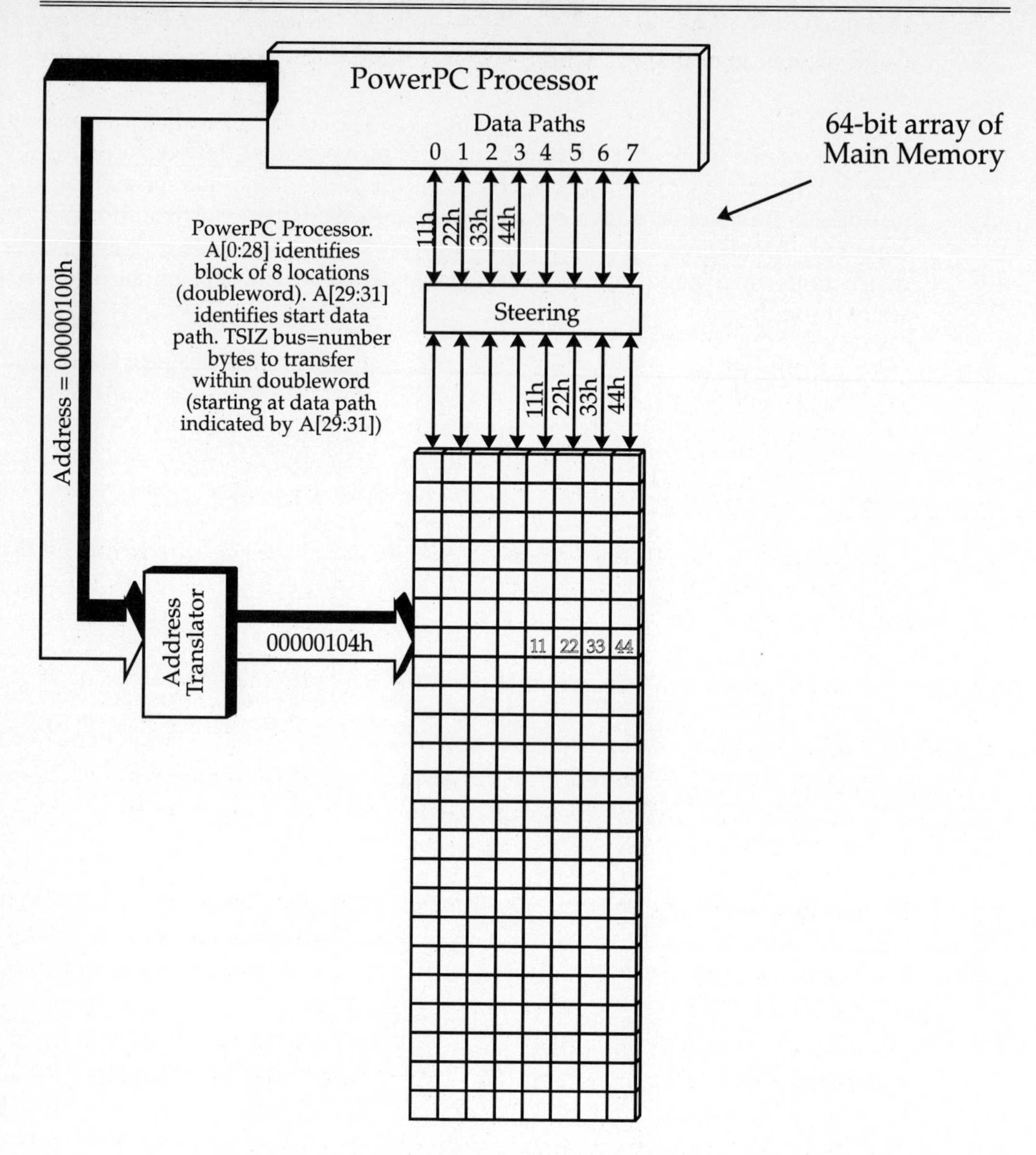

Figure 23-9. Before/After Address Translation/Data Bus Steering

Processor Operating in Little-Endian Storage Mode

If the processor is operating in little-endian storage mode when it writes the CDB into memory, the data is stores in main memory in the format expected by the SCSI HBA, so no action is necessary.

Receiving Data from Bus Masters through Memory

Bus masters pass data back to the processor by writing it into main memory. When the master has completed writing the data into memory, the processor may then perform memory reads to access it. The addressing format used by the bus master is virtually always little-endian in the PC environment.

Processor Operating in Big-Endian Storage Mode

If the processor is operating in big-endian storage mode when it reads the data from memory, one of two scenarios must be implemented to ensure that the processor accesses the data in the correct format.

- The little-endian addressing/data path usage of the bus master when it writes the data to main memory must be altered to store the data in big-endian format.
- The address issued by the processor when it reads the data from main memory must be translated to little-endian and the data steered to the proper paths as it is delivered to the processor.

Processor Operating in Little-Endian Storage Mode

If the processor is currently operating in little-endian storage mode when it reads the data from memory, no action is necessary.

Accessing Little-Endian Memory-Mapped I/O Ports

As mentioned earlier in this chapter, the PPC 601 processor has eight data paths that are used to transfer data to/from target locations. The eight data paths are identified as indicated in table 23-9.

Table 23-9. PPC 601 Data Path Assignment

Path	Signals	Corresponding location in addressed doubleword
0	DH[0:7]	0
1	DH[8:15]	1
2	DH[16:23]	2
3	DH[24:31]	3
4	DL[0:7]	4
5	DL[8:15]	5
6	DL[16:23]	6
7	DL[24:31]	7

The PPC 601 uses A[0:28] to identify a group of eight locations (the target doubleword), A[29:31] to identify the start location within the group of eight, and the TSIZ[0:2] bus to indicate the number of bytes to be transferred. As an example, assume the following:

- **contains 00000100h**. The target doubleword consists of locations 00000100h – 00000107h.
- **contains 100b**. The binary-weighted value of this field is four. The start location within the doubleword in four (i.e., location 00000104h). This also indicates that data path four is the first data path to be used (paths 0:3 will not be used during this transfer).
- **TSIZ[0:2] contains 100b**. The binary-weighted value of this field is four. Four bytes will be transferred to or from locations 00000104h – 00000107h. The bytes will be transferred over data paths 4:7.

Assume that the following conditions are true:

- The processor is in little-endian mode.
- GPR 1 contains 12345678h.
- GPR 2 contains 00000100h.
- Data address translation is disabled (MSR[DT] = 0).
- The instruction "***stw r1, 0, r2***" is executed.
- A 32-bit I/O port is implemented at word address 00000100h. It is a command port for the I/O device.
- The I/O port is organized in little-endian byte order and is connected to little-endian data paths 0:3. It expects to receive the byte for location 00000100h over data path 0, the byte for location 00000101h over data path 1, etc.

- The data in GPR 1 must be written to the device over data paths 0:3 in little-endian byte order: 78h to location 00000100h, 56h to location 00000101h, etc.

The target word address, 00000100h, is the first word in the doubleword of space consisting of locations 00000100h – 00000107h. When the instruction is executed, the lower three bits of the effective address, 00000100h, are exclusive-OR'd with 100b. When the store transaction appears on the PPC 601 bus, the doubleword address on A[0:28] is not modified (it is 00000100h), but A[29:31] are changed to 100b (due to the little-endian bit-twisting). The address bus then contains the following information:

- doubleword address 00000100h on A[0:28].
- start address of the operand (the target word) within the doubleword has been altered from 00000100h to 00000104h.
- the size of the operand to be transferred is encoded as 100b (4d) on the TSIZ[0:2] bus. In other words, a word (4 bytes) is to be transferred over data paths 4:7 to the last four locations (00000104h – 00000107h) in the currently-addressed doubleword.

During the data phase of the transaction, the four bytes from the source register, GPR 1, are driven out onto the upper four data paths in the following order:

- path 4 contains 12h (MSB from GPR 1), destined for location 00000104h.
- path 5 contains 34h ,destined for location 00000105h.
- path 6 contains 56h, destined for location 00000106h.
- path 7 contains 78h (LSB from GPR 1), destined for location 00000107h. This is big-endian byte ordering (the MSB of the word is stored in the start address, 00000104h).

There are problems related to both the address and data that must be fixed by logic residing between the processor and the little-endian device:

- The address on A[29:31], 100b, must be converted back to 000b so that location 00000100h is addressed rather than 00000104h. This can be accomplished by externally re-applying the exclusive-or process: 100b exclusive-OR'd with 100b yields 000b (address 00000100h rather than 00000104h).
- The data byte on path 4, 12h, must be copied, or steered, to path 3.
- The data byte on path 5, 34h, must be copied, or steered, to path 2.

- The data byte on path 6, 56h, must be copied, or steered, to path 1.
- The data byte on path 7, 78h, must be copied to, or steered, path 0.

The data steering would be handled by a set of external transceivers built into the bridge.

Volume Two
The PPC 601 Processor

The second volume of this book consists of part four. This part focuses specifically on the PPC 601 processor and describes how it fits within or deviates from the specification. This part also provides a complete description of the PPC 601 processor's external bus structure and operation. It is important to note that the external bus that a PowerPC processor uses to communicate with the rest of the machine is outside the scope of the PowerPC processor specification. As an example, it would be perfectly "legal" to build a PowerPC processor that glues right onto the PCI bus. It would be possible to build a processor with the same bus structure as an Intel Pentium processor.

Part Four

The PowerPC 601 Processor

Part four describes how the PPC 601 processor adheres to or deviates from the PowerPC processor specification (described in parts two and three). The bus structure and protocol are defined. The processor's relationship to the L2 cache is defined. A summary of the PPC 601 processor's multiprocessing support mechanisms is provided. The remainder of the processor's interface signals are discussed.

The chapters that comprise part four are:

- PPC 601 Microarchitecture Overview
- 601 User Register and Instruction Set
- 601 OS Register and Instruction Set
- 601 Processor Startup State
- PPC 601 Interrupts
- PPC 601 MMU Operation
- 601 Cache and Memory Unit
- Bus Transaction Causes
- PPC 601 Split-Bus Concept
- PPC 601 Memory Address Phase
- PPC 601 Data Phase
- PPC 601 I/O Transactions
- 601 External Control Transaction
- 601 Relationship with the L2 Cache
- 601 Multiprocessor Support
- Other PPC 601 Bus Signals

Chapter 24

The Previous Chapter

The previous chapter provided a detailed description of the PowerPC processor operation in both its native big-endian storage mode and when operating in little-endian storage mode. This included a discussion of necessary external hardware support mechanisms.

This Chapter

This chapter begins part four of the book — the discussion of the PPC 601 processor. This chapter provides a discussion of the PPC 601 processor's microarchitecture and the relationships of the processor's functional units to each other.

The Next Chapter

The next chapter defines the PPC 601 processor's implementation of the user mode register and instruction set.

Introduction

The PPC 601 processor is a superscalar implementation of the PowerPC architecture. The instruction issue logic is capable of issuing three instructions simultaneously to the three execution units:

- Integer unit, or IU
- Floating-point unit, or FPU
- Branch processor unit, or BPU

The integer and floating-point units implement internal pipelines, enabling them to handle multiple instructions at one time. The following paragraphs provide a brief description of each unit and its relationship to the other units.

The PPC601 block diagram in figure 24-1 illustrates the relationships of the units to each other.

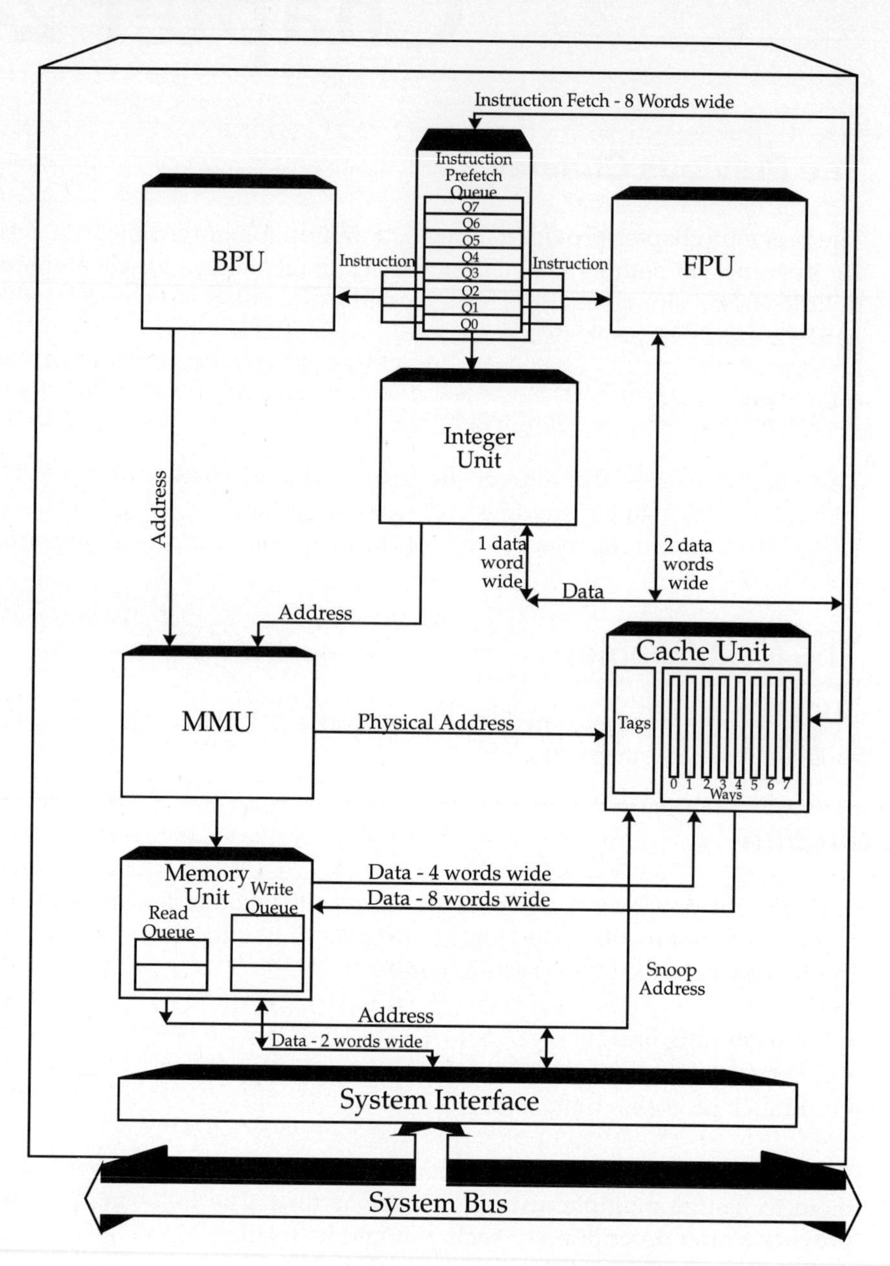

Figure 24-1. PPC601 Block Diagram

Instruction Unit

General

The instruction unit maintains an eight-entry prefetch queue (one word per entry) that fetches instruction words from memory sequentially (using speculative fetching). The eight queue entries are referred to as Q0 (bottom) – Q7 (top). When the BPU decides that a branch will take place, it instructs the prefetcher to alter program fetching to the predicted branch target address (see the section on branch prediction in the chapter entitled "Address Modes, Branch Prediction"). If the branch prediction is correct, the processor core doesn't stall when the branch instruction is executed (because the correct instructions are already in the instruction pipeline immediately following the branch instruction). In the event of a misprediction, the queue is flushed and fetching resumes at the new target address. Due to the 256-bit width of the data path between the instruction unit and the cache, the prefetcher can load up to 8 words (32 bytes) into the queue from the cache simultaneously (in the event of a cache hit). The BPU and FPU can extract instructions from the bottom four queue entries, Q0–Q3, while the IU extracts instructions only from Q0. When Q0 holds an integer instruction, it acts as a one instruction buffer for the integer unit.

Instruction Dispatcher (Prefetch Queue Logic)

The instruction dispatcher can handle the simultaneous dispatch of instruction words to the IU, BPU and FPU. Figure 24-2 illustrates the relationship of the instruction dispatch logic to the branch, integer and floating-point units. As the branch or floating-point units become available to accept another instruction, each may extract the next instruction related to their unit from queue position Q0 – Q3. The instructions above the now empty queue position shift down one position to fill the gap and new instructions are shifted into the upper queue positions as they are fetched. The integer unit can only extract instructions from queue position Q0. A detailed description of the instruction dispatch logic can be found in the publication entitled *PowerPC 601 RISC Microprocessor User's Manual.*

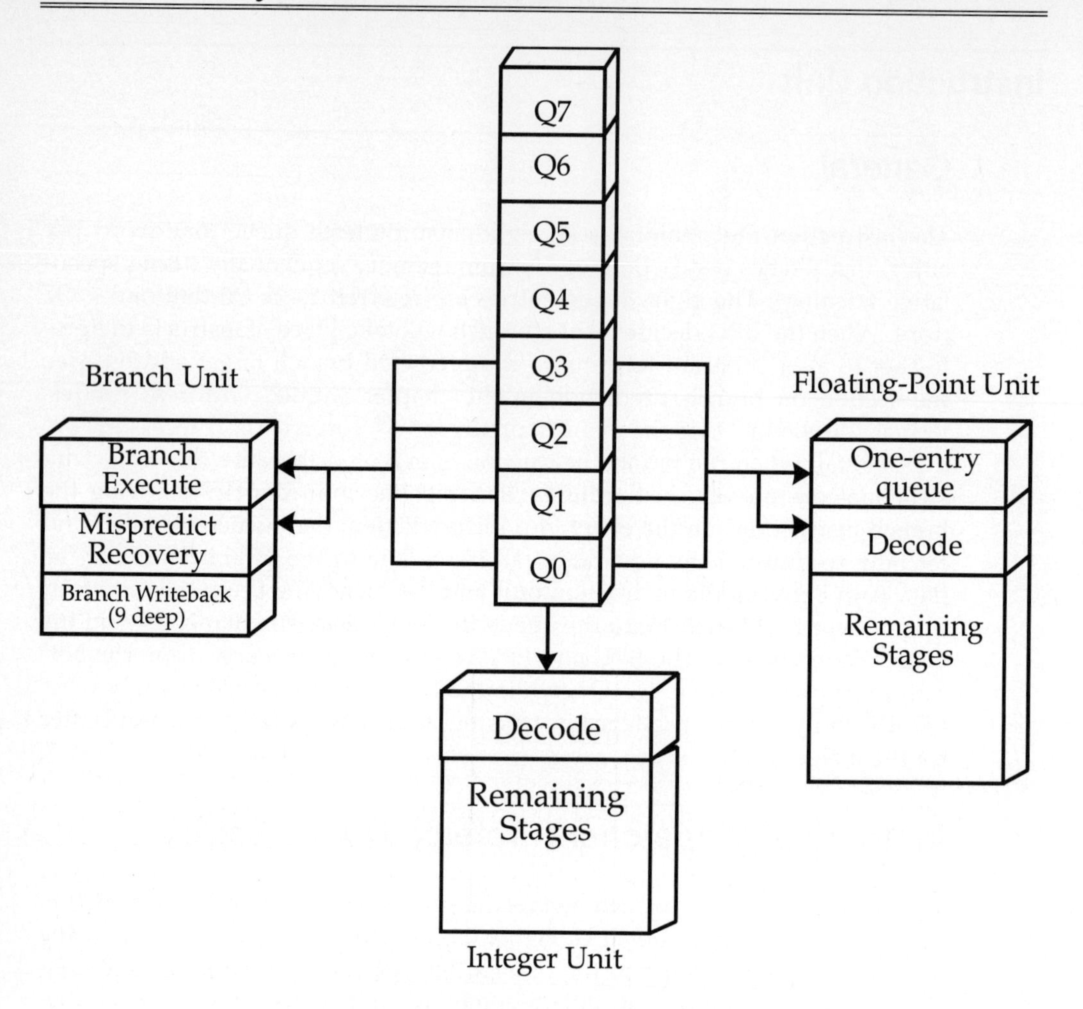

Figure 24-2. Instruction Issue (Dispatch) Logic

Branch Processor Unit (BPU)

Refer to figure 24-2 during the following discussion. The branch unit uses static branch prediction to predict whether or not a branch will be taken. In other words, it does not dynamically maintain a history of branch execution, but rather receives hints encoded in conditional branch instructions by the compiler. For a discussion of PowerPC static branch prediction, refer to the chapter entitled "Address Modes, Branch Predition." It should be noted that the PowerPC processor specification does not preclude the implementation of dynamic branch prediction. Using this method, the processor maintains a branch target buffer, or BTB, in which execution history is continually updated for each conditional branch instruction. The Pentium and PPC 604 processors both use dynamic branch prediction.

The branch unit recognizes unconditional branches in the queue and immediately instructs the instruction prefetcher to alter the flow of program fetching. The branch instruction is immediately discarded from the queue. This is referred to as branch folding. In the case of a conditional branch where the branch condition has already been resolved by one of the execution units, the branch unit will also fold the branch and immediately alter the flow of instruction prefetching.

As an example of the PPC 601 processor's static branch prediction, the branch prediction logic always predicts backward conditional branches as taken unless the compiler has set a special bit in the instruction to indicate that it probably won't be. Since most backward conditional branches are found at the end of loops and are usually taken, the default prediction mechanism is usually correct.

Conditional branch instructions enter the execute and mispredict recovery stages simultaneously, while unconditional branches only occupy the branch execute stage. The branch execute stage of the branch unit calculates or predicts the branch target address. The unpredicted branch target address of a conditional branch remains in the recovery stage until the condition is resolved. If the branch prediction was correct, the unpredicted branch target address is discarded. If the branch was incorrectly predicted, however, all instructions that were fetched into the queue after the incorrectly-predicted branch are flushed and the correct instructions are fetched starting at the address supplied by the mispredict recovery stage of the branch processor unit. While the unpredicted branch target address of a conditional branch is waiting for branch resolution in the mispredict recovery stage, an unconditional branch can enter the branch execute stage.

If the execution of a branch instruction updates the link (to store a return address) or count (to decrement it) registers, the instruction is shifted into the branch write-back stage. This stage can hold up to nine branches awaiting access to the link or count registers.

Floating-Point Unit (FPU)

The FPU contains the FPSCR, a single-precision multiply/add array, and the FPR register file. When performing a floating-point load or store, it uses the two-word-wide data bus illustrated in figure 24-1 to load or store a 64-bit data operand. Figure 24-3 illustrates the FPU's internal pipeline. The FPU can extract two instructions from the queue simultaneously, placing one into its first stage (F1, a one instruction buffer) and the other in its decode stage, FD. This permits the FPU to accept additional instructions even when busy. The removal of these instructions from the prefetch queue permits other instructions to shift downward in the queue. The following sections provide a brief description of the FPU's internal pipeline stages. An instruction occupies each pipeline stage for one or more clock cycles, depending on the instruction type.

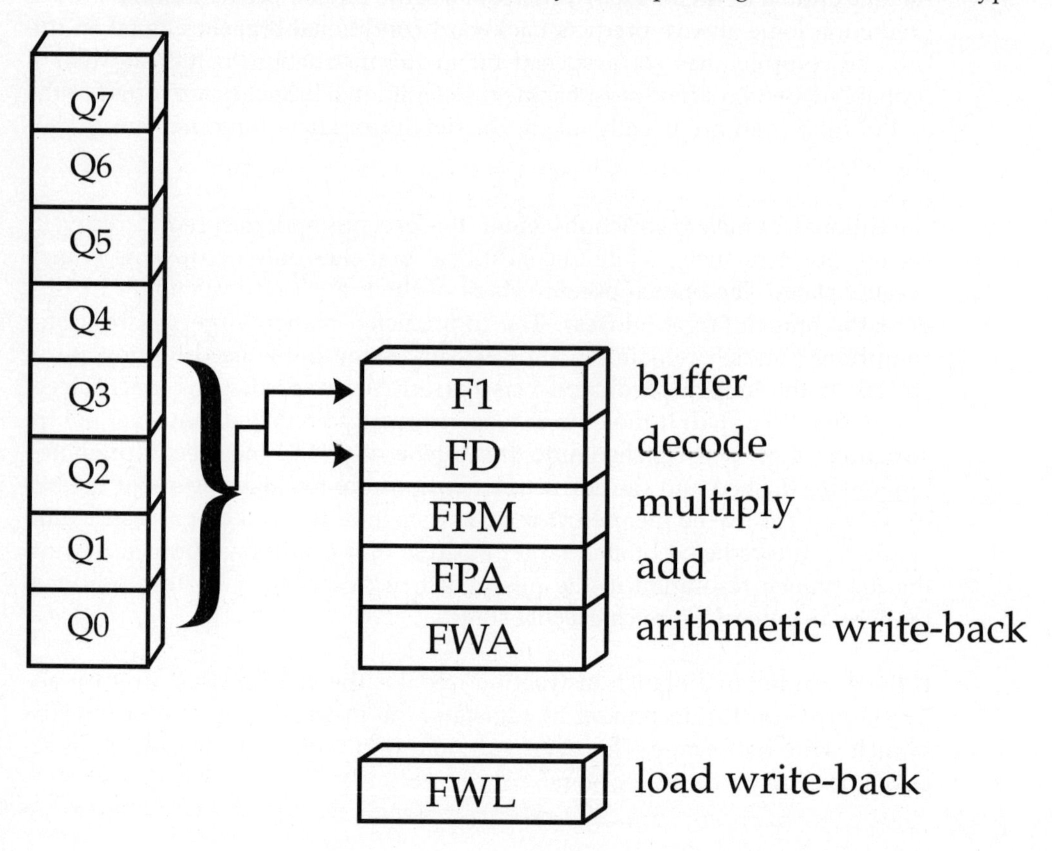

Figure 24-3. FPU's Internal Instruction Pipeline

F1 Stage

The F1 stage serves a one instruction buffer. If a floating-point instruction already occupies the FD stage and another floating-point instruction has entered the bottom half of the prefetch queue, the FPU can extract the instruction from the queue and place it into the F1 stage. This opens up a hole in the queue, permitting another instruction to drop into the lower half (where it becomes visible to the BPU and FPU). When the instruction currently in the FD stage moves on to a subsequent stage, the instruction in the F1 stage can immediately shift into the FD stage.

Floating-Point Decode Stage (FD)

In this stage, the instruction is decoded and the specified operand(s) are fetched from the FPR register set. An illegal instruction can cause a program interrupt at this stage. After completing the FD stage, the instruction moves to the FPM stage.

Floating-Point Multiply Stage (FPM)

This stage performs the first stage of a multiply operation. The multiplication is completed in the FPA stage.

Floating-Point Add Stage (FPA)

In this stage, an addition is performed (if necessary). An addition would be completed in this stage to complete a multiplication operation begun in the FPM stage , or to complete a an accumulate instruction.

Floating-Point Arithmetic Write-Back Stage (FWA)

Normalization and rounding are performed in the FWA stage. FPRs are update. If a store is being executed, the data is sent to the cache and/memory unit. The appropriate condition bits are set in the FPSCR. Data written to the FPRs in the FWA stage is made available to the FD stage (if necessary) in the next clock cycle.

Floating-Point Load Write-Back Stage (FWL)

If a floating-point load is being executed, the data loaded from memory is written into the target FPR. If the instruction currently in the FD stage requires the data as an operand, the data is also made available to the FD stage.

Integer Unit (IU)

The IU can complete one instruction during each clock. It contains the ALU, a multiplier, a divider, the integer exception register, XER, and the GPR register file. Since the floating-point load and stores use indirect addressing through the integer unit's GPR registers, the integer unit performs memory accesses for the FPU. This explains why figure 24-1 only shows the integer and branch units with address connections to the MMU. Figure 24-1 also illustrates the one-word-wide data path between the integer unit and the cache. The integer unit is only capable of loading or storing objects up to one word wide. Figure 24-4 illustrates the integer unit's internal pipeline. An instruction occupies each pipeline stage for one clock cycle.

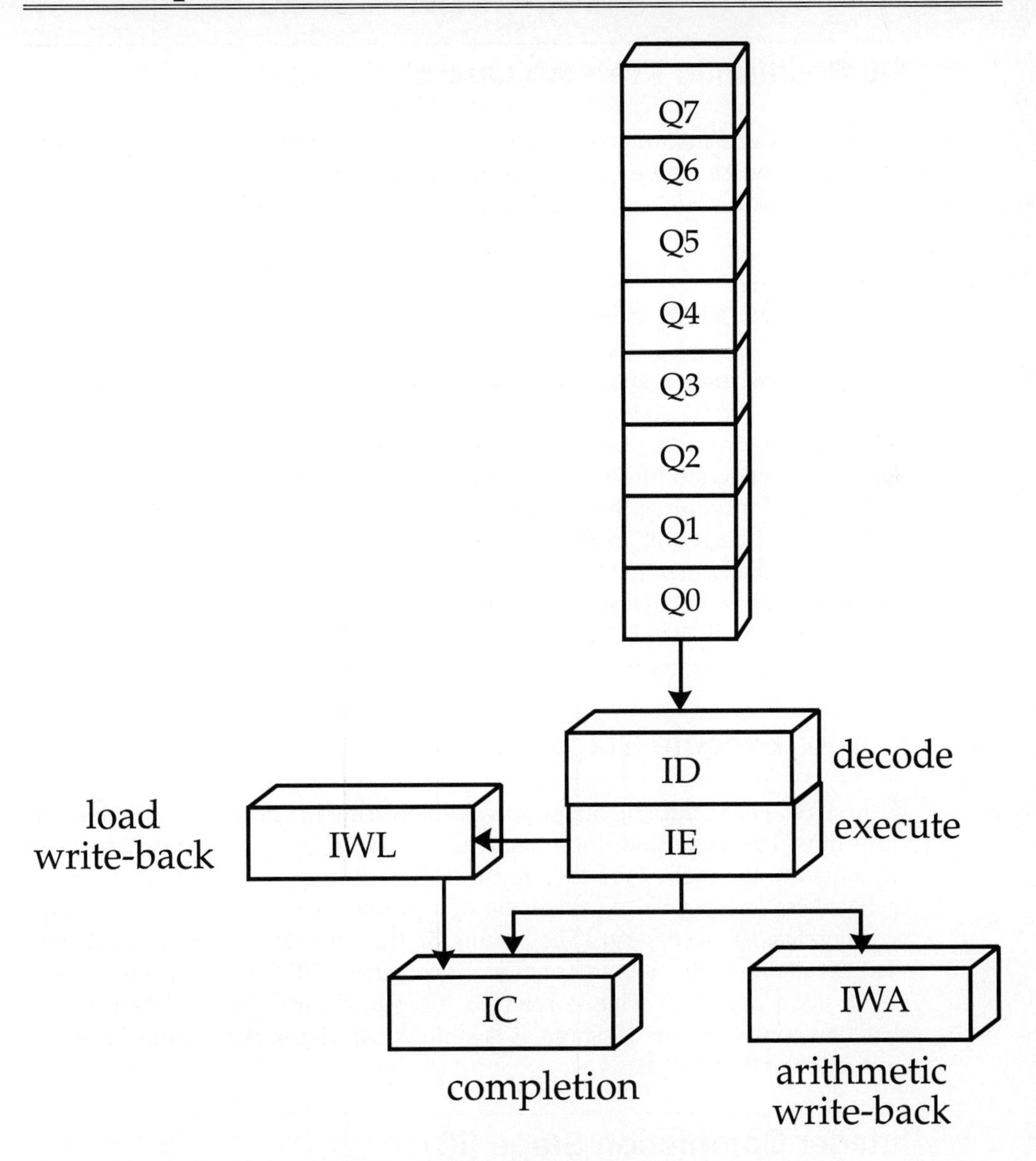

Figure 24-4. Integer Unit's Internal Pipeline

Q0 Position in Prefetch Queue

Q0 acts as a one instruction buffer for the integer unit's decode stage. When the integer unit's decode stage becomes available to accept the instruction from Q0, the instruction is shifted from Q0 into the integer unit's decode stage.

Integer Decode Stage (ID)

An integer instruction enters the integer decode stage at the same time that it enters Q0. In the ID stage, the instruction is decoded and the specified operands are read from the GPRs indicated in the instruction. An illegal opcode will cause a program interrupt at this stage. An instruction may stall in the IE stage (e.g., if it requires that an operand be loaded from memory). If another instruction is currently in the decode stage awaiting completion of the instruction in the IE stage, it, too, is stalled (in the ID stage). While this instruction is stalled in the ID stage, another integer instruction can enter the Q0 stage. When the IE stage becomes available, the next instruction is shifted into IE from ID, and the instruction in Q0 enters the ID stage.

Integer Execute Stage (IE)

In the IE stage, arithmetic operations are performed if necessary. If a load or store must be performed, the effective address is calculated, translated and submitted to the cache for a lookup (if the WIM bits indicate the access is in a cacheable memory area). In the event of a problem, the appropriate interrupt is generated (if necessary). The results of this instruction are immediately made available to the next instruction that enters the IE stage (if it requires the result as an operand). This is referred to as feed-forwarding. When the instruction completes the IE stage, it is shifted into the IC stage, and, if necessary, into the IWA stage.

Integer Completion Stage (IC)

In the instruction completion stage, the results of the instruction are made available for use by other logic.

Integer Arithmetic Write-Back Stage (IWA)

If necessary, the specified GPR is updated with the results of an arithmetic operation.

Integer Load Write-Back Stage (IWL)

If a load instruction is being executed, the data loaded from memory is loaded into the target GPR in this stage (when the data is supplied by the cache or memory). If the data must be loaded from external memory, the instruction resides in the IWL stage until the requested data is received. The instruction then proceeds to the IC stage.

Memory Management Unit (MMU)

The MMU handles memory block/page and I/O address translation and checks for access violations. It translates effective, or logical, addresses presented by the integer or instruction units to physical memory or I/O addresses. If the access is within a cacheable page or block in memory, the physical memory address is then presented to the cache for a lookup. A detailed description of the MMU can be found in the chapter entitled "601 Cache and Memory Unit."

Cache Unit

The PPC 601 incorporates a 32KB, eight-way set-associative, unified code/data cache. The inclusion of eight cache ways makes the processor ideal for multitasking operating systems (because the cache can maintain copies of information from the same relative position within eight different memory pages without having to overwrite any of them). The cache receives 32-bit physical memory addresses from the MMU and uses them to perform a lookup. In the event of a hit on a load or instruction fetch, no external memory access is necessary. In the event of a miss, a memory access request is posted to the memory unit, or MU, to read the 32-byte sector from memory and store it in the cache. When the MU has read the first 16 bytes from memory, it forwards them to the cache. This explains the four-word-wide data bus between the MU and cache in figure 24-1. There are two cases where the cache has to write a modified sector back to memory:

- When the cache has to cast out a modified sector to make room for a new sector being read into the cache, the modified sector is forwarded to the MU over the eight-word-wide data bus illustrated in figure 24-1.
- In the event of a snoop hit on a modified sector, the modified sector has to be written back to memory. It is forwarded to the MU over the eight-word-wide data bus.

A complete description of the cache can be found in the chapter entitled "601 Cache and Memory Unit."

Memory Unit (MU)

The MU implements a two-deep read access queue and a three-deep write access queue. It decouples the cache and the processor core from the external bus. In figure 24-1, the MU uses the two-word-wide data bus to read or write eight bytes at a time between itself and the system interface. A complete description of the MU can be found in the chapter entitled "601 Cache and Memory Unit."

System Interface

The system interface provides the processor's interface to the outside world. The bus is used to communicate with memory and I/O devices, and to ensure that each processor's cache is kept informed of all memory-related operations performed by other bus masters. Separate address and data buses with separate arbitration permits transaction pipelining (two transactions may be in progress at a given instant in time). A detailed description of the bus operation can be found in the chapter entitled "The PPC 601 Split-Bus Concept."

Chapter 25

The Previous Chapter

The previous chapter began part four of the book — the discussion of the PPC 601 processor. It provided a discussion of the PPC 601 processor's microarchitecture and the relationships of the processor's functional units to each other.

This Chapter

This chapter defines the PPC 601 processor's implementation of the user mode register and instruction set.

The Next Chapter

The next chapter defines the PPC 601 processor's implementation of the supervisor mode register and instruction set.

Introduction

This chapter defines cases where the PPC 601 user register set is non-compliant with the specification. It identifies user instructions that are defined by the architecture but are not implemented in the PPC 601. It also identifies user instructions that are a superset of the architecture.

User Mode Registers

Figure 25-1 illustrates the user-accessible registers. The special purpose register numbers that correspond to each are also indicated. The following sections define the user mode registers that are non-compliant with the PowerPC specification or that are processor-specific and therefore fall outside the scope of the specification.

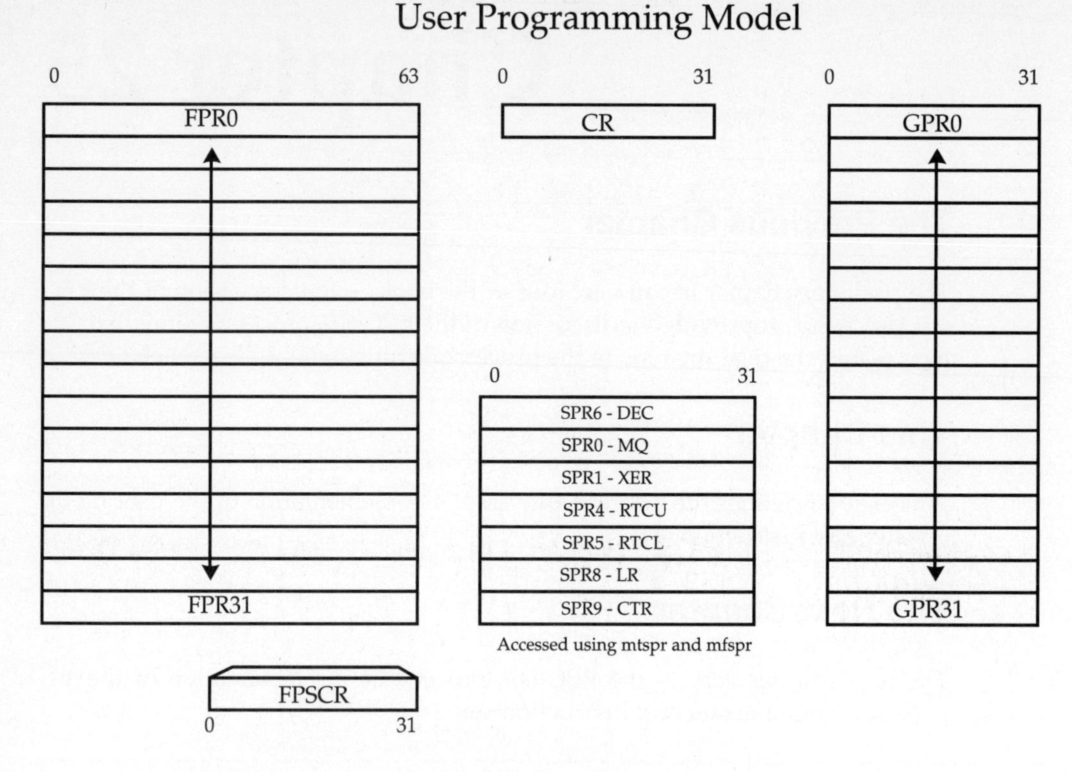

Figure 25-1. User Registers

MQ Register

The MQ (multiplier and quotient) register is outside the scope of the specification. It holds the product for multiply operations and the divisor for divide operations. It also acts as the operand for long rotate and shift operations. The multiply and divide instructions are PowerPC instructions while some of the long rotate and shift instructions are outside the scope of the specification.

Real-Time Clock (RTC) Register

As described earlier in this publication, the specification defines a timebase register that is utilized to track the passage of time. The RTC register is non-compliant with the specification in the following respects:

- The RTC keeps track of the passage of time in seconds and nanoseconds since the last second ticked. The timebase frequency is processor implementation-dependent and doesn't use any specification-defined defined frequency.
- The RTC increments up to a maximum value of all nines and then rolls over to zero. The timebase increments up to a maximum value of all F's and then rolls over to zero.
- The programmer uses the mftb and mttb instructions to access the timebase, while the mfspr and mtspr instructions are used to access the RTC. When the processor is operating at the user privilege level, RTCU is SPR 4 and RTCL is SPR 5.

The RTC register is divided into two halves referred to as RTC upper, or RTCU, and RTC lower, or RTCL. RTCU contains the number of seconds that have elapsed since the register was initialized. It is implemented as a 32-bit binary counter. When it is incremented past its maximum count of FFFFFFFFh, it rolls over to zero.

RTCL contains the number of nanoseconds that have elapsed since the start of the current second. It is implemented as a 23-bit counter (bits 0:1 and 25:31 are not implemented). It counts to a maximum value of 999,999,872 (999,999,999-128ns) and then rolls over to zero and RTCU is then incremented.

When in user mode, the programmer can only read from the RTC registers. The RTCU register is read using the mfspr instruction and its SPR number is 4. The RTCL register is also read from using the mfspr instruction and its SPR number is 5.

FPSCR Register

With the following exceptions, the FPSCR is compliant with the specification:

- The FPSCR[29], non-IEEE, or NI, mode bit is not implemented.
- The FPSCR[21], VXSOFT bit is not implemented.
- The FPSCR[22], VXSQRT bit is not implemented.

Figure 25-2 illustrates the PPC 601 FPSCR register.

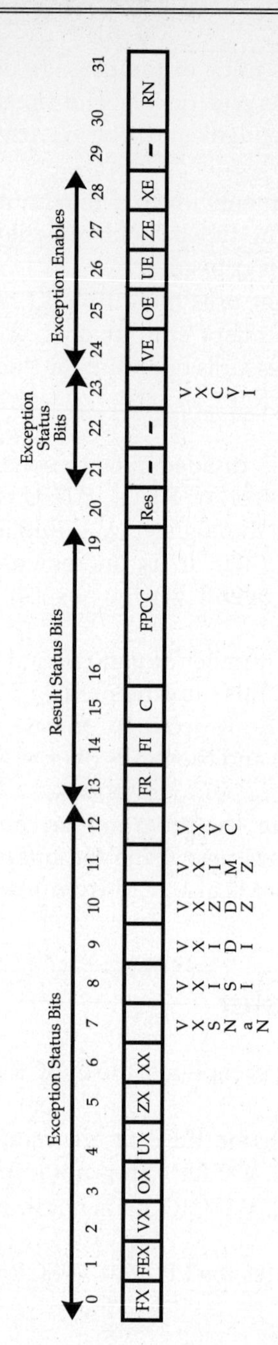

Figure 25-2. PPC601 FPSCR Register

DEC Register

The PPC 601 processor's implementation of the decrementer register has the following operational characteristics (the register is illustrated in figure 25-3):

- The specification defines the DEC register as supervisor-only access. However, the PPC 601 DEC register may be read in user mode using the mfspr instruction. This capability was included for compliance with the POWER architecture.
- The DEC register is SPR number 6 when the processor is operating at the user privilege level and SPR 22 at the supervisor privilege level.
- Decrements using the 7.8125MHz RTC input clock and therefore decrements at the rate of one tick every 128ns.
- Cleared to zero by the assertion of the processor's hard reset input.
- Unless disabled by cleared MSR[EE], generates a decrementer interrupt when its count is exhausted.
- If the programmer moves a value into the DEC register that sets bit zero to a one, the decrementer interrupt is generated. It should be noted that the programmer can only write to the DEC register if the processor is operating at the supervisor privilege level.
- The lower seven bits in the DEC register are not implemented (because the DEC counts in nanoseconds and the RTC decrements the DEC once every 128ns), so bit 24 serves as the lsb of the DEC register.
- The maximum interval count that can be loaded in the upper 25 bits of the register is 1FFFFFFh, or 33,554,432 in decimal. At a tick rate of 128ns, this yields a maximum interval of 4.29 seconds.
- The RTC is sampled using the processor's PCLK. If the PCLK frequency is less than twice the RTC frequency, sampling errors may occur.

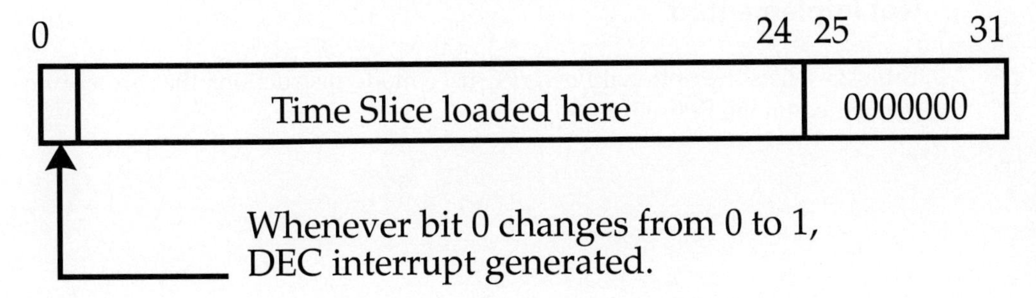

Figure 25-3. PPC601 Decrementer (DEC) Register

User Mode Instructions

This section identifies user mode instructions that are defined by the architecture but are not implemented in the PPC 601. It also identifies user instructions that are a superset of the architecture.

Missing Instructions

The PPC 601 does not implement the full PowerPC user mode instruction set. It does not implement the instructions intended for use only on 64-bit processors. This includes all of the integer doubleword-oriented instructions.

Superset instructions

The mtspr and mfspr instructions are used to access the MQ, while the mfspr instruction is used to read from the RTCU and RTCL registers.

The PPC 601 processor provides a group of POWER-compliant instructions. For a listing of these instructions, refer to the PPC 601 documentation.

Optional Instructions

Implemented

The PPC 601 implements the following PowerPC optional user mode instructions: eciwx and ecowx.

Not Implemented

Table 25-1 lists the optional PowerPC user mode instructions that are not implemented on the PPC 601.

Table 25-1. Optional PowerPC User Mode Instructions Not Implemented On 601

Mnemonic	Instruction
fres	Floating-point reciprocal estimate single-precision.
frsqrte	Floating-point reciprocal square root estimate.
fsel	Floating-point select.
fsqrt	Floating-point square root.
fsqrts	Floating-point square root single-precision.
mfspr	Move from special purpose register (the instruction is implemented, but only for the SPR register numbers that are valid for this processor).
mtspr	Move to special purpose register (the instruction is implemented, but only for the SPR register numbers that are valid for this processor).
stfiwx	Store floating-point as integer word indexed.

Chapter 26

The Previous Chapter

The previous chapter defined the PPC 601 processor's implementation of the user mode register and instruction set.

This Chapter

This chapter defines the PPC 601 processor's implementation of the supervisor mode register and instruction set.

The Next Chapter

The next chapter defines the startup state of the PPC 601 processor (after hard reset is removed from the processor by the platform logic).

Introduction

This chapter defines cases where the PPC 601 supervisor register set is non-compliant with the specification. It identifies supervisor instructions that are defined by the architecture but are not implemented in the PPC 601. It also identifies supervisor instructions that are a superset of the architecture.

Supervisor Mode Registers

The supervisor-accessible registers are illustrated in figure 26-1. The following sections define the user mode registers that are non-compliant with the PowerPC specification or that are processor-specific and therefore fall outside the scope of the specification.

Special-Purpose Registers

SPR	0 — 31
SPR18	DSISR (DAE/source instruction service)
SPR19	DAR (Data Address)
SPR20	RTCU (Real-time clock upper)
SPR21	RTCL (Real-time clock lower)
SPR22	DEC (Decrementer)
SPR25	SDR1 (Table Search Description)
SPR26	SRR0 (Save/restore register 0)
SPR27	SRR1 (Save/restore register 1)
SPR272	SPRG0 (Pointer to exception memory)
SPR273	SPRG1 (Exception handler scratch)
SPR274	SPRG2 (For OS use)
SPR275	SPRG3 (SPR General 3, for OS use)
SPR282	EAR (External Access)
SPR287	PVR (Processor Version)
SPR528	IBAT0U
SPR529	IBAT0L
SPR530	IBAT1U
SPR531	IBAT1L
SPR532	IBAT2U
SPR533	IBAT2L
SPR534	IBAT3U
SPR535	IBAT3L
SPR1008	HID0 (Checkstop sources/enables)
SPR1009	HID1 (Debug modes)
SPR1010	HID2, IABR (Instruction address breakpoint)
SPR1013	HID5, DABR (Data/address breakpoint)
SPR1023	HID15, PIR

SPRs are accessed using mfspr and mtspr instructions

Segment Registers

0 — 31
Segment Register 15 (SR15)
Segment Register 14 (SR14)
Segment Register 13 (SR13)
Segment Register 12 (SR12)
Segment Register 11 (SR11)
Segment Register 10 (SR10)
Segment Register 9 (SR9)
Segment Register 8 (SR8)
Segment Register 7 (SR7)
Segment Register 6 (SR6)
Segment Register 5 (SR5)
Segment Register 4 (SR4)
Segment Register 3 (SR3)
Segment Register 2 (SR2)
Segment Register 1 (SR1)
Segment Register 0 (SR0)

0 — 31
Machine State Register (MSR)

Supervisor Programming Model

Figure 26-1. Supervisor Registers

RTC

The PPC 601 RTC registers are not compliant with the specification. At the supervisor level, the RTC registers are read/writable using the mtspr and mfspr instructions. At the supervisor privilege level, the RTCU register's SPR number is 20, while the RTCL lower register's SPR number is 21.

The RTC register is divided into two halves referred to as RTC upper, or RTCU, and RTC lower, or RTCL. RTCU contains the number of seconds that have elapsed since the register was initialized. It is implemented as a 32-bit binary counter. When it is incremented past its maximum count of FFFFFFFFh, it rolls over to zero.

RTCL contains the number of nanoseconds that have elapsed since the start of the current second. It is implemented as a 23-bit counter (bits 0:1 and 25:31 are not implemented). It counts to a maximum value of 1,000,000,000 minus 128ns and then rolls over to zero and RTCU is then incremented.

Machine State Register (MSR)

The MSR is illustrated in figure 26-2. It defines the current state of the processor. The PPC 601 processor's MSR register is non-compliant with the specification on the following points:

- MSR[13], the POW, or power management, bit is not implemented.
- MSR[15], ELE (also referred to as ILE bit), the interrupt little-endian bit is not implemented.
- MSR[22], the BE, or branch trace enable, bit is not implemented.
- MSR[30], the RE (also referred to as RI bit), the recoverable exception bit is not implemented.
- MSR[31], LE, the little-endian bit is not implemented in the MSR register. Rather, it is implemented in bit 28 of the checkstop sources/enables register, HID0.

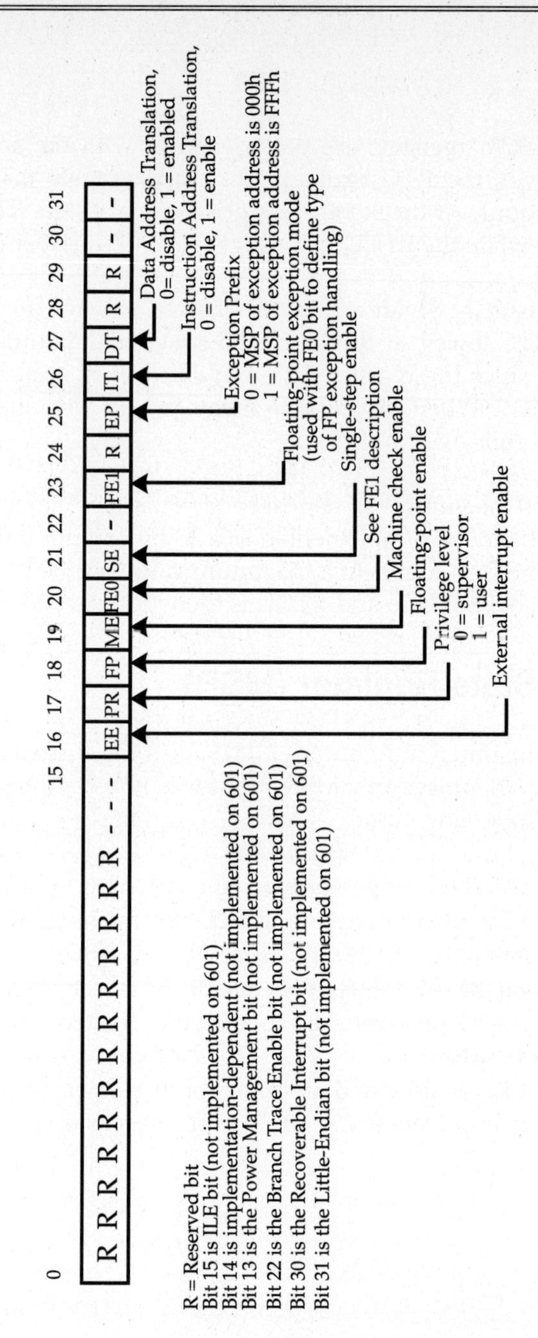

Figure 26-2. Machine State Register

Decrementer Register (DEC)

The DEC can be used to cause an interrupt after a programmed delay. The amount of delay resolution is based on the 7.8125MHz RTC (128ns per tick). The PPC 601 processor deviates from the specification in that the DEC register may be read from in user mode. This feature was included for compatibility with the POWER architecture. For more information on the DEC register, refer to the chapter entitled "601 User Register and Instruction Set."

Segment Registers and Page Translation

The format of the segment registers is illustrated in figure 26-3. The I/O segment descriptor differs from that specified in the specification. In the specification, bits [12:31] of the I/O segment descriptor are generally described as a "controller-specific" field. In the PPC 601, bits [12:27] are controller-specific, while bits[28:31] supply the upper hex digit of the I/O port address that is output to the I/O controller during transmission of address packet one in an I/O transaction.

When a segment register contains an I/O descriptor (T = 1) and the controller ID is 7Fh, any access within the segment results in a memory transaction rather than an I/O transaction. This is referred to as memory-forced I/O and it is outside the scope of the specification. The target memory address is formed as follows — the upper hex digit of the address is supplied by bits[28:31] from the segment register, while the lower seven digits of the address are supplied by the lower seven digits of the effective address. The memory access is performed with an assumed WIM bit setting of 011b: non-cacheable, memory coherency required.

For a detailed description of the I/O transaction, refer to the chapter entitled "PPC 601 I/O Transactions."

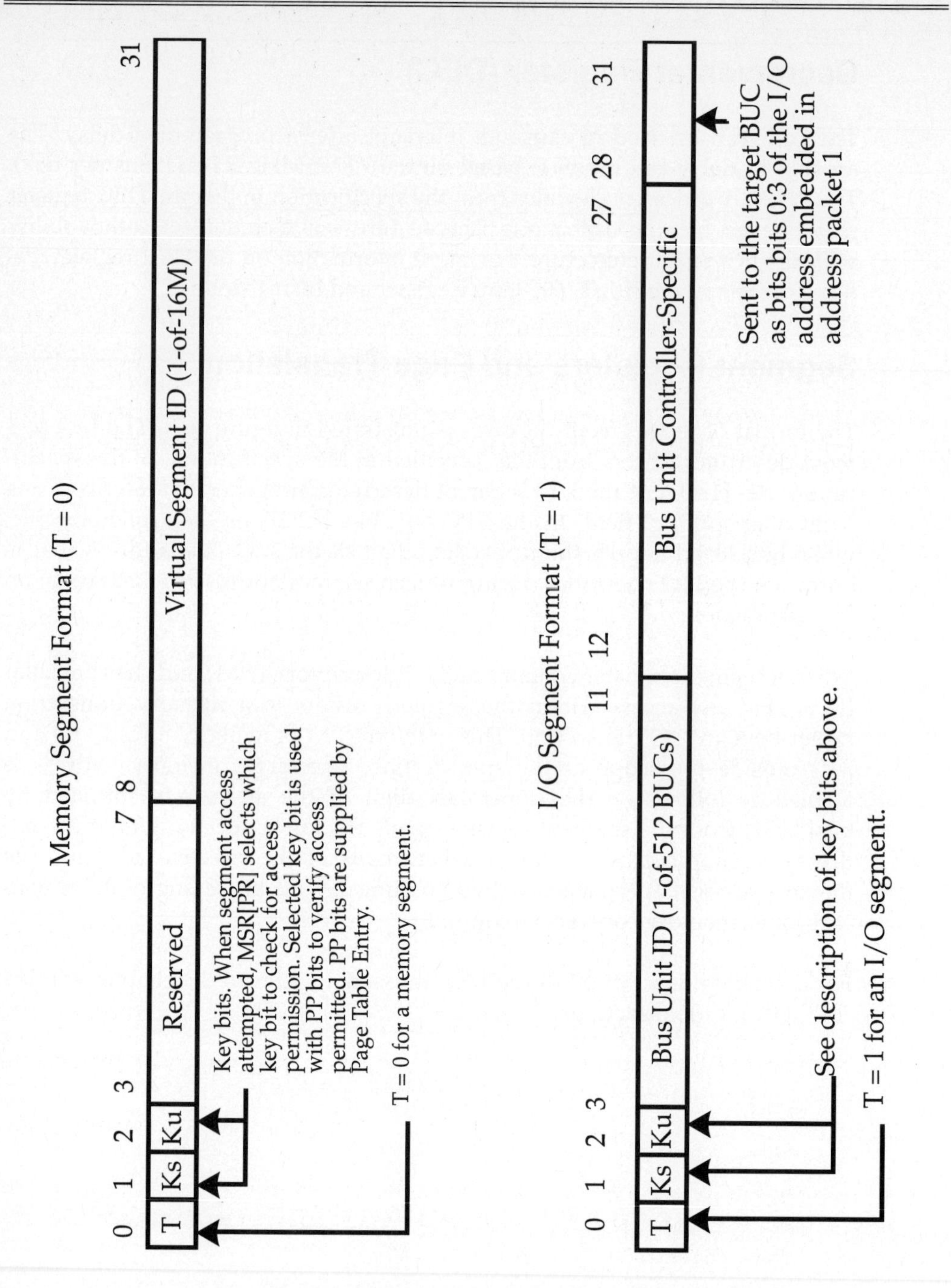

Figure 26-3. Segment Register

External Access Register (EAR)

The PPC 601 processor implements the optional EAR register and the ecowx and eciwx instructions. During the execution of ecowx and eciwx instructions, if the EAR enable bit is set, the resource ID of a special external target device is output from the EAR to the concatenated field created from TBST# | | TSIZ[0:2]. When the special device detects an ecowx or eciwx transaction in progress, it compares the resource ID on TBST#| |TSIZ[0:2] to its ID. If it matches, it is the target of the transaction. The EAR is illustrated in figure 26-4. The specification states that the RID field consists of bits 26:31, while the PPC 601 only implements bits 28:31. This restricts the number of possible RIDs to 16 rather than 64. A detailed description of the bus transactions that result from execution of the ecowx or eciwx instructions can be found in the chapter entitled "601 External Control Transaction."

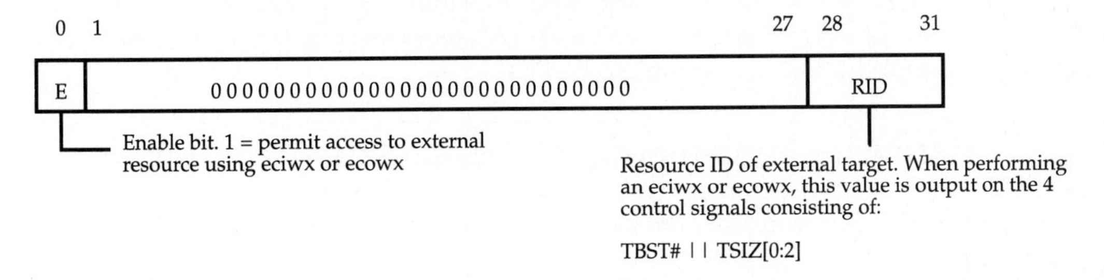

Figure 26-4. External Address Register (EAR)

BAT Registers

The PPC 601 processor's BAT register set is non-compliant with the specification in the following respects:

- The four DBAT register pairs are missing.
- The four IBAT register pairs are actually used for both load/store and instruction address translation.
- The layout of the fields within the IBAT registers is non-compliant with the specification.
- The IBAT registers may be used to define a block from 128KB to 8MB in size, rather than from 128KB to 256MB as stated in the specification.
- The G, or guarded, bit is not implemented.

For a more detailed discussion of block address translation in the PPC 601 processor, refer to the chapter entitled "601 Cache and Memory Unit."

DSISR Register

The DSISR register contains status after the occurrence of a data storage or an alignment interrupt. The bit definition of DSISR is different for these two events. The 601 implementation of the DSISR register is 100% compliant with the specification for the alignment interrupt, but exhibits the following differences for the data storage interrupt:

- Bit 0 is reserved on the 601 (in the specification, bit 0 is set if the target address is within an I/O segment).
- Bit 5 is set under all of the conditions cited in the specification, but additionally is set upon the attempted execution of an lscbx instruction specifying a target address within an I/O segment. The lscbx instruction is a POWER instruction (not PowerPC).

Hardware Implementation Dependent (HID) Registers

The PPC 601 processor contains the following processor-specific registers:

- Checkstop Sources and Enables Register, or HID0.
- Debug Modes Register, or HID1.
- Instruction Address Breakpoint Register (IABR), or HID2.
- Data Address Breakpoint Register (DABR), or HID5.
- Processor ID Register (PIR), or HID15.

The following sections provide a description of each of these registers.

Checkstop Sources and Enables Register (HID0)

HID0 contains four groups of bits:

- Checkstop enable/disable bits.
- Checkstop status bits.
- Bits used to enable/disable miscellaneous features.
- HID0[30] is the cache initialization error bit. If no error occurred during the power-on self-test and initialization of the L1 cache, this bit is cleared to zero. Otherwise, it is set to one.

Checkstop Enable/Disable and Status Bits

The PPC 601 processor contains self-check logic. The operating system programmer can selectively enable/disable portions of this logic with bits in the HID0 register. If a portion of the self-check logic has been enabled and it detects a failure, the processor will enter the checkstop state. The contents of all registers are frozen within two clock cycles. The corresponding checkstop status bit is set in the HID0 register. The processor can typically only be restarted by resetting it. Upon entering the checkstop state, the processor asserts its CKSTP_OUT# output.

HID0[0] is the master checkstop enable, or CE, bit. When set to a one, the processor will checkstop if a failure is detected and the corresponding checkstop enable/disable bit is also set to a one. The HID0[15:25] bit field contains the enable/disable bits. They are defined in table 26-1. All but two of the checkstop enable bits are disabled by the assertion of the processor's hard reset input, HRESET#. The two that are always enabled when HRESET# is removed are bits 15 and 24. In other words, when reset is removed and the processor begins to executes its BIST out of the microcode ROM embedded within the processor, it will checkstop if a microcode parity error is detected or an invalid microcode opcode.

Table 26-1. Checkstop Enable/Disable Bits

HID0 Bit	Description
0, CE	1 = Master checkstop enable.
15, ES	1 = Enable microcode checkstop. Enables logic that tests for bad microcode being fetched from the processor's internal microcode ROM when the BIST is being executed. If ES and CE = 1, the processor freezes on a microcode error. This checkstop is enabled when reset is removed. The microcode checkstop status bit HID0[1], the S bit is set on error.
16, EM	1 = Enable machine check checkstop. If EM and CE = 1 and external logic asserts the processor's TEA# (transfer error acknowledge) input during a bus transaction, the processor freezes. This checkstop is disabled when reset is removed.
17, ETD	1 = Enable TLB checkstop. If ETD and CE =1 and the MMU's paging unit's TLB experiences a double hit when performing a PTE lookup in the TLB, the processor freezes. This checkstop is disabled when reset is removed. The HID0[3] TD status bit is set.
18, ECD	1 = Enable cache checkstop. If ECD and CE =1 and the processor's L1 cache experiences a double hit, the processor freezes. This checkstop is disabled when reset is removed. The HID0[4] CD status bit is set.
19, ESH	1 = Enable sequencer timeout checkstop. If ESH and CE =1 and the processor's sequencer times out, the processor freezes. This checkstop is disabled when reset is removed. The HID0[5] SH status bit is set.
20, EDT	1 = Enable dispatch timeout checkstop. If EDT and CE =1 and the processor's dispatcher times out, the processor freezes. This checkstop is disabled when reset is removed. The HID0[6] DT status bit is set.
21, EBA	1 = Enable address bus parity checkstop. If EBA and CE =1 and the processor experiences a parity error when snooping an address, the processor freezes. This checkstop is disabled when reset is removed. The HID0[7] BA status bit is set.
22, EBD	1 = Enable data bus parity checkstop. If EBD and CE =1 and the processor experiences a parity error when reading data from an external device, the processor freezes. This checkstop is disabled when reset is removed. The HID0[8] BD status bit is set.
23, ECP	1 = Enable cache parity checkstop. If ECP and CE =1 and the processor's L1 cache experiences a parity error when reading from the cache directory or data storage, the processor freezes. This checkstop is disabled when reset is removed. The HID0[9] CP status bit is set.
24, EIU	1 = Enable invalid microcode instruction checkstop. If EIU and CE =1 and the processor reads an invalid microcode instruction from its internal microcode ROM, the processor freezes. This checkstop is enabled when reset is removed. The HID0[10] IU status bit is set.
25, EPP	1 = Enable I/O protocol checkstop. If EPP and CE =1 and the processor detects an I/O protocol error during an I/O bus transaction, the processor freezes. This checkstop is disabled when reset is removed. The HID0[11] PP status bit is set.

When a checkstop occurs, the HID0 register (and any of the processor's other registers) can be accessed via the boundary scan interface. This will typically only occur in the engineering, manufacturing test, or depot test environments. If external logic asserts TEA# during a transaction, MSR[ME] is cleared, and HID0[CE] is cleared, the processor will take the machine check interrupt (regardless of the cleared state of MSR[ME]).

If external logic asserts TEA# during a transaction with MSR[ME] cleared, and HID0[CE] set and HID0[EM] cleared, the processor will take the machine check interrupt (regardless of the cleared state of MSR[ME]).

Figure 26-5 illustrates HID0.

HID0 Bits Used to Enable/Disable Miscellaneous Features

In addition to the checkstop enable/disable and status bits, the HID0 register also contains bits that control the following processor features:

- Enable high-priority snoop request feature bit (HID0[EHP]). For additional information on high-priority snoop request, refer to the chapter entitled "601 Cache and Memory Unit."
- Enable precharge of snoop result signals bit (HID0[PAR]). The default state of the PAR bit after rest is zero (enabled). When deasserting ARTRY# and/or SHD#, the processor tri-states them for one bus clock cycle, drives them high for a half-cycle of the bus clock and then tri-states them. If the feature is disabled (PAR = 1), the signals are tri-stated. The system is then responsible for precharging these signals.
- Big/little-endian mode select bit (HID0[LE]). When cleared to zero, the processor uses the big-endian storage method, while it uses the little-endian method when set to one. For more information, refer to the chapter entitled "Big vs. Little-Endian."
- Enable optional reload of alternate sector on load/store miss (HID0[DRL]). For more information refer to the chapter entitled "601 Cache and Memory Unit."
- Enable optional reload of alternate sector on instruction fetch miss (HID0[DRF]). For more information refer to the chapter entitled "601 Cache and Memory Unit."

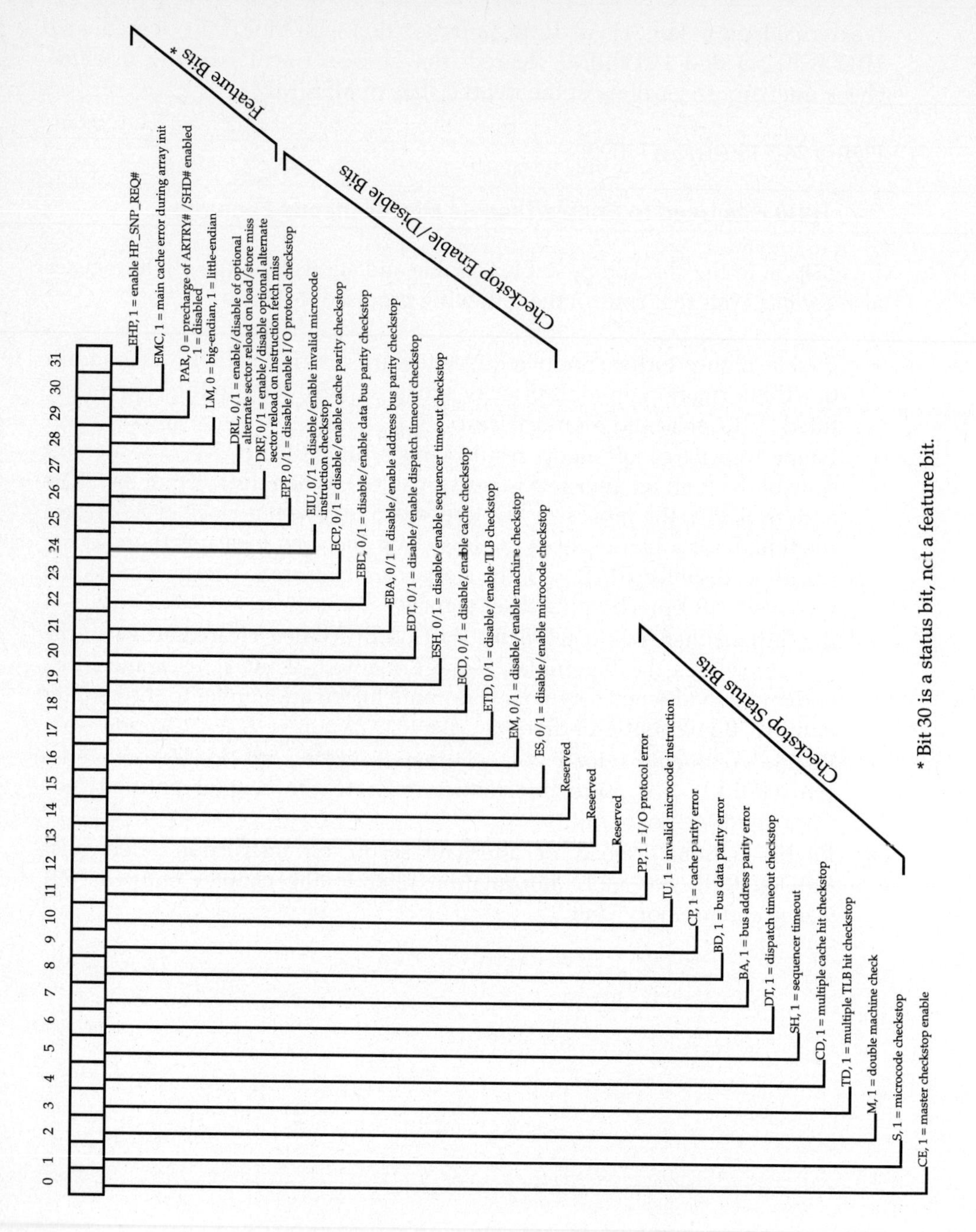
0 1 2 3 4 5 6 7 8 9 10 11 12 13 14 15 16 17 18 19 20 21 22 23 24 25 26 27 28 29 30 31
Feature Bits *
Checkstop Enable/Disable Bits
Checkstop Status Bits
EHP, 1 = enable HP_SNP_REQ#
EMC, 1 = main cache error during array init
PAR, 0 = precharge of ARTRY# /SHD# enabled
1 = disabled
LM, 0 = big-endian, 1 = little-endian
DRL, 0/1 = enable/disable of optional
alternate sector reload on load/store miss
DRF, 0/1 = enable/disable optional alternate
sector reload on instruction fetch miss
EPP, 0/1 = disable/enable I/O protocol checkstop
EIU, 0/1 = disable/enable invalid microcode
instruction checkstop
ECP, 0/1 = disable/enable cache parity checkstop
EBD, 0/1 = disable/enable data bus parity checkstop
EBA, 0/1 = disable/enable address bus parity checkstop
EDT, 0/1 = disable/enable dispatch timeout checkstop
ESH, 0/1 = disable/enable sequencer timeout checkstop
ECD, 0/1 = disable/enable cache checkstop
ETD, 0/1 = disable/enable TLB checkstop
EM, 0/1 = disable/enable machine checkstop
ES, 0/1 = disable/enable microcode checkstop
Reserved
Reserved
Reserved
PP, 1 = I/O protocol error
IU, 1 = invalid microcode instruction
CP, 1 = cache parity error
BD, 1 = bus data parity error
BA, 1 = bus address parity error
DT, 1 = dispatch timeout checkstop
SH, 1 = sequencer timeout
CD, 1 = multiple cache hit checkstop
TD, 1 = multiple TLB hit checkstop
M, 1 = double machine check
S, 1 = microcode checkstop
CE, 1 = master checkstop enable
* Bit 30 is a status bit, nct a feature bit.

Figure 26-5. Checkstop Enable/Disable Register (HID0)

Debug Modes Register (HID1)

HID1 is used to specify the type of breakpoint monitoring to perform and the action to take when a breakpoint hit is detected. Its SPR number is 1009. Using this register, the OS programmer may enable the following types of breakpoints:

- Limited instruction address compare.
- Single-step.
- Full instruction address compare.
- Full branch target address compare.

When a breakpoint match occurs (or a single-step), this register can be used to instruct the processor to stop or to trap to the run mode interrupt handler. For a full description of HID1, refer to the PPC 601 reference manuals. HID1 is used in conjunction with HID2 and HID5. Table 26-2 defines the debug modes that may be selected via HID1[1:3].

Table 26-2. Debug Modes

HID1[1:3]	Mode	Description
000b	Normal	Breakpoint detection turned off.
001b	Do not use	
010b	Limited instruction address compare	Program execution proceeds at full speed. Address compare is only performed in Q0. Branches and FPU operations and their associated addresses may not make it to Q0.
011b	Do not use	
100b	Single-step	Interrupt after successful completion of each instruction. See warning in 601 manual.
101b	Do not use	
110b	Full instruction address compare	All instructions are forced through Q0 for the compare. This degrades CPU performance. Breakpoint occurs on instruction address match.
111b	Full branch target address compare	All instructions are forced through Q0 for the compare. This degrades CPU performance. Breakpoint occurs on branch target address match.

Instruction Address Breakpoint Register (IABR or HID2)

When an instruction breakpoint has been enabled in HID1, the breakpoint compare address is specified in HID2.

Data Address Breakpoint Register (DABR or HID5)

HID5 is used to enable a data access breakpoint and to set the breakpoint compare address.

Processor ID Register (PIR or HID15)

HID15 contains a 4-bit processor ID in bits [28:31]. This provides the sender ID during I/O load/store transactions, and provides the receiver ID during I/O reply transactions. For more information regarding I/O transactions, refer to the chapter entitled "PPC 601 I/O Transactions."

Unimplemented Registers

The ASR register is only associated with 64-bit processors and is not implemented on the PPC 601 processor.

The DBAT register pairs are not implemented on the PPC 601 processor.

Supervisor Mode Instructions

Missing Instructions

The PPC 601 does not implement the full PowerPC supervisor mode instruction set. It does not implement the instructions intended for use only on 64-bit processors. This includes the SLB management instructions. In addition, the PPC 601 does not implement the supervisor-level instructions listed in table 26-3

Table 26-3. Optional PowerPC Supervisor Mode Instructions Not Implemented on 601

Mnemonic	Instruction
mftb	move from time base.
tlbia	translation lookaside buffer invalidate all.
tlbsync	translation lookaside buffer synchronize.

The PPC 601 processor does not implement the tlbsync instruction. A sync instruction should be used to synchronize the completion of a broadcast tlbie instruction.

Superset Instructions

The mfspr and mtspr instructions are used to read from and write to the RTCU and RTCL registers.

The PPC 601 processor provides a group of POWER-compliant instructions. For a listing of these instructions, refer to the PPC 601 documentation.

Instructions with Modified Operational Characteristics

Because the 601 implements a unified code/data cache, the icbi instruction acts as a no-op. The MMU doesn't even validate the target address.

Treatment of Invalid Instruction Forms

The PowerPC processor specification states that invalid instruction forms will cause a program interrupt. The PPC 601 processor does not generate an interrupt for invalid instruction forms (e.g., a load string with both rA and rB set to zero).

Chapter 27

The Previous Chapter

The previous chapter defined the PPC 601 processor's implementation of the supervisor mode register and instruction set.

This Chapter

This chapter defines the startup state of the PPC 601 processor (after hard reset is removed from the processor by the platform logic). It may seem counterproductive to include this brief a chapter, but the author considers knowledge of a processor's initial startup state to be crucial to understanding how it operates at startup time.

The Next Chapter

The next chapter provides a description of the PPC 601 processor's implementation of interrupts. Any deviations from the architecture specification are described.

Processor State after Hard Reset Removed

When the system is first powered up, the system reset logic keeps the PPC 601 processor's hard reset (HRESET#) input active until the power has stabilized. HRESET# is then removed. While HRESET# was asserted, it forced the values indicated in table 27-1 into the processor's register set. The first instruction is fetched from memory location FFF00100h.

Table 27-1. Register Contents After Reset

Register	Contents	Comments
GPRs	zeros	
FPRs	zeros	
FPSCR	zeros	All floating-point exceptions masked.
CR	zeros	
SRs	zeros	
MSR	00001040h	External and decrementer interrupts masked. Supervisor mode. Floating-point unit disabled. Machine check interrupt enabled. All floating-point interrupts disabled. Single-step interrupt disabled. Upper three hex digits of interrupt handler addresses are FFFh. Address translation disabled.
MQ	zeros	
XER	zeros	
RTCU	zeros	If RTC clock input is running, will increment.
RTCL	zeros	If RTC clock input is running, will increment.
LR	zeros	
CTR	zeros	
DSISR	zeros	
DAR	zeros	
DEC	zeros	If RTC clock input is running, will decrement.
SDR1	zeros	
SRR0	zeros	
SRR1	zeros	
SPRGs	zeros	
EAR	zeros	ecowx and eciwx cannot be executed (no resource ID set up).
PVR	00010001h	Processor version 0001h, revision 0001h. The revision may change (early chips were rev 0).
IBATs	zeros	No blocks set up.
HID0	80010080h	Master checkstop enable active. Microcode checkstop enabled. Invalid microcode checkstop enabled. High-priority snoop disabled. If HID0[30] = 0, no cache init error detected. Precharge of ARTRY# and SHD# enabled. Big-endian mode selected.
HID1	zeros	No debug breakpoints enabled.
HID2	zeros	
HID5	zeros	
HID15	zeros	Processor ID = 0.
TLBs	zeros	TLB empty.
Cache	zeros	Cache empty.
Tag directory	zeros	Cache empty.

Chapter 28

The Previous Chapter

The previous chapter defined the startup state of the PPC 601 processor (after hard reset is removed from the processor by the platform logic).

This Chapter

This chapter provides a description of the PPC 601 processor's implementation of interrupts. Any deviations from the architecture specification are described.

The Next Chapter

The next chapter provides a description of the PPC 601 processor's MMU implementation and describes any deviations from the architecture specification.

Location of Interrupt Table

When an interrupt occurs, the processor saves the instruction pointer in SRR0 and the machine state and interrupt status information in SRR1. Having done this, the processor then jumps to the interrupt handler entry point associated with the interrupt currently being serviced. The base address of the interrupt table is selected by the state of the interrupt prefix, or IP, bit in MSR. With IP = 0, the interrupt table base address is 00000000h. With IP = 1, the base address is FFF00000h.

The processor forms the address to jump to by adding the offset associated with the interrupt type to the base address. At startup time after hard reset, HRESET#, is removed, IP is set to one.

Interrupt Handler Entry Points

The interrupt handler entry points are listed in table 28-1. The PPC 601:

- does not implement the optional trace interrupt.
- does not implement the optional floating-point assist interrupt.
- implements an I/O controller interface error interrupt.
- implements a run mode/trace interrupt.

Table 28-1. PPC 601 Interrupt Handler Entry Points

Interrupt Type	Interrupt Table Offset
Reserved	00000h
System reset	00100h
Machine check	00200h
Data Storage	00300h
Instruction storage	00400h
External	00500h
Alignment	00600h
Program	00700h
Floating-point unavailable	00800h
Decrementer	00900h
I/O Controller Interface Error	00A00h
Reserved	00B00h
System call	00C00h
Not used (Trace)	00D00h
Not used (Floating-point assist)	00E00h
Reserved	00E10h – 00FFFh
Reserved	01000h – 01FFFh
Run mode/Trace	02000h
Reserved	02001h –03FFFh

Architecture-Defined Interrupts

System Reset Interrupt

This interrupt is invoked when the processor's hard reset, HRESET#, or soft reset, SRESET#, input is asserted by external logic. This interrupt is not maskable.

Hard Reset

If HRESET# is asserted, the reset interrupt entry point is always FFF00100h (regardless of the state of the MSR[IP] bit). Refer to the chapter entitled "601 Processor Startup State" for more information on the effects of hard reset. Since address translation is disabled, all data and code accesses to memory are considered cacheable (the assumed WIM bit setting is 001b).

Soft Reset

If SRESET# is asserted, the reset interrupt entry point is determined by the state of MSR[IP]. If MSR[IP] = 0, then the handler's entry point is 00000100h. if MSR[IP] = 1, then the handler's entry point is FFF00100h. The only registers affected by soft reset are SRR0, SRR1 and MSR.

Machine Check Interrupt

Assertion of TEA#, transfer error acknowledge, by external logic causes the processor to immediately terminate any transaction it is performing on the bus. One processor clock tick after TEA# is asserted, the processor floats the data bus. It does not, however, invalidate data that may have already been read into a GPR or the cache.

If the machine check interrupt is enabled (MSR[ME] = 1), the processor suspends execution of the currently-running program and invokes the machine check interrupt handler at offset 00200h in the interrupt entry point table.
If the machine check interrupt is disabled (MSR[ME] = 0) and the machine check checkstop is disabled (HID0[CE] = 0, or HID0[CE] = 1 but HID0[EM] = 0), the machine check interrupt is taken (machine check checkstop disabled implies "don't stop").

If the machine check checkstop is enabled (HID0[CE] = 1 and HID0[EM] = 1) and MSR[ME] = 0, the processor will checkstop (freeze) if TEA# is asserted by external logic. For more information regarding checkstop, refer to the chapter entitled "601 OS Register and Instruction Set."

If another machine check (TEA# assertion) occurs while the processor is executing the machine check handler and it has not yet re-enabled the machine check interrupt (MSR[ME] = 1), the processor will enter the checkstop state after setting the double machine check status bit in HID0.

Data Storage, or Access, Interrupt

The entry point for the data storage interrupt handler is 00300h in the entry point table. For a detailed discussion of the data storage interrupt, refer to the chapter entitled "Interrupts."

In the PPC 601 processor, the following additional conditions can cause a data storage interrupt:

- Attempted execution of a lwarx, stwcx or lscbx instruction where the specified effective address maps into an I/O segment (T = 1 in the segment register) and the I/O controller number is not 7Fh (in other words, an I/O access).
- The effective address matches the address specified in the data access breakpoint register, or DABR (HID5) and data access breakpoints are enabled in the debug mode register, HID1.

DSISR[0] is reserved on the PPC 601. In the specification, this bit is used to signal an I/O controller interface error. In the event that an I/O reply is received with the error bit set in address packet 0, the PPC 601 takes the I/O controller interface error interrupt instead (see section on this subject in this chapter).

Any instruction that would cause a data storage interrupt if the effective address maps to an I/O segment (e.g., an instruction fetch or semaphore load/store) will do so on the PPC 601 if the segment register's T = 1 and the I/O controller number in the segment register is 7Fh (i.e., a memory-forced I/O segment).

Instruction Storage Interrupt

The entry point for the instruction storage interrupt handler is 00400h in the entry point table. For a detailed discussion of the instruction storage interrupt, refer to the chapter entitled "Interrupts."

The specification defines SRR1[3] as set if an instruction fetch attempted to access an I/O segment (segment register T = 1). When the PPC 601 detects this condition, it clears SRR1[0:15].

External Interrupt

The entry point for the external interrupt handler is 00500h in the entry point table. For a detailed discussion of the external interrupt, refer to the chapter entitled "Interrupts."

In revision 0000h PPC 601 processors, the processor's INT# input is level-sensitive. When asserted by the external interrupt controller, it must remain asserted until reset by the interrupt handler. An external pullup resistor should be added to ensure that noise doesn't generate a phantom interrupt.

Alignment Interrupt

The entry point for the alignment interrupt handler is 00600h in the entry point table. For a detailed discussion of the alignment interrupt, refer to the chapter entitled "Interrupts."

When an alignment interrupt is taken, DSISR[12:13] are cleared on the PPC 601. In a 64-bit processor, these bits can be set by several of the 64-bit instructions. These instructions are not supported by the PPC 601.

The PPC 601 will take the alignment interrupt within a memory-forced I/O segment (segment register T = 1 and I/O controller number = 7Fh) if a segment boundary is crossed. Memory-forced I/O segments are outside the scope of the PPC processor specification.

If an instruction causes multiple-accesses and a 4KB (page) boundary is crossed within the bounds of a block defined in the BAT registers, the PPC 601 takes the alignment interrupt.

The specification supports floating-point loads and stores within an I/O segment. An attempt to perform one on the PPC 601 will result in an alignment interrupt.

Any attempt to execute a load/store multiple or load/store string instruction while the processor is operating in little-endian mode results in an alignment interrupt.

Program Interrupt

The entry point for the program interrupt handler is 00700h in the entry point table. For a detailed discussion of the program interrupt, refer to the chapter entitled "Interrupts."

The PPC 601 handles all floating-point interrupts in a precise manner (see the chapter entitled "Interrupts").

The program interrupt is taken when the PPC 601 attempts execution of an instruction with an illegal opcode or an illegal combination of opcode and extended opcode fields (this includes PowerPC instructions not implemented in the PPC 601), or when it attempts execution of an unimplemented optional instruction.

The MSR[FE0] and MSR[FE1] bits are ORed in the PPC 601. Because of this, the processor is enabled to report precise floating-point interrupts if either bit (or both bits) is set to one.

Floating-Point Unavailable Interrupt

The entry point for the floating-point unavailable interrupt handler is 00800h in the entry point table. For a detailed discussion of this interrupt, refer to the chapter entitled "Interrupts."

This interrupt is compliant with the specification.

Decrementer Interrupt

The entry point for the decrementer interrupt handler is 00900h in the entry point table. For a detailed discussion of the decrementer interrupt and operation, refer to the chapter entitled "Interrupts."

This interrupt can be masked by clearing MSR[EE] to zero. When the value in the DEC register decrements and its count is exhausted, the decrementer interrupt is generated (if it is currently unmasked). The DEC decrements at the same rate that the RTC increments. It is driven by the 7.8125MHz RTC input, so it decrements once every 128ns. This interrupt is compliant with the specification, but the format and operation of the DEC register is not. For additional information, refer to the discussion of the DEC register in the chapter entitled "601 User Register and Instruction Set."

System Call Interrupt

The entry point for the system call interrupt handler is 00C00h in the entry point table. For a detailed discussion of the system call interrupt, refer to the chapter entitled "Interrupts."
This interrupt is compliant with the specification.

Processor-Specific Interrupts

I/O Controller Interface Error Interrupt

The entry point for the I/O controller error interrupt handler is 00A00h in the entry point table. This is a processor-specific interrupt. In the specification, an I/O controller error will normally result in a data storage interrupt with DSISR[0] set to one.

This interrupt results when the error bit is set to one in address packet zero returned by the I/O controller in the load or store reply transaction. For a detailed discussion of I/O transactions, refer to the chapter entitled "PPC 601 I/O Transactions."

When this interrupt occurs, it has the following effects on registers:

- SRR0 points to the instruction that follows the load/store that attempted the I/O access.
- SRR1[0:15] are cleared.
- SRR1[16:31] are loaded from MSR[16:31].
- In MSR, the following bits are cleared: EE, PR, FP, FE0, FE1, SE, IT, and DT. The value of ME and IP are not altered.
- DAR points to either the first byte of the operand (for scalar load/stores), or to the first byte in the last word (for multiple string load/stores).
- Refer to the PPC 601 manual for the state of the GPRs.

Run Mode/Trace Interrupt

The entry point for the run mode/trace interrupt handler is 02000h in the entry point table. This is a processor-specific interrupt. This interrupt is enabled under the following circumstances:

- MSR[SE] = 1 enables the single-step (trace)interrupt. When enabled, the trace interrupt is taken on the completion of each instruction that doesn't cause an interrupt or a context change. Examples of instructions that complete without causing the trace interrupt are sc, trap, or rfi.
- HID1[8:9] = 10b enables the run mode interrupt. HID1 is the debug mode register. This bit combination enables the debug breakpoint logic to generate a run mode interrupt if one of the following two conditions are detected: instruction address compare, or branch target address compare.

When the run mode/trace interrupt is taken, the registers settings are:

- SRR0 contains the address of the instruction that caused the interrupt.
- SRR1 loaded from MSR[0:31].
- The following MSR bits are cleared to zero: EE, PR, FP, FE0, FE1, SE, IT, and DT.
- The following MSR bits are unaffected: ME and IP.

The debug mode, also referred to as the run mode, is selected via HID1[1:3]. Table 28-2 defines the available modes.

Table 28-2. Debug Modes

HID1[1:3]	Mode	Description
000b	Normal	Breakpoint detection turned off.
001b	Do not use	
010b	Limited instruction address compare	Program execution proceeds at full speed. Address compare is only performed in Q0. Branches and FPU operations and their associated addresses may not make it to Q0.
011b	Do not use	
100b	Single-step	Interrupt after successful completion of each instruction. See warning in 601 manual.
101b	Do not use	
110b	Full instruction address compare	All instructions are forced through Q0 for the compare. This degrades CPU performance. Breakpoint occurs on instruction address match.
111b	Full branch target address compare	All instructions are forced through Q0 for the compare. This degrades CPU performance. Breakpoint occurs on branch target address match.

MSR Recoverable Interrupt Bit

The specification defines the recoverable interrupt bit (RI) in the MSR register. The PPC 601 doesn't implement this bit. For a revue of the recoverable interrupt bit, refer to the chapter entitled "Interrupts."

Since the MSR[RI] bit is not implemented on the PPC 601, the programmer must utilize some other method to ensure that an interrupt is recoverable.

Interrupt Processing Endian Mode

The specification defines MSR[ILE] to permit the operating system programmer to select the endian mode to operate in when an interrupt handler is entered. When an interrupt occurs, a spec-compliant PowerPC processor copies MSR[ILE] to MSR[LE] after saving LE in SRR1. This automatically places the processor in the desired endian mode for interrupt handling.

The PPC 601 doesn't implement the MSR[ILE] bit. It is therefore up to the programmer that writes an interrupt handler to select the desired endian mode upon entering the interrupt handler.

A complete discussion of endian-related issues can be found in the chapter entitled "Big vs. Little-Endian."

Chapter 29

The Previous Chapter

The previous chapter provides a description of the PPC 601 processor's implementation of interrupts. Any deviations from the architecture specification are described.

This Chapter

This chapter provides a description of the PPC 601 processor's MMU implementation and describes any deviations from the architecture specification.

The Next Chapter

The next chapter provides a detailed description of the PPC 601 processor's cache and MU implementation.

MMU's Relationship to Other Units

Figure 29-1 picture illustrates the relationship of the instruction unit, memory management unit (MMU), integer unit and the unified code/data cache. The floating-point unit is capable of performing floating-point load and store operations, but it uses addresses specified in the integer unit's GPR register set. This being the case, the floating-point unit depends on the integer unit to submit memory addresses to the MMU for it.

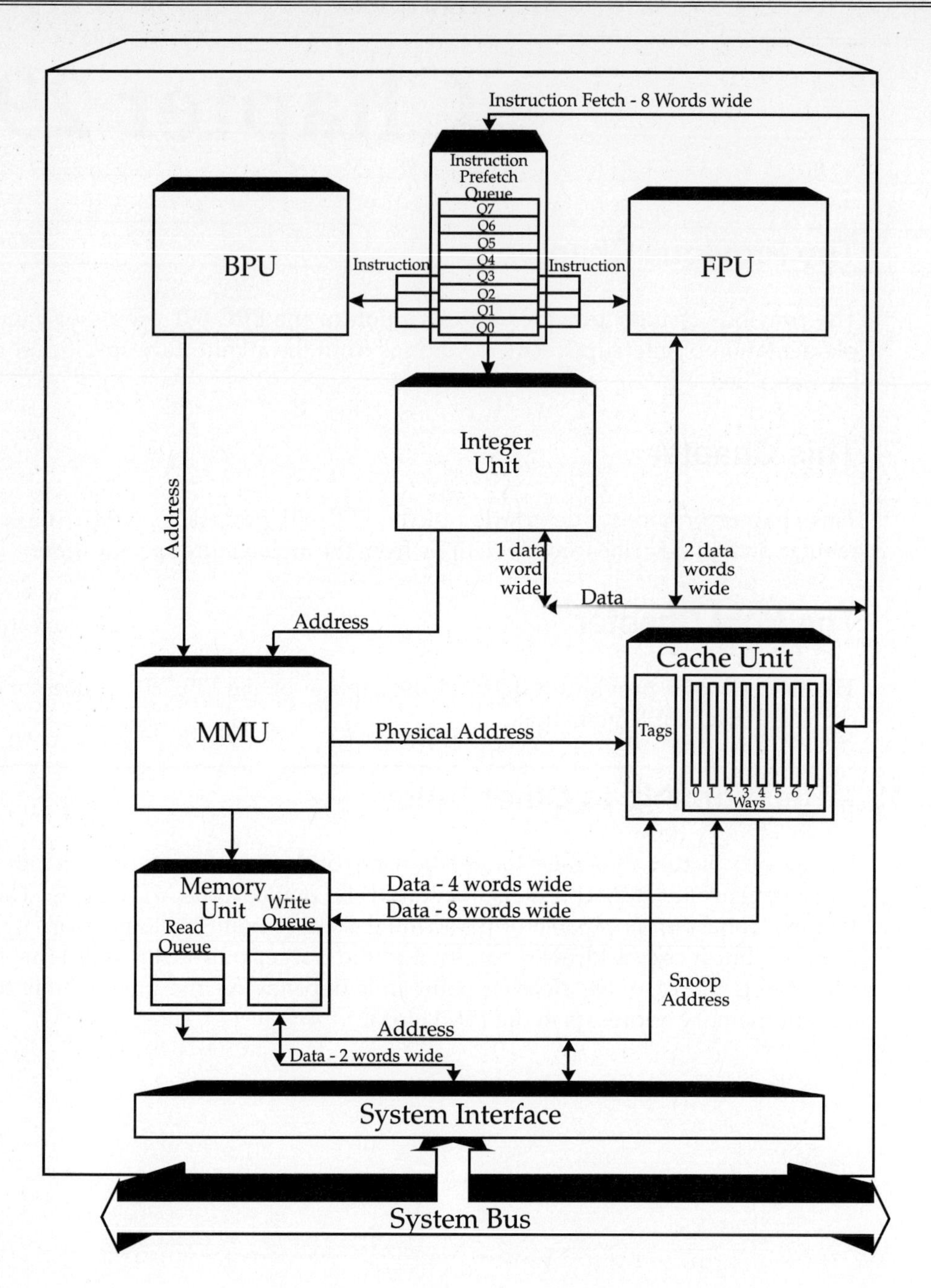

Figure 29-1. Relationship of MMU to Other Units

Chapter 29: PPC 601 MMU Operation

PPC 601 MMU Overview

A complete description of the block address translation process may be found in the chapter entitled "Block — Large Memory Region." A complete description of the page address translation process may be found in the chapter entitled "Virtual paging." The PPC 601 MMU contains the following major elements:

- ITLB (*601 processor-specific; outside scope of PowerPC architecture specification*).
- Page translation logic.
- Block translation logic.

Figure 29-2 illustrates the relationship of the ITLB to the BAT and page address translation logic.

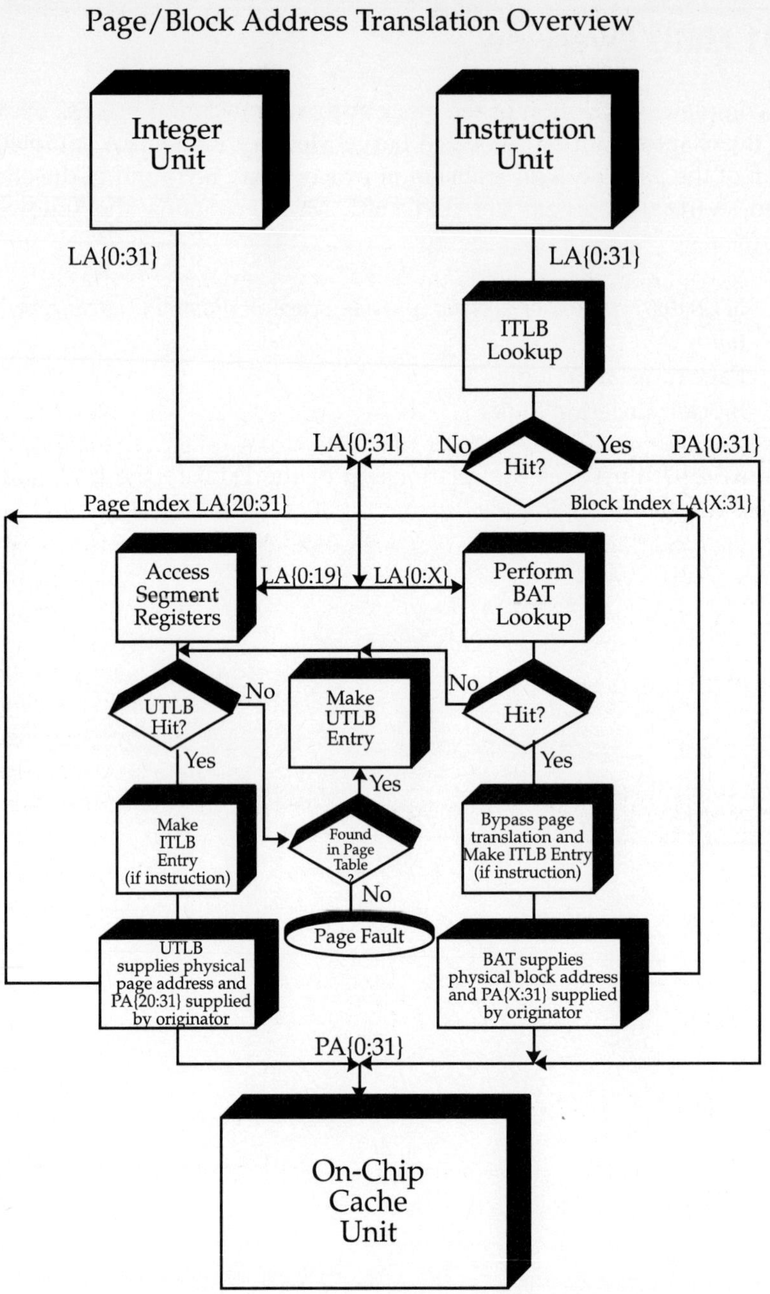

Page/Block Address Translation Overview

Integer Unit
Instruction Unit
LA{0:31}
LA{0:31}
ITLB Lookup
LA{0:31}
No
Hit?
Yes
PA{0:31}
Page Index LA{20:31}
Block Index LA{X:31}
Access Segment Registers
LA{0:19}
LA{0:X}
Perform BAT Lookup
UTLB Hit?
No
Make UTLB Entry
No
Hit?
Yes
Yes
Yes
Make ITLB Entry (if instruction)
Found in Page Table ?
No
Bypass page translation and Make ITLB Entry (if instruction)
Page Fault
UTLB supplies physical page address and PA{20:31} supplied by originator
BAT supplies physical block address and PA{X:31} supplied by originator
PA{0:31}
On-Chip Cache Unit

Figure 29-2. 601 MMU's Address Translation Logic

ITLB

The instruction translation lookaside buffer, or ITLB, is a performance enhancement tool outside the scope of the PowerPC processor specification. It is a small, very fast lookaside cache that can hold up to four entries. Each entry can contain either:

- a copy of the block address translation information from a BAT register pair, or
- a page table entry, or PTE.

When the instruction fetcher generates an effective address to request the next instruction from memory, the effective address is submitted first to the ITLB for a lookup. In the event of a hit on the ITLB, the information (previously copied from a BAT or a PTE) from the entry is used to perform the effective to physical address translation and also supplies the access rights and caching rules (WIM bits). This leaves the BAT and page translation logic available to simultaneously service an address translation request from the integer unit.

When there is a miss on the ITLB, the BAT or page logic performs the translation of the address from effective to physical address. When a match is found on a BAT register pair or a page table entry, the BAT or PTE contents are copied into the ITLB to service subsequent instruction fetch requests. Although the ITLB is quite small, it can yield a very high hit rate for instruction accesses. This is due to the fact that most program execution is sequential in nature, so a block or page mapping in the ITLB will typically yield a high hit rate as the prefetcher issues instruction fetch requests from sequential word addresses.

Block Address Translation (BAT) Logic

Compliancy with Specification

The PPC 601's block translation logic is non-compliant with the specification in the following respects:

- The four DBAT register pairs are missing.
- The four IBAT register pairs are actually used for both load/store and instruction address translation (in effect, they are really universal BATs, or UBATs).
- The layout of the fields within the IBAT registers is non-compliant with the specification.
- The IBAT registers may be used to define a block from 128KB to 8MB in size, rather than from 128KB to 256MB as stated in the specification.
- The G, or guarded, bit is not implemented.

Upper BAT Register

The upper BAT register format is defined in figure 29-3. The BLPI field (block logical page index) defines the effective start address of the block. It is a rule that a block must start on an address divisible by its size. The WIM bits define the cache-related rules within the block. The key bit selected by the privilege level of the currently-running program is used in conjunction with the PP bit field to define the access rights of the current program within the block. If a user program is currently running, MSR[PR] = 1 selects the Ku bit to be used with the PP bits. If a supervisor program is currently running, MSR[PR] = 0 selects the Ks bit to be used. Table 29-1 defines the access rights within the block.

Table 29-1. Access Rights Within Block

Key Bit	PP Bits	Access Rights
0	00b	Read/write.
0	01b	Read/write.
0	10b	Read/write.
0	11b	Read-only.
1	00b	None.
1	01b	Read-only.
1	10b	Read/write.
1	11b	Read-only.

Lower BAT Register

The upper BAT register format is defined in figure 29-4. The physical block number field is used to specify the physical start address of the block in memory. The start address of the block must be on address divisible by the block size. The block size is specified in the block size mask field (BSM). The block size may be specified in the range from 128KB to 8MB. In order for the BAT logic to compare an effective address to the block defined in any of the four BAT register pairs, a BAT register pair must contain a valid block definition. When the operating system programmer sets up a valid block definition in a BAT register pair, the V, or valid, bit must be set to one.

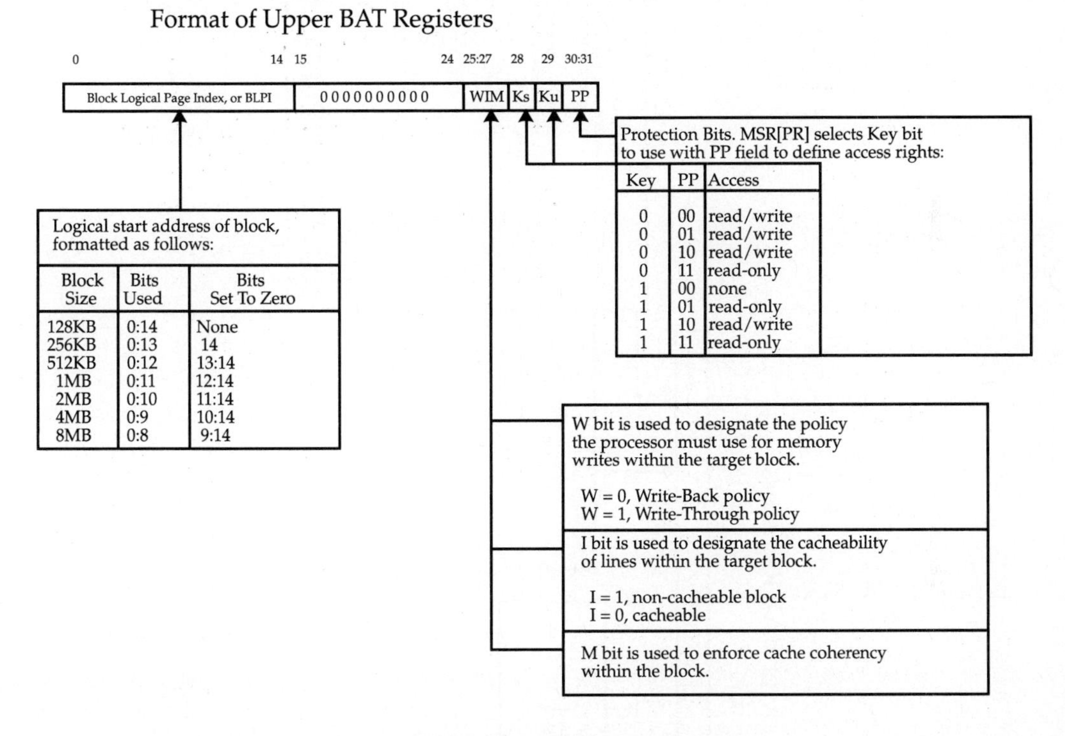

Figure 29-3. Upper BAT Register

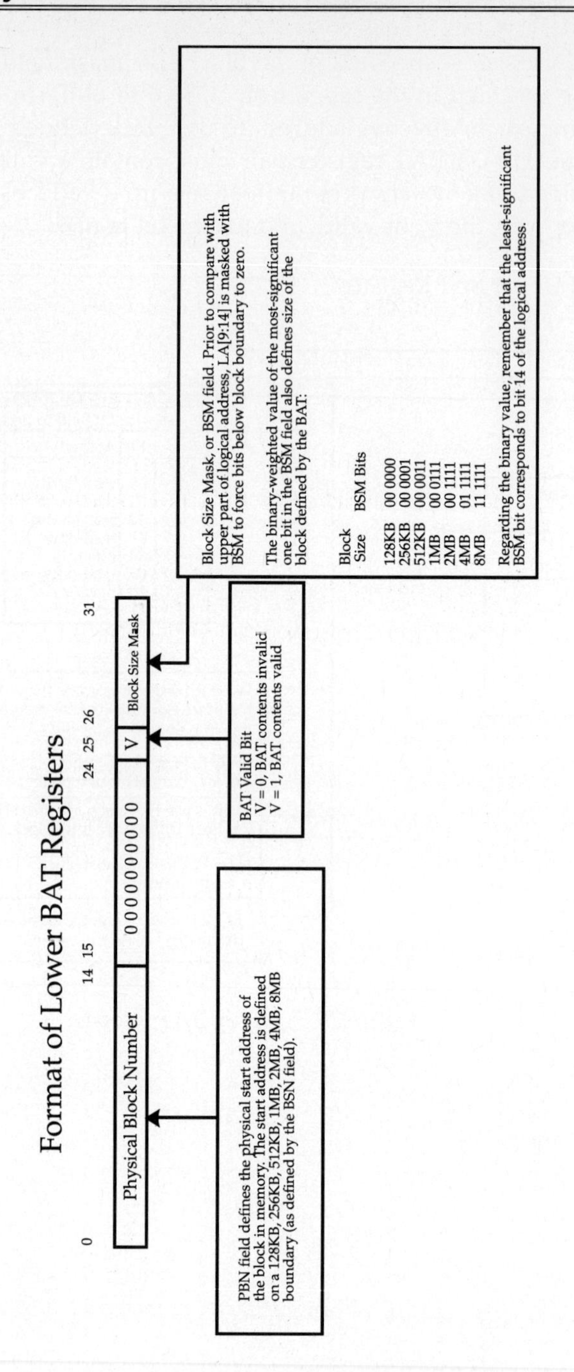

Format of Lower BAT Registers
0
14 15
24 25 26
31
Physical Block Number
0000000000
V
Block Size Mask
PBN field defines the physical start address of the block in memory. The start address is defined on a 128KB, 256KB, 512KB, 1MB, 2MB, 4MB, 8MB boundary (as defined by the BSN field).
BAT Valid Bit
V = 0, BAT contents invalid
V = 1, BAT contents valid
Block Size Mask, or BSM field. Prior to compare with upper part of logical address, LA[9:14] is masked with BSM to force bits below block boundary to zero.
The binary-weighted value of the most-significant one bit in the BSM field also defines size of the block defined by the BAT:
Block Size
BSM Bits
128KB 00 0000
256KB 00 0001
512KB 00 0011
1MB 00 0111
2MB 00 1111
4MB 01 1111
8MB 11 1111
Regarding the binary value, remember that the least-significant BSM bit corresponds to bit 14 of the logical address.

Figure 29-4. Lower BAT Register

Paging Logic

Segment Registers

The PPC 601 segment registers are compliant with the specification. Figure 29-5 illustrates the contents of the segment register for both a memory and an I/O segment. When defining an I/O segment, the following characteristics should be noted:

- The lower hex digit in the segment register supplies the upper hex digit of the I/O port address supplied to the I/O controller in address packet one of the I/O transaction. The lower seven hex digits of the I/O port address supplied in address packet one are supplied from the lower seven digits of the effective address.
- If the I/O bus unit controller (BUC) number in the segment register is 7Fh, the access performed is a memory access rather than an I/O access. This is referred to as a memory-forced I/O operation.

For a detailed discussion of I/O and memory-forced I/O transactions, refer to the chapter entitled "PPC 601 I/O Transactions."

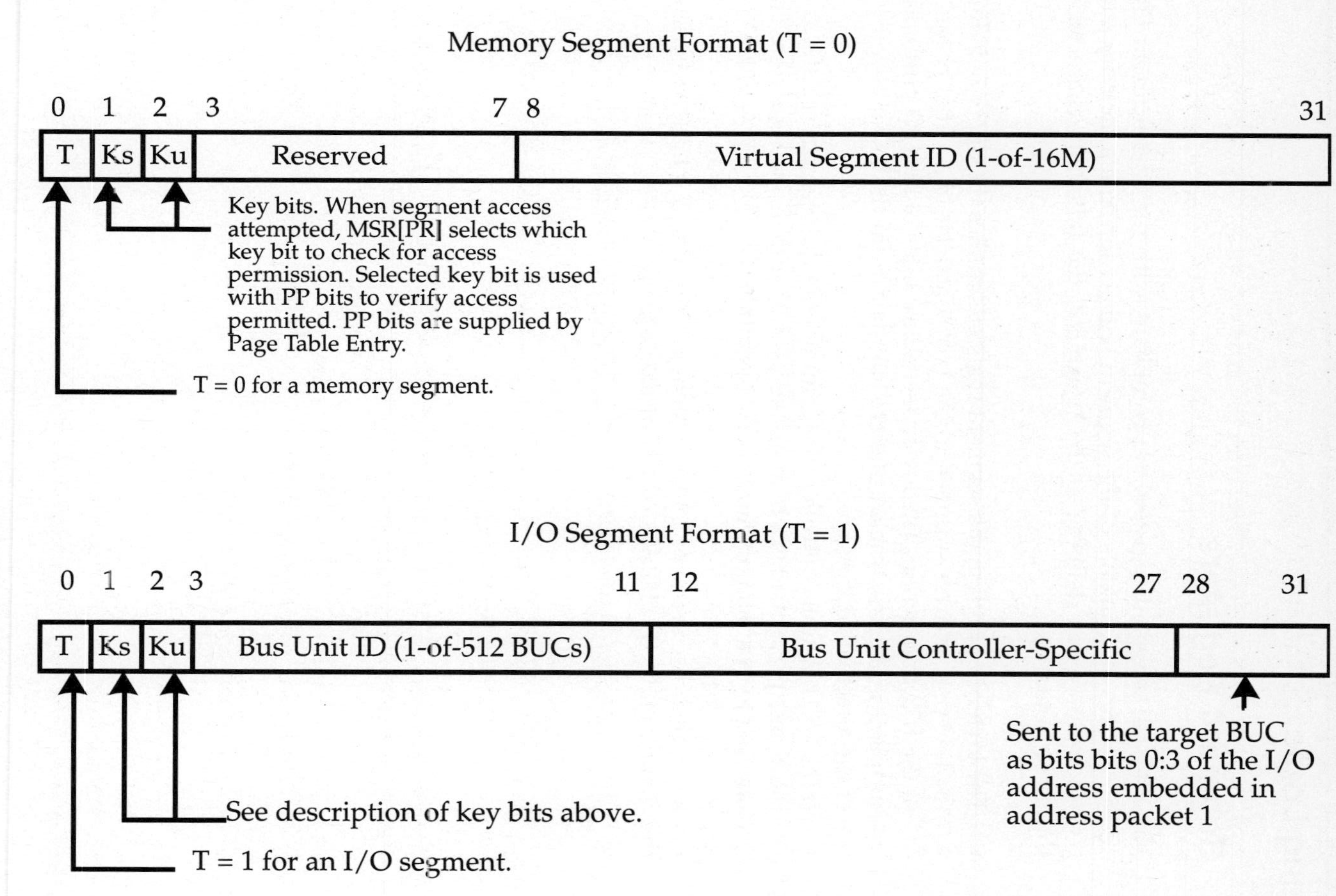

Figure 29-5. Segment Register Format

Page Table Entry (PTE) Format

Each PTE is comprised of a two word entry in the page table. Bits 25:28 in the second doubleword are designated as the WIMG bits in the specification. The G bit is not implemented in the 601 and bit 28 of the entry must therefore be zero.

Page Address Translation

The PPC 601 processor's page address translation logic is compliant with the specification and operates as described in the chapter entitled "Virtual Paging." The only exception is that the G bit is not implemented, so a page of memory space may not be marked as guarded.

TLB

It implements a TLB to provide a fast access cache for page table entries. It is implemented as a universal TLB, or UTLB — i.e., it is used to cache both data and code page table entries. The PPC 601's paging logic is illustrated in figure 29-6. The UTLB is implemented as a two-way set-associative cache with 128 entries per cache bank (or way). This means that it can hold a total of 256 PTEs at a given instant in time.

The lower seven bits of the page address are used to select a pair of UTLB entries to compare the target virtual segment ID and page number to. If a match occurs, the PTE entry from the UTLB supplies the 20-bit physical memory page address. The lower 12 bits of the effective address supply the lower 12 bits of the physical memory address and indicate the exact start location of the operand within the memory page. The WIM bits from the UTLB entry define the caching rules, while the selected Key bit from the segment register and the PP bits from the UTLB entry are used to check for an access violation.

When TLB Miss Occurs

When a memory address is submitted to the TLB resulting in a TLB miss, the virtual segment ID from the segment register and the page number from the effective address, EA[4:19], must be scanned for in the memory-based page table to determine if the target page is currently-resident in physical memory. A detailed description of the page table scan process can be found in the chapter entitled "Virtual Paging."

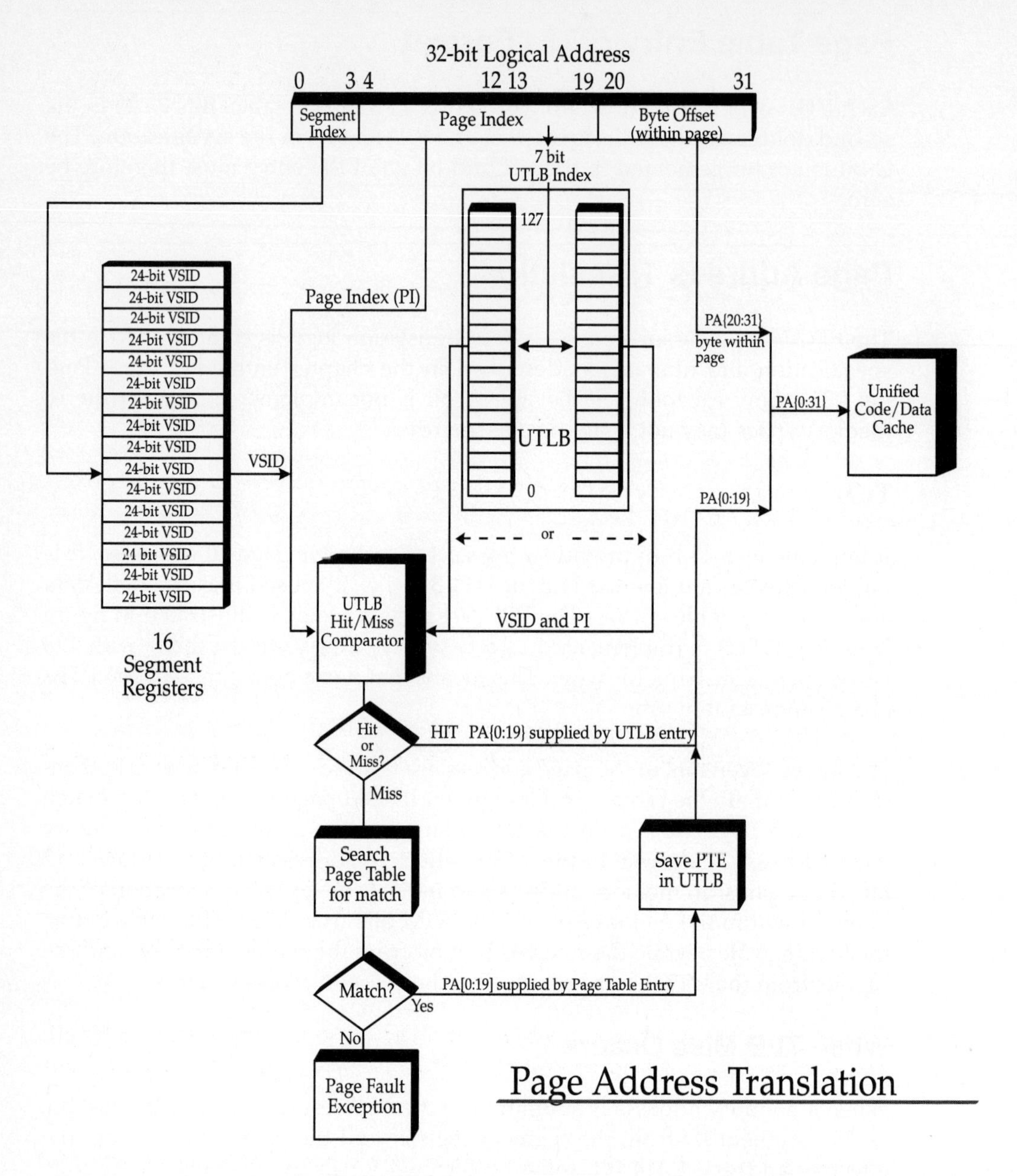

Figure 29-6. Page Address Translation Process

Chapter 30

The Previous Chapter

The previous chapter provided a description of the PPC 601 processor's MMU implementation and described any deviations from the architecture specification.

This Chapter

This chapter provides a detailed description of the PPC 601 processor's cache and MU implementation.

The Next Chapter

The next chapter provides a detailed description of every condition and/or instruction that can cause the PPC 601 processor to perform a transaction on the external bus.

Cache View of Memory Space

Figure 30-1 illustrates the PPC 601 processor's L1 cache view of memory space. The cache views the 4GB memory space as being subdivided into one million pages, each of which is 4KB in length. Each page starts on an address boundary divisible by 4K. The pages are numbered from page zero through page 2^{20} (1M pages).

Each page is in turn divided into 64 lines, each of which is 64 bytes in length. Each line starts on an address boundary divisible by 64. The lines are numbered from 0 – 63.

Each line is divided into two sectors, each of which is 32 bytes in length. Each sector starts on an address boundary divisible by 32. The sectors are numbered as sector 0 and sector 1.

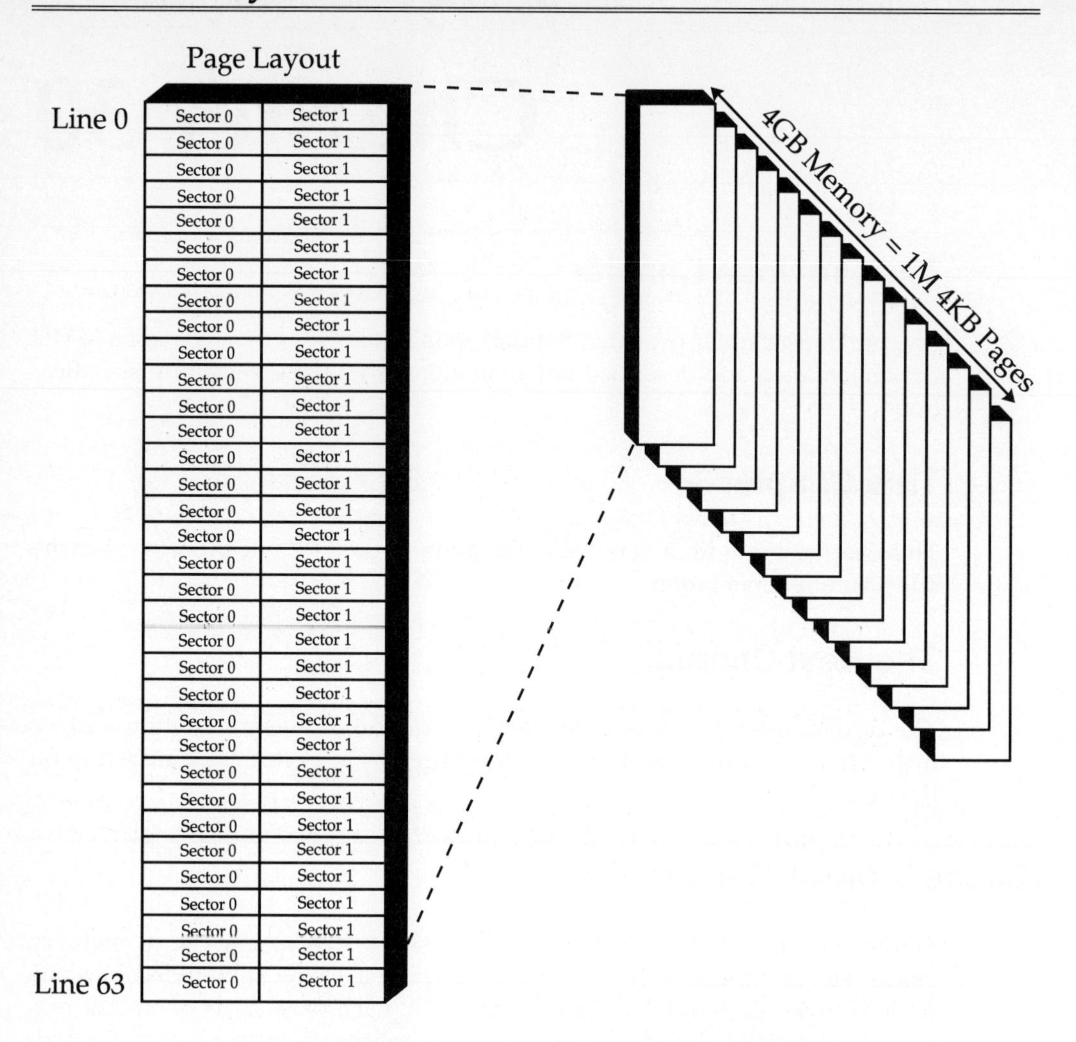

Figure 30-1. Cache's View of Memory Space

Cache Interpretation of Physical Memory Address

Assuming that the currently-addressed operand or instruction is within a page or block that is cacheable (I = 0), the physical memory address produced by the MMU is submitted to the cache for a lookup. From the cache's perspective, the location currently being addressed lies within a sector that lies within a line that lies within a page. At this instant in time, the target sector is either present in the cache or absent. In order to determine this, the cache must search the cache, or a portion of the cache, for a match on the page, line and sector. The physical memory address, or PA, is interpreted as follows:

- The upper 20 bits of the physical address, PA[0:19], identify one of the 1M pages as the target page.
- The next lower six bits, PA[20:25], identify one of 64 lines within the page as the target line.
- The next bit, PA[26], identifies the target sector within the line (sector 0 or sector 1).

Cache Organization

Figure 30-2 illustrates the overall organization of the cache. It is an 8-way, set-associative, unified code/data cache. It caches both code and data. It is organized into eight banks, or ways. The ways are referred to as way zero through way seven.

Each way contains a storage array to store sectors in, a directory to keep track of which sectors are currently stored in each array entry, the source of each sector (the tag field in the figure), and the current state of each sector (the current state of a sector may be M, E, S, or I).

Each of the storage arrays are organized in exactly the same manner as a page in memory — it is divided into 64 lines, each consisting of sector 0 and sector 1. When the cache fetches a new sector from memory and stores it in one of the eight ways, the sector will be stored in precisely the same position within the selected way as it occupied within its source memory page. The source page address is stored in the directory entry as a tag (in the tag field). The sector's state bits are set to indicate its current state (M, E, S, or I).

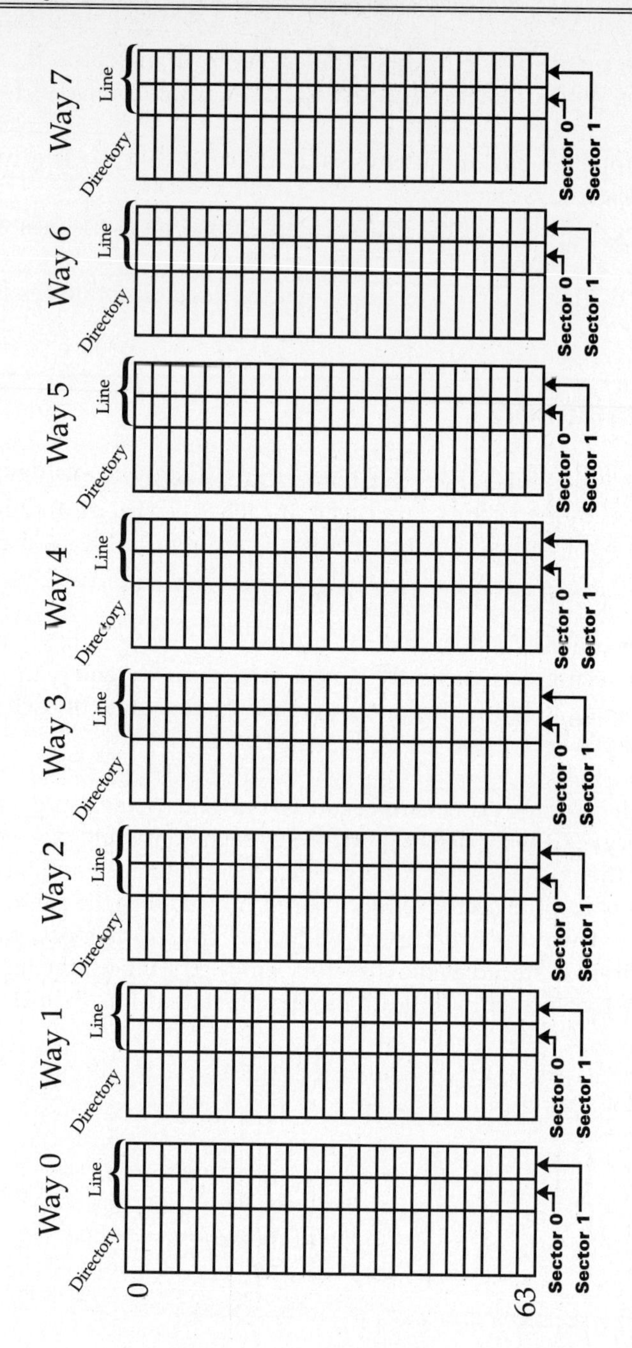

Figure 30-2. Basic Cache Organization

Intro to Cache Lookup Mechanism

One approach that the cache designer could take would be to compare the target page, line and sector number to every entry in the cache until either a match is found or the end of the cache is reached. This implies terrible performance and this not the way it is done in the PPC 601.

Rather than search the entire cache, it indexes into the cache and picks a relatively small subset of entries to compare against. The designer could use the target page number as the index into the directory. If this were the case, the cache directory would have to be 1M, or 2^{20}, deep (because the page number can be any of 1M numbers). Since this approach results in a huge cache directory, the target page number is not used as the index. Rather, the target line number is used as the index. Since this number will only range from 0 – 63, the cache directory only has to be 64 deep. This is a reasonable size.

Index into Cache Directory

The cache uses the target line number to index into the directories of all eight cache ways simultaneously. This selects a set of eight directory entries to compare against.

As an example, if the target line were five, the cache would select entry five in each way's directory to compare against. Entry five in each cache way will only be used to store a copy of the sectors comprising line five from a page. Since there is an entry five in each way's directory, the cache could have a copy of line 5 (sector 0, sector 1, or both sectors) from eight different pages in memory stored in the cache at a given instant in time (one in entry five within each cache way).

Composition of Valid Entry

The cache has a copy of a sector from memory if the sector's state bits are set to the M, E, or S state. It does not have a copy if the state bits are set to the I state. If the copy is valid, the page number it was fetched from is stored in the tag field corresponding to the line in this way.

Exclusive (E) State

The cache marks a copy of a sector as exclusive if it has the only copy of the sector and the sector has not been modified since it was read from memory. The memory and cache sectors are mirror image of each other.

Shared (S) State

The cache marks a copy of a sector as shared under two sets of circumstances:

- One or more other caches indicated that they also had a copy of the sector when this processor was reading the sector into its cache.
- When this processor read the sector from memory, it originally marked it exclusive because no other cache indicated that it had a copy. Subsequently, however, another processor indicated that it was reading a copy of the sector from memory, so this processor changed the state of its copy from E to S.

The sector has not been modified since it was read from memory. The memory and cache sectors are mirror image of each other.

Modified (M) State

The cache marks a copy a sector as modified if it has modified the sector since it was read from memory. This means that the sector in memory is currently stale.

Cache Lookup

Figure 30-3 illustrates one cache way and its directory. The cache simultaneously compares for the following in the selected set of directory entries:

- the target page number is compared to the page number stored in the selected tag field within each way's directory (the term tag is synonymous with the term page).
- the target sector within the line must be valid (M, E, or S).

The lookup results in either a hit or a miss. A hit results if the page matches and the target sector is marked valid (M, E or S). In the event of a miss, the cache issues a request to the memory unit, or MU, to read the target sector from memory. The MU in turn issues a request to the system interface. The system interface will acquire the bus and transfer the sector from memory. As it is read, it will be passed back to the cache. This process is described in the next section of this chapter.

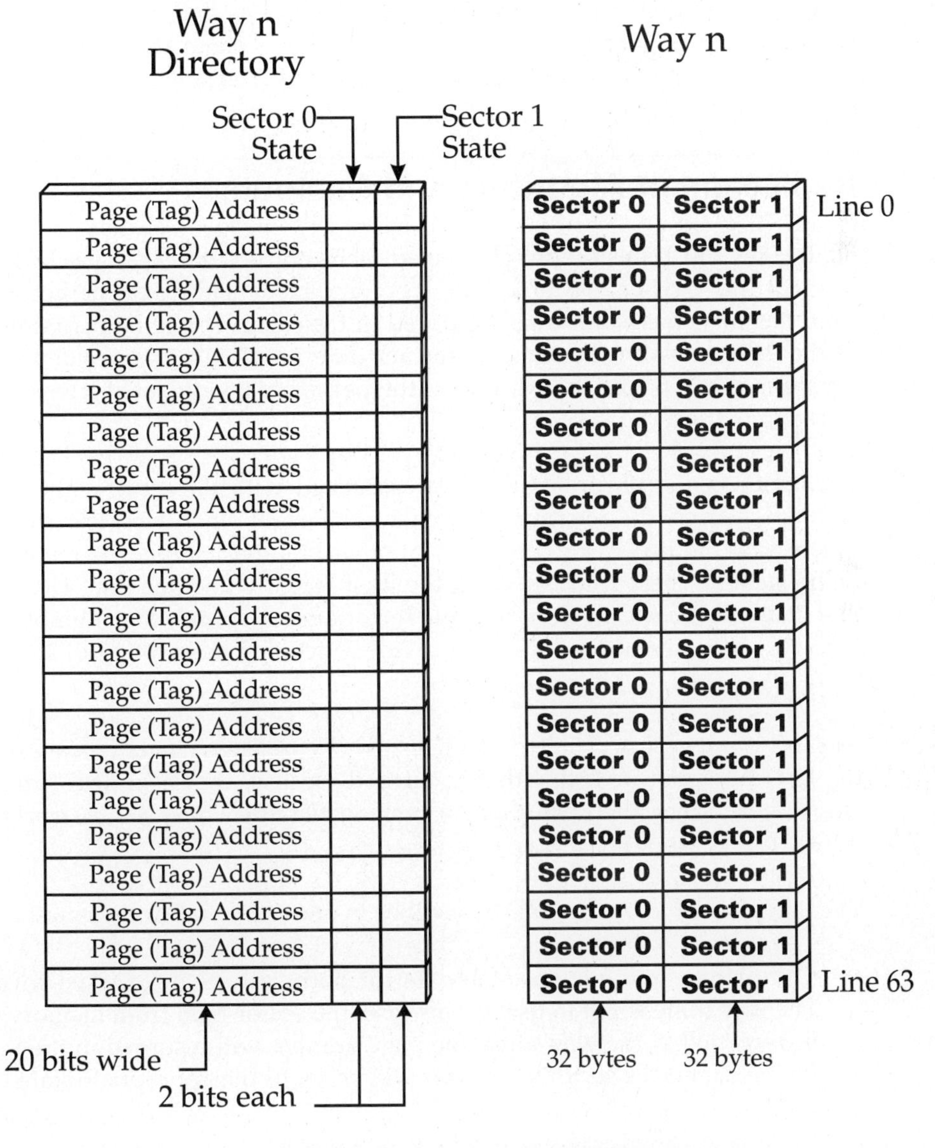

Figure 30-3. Structure of Single Cache Way

Cache Sector Fill Operation

The process of reading a sector from memory and placing it in the cache is referred to as a cache sector fill operation. A sector fill is initiated when a miss occurs in the cache. This section describes this process. It should be noted that a detailed discussion of the PPC 601 processor's bus and transaction timing can be found in subsequent chapters. The discussion in this chapter of the memory read operation to fetch the target sector from memory is general in nature.

Replacement Algorithm and Castouts

Figure 30-4 illustrates the set of selected cache entries that were checked for a hit or a miss. When the processor has completed reading the target sector from memory, the sector must be stored in the cache. It will be placed in one of the eight ways in the same sector and line number that it resided in the source memory page. The address of the page that it originated from will be stored in that way's tag field.

The least-recently used, or LRU, bits associated with the set of eight entries will be checked to determine which of the eight lines was least-recently touched by the processor core or by another bus master (via snooping). The cache makes a "best effort" to track the least-recently touched line. This is the line that will be used to store the new sector and its source page number. The PPC 601 documentation does not provide a detailed description of the LRU bit field.

At this instant in time, some of the lines may be in use while others are not. If the LRU bits point to a line that is currently in use, the cache will store the new sector in that line ***even if one or more of the other lines are currently not in use***.

The line pointed to by the LRU bits will be in one of the following states:

- **Completely invalid**. The state bits for both sectors are marked invalid. The way's line is not in use. In this case, the sector read from memory will be recorded in the way's line, the page number will recorded in the way's tag field, and the sector's state bits will be set to the appropriate state (E, S or M).

- **In use, but the line is from a different page**. In this case, the page number currently in the way's tag field must be overwritten with the new page number. The one or two sectors from the line in the old page must be cast out of the cache. If neither has been modified since being read into the cache, both are invalidated. If either or both have been modified, they will be immediately cast out to the MU to be written back to memory. This frees up the targeted cache entry to receive the new sector being read from memory by the MU. The new line is read from memory, placed in the proper sector in the way's line, and the sector's state bits are set to the appropriate state (E, S, or M).
- **In use and the line is from the target page**. In this case, the new line is read from memory, placed in the proper sector in the way's line, and the sector's state bits are set to the appropriate state (E, S, or M).

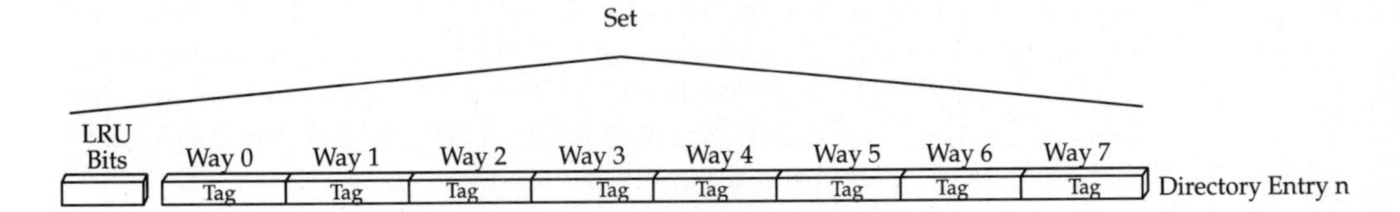

Figure 30-4. Selected Set

Memory Read Bus Transaction Initiation

In order to read the target sector from memory, the processor must first acquire the address bus to broadcast the address and transaction type. A detailed description of this process may be found in the chapter entitled "PPC 601 Memory Address Phase."

After acquiring ownership of the address bus, the PPC 601 broadcasts the address and transaction type. The PPC 601 processor uses a doubleword address bus and has a doubleword-wide data bus. Using its address bus, it identifies a block of eight memory locations starting at an address divisible by eight. In this case, the transaction type will be a burst memory read transaction. By definition, a burst read is a 32 byte read.

In addition to the address and transaction type, the PPC 601 also indicates whether other processors should snoop the memory address in their caches. If the WIM bit setting for this page or block has M = 1, the processor asserts its GBL# output. This is the snoop command signal that instructs all other processors/caching entities to perform a lookup in their caches and to report the result of the snoop back to the processor that initiated the memory read.

Snoop and Snoop Result

Upon detecting GBL# asserted, all other processors/caching entities perform a cache lookup. Using a common set of snoop result signals, they will report one of the following indications back to the processor that initiated the transaction:

- **Snoop miss**. None of the snoopers have a copy of the target sector in their caches. The processor that initiated the memory read can proceed to read the sector from memory. Upon completing the memory read, the sector should be placed in the cache in the exclusive state (because no other cache has copy).
- **Snoop hit on a clean sector**. This indicates that one of the snoopers has copy of the sector in the exclusive state, or that one or more of the snoopers' caches have a copy of the target sector in the shared state. In other words, it has not been modified since being read into the snooper's cache. The processor that initiated the memory read can proceed to read the sector from memory. Upon completing the memory read, the sector should be placed in the cache in the shared state (because other caches have copies).
- **Snoop hit on a modified sector**. This indicates that the snooper's cache has a copy of the target sector in the modified state. In other words, it has been modified since being read into the snooper's cache. The processor that initiated the memory read will not perform the data read from memory. It will retry the transaction later.
- **Snooper(s) busy**. One or more of the snoopers cannot currently snoop the address. It would be dangerous for the memory read to proceed (because one of the busy snoopers may have a copy of the target sector in the modified state). The processor that initiated the memory read will not perform the data read from memory. It will retry the transaction later.

Data Transfer Sequence

When the cache experiences a cache miss and reads a sector from memory, it uses a four-beat burst read transaction. Since the sector consists of 32 bytes of information and the PPC 601 can only read eight bytes at a time (because it only has eight data paths), it must perform four data transfers in order to transfer all 32 bytes from memory. The processor only issues a start address for the burst transaction.

Every sector in memory starts on a address divisible by 32 and consists of four groups of eight bytes each. The processor could have been designed to always read the sector from memory in sequential order.

For example, if the start address of the sector were 00000100h, it would consists of the following four doublewords in memory:

- 00000100h – 00000107h
- 00000108h – 0000010Fh
- 00000110h – 00000117h
- 00000118h – 0000011Fh

If a miss occurred on the cache anywhere in this memory address range, the processor could be designed to read the four doublewords from memory in sequential order. This would result in good performance if the data or code item originally requested resided in the first doubleword, but would result in poor to very poor performance if the requested item were in any of the last three doublewords that comprise the sector.

Optimally, the processor would be designed to always request the doubleword first that contains the item that the integer, floating-point or instruction unit is stalled on. The PPC 601 considers the four doublewords that comprise the sector to be organized as two pairs of doublewords. In the earlier example, doublewords 00000100h and 00000108h comprise the first pair, while doublewords 00000110h and 00000118h comprise the second pair. On a cache miss, the processor always reads the two pairs from memory in the following order: the pair containing the desired item is fetched first, in sequential order; followed by the other pair in sequential order. The start address placed on the address bus is the quadword-aligned start address of the first pair to be transferred.

Table 30-1 defines the doubleword transfer order. The cases documented in the first and third rows result in excellent performance. The desired item is transferred back to the processor immediately in the first doubleword. The cases documented in the second and fourth rows, however, result in less than optimal performance — the processor core is stalled while the first doubleword is transferred. The load or instruction fetch that resulted in the cache miss cannot complete until the second doubleword is read.

Table 30-1. Sector Fill Order

If Desired Item Is In DW	1st DW Transferred Is	2nd DW	3rd DW	4th DW
00000100h	00000100h	00000108h	00000110h	00000118h
00000108h	00000100h	00000108h	00000110h	00000118h
00000110h	00000110h	00000118h	00000100h	00000108h
00000118h	00000110h	00000118h	00000100h	00000108h

The MU accumulates the first two doublewords read and then forwards them to the cache. It then accumulates the second two doublewords and forwards them to the cache. Once the entire cache sector has been transferred to the cache, it can record the sector into the cache.

Entering Sector in Cache

Figure 30 5 illustrates the structure of a cache way. The sector just read from memory is recorded in the cache way selected by the current LRU bit setting. It is recorded in the same line it resided in within its source memory page and in its same sector position within the line. The page address it was read from is stored in the line's tag field. The sector's state bits are set to the state indicated by the snoop result (exclusive or shared). The PPC 601 documentation does not define the encoding of the state bits, but does state that there two state bits for each sector. This makes sense, since a sector can be in one of four possible states: M, E, S or I.

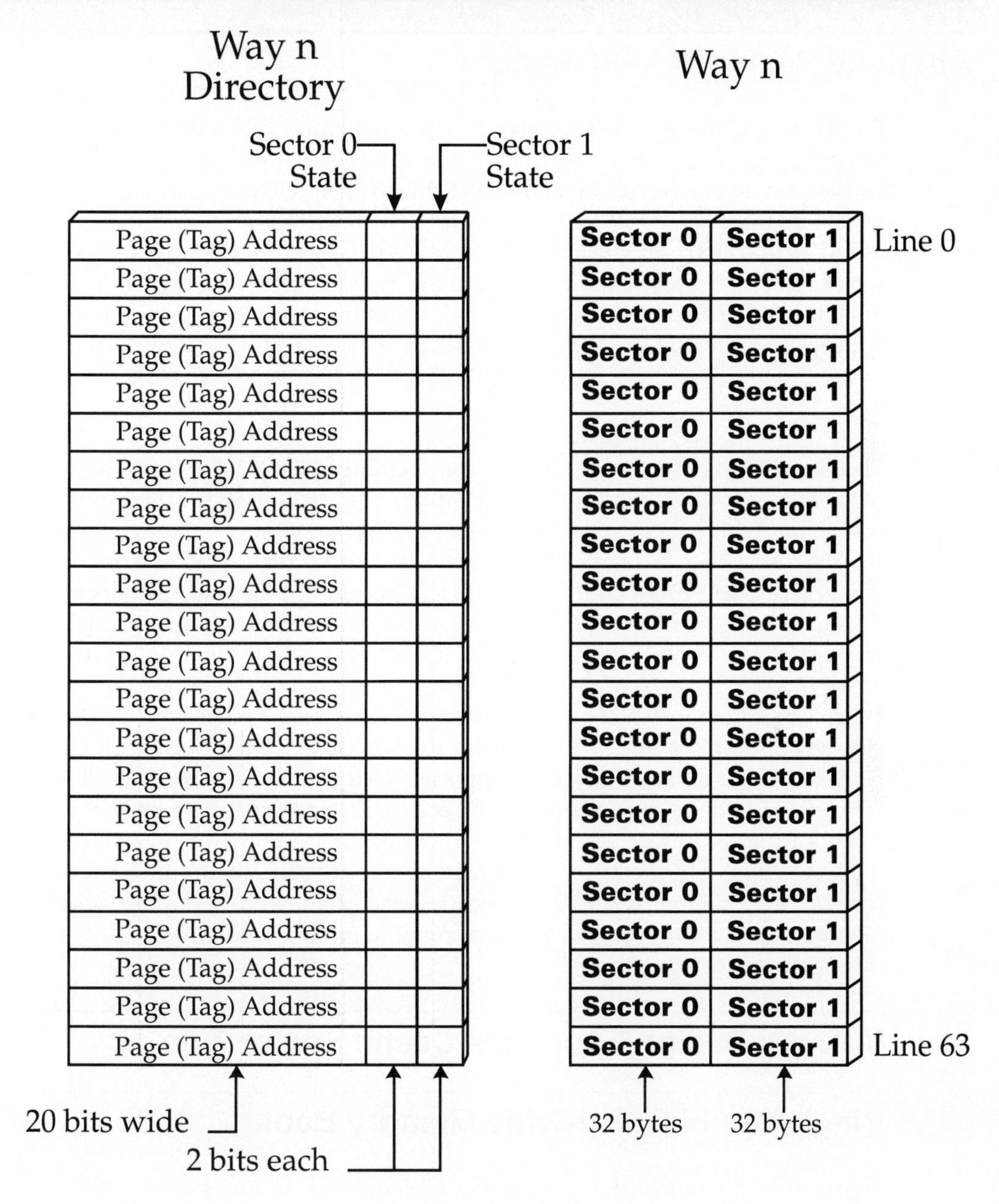

Figure 30-5. Structure of Cache Way

Alternate Sector Reload Feature

Bits 26 and 27 in the HID0 register are feature control bits that the operating system programmer may utilize to enable/disable the alternate sector reload feature. Bit 26 is referred to as the DRF bit (disable reload on fetch) and controls alternate sector reload on an instruction fetch cache miss. Bit 27 is referred as the DRL bit (disable reload on load/store) and controls alternate sector reload on a load or store cache miss. The default state of these two bits after removal of reset is cleared (zero), enabling alternate sector reload for both instruction fetch and load/store cache misses. Setting the respective bit to a one will disable alternate sector reload for the respective type of cache miss.

The process used to read a sector from memory after a cache miss was described in previous sections of this chapter. The cache issues a high-priority full-sector read request to the MU (memory unit) to read the sector containing the requested data (or code) from memory. This sector is one of a pair that comprise a 64 byte line in the cache. At this instant in time, the other sector of the line may not yet be in the cache (because nothing from that sector has been requested yet).

When the alternate sector reload feature is enabled (respective HID0 bit cleared to zero), the MU will automatically schedule a low-priority full-sector read in its read buffer to read the opposing sector into the cache as well. It is scheduled as a low-priority operation because the processor core has not indicated a need for any of the information within this sector. If, before this read request is issued to the bus, a higher-priority read request from the processor core occurs (due to a cache miss) and the read queue is full, the low-priority read for the alternate sector is purged from the read queue and is replaced by the high-priority read request.

Main Memory Design Expedites Cache Sector Fills

Single Doubleword-Wide Memory Bank

Figure 30-6 illustrates main memory implemented as one bank of doubleword-wide DRAM. If the main array of DRAM memory were organized in this manner, the DRAM controller would have to perform four DRAM accesses to read each of the four doublewords and send them to the processor. Multiple wait states would be inserted into each of the four data beats of the

4-beat burst read transaction. This results in less than optimal performance when performing cache block fill, push-back and cast out operations.

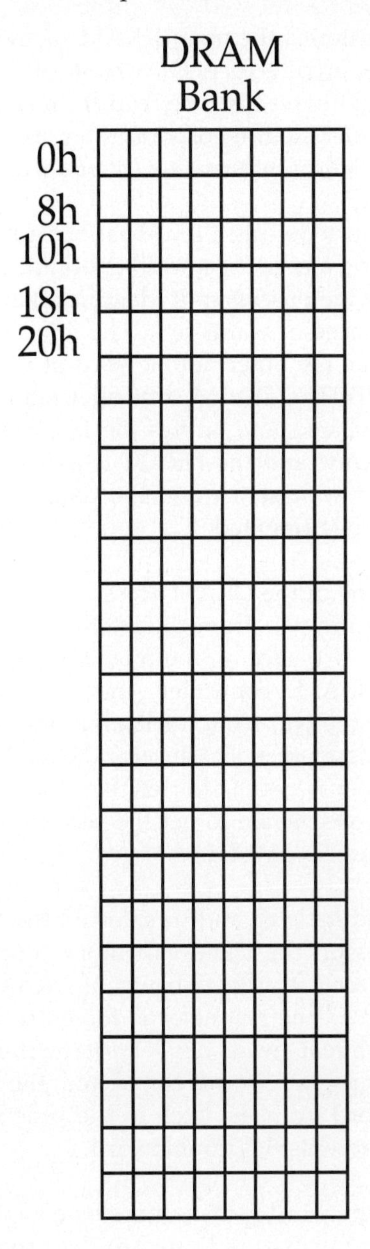

Figure 30-6. Single Main Memory DRAM Bank

2-Way Interleaved Memory

Figure 30-7 illustrates the main DRAM memory organized in a 2-way, interleaved memory architecture. Each bank of DRAM is 64-bits wide — a doubleword, or eight bytes, may be read from each DRAM bank with one access. The memory subsystem incorporates a data latch that can hold two doublewords, or 16 bytes, of information (in other words, half of a sector).

When the memory detects a four-beat burst read, this indicates that a processor is performing a cache sector fill operation. Using the start doubleword address issued by the processor, it identifies the start address of the doubleword pair that the processor wants first. The first doubleword of the selected pair is in bank A, while the other doubleword of the pair is in the adjacent doubleword of bank B. The DRAM controller simultaneously performs a memory read from both banks and latches the 16 bytes of data. Since this involves accessing the DRAM and the DRAM is a slow access device, the processor is forced to insert wait states into the data access while it waits for the first doubleword to be presented.

Upon completion of the DRAM access, the DRAM controller outputs the first doubleword of the pair from the latch to the requesting processor and indicates the data's presence on the bus. The processor accepts the first doubleword. The DRAM controller then immediately outputs the second doubleword of the pair from the latch to the processor and indicates its presence. The processor accepts the second doubleword. The duration of the second data transfer is much shorter than the first because the DRAM did not have to be accessed again to get the second doubleword. Rather, it was supplied by a fast access data latch.

Having emptied its latch and transferred the first doubleword pair to the requesting processor, the DRAM memory controller immediately initiates another memory read from both banks of DRAM to read the other doubleword pair into its latch. The processor is forced to insert wait states into the third data transfer while it awaits delivery of the third doubleword of the cache sector. When the memory read is completed, the memory subsystem outputs the third doubleword from the latch to the processor and indicates its presence. The processor accepts this doubleword.

The fourth doubleword is then immediately output from the latch to the processor and its presence is indicated to the processor. The processor accepts it.

The transfer of the fourth doubleword completes very quickly because the DRAM was accessing the fast data latch rather than slow DRAM memory.

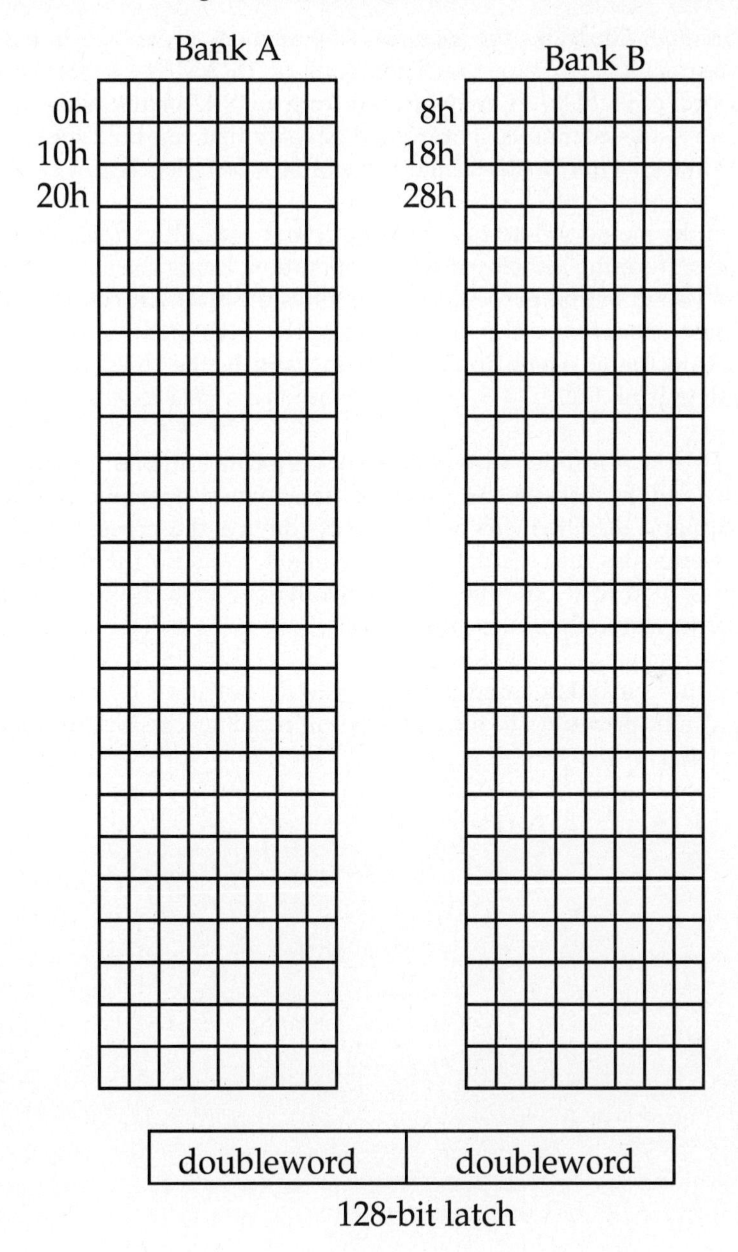

Figure 30-7. 2-Way Interleaved Memory Architecture

4-Way Interleaved Memory

Figure 30-8 illustrates the main DRAM memory organized in a 4-way, interleaved memory architecture. Each bank of DRAM is 64-bits wide — a doubleword, or eight bytes, may be read from a DRAM bank with one access. The memory subsystem incorporates a data latch that can hold four doublewords, or 32 bytes, of information (in other words, a complete sector).

When the memory detects a four-beat burst read, this indicates that a processor is performing a cache sector fill operation. Using the start doubleword address issued by the processor, it identifies the start address of the sector that the processor wants. The first doubleword of the sector is in bank A, the second is in the adjacent doubleword in bank B, the third in bank C and the fourth in bank D.

The DRAM controller simultaneously performs a memory read from all four banks and latches the 32 bytes of data. Since this involves accessing the DRAM and the DRAM is a slow access device, the processor is forced to insert wait states into the data access while it waits for the first doubleword to be presented to it. The memory controller presents the four doublewords to the processor in the order expected.

Since the remaining three doublewords do not have be read from memory, they can be presented to the processor in rapid succession from the fast access data latch.

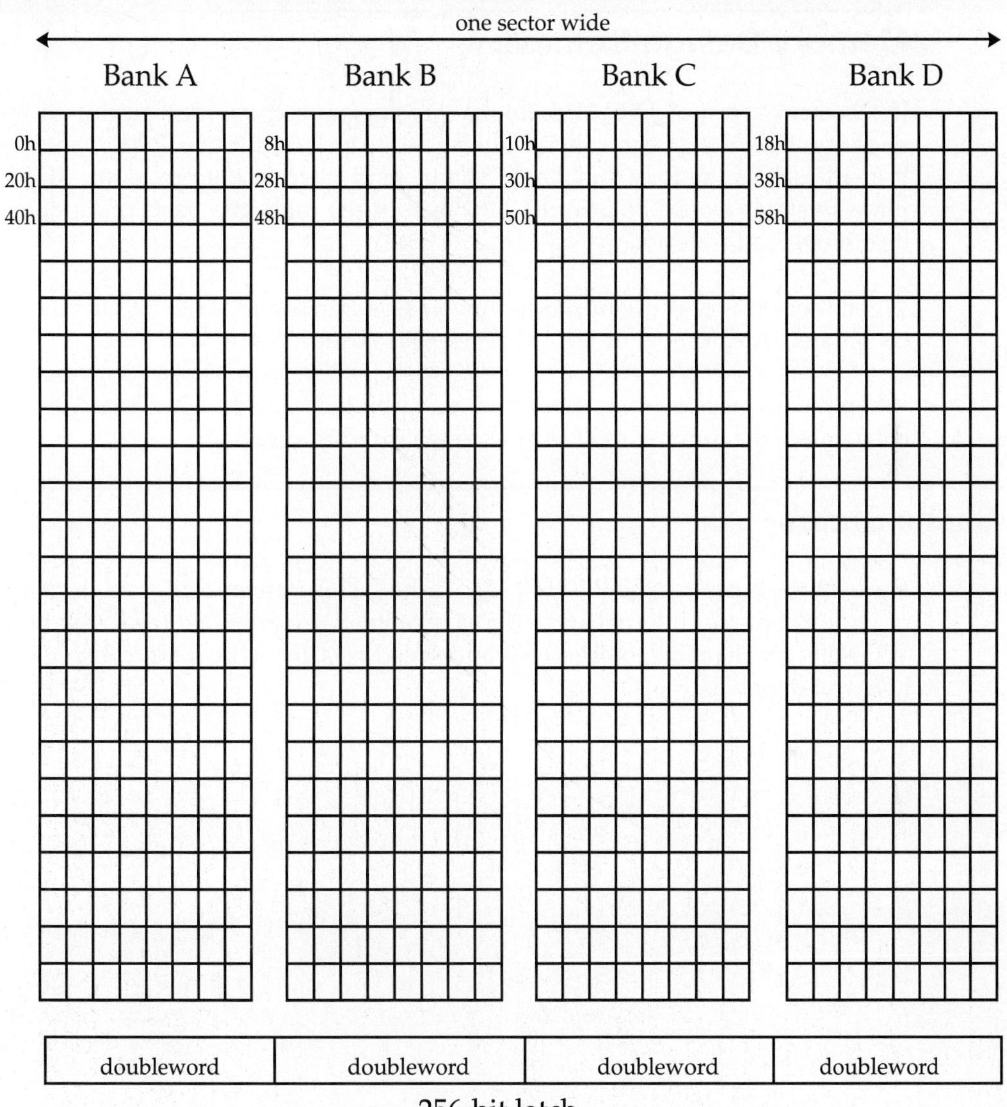

Figure 30-8. 4-Way Interleaved Memory Architecture

Memory Design Summary

If the main array of DRAM memory were organized as one bank of 64-bit memory, the DRAM controller would have to perform four DRAM accesses to read each of the four doublewords and send them to the processor. Multiple wait states would be inserted into each of the four data beats of the four-beat burst read transaction.

When the memory is organized into two 64-bit banks and a 128-bit latch is incorporated, the number of DRAM accesses is reduced to two.

When the memory is organized into four 64-bit banks and a 256-bit latch is incorporated, the number of DRAM accesses is reduced to one.

Cache States

Figure 30-9 illustrates the PPC 601's L1 cache sector state transitions as a result of various types of internal and external events. It assumes that the state of the WIM bits for the page/block being addressed is 001b: write-back, caching enabled, and global.

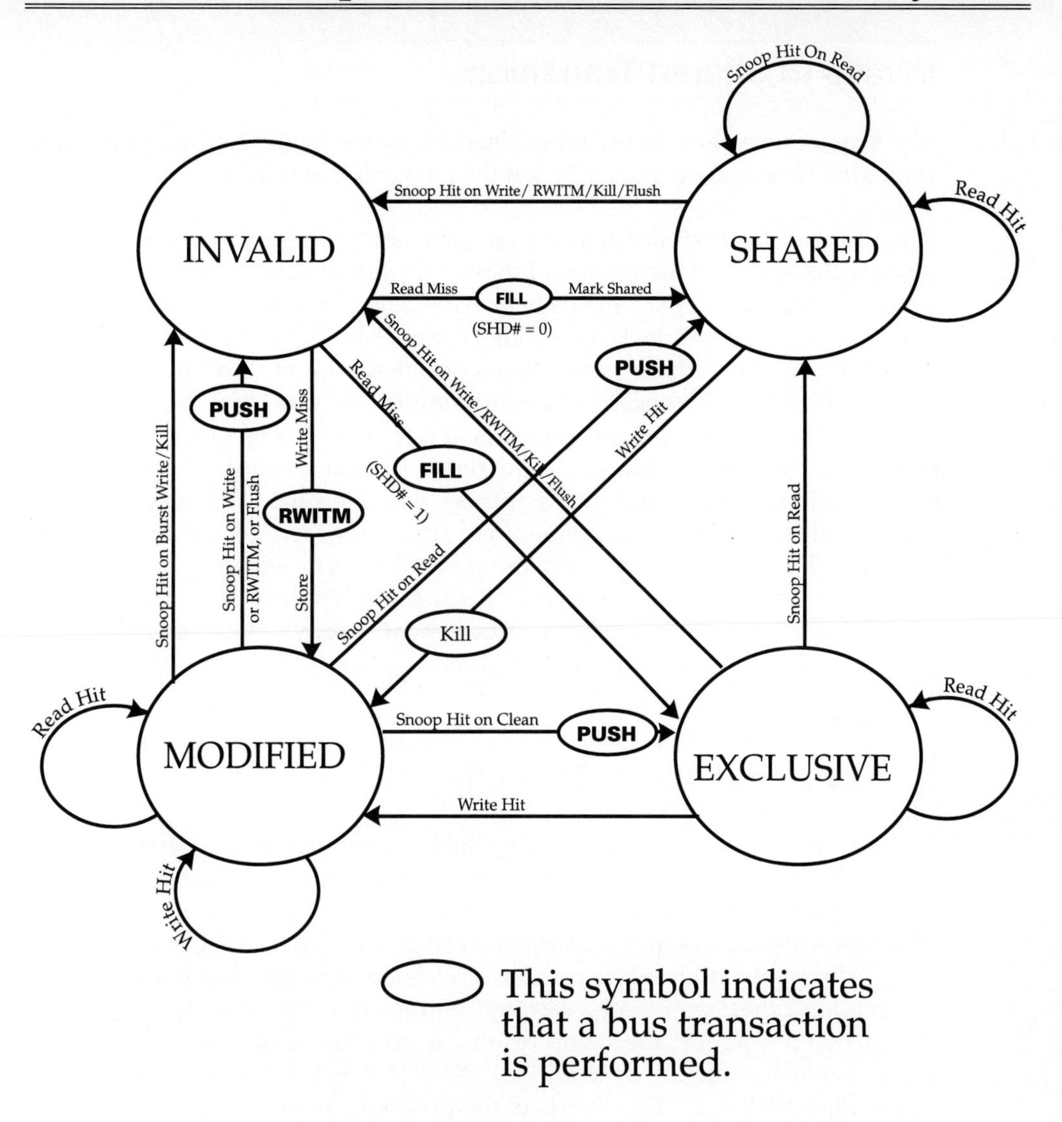

Figure 30-9. MESI State Transitions (WIM = 001b)

Invalid to Shared Transition

The state of a sector will be transitioned from the invalid to the shared state under the circumstances described in the paragraph that follows.

When a load, instruction fetch or page table entry read miss occurs the processor initiates a burst memory read to read the target sector from memory and place it in the cache. Since the page or block's M attribute indicates that other processors also access the target memory area (M = 1), the GBL# output is asserted during the address transaction associated with the read burst. This instructs all other processors/caching entities on the bus to snoop the transaction and report the snoop results. If one other processor has copy of the sector in the exclusive state, or if more than one other processor have copies of the sector in the shared state, each of them will assert the SHD# signal to indicate that they possess clean (unmodified since they were read from memory) copies of the sector. This instructs the processor performing the burst read to store the sector in the shared state when the burst read has completed. If SHD# was asserted by one other processor with a copy of the sector in the exclusive state, that processor will transition the state of its copy from exclusive to shared.

Invalid to Exclusive Transition

When a load, instruction fetch, or page table entry read miss occurs, the processor initiates a burst memory read to read the target sector from memory and place it in the cache. Since the page or block's M attribute indicates that other processors also access the target memory area (M = 1), the GBL# output is asserted during the address transaction associated with the read burst. This instructs all other processors/caching entities on the bus to snoop the transaction and report the snoop results. If no other cache has a copy of the sector in any form (clean or modified), the SHD# and ARTRY# signals remain deasserted (both = 1). This instructs the processor performing the burst read to store the sector in the exclusive state when the burst read has completed.

Invalid to Modified Transition

The PPC 601 cache uses an allocate-on-write policy on store misses within a page or block with WIM attributes of 001b (write-through, cacheable, memory coherency required). If a store generated within this processor misses the cache, the processor reads the sector into its cache, performs the store into it, and immediately marks it modified. There are two possible scenarios:

- Another processor/caching entity has a copy of the sector in the modified state.
- No other processor/caching entity has a copy of the sector in the modified state.

Another Cache Has Modified Copy of Sector

The processor initiates a burst read with intent to modify, or rwitm, transaction. Since the page or block is marked shared (M = 1), the GBL# output is asserted during the address transaction. This instructs all other processors/caching entities on the bus to snoop the transaction and report the snoop results. If another cache has a modified copy of the sector, it asserts both SHD# and ARTRY#. This instructs the processor that has initiated the burst rwitm that it is about to read a stale sector from memory. The processor does not proceed with the data transfer, but instead surrenders the bus.

At the same time that it indicates a hit on a modified sector (SHD# and ARTRY# asserted), the processor with the modified sector asserts BR# to request access to the address bus in order to perform the snoop push back burst write to deposit the fresh sector in memory. The arbiter grants it the bus and it initiates the burst write. Upon completion of the snoop push back, it transitions the sector from modified to invalid (because the processor that attempted the rwitm will re attempt the operation, successfully complete it, and then modify the sector internally).

Upon completion of the snoop push back, the first processor reattempts the rwitm with GBL# asserted. The transaction is once again snooped by all processors/caching entities, now resulting in a snoop miss (SHD# and ARTRY# remain deasserted). The sector is read into the cache, the store is completed, and the sector is marked modified.

No other Cache Has Modified Copy of Sector

The processor initiates a burst read with intent to modify, or rwitm, transaction. Since the page or block is marked shared (M = 1), the GBL# output is asserted during the address transaction. This instructs all other processors/caching entities on the bus to snoop the transaction and report the snoop results. If no other cache has a modified copy of the sector, SHD# and

ARTRY# remain deasserted. Any other cache that has a copy of the sector in the shared or the exclusive state invalidates its copy of the sector (because the sector will be immediately modified when the processor performing the rwitm completes reading the sector from memory). In this case, the processor performing the rwitm ignores the fact that SHD# was asserted (because all other processors with copies in the exclusive or shared state invalidate their copies). The processor proceeds with the burst read. The sector is read into the cache, the store is completed, and the sector is marked modified.

Shared to Invalid Transition

A sector currently in the shared state will be transitioned to the invalid state under the following conditions:

- The processor experiences a snoop hit while another processor is performing a burst write to memory. The burst write could be due to: a snoop push back; another cache casting a modified sector out to make room for a new sector; an intelligent bus master subsystem may be bursting data into memory with GBL# asserted. Upon completion of the burst write into memory by the current bus master, the sector in the snooping processor's cache is stale.
- The processor experiences a snoop hit while another processor is performing a single-beat write to memory. The write could be due to: an intelligent bus master subsystem writing data into memory with GBL# asserted; a processor that does not cache from this area of memory performing a store into memory; a processor that utilizes a write-through policy in this area of memory performing a store. Upon completion of the single-beat write, the sector in snooping processor's cache is stale.
- The processor experiences a snoop hit while another processor is performing a flush sector transaction. The other processor would be performing a flush sector transaction because it is executing a dcbf instruction that either missed its cache or was a hit on a sector in the shared state, and M = 1.
- The processor experiences a snoop hit while another processor is performing a kill sector transaction. The other processor would be performing a kill sector transaction for one of the following reasons: it had a store hit on a shared sector in its cache (memory area with WIM = 001b); it is executing a dcbz instruction on the target sector and the sector is not present in its cache (but may be in other caches), or the sector is in its cache in the shared state.

- The processor experiences a snoop hit while another processor is performing a rwitm transaction. The other processor is performing a rwitm because it experienced a store miss and uses a write-back, cacheable, memory coherency required policy when performing accesses in this area of memory. When the rwitm has completed, the bus master will store into the sector just read from memory and mark it modified.

Shared to Modified Transition

A sector currently in the shared state will be transitioned to the modified state under the following circumstance.

The processor experiences a store hit on the sector in the shared state and M = 1 in this area of memory. Before performing the store into the sector, it must gain exclusive ownership of the sector. This is accomplished by broadcasting an address-only kill transaction to the other caching entities. They all snoop the transaction and transition the sector from the shared to the invalid state in the event of a hit on a sector in the shared state. Note that none of them will have a copy in the exclusive (this processor has copy in the shared state, so any copies residing in other processors would also be marked shared) or modified state (this processor has a copy in the shared state, indicating that no other processor has modified its copy). The processor that initiated the kill transaction then completes the store into the sector and transitions it from the shared to the modified state.

Exclusive to Invalid Transition

A sector currently in the exclusive state will be transitioned to the invalid state under the following circumstances:

- The processor experiences a snoop hit on a sector in the exclusive state while an intelligent bus master subsystem is performing a single beat write transaction with GBL# asserted. When the write has completed, the copy of the sector in the cache is stale.
- The processor experiences a snoop hit on a sector in the exclusive state while another processor is performing a single-beat write within the address range encompassed by the sector. The single-beat write could be the result of: a store by another processor that doesn't cache from this area of memory, but M = 1; a store by another processor that uses a write-through policy for stores in this area of memory and M = 1.

- The processor experiences a snoop hit on a sector in the exclusive state while another processor is performing a kill transaction. The other processor initiated the kill transaction due to execution of a dcbz instruction where the target sector is invalid and M = 1. The processor executing the dcbz instruction is modifying the entire sector by setting it to zeros, rendering this copy of the sector stale.
- The processor experiences a snoop hit on a sector in the exclusive state while another processor is performing a rwitm transaction. The other processor would perform a rwitm transaction due to a store miss on its cache and WIM = 001b. Upon completion of the rwitm, the other processor performs a store into the sector and marks its copy modified, rendering this processor's copy of the sector stale.
- The processor experiences a snoop hit on a sector in the exclusive state while another processor is performing a flush transaction. The other processor performed the flush transaction due to execution of a dcbf instruction where the target sector is invalid and M = 1. This instruction should cause any cache with the sector in the modified state to push it to memory and then invalidate it. It causes all caches with the sector in the shared or exclusive state to invalidate their copies of the sector.
- This processor is executing a dcbf instruction that results in a hit on a sector in the exclusive state. It invalidates the sector.
- The processor experiences a snoop hit on a sector in the exclusive state while an intelligent bus master subsystem is performing a burst write transaction with GBL# asserted. Upon completion of the burst write to memory, the entire sector in memory has been updated, rendering all copies of the sector currently marked shared or exclusive stale.
- The processor is executing a dcbi instruction that results in a hit on a sector in the exclusive state. It invalidates the sector.

Exclusive to Modified Transition

A sector currently in the exclusive state will be transitioned to the modified state under the following circumstances:

- A store hit on a sector in the exclusive state results in a store into the cache sector and a transition from the exclusive to the modified state.
- Execution of a dcbz instruction that results in a hit on a sector in the exclusive state causes the processor to zero out the sector and mark it modified.

Modified to Invalid Transition

A sector currently in the modified state will be transitioned to the invalid state under the following circumstances:

- The processor executes a dcbf instruction resulting in a hit on a modified sector. The modified sector is pushed back to memory and is then marked invalid.
- The processor executes a dcbi instruction resulting in a hit on a modified sector. The sector is marked invalid.
- The processor experiences a snoop hit on a modified sector while another processor is performing a rwitm transaction. The other processor is issued an address retry (ARTRY# and SHD# asserted) and this processor then performs a burst write to push the modified sector to memory. After completion of the push back, the sector is marked invalid (because the other processor will immediately retry the transaction, read the sector into its cache, store into it and mark its copy modified).
- The processor experiences a snoop hit on a modified sector while snooping a flush transaction generated by another processor that is executing a dcbf instruction (and had a miss in its cache). As a result, this processor performs a burst write to push the modified sector to memory. After completion of the push back, the sector is marked invalid.
- The processor experiences a snoop hit on a modified sector while snooping a single-beat write transaction initiated by an intelligent bus master subsystem. The bus master is issued an address retry (ARTRY# and SHD# asserted) and this processor then performs a burst write to push the modified sector to memory. After completion of the push back, the sector is marked invalid (because the bus master will then modify the sector in memory).
- The processor experiences a snoop hit on a modified sector while snooping a burst write transaction initiated by an intelligent bus master subsystem. The sector is marked invalid (because the bus master will modify the entire sector in memory).

Modified to Shared Transition

A sector currently in the modified state will be transitioned to the shared state under the following circumstances:

- The processor experiences a snoop hit on a burst read initiated by another processor. The other processor is issued an address retry (ARTRY# and SHD# asserted) and this processor then performs a burst write to push the modified sector to memory. After completion of the push back, the sector is marked shared (because the other processor then reinitiates the burst read and places the sector in its cache). The sector is stored in the shared state in the other processor because this processor then asserts SHD# during the retry of its burst read.
- The processor experiences a snoop hit on a single-beat read initiated by an intelligent bus master subsystem or a processor that treats this as non-cacheable memory. The bus master is issued an address retry (ARTRY# and SHD# asserted) and this processor then performs a burst write to push the modified sector to memory. After completion of the push back, the sector is marked shared. The PPC 601 always a marks the sector shared on a snoop read hit after the push back. Technically, this isn't necessary upon detection of a snoop hit on a single-beat read because the other entity obviously isn't reading the whole sector to make a cache entry. This action is probably taken to simplify the design of the processor.

Modified to Exclusive Transition

A sector currently in the modified state will be transitioned to the exclusive state under the following circumstances:

- The processor is executing a dcbst instruction resulting in a hit on a modified sector. The sector is pushed back to memory and is then marked exclusive. No other cache should have a copy of the sector Their copies would have been invalidated when this sector was first modified (when this processor broadcast the kill sector transaction).
- The processor experiences a snoop hit on a modified sector while snooping a clean sector transaction initiated by another processor. The other processor is broadcasting a clean transaction because it is executing a dcbst instruction and had a miss in its cache. In response, this processor performs a burst write to push back the modified sector into memory and then marks the sector exclusive.

Memory Unit (MU)Operation

General

The MU acts as a posted memory read/write buffer. This includes loads and stores in cacheable memory space and in non-cacheable memory space. Address-only transactions are also posted (in the read buffer). I/O transactions are not posted. Once a transaction has been posted in the MU, the MU issues a request to the processor's system interface. The system interface arbitrates for ownership of the external bus and then performs the transaction or transactions currently posted in the MU. The following sections define the operation of the MU.

Posted-Write Buffer

The MU's posted write buffer has three entries that it uses to memorize memory-oriented writes. Each buffer entry can hold either a single-beat write or an entire sector of data to be written back to memory as well as the target address it is to be written to. Two of the three buffer entries are used to post any type of memory write operation. This would include:

- Stores to non-cacheable memory that result in single-beat memory write transaction.
- Stores to cacheable, write-through pages or blocks of memory that result in a single-beat write transaction.
- Castout of a modified sector or sectors to make room for a new sector being read into the cache due to a load miss in a page or block marked as cacheable by the operating system.
- Castout of a modified sector or sectors to make room for a new sector being read into the cache due to a store miss in a page or block marked as cacheable and write-back by the operating system.
- Snoop push-back operation as a result of a snoop hit on a modified cache block.

The third buffer entry is referred to as the snoop entry. It is only used to hold a modified sector that must be written back to memory as the result of a snoop hit on a modified sector. For more information regarding the use of this entry, refer to the section in this chapter entitled "High-Priority Snoop Request."

Stores to Non-Cacheable Memory

Stores to non-cacheable memory result in between one and eight bytes of data being written to memory. The store bypasses the cache and is recorded in the MU's write buffer.

Stores to Cacheable, Write-Through Memory

Stores to cacheable, write-through memory (WIM = 10xb) update the cache in the event of a hit, but also write the specified data through to memory as well. This results in between one and eight bytes of data being written to memory. The store is recorded in the MU's write buffer.

Modified Sector Castout Due to Load or Instruction Fetch Miss

When a load or an instruction fetch results in a cache miss, the cache must fetch the sector containing the requested information from memory. If the LRU algorithm specifies replacement of a line with one or both sectors marked modified, the modified sector(s) must be cast back to memory. The modified sector(s) are posted in the MU's write buffer to be written to memory.

Modified Sector Castout Due to Store Miss In Cacheable, Write-Back Memory

When a store miss occurs in a page or block of memory marked as cacheable, write-back, the cache must read the sector to be updated into the cache and then store into it. If the LRU algorithm specifies replacement of a line with one or both sectors marked modified, the modified sector(s) must be cast back to memory. The modified sector(s) are posted in the MU's write buffer to be written to memory.

Snoop Push-Back Operation

When another bus master attempts a memory read or write in a page or block of memory with M = 1, it asserts GBL# to instruct all processors to snoop the target address in their L1 caches. If a processor experiences a snoop hit on a modified sector, it issues an ARTRY# to the bus master attempting the access. The modified sector is posted in the MU's write buffer to be written back to memory. For additional information on snoop push-back operations, refer to the section in this chapter entitled "High-Priority Snoop Request" and to the section entitled "Data Bus Write-Only Feature" in the chapter entitled "PPC 601 Split-Bus Concept."

Write Buffer Snooping

When another bus master attempts a memory read or write in a page or block of memory with M = 1, it asserts GBL# to instruct all processors to snoop the target address in their L1 caches and in their write buffers. If a processor experiences a snoop hit on a modified sector in either the cache or write buffer, it issues an ARTRY# to the bus master attempting the access. Only modified sectors currently resident in the write buffer are snooped (in addition to the cache snoop). Single-beat writes are not (because the area is not cached from or is marked write-through).

High-Priority Snoop Request

The MU's posted-write buffer has a third entry that can only be used for snoop push-back operations. A feature bit, HID0[31], controls the usage of this queue entry. This is known as the high-priority snoop request feature control bit.

The default state of this bit is zero, disabling the feature. When disabled, the snoop entry in the MU may be used whenever the processor snoops a memory transaction performed by another master. If the snoop results in a snoop hit on a modified cache block, the master is issued an ARTRY#, causing it to abort its data transfer. The modified sector is immediately placed in the MU's snoop entry to be written back to memory.

If the feature bit is set to one by the operating system, the snoop entry is only made available for snoops performed for a master that asserts HP_SNP_REQ# to the processor during performance of its address transaction. If the snoop results in a hit on a modified cache block, the modified sector is pushed into the snoop entry and scheduled to be written back to memory immediately. If a master asserts GBL#, instructing the processor to snoop its transaction, but does not assert HP_SNP_REQ# during the performance of its address transaction, the snoop entry in the MU is not available in the event of a hit on a modified cache block. The modified cache block must be pushed into one of the MU's two regular posted-write entries. In the event that neither of the entries is currently available (due to previously-posted writes), the processor will not be able to post the push-back of the modified sector until one of the two regular entries is freed up by the performance of one of the previously-posted writes on the bus. This would result in prolonged latency in accomplishing the push-back of the modified sector to memory. The master that was issued the ARTRY# will probably receive additional retries before achieving success.

This feature would be useful in a system where the system designer wanted to ensure that a particular processor was guaranteed an expeditious completion of a push-back to memory by another processor that had issued a retry to it. Whenever it runs a transaction that must be snooped by other processors, it asserts GBL# and HP_SNP_REQ#. If a snooper experiences a hit on a modified cache block and detects HP_SNP_REQ# asserted, it will assert ARTRY# and immediately post the push-back of the modified cache block in the snoop entry in its MU and then perform the burst write to deposit the block into memory. This will minimize the latency experienced by the master that was issued the retry.

For additional information on snoop push-back operations, refer to the section entitled "Data Bus Write Only Feature" in the chapter entitled "PPC 601 Split-Bus Concept."

Posted-Read Buffer

The MU's read buffer contains two entries. They are used to post memory read requests and address-only transactions. The following types of requests are posted in the read buffer:

- High-priority full sector read as a result of a load or instruction fetch miss on the cache.
- High-priority full sector read with intent to modify as a result of a store miss within a page or block marked as cacheable, write-back.
- High-priority full sector read as a result of an MMU miss on the cache when attempting to read a page table entry from the page table (assuming that the page table is cacheable).
- High-priority eight byte read as a result of MMU read of a page table entry (assuming that the page table is non-cacheable).
- Low-priority full sector read as a result of the execution of a dcbt or dcbtst instruction.
- High-priority one-to-eight byte, single-beat read as a result of a load within a non-cacheable area of memory (I = 1).

- Address-only kill request as a result of one of the following: the execution of a dcbz instruction that misses the cache or hits on a sector in the shared state with M = 1; store hit on a shared sector with M = 1; execution of a dcbi instruction that hits on a shared sector with M = 1 or that misses the cache with M = 1.
- Address-only flush request as a result of the execution of a dcbf instruction that misses the cache (M = 1) or that hits on a shared sector (M = 1).
- Address-only clean request as a result of the execution of a dcbst instruction that misses the cache (M = 1).

The PPC 601 MU read buffer implementation imposes the following constraints:

- The buffer may not contain two simultaneous load requests.
- The buffer may not contain two simultaneous read with intent to modify (rwitm) requests.

Relationship of Read and Write Buffers

In order to ensure that all memory reads and writes are completed in the proper order in memory, the MU follows the following rules:

- The addresses for currently-posted reads and writes are compared and, in the event of an address match, the MU always performs the write before the read associated with the same address. This ensures that the read always receives the fresh data.
- Cacheable read requests (loads, rwitm, and instruction fetch) have priority over single beat writes. If a posted write is to a non-cacheable area of memory, then it cannot be associated with any of the posted reads from cacheable memory. If a posted write is to cacheable memory, it is in a write-through area of memory and the data has already been updated in the cache.

Forcing MU to Perform Reads and Writes In Defined Order

Refer to the chapter entitled "Access Order" for a description of the mechanisms used to ensure that posted memory accesses occur in a defined order.

Priority of Posted Operations

At a given instant in time the MU may have a number of posted memory read and/or write accesses. In addition, the system interface may have an I/O access pending. In order to minimize stalling of the processor core, the PPC 601 processor adheres to the following priority scheme (listed in highest-to-lowest priority):

1. High-priority snoop push back. This is the highest priority because the master that was issued an ARTRY# cannot complete its memory access until this processor is successful in depositing the modified sector into memory. The retried master asserted HP_SNP_REQ# during its address transaction to request that the push back be performed expeditiously.
2. Normal snoop push back. The retried master did not assert HP_SNP_REQ# or it did but the associated feature bit in HID0[0] was cleared to zero.
3. I/O accesses that haven't been retried. If the I/O access is initiated on the bus and receives a retry (ARTRY#), it is then moved to the lowest priority (because the I/O controller has a buffer full or empty condition and it could take an extended period of time for this condition to be alleviated). See entry 10 in this list.
4. Cache instruction accesses (i.e., address-only transactions used to maintain cache consistency: flush, kill, clean, TLB invalidate).
5. Read requests (i.e., load, rwitm, instruction fetch).
6. Single-beat write.
7. Address-only sync transaction resulting from execution of a sync instruction.
8. Alternate sector reload or touch request. These operations are assigned very low priority because it is not critical to the processor core that they be carried out. If one of these operations is posted in the MU's read buffer and the buffer space is needed for a high-priority read requests (e.g., load or instruction fetch miss, rwitm, TLB miss, etc.), the MU will purge the low-priority request and replace it with the higher-priority request.
9. Cast-out of a modified sector to make room for a new sector being read into the cache. No other processor has requested data in the modified sector, so it's not considered a high-priority operation to write it to memory. In other words, it must be performed, but there is no rush.
10. I/O accesses that have been retried.

Non-Queueable Operations

Some operations cannot be placed in the MU buffers (because they require synchronization with respect to the execution units, cache, or the MU). They are:

- TLB invalidate transaction as a result of the execution of a tlbie instruction.
- Sync transaction as a result of the execution of a sync instruction.
- Sync transaction as a result of the execution of a eieio instruction.
- A store hit on a shared sector and M = 1. Before storing into the sector, the processor must first issue an address-only kill transaction to kill copies of the sector in the caches of all other processors.

Chapter 31

The Previous Chapter

The previous chapter provided a detailed description of the PPC 601 processor's cache and MU implementation.

This Chapter

This chapter provides a detailed description of every condition and/or instruction that can cause the PPC 601 processor to perform a transaction on the external bus.

The Next Chapter

The next chapter provides a detailed description of the PPC 601 processor's split-bus architecture. It covers acquisition and usage of the address and data buses in both coupled and uncoupled designs. The data bus write-only feature is also covered.

Transaction Types

The PPC 601 processor is capable of performing four types of bus transactions:

- **Cache management transactions**. These transactions only involve the broadcast of the address and transaction type. No data is transferred to or from memory. They are referred to as address-only transactions.
- **Memory access**. These transactions transfer data to or from memory. There are two types: single and four-beat transfers. A single-beat transfer reads or writes between one and eight bytes of data, while a four-beat transfer reads or writes a cache block (32 bytes; referred to as a sector).
- **I/O transactions**.
- **External control transactions**. Only generated by execution of the ecowx and eciwx instructions.

Table 31-1 lists the transaction types by category (a double line separate the four categories: cache, memory access, I/O, and external control). The sections that follow define the instructions and/or conditions that can cause each type of transaction to be performed on the bus.

Table 31-1. Transaction Types

Type	Category	Description
Clean sector	Cache	Commands all caches to perform lookup in data cache. If hit on modified block, write block to memory and mark exclusive.
Sync	Cache	Forces the L2 cache to perform any posted writes currently pending.
Kill sector	Cache	Commands all caches to perform lookup in data and code caches. If hit on block in E, S or M, invalidate.
TLB invalidate	Cache	Commands all processors to perform lookup in paging TLB. Invalidate on hit.
Single-beat write (write with flush)	Memory access	Master is writing between one and eight bytes into memory.
Single-beat write atomic (write with flush atomic)	Memory access	Master is writing between one and eight bytes into memory as a result of execution of a memory semaphore update.
Four-beat write (write with kill)	Memory access	Master is writing an entire cache block (32 bytes) into memory.
Single-beat read	Memory access	Master is reading between one and eight bytes from memory.
Single-beat read atomic	Memory access	Master is reading between one and eight bytes from memory as a result of execution of a memory semaphore read.
Four-beat read atomic	Memory access	Master is reading an entire cache block from memory as a result of execution of a memory semaphore read that missed the cache.
Read with intent to modify (rwitm)	Memory access	Master is reading an entire cache block from memory to perform a store into it and mark it modified.
Read with intent to modify atomic (rwitma)	Memory access	Master is reading an entire cache block from memory to perform a store into it and mark it modified. Due to performance of memory semaphore update.
I/O load request	I/O	Master initiating an I/O load sequence.
I/O load immediate	I/O	Master performing an intermediate load of load sequence.
I/O load last	I/O	Master performing last load of load sequence.
I/O load reply	I/O	I/O controller reply to load operation.
I/O store immediate	I/O	Master performing first or an intermediate store of a store sequence.
I/O store last	I/O	Master performing last store of store sequence.
I/O store reply	I/O	I/O controller reply to store operation.
External control out	External control	Master is executing an ecowx instruction.
External control in	External control	Master is executing an eciwx instruction.

Cache Management Transactions

Clean Sector Transaction

Generated by PPC 601 Processor

In the table, the clean sector transaction is defined as follows — commands all caches to perform a lookup in their data caches. If the lookup results in a hit on a modified block, the block must be written to memory and marked exclusive. Processors must also snoop their internal posted write queues for a modified block.

A PPC 601 processor will generate a clean sector transaction when it executes a dcbst (data cache block store) instruction and the address specified by the programmer misses in the processor's L1 data cache. The address is within an area of memory that may be accessed by other processors/caching entities (M = 1).

Since another processor may have a copy of the block in the modified state, the processor executing the dcbst instruction broadcasts the specified address and the clean sector transaction type to command all processors/caching entities to perform a lookup in their data caches. In the event of a hit on a modified block, the cache that experienced the hit should perform a four-beat write to deposit the modified block in memory (i.e., make the block in memory clean, or fresh). It should then mark its copy exclusive.

Generated by Look-Through, Write-Back L2 Cache

In a system with a look-through L2 cache incorporated into the host/PCI bridge, the L2 cache may generate the clean transaction under the following circumstance.

When a PCI master attempts to read from cacheable memory, the L2 cache snoops the transaction in its cache. In the event of a cache hit on a modified block, the L2 cache instructs the cacheable memory target to issue a retry to the PCI master (because it was about to read a stale block from memory). The block is marked modified in the L2 cache, but is really stale. At some earlier point in time, the processor had issued a kill to the L2 prior to modifying its copy of the block. When the L2 cache detected the kill, it had marked its copy modified (but the processor hadn't written the data modification through to the L2 cache).

After issuing the retry to the cacheable PCI memory target, the L2 cache generates a flush transaction on the host bus using the memory address specified by the PCI bus master. It also asserts GBL# to command the host processor(s) to snoop the transaction. The processor(s) performs a lookup in its L1 cache (and its posted-write buffer), resulting in a hit on the modified block. The processor then initiates a four-beat write transaction to deposit the modified block into memory. The processor then marks its copy invalid.

The host/PCI bridge passes the data to the cacheable memory target to be subsequently read from memory by the PCI master when it retries its memory read transaction. The L2 cache snarfs the updated data into its cache and, as the processor is pushing its modified copy into memory, changes the state of its block from modified to exclusive.

When the PCI master retries the memory read, the L2 cache snoops the transaction again, resulting in a snoop hit on a clean block (exclusive state). The L2 cache doesn't intervene in the PCI master's read and it is permitted to read the data from memory.

Sync Transaction

The sync transaction is generated by the PPC 601 processor whenever it executes a sync or an eieio instruction. If the system incorporates a look-through L2 cache with a posted-write buffer, the L2 cache should perform all posted memory writes to memory when it detects the sync transaction. There is no address associated with the sync transaction.

Kill Sector Transaction

Generated by PPC 601 Processor

The kill sector transaction commands all caches to perform a lookup in their data and code caches. If the lookup results in a hit on a block in the exclusive, shared or modified state, the block must be invalidated. The PPC 601 processor generates a kill transaction under the circumstances described in the following sections.

Execution of dcbi Instruction

When the processor executes a dcbi (data cache block invalidate) instruction, it performs a lookup in its own data cache and, if a hit occurs, it invalidates its copy of the block. It also performs a lookup in its posted-write buffer and invalidates the block posted in the queue if a hit occurs. If the address specified is within a page or block with M = 1, it also broadcasts a kill transaction using the address specified by the programmer and asserts GBL#. All other processors/caching entities snoop the transaction in their caches (and posted-write buffers) and, in the event of a hit, invalidate their copy of the block.

Execution of icbi Instruction

When the processor executes an icbi (instruction cache block invalidate) instruction, it performs a lookup in its own code cache and, if a hit occurs, it invalidates its copy of the block. If the address specified is within a page or block with M = 1, it also broadcasts a kill transaction using the address specified by the programmer and asserts GBL#. All other processors/caching entities snoop the transaction in their caches and, in the event of a hit, invalidate their copy of the block. It should be noted that the icbi instruction is treated as a no-op by PowerPC processors with a unified code/data cache (such as the PPC601).

Execution of Store within Write-Back Area

When the processor executes a store that hits on a block in its data cache in the shared state and WIM = 001b within the page or block, the processor must first kill copies of the block in all other caches before it performs the store into its copy and marks it modified. The kill is performed on the bus using the specified block address and GBL# is asserted. All other processors/caching entities snoop the transaction in their caches and, in the event of a hit, invalidate their copy of the block.

Execution of dcbz Instruction

The processor executes a dcbz (data cache block zero) instruction that misses its data cache or hits on a block in the shared state (WIM = 001b within the page or block).

If the dcbz misses the processor's data cache, the processor first generates a kill transaction to kill copies of the block that may currently reside in other caches. It then creates a block in its data cache containing all zeros and marks it modified.

If the dcbz hits on a block in the shared state in this processor's data cache, the processor first generates a kill transaction to kill copies of the block that currently reside in other caches. It then sets its copy of the block in its data cache to all zeros and marks it modified.

Generated by Look-Through L2 Cache

If a PCI bus master issues a memory write and invalidate command, it is indicating that it will overwrite an entire block in memory. The L2 cache snoops the transaction. In the event of a cache hit, it invalidates it copy. It also generates a kill transaction (with GBL# asserted) using the block start address specified by the PCI master. The processor snoops the address in its L1 cache. In the event of a cache hit, it invalidates the block in its cache.

TLB Invalidate Transaction

The PPC 601 processor will generate a TLB invalidate transaction when it executes a tlbie instruction. The processor performs a lookup in its own TLB and invalidates the TLB entry if a hit occurs. It also generates a TLB invalidate transaction with GBL# asserted. All other processors perform a lookup in their TLBs and invalidate the entry if a hit occurs.

Memory Access Transactions

Single-Beat Write (Write with Flush)

Generated by PPC 601 Processor

The PPC 601 processor generates a single-beat write transaction when executing a store into an area of memory that is designated non-cacheable (I = 1) or that is cacheable with a write-through policy (I = 0, W = 1). In both cases, it generates a single-beat memory write transaction to write from one to eight bytes into memory.

If M = 1, the processor asserts GBL# and all other processors/caching entities snoop the transaction. One of the following will result:

- A snooping cache has a snoop miss. There is no effect on the cache.
- A snooping cache has a snoop hit on a block in the exclusive or shared state. The cache invalidates, or flushes, its copy (because the write transaction is altering the block in memory).
- A snooping cache has a snoop hit on a block in the modified state. The master is attempting to update a portion of a stale block in memory. The cache issues a retry to the processor attempting the write, deposits the modified block in memory, and then permits the master to retry its transaction successfully.

Generated by Intelligent Bus Master

An intelligent master can utilize a single-beat memory write transaction to write from one to eight bytes of data into memory. Since it does not have access to the WIM bits in the page table entries or BAT registers, it must assume that one or more processors have been caching from the area of memory being accessed and must therefore assert GBL# to force a snoop. The actions taken by the snoopers is identical to those described in the previous section.

Single-Beat Write Atomic (Write with Flush Atomic)

The only difference between this transaction and the single-beat write is that this one is the result of the processor's execution of a stwcx instruction to update a memory semaphore. For more information regarding semaphores, refer to the chapter entitled "Shared Resource Acquisition."

Four-Beat Burst Write (Write with Kill)

Generated by PPC 601 Processor

The processor generates a four-beat write transaction in order to deposit a modified cache block into memory. Since the PPC 601 processor's data bus is only eight bytes wide and a cache block is 32 bytes long, the processor must perform four eight byte data writes to deposit the block into memory. If the WIM bit setting for this area of memory has M = 1, the processor asserts GBL# when it performs the write. This forces all other caches to snoop the transaction. In the event of a cache hit, the cache block should be invalidated (killed). The processor performs a four-beat memory write under the following circumstances:

- If the processor executes a dcbst instruction and it hits on a cache block in the modified state, the processor performs a four-beat memory write to store the block into memory. It then marks its copy exclusive.
- If the processor executes a dcbf instruction and it hits on a cache block in the modified state, the processor performs a four-beat memory write to store the block into memory. It then marks its copy invalid.
- If the processor snoops another master's memory access transaction and has a hit on a modified cache block, it must issue a retry to the other master and then perform a snoop push-back operation to write the modified block into memory for the other master. It will mark its copy invalid (if it snooped a write) or shared (if it snooped a read).
- If the processor has a load miss on its data cache, it must read the target block into its cache. If the cache logic determines that the new cache block must overwrite a modified block, the modified cache block must be written back to memory. This is referred to as a cast-out.

Generated by Intelligent Bus Master

An intelligent master can utilize a four-beat memory write transaction to write 32 bytes of data into memory. Since it does not have access to the WIM bits in the page table entries or BAT registers, it must assume that one or more processors have been caching from the area of memory being accessed and must therefore assert GBL# to force a snoop. All other processors/caching entities snoop the transaction. One of the following will result:

- A snooping cache has a snoop miss. There is no effect on the cache.
- A snooping cache has a snoop hit on a block in the exclusive, shared or modified state. The cache invalidates its copy (because the write transaction is altering the block in memory).

Single-Beat Read Transaction

Generated by PPC 601 Processor

The processor generates a single-beat read to read between one and eight bytes of data from memory. This will occur on a load or instruction fetch miss within a non-cacheable area of memory (I = 1). If M = 1 for this area of memory, the processor asserts GBL# to force other processors/caching entities to snoop the transaction. In the event of a snoop hit on a modified block, the processor receives a retry, the cache with the modified block performs a four-beat memory write to deposit the modified block into memory and then marks its copy shared. The processor is then permitted to retry its single-beat read to read the data from memory. The transaction is snooped again, but no retry is issued (because the block is shared, not modified). The data is successfully read from memory.

Generated by Intelligent Bus Master

An intelligent master can utilize a single-beat memory read transaction to read from one to eight bytes of data from memory. Since it does not have access to the WIM bits in the page table entries or BAT registers, it must assume that one or more processors have been caching from the area of memory being accessed and must therefore assert GBL# to force a snoop. All other processors/caching entities snoop the transaction. The snoop results are the same as those listed in the chapter entitled "PPC 601 Memory Address Phase."

Single-Beat Read Atomic Transaction

Generated by execution of a lwarx instruction to read a memory semaphore from non-cacheable memory (I = 1). Refer to the previous section and to the chapter entitled "Shared Resource Acquisition."

Four-Beat Burst Read Transaction

Generated by PPC601 Processor

The PPC 601 generates a four-beat burst read transaction under the following circumstances:

- Load miss in a page or block marked as cacheable by the operating system (I = 0).
- Instruction fetch miss in a page or block marked as cacheable by the operating system (I = 0).
- TLB miss in a page or block marked as cacheable by the operating system (I = 0).

Generated by Intelligent Bus Master

An intelligent master can utilize a four-beat memory read transaction to read 32 bytes from memory. Since it does not have access to the WIM bits in the page table entries or BAT registers, it must assume that one or more processors have been caching from the area of memory being accessed and must therefore assert GBL# to force a snoop. All other processors/caching entities snoop the transaction. The snoop results are the same as those listed in the chapter entitled "PPC 601 Memory Address Phase."

Four-Beat Burst Read Atomic

Generated by execution of a lwarx instruction to read a memory semaphore from cacheable memory (I = 0) that resulted in a miss on the cache. The processor initiates a four-beat memory read transaction to read the block containing the semaphore from memory to place into the data cache.

If M = 1 for this area of memory, the processor asserts GBL# to force other processors/caching entities to snoop the transaction.

- If the snoop results in a snoop miss, the block is stored in the cache in the exclusive state.
- If it results in a snoop hit on a cache block in the exclusive or the shared state, the block is stored in the cache in the shared state.
- In the event of a snoop hit on a modified block, the processor receives a retry, the cache with the modified block performs a four-beat memory write to deposit the modified block into memory and then marks its copy shared. The processor is then permitted to retry its four-beat read to read the data from memory. The transaction is snooped again, but no retry is issued (because the block is shared, not modified). The data is successfully read from memory and placed into the data cache.

Refer to the chapter entitled "Shared Resource Acquisition."

Read with Intent to Modify (rwitm) Transaction

The processor will perform a rwitm transaction if the area of memory has a WIM setting of 00xb and a store miss occurs on the data cache. The processor will generate a four-beat rwitm transaction to read the target block from memory into the cache in preparation for storing into it and marking it modified. If M = 1, other processors/caching entities will snoop the transaction.

- If the snoop results in a snoop miss, it has no effect on the snooper.
- If it results in a snoop hit on a cache block in the exclusive or the shared state, the block is invalidated (because the processor reading the block will immediately modify it upon completion of the read).
- In the event of a snoop hit on a modified block, the processor receives a retry, the cache with the modified block performs a four-beat memory write to deposit the modified block into memory and then marks its copy invalid. The processor is then permitted to retry its four-beat rwitm to read the data from memory. The transaction is snooped again, but no retry is issued (because the block is invalid). The data is successfully read from memory and placed into the data cache. The processor then performs the store into the cache block and marks it modified.

Read with Intent to Modify Atomic (rwitma) Transaction

Has the same effects as the rwitm, but it is caused by a store miss originated by the execution of a stwcx instruction to update a memory semaphore. For more information, refer to the chapter entitled "Shared Resource Acquisition."

I/O Transactions

The processor performs an I/O transaction if a load or store is performed within an I/O segment (T = 1 in the selected segment register). Refer to the chapter entitled "PPC 601 I/O Transactions" for additional information.

Load I/O Sequence

If the processor performs a single load from an I/O segment, the following I/O transaction sequence results:

- The processor generates an I/O load request transaction.
- The processor generates an I/O load last transaction.
- The I/O controller responds with an I/O load reply transaction.

If the processor performs a load multiple within an I/O segment, the following I/O transaction sequence results:

- The processor generates an I/O load request transaction.
- The processor generates one or more I/O load immediate transactions.
- The processor generates an I/O load last transaction.
- The I/O controller responds with an I/O load reply transaction.

Store I/O Sequence

If the processor performs a single store into an I/O segment, the following I/O transaction sequence results:

- The processor generates an I/O store last transaction.
- The I/O controller responds with an I/O store reply transaction.

If the processor performs a store multiple into an I/O segment, the following I/O transaction sequence results:

- The processor generates one or more I/O store immediate transactions.
- The processor generates an I/O store last transaction.
- The I/O controller responds with an I/O store reply transaction.

External Control Transactions

External Control Out Transaction

The processor performs an external control out transaction in response to execution of an ecowx instruction with a valid resource ID set up in the EAR register. For more information about external control transactions, refer to the chapter entitled "601 External Control Transaction."

External Control In Transaction

The processor performs an external control out transaction in response to execution of an eciwx instruction with a valid resource ID set up in the EAR register. For more information about external control transactions, refer to the chapter entitled "601 External Control Transaction."

Chapter 32

The Previous Chapter

The previous chapter provided a detailed description of every condition and/or instruction that can cause the PPC 601 processor to perform a transaction on the external bus.

This Chapter

This chapter provides a detailed description of the PPC 601 processor's split-bus architecture. It covers acquisition and usage of the address and data buses in both coupled and uncoupled designs. The data bus write-only feature is also covered.

The Next Chapter

The next chapter provides a detailed description of the address bus, including bus acquisition, use and transaction termination. Bus snooping is covered, as well. Heavily-annotated timing diagrams are utilized throughout the discussion.

Bus Clock

The bus clock is referenced frequently in this and other chapters. A detailed discussion of the bus clock can be found in the chapter entitled "Other PPC 601 Bus Signals."

Split-Bus Concept

Figure 32-1 illustrates the PPC 601 bus structure. The PPC 601 processor's bus is split into two separate and distinct buses: the address bus and the data bus. All transactions begin with a request for ownership of the address bus (BR#) issued to the external bus arbiter. If the arbiter has parked the address bus on the PPC 601, address bus grant (BG#) will already be present. The PPC 601 may initiate its address transaction if the address bus isn't busy (ABB# deasserted) and if the previous master's address transaction did not receive a retry (ARTRY# deasserted). If the grant is not already present, the PPC 601 must sample its grant input on each subsequent bus clock to determine when it has been granted the bus. When the address bus has been acquired, the PPC 601 uses the address bus to transfer the target address, the transfer size and the transfer type to the target device.

During this period of time, another processor may still own the data bus and may be using it to complete a data transfer with a previously-addressed target device. This ability to overlap the data transfer of one transaction with the address portion of another transaction is referred to as transaction pipelining.

The transaction initiated on the address bus may or may not require the subsequent transfer of data between the PPC 601 and the target device. In the event that it does not, the PPC 601 does not acquire the data bus. If the transaction will require use of the data bus, the external bus arbiter recognizes this fact from the transaction type. In other words, *the request for ownership of the data bus is implicit in the transaction type.*

When the bus arbiter determines that the PPC 601 will be the next owner of the data bus, it issues a data bus grant to the PPC 601. The bus arbiter may park the data bus on the PPC 601 by keeping its data bus grant signal, DBG#, asserted. In this event, the PPC 601 has immediate access to the data bus. When the PPC 601 determines that it has received the data bus grant (DBG# asserted), the data bus is not busy (DBB# deasserted), DRTRY# is not being asserted by the previous master, and the address transaction completed successfully (ARTRY# deasserted), it has acquired ownership of the data bus and may use it to transfer data with the target.

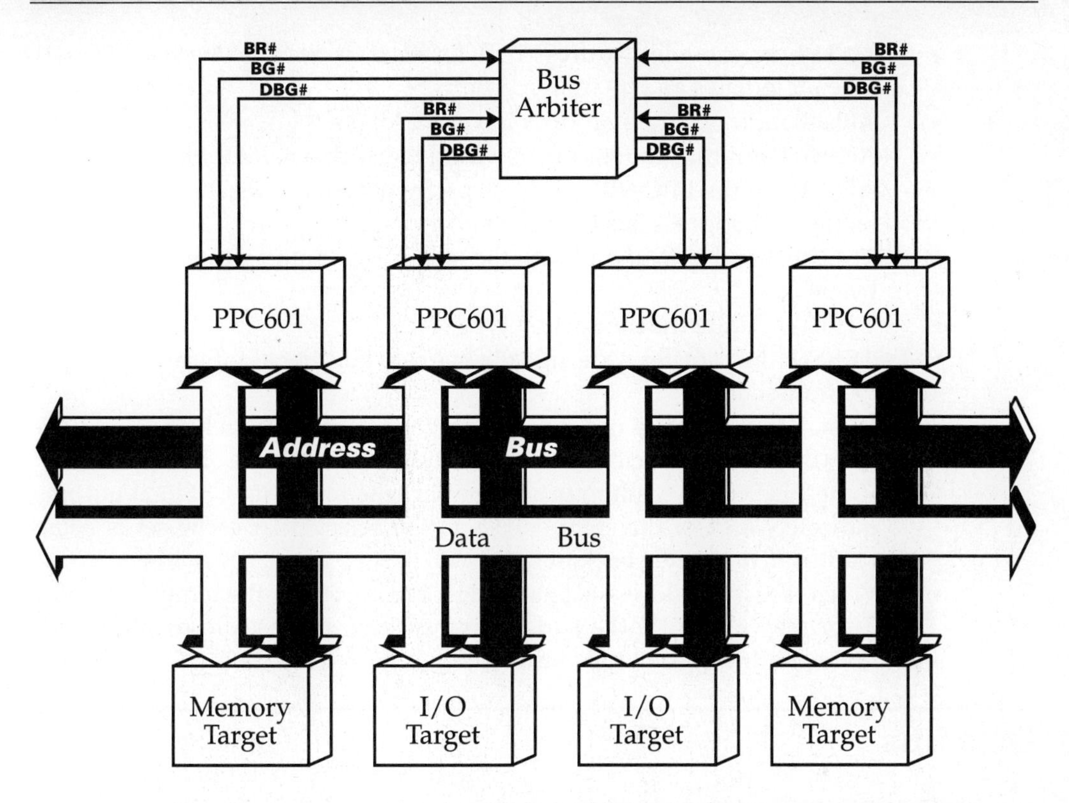

Figure 32-1. PPC601 Address and Data Buses May Be Used by Different Masters

Address Bus

The PPC 601's main address bus-related signals consist of the following signal groups:

- **BR#** is the address bus request signal from the PPC 601 to the arbiter.
- **BG#** is the address bus grant signal from the arbiter.
- **ABB#** is the address bus busy signal. Before the PPC 601 takes ownership of the address bus it must sample ABB# to determine that the previous address bus master is no longer driving the bus and its BR# input to determine if has been granted access to the bus by the arbiter. The PPC 601 asserts ABB# to indicate that it has taken ownership and begins to drive an address and transaction type onto the bus.
- **TS#**, or transfer start, is asserted by the PPC 601 when it initiates a memory-oriented transaction.

- **XATS#**, or extended address transfer start, is asserted by the PPC 601 when it initiates an I/O transaction.
- **A[0:28]** indicates the start doubleword address.
- **A[29:31]** indicates the start byte within the addressed doubleword.
- **AP[0:3]** are the PPC 601's address parity outputs. They force odd parity on the four address bus byte lanes.
- **TSIZ[0:2]** and **TBST#** indicate the size of the data transfer (number of bytes).
- **TT[0:3]** indicate the transaction type.
- **TC[0:1]**, the transfer code signals, indicate additional information about the transaction.
- **WT#, CI# and GBL#** indicate the operating system's cache-related policies (the WIM bits) within the currently-addressed page or block.
- If the PPC 601 is reading or writing a cache block, its **CSE[0:2]** outputs indicate which of the eight entries in the selected L1 cache set is being read from or written back to memory.
- When **AACK#**, address acknowledge, is asserted by the target, the processor may terminate the address transaction. It ceases to drive the address and transaction type information onto the bus.

Data Bus

The PPC 601's data bus-related signals consist of the following signal groups:

- **DBG#** is asserted by the arbiter to grant data bus ownership to the PPC 601. The PPC 601 may not take ownership until its DBG# is sampled asserted, while DBB#, DRTRY# and ARTRY# are sampled deasserted.
- **DBB#** is sampled by the PPC 601 after DBG# to determine if the previous data bus master has surrendered control of the data bus. **DBB#** is asserted by the PPC 601 when it acquires ownership of the data bus.
- **DRTRY#** is asserted by the target if the data just forwarded back to the PPC 601 on a read was bad and should be discarded by the processor. The target then keeps DRTRY# asserted until one clock after it has presented the correct data item on the data bus. It then deasserts DRTRY#, indicating to the PPC 601 that it latched the correct data from the data bus on the previous clock.
- **DL[0:31] and DH[0:31]** represents the lower and upper four data paths that the PPC 601 uses to perform data transfers.
- **DP[0:7]** are the PPC 601's data parity input/outputs. On a write, the PPC 601 sets the appropriate DP bit to force odd parity on the respective data

path. On a read, the PPC 601 samples each of the data paths that contain valid data to test for odd parity on the data byte(s) being received.

- **TA#**, or transfer acknowledge, is asserted by the target device to acknowledge receipt of data on a write, or to indicate the presence of the requested data on the data bus during a read transaction. On a read, the read data delivered with TA# must be validated on the next clock by sampling DRTRY# deasserted.
- **TEA#**, or transfer error acknowledge, is asserted by the target to indicate that the current data transfer must be terminated abnormally due to a transaction error. This causes a PPC 601 machine check interrupt or checkstop (if the machine check is disabled).

Uncoupled Address/Data Buses

Figure 32-2 illustrates an address/data transaction where the buses are uncoupled. Using the uncoupled buses, the address transaction of the next transaction may be overlapped with the data transfer portion of the previous transaction. The target asserts AACK# to terminate the address transaction when it is has accepted the address and transaction information from the master. It does not wait until the final data item has been transferred.

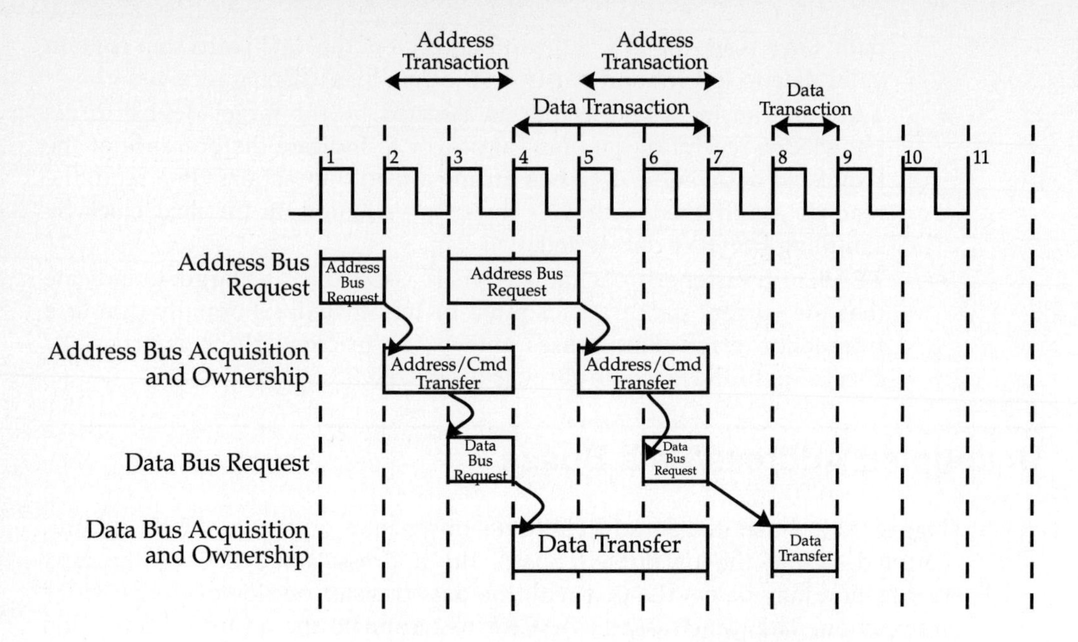

Figure 32-2. Uncoupled Address/Data Buses

Figure 32-3 illustrates an example of a bus arbitration scheme that may be used to support uncoupled use of the address and data buses. The following sections describe the operation of this example arbitration scheme.

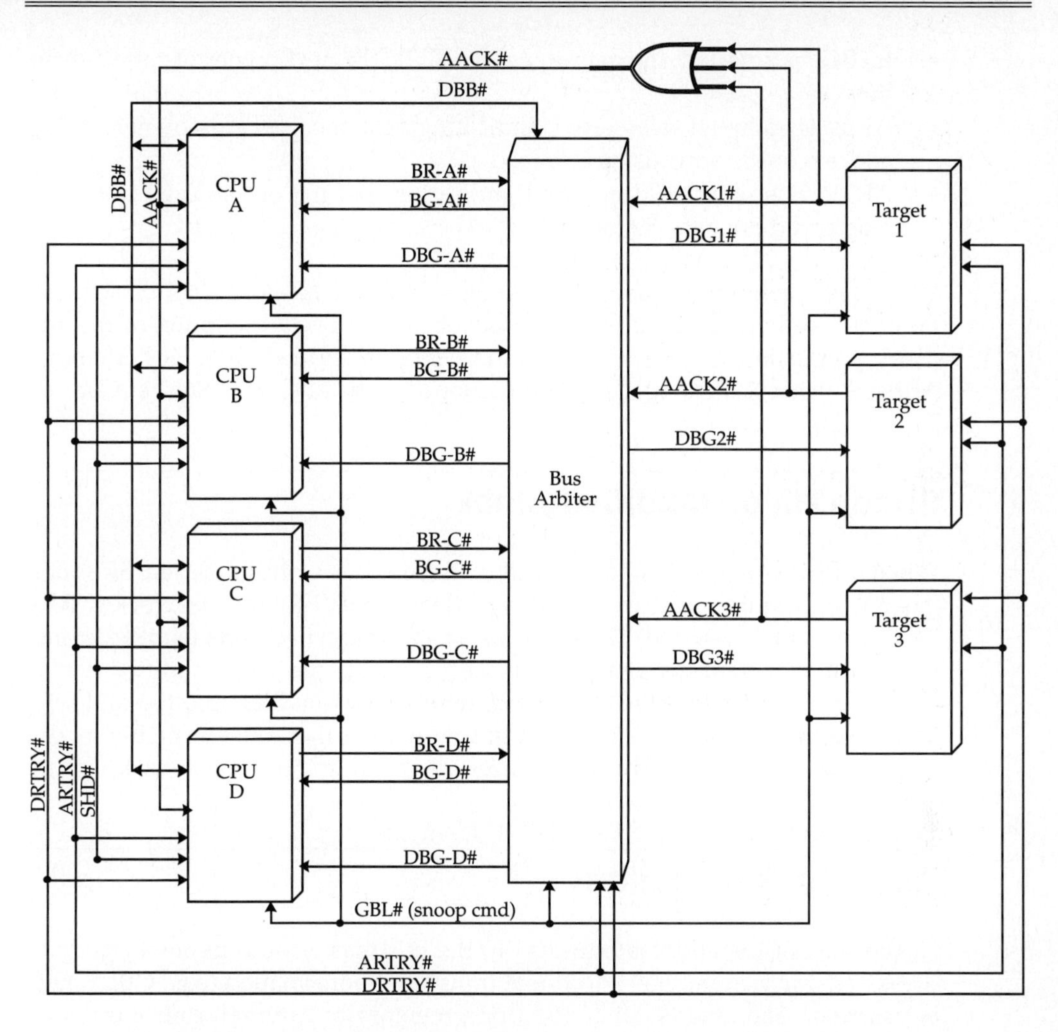

Figure 32-3. Example Bus Arbitration Scheme for Uncoupled Bus Transactions

Address Bus Arbitration

When a PPC 601 processor requires the use of the address bus, it asserts BR# to the arbiter. When the arbiter decides it's the requesting processor's turn to use the address bus, it asserts BG#. The processor may not begin using the address bus until:

- Its BG# is asserted, indicating that it will be the next owner of the address bus.
- ABB# is sampled deasserted, indicating that the previous owner of the address bus is done using it.
- ARTRY# is sampled deasserted, indicating that the previous address bus master did not experience a retry.

When these conditions have been met, the PPC 601 has address bus acquisition and can initiate an address transaction. A detailed description of the address transaction may be found in the chapters entitled "PPC 601 Memory Address Phase," "PPC 601 I/O Transactions," and "PPC 601 External Control Transactions."

Snoop Hit on Modified Block

When a PPC 601 requires access to the address bus (it has asserted BR#) but has not yet acquired ownership, it must deassert its BR# for one clock if ARTRY# is sampled asserted. The only bus master that will asserts its BR# during this clock is the master that experienced a snoop hit on a modified cache block. This ensures that the arbiter will detect only one BR# asserted and will therefore grant the address bus next to the snooper that must write the modified block back to memory (i.e., it must perform a snoop push-back operation).

Address Transaction

At the start of the address transaction, the bus master outputs the target address, the transaction type, additional transaction information (e.g., GBL# may be asserted), and asserts either TS# (for a memory or external control transaction) or XATS# (for an I/O transaction).

The bus master must continue to output this information until a target acknowledges receipt of the transaction. When a target has decoded the address, it acknowledges receipt of the transaction by asserting its AACK# signal. This is visible to the arbiter (refer to figure 32-3). Since the arbiter has individual AACK# inputs from each target and it also knows which master initiated the transaction, it can keep track of the two parties that will be involved in the subsequent data transfer (if one is required). In addition, assertion of the target's AACK# signal causes the OR gate (it's actually an AND gate performing an OR function — if any input goes low, the output goes low) to assert

AACK# to the master that initiated the transaction. Upon detection of AACK# asserted, the master terminates the address transaction.

Snooping

If the master had instructed all other processors to snoop the transaction (by asserting GBL#) in their L1 caches and report back the snoop result, the master will sample the snoop result (on SHD# and ARTRY#) one bus clock cycle after AACK# is sampled asserted. If ARTRY# is sampled deasserted, the address transaction completed without the need for a later retry (the snoop result indicated that none of snoopers were busy and that none of them experienced a hit on a modified cache block).

If ARTRY# is asserted by a snooper, it indicates either that one or more of the snoopers were busy and could not snoop right now or that one of the snoopers experienced a snoop hit on a modified cache block. In either event, the bus master that performed the address transaction may be accessing a stale area of memory and must therefore retry the address transaction again later. When the target detects the ARTRY#, it recognizes that the pending data transfer has been canceled. The arbiter cancels the pending data bus request associated with the transaction.

Assuming that the transaction requires a subsequent data transfer with the target and that ARTRY# was not asserted, the master must await data bus acquisition before using the data bus to perform the required data transfer.

Data Bus Arbitration

When the PPC 601 processor performs an address transaction, it may or may not require that a data transfer be performed after completion of the address transaction. The need for the data bus is implied in certain transaction types. If the arbiter determines that a bus master will require the data bus (by examining the transaction type), it takes one of the following courses of action:

- In most cases, the arbiter will grant the data bus to the master that just completed the address transaction. If this is the case, the arbiter will assert DBG# to the bus master that just completed the address transaction and to the target of the transaction.
- In some cases, the arbiter may decide to defer granting permission to the master and target for the data transfer associated with the address trans-

action just completed. It may permit another bus master to perform a data transfer before permitting the deferred data transfer to take place. In this case, the arbiter will remember the two parties (master and target) involved in the address transaction until such time as it decides to permit the deferred data transfer. When the arbiter decides to permit the data transfer to take place, it asserts DBG# to the master.

When the arbiter detects DBB# deasserted by the current data bus master and DRTRY# not asserted, indicating that the previous data bus master has completed using the data bus, it must also check ARTRY# to ensure that the address transaction has not received a retry. Assuming there wasn't a retry issued, the arbiter then asserts DBG# to the target that accepted the address transaction. The bus master asserts its DBB# output to signal its ownership of the data bus. A complete description of the data bus transaction may be found in the chapter entitled "PPC 601 Data Phase."

Write Transaction

If a write transaction was initiated, the PPC 601 drives the data onto the data bus at the same time that it asserts DBB#. The target asserts TA# when it has accepted the data item. The master ceases to drive the write data and deasserts DBB# to indicate its surrender of data bus ownership.

Read Transaction

If a read transaction was initiated, the target may utilize the assertion of its DBG# (by the arbiter) to gate the requested data onto the data bus and asserts TA# to indicate its presence. If the target requires more time to place the requested data on the data bus, it may keep TA# deasserted until the requested data is present on the data bus. The bus master inserts wait states in the data phase until TA# is sampled asserted. When the master samples TA# asserted, it latches the read data. One bus clock tick later, the master samples DRTRY# to determine if the read data was good (DRTRY# deasserted indicates that the data is good) and can be forwarded to the processor core.

Single-Beat Write Transaction

If the transaction involves the transfer of a single doubleword (or a subset of a doubleword), it is referred to as a single-beat transaction. When TA# is sampled asserted, the data item is transferred. If it is a write transaction, the master then deasserts DBB# and gives up control of the data bus.

Single-Beat Read Transaction

If it is a read transaction, the bus master latches the read data when TA# is sampled asserted. It also deasserts DBB#. The master then samples DRTRY# one tick after TA# is sampled asserted to determine if the latched data is good and can be forwarded to the processor core. If DRTRY# is sampled deasserted, the data is good and the transaction is over. If DRTRY# is sampled asserted, the data is bad and the processor discards it. It then samples the data on the bus on each subsequent rising-edge of the bus clock along with the state of the DRTRY# signal to determine when the correct data has been latched from the bus. The continued assertion of DRTRY# causes the processor to insert wait states in the data phase. When DRTRY# is subsequently sampled deasserted, this indicates that the correct data was sampled on the previous bus clock rising-edge and that the single-beat read is over. A complete description of DRTRY# usage can be found in the chapter entitled "PPC 601 Data Phase" under the heading "Burst With Data Retry."

Four-Beat Burst Write Transaction

If the bus master asserted TBST# during the address transaction, this indicates that the bus master will transfer four doublewords (a 32-byte cache block) to or from the target. If a write burst transaction, the processor outputs the second doubleword when it samples TA# asserted for the first doubleword. It continues to drive the second doubleword until TA# is sampled asserted again. It then begins to drive the third doubleword and continues to drive it until the third TA# is sampled. It then outputs the final doubleword and continues to drive it until TA# is sampled asserted for the fourth time. The master then ceases to drive the fourth doubleword and deasserts DBB# to indicate its surrender of the data bus.

Four-Beat Burst Read Transaction

If the master is performing a four-beat burst read transaction, four doublewords (an entire 32-byte cache block) will be read from the target. Each time that the target places a doubleword on the data bus, it asserts TA# to indicate its presence. Just as with the single-beat read transaction, the master latches the doubleword when TA# is sampled asserted. On the bus clock rising-edge after TA# is sampled asserted and a doubleword is latched, the processor samples both TA# and DRTRY#. One of the following combinations will be detected:

- **TA# asserted and DRTRY# deasserted**. This combination indicates that the doubleword that was latched on the previous clock was good and that the next doubleword is being presented on the data bus by the target. The processor latches the next doubleword and validates it on the next clock by sampling DRTRY# again.
- **TA# deasserted and DRTRY# asserted**. The doubleword latched on the previous clock was bad (DRTRY# asserted) and is discarded by the processor. The next doubleword is not yet present on the bus (TA# deasserted). The processor must continue to latch data and the state of DRTRY# and TA# on each clock. On the clock where DRTRY# is sampled deasserted and TA# is sampled asserted, the doubleword latched on the previous clock was good (DRTRY# then transitioned from asserted to deasserted) and the next doubleword was latched on this clock (TA# was sampled asserted).

During the fourth beat of the burst read transaction, the processor samples TA# until the presence of the last doubleword is indicated (TA# asserted). The doubleword is latched and DBB# is deasserted by the master. The last doubleword is validated on the next clock by sampling DRTRY# again. If DRTRY# is sampled deasserted, the final doubleword was good and the data transaction completed. If DRTRY# is sampled asserted, the doubleword is bad and is discarded. The processor continues to sample DRTRY# and latch data on each clock until DRTRY# is sampled deasserted. When it is, the doubleword latched on the previous clock was good and the transaction is over.

Data Bus Write-Only Feature

Assume that a PPC 601 processor (referred to as master A in this discussion) initiates a memory read transaction and completes its address phase without receiving a retry (ARTRY# not asserted). When master A completes its memory read address transaction without receiving a retry, it is then awaiting assertion of its DBG# by the arbiter so that it may transfer the read data from memory. The memory target that acknowledged receipt of the read request now begins to access its memory in preparation for the pending data bus transaction.

During the address phase of master A's memory read transaction, another bus master (referred to as master B in this discussion) receives BG# from the bus arbiter to run a memory read or write address transaction. When bus master A completes its address transaction, master B initiates its transaction and asserts GBL#, instructing all other processors to snoop its transaction and report back the snoop result. Bus master A experiences a snoop hit on a modified sector and issues a retry to master B by asserting ARTRY#. This causes bus master B to terminate its memory access attempt without performing the data transfer with memory. Master B will re attempt its memory access later.

When it experienced the snoop hit on the modified sector, master A immediately asserted its BR# so that it can perform the snoop push-back of the modified sector to memory. The highest-priority write that is present in the write queue of master A's MU at this moment is the push-back operation. Because the ARTRY# was visible to all other masters, each of them cancels any pending bus requests (they each deassert their respective BR# signals). The arbiter thus only detects the BR# signal asserted from the master that experienced the snoop hit on the modified sector. The arbiter therefore grants the address bus to master A by asserting its BG# signal.

Master A assumes ownership of the address bus and initiates its snoop push-back memory write transaction. When it completes its address transaction, the arbiter grants it ownership of the data bus by asserting its DBG# signal. In addition, the arbiter asserts DBWO# to permit it to use the data bus to write the modified data to memory.

Prior to the initiation of the push-back transaction, master A had successfully completed the address portion of a memory read and was awaiting ownership of the data bus to read the requested data from memory. Ordinarily, the PPC 601 must perform this memory read data transfer when it receives its next data bus grant. The assertion of DBWO# along with the DBG#, however, gives the PPC 601 permission to use the data bus to write the modified sector to memory — in other words, the PPC 601 is permitted to perform the write data operation out-of-order. If the arbiter had not asserted DBWO# to master A along with its DBG#, master A does not have permission to perform an out-of-order data transfer. It would have to use the data bus to read the previously-requested data from memory.

When the PPC 601 receives ownership of the data bus along with DBWO# asserted, it asserts DBB# and performs the highest-priority write operation pending in its MU — the four-beat burst write of the modified sector to memory. Upon completion of the burst write, the arbiter would typically grant ownership of the address bus to the bus master that experienced the retry earlier (master B) so that it may now retry its memory access. Bus master B now reinitiates its memory access and completes it successfully (without a retry). The arbiter then asserts DBG# to master A (and to the memory target it had previously issued the memory read request to) so that it may read the data previously-requested from memory. The arbiter must "remember" the target and master so that it may re-establish this connection to permit the data transfer to take place.

Coupled Address/Data Buses

In order to simplify the design of the host bus arbiter, the system board designer may choose to tightly couple the address and data buses. In this scenario, the arbiter will not permit the bus master to relinquish ownership of the address bus until the final doubleword of data has been transferred successfully. Figure 32-5 illustrates the bus arbitration logic.

The snoopers must make the snoop result available two clocks after TS# is sampled asserted from the master. If the arbiter detects that a snooper has asserted ARTRY#, it will assert AACK# to the master to terminate the address transaction and force the master to sample the snoop result one clock after AACK# is sampled asserted. When the master detects ARTRY# asserted, it will abort the subsequent data transfer associated with the address transaction. When the target samples ARTRY# asserted, it will recognize that the data transfer has been canceled.

In this scenario, there can be one common AACK# signal between the arbiter and all targets. When a target asserts AACK#, the arbiter can choose to pass it through to the master in the event of an ARTRY# (as just described) or to defer assertion of AACK# to the master until the data transaction has concluded.

Figure 32-4 illustrates address/data transactions where the buses are coupled together.

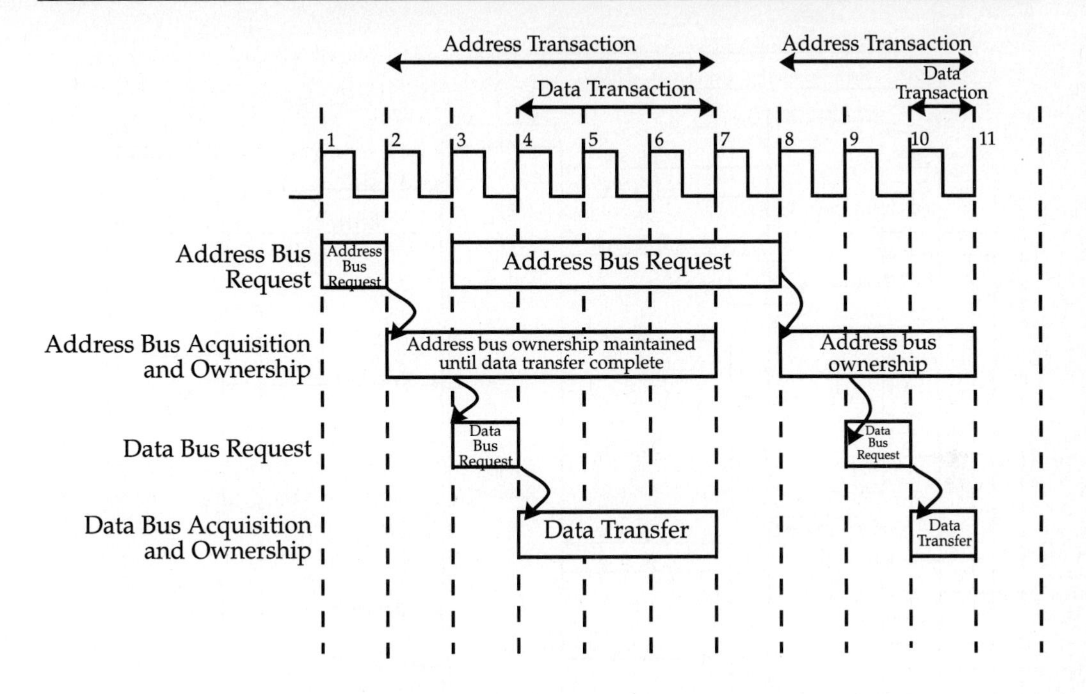

Figure 32-4. Coupled Address/Data Buses

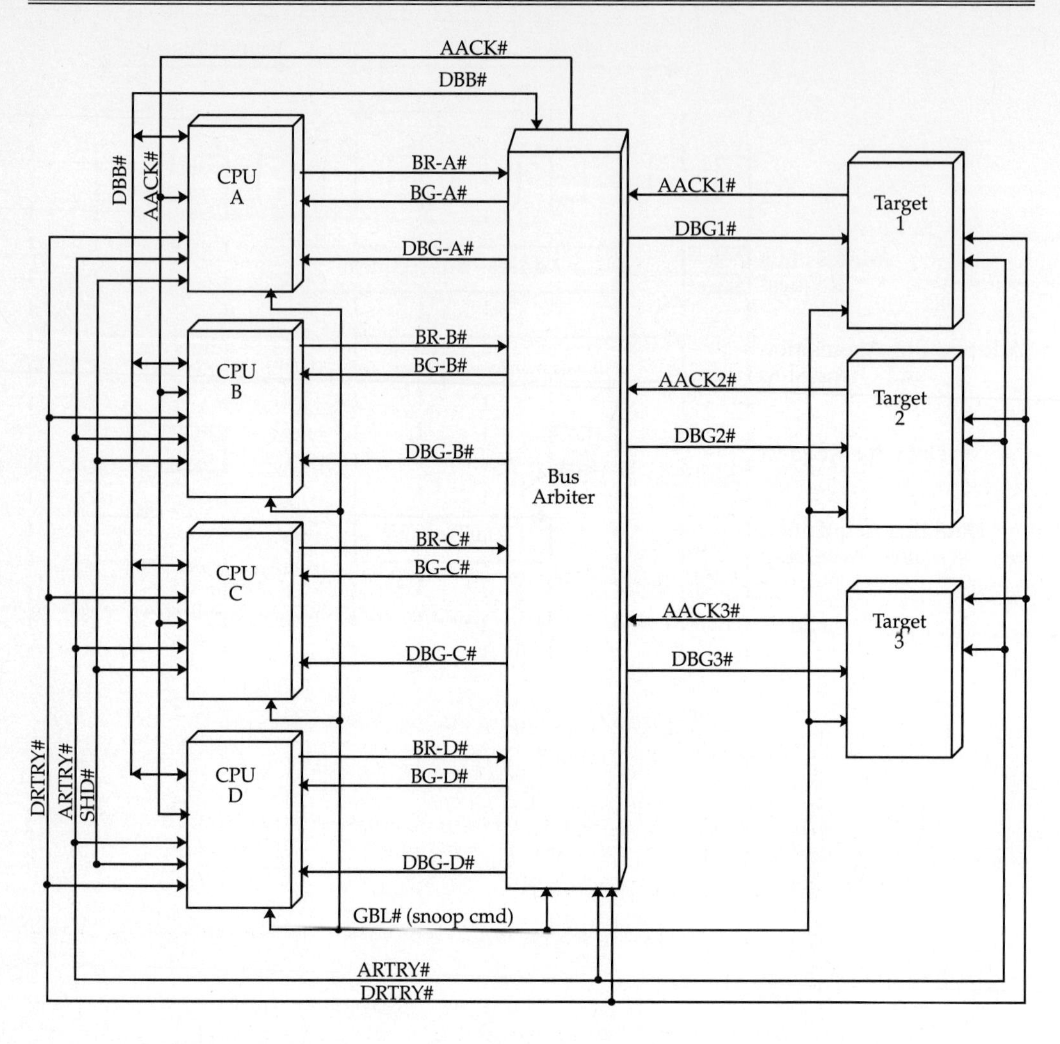

Figure 32-5. Example Bus Arbitration Scheme for Coupled Bus Transactions

Chapter 33

The Previous Chapter

The previous chapter provided a detailed description of the PPC 601 processor's split-bus architecture. It covered acquisition and usage of the address and data buses in both coupled and uncoupled designs. The data bus write-only feature was also covered.

This Chapter

This chapter provides a detailed description of the address bus as used during memory-oriented transactions, including bus acquisition, use and transaction termination. Bus snooping is covered, as well. Heavily-annotated timing diagrams are utilized throughout the discussion.

The Next Chapter

The next chapter provides a detailed description of the data bus, including bus acquisition, use and transaction termination. Heavily-annotated timing diagrams are utilized throughout the discussion.

Background

The PPC601 bus permits any device with bus master capability to acquire bus ownership and run a transaction to communicate with either a target device (memory, I/O or external) and/or all processors and caching entities on the bus. Basically, there are two types of transactions that can be performed once the bus has been acquired:

- **Address-only transaction**. A bus master uses the address-only transactions to enforce consistency with other processors/caching entities in the system. The PPC601 transactions that fall into this category are: clean, flush, kill, sync, and TLB invalidate.

- **Address transaction followed by a data transaction**. When a bus master must transfer data to or from a target device (memory, I/O or external), it must first acquire ownership of the address bus and then perform an address transaction to inform the target device of the start address, transaction type and the size of the data operand to be transferred. After the target acknowledges receipt of this information, the master must then acquire ownership of the data bus in order to transfer the data to or from the target device.

Timing Diagrams

This chapter focuses on the acquisition of the address bus, the performance and receipt of the address transaction, and testing the snoop result of the transaction snoop (if applicable). Timing diagrams are referenced throughout this chapter. The timing of all bus transaction is synchronized to the bus master's internal bus clock signal. The bus clock is always shown at the top of the timing diagrams. The only time that the processor samples signals is on the rising-edge of the bus clock. A dotted line has been aligned with each rising-edge of the bus clock and these edges have been numbered for easy reference within the text that accompanies each timing diagram. A complete description of the bus clock can be found in the chapter entitled "Other PPC 601 Bus Signals."

Address Bus Acquisition

Before performing any type of transaction, a bus master must first acquire ownership of the host bus. To initiate this process, the bus master must start by asserting its address bus request signal, BR#. This point-to-point signal is issued to the host bus arbiter (as illustrated in figure 33-1).

Chapter 33: PPC 601 Memory Address Phase

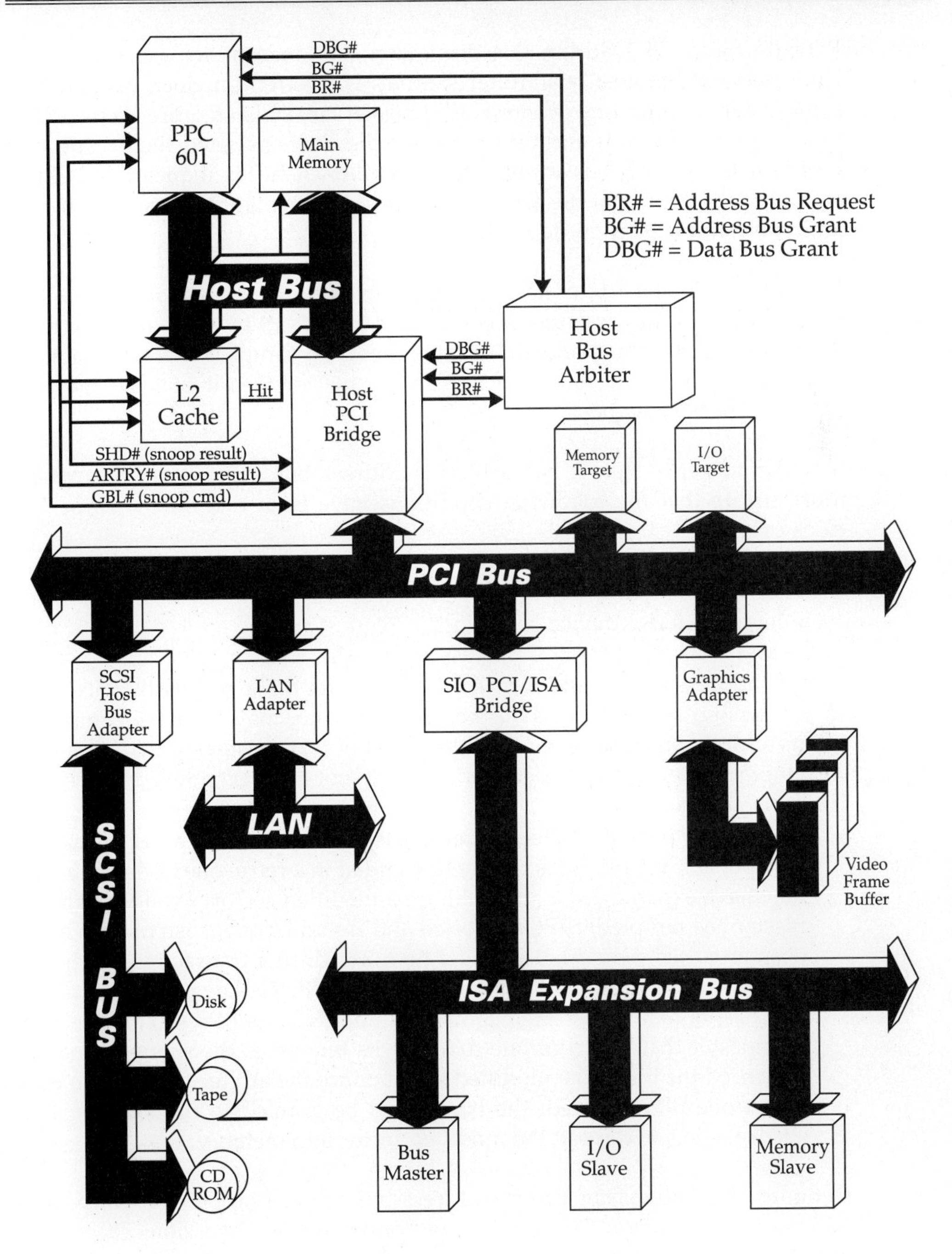

Figure 33-1. Sample System

Refer to figure 33-2 during this discussion. The bus master asserts BR# on clock one and the host bus arbiter samples it asserted on clock two. At this same instant in time, one or more other masters may also require access to the bus to run transactions and may therefore also have asserted their respective BR# signals. The host bus arbiter evaluates all outstanding requests and issues a grant to the winner of the arbitration. The decision algorithm utilized by the arbiter is platform design-dependent.

In this example, the arbiter has decided to grant ownership of the address bus to this master. It has asserted BG# (address bus grant) to the requesting master prior to clock three and the master therefore samples its BG# input asserted on clock three. This indicates to the master that it may be the next owner of the address bus.

In order to verify that it has achieved address bus acquisition, the master must ensure that the following conditions have been met on the same bus clock edge:

- **Address bus grant, BG#, still asserted**. If the bus arbiter determines that a higher-priority device has issued a request for the address bus, it may deassert this master's BG# and assert the other master's BG#.
- The **address bus is not busy (ABB# deasserted)**. The master that acquired ownership of the address bus before this master may not have completed its address bus transaction yet (the target of that master's transaction may employ a slow address decoder and may not have acknowledged receipt of the transaction).
- **No backoff issued to the previous master** (ARTRY# not asserted by any snoopers). If the previous transaction ended in a retry, one of the snoopers may have experienced a snoop hit on a modified sector. Even though this master has sampled its BG# asserted and the address bus isn't busy (ABB# deasserted), it should not proceed with its address transaction. Rather, it must ignore its grant and deassert its request (BR#). Any other bus master that has its request asserted should also deassert its BR# signal. The only bus master that will continue to assert its request is the snooper that experienced the hit on the modified sector. Since the arbiter would then only detect one BR# asserted, the bus would be granted to the snooper that needs the bus to deposit the modified sector into memory.

In figure 33-2, the master detects address bus acquisition on clock three and initiates the transaction. The next section continues this discussion.

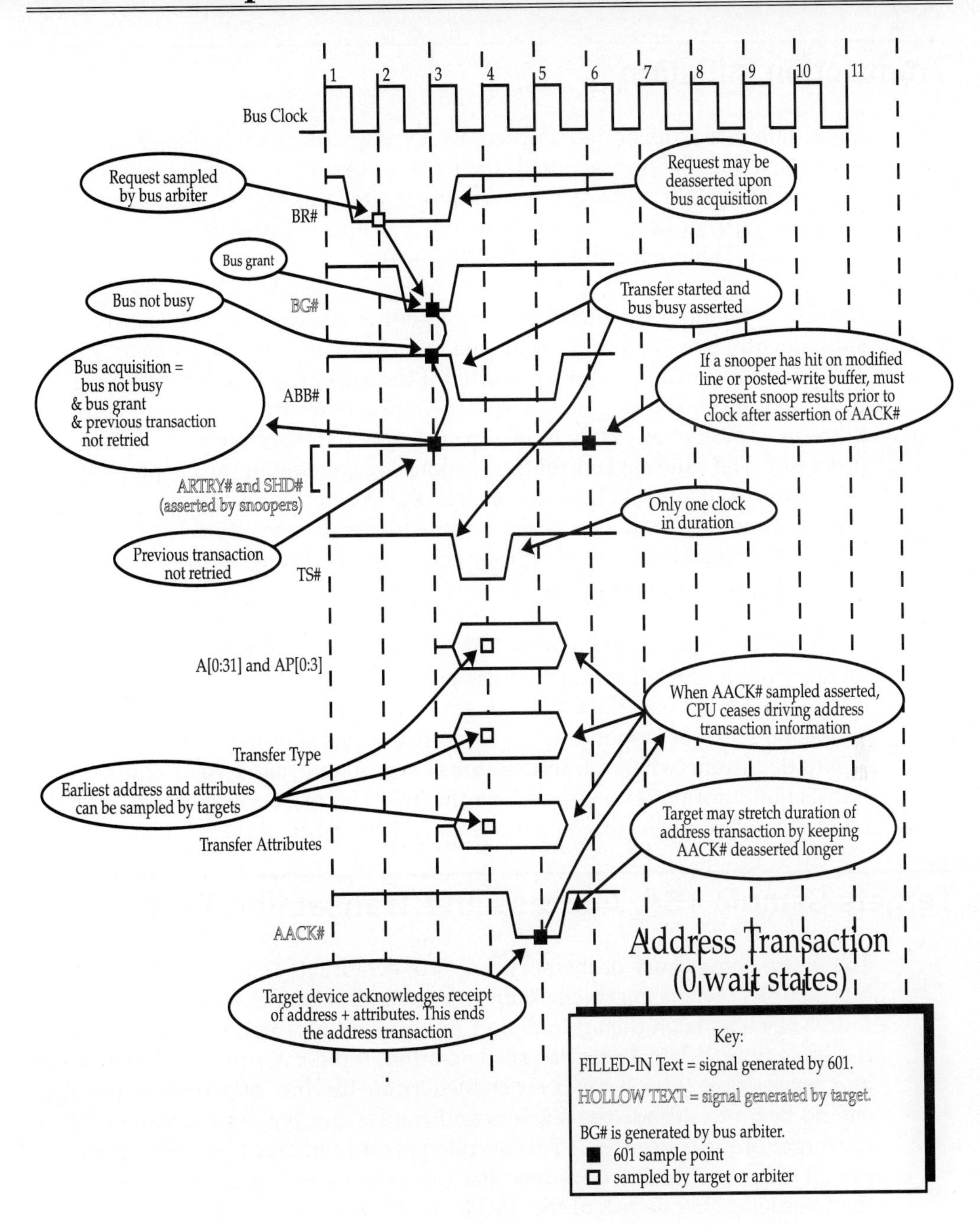

Figure 33-2. Zero Wait State Address Transaction

Transaction Initiation

Once data bus acquisition has been achieved (clock three in figure 33-2), the master initiates the transaction. If the master does not require the address bus to perform another address bus transaction after this one, it deasserts its BR# when the current transaction is initiated. If it will require the bus to perform another transaction, it will keep its BR# asserted.

If this is a memory-oriented transaction (either address-only or one that will subsequently involve a transfer of data to or from memory), the master asserts TS# (transfer start). TS# is also asserted if the master will perform an external control in or out transaction. These two transactions are only run in response to the execution of an eciwx or ecowx instruction, respectively, by a PowerPC processor. The external control transactions are covered in the chapter entitled "601 External Control Transaction." If the master is performing an I/O-oriented transaction, it asserts extended address transfer start, XATS#, rather than TS#. Discussion of the I/O transaction can be found in the chapter entitled "PPC 601 I/O Transactions."

In figure 33-2, the master asserts TS# on clock three, indicating that either a memory or an eco/eci transaction has been initiated. TS# will only be asserted by the master for one clock tick. This means that all memory targets and the special targets that respond to eco/eci transactions should continually sample TS# to determine when a transaction has begun and that a valid address and transaction information is present on the bus. The master also asserts address bus busy, ABB#, indicating that it has taken ownership of the address bus.

Targets Sample TS#, Address and Transaction Type

The entire community of memory and eco/eci targets that reside on the host bus sample TS# on every clock until it is finally sampled asserted on clock four. They also latch the address and transaction information from the bus at the same time. When TS# is sampled asserted, it indicates that a valid address and transaction type have been latched from the bus and that each target should begin to decode the address and transaction type to determine if it is the target of the transaction. This decode process can take some time (because not all targets will have decoders that can determine if they are the target of the transaction in one tick of the clock).

Memory Transaction Types

When the master initiates an address-only, memory read/write or external control transaction, it asserts TS# and drives the transaction type onto the transaction type bus, TT[0:3]. Table 33-1 defines the memory and external control-oriented transactions. The I/O transaction types are defined in the chapter entitled "PPC 601 I/O Transactions." The sections that follow define the address-only, memory read/write and external control transactions. Table 33-2 provides individual definitions of the TT[0:3] outputs.

Table 33-1. Transaction Types (Exclusive of I/O)

TT0	TT1	TT2	TT3	Transaction Type
0	0	0	0	***Clean sector operation***. Address-only.
0	0	0	1	***Write With Flush***. Single-beat write.
0	0	1	0	***Flush Sector***. Address-only.
0	0	1	1	***Write With Kill***. Burst Write.
0	1	0	0	***Sync***. Address-only.
0	1	0	1	***Read***. Single or four-beat burst read.
0	1	1	0	***Kill Sector***. Address-only.
0	1	1	1	***Read With Intent To Modify***. Burst read.
1	0	0	0	Reserved.
1	0	0	1	***Write With Flush Atomic***. Single-beat write.
1	0	1	0	***External Control Out***. Single-beat write.
1	0	1	1	Reserved.
1	1	0	0	***TLB Invalidate***. Address-only.
1	1	0	1	***Read Atomic***. Single or four beat burst read.
1	1	1	0	***External Control In***. Single-beat read.
1	1	1	1	***Read With Intent To Modify Atomic***. Burst read.

Table 33-2. Definition of TT Bits (TT[0:4])

TT Bit	Description
TT0	Asserted whenever a transaction is run in response to a ***lwarx/stwcx instruction pair,*** a ***tlbie*** (Translation Lookaside Buffer Invalidate) operation, or either an ***eciwx or ecowx*** instruction.
TT1	***Read or Write*** operation. 1 = read, 0 = write. This assumes that the transaction is not an address-only operation (see TT3).
TT2	TT2 = 1 indicates an ***Invalidate*** Operation. When asserted with GBL#, TT2 indicates all other caches in the system should snoop the transaction and invalidate entries that have a snoop hit. If the snoop hits on a modified line, the respective cache should perform a push back operation before invalidating the line.
TT3	***Memory Data Transfer or Address-Only Operation.*** TT3 = 1 indicates that a memory data transfer will occur, while TT3 = 0 indicates that this is an address-only transaction. The single-beat external control operations, eciwx and ecowx, are an exception. In this case, TT3 = 0, but a data transfer will take place.
TT4	***Reserved*** for future use. Always set low by the PPC601.

Address-Only Transactions

The following transactions do not involve a data transfer and therefore do not require access to the data bus (for a list of the events that cause each transaction type, refer to the chapter entitled "Bus Transaction Causes"):

- **Clean sector**. Causes any processor with a copy of the addressed sector in the modified state to write the sector into memory and then mark its copy exclusive. Caused by the execution of a dcbst instruction.
- **Flush sector**. Causes any processor with a copy of the addressed sector in the modified state to write the sector into memory and then invalidate its copy. Caused by the execution of a dcbf instruction.
- **Kill sector**. Causes any processor with a copy of the addressed sector to invalidate its copy (even if in the modified state). Caused by execution of a dcbi or dcbz instruction, or a store hit on a sector in the shared state within a page or block with M = 1.
- **Sync**. Causes a look-through L2 cache with a posted-write buffer to perform all of its posted writes. Caused by execution of a sync instruction.
- **TLB invalidate**. Causes all processors to perform a lookup in their TLBs and invalidate the indicated pair of page table entries. Caused by execu-

tion of a tlbie instruction. The TLB index field, EA[12:18], is output onto the address bus.

This chapter contains a detailed description of the address transaction.

Memory Read/Write Transactions

The following transactions perform memory data reads or writes and therefore require access to the data bus:

- **Single-beat read**. Used to read between one and eight bytes from memory. Caused by a load or instruction fetch in a non-cacheable memory area (I = 1).
- **Single-beat read atomic**. Used to read a memory semaphore into the processor. Caused by execution of an lwarx instruction in a non-cacheable memory area.
- **Single-beat write**. Used to write between one and eight bytes into memory. Caused by one of the following: store in a non-cacheable memory area; store hit or miss in a cacheable memory area with a write-through policy.
- **Single-beat write atomic**. Used to update a memory semaphore in memory. Caused by execution of a stwcx instruction in a non-cacheable memory area or a cacheable memory area with a write-through policy.
- **Four-beat burst read**. Used to read a cache sector from memory into the L1 cache. Caused by a load miss on the cache in a memory area designated as cacheable.
- **Four-beat burst read atomic**. Used to read a cache sector containing a memory semaphore into the L1 cache. Caused by execution of an lwarx instruction that results in an L1 miss within an area of memory designated as cacheable.
- **Four-beat burst write**. Used to write a modified cache sector back to memory. Caused by one of the following: cast out of a modified cache sector to make room for a new sector being copied into the L1 cache; snoop push-back of a modified sector to memory as a result of a snoop hit on the modified sector.
- **Read with intent to modify (rwitm)**. Used to read a cache sector into the cache in order to store into it. Caused by a store miss in a cacheable memory area with a write-back policy.
- **Read with intent to modify atomic (rwitma)**. Used to read a cache sector containing a memory semaphore into the cache in order to update the

semaphore. Caused by the execution of a stwcx instruction resulting in a store miss in a cacheable memory area with a write-back policy

The address phase of these transactions is covered in this chapter, while the data phase of the transaction is covered in the chapter entitled "PPC 601 Data Phase."

External Control Transactions

The following transactions perform data transfer to or from a special external device and therefore require access to the data bus:

- External control in. Caused by execution of an eciwx instruction.
- External control out. Caused by execution of an ecowx instruction.

The address and data phase of these transactions are covered in the chapter entitled "601 External Control Transaction."

Address and Transaction Information

When the master initiates the address bus transaction, it outputs the following information:

- Start doubleword address, start byte within the doubleword and the size of the operand to be transferred.
- Transaction Type.
- Other transaction attributes.

Rather than impede the flow of this discussion, a description of the addressing scheme and transaction attributes can be found in this chapter in the sections entitled "Addressing Scheme" and "Additional Transaction Attributes Output by Master." A detailed description of each transaction type can be found in the chapter entitled "Bus Transaction Causes."

Target Claims Transaction

When the target of the current transaction has determined that it is the target, it acknowledges receipt of the address and transaction information by asserting address acknowledge, or AACK#. In figure 33-2, a target with a very fast decoder has claimed the transaction. It latched the transaction information on clock four, decoded it, and asserted AACK# before clock five. If the target had a relatively slow decoder, AACK# would not have been asserted so quickly. Refer to the section in this chapter entitled "Slow, Non-Existent or Broken Target" for a discussion of this subject.

When the master detects AACK# asserted by the target (on clock five), it ceases to drive the address and transaction information onto the bus. It also deasserts ABB#, indicating that it has given up address bus ownership.

Snoop Results Sampled by Bus Master

When the master is performing a bus access within a page or block with M = 1, it must assert GBL# to instruct all other processors and caching entities on the host bus to snoop its transaction. At the conclusion of its address bus transaction, all of the snoopers must report back the results of the snoop. The snoop result will be sampled by the master one tick after it has sampled AACK# asserted and surrendered ownership of the address bus. The master will only assert GBL# to instruct all other processors/caching entities to snoop its transaction under the following circumstances:

- The master is a PPC601 processor performing an access in a page or block of memory that the OS has indicated (by setting M = 1 in the page table entry or the BAT register) may be accessed by other masters.
- The master is an intelligent bus master or DMA controller accessing memory and it does not have access to the page table entries or to the processor's internal BAT registers. It must therefore assume that one or more processors/caching entities have been caching from the target memory area.
- The master is a PPC601 processor operating in real address mode (its MMU is turned off). The processor then assumes the WIM bits for the access are set to 001b, indicating that the target memory is cacheable, a write-back policy should be used and other processors/caching entities may also access the area of memory being accessed.

The snoop result is reported back to the master on the shared, SHD#, and address retry, ARTRY#, signals. The following sections define the actions taken (as defined by the snoop result). The master samples the snoop result on clock eight in figure 33-3. The following sections discuss the various forms of snoop results that may be reported.

Neither SHD# Nor ARTRY# Asserted — Snoop Miss

All of the snoopers have successfully completed the snoop and none of them experienced a hit on the target cache sector. If the bus master is performing a burst read to read a sector from memory, the cache sector should be stored in the L1 cache in the exclusive state when the read is completed.

SHD# Asserted — Someone Has Copy of Target Sector in Exclusive or Shared State

This indicates the existence of one of the following conditions:

- One of the snoopers has experienced a hit on a cache sector in the exclusive state (and is asserting SHD#).
- Two or more of the snoopers have experienced a hit on a cache sector in the shared state (and are asserting SHD#).

In either case, if the master is performing a burst read to read a sector from memory, the cache sector should be stored in the L1 cache in the shared state.

Just ARTRY# Asserted — One or More of the Snoopers Are Busy

One or more of the snoopers are currently busy and cannot snoop (and are asserting ARTRY# to indicate a snooper busy condition). The assertion of ARTRY# instructs the master to retry the address transaction again later. If the master were to proceed with the transaction, there is the danger that a stale sector will be accessed in memory. Figure 33-4 illustrates the master sampling ARTRY# asserted on clock six.

Both SHD# and ARTRY# Asserted

Refer to figure 33-4. This indicates the existence of one of the conditions described in the sections that follow.

Snoop Hit on Modified Copy of Sector

One of the snooping devices has experienced a snoop hit on a modified cache sector. If the master is attempting to perform a memory read or write, this indicates that it is about to access a stale sector in memory. The master should not proceed with the data transfer and should re attempt the address transaction again later. Any other master that is requesting access to the address bus must deassert its request (BR#) to permit the snooper that experienced the hit to acquire the bus. The snooper that experienced the hit asserts its BR# and the arbiter grants it the bus (because all other requesters have deasserted their requests). Upon acquiring the address bus, the snooper performs a burst memory write transaction to deposit the modified cache sector into memory. Upon completion of the memory write, the snooper takes one of the two actions described in the next two sections.

If Snooped Transaction Was Read

If the transaction that was aborted was a memory read attempt, the snooper now changes the state of its copy of the cache sector from modified to shared (because the master that experienced the retry will now re acquire the bus and read the newly-deposited sector into its cache). The master that experienced the retry then reacquires the bus and reattempts its previously aborted memory read access. Because it once again asserts GBL#, the transaction is again snooped, this time resulting in a snoop hit on a shared sector. The snooper asserts SHD#, but not ARTRY#. The master is permitted to complete the read and places the sector into its cache in the shared state.

If Snooped Transaction Was Write

If the transaction that was aborted was a memory write, the snooper changes the state of its cache sector from modified to invalid after completing the snoop push back of the modified sector to memory (because the master that experienced the retry will overwrite all or a portion of the sector in memory when it reattempts the previously-aborted memory write). The master that experienced the retry then reacquires the bus and reattempts its previously aborted memory write access. Because it once again asserts GBL#, the transaction is again snooped, this time resulting in a snoop miss (the snooper asserts neither SHD#, nor ARTRY#). The master is permitted to complete the write.

Snooper(s) Busy and One other Cache Has Exclusive Copy of Sector

One of the snoopers has experienced a hit on a cache sector in the exclusive state (and is asserting SHD#) and one or more of the other snoopers are currently busy and cannot snoop (and are asserting ARTRY#). Because a busy snooper may have a copy of the sector in the modified state, the master must abort the transaction and retry the address portion of the transaction again later. It should be noted that it is highly unlikely that any snooper has a copy of the sector in the modified state because one of the processors has a copy in the exclusive state. This copy would have been killed by the other processor before it modified its copy of the sector.

Snooper(s) Busy and One or more other Caches Have Shared Copies of Sector

One or more of the snoopers have experienced a hit on a cache sector in the shared state (and are asserting SHD#) and one or more of the other snoopers are currently busy and cannot snoop (and are asserting ARTRY#). Because a busy snooper may have a copy of the sector in the modified state, the master must abort the transaction and retry the address portion of the transaction again later. It should be noted that it is highly unlikely that any snooper has a copy of the sector in the modified state because two or more of the processors have copies in the shared state. These copies would have been killed by the other processor before it modified its copy of the sector.

Slow, Non-Existent or Broken Target

Figure 33-3 illustrates an address transaction with wait states inserted by a slow target. The master is obliged to keep driving the address and transaction information onto the bus until a target acknowledges receipt of the information (clock seven in the example). In this example, the master samples AACK# deasserted on clocks five and six, forcing two wait states to be inserted into the address transaction. If the currently-addressed target were non-existent or broken, the address transaction could be stretched out forever. The platform designer might want to consider including some type of bus monitoring logic to automatically terminate an abnormally-extended transaction. This could be accomplished by asserting transfer error acknowledge, or TEA#, to the master. This would cause the master to immediately terminate the transaction.

identify the size (number of bytes) of the operand to be transferred to or from the currently-addressed target. The processor also utilizes four address parity outputs, AP[0:3], to indicate odd parity for the address.

Doubleword Address Bus

The processor uses A[0:28] as its doubleword address bus. This portion of the address identifies the doubleword of address space (an address divisible by eight).

Start Address of Operand Within Currently-Addressed Doubleword

A[29:31] identifies the start address of the operand within the currently-addressed doubleword. Table 33-3 defines the possible values contained in this field.

Table 33-3. Operand Start Address

A[29:31]	Start Address of Operand Within Doubleword
000b	Location 0 in the currently-addressed doubleword.
001b	Location 1 in the currently-addressed doubleword.
010b	Location 2 in the currently-addressed doubleword.
011b	Location 3 in the currently-addressed doubleword.
100b	Location 4 in the currently-addressed doubleword.
101b	Location 5 in the currently-addressed doubleword.
110b	Location 6 in the currently-addressed doubleword.
111b	Location 7 in the currently-addressed doubleword.

Size of Operand

The processor uses its transfer size bus, TSIZ[0:2} to indicate the size of the operand to be transferred. Table 33-4 defines the encoding of this value. If TBST# is asserted, the entire doubleword (and the three additional doublewords that make up the cache sector) will be transferred. The state of the TSIZ bus is meaningless.

Table 33-4. Transfer Size (Operand Size)

TSIZ[0:2}	Operand Size
000b	8 bytes
001b	1 byte
010b	2 bytes
011b	3 bytes
100b	4 bytes
101b	5 bytes
110b	6 bytes
111b	7 bytes

Address Parity

The four address parity signals are AP[0:3]. When the 32-bit address is driven onto the bus, the processor calculates and supplies a parity bit for each group of eight address lines. Odd parity is used (the parity bit is set to the appropriate state to force an odd number of one bits in the nine bit group). Whether or not the address parity is checked for correctness is platform design-dependent.

Additional Transaction Attributes Output by Master

As already noted, during the address transaction the processor outputs the doubleword address, operand start address within the currently-addressed doubleword and the operand size. The transaction type is also output. In addition, the processor also provides additional detail regarding the transaction in progress. This includes:

- The WIM bits that define the caching rules within the page or block of memory being addressed.
- On a memory read transaction, the transaction is identified as a code or a data read (with TC0).
- On a write transaction where an entire modified cache sector is being written back to memory, the processor identifies (with TC0) whether the cache sector will be marked invalid in its L1 cache after the modified cache sector has been written to memory.
- On a memory read that will read one of the cache sectors from a line into the cache, the processor indicates (with TC1) whether it has also internally posted a read to fetch the line's other sector from memory (for more in-

formation regarding alternate sector reload, refer to the chapter entitled "601 Cache and Memory Unit").

- If the processor is performing a burst memory read to read a cache sector into the L1 cache, it will indicate (using CSE[0:2]) which of the eight entries in the selected L1 cache set it will use to record the sector. If the processor is performing a burst memory write to write a modified cache sector back to memory, it will indicate which of the set of eight entries the cache sector is originating from.
- On a memory read or write operation, the processor indicates (using TBST#) whether it is performing a single-beat vs a four-beat burst read or write.

The following sections provide a detailed description of these transaction attributes.

WIM Outputs (WT#, CI# and GBL#)

Whenever the PPC601 processor initiates a memory-oriented transaction, it outputs the WIM bits applicable to the page or block of memory space being accessed. As described earlier, the WIM bits are supplied either from the page table entry or from the BAT register. The following sections describe the signal lines that the WIM bits are output on and their interpretation by external logic.

W, or Write-Through, Bit (WT#)

The W bit is output on the processor's WT# signal line. When deasserted (set to one) during a memory write transaction, WT# indicates that the L2 cache is to use a write-back policy in dealing with the memory write. In other words, the L2 cache doesn't have to write the data through to the memory target being addressed.

When asserted (cleared to zero) during a memory write transaction, WT# indicates that the L2 cache is to use a write-through policy in dealing with the memory write. In other words, the L2 cache must write the data through to the memory target being addressed.

I, or Cache Inhibit, Bit (CI#)

The I bit is output on the processor's CI# output. When deasserted (set to one) during a memory read burst, the L2 cache is permitted to cache from the memory area being addressed. When asserted (cleared to zero), the L2 cache is not permitted to keep copies of information from the memory area being addressed. The requested information should be read from the target memory and passed back to the processor without making a copy in the L2 cache.

M, or Memory Coherency Required, Bit (GBL#)

The M bit is output on the processor's GBL# output. When deasserted (set to one) during a memory-oriented transaction, the processor is accessing an area of memory that no other processor accesses. Other processors therefore do not have to snoop the current transaction and the processor that initiated the transaction will not check snoop results.

When asserted (cleared to zero) by the processor, the processor is accessing an area of memory that may be accessed by other processors. Other processors therefore must snoop the current transaction and report their collective snoop result back to the processor that initiated the transaction. The processor that initiated the transaction will sample the snoop result at the conclusion of the current address transaction.

Code or Data Read (TC0)

During a memory read transaction, the processor clears its TC0 output (TC stands for transfer code) to zero if a data read is in progress, or sets it to one to indicate that a code read is in progress.

This signal is supplied to the L2 cache. If the L2 cache has been implemented as a split-cache, the TC0 state indicates which of the two external caches, code or data, should perform a lookup (assuming that CI# is set to one, indicating that the access is cacheable). If a code read is in progress and it results in a miss on the L2 code cache, the code cache will read the target cache sector from memory, make a copy of it, and also pass it back to the L1 cache. The code cache may also be designed to take advantage of the predictability of code fetches and may fetch additional code sectors into its L2 code cache (on the assumption that the processor will continue to fetch instructions from memory in a linear manner).

Invalidate on Completion of Modified Cache Sector Write-back (TC0)

When the processor is performing a four-beat burst write transaction to write a modified cache sector back to memory, it will use TC0 to indicate to the L2 cache whether or not it will mark the cache sector invalid in its L1 cache after the write-back has been completed. TC0 cleared to zero indicates that the cache sector will not be invalidated, but will be marked exclusive or shared. This would occur under the following circumstances:

- The processor is executing a dcbst instruction that resulted in a hit on a modified sector in the data cache. The cache sector is written back to memory and then marked exclusive.
- The processor is performing a snoop push-back operation in response to a snoop hit on a modified cache sector on a read attempt by another bus master. The processor backed the other master off the bus (ARTRY# asserted) and then initiated the write-back of the modified cache sector to memory. Upon completion of the write-back, the processor will mark the cache sector shared (because it will be read from memory by the other master when it retries its read).

TC0 set to one indicates that the cache sector will be marked invalid. The processor is casting a modified cache sector back to memory to make room for a new cache sector that has been read from memory. The processor has marked the cache sector invalid.

Alternate Sector Reload (TC1)

If the processor is currently performing a burst read to fetch a cache sector from a line and the processor's memory unit has a read posted to fetch the opposing sector as well, it will assert TC1 = 1 to indicate this. This information can cause a look-through L2 cache to initiate a memory read to fetch the other sector before it is actually asked for.

Cache Set Element Being Read from or Written Back to Memory (CSE[0:2])

When the processor is performing a burst transfer to read a sector into its cache or to write a modified sector back to memory, it will use its cache set element bus, CSE[0:2], to indicate which of the eight entries in the selected set of the L1 cache is being read into or written back. This information can be used by the L2 cache to maintain cache consistency.

Single-Beat vs. Four-Beat Burst Transaction (TBST#)

The processor deasserts its burst transfer output, TBST#, if it is performing a single beat data transfer and asserts it when performing a four-beat burst transfer.

Chapter 34

The Previous Chapter

The previous chapter provided a detailed description of the address bus as used during memory-oriented transactions, including bus acquisition, use and transaction termination. Bus snooping was covered, as well. Heavily-annotated timing diagrams were utilized throughout the discussion.

This Chapter

This chapter provides a detailed description of the data bus, including bus acquisition, use and transaction termination. Heavily-annotated timing diagrams are utilized throughout the discussion.

The Next Chapter

The next chapter provides a detailed description of the PPC 601 processor's implementation of I/O bus transactions. Timing diagrams are utilized to illustrate the use of the bus.

General

When a transaction requires the transfer of data, the data bus must be used. It consists of a low half, DL[0:31] and a high half, DH[0:31]. Each half is subdivided into four 8-bit data lanes, for a total of eight data lanes. They are frequently referred to as data lanes (paths) 0 – 7 and are illustrated in figure 34-1. The processor always places an address divisible by eight (referred to as a doubleword address) on A[0:28] when initiating a transaction. This identifies a block of eight memory locations. The combination of TSIZ[0:2], TBST# and A[29:31] identify which of the eight locations within the doubleword will be transferred. The contents of the first location (the lowest address in the doubleword) is always transferred over data lane 0, the second location's contents over data lane 1, etc.

As with the address bus transaction, the data bus transaction consists of three events:

- Data bus acquisition.
- The data transfer (consisting of one or four data beats).
- Transaction termination.

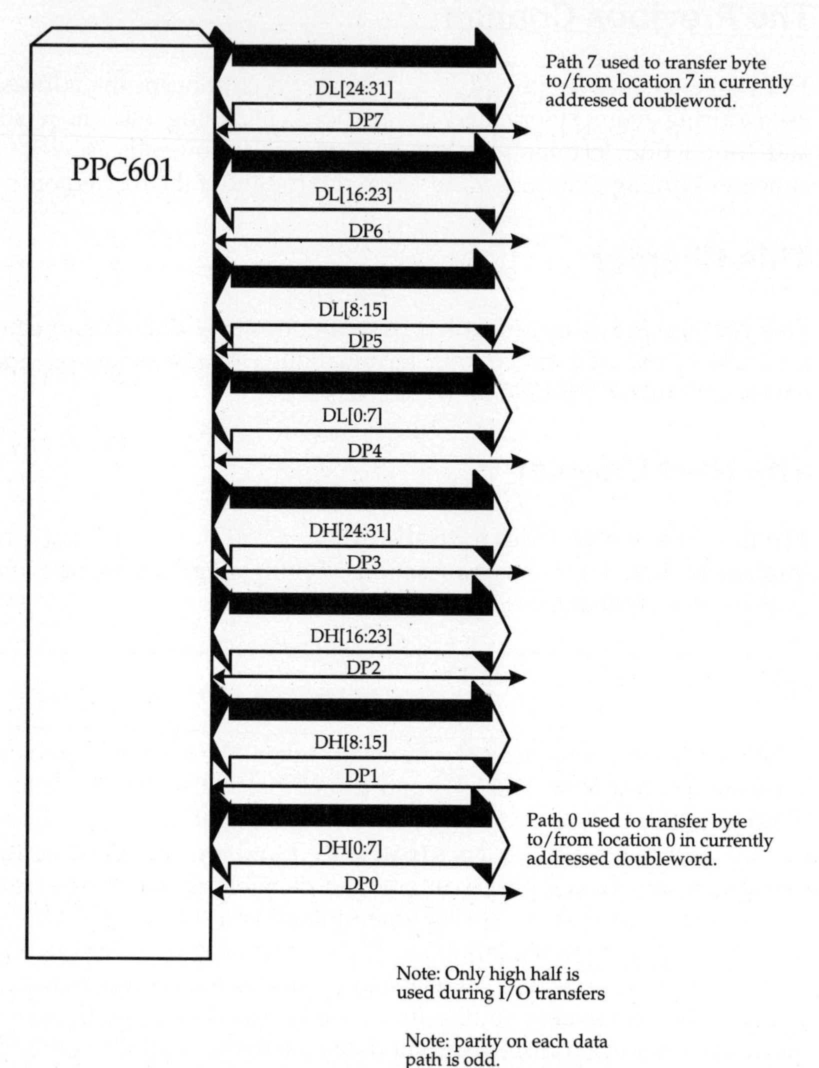

Figure 34-1. Data Paths

Data Bus Acquisition

Prior to performing a data transfer, the processor must acquire the address bus and deliver the address/transaction information to the target device. The following conditions act as a data bus request:

- **Assertion of TS# or XATS#.** Acquisition of the address bus is implied by the assertion of TS# or XATS#.
- **TT3 = 1** indicates that the current transaction requires a data transfer. In other words, it is **not** an **address-only transaction**.

The processor has acquired the data bus if the following conditions are met:

- **DBG# asserted**. Indicates the arbiter has granted the data bus to the requesting processor.
- **DBB# deasserted**. Indicates that the data bus is not currently in use (busy). In other words, the previous data bus owner has completed its data transfer (this must be qualified by DRTRY# deasserted).
- **DRTRY# deasserted**. The last data transfer of the previous data bus transaction completed without receiving a retry from the target. For additional discussion, refer to the section in this chapter entitled "Target Verifies Validity of Data Read by Master."
- **ARTRY# deasserted**. The address transaction associated with this data transfer completed without receiving a retry.

Data Transaction Initiation

The bus master indicates that it has taken ownership of the data bus by asserting data bus busy (DBB#). If this is a write transaction, the master also begins to drive the data to be written onto the appropriate data paths.

Target Acknowledges Receipt or Presence of Data

When the target has accepted a data item presented to it on a write or has placed the requested data on the data bus on a read, it asserts transfer acknowledge, TA#. When the processor samples TA# asserted during a write, it ceases to drive the data item. On a read, the processor latches the read data. It may not utilize the read data until it has been verified as correct by the target, however. This subject is discussed in the section that follows.

Target Verifies Validity of Data Read by Master

Background

This section describes the purpose of the data retry signal, DRTRY#. It should be noted that the processor only samples DRTRY# during read transactions.

The system designer may include an external L2 cache in order to expedite the delivery of cacheable data requested from memory. In the event of a load or instruction fetch miss on the L1 cache, the processor initiates a burst read transaction to fetch the target cache block from main memory. A detailed description of the four-beat burst read transaction may be found later in this chapter. When the L2 cache detects the read, it uses the target memory address to index into the cache. The designer may implement the L2 cache as a direct-mapped cache comprised of one bank of static RAM memory.

The memory address emitted by the processor is immediately used to select an entry in the cache, the first doubleword of the entry is forwarded back to the processor, and TA# is asserted to indicate its presence. The processor latches the doubleword, but should not yet forward the data to the processor core because the cache has not yet determined whether the cache entry being forwarded back to the processor is valid. This is accomplished in the clock cycle following TA# assertion.

Target Verifies Data Read Is Good

If the L2 cache determines that the data forwarded to the processor is good, it keeps DRTRY# deasserted to indicate that the data latched on the previous rising-edge of the bus clock may be forwarded to the processor core and utilized.

Target Issues Retry to Indicate Read Data Bad

If, on the other hand, the cache entry is invalid, the L2 cache asserts DRTRY# to indicate to the processor that the data latched on the previous clock must be discarded. Since the L2 cache does not have a valid copy of the requested cache block, the block must be read from memory. DRTRY# will be kept asserted until one bus clock after the first valid doubleword is presented to the processor. The processor must latch data from the bus on each bus clock rising-edge until DRTRY# is sampled deasserted again. When this occurs, the data latched on the edge prior to that on which DRTRY# is sampled deasserted is the first valid doubleword from memory.

If L2 Is Look-Aside

If the L2 cache is implemented as a look-aside cache and main memory resides on the host bus with the processor and the L2 cache, the memory read initiated by the processor will be permitted to proceed unhindered by the L2 cache (because of the L2 miss). DRTRY# will remain asserted until one bus clock after the first valid doubleword is presented on the data bus. When DRTRY# is sampled deasserted, the doubleword latched on the previous rising-edge is validated and may be forwarded to the processor core. On this same clock edge, the memory subsystem may also assert TA# again, indicating that the second doubleword is present on the bus and may be latched by the processor. It should be noted that, once again, the latched data may not be forwarded to the processor core unless DRTRY# is sampled deasserted on the next bus clock rising-edge. The third and fourth doublewords are transferred and validated in the same manner as the first two.

If L2 Is Look-Through

If the L2 cache is implemented as a look-through cache and it experiences a cache miss, it must assert DRTRY# to force the processor to discard the doubleword latched on the previous clock. The L2 cache must then keep DRTRY# asserted and access DRAM memory to fetch the requested cache block from memory. When the correct doubleword has been fetched from memory, the L2 cache presents it to the processor during one clock and then deasserts DRTRY# during the next clock. When the processor samples DRTRY# deasserted, this indicates that the doubleword latched on the previous clock is the valid doubleword. If the L2 cache has also fetched the second doubleword of the cache block from DRAM memory, it will drive it onto the data bus at the same time that it deasserts DRTRY# and will assert TA# to indicate its presence. When the processor samples DRTRY# deasserted and TA# asserted, it forwards the first doubleword to the processor core and also latches the second doubleword. The processor must validate the second doubleword on the next clock by sampling DRTRY# again. If it is deasserted, the second doubleword is good and can be forwarded to the processor core. The third and fourth doublewords are transferred and validated in the same manner as the first two.

Completion of Cache Block Read

As the processor reads and validates the four doublewords from memory, the L2 cache has also acquired each of the doublewords. Both the L2 and the L1 caches will then record the cache block.

Single-Beat Read or Write Transaction

General

Figure 34-2 illustrates a single-beat read or write transaction. The processor performs a single-beat memory read transaction under the following circumstances:

- When the instruction fetcher reads an instruction from a non-cacheable area of memory (as defined by the page table entry or BAT register's I bit set to one).
- When the integer or floating-point unit performs a load from a non-cacheable area of memory (as defined by the page table entry or BAT register's I bit set to one).

The processor performs a single-beat memory write transaction under the following circumstances:

- When executing a store operation in an area of memory designated as non-cacheable the processor will only read the byte or bytes specified, not an entire cache block.
- When executing a store operation in an area of memory designated as cacheable and write-through, the processor will perform a single-beat memory write to deposit the specified byte or bytes into memory.

Timing Diagram

Address Phase

Figure 34-2 illustrates a single-beat memory read or write transaction. The address-portion of the transaction was described in the chapter entitled " PPC 601 Memory Address Phase." The address output by the processor is a doubleword address. The least-significant three address bits, A[29:31], identify the start location of the target operand within the doubleword and the data path the byte will be transferred over. The TSIZ[0:2] bus identifies the size of the operand to be transferred and the number of data paths, starting at the data path indicated by A[29:31], that will be utilized to transfer the target operand to or from the processor. The address phase is terminated when the target asserts AACK#.

Data Phase

The arbiter determines that the master requires ownership of the data bus to perform a data transfer with the target by sampling a one on TT3. When it decides that it is this master's turn to use the data bus, it asserts DBG# to the master. When the arbiter has determined that bus acquisition has occurred (DBG# asserted, DBB# and DRTRY# deasserted and no ARTRY# on the associated address transaction), it also asserts DBG# to the addressed target. In figure 34-2, the address transaction is lightly shaded, while the data transaction is more darkly shaded. Data bus acquisition occurs on clock five. The master asserts DBB# to indicate that it has taken ownership of the data bus.

Data Read Transaction

If it is a read transaction, the target drives the requested doubleword (or the requested subset of the doubleword) onto the data bus and asserts TA# on clock six to indicate its presence. The master latches the data from the data bus on clock six. The master then deasserts DBB# to indicate that it may be surrendering ownership of the data bus. On clock seven, the master samples DRTRY# to determine if the data latched on clock six was good and can be used. If it sampled deasserted, the data is good and the master really has surrendered control of the data bus.

Data Write Transaction

If it is a write transaction, the master begins to drive the data item onto the data bus when it has acquired bus ownership (on clock five). The target asserts TA# when it has latched the data from the bus. This completes the single-beat write transaction. The master deasserts DBB#, indicating that is surrendering ownership of the data bus. The master does not sample DRTRY# on write transactions.

Data Phase with Wait States

Figure 34-3 illustrates a single-beat data transfer where the target kept TA# deasserted until is ready to end the data transfer. This forces the master to insert one wait state in the data phase until the target gives it permission to terminate the transfer (by asserting TA#).

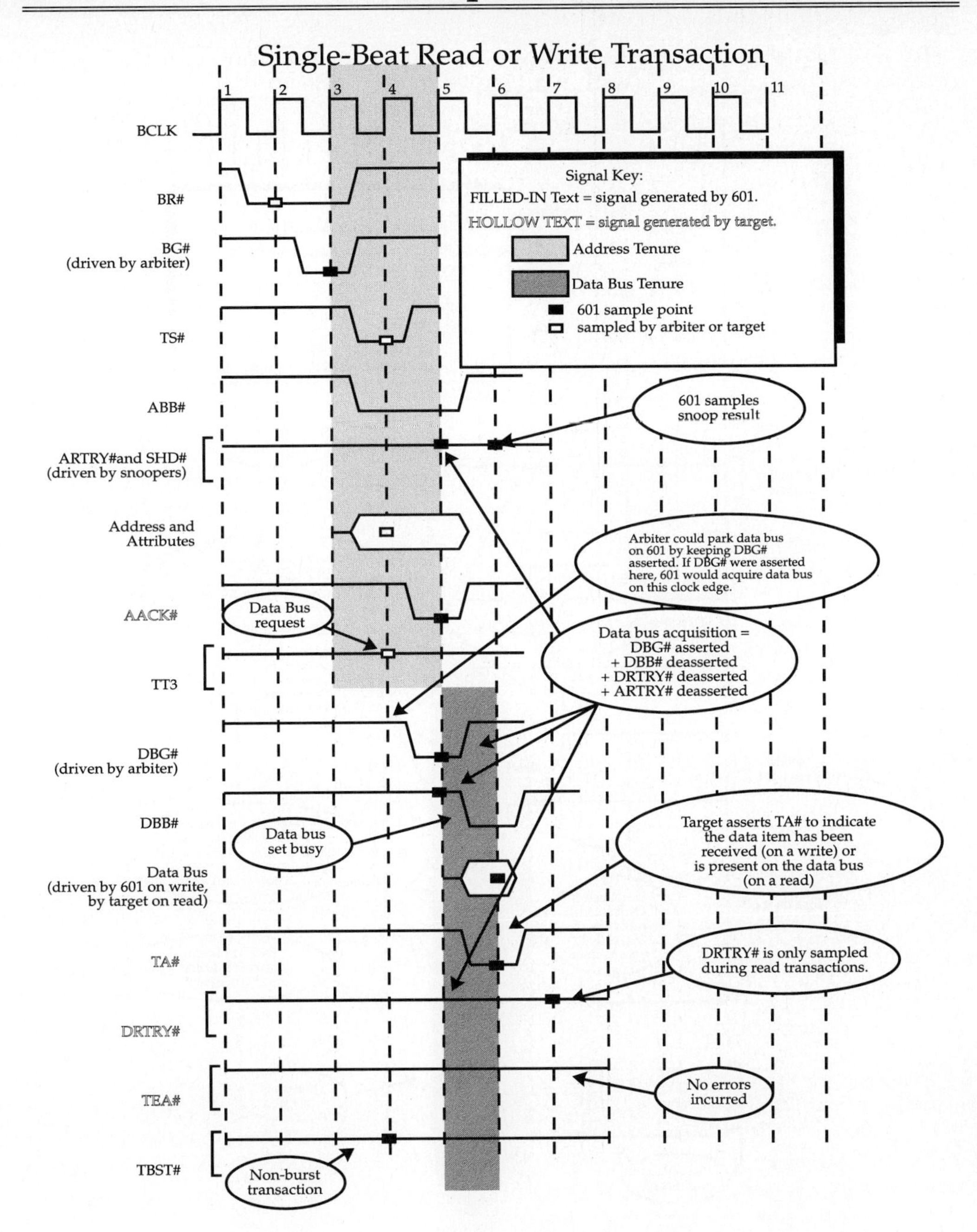
Single-Beat Read or Write Transaction
1
2
3
4
5
6
7
8
9
10
11
BCLK
BR#
BG#
(driven by arbiter)
TS#
ABB#
ARTRY#and SHD#
(driven by snoopers)
Address and
Attributes
AACK#
TT3
DBG#
(driven by arbiter)
DBB#
Data Bus
(driven by 601 on write,
by target on read)
TA#
DRTRY#
TEA#
TBST#
Signal Key:
FILLED-IN Text = signal generated by 601.
HOLLOW TEXT = signal generated by target.
Address Tenure
Data Bus Tenure
601 sample point
sampled by arbiter or target
601 samples
snoop result
Arbiter could park data bus
on 601 by keeping DBG#
asserted. If DBG# were asserted
here, 601 would acquire data bus
on this clock edge.
Data Bus
request
Data bus acquisition =
DBG# asserted
+ DBB# deasserted
+ DRTRY# deasserted
+ ARTRY# deasserted
Data bus
set busy
Target asserts TA# to indicate
the data item has been
received (on a write) or
is present on the data bus
(on a read)
DRTRY# is only sampled
during read transactions.
No errors
incurred
Non-burst
transaction

Figure 34-2. Zero Wait State Single-Beat Read or Write Transaction

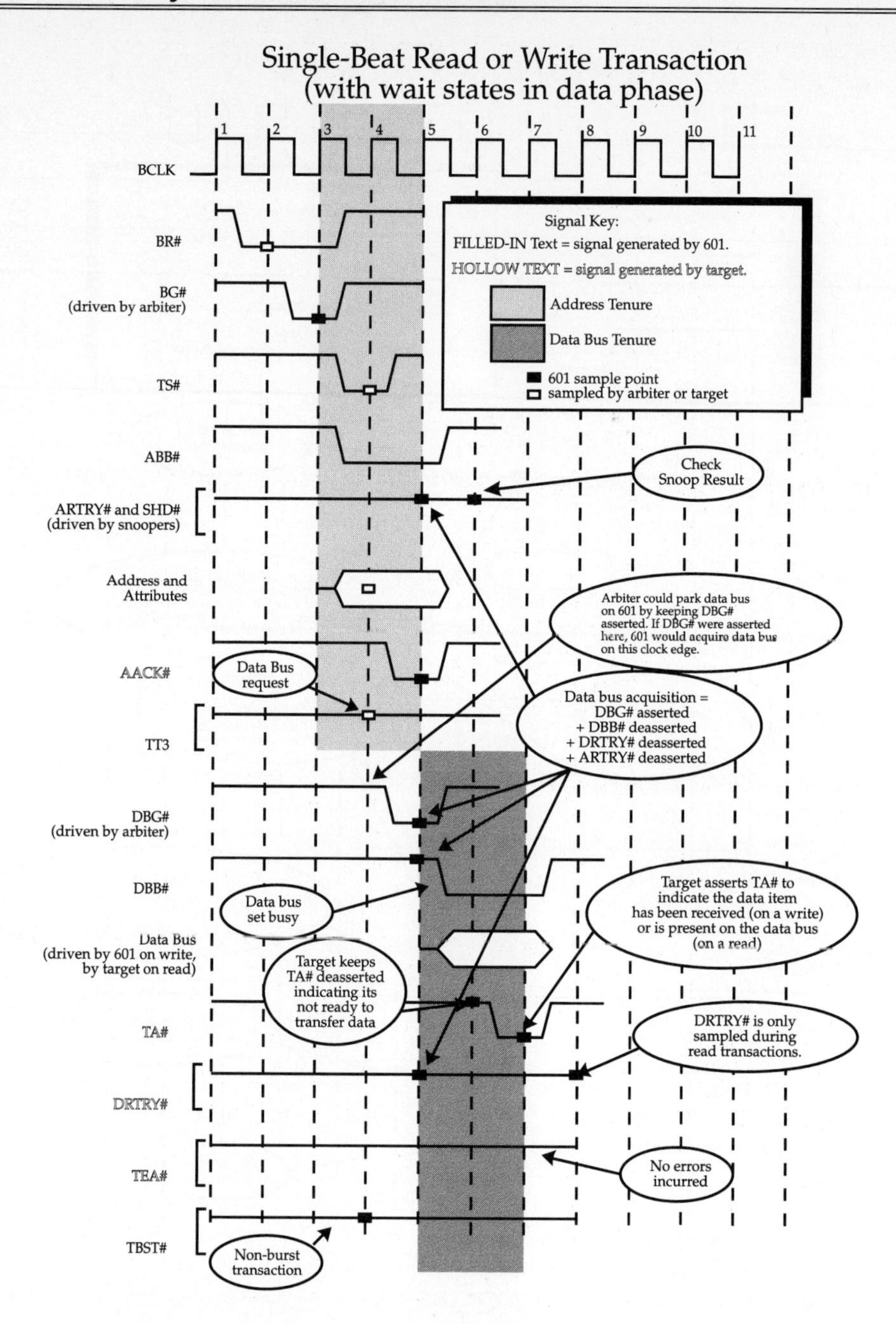

Figure 34-3. Single-Beat Read or Write Transaction with One Wait State

Four-Beat Burst Read or Write Transaction

Typically Indicates Cache Fill, Castout or Snoop Push Back

The PowerPC processor only performs four-beat burst reads or writes to read or write a sector of information. A burst read is performed under the following circumstances:

- Load miss on the L1 cache in a page or block marked cacheable by the operating system (I = 0).
- Instruction fetch miss in a page or block marked cacheable by the operating system (I = 0).
- TLB miss in a page or block marked cacheable by the operating system (I = 0).
- Store miss on the cache in a page or block marked cacheable, write-back by the operating system (I = 0 and W = 0).

A burst write is performed under the following circumstances:

- Cast out of a modified sector to make room for a new sector to be read into the cache.
- Snoop push-back of a modified sector into memory.

It should be noted that an intelligent bus master might utilize four-beat burst reads or writes to transfer a block of data to or from memory rapidly. Because the bus master would not know the WIM bit settings that define the usage of the area of memory, it must always assert GBL# during the address phase to force a snoop of the transaction.

Burst without Wait States (Fast L2 Cache Supplies/Accepts Data)

When the processor performs a burst read or write transaction and the TA# signal remains asserted for four clocks of the data transaction, this permits the master to transfer all 32 bytes to/from memory in four clocks. The only device fast enough to source a sector to the master or accept a sector from the master this quickly is the L2 cache.

Figure 34-4 illustrates a four-beat burst read or write transaction. On the bottom of the timing diagram, the master asserts TBST# during the address transaction to indicate that this is a four-beat burst operation.

If it's a read burst, the processor latches a doubleword on clocks six, seven, eight and nine. The data is validated by sampling DRTRY# deasserted on clocks seven, eight, nine and ten.

If it's a write burst, the processor outputs the first doubleword and asserts DBB# on clock five. The L2 cache keeps TA# asserted for clocks five – nine. On clocks six, seven and eight the processor samples TA# asserted, indicating that the L2 cache has accepted each of the doublewords. As each doubleword is accepted, the processor starts to drive the next doubleword onto the data bus. When the final TA# is sampled asserted on clock nine, the processor ceases to output the final doubleword and deasserts DBB# output to indicate that it is surrendering ownership of the data bus. The processor does not sample DRTRY# on a write.

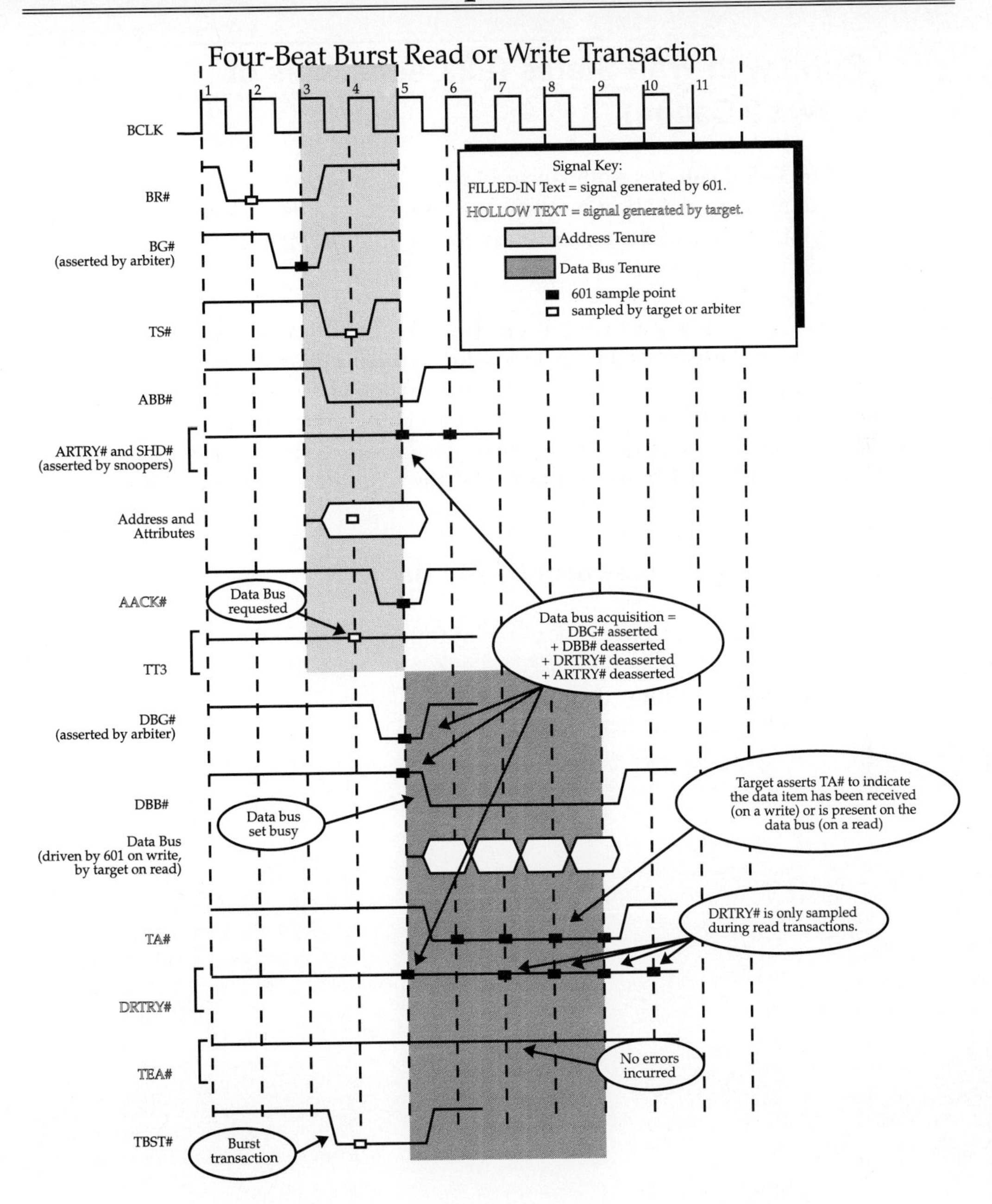

Figure 34-4. Zero Wait State Four-Beat Burst Read or Write Transaction

Burst with Wait States (L2 Cache Miss or Slow L2 Cache)

Figure 34-5 illustrates a four-beat burst read or write with one wait state inserted into each data beat by the target. A target that is only inserting one wait state into each data beat at a bus speed of 33 or 40MHz is almost certainly a slightly-slow L2 cache.

If this were a miss on the L2 cache resulting in an access to DRAM memory, the number of wait states incurred in each data beat would depend on the DRAM access time and the design of the DRAM memory subsystem. In the chapter entitled "601 Cache and Memory Unit," several memory architecture designs were discussed. Using these designs as examples, the following descriptions would be representative of the wait states incurred in each data beat.

One 64-bit (Doubleword) DRAM Bank

Memory laid out as one bank of 64-bit (doubleword) memory. The processor would have to access the DRAM bank four separate times (once for each doubleword), resulting in poor performance (multiple wait states) for each doubleword data transfer.

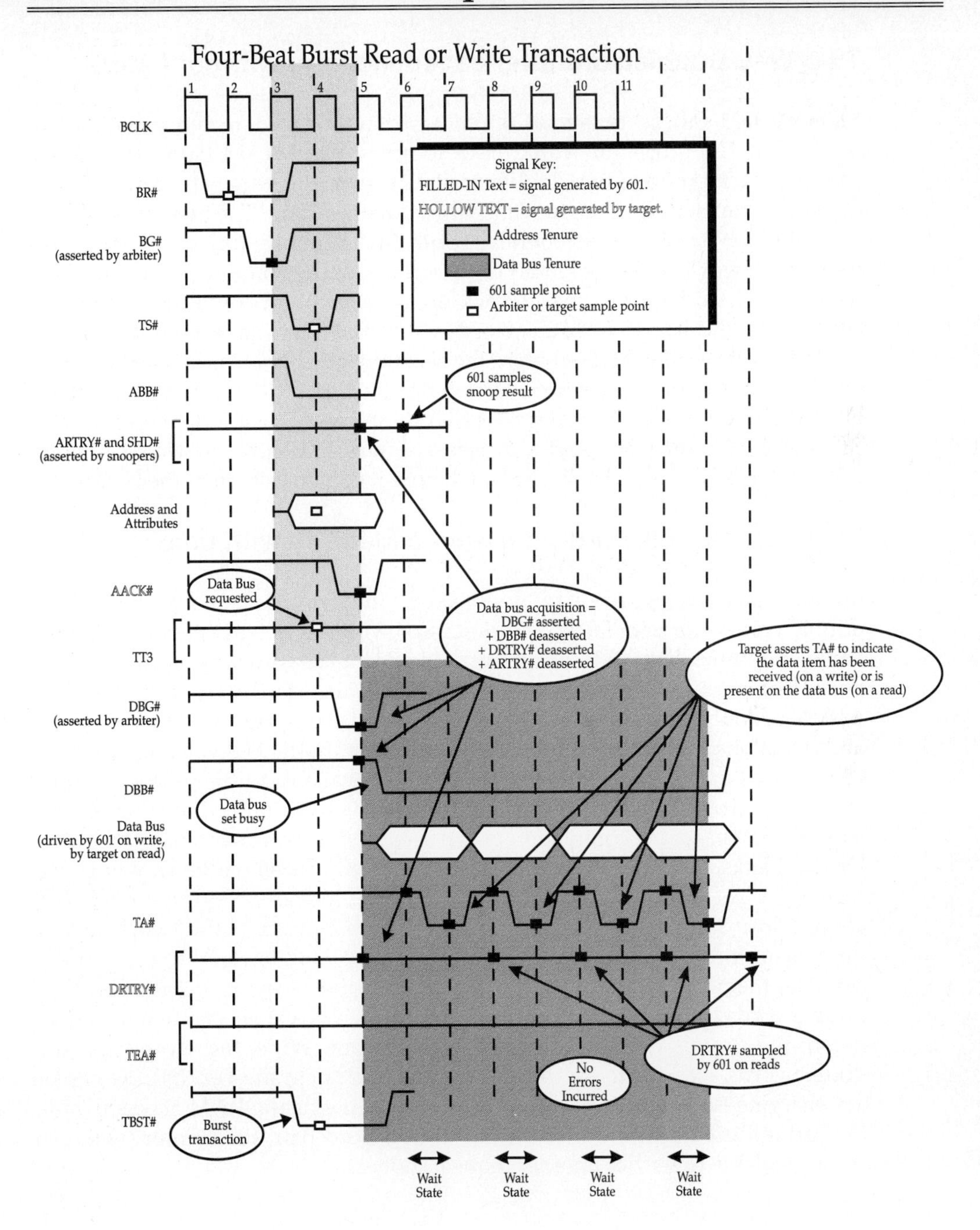

Figure 34-5. Four Beat Burst Read or Write with Wait States

Two-Way Doubleword-Interleaved Memory without Latch

Memory laid out as two-way, doubleword interleaved memory without a data latch. The processor would have to access the DRAM banks two times (once for each group of two doublewords), resulting in very poor performance (multiple wait states) in the first and third data transfers. The memory controller would have to continue to address both DRAM banks until both of the first two doublewords were delivered to the processor. It would then have to wait for both DRAM banks to charge back up again before it could initiate the access to get the last two doublewords. It would then have to wait for the DRAM access time to elapse before the second two doublewords were output. Once again, the memory controller would have to continue to address both DRAM banks until both of the first two doublewords were delivered to the processor. It could then end the access, but would have to wait for both DRAM banks to charge back up again before it could service another request.

Two-Way Doubleword-Interleaved Memory with Latch

Memory laid out as two-way, doubleword interleaved memory with a two doubleword-wide data latch. The processor would have to access the DRAM banks two times (once for each group of two doublewords), resulting in poor performance (multiple wait states) in the first and third data transfers. The first two doublewords are simultaneously read from the two DRAM banks and are latched for presentation to the processor. Both DRAM banks begin to charge back up. The first doubleword is made available to the processor from the latch. After it is taken, the second doubleword is immediately available from the latch. At the completion of the second doubleword transfer, the two DRAM banks are either completely recharged or are well on the way to being recharged. As soon as they are fully charged the memory controller reads the second two doublewords into the latch. The charge up of the two banks is once again hidden behind the transfer of the two doublewords to the processor. The memory controller could then initiate the access to get the last two doublewords. It would then have to wait for the DRAM access time to elapse before the second two doublewords were output. While the second pair of doublewords are sent to the processor from the latch, the two DRAM banks are charging back up. Since the charge up after the final DRAM access is hidden behind the transfer of the second doubleword pair, the memory will become available to service another request sooner.

Four-Way Doubleword-Interleaved Memory without Latch

Memory laid out as four-way, doubleword interleaved memory without a data latch. The processor would have to access the DRAM banks one time (to read all four doublewords), resulting in very poor performance (multiple wait states) in the first data transfer. The memory controller would have to continue to address the four DRAM banks until all four of the doublewords were delivered to the processor. It would then have to wait for all four DRAM banks to charge back up again before it could service another request.

Four-Way Doubleword-Interleaved Memory with Latch

Memory laid out as four-way, doubleword interleaved memory with a four doubleword-wide data latch. The processor would have to access the DRAM banks one time (to read all four doublewords), resulting in very poor performance (multiple wait states) in the first data transfer. The memory controller then transfers each of the four doublewords back to the processor from the latch while the DRAM banks are recharging. Since the DRAM charge up is hidden behind the transfers from the latch, the memory becomes available sooner to service a subsequent request.

Burst with Data Retry

Figure 34-6 illustrates a cache sector fill that experiences a cache miss on the L2 cache. The L2 cache is implemented as a direct-mapped cache and may be implemented as either a look-through or a look-aside cache. The main DRAM memory must be accessed. This memory is implemented as four-way, doubleword-interleaved memory with the ability to read an entire sector (four doublewords) from memory at one time. The four doublewords are then stored in a fast-access latch in the memory controller and are delivered to the processor very rapidly. The L2 cache also makes a copy of the cache sector as it is read from memory.

The start memory address issued by the master is used to select a cache entry and the first doubleword of the entry is immediately output to the master on clock five without waiting to check the state of the cache entry. TA# is asserted by the L2 cache to indicate the presence of the doubleword on the bus. The processor latches the doubleword when it samples TA# asserted on clock six. It checks the validity of the data by sampling DRTRY# on clock seven. DRTRY# is sampled asserted, indicating that the L2 cache has determined that the cache entry is invalid. The L2 cache will keep DRTRY# deasserted until the clock after it has presented the valid data to the processor. The processor samples the data on the bus and the state of DRTRY# on clocks seven and eight. In effect, the first data transfer is being extended by DRTRY#. Between clocks seven and eight, the good doubleword is presented on the bus and is latched by the processor on clock eight. Between clocks eight and nine, the second doubleword is presented to the processor and DRTRY# is deasserted and TA# asserted. When the processor samples DRTRY# deasserted on clock nine, this indicates that the correct first doubleword was latched on clock eight. The assertion of TA# indicates that the second doubleword is now present on the bus. The processor latches the second doubleword. The third and fourth doublewords are latched on clocks 10 and 11. Doublewords two, three and four are validated by sampling DRTRY# deasserted on clocks 10, 11 and 12. This completes the cache sector fill operation.

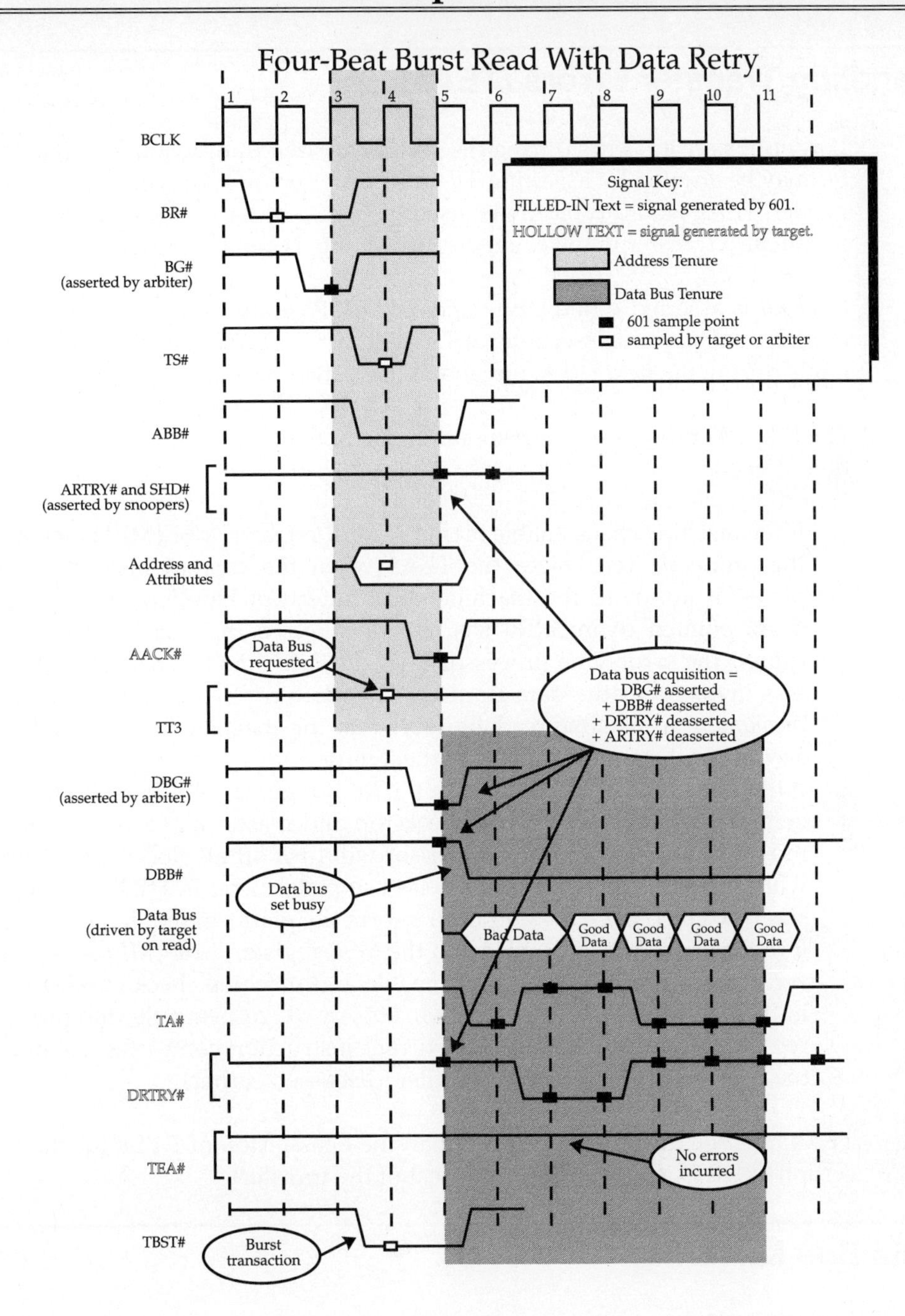

Figure 34-6. Cache Sector Fill with Data Retry

Handling Transfer Errors (TEA#)

If a serious error occurs during the data phase of a transaction, the data transfer may be aborted by asserting TEA# (transfer error acknowledge) to the bus master. TEA# would typically be used by ECC or parity-protected memory to terminate a transfer in the event corrupted data is being transferred.

If TEA# is asserted while DBB# and/or DRTRY# are asserted, the master ignore any subsequent assertions of TA# and/or DRTRY#. The master deasserts DBB# during the next clock and aborts the transaction.

The PPC 601 processor will respond in one of the following ways to the assertion of TEA#:

1. If the machine check enable bit in the MSR register, MSR[ME] is set to one, the processor recognizes the TEA# when the current instruction completes. It jumps to the machine check interrupt handler. The return address pointed to in SRR0 has no relevance to the bus transaction that caused the error. The processor does not latch the address of target that was involved in the data transfer. The platform designer may choose to implement a machine-readable port that the machine check handler can access to determine the cause of the failure.
2. If the machine check enable bit in the MSR register, MSR[ME] is cleared to zero, and the machine check checkstop and master checkstop enable bits in HID0 are set to one, the processor will turn off all clocks and freeze. It will also set the machine check checkstop status bit in HID0 and will assert its CHKSTP_OUT# output to inform the platform that it has frozen.
3. If the machine check enable bit in the MSR register, MSR[ME] is cleared to zero, and the master checkstop enable and machine check checkstop bits in the HID0 register are set to 10b, 00b, or 01, respectively, the processor recognizes the TEA# when the current instruction completes. It jumps to the machine check interrupt handler (discussed earlier).

TEA# must be deasserted no later than the deassertion of DBB# (or the deassertion of DRTRY# on the last data beat of the transfer).

Data Bus Mirroring

The PPC 601 processor does not support devices less than 64-bits wide (in other words, 32, 16 or 8 bit devices). When performing stores in non-cacheable memory, however, it acts as indicated in table 34-1. The practice of duplicating data on normally unused data paths is referred to as data bus mirroring. If a device with less than a 64-bit data width is only connected to a subset of the data bus, it may be able to utilize the mirrored data if the other data paths are not available to it.

It should be noted that data mirroring may not be supported on future versions of the PPC 601 processor or on other PowerPC processors. It should also be noted that the PPC 601 processor only utilizes data mirroring when performing stores within pages or blocks marked as non-cacheable by the operating system (I = 1). This may make it useful when storing data to memory-mapped I/O ports (they are never marked as cacheable).

Table 34-1. Data Mirroring

Size of Data Item and Paths Used	Data Also Mirrored On Paths
byte on path 0	path 4
byte on path 1	path 5
byte on path 2	path 6
byte on path 3	path 7
byte on path 4	path 0
byte on path 5	path 1
byte on path 6	path 2
byte on path 7	path 3
halfword on paths 0 and 1	paths 4 and 5
halfword on paths 2 and 3	paths 6 and 7
halfword on paths 4 and 5	paths 0 and 1
halfword on paths 6 and 7	paths 2 and 3
word on paths 0, 1, 2 and 3	paths 4, 5, 6 and 7
word on paths 4, 5, 6 and 7	paths 0, 1, 2 and 3

Chapter 35

The Previous Chapter

The previous chapter provided a detailed description of the data bus, including bus acquisition, use and transaction termination. Heavily-annotated timing diagrams were utilized throughout the discussion.

This Chapter

This chapter provides a detailed description of the PPC 601 processor's implementation of I/O bus transactions. Timing diagrams are utilized to illustrate the use of the bus.

The Next Chapter

The next chapter provides a detailed description of the external control transactions generated by the PPC 601 processor when it executes an ecowx or eciwx instruction. This includes a discussion of software-related issues.

I/O Segment Descriptor

I/O addresses reside within a segment with the T bit set to one. Figure 35-1 illustrates the contents of an I/O segment register when the segment type bit is set to one. When the effective address specified for a load or store is submitted to the MMU for address translation, it is first determined that it doesn't map into any blocks currently defined by the BAT registers. Assuming that it doesn't, the upper hex digit of the effective address, EA[0:3], is used to select the segment register that describes the target segment. If the T bit, bit 0, is set to one, the access falls within an I/O segment. The access is by definition noncacheable and also bypasses the posted read/write buffers in the MU. The processor must acquire the PPC 601 bus and perform a series of I/O transactions to accomplish the specified data transfer.

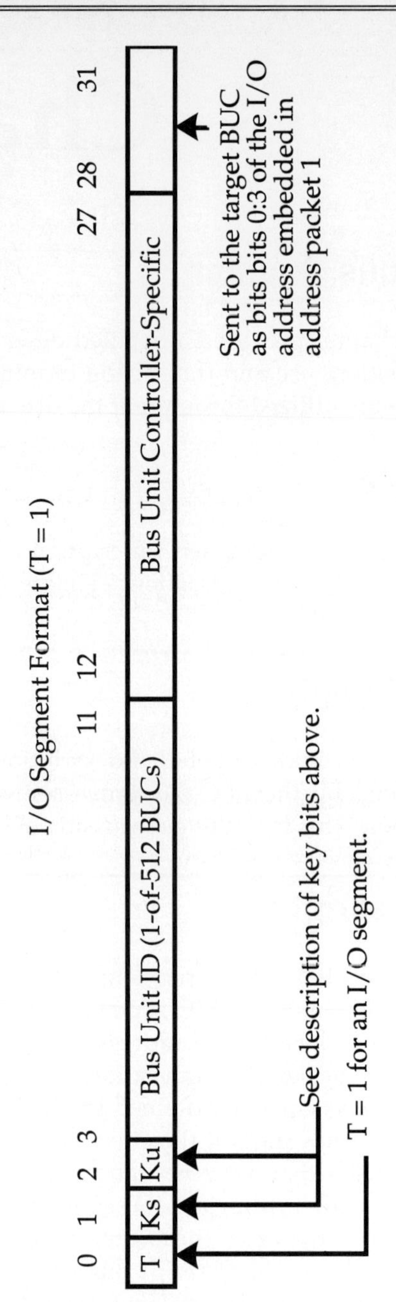

Figure 35-1. Segment Register Containing I/O Segment Descriptor

I/O Device Hierarchy

All I/O devices that reside on the PPC 601 bus have the following structure:

- One or more I/O bus unit controllers, or BUCs, may reside on the PPC 601 bus. The PPC 601 processor is capable of mapping any load or store within a 256MB segment of effective address space to one of up to 512 BUCs.
- Each BUC may control access within a 4GB I/O space.

In order to access an I/O port, the processor must address the BUC specified in the segment register and then address the I/O port within the BUC.

Data Path Usage

The PPC 601 processor only uses data paths 0:3 (the DH portion of the data bus) when transferring data to/from an I/O device.

I/O Transaction Types

The I/O transaction types may be divided into two categories: those associated with performing load operations and those associated with performing store operations. Tables 35-1 and 35-2 list the transactions within each category.

Table 35-1. Load-Oriented Transactions

Transaction Type	Description
Load Request	Issued by the PPC 601 processor to initiate a series of one or more load word operations. This is an address-only transaction. It identifies the originating processor, the target BUC, the target I/O port, and the byte transfer count.
Load Immediate	Issued by the PPC 601 processor to load one word from the I/O device into the processor. This transaction consists of both an address and a data transaction.
Load Last	Issued by the PPC 601 processor to load the last word of a series from the I/O device into the processor. This transaction consists of both an address and a data transaction.
Load Reply	Issued by the BUC to deliver completion status information to the processor at the end of a load series. This is an address-only transaction.

Table 35-2. Store-Oriented Transactions

Transaction Type	Description
Store Immediate	Issued by the PPC 601 processor to store one word to the I/O device. The word is one of a series and is not the last word. This transaction consists of both an address and a data transaction. It identifies the originating processor, the target BUC, the target I/O port, and the byte transfer count.
Store Last	Issued by the PPC 601 processor to store the last of a series of words to the I/O device. This transaction consists of both an address and a data transaction.
Store Reply	Issued by the BUC to deliver completion status information to the processor at the end of a store series. This is an address-only transaction.

Transactions Generated by Load Word Operation

In order to load a single word (for a load word instruction) from an I/O device into the processor, the following transaction series must be performed:

- Processor performs an address-only load request transaction, identifying the originating processor, the target BUC, the target I/O port, and the byte transfer count.

- Processor performs an address/data load last transaction to load the word from the I/O device.
- Target BUC performs an address-only load reply transaction to send completion status to the originating processor.

The master or BUC must perform a separate arbitration for the bus to perform each of these transactions.

Transactions Generated by Load Multiple Word Operation

In order to load multiple words (for a load multiple word instruction) from an I/O device into the processor, the following transaction series must be performed:

- Processor performs an address-only load request transaction, identifying the originating processor, the target BUC, the target I/O port, and the byte transfer count.
- Processor performs a separate address/data load immediate transaction for each word except the last word to be loaded.
- Processor performs an address/data load last transaction to load the word from the I/O device.
- Target BUC performs an address-only load reply transaction to send completion status to the originating processor.

Transactions Generated by Store Word Operation

In order to store a single word (for a store word instruction) to an I/O device, the following transaction series must be performed:

- Processor performs an address/data store last transaction to store the word to the I/O device.
- Target BUC performs an address-only store reply transaction to send completion status to the originating processor.

Transactions Generated by Store Multiple Word Operation

In order to store multiple words (for a store multiple word instruction) to an I/O device, the following transaction series must be performed:

- Processor performs a separate address/data store immediate transaction for each word except the last word to be stored.
- Processor performs an address/data store last transaction to store the word to the I/O device.
- Target BUC performs an address-only store reply transaction to send completion status to the originating processor.

Address Bus Arbitration

Address bus arbitration for I/O transactions is identical to that used for memory-oriented transactions.

Address Transaction

The I/O address transaction differs substantially from that used when performing a memory-oriented transaction. The differences are:

- The signals used to indicate the transaction type are different.
- The master sends two packets of address information to the target BUC, not one.
- XATS# is asserted, rather than TS#.

Refer to figure 35-2. When the master (or the BUC, if performing a load or store reply transaction) has acquired ownership of the address bus, it asserts XATS# for one clock to indicate that an I/O transaction has begun. It also outputs the transaction type and address packet 0 for one clock. The BUCs must latch address packet 0 when XATS# is asserted because packet 0 is only presented for one clock. The transaction type is encoded on eight signal lines: TT[0:3], TBST#, and TSIZ[0:2]. The transaction type is referred to as the extended address transfer code (XATC) or as the I/O opcode. Table 35-3 lists the I/O transaction types.

Table 35-3. I/O Transaction Type Encoding

TT[0:3], TBST#, TSIZ[0:2]	Transaction Type
40h	Load request
50h	Load immediate
70h	Load last
10h	Store immediate
30h	Store last
C0h	Load reply
80h	Store reply

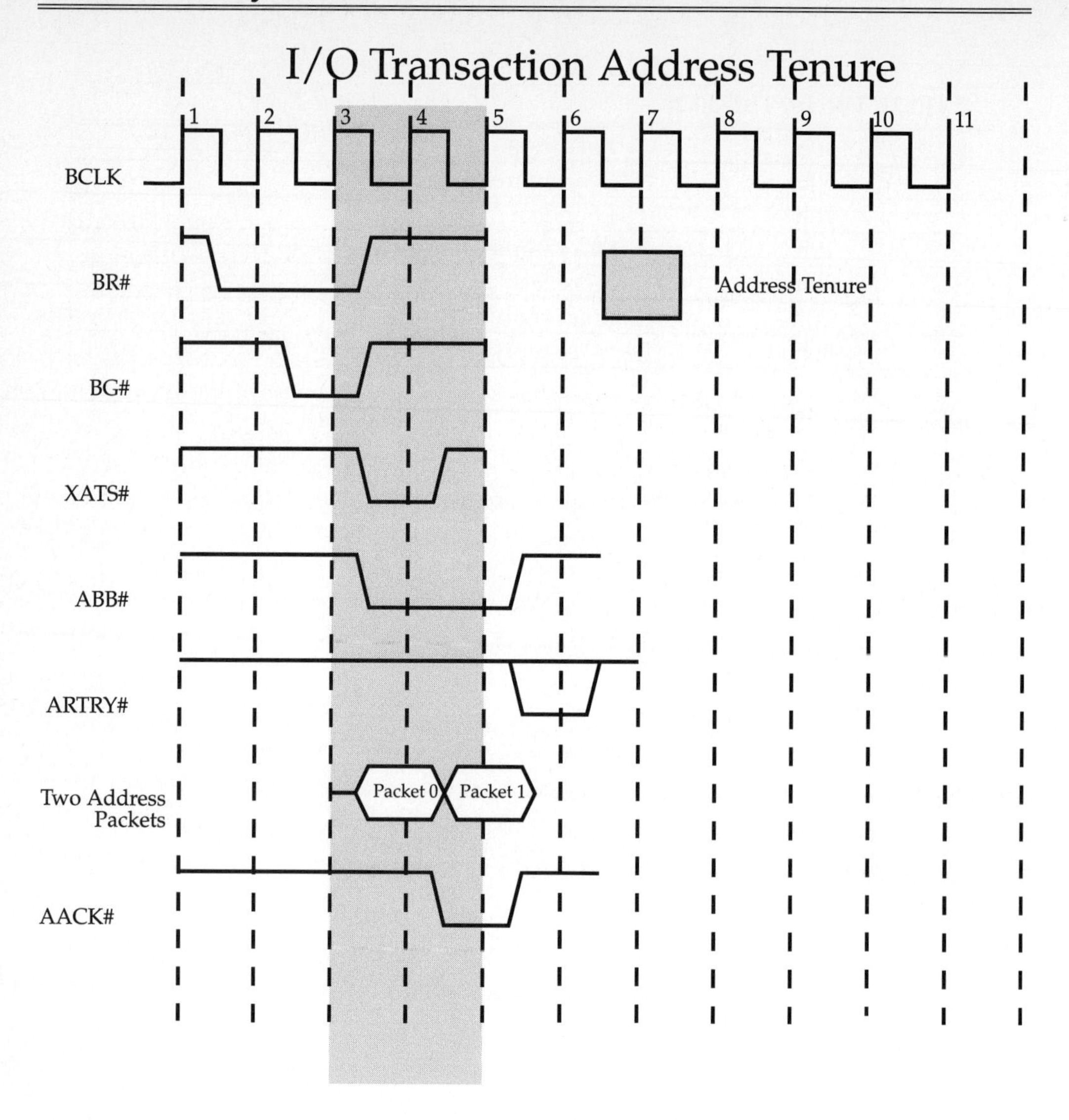

Figure 35-2. I/O Address Transaction

The information output by the processor in address packet 0 is illustrated in figure 35-3. The following information is output:

- The **Key bit** from the segment register. The operating system programmer could use the two key bits in the segment register to permit or deny applications programs to access the BUC. The privilege level of the currently program selects either the Ks (supervisor program is running) or the Ku bit (user program is running) to output to the BUC. The Ks bit in the segment register could be set to 1 while the Ku bit could be set to 0. If the BUC detects an access attempt with the selected key bit = 0, it could deny access.

- The **BUC number** from the segment register. The target BUC number is decoded by each BUC to determine if it is the target of the I/O transaction. The targeted BUC will assert AACK# after latching address packet 1.
- **Bits 12:27 from the segment register**. This bit field may or may not be used by the target BUC.
- The originating **processor's ID** from the processor identification register, PIR or HID15. Also referred to as the sender ID, this number will be used during the I/O reply transaction (load or store) to re-address the originating processor.

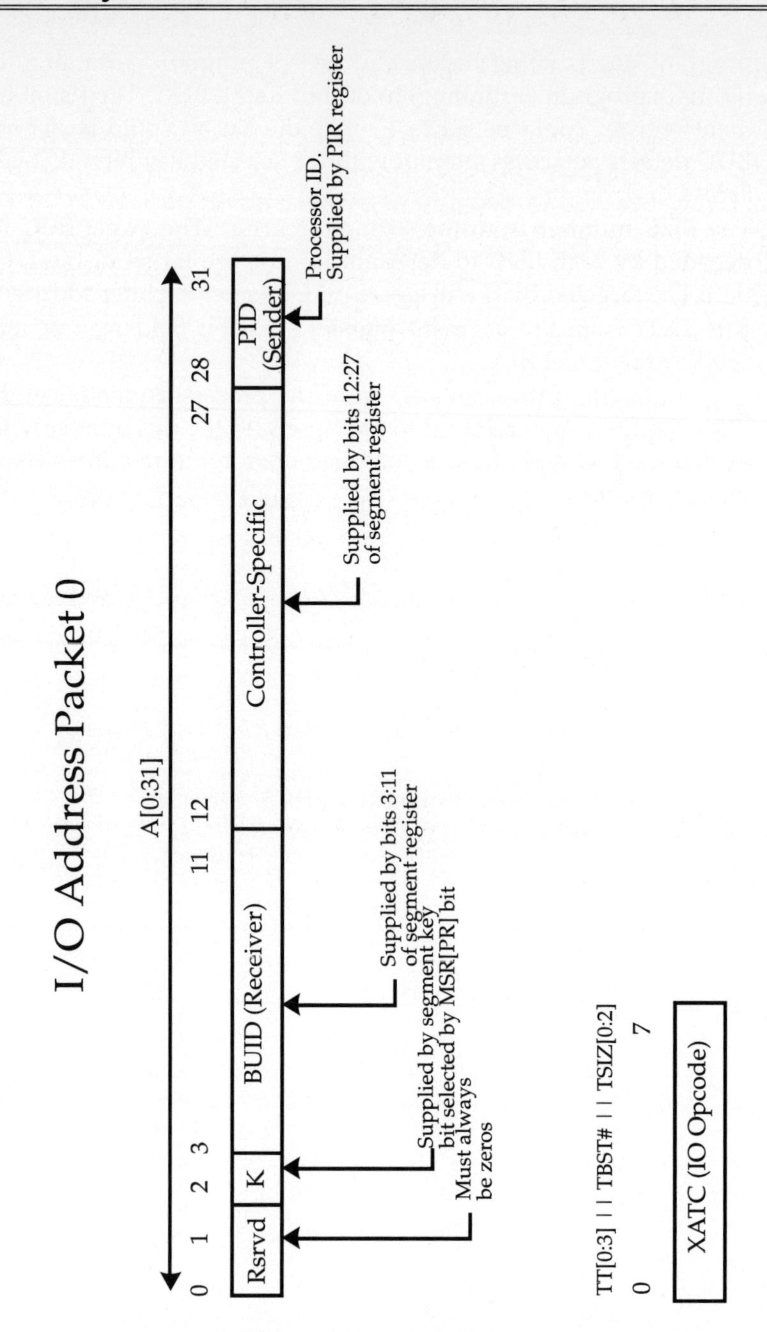

Figure 35-3. I/O Address Packet 0

At the end of the first clock, the processor ceases to output address packet 0 and begins to output address packet 1. In addition, the processor ceases to output the transaction type and instead outputs the byte transfer count in its place. For a load request transaction, the total number of bytes to be transferred is specified (the maximum byte transfer count is 128). For a load immediate, load last, store immediate, or store last transaction, a transfer count of one to four bytes is indicated. The byte transfer count is encoded in the binarily-weighted field consisting of the lower seven bits of TT[0:3], TBST# and TSIZ[0:2]. Address packet 1 is pictured in figure 35-4 and contains the following information:

- The least-significant hex digit from the segment register, bits 28:31, supply the upper hex digit of the I/O port address.
- The lower seven digits of the I/O port address are supplied from the lower seven digits of the effective address.

The target BUC may delay acceptance of address packet 1 by keeping AACK# deasserted. The processor will continue to drive address packet 1 until AACK# is received from the BUC.

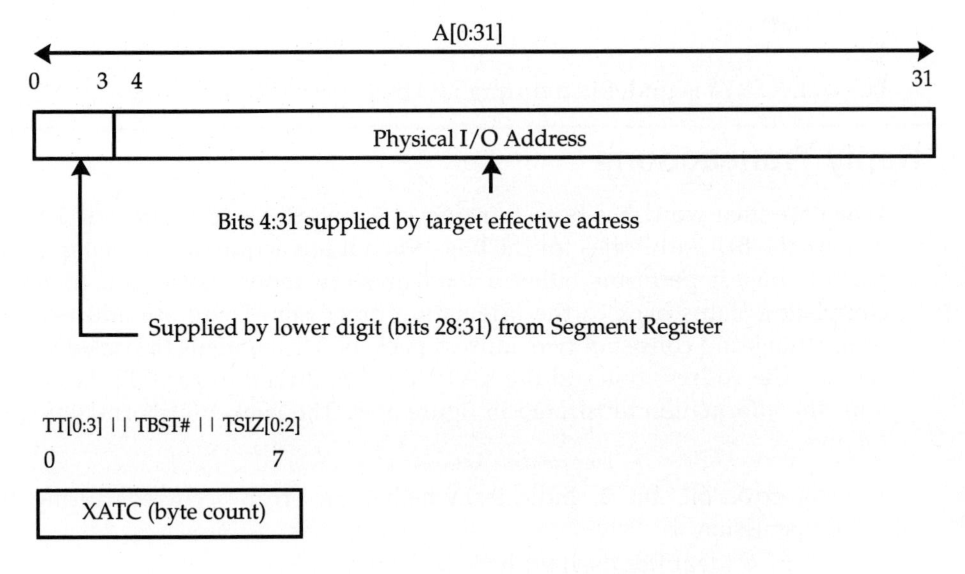

Figure 35-4. I/O Address Packet 1

ARTRY# Usage

The target BUC may assert ARTRY# one clock after AACK# to force the processor to retry the transaction again later. This method can be used to free up the bus if the BUC has a temporary buffer empty condition on a load or a temporary buffer full condition on a store.

Data Transaction

The following I/O transactions each involve a single-beat data transaction:

- Load immediate.
- Load last.
- Store immediate.
- Store last.

With the following exceptions, the I/O data transaction is identical to that already described for the single-beat memory data transfer — only one word may be transferred at a time over data paths 0:3.

DRTRY# Use

Use of DRTRY# is undefined during I/O bus operations.

I/O Reply Transactions

When the final word has been transferred (using the load or store last transaction), the BUC arbitrates for the bus. When it has acquired ownership of the address bus, it performs either a load or store reply transaction to report completion status back to the originating processor. These are address-only transactions and consist of two address packets. The contents of packet 1 is reserved. The address bus and the XATC bus are driven to zero. Packet 1 contains the information illustrated in figure 35-5. The packet 0 information is as follows:

- The error bit, bit 2, indicates whether an error occurred during the transmission.
- The BUC identifies itself with its BUC number in bits 3:11.
- Bits 12:27 of packet 0 are BUC-specific and are not used by the processor.
- The BUC uses bits 28:31 to identify the originating processor.

If the processor detects that the error bit is set, it completes the instruction that caused the I/O access. If it was a load operation, the data is forwarded to the GPR registers. An I/O protocol interrupt is generated. This is outside the scope of the PowerPC architecture. The interrupt vector offset is 00A00h.

If a processor receives a reply with a processor ID that matches its own at a point that it wasn't expecting a reply, the processor will checkstop (freeze). The platform designer must supply logic to assert AACK# for the processor in response to an I/O reply transaction. The processor checks address parity when it receives an I/O reply transaction.

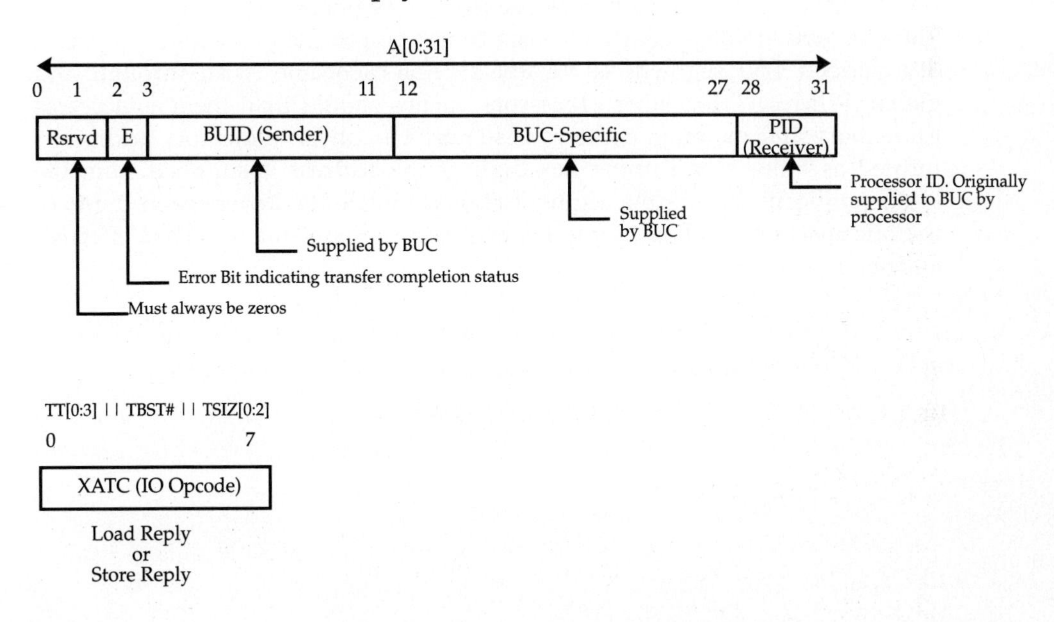

Figure 35-5. I/O Reply Address Packet 0

Effect of TEA# Assertion

If TEA# is asserted during an I/O transaction and the MSR[ME] bit is cleared, the processor will enter the checkstop state. If MSR[ME] is set, the processor will note the fact that a machine check condition was detected but will continue with the I/O transaction series associated with the currently-executing instruction. TEA# must then be reasserted for each subsequent immediate operation. If TEA# is not asserted for each of the subsequent immediate operations, the result of TEA# assertion is unpredictable (either a machine check interrupt or a checkstop will result). The BUC must not perform the load or store last operation. If performed, the processor enters the checkstop state. When the I/O transaction series has completed up to but not including the last operation and TEA# was reasserted for each immediate operation, the processor then completes the instruction that caused the transaction series and takes the machine check interrupt.

Memory-Forced I/O Segment

If the BUC in the segment register is equal to 7Fh, it should be noted that the processor is accessing a memory-mapped I/O segment , not an I/O segment. These accesses bypass page and block translation in the processor. The memory-mapped I/O segment is treated as non-cacheable, write-through and global (WIM = 111b). Other processors/caches should treat them as accesses to memory and maintain cache consistency. The physical memory address is formed as follows: the upper hex digit of the address is supplied from the least-significant digit in the segment register, while the lower seven digits of the address are supplied by the lower seven digits of the specified effective address.

Any BUC other than 7Fh results in an I/O access. *The memory-forced I/O feature of the PPC601 processor is outside the scope of the PowerPC architecture.*

Chapter 36

The Previous Chapter

The previous chapter provided a detailed description of the PPC 601 processor's implementation of I/O bus transactions. Timing diagrams were utilized to illustrate the use of the bus.

This Chapter

This chapter provides a detailed description of the external control transactions generated by the PPC 601 processor when it executes an ecowx or eciwx instruction. This includes a discussion of software-related issues.

The Next Chapter

The next chapter provides a detailed discussion of the implementation of L2 caches in platforms incorporating the PPC 601 processor. This includes a detailed description of both single and multi-processor systems using both lookaside and look-through L2 caches. The write-through and write-back policies are also described.

General

Memory transactions are used to communicate with memory. I/O transactions are used to communicate with I/O devices. The external control instructions are used to transfer one word between the processor and a special external device. The system designer may include up to 64 of these devices, each with its own address, or resource ID. The resource ID must be set up in the External Address Register, or EAR. This register can only be accessed by the operating system. As implemented in the PPC 601 processor, the resource ID field in the EAR is only four bits wide and the processor therefore only supports up to 16 devices. The PowerPC processor architecture states that the implementation of the ecowx and eciwx instructions and the EAR register are optional, but they are implemented and supported in the PPC 601 processor.

Example Usage

The system designer may utilize the ecowx and eciwx instructions to communicate with a graphics adapter. The ecowx instruction can be used to specify the graphics adapter as the target external device, or resource, deliver the start address of a graphics frame buffer to it, and also deliver a command or request to it. The eciwx instruction could be used to check the graphics adapter's status.

EAR Must Be Initialized

Before the ecowx and eciwx instructions can be successfully executed, the operating system programmer must initialize the PPC 601's EAR register with the resource ID of the target device and set the enable bit in the EAR to indicate that it has been initialized with a valid ID. Figure 36-1 illustrates the PPC 601's EAR register. If an attempt is made to execute either instruction when the EAR's enable bit is zero, the processor will take the data storage interrupt and set DSISR[11] to one to indicate the cause of the interrupt.

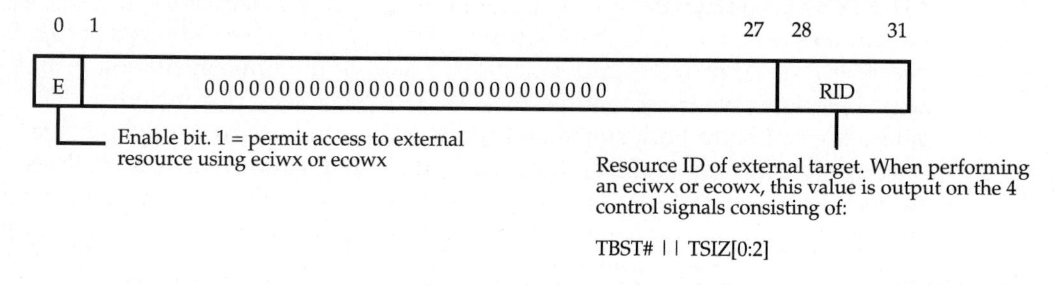

Figure 36-1. PPC 601's EAR Register

Instruction Format

The eciwx and ecowx instructions take any of the following forms:

```
ec*wx       r1,r2,r3
ec*wx       r1,0,r2
ec*wx       r1,d(r2)
```

where * can be either "o" or "i." The target effective address is formed as previously described in the chapter entitled "Address Modes, Branch Prediction."

The address specified should be word-aligned. For more information on alignment-related issues, refer to the section in this chapter entitled "Alignment Issues."

Access Must Be in Memory Segment or Block

When an ecowx or eciwx instruction is executed, it should map to a memory segment or a block defined by one of the BAT registers. If it maps to an I/O segment, the instruction acts as a no-op. When performed in a memory segment, the access assumes a WIM bit setting of x1Mb (the access is non-cacheable and the M bit from the page table entry or BAT register supplies the state of the GBL# signal).

Address Translation Modes Supported

The PowerPC architecture only supports execution of the ecowx and eciwx instructions with data address translation enabled (MSR[DT] = 1), but the PPC 601 supports execution with translation turned off, as well. When translation is disabled, the effective address is the physical address that is output during the address transaction. A WIM bit setting of x11b is assumed (non-cacheable, memory coherency required).

When translation is enabled, the effective address is translated to a physical address by either the BAT or paging logic. The WIM bit setting is still assumed to be x1Mb (the access is non-cacheable and the M bit from the page table entry or BAT register supplies the state of the GBL# signal).

Address Transaction

The processor will arbitrate for ownership of the address bus as already defined for memory and I/O transactions. Upon acquiring ownership of the address bus, the processor outputs the following information:

- The target physical address is output on A[0:31].
- TS# is asserted.
- The transaction type indicated on TT[0:3] will either be an eco or eci transaction.
- The four-bit address of the target external resource is supplied by bits 28:31 of the EAR register and is output on the four bit bus comprised of

TBST# and TSIZ[0:2] (TBST# carries bit 28, the msb of the ID, while TSIZ carries bits the lsbs of the ID from bits 29:31 of the EAR).

Alignment Issues

The PowerPC processor architecture does not specify that the target effective address must be word-aligned, but the PPC 601 documentation does impose this constraint. It states that the results will be boundedly-undefined. This means that although the result is not defined, it will always be the same.

If the programmer should specify an address that is not word-aligned, the PPC 601 processor will perform one or two bus transactions (each consisting of an address and a data transaction) to transfer the specified word. One eco or eci bus transaction will result if the entire word resides within a single doubleword. Two transactions will be performed if the word crosses over a doubleword address boundary.

If the word straddles two doublewords, the processor must perform two transactions (because it is only capable of addressing one doubleword at a time). Table 36-1 defines the address and number of bytes transferred for each possible case.

Table 36-1. Addressing and Byte Transfer Count When an eco or eci Transactions Cross Doubleword Address Boundary

A[29:31] of Effective Address	A[29:31] in 1st Transaction	# Bytes Transferred In 1st Transaction	A[29:31] in 2nd Transaction	# Bytes Transferred In 2nd Transaction
101b	101b	3	000b	1
110b	110b	2	000b	2
111b	111b	1	000b	3

As an example, if the target address were 00000105h, the four bytes to be transferred reside in locations 00000105h – 00000108h. 00000105h – 00000107h reside in the doubleword that starts at address 00000100h, while location 00000108h is the first location in the doubleword that starts at address 00000108h. During the first transaction, the address placed on the bus would be 00000105h (A[29:31] = 101b). The implied size of the transfer is three bytes (the contents of the last three locations in the currently-addressed doubleword (00000105h – 00000107h). During the second transaction, the address placed on the bus would be 00000108h (A[29:31] = 000b). The implied size of the transfer is one byte (the contents of location 00000108h).

Although the PPC 601 processor is capable of performing these two transactions as a result of a word transfer that crosses doubleword address boundaries, the platform logic external to the processor might not support this scenario and may generate a TEA# in response. An unaligned transfer series with an external control device is generally considered to be a programming error. It should also be noted that the two bus transactions are not guaranteed to occur atomically. Another bus master may gain ownership of the bus after the first transaction and before the second. Also, once the processor starts the first transaction in the pair, it permits subsequent instructions (that follow the ecowx or eciwx) to execute. If one of these instructions is an aligned eciwx or ecowx, the transaction generated as a result of that instruction may be enveloped between the two transfers associated with the misaligned transfer. This could cause problems with the target device (i.e., confusion).

Data Transaction

As with memory-oriented transactions, TT3 = 1 implies a need for the data bus. The data bus is acquired in the same manner as that already described for memory and I/O transactions. If executing an ecowx instruction, the word from the specified source register supplies the data driven onto the data bus. The data paths the data is driven onto depends on the start address specified within the currently-addressed doubleword.

Chapter 37

The Previous Chapter

The previous chapter provided a detailed description of the external control transactions generated by the PPC 601 processor when it executes an ecowx or eciwx instruction. This included a discussion of software-related issues.

This Chapter

This chapter provides a detailed discussion of the implementation of L2 caches in platforms incorporating the PPC 601 processor. This includes a detailed description of both single and multi-processor systems using both lookaside and look-through L2 caches. The write-through and write-back policies are also described.

The Next Chapter

The next chapter collects all aspects of the PPC 601 processor's design that facilitate its usage in multiprocessor systems. The discussion of each topic references the detailed descriptions found in other parts of the book.

Single-Processor System

Single-Processor System with Look-Aside L2 Cache

General

Figure 37-1 illustrates the basic relationships in a system with the L2 cache implemented as a look-aside cache. The processor's L1 cache and the L2 cache only cache information from the main array of DRAM memory. Both caches only keep copies of information accessed by the host processor. They do not keep copies of information accessed by PCI masters. Main memory resides on the processor's host bus along with the L2 cache. Whenever the host processor initiates a memory access, the access is immediately visible to both the L2 cache and main memory.

In addition, the host/PCI bridge resides in between the host processor bus and the PCI bus. Whenever a PCI bus master initiates an access to main memory, the bridge must recognize that the target memory address is within the range assigned to main memory and must bridge the transaction over onto the host bus. The transaction is then visible to main memory, the L2 cache and the processor. Conversely, the bridge must recognize when the host processor initiates a transaction that targets a device on the PCI side and must then bridge the host bus transaction over onto the PCI bus. This section describes the interaction between the host processor, main memory, the L2 cache and PCI bus masters.

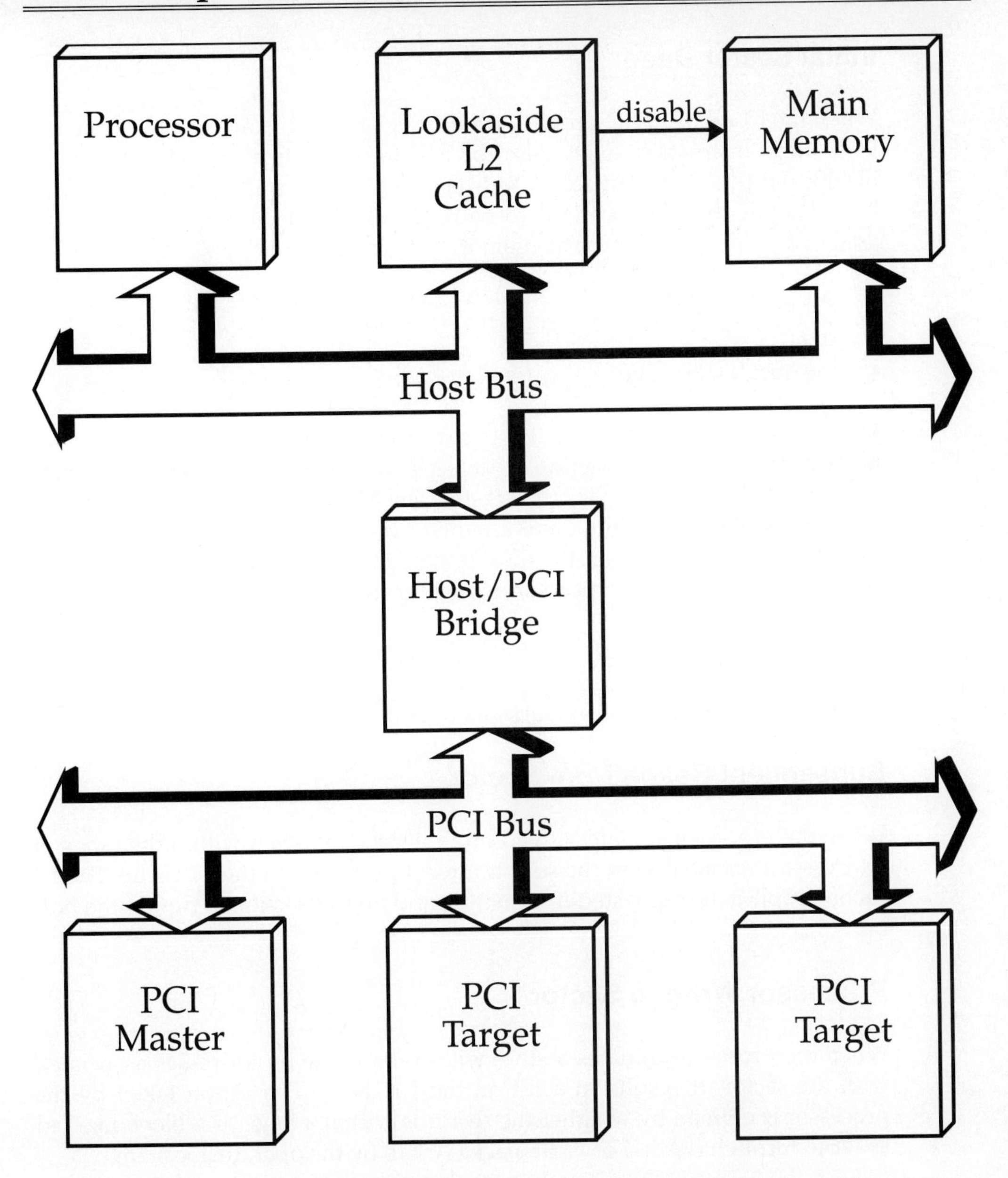

Figure 37-1. Single Processor System with Look-Aside L2 Cache

Initial Sector Read

When the L1 cache in the processor must read a sector from memory (due to a load miss, instruction fetch miss, or a store miss in a write-back page or block), the processor initiates a four-beat burst read transaction on the host bus. Assume that the locations to be read fall within the range of addresses assigned to main memory. The memory read is immediately visible to:

- the main memory.
- the L2 cache.
- the host/PCI bridge.

The host/PCI bridge ignores the transaction because the target memory is main memory. The transaction is detected by both the L2 cache and main memory, but the L2 cache is much faster. The L2 cache performs a lookup and determines that it does not have a copy of the requested sector. As a result, the L2 cache does not assert the disable signal to main memory. The requested sector is supplied to the processor by main memory.

The L2 cache quietly snarfs a copy of the sector from the bus as it is read by the processor. It marks its copy exclusive (because it's the same as the data in memory). The processor also marks its copy of the sector exclusive.

Subsequent Reads from Sector

When the processor initiates a load or an instruction fetch within the range of addresses associated with the sector, it results on a hit on the L1 cache. The L1 cache supplies the requested information and no transaction is run on the host bus.

Processor Write to Sector

When the processor initiates a store within the range of addresses associated with the sector, it results in a hit on the L1 cache. The action taken by the processor is defined by whether the sector is within a page or a block marked as write-through (W = 1) or write-back (W = 0) by the operating system.

In Write-Through Page or Block (W = 1)

If the page or block is marked as write-through, the store hit on the cache results in two actions:

- The data is updated in the L1 cache and the sector stays in the same state (exclusive).
- The processor initiates a single-beat write transaction to update the byte of bytes in main memory. It asserts its WT# output to instruct the L2 cache to also use a write-through policy.

When the single-beat memory write transaction appears on the host bus, it is visible to both the L2 cache and main memory.

If the sector is not in the L2 cache (it was cast out to make room for another sector), the data is updated in memory and the memory write does not complete until the main memory controller returns the TA# signal.

If the sector is in the L2 cache, the data is updated in the L2 cache. The memory write to main memory is permitted to proceed (if the L2 cache is implemented as a write-back cache, the assertion of the processor's WT# output instructs L2 to permit the data to be written to memory) and terminates when main memory has accepted the write data (main memory controller asserts TA#).

In Write-Back Page or Block (W = 0)

If the page or block is marked as write-back (W = 0), the store hit on the L1 cache causes the L1 cache to accept the write data and to mark the sector as modified. The data in the L1 cache has been updated, but the copies of the sector in the L2 cache and main memory are now stale.

PCI Bus Master Read from Sector

When a PCI bus master initiates a memory read transaction on the PCI bus, the host/PCI bridge determines if the address falls within the range of addresses assigned to main memory. If it does, the bridge acts as the PCI memory target. It acquires ownership of the host bus and initiates a memory read transaction. It asserts GBL# during the address phase of the memory read to force the processor to snoop the transaction and to report snoop results.

Snoop Miss on L1

If the memory read attempt by the PCI bus master results in a snoop miss on the L1 cache (SHD# and ARTRY# sampled high), the bridge is permitted to read the data from main memory. There is no effect on a copy of the sector in the L2 cache.

Snoop Hit on Clean Sector in L1

If the memory read attempt by the PCI bus master results in a snoop hit on a clean sector (exclusive state; SHD# sampled asserted and ARTRY# deasserted), the bridge is permitted to read the data from memory. The L1 cache changes the state of its sector from exclusive to shared when it detects another master reading from the same area. There is no effect on a copy of the sector in the L2 cache.

Snoop Hit on Modified Sector in L1

If the memory read attempt by the PCI bus master results in a snoop hit on a modified sector, the processor asserts ARTRY# to the bridge. The bridge terminates its memory read without proceeding with the memory read. The ARTRY# is also visible to the main memory controller, causing it to abort the data transfer, as well. The bridge, acting as the PCI memory target, issues a retry to the PCI bus master. This forces it to retry the memory read again later.

The processor then performs a four-beat burst memory write (a snoop pushback) to deposit the modified data into main memory. To keep its copy of the sector updated, the L2 cache snarfs the data off the bus as it is being written to memory. The L2 cache keeps its copy of the sector in the exclusive state. In the event that the L2 cache had previously cast out its copy of the sector to make room for another sector, it would snarf the modified sector from the bus as the processor writes it to memory. It would then enter the snarfed sector into its cache and mark it exclusive.

After depositing the modified sector into memory, the L1 cache changes the state of the sector from modified to shared (because the PCI master will then read the data from memory). The PCI bus master then retries the memory read and forces the processor to snoop it again. This time, it results in a hit on a clean sector (SHD# sampled asserted and ARTRY# deasserted). The PCI master is permitted to read the requested data from memory.

PCI Bus Master Write to Sector

When a PCI bus master initiates a memory write transaction on the PCI bus, it may utilize either the PCI memory write or the memory write and invalidate transaction type. If it uses a memory write, there is no guarantee that the master is going to write an entire sector into memory, while a sector write is guaranteed if the memory write and invalidate transaction is used. The host/PCI bridge determines if the address falls within the range of addresses assigned to main memory. If it does, the bridge acquires ownership of the host bus and initiates a memory write transaction. It may use either a single-beat write (if the PCI master is using the memory write command) or a four-beat burst write (if the PCI master is using the write and invalidate command). The bridge asserts GBL# during the address phase of the memory write to force the processor to snoop the transaction and to report snoop results.

Snoop Miss on L1

If the memory write attempt by the PCI bus master results in a snoop miss on the L1 cache (SHD# and ARTRY# sampled high), the bridge is permitted to write the data to main memory. If the L2 cache has a copy of the sector, it will take one of two actions:

- Invalidate its copy (because the PCI master is overwriting all or a portion of the sector in memory).
- Snarf the write data from the bus to keeps its copy of the sector updated. In this case, it will keep its copy of the sector in exclusive state.

If the L2 cache does not a have copy of the sector and the bridge is performing a single-beat memory write, the L2 ignores the transaction. If the bridge is performing a four-beat burst write, the L2 cache can snarf the sector from the bus as it is written to memory by the bridge. The sector is then entered in the L2 cache in the exclusive state.

Snoop Hit on Clean Sector in L1

If the memory write attempt by the PCI bus master results in a snoop hit on a clean sector in L1 (exclusive state; SHD# sampled asserted and ARTRY# deasserted), the bridge is permitted to write the data to memory. The L1 cache changes the state of its sector from exclusive to invalid when it detects another master writing to the same area. It has no way of snarfing the write data from the bus during the memory data write by the other bus master.
If the L2 cache has a copy of the sector, it will take one of two actions:

- Invalidate its copy (because the PCI master is overwriting all or a portion of the sector in memory).
- Snarf the write data from the bus to keeps its copy of the sector updated. In this case, it will keep its copy of the sector in exclusive state.

If the L2 cache does not a have copy of the sector and the bridge is performing a single-beat memory write, the L2 ignores the transaction. If the bridge is performing a four-beat burst write, the L2 cache can snarf the sector from the bus as it is written to memory by the bridge. The sector is then entered in the L2 cache in the exclusive state.

Snoop Hit on Modified Sector in L1

If the memory write attempt by the PCI bus master results in a snoop hit on a modified sector, the processor takes one of two actions:

1. **Bridge Is Using a Single-Beat Write**. If the bridge has initiated a single-beat memory write transaction (because the PCI master has initiated a memory write transaction, not a write back and invalidate), the processor asserts ARTRY# to the bridge. The bridge terminates its memory write without proceeding with the memory write. The ARTRY# is also visible to the main memory controller, causing it to abort the data transfer, as well. The bridge, acting as the PCI memory target, issues a retry to the PCI bus master. This forces it to retry the memory write again later. The processor then performs a four-beat burst memory write (a snoop push-back) to deposit the modified data into main memory.

   The L2 cache snarfs the data off the bus as it is being written to memory. The L2 cache keeps its copy of the sector in the exclusive state. In the event that the L2 cache had previously cast out its copy of the sector to make room for another sector, it would snarf the modified sector from the bus as the processor writes it to memory. It would then enter the snarfed sector into its cache and mark it exclusive.

   After depositing the modified sector into memory, the L1 cache changes the state of the sector from modified to invalid (because the PCI master will then write the data to memory). The PCI bus master then retries the memory write and forces the processor to snoop it again. This time, it results in a miss (SHD# and ARTRY# sampled deasserted). The PCI master is permitted to write the requested data to memory. The L2 snarfs the write data from the bus to keep its copy of the sector updated. The L2 copy stays in the exclusive state.

2. **Bridge Is Using a Burst Write**. If the PCI master initiates a memory write and invalidate transaction, it is guaranteeing that it will write an entire sector into memory. The bridge can use a four-beat burst write to write the sector into main memory for the PCI master. If the host processor snoop results in a snoop hit on a modified sector, the processor invalidates its copy of the sector even though it's marked modified (because the performance of the four-beat burst write on the host bus guarantees that the bridge will overwrite the entire sector of information in main memory).

   The L2 cache can snarf the sector from the bus as it is written to memory by the bridge. If the sector was already in the L2 cache, it is just overwritten and stays in the exclusive state. If the sector was not in the L2 cache, the sector is then entered in the L2 cache in the exclusive state.

Sector Cast Out from L1 Cache

When a miss occurs in the L1 cache, the processor will read a new sector into the L1 cache from memory. The L1 cache uses its LRU algorithm to select which member of the set of eight entries to replace with the new sector being read from memory.

Clean Sector Castout

If the sector selector for cast out is in the invalid, exclusive or shared state in L1, it is just overwritten with the new sector and the tag (page) address is updated with the new source page number. If the L2 cache has a copy of the sector being cast out, it remains in the L2 cache until it is cast out by the L2 LRU algorithm.

Modified Sector Castout

If the sector selected for cast out is in the modified state in L1, the processor performs a four-beat burst write to cast the modified sector back to memory. The L2 cache can snarf the sector as it is written back to memory and update its copy.

Advantages of Look-Aside L2 Cache

The look-aside L2 cache has two distinct advantages over the look-through L2 cache implementation:

- There is **no look up penalty**. Since the processor's memory accesses are instantly visible to both the L2 cache and main memory, in the event of an L2 cache miss there is no delay in making the access visible to main memory.
- **Simple to implement**. The look-aside L2 implementation need only implement the invalid and exclusive states. It also doesn't act as a snoop filter for the host processor. All memory accesses performed by other bus master are visible to the L1 cache in the processor.

Disadvantages of Look-Aside L2 Cache

All PCI master memory accesses must use the host bus, making the host bus less available to the processor. In addition, PCI bus masters may not access main memory while the host processor is using the host bus to access main memory.

Single-Processor System with Look-Through L2 Cache

Figure 37-2 illustrates the basic relationships in a system with the L2 cache implemented as a look-through cache. The processor's L1 cache and the L2 cache integrated into the bridge only cache information from the main array of DRAM memory. Both caches only keep copies of information accessed by the host processor. They do not keep copies of information accessed by PCI masters. Main memory resides on a separate memory bus and the bridge controls access to main memory. It can permit either a PCI master or the host processor to access main memory, but not both simultaneously. This section describes the interaction between the host processor, main memory, the L2 cache and PCI bus masters.

Bus Concurrency

Whenever the host processor initiates a memory access, it is immediately visible only to the L2 cache. If the processor is attempting to access a memory location within the range of addresses associated with main memory, the L2 cache performs a lookup to determine if the access can be satisfied by the L2 cache. If it can, the bridge needn't utilize the memory bus to access main memory. As long as all of the processor's memory accesses can be serviced by the L2 cache, the bridge may permit PCI bus masters to perform data transfers with main memory or PCI target devices. The system is thus able to use the PCI and host buses simultaneously, yielding higher throughput.

Host-to-PCI Transaction Bridging

When the processor attempts a memory access from memory outside the range of addresses associated with main memory, the bridge must propagate the memory access onto the PCI bus. When the processor attempts to access an I/O address outside the range of I/O port addresses that may be implemented within the bridge itself, the bridge must propagate the I/O access onto the PCI bus.

PCI-to-Main Memory Transaction Bridging

Whenever a PCI bus master initiates an access to main memory, the bridge must recognize that the target memory address is within the range assigned to main memory and must bridge the transaction over onto the memory bus. The transaction is then visible to main memory.

Policy of Inclusion

All sectors that reside in the L1 cache get into the L1 cache when they are initially read from main memory by the L2 cache. At any given moment in time, the L2 cache therefore contains a copy of each sector that is currently resident in the L1 cache. This is referred to as the policy of inclusion.

The L2 cache is substantially larger than the L1 cache. Although a cache sector is initially copied into both the L1 and L2 caches, the replacement, or LRU, algorithm in the L1 cache casts out sectors in the L1 when the space is needed to store new sectors that are needed from memory. Although the sector no longer resides in the L1 cache, a copy of it probably still resides in the L2 cache and is available to service processor memory access requests. It should be noted, however, that the L2 cache also implements an LRU algorithm and will eventually cast out the sector in L2 when it needs the space to store a new sector requested by the processor. The sector being cast out of L2 may still be in the L1 cache, so the L2 must force the L1 to cast out its copy as well. This is necessary because, once the L2 has its copy of the sector out, it can no longer perform snooping of that sector for accesses performed by PCI bus masters.

L2 Acts as Snoop Filter for Processor

In the earlier discussion of the look-aside implementation of the L2 cache, one of the disadvantages stated was that every PCI bus master access to main memory must utilize the host bus and the host processor must snoop every access to main memory performed by PCI bus masters. In an environment where PCI bus masters are performing large numbers of main memory accesses, the processor and the bridge must compete for ownership of the host bus. In addition, the processor must snoop each and every one of the bridge's main memory accesses. When the L2 cache is implemented as a look-through cache, the L2 acts as a snoop filter — it only forces the L1 cache to snoop PCI accesses to main memory that are hits on the L2 cache. This can significantly diminish the number of snoops sent to the processor, resulting in more host bus availability to the processor for L2 cache look-ups.

Whenever a PCI master attempts an access to main memory, the L2 cache must snoop the memory address that the PCI master is attempting to access. If the snoop results in a miss on the L2 cache, the PCI master is accessing an area of memory that neither the L1 nor the L2 cache have a copy of in any state. On the other hand, if the snoop results in a snoop hit in the L2 cache, the PCI master is accessing an area of memory that either just the L2, or both the L1 and L2 have copies of. In these cases, the L2 cache may need to inform the processor's L1 cache of the memory access being attempted by the PCI bus master. In other words, the processor's L1 cache must be forced to snoop the transaction, as well.

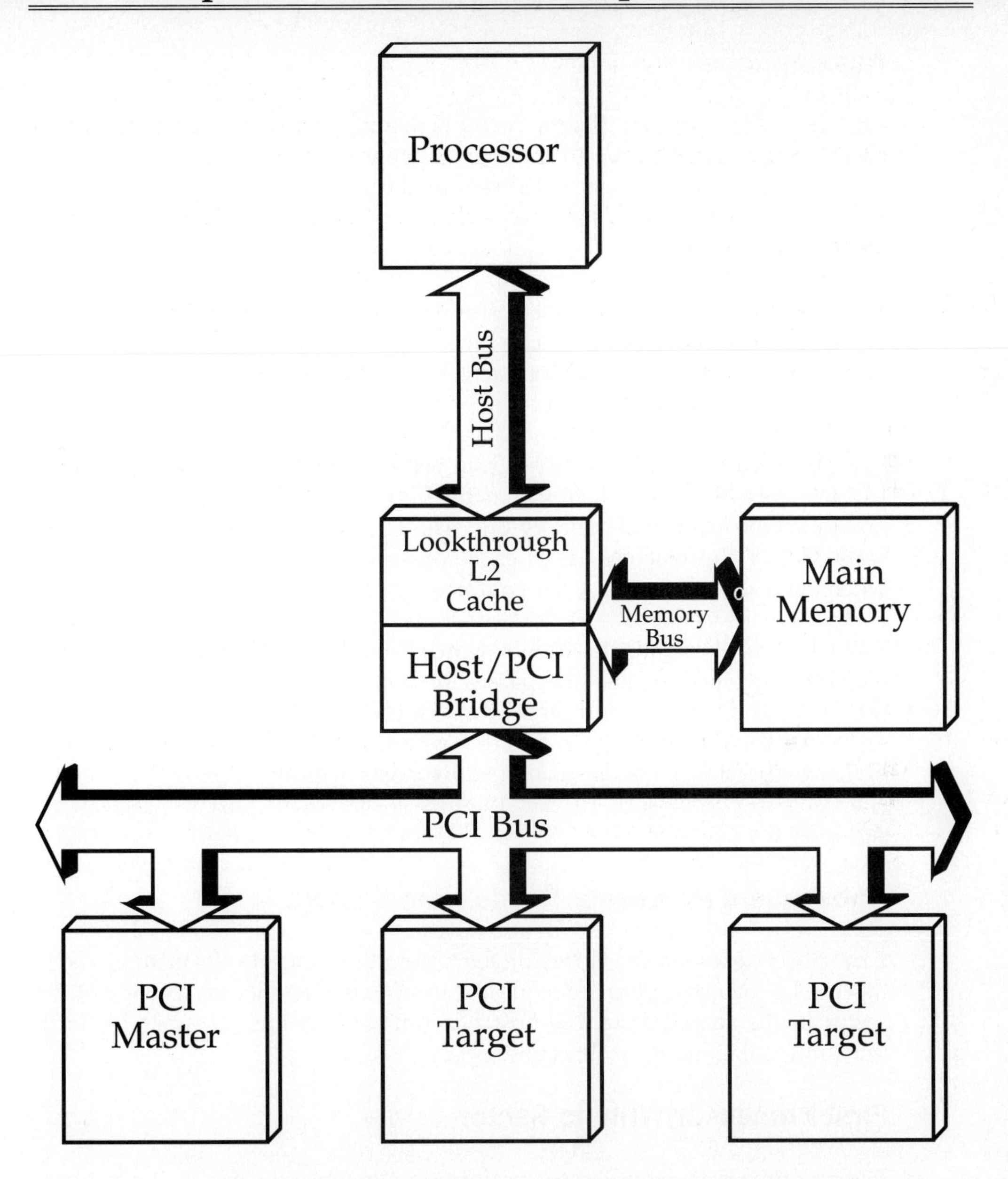

Figure 37-2. Single-Processor System with Look-Through L2 Cache

Assumptions

This discussion assumes that the sector is in a page or block marked as write-back (W = 0), cacheable (I = 0) and memory coherency required (M = 1). It also assumes that the only device with associated caches is the host processor.

Initial Sector Read

The first time that the processor performs a load or an instruction fetch from the sector, it results in an L1 cache miss. As a result, the processor initiates a four-beat burst memory read transaction and asserts GBL# to instruct the L2 cache to report the snoop result.

Since the sector has not been read from before, the read attempt results in an L2 cache miss. The L2 cache instructs the bridge to read the target sector from main memory using the memory bus. The L2 cache asserts SHD# and deasserts ARTRY#, instructing the L1 cache to store the sector in the shared state when the read from memory has completed.

As each group of eight bytes (doubleword) is read from memory, the L2 cache latches a copy for itself and also passes the doubleword to the processor. It asserts TA# to instruct the processor to latch the doubleword. When the entire sector has been read and passed to the processor, the L2 cache marks its copy exclusive (because no other caching entity exists behind the bridge on the PCI side) and the processor's L1 cache marks it shared (because SHD# was asserted by the L2 cache).

Subsequent Processor Reads from Sector

Any subsequent load or instruction fetch from the sector results in an L1 cache hit. The L1 cache supplies the requested information and leaves its copy of the sector in the shared state. No host bus transactions are necessary to fulfill these internal memory read requests.

First Processor Write to Sector

The first time that the processor performs a store into the sector, it must first inform the L2 cache that an internal modification will be made to the sector in the L1 cache (the processor knows that this notification is necessary because M = 1 and the sector is marked shared, indicating that at least one cache external to the processor also has a copy of the sector).

Before accepting the data to be stored into its copy of the sector, the processor first broadcasts an address-only kill transaction. The memory address specified is the start address of the sector to be modified in the L1 cache. When the L2 cache detects the kill transaction, it recognizes that the processor is about to internally modify its copy of the sector. The kill results in a hit on the L2 cache. The L2 cache marks its copy of the sector modified. Although the processor has not propagated the write data through to the L2 cache (because the processor uses a write-back policy in this area of memory), the L2 cache must mark its copy as modified in order to accurately PCI bus master main memory accesses for the host processor. After successfully broadcasting the kill transaction, the processor accepts the store data into its copy of the sector and marks its copy modified. This means that it doesn't have to inform the L2 cache of any subsequent changes it makes within the sector.

Subsequent Processor Writes to Sector

Any subsequent stores that the processor performs within the sector result in the update being made to the sector in the L1 cache with no notification to the L2 cache. The sector stays in the modified state.

L1 Castout of Modified Sector

If the processor experiences a miss on its L1 data cache for some other sector and has to read the target sector from external memory, the L1 cache's LRU algorithm may force the L1 cache to overwrite a modified sector. Since the modified sector represents the "freshest" copy of the sector, the processor must place the modified sector into the MU's write queue and schedule it to be written back to memory. The memory read is performed to fetch the new sector to put into the L1 cache entry freed up by the cast out of the modified sector.

After the memory read is completed, the processor performs a four-beat burst write transaction on the host bus to write the modified sector to memory. During this memory write, the processor asserts TC0 (TC0 = 1), indicating that it is eliminating its copy of the sector when the write completes. The L2 cache also has a copy of the sector in the modified state, but it contains stale data (because the processor had issued a kill but not the update data when it initially stored into the L1 copy of the sector). The L2 cache latches the sector and overwrites its stale copy of the sector. After absorbing the "freshest" copy of the sector from the processor, the L2 cache may be implemented to handle the state of the sector in one of two ways:

- **Leave it marked modified**. The L2 cache would not know if had the "freshest" copy of the sector, so, in the event of an L2 snoop of a PCI master's memory access, the L2 would therefore have to force the processor to perform a snoop. If the processor's L1 cache had a copy of the sector in the modified state, the processor would perform the snoop push-back. If the processor didn't have a copy, the L2 cache has the latest version of the sector and would perform the snoop push-back of its copy.
- May **mark it as "modified/exclusive."** The exact terminology for this state will vary. It indicates that the L2's copy of the sector is not the same as memory and that the processor does not have a copy of the sector. In the event of an L2 snoop of a PCI master's memory access, the L2 could therefore immediately perform the snoop push-back without generating a snoop back to the processor.

PCI Bus Master Read from Sector

When a PCI master initiates a memory read from main memory, the L2 cache snoops the memory address being accessed. The possible results and actions taken are covered in the following sections.

Snoop Miss on L2 Cache

If the snoop results in a snoop miss on the L2 cache, the PCI bus master is permitted to read the requested data from memory. There is no effect on the L2 cache and the processor is not informed of the access attempt.

Snoop Hit on Sector in Exclusive State in L2

If the snoop results in a snoop hit on a sector in the exclusive state, the PCI bus master is about to read good data from memory. The L2 cache permits the access. The L2 cache does not change the state of its copy of the sector and the host processor is not informed of the access.

Snoop Hit on L2 Sector in Modified State

If the snoop results in a snoop hit on a modified sector, the PCI bus master is attempting to read stale data from memory. The L2 cache instructs the bridge to issue a retry to the PCI bus master, causing the PCI master to abort its transaction with no data transferred. The PCI master will re attempt the memory access at a later time.

If the L2 cache's copy is marked modified, it must force the processor to perform a snoop in its L1 data cache. The L2 cache can accomplish this by performing an address-only flush sector transaction on the processor's host bus with GBL# asserted. If the L1 cache experiences a snoop hit on a modified copy of the sector, the L1 cache has the "freshest" copy of the sector and must write the sector to memory and then marks its copy invalid. The L2 cache passes the sector being written back to memory through to main memory and also latches the data to update its copy of the sector. Because its copy is now the same as the one in memory, it marks its copy exclusive.

If the L2's copy of the sector is marked modified/exclusive (see the section in this chapter entitled "Cast Out of Modified Sector"), it has the latest copy of the sector. It does not have to force the processor to snoop the address in the L1 cache. The L2 cache performs the snoop push-back of its copy of the sector to main memory.

PCI Bus Master Write to Sector

When a PCI master initiates a memory write to main memory, the L2 cache snoops the memory address being accessed. The possible results and actions taken are covered in the following sections.

Snoop Miss on L2 Cache

If the snoop results in a snoop miss on the L2 cache, the PCI bus master is permitted to write to memory. There is no effect on the L2 cache and the processor is not informed of the access attempt.

Snoop Hit on Sector in Exclusive State in L2

If the snoop results in a snoop hit on a sector in the exclusive state, the PCI bus master is about to write data to a clean area of memory. The L2 cache permits the access. The L2 cache invalidates its copy of the sector and, using the host bus, generates an address-only kill transaction with GBL# asserted to force the processor to kill its copy of the sector. It should be noted that the L2 cache could also snarf the data being to written to memory by the PCI bus master and thereby update its copy of the sector. In this case, it would still kill the processor's copy, but would keep its updated copy and leave it marked exclusive (because it's the same as memory).

Snoop Hit on L2 Sector in Modified State

If the snoop results in a snoop hit on a modified sector, the PCI bus master is attempting to write data to a stale sector in memory. The L2 cache instructs the bridge to issue a retry to the PCI bus master, causing the PCI master to abort its transaction with no data transferred. The PCI master will re attempt the memory access at a later time.

If the L2 cache's copy is marked modified, it must force the processor to perform a snoop in its L1 data cache. The L2 cache can accomplished this by performing an address-only flush sector transaction on the processor's host bus with GBL# asserted. If the L1 cache experiences a snoop hit on a modified copy of the sector, the L1 cache has the "freshest" copy of the sector and must write the sector to memory and then marks its copy invalid. The L2 cache passes the sector being written back to memory through to main memory. Because the PCI bus master will then write into the sector in memory, the L2 cache marks its copy invalid.

If the L2's copy of the sector is marked modified/exclusive (see the section in this chapter entitled "Cast Out of Modified Sector"), it has the latest copy of the sector. It does not have to force the processor to snoop the address in the L1 cache. The L2 cache performs the snoop push-back of its copy of the sector to main memory and then invalidates its copy.

L1 Cast Out

This subject is covered in the section earlier in this chapter entitled "L1 Cast Out of Modified Sector."

L2 Cast Out

If the L2 cache must cast out a sector to make room for a sector requested by the processor, one of the following conditions will be true:

- The sector to be cast out is in the exclusive state in the L2 cache. In this case, the L2 cache eliminates its copy of the sector and also generates a kill transaction to kill the processor's copy of the sector. It is necessary to kill the processor's copy because the L2 cannot snoop the sector for the L1 cache anymore.
- The sector to be cast out is in the modified state in the L2 cache. If the L2 cache's copy is marked modified, it must force the processor to perform a

snoop in its L1 data cache. The L2 cache can accomplished this by performing an address-only flush sector transaction on the processor's host bus with GBL# asserted. If the L1 cache experiences a snoop hit on a modified copy of the sector, the L1 cache has the "freshest" copy of the sector and must write the sector to memory and then marks its copy invalid. The L2 cache passes the sector being written back to memory through to main memory and invalidates its copy.

If the L2's copy of the sector is marked modified/exclusive (see the section earlier in this chapter entitled "L1 Cast Out of Modified Sector"), it has the latest copy of the sector. It does not have to force the processor to snoop the address in the L1 cache. The L2 cache performs the cast out of its copy of the sector to main memory and then invalidates its copy.

Disadvantages of Look-Through L2 Cache

There are two disadvantages associated with the look-through cache:

- Design is more substantially more complex than that of a look-aside cache.
- There is a lookup penalty inherent in accesses initiated by the host processor. The L2 cache will not initiate an access to main memory until it has checked for a miss in the cache. This injects some latency before the memory access is made visible to main memory.

Advantages of Look-Through L2 Cache

The look-through cache offers two advantages:

- As the L2 cache hit rate increases, the processor becomes decoupled from the memory bus, leaving it more available for use by PCI bus masters. This permits the host bus and the memory bus to be used concurrently.
- The L2 cache acts as a snoop filter for the host processor, decreasing the number of PCI memory accesses that must be snooped by the host processor.

Multiprocessor System

Multiprocessor System with Shared Look-Aside L2 Cache

The system illustrated in figure 37-3 consists of an array of four host processors with the host bus, main memory and a look-aside L2 cache in common. The relationship between each of the processors and the L2 cache is the same as that already described in the section in this chapter entitled "Single-Processor System with Look-Aside L2 Cache."

When any of the processors initiates a memory transaction, it is immediately visible to the other processors in the array, to main memory and to the L2 cache. A memory transaction initiated by any of the processors will be snooped by the other processors if the initiator asserts GBL# during the transaction. If any PCI bus master attempts an access to main memory, the bridge acquires ownership of the host bus and propagates the memory access onto the host bus so it can be seen by main memory. When performing a memory access on the host bus for a PCI master, the bridge always asserts GBL# to force the L2 cache and the host processor array to snoop the transaction.

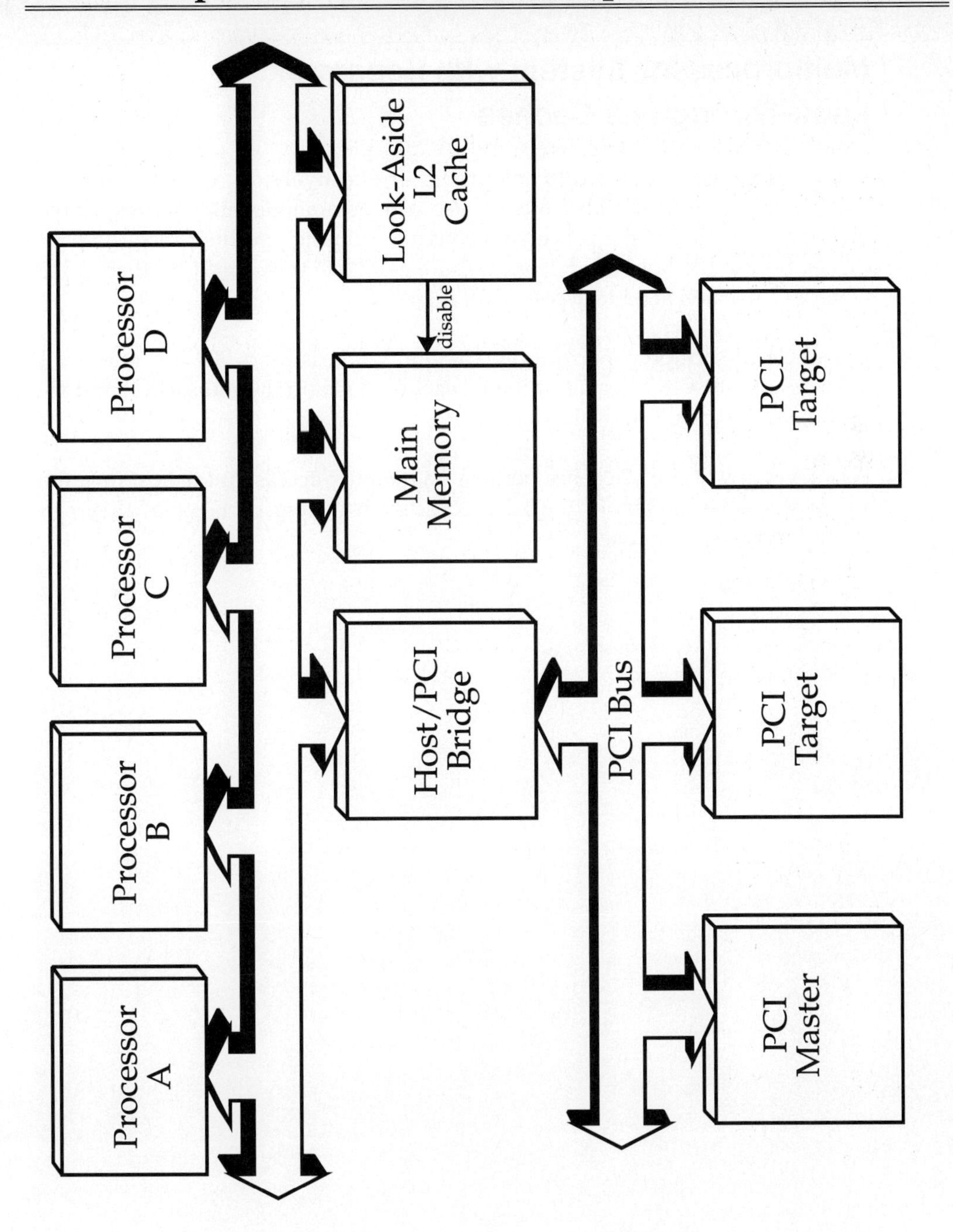

Figure 37-3. Multiprocessing System with Shared Look-Aside L2 Cache

Multiprocessor System with Separate Look-Through L2 Caches

The L2 cache associated with each processor effectively decouples its respective processor from the host bus. It also acts as a snoop filter its respective processor. As each of the processors continue running and their respective L2 caches fill up, the host bus becomes more available to be used by the bridge when PCI masters need to access main memory.

Whenever the bridge is performing a memory access for a PCI bus master, it must assert GBL# to force all of the L2 caches to snoop the transaction and report the snoop result to the bridge.

Whenever any of the L2 caches performs a memory access on the host bus, the access is visible to each of the L2 caches. By watching each other, they can maintain cache consistency.

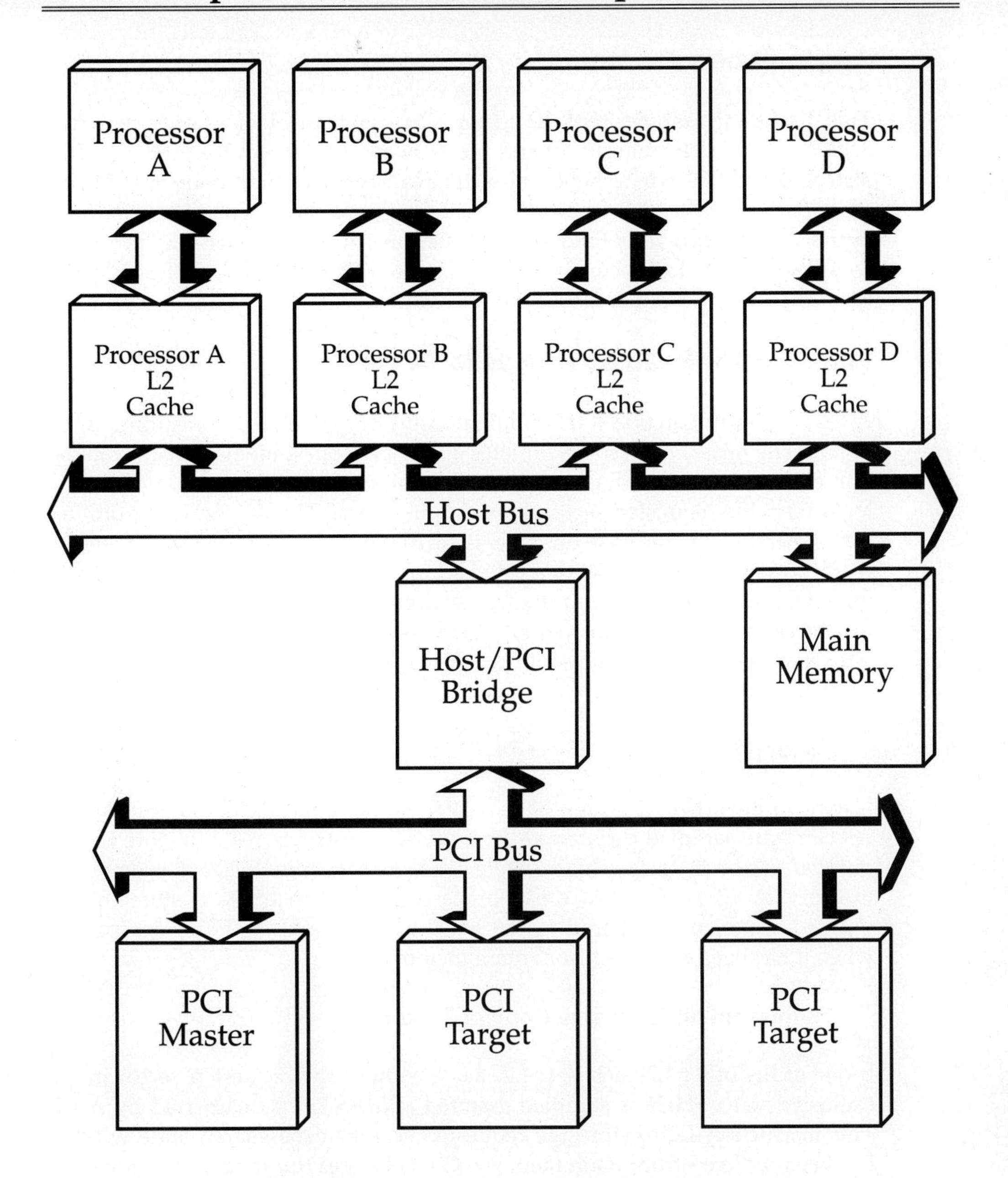

Figure 37-4. Multiprocessing System with Separate Look-Through L2 Caches

Assumptions

This discussion assumes that the sector is in a page or block marked as write-back (W = 0), cacheable (I = 0) and memory coherency required (M = 1). It is also assumed that when the initial sector read is performed, none of the processors or their respective L2 caches has a copy of the target sector. Refer to figure 37-4 during the following discussion. In this discussion, processor complex A refers to processor A and its related L2 cache. A-L1 refers to processor A's L1 cache. A-L2 refers to its L2 cache.

Initial Sector Read by Processor A

A load or an instruction fetch is initiated inside processor A, resulting in an A-L1 cache miss. Processor A initiates a four-beat burst memory read transaction on its local bus and asserts its GBL# output. The A-L2 cache performs a lookup for the requested sector, resulting in a miss. The A-L2 cache arbitrates for ownership of the host bus and then initiates a four-beat burst memory read transaction to read the requested sector from memory. It asserts GBL# to force the other L2's to snoop the transaction. A-L2 keeps AACK# deasserted to processor A until main memory acknowledges receipt of the transaction with AACK#. A-L2 then presents processor A with the snoop result from the other L2 caches.

Snoop Miss

If none of the other L2 caches have a copy of the requested sector, SHD# and ARTRY# are sampled deasserted by A-L2. This instructs A-L2 to store the requested sector in the exclusive state when it has been received from main memory. A-L2 asserts AACK# to processor A and instructs it store the requested sector in the shared state (SHD# asserted and ARTRY# deasserted) when it has been delivered from main memory.

Snoop Hit on Exclusive Copy of Sector

If one of the other L2 caches, C-L2, has a copy of the requested sector in the exclusive state, SHD# is sampled asserted and ARTRY# deasserted by A-L2. This instructs A-L2 to store the requested sector in the shared state when it has been received from main memory. C-L2 changes the state of its copy from exclusive to shared (because it has detected another cache reading a copy of the sector into its cache). C-L1 is not informed of the access. A-L2 asserts AACK# to processor A and instructs it store the requested sector in the shared state (SHD# asserted and ARTRY# deasserted) in A-L1 when it has been delivered from main memory.

Snoop Hit on Shared Copies of Sector

If more than one of the other L2 caches, C-L2 and B-L2, have copies of the requested sector in the shared state, SHD# is sampled asserted and ARTRY# deasserted by A-L2. This instructs A-L2 to store the requested sector in the shared state when it has been received from main memory. C-L2 and B-L2 leave the state of their copies in the shared state. C-L1 and B-L1 are not informed of the access. A-L2 asserts AACK# to processor A and instructs it store the requested sector in the shared state (SHD# asserted and ARTRY# deasserted) in A-L1 when it has been delivered from main memory.

Snoop Hit on Modified Copy of Sector

If one of the other L2 caches, D-L2, has a modified copy of the target sector, A-L2 samples ARTRY# and SHD# asserted. This forces A-L2 to abort the memory read attempt and retry it later. A-L2 issues a retry to A-L1 (by asserting ARTRY# on processor A's local bus).

In D-L2, one of two things is currently true:

- The copy of the target sector is currently marked modified/exclusive (because the D-L1 copy of the modified sector had been cast out of D-L1 by the LRU algorithm at an earlier point in time; D-L2 had then latched this copy during the D-L1 cast out operation and had marked its copy modified/exclusive). D-L2 therefore knows that processor D does not have a copy of the requested sector in D-L1. D-L2 arbitrates for ownership of the host bus and then performs a four-beat burst memory write transaction, a snoop push-back, to write the requested sector to memory. Upon completion of the push-back, D-L2 changes the state of its copy from modified to shared (because A-L2 will then read it from memory when it retries its read transaction). When the read has completed, the sector resides in A-L1, A-L2, and D-L2 and all are marked shared.
- The copy of the target sector is currently marked modified. In this case, D-L1 has the "freshest" copy of the sector and it must be forced to write it back to memory. D-L2 performs an address-only flush sector transaction with GBL# asserted on processor D's local bus. D-L1 performs a lookup and experiences a hit on the modified sector. As instructed by the flush sector transaction, processor D performs a four-beat burst memory write

transaction on its local bus to place the modified sector into memory and it also invalidates its copy of the sector. D-L2 writes the sector into main memory using the host bus and also latches the updated copy of the sector during the push-back operation. The new D-L2 copy is then marked shared (because A-L2 will retry the memory read and read the sector into its cache). Processor A retries the memory read, causing A-L2 to retry the read on the host bus. The snoop result reported back to A-L2 is now SHD# asserted and ARTRY# deasserted, instructing A-L2 to proceed with the memory read and then mark its copy of the sector as shared. A-L2 also passes the sector being read from main memory back to the processor and instructs A-L1 to store its copy in the shared state. When the read has completed, the sector resides in A-L1, A-L2, and D-L2 and all copies are marked shared. The D-L1 copy has been invalidated.

Subsequent Processor A Reads from Sector

Any subsequent load or instruction fetch from the A-L1 sector by processor A's core results in an A-L1 cache hit. The A-L1 cache supplies the requested information and leaves its copy of the sector in the shared state. No local bus or host bus transactions are necessary to fulfill these internal memory read requests.

First Processor A Write to Sector

The first time that processor A performs a store into the sector, it is forced to perform an address-only kill sector transaction on its local bus (because M = 1 and the sector is marked shared). When A-L2 detects the kill sector transaction on processor A's local bus, it takes one of the following actions:

- If the sector is marked shared in A-L2, other caches have copies of the sector. A-L2 broadcasts the kill sector transaction on the host bus to kill copies of the sector in all other caches. Until the host bus kill transaction completes without a retry, A-L2 keeps AACK# deasserted on processor A's local bus, preventing it from completing its kill transaction. All other L2 caches that have copies of the sector kill their copies. They also broadcasts the kill transaction to their respective processors on the processors' local buses, causing all other L1 caches to kill their copies of the sector as well. When the host bus kill has completed without retry (indicating that none of the snoopers were busy and each has acted upon the kill), A-L2 changes the state of its sector from the shared to the modified state. A-L2 asserts AACK# to processor A with both SHD# and ARTRY# deasserted (no retry on the kill). Internally, A-L1 then stores into the sector in A-L1 and marks it modified. Only A-L1 and A-L2 now have copies of the sector and both are now marked modified, but the A-L1 copy is the freshest copy.

- If the sector is marked exclusive in A-L2, no other caches have copies of the sector, so A-L2 does not have to broadcast the kill on the host bus. A-L2 changes the state of its sector from the shared to the modified state. A-L2 asserts AACK# to processor A with both SHD# and ARTRY# deasserted (no retry on the kill). Internally, A-L1 then stores into the sector in A-L1 and marks it modified. Only A-L1 and A-L2 now have copies of the sector and both are now marked modified, but the A-L1 copy is the freshest copy.

Subsequent Processor A Writes to Sector

Any subsequent stores that processor A performs within the sector result in the update being made to the sector in A-L1 with no notification to the L2 cache. The A-L1 copy of the sector stays in the modified state.

L1 Castout of Modified Sector

If a processor experiences a miss on its L1 data cache for some other sector and has to read the target sector from external memory, the L1 cache's LRU algorithm may force the L1 cache to overwrite a modified sector. Since the modified sector represents the "freshest" copy of the sector, the processor must place the modified sector into the MU's write queue and schedule it to be written back to memory. The memory read is performed to fetch the new sector to put into the L1 cache entry freed up by the cast out of the modified sector.

After the memory read is completed, the processor performs a four-beat burst write transaction on its local bus to write the modified sector to memory. During this memory write, the processor asserts TC0 (TC0 = 1), indicating that it is eliminating its copy of the sector when the write completes. The L2 cache also has a copy of the sector in the modified state, but it contains stale data (because the processor had issued a kill but not the update data when it initially stored into the L1 copy of the sector). The L2 cache overwrites its stale copy of the sector with the new data. After absorbing the "freshest" copy of the sector from the processor, the L2 cache may be implemented to handle the state of the sector in one of two ways:

- **Leave it marked modified**. The L2 cache would not know if had the "freshest" copy of the sector, so, in the event of an L2 snoop of a another master's memory access, the L2 would therefore have to force its processor to perform a snoop. If its processor's L1 cache had a copy of the sector in the modified state, the processor would perform the snoop push-back. If the processor didn't have a copy, the L2 cache has the latest version of the sector and would perform the snoop push-back of its copy to memory.
- May **mark it as "modified/exclusive."** The exact terminology for this state will vary. It indicates that the L2's copy of the sector is not the same as memory and that the processor related to this L2 does not have a copy of the sector (because of a previous cast out). In the event of an L2 snoop of another master's memory access, the L2 could therefore immediately perform the snoop push-back without generating a snoop back to the processor.

PCI Bus Master Read from Sector

When a PCI master initiates a memory read from main memory, the L2 caches snoop the memory address being accessed (because the bridge asserts GBL#). The possible results and actions taken are covered in the following sections.

Snoop Miss on L2 Caches

If the snoop results in a snoop miss on the L2 caches, the PCI bus master is permitted to read the requested data from memory. There is no effect on the L2 caches and the processors are not informed of the access attempt.

Snoop Hit on Sector in Exclusive State in L2

If the snoop results in a snoop hit on a sector in the exclusive state, the PCI bus master is about to read good data from memory. The L2 cache with the exclusive copy of the sector permits the access (no retry issued). The L2 cache does not change the state of its copy of the sector and the related processor is not informed of the access.

Snoop Hit on Sector in Shared State in L2

If the snoop results in a snoop hit on two more of the L2 caches with copies of the sector in the shared state, the PCI master read is permitted (no retry issued) and the read does not change the state of the L2 cache copies of the sector. None of the L2 caches inform their respective processors of the memory access.

Snoop Hit on L2 Sector in Modified State

If one of the L2 caches, D-L2, has a modified copy of the target sector, the bridge samples ARTRY# and SHD# asserted. This forces the bridge to abort the memory read attempt and retry it later. The bridge, in turn, issues a retry to the PCI bus master.

In D-L2, one of two things is currently true:

- The copy of the target sector is currently marked modified/exclusive (because the D-L1 copy of the modified sector had been cast out of D-L1 by the LRU algorithm at an earlier point in time; D-L2 had then latched this copy during the D-L1 cast out operation and had marked its copy modified/exclusive). D-L2 therefore knows that processor D does not have a copy of the requested sector in D-L1. D-L2 arbitrates for ownership of the host bus and then performs a four-beat burst memory write transaction, a snoop push-back, to write the requested sector to memory. Upon completion of the push-back, D-L2 changes the state of its copy from modified to shared (because the bridge will then read it from memory when it retries its read transaction; it should be noted that the L2 cache performing the snoop push-back does not know that the device it retried was the bridge and that it doesn't have a cache). When the read is retried and has completed, the sector resides only in D-L2 and is marked shared.
- The copy of the target sector is currently marked modified. In this case, D-L1 has the "freshest" copy of the sector and it must be forced to write it back to memory. D-L2 performs an address-only flush sector transaction with GBL# asserted on processor D's local bus. D-L1 performs a lookup and experiences a hit on the modified sector. As instructed by the flush sector transaction, processor D performs a four-beat burst memory write transaction on its local bus to place the modified sector into memory and it also invalidates its copy of the sector. D-L2 writes the sector into main memory using the host bus and also latches the updated copy of the sector. The new D-L2 copy is then marked shared (because the bridge will retry the memory read and read the sector). The bridge retries the memory read. The snoop result reported back to the bridge is now SHD# asserted and ARTRY# deasserted, permitting the bridge to proceed with the memory read. The bridge passes the requested data back to the PCI master.

When the read has completed, the sector resides only in D-L2 and is marked shared. The D-L1 copy has been invalidated.

PCI Bus Master Write to Sector

When a PCI master initiates a memory write to main memory, the L2 caches snoop the memory address being accessed (because the bridge asserts GBL#). The possible results and actions taken are covered in the following sections.

Snoop Miss on L2 Cache

If the snoop results in a snoop miss on the L2 cache, the PCI bus master is permitted to write to memory. There is no effect on the L2 caches and the processors are not informed of the access attempt.

Snoop Hit on Sector in Exclusive State in L2

If the snoop results in a snoop hit on a sector in the exclusive state in one of the L2 caches, the PCI bus master is about to write data to a clean area of memory. The L2 cache that experienced the hit permits the access. The L2 cache invalidates its copy of the sector and, using its processor's local bus, generates an address-only kill transaction with GBL# asserted to force its processor to kill its copy of the sector. It should be noted that the L2 cache could also snarf the data being to written to memory by the PCI bus master and thereby update its copy of the sector. In this case, it would still kill the processor's copy, but would keep its updated copy and leave it marked exclusive (because it's the same as memory).

Snoop Hit On Sector in the Shared State in L2

If the snoop results in a hit on shared copies of the sector in two or more of the L2 caches, the memory write is permitted. Each of the L2 caches with a copy of the sector will invalidate its copy and will also send a kill transaction back to its respective processor to force each of the L1 caches to kill their copies, as well. It should be noted that the L2 caches could also snarf the data being to written to memory by the PCI bus master and thereby update their copies of the sector. In this case, each of the L2 caches would still kill their processor's copy, but would keep its updated copy and leave it marked shared (because it's the same as memory).

Snoop Hit on an L2 Sector in the Modified State

If the snoop results in a snoop hit on a modified sector, the PCI bus master is attempting to write data to a stale sector in memory. The L2 cache that experienced the hit on the modified copy instructs the bridge to issue a retry to the PCI bus master, causing the PCI master to abort its transaction with no data transferred. The PCI master will re attempt the memory access at a later time.

If the L2 cache's copy is marked modified, it must force its processor to perform a snoop in its L1 data cache. The L2 cache can accomplished this by performing an address-only flush sector transaction on its processor's local bus with GBL# asserted. If the L1 cache experiences a snoop hit on a modified copy of the sector, the L1 cache has the "freshest" copy of the sector and must write the sector to memory and then marks its copy invalid. The L2 cache passes the sector being written back to memory through to main memory. Because the PCI bus master will then write into the sector in memory, the L2 cache marks its copy invalid.

If the L2's copy of the sector is marked modified/exclusive (see the section in this chapter entitled "Cast Out of Modified Sector"), it has the latest copy of the sector. It does not have to force the processor to snoop the address in the L1 cache. The L2 cache performs the snoop push-back of its copy of the sector to main memory and then invalidates its copy.

L1 Cast Out

This subject is covered in the section in this chapter entitled "Cast Out of Modified Sector."

L2 Cast Out

If an L2 cache must cast out a sector to make room for a sector requested by its processor, one of the following conditions will be true:

- The sector to be cast out is in the exclusive state in the L2 cache. In this case, the L2 cache eliminates its copy of the sector and also generates a kill transaction on its processor's local bus to kill its processor's copy of the sector. It is necessary to kill the processor's copy because the L2 cannot snoop the sector for the L1 cache anymore.
- The sector to be cast out is in the modified state in the L2 cache. If the L2 cache's copy is marked modified, it must force its processor to perform a

snoop in its L1 data cache. The L2 cache can accomplished this by performing an address-only flush sector transaction on the processor's local bus with GBL# asserted. If the L1 cache experiences a snoop hit on a modified copy of the sector, the L1 cache has the "freshest" copy of the sector and must write the sector to memory and then marks its copy invalid. The L2 cache passes the sector being written back to memory through to main memory and invalidates its copy.

If the L2's copy of the sector is marked modified/exclusive (see the section in this chapter entitled "Cast Out of Modified Sector"), it has the latest copy of the sector. It does not have to force its processor to snoop the address in its L1 cache. The L2 cache performs the cast out of its copy of the sector to main memory and then invalidates its copy.

Chapter 38

The Previous Chapter

The previous chapter provided a detailed discussion of the implementation of L2 caches in platforms incorporating the PPC 601 processor. This included a detailed description of both single and multi-processor systems using both lookaside and look-through L2 caches. The write-through and write-back policies were also described.

This Chapter

This chapter presents a collection of all aspects of the PPC 601 processor's design that facilitate its usage in multiprocessor systems. The discussion of each topic references the detailed descriptions found in other parts of the book.

The Next Chapter

The next chapter provides a description of signals not covered elsewhere in the book. This includes:

- The clock-related signals.
- External interrupt input.
- Checkstop input signal.
- SC_DRIVE# input signal.
- Test-related signals.
- Signals related to the system quiesce feature.

MESI Cache Protocol

The PPC 601 processor's L1 cache implements the MESI protocol. The MESI state bits in concert with the processor's bus snooping capability and its ability to use address-only transactions to transmit cache information between processors ensures that multiple caching processors will always be dealing with fresh copies of data and code. The MESI protocol permits the PPC 601 to indicate that the current state of a sector in its L1 cache is:

- **Invalid**. The L1 cache does not currently have a copy of the sector.
- **Exclusive**. The L1 cache is currently the only cache in the system with a copy of the sector. Its copy of the sector has not been modified since it was read from memory.
- **Shared**. The L1 cache has a copy of the sector and at least one other cache in the system has a copy of the sector, as well. None of the caches with copies of the sector have modified their respective copies since reading it from memory.
- **Modified**. The L1 cache has a copy of the sector and has modified one or more of the bytes within it since the sector was read from memory. No other cache has a copy of the sector.

A complete description of the cache states can be found in the chapter entitled "601 Cache and Memory Unit."

M Bit Use

The operating system programmer can identify areas of memory that are accessed by and cached from by multiple processors. It can also identify other areas of memory as solely accessed by one processor. This designation is accomplished via the M bit (memory coherency required) in the each page table entry and each of the BAT registers. For a complete description of the M bit, refer to the chapter entitled "Memory Usage Bits (WIMG)."

Snooping Mechanism

Whenever a PPC 601 processor is accessing an area of memory that the operating system programmer has identified as one that multiple processors cache from (M = 1), it asserts the GBL# signal. This instructs all other caching entities on the bus to perform a snoop in their respective caches and to report the snoop result back to the processor that originated the memory access. A complete description of the snooping mechanism can be found in the chapter entitled "PPC 601 Memory Address Phase."

Address-Only Transactions

The PPC 601 processor uses address-only transactions to broadcast cache management instructions to other caches in the system. These transactions are:

- **Clean sector**. Causes any processor with a copy of the addressed sector in the modified state to write the sector into memory and then mark its copy exclusive. Caused by the execution of a dcbst instruction.
- **Flush sector**. Causes any processor with a copy of the addressed sector in the modified state to write the sector into memory and then invalidate its copy. Caused by the execution of a dcbf instruction.
- **Kill sector**. Causes any processor with a copy of the addressed sector to invalidate its copy (even if in the modified state). Caused by execution of a dcbi or dcbz instruction, or a store hit on a sector in the shared state within a page or block with M = 1.
- **Sync**. Causes a look-through L2 cache with a posted-write buffer to perform all of its posted writes. Caused by execution of a sync instruction.
- **TLB invalidate**. Causes all processors to perform a lookup in their TLBs and invalidate the indicated pair of page table entries. Caused by execution of a tlbie instruction. The TLB index field, EA[12:18], is output onto the address bus.

A complete description of the address-only transactions can be found in the chapters entitled "PPC 601 Memory Address Phase" and "Bus Transaction Causes."

Ensuring Unified View of Page Table

Whenever the operating system programmer modifies a page table entry by performing a store into it, one of two actions will take place:

- If the processor performing the store experiences a store hit on a sector in the shared state, it will first broadcast a kill transaction to kill copies of the sector in the caches of other processors. When the kill transaction has completed, the processor performs the store into the sector modifying the page table entry in the sector and marking the sector modified.
- If the processor performing the store experiences a store miss on its cache, it will utilize a rwitm bus transaction to read the sector containing the page table entry into its cache. Other processors observing (snooping) the

rwitm will kill their copies of the sector. When the sector has been read into the cache, the processor stores into it and marks it modified.

Because this and other processors may have an unmodified copy of the page table entry in their TLBs, the programmer executes an tlbie instruction. The processor uses the lower seven bits of the page number portion of the specified effective address, EA[13:19], as an index into the TLB to select a pair of TLB entries to invalidate. Execution of the tlbie instruction causes the processor executing it to invalidate a pair of entries in its TLB. The processor also broadcasts an address-only TLB invalidate transaction to cause all other processors to perform a lookup and invalidation in their TLBs, as well.

If the operating system programmer wishes to delete a page table entry (by marking it invalid), the following actions must be taken:

- Use a store instruction to clear the entry's valid bit.
- Use a dcbst instruction to force the update to be written to memory. This will kill copies of the sector in all other caches.
- Use a tlbie instruction to kill all copies of the page table entry that are currently-resident in TLBs.

If the operating system programmer is changing the pointer in the SDR1 register to point to a new page table, all vestiges of the old table must be blown out of the TLB and the data cache. This would be accomplished by putting a tlbie instruction in a spin loop that increments the lower seven bits of the page number in the effective address once for each pass. This causes the processor to invalidate all 128 of its TLB pairs and to broadcast 128 TLB invalidate transactions to delete the entries in the TLBs of the other processors. The programmer would also execute a dcbi instruction in a spin loop that increments the sector number once for each pass. This causes the processor to eliminate all sectors of the page table from its data cache and to generate one kill transaction for each of the sectors, as well. This causes all other processors to eliminate sectors of the page table from their data caches.

Split-Bus

The system designer may implement a loosely-coupled bus structure to allow efficient performance of transactions by two processors at a time. A complete description of the split-bus architecture can be found in the chapter entitled "PPC 601 Split-Bus Concept."

L1 Cache's LRU Algorithm

When a new sector must be read into the PPC 601's L1 cache, the LRU bit field associated with the selected set of eight entries is consulted to determine which of the set of eight is the least-recently touched. Even if one or more of the entries are currently not in use, the processor may store the new sector in one of the entries currently in use. On the surface, it would seem that the processor should store the new sector in one of the unused entries. The PPC 601 processor, however, keeps track of the sector ***least-recently touched by any processor***. One of the unused entries may have recently been invalidated by an action initiated by another processor in a multiprocessing environment.

Shared Resource Acquisition — Semaphore Operations

The PPC 601 processor implements the lwarx and stwcx instructions, permitting a programmer to test for availability of a resource shared among multiple processors and to acquire ownership of the resource if it is not currently in use by another processor. A complete description of the memory semaphore access mechanisms can be found in the chapter entitled "Shared Resource Acquisition."

Providing Separate Stack for Each Processor

In a multiprocessing environment, the operating system programmer assigns a separate stack area to the interrupt handlers for each processor by placing the start address of a separate stack into each processor's SPRG0 register. This subject is covered in the chapter entitled "Interrupts."

Processor ID Register

In a multiprocessing environment, the operating system programmer can assign a separate ID to each processor by placing mutually-exclusive IDs into their respective PIR (processor identification) registers. Operating system software can then use this ID to identify which processor its is running on. The PPC 601 processor uses the processor ID when running I/O transactions. For a complete description of the I/O transaction protocol, refer to the chapter entitled "PPC 601 I/O Transactions."

Processor Clock and Bus Clock Synchronization

The system designer can ensure that the internal processor clock and bus clock in each of the processors are in sync with each other using the PCLK_EN# signal. A complete description of this capability can be found in the chapter entitled "Other PPC 601 Bus Signals."

Real-Time Clock Synchronization

The system designer can ensure that the RTC signals used by all processors are in sync with each other by providing a machine-writable port that can be used to gate/de-gate the RTC input to the processors. The operating system programmer could write to the port to de-gate the RTC, initialize the RTC registers in each processor to the same startup value, and then write to the port again to re-enable the RTC to the processors.

Chapter 39

The Previous Chapter

The previous chapter presented a collection of all aspects of the PPC 601 processor's design that facilitate its usage in multiprocessor systems. The discussion of each topic referenced the detailed descriptions found in other parts of the book.

This Chapter

This chapter provides a description of signals not covered elsewhere in the book. This includes:

- The clock-related signals.
- External interrupt input.
- Checkstop input signal.
- SC_DRIVE# input signal.
- Test-related signals.
- Signals related to the system quiesce feature.

Introduction

Figure 39-1 illustrates all of the signal lines that the PPC 601 processor uses to interface with the external environment. The sections that follow provide a description of the signals that have not been described elsewhere in this document.

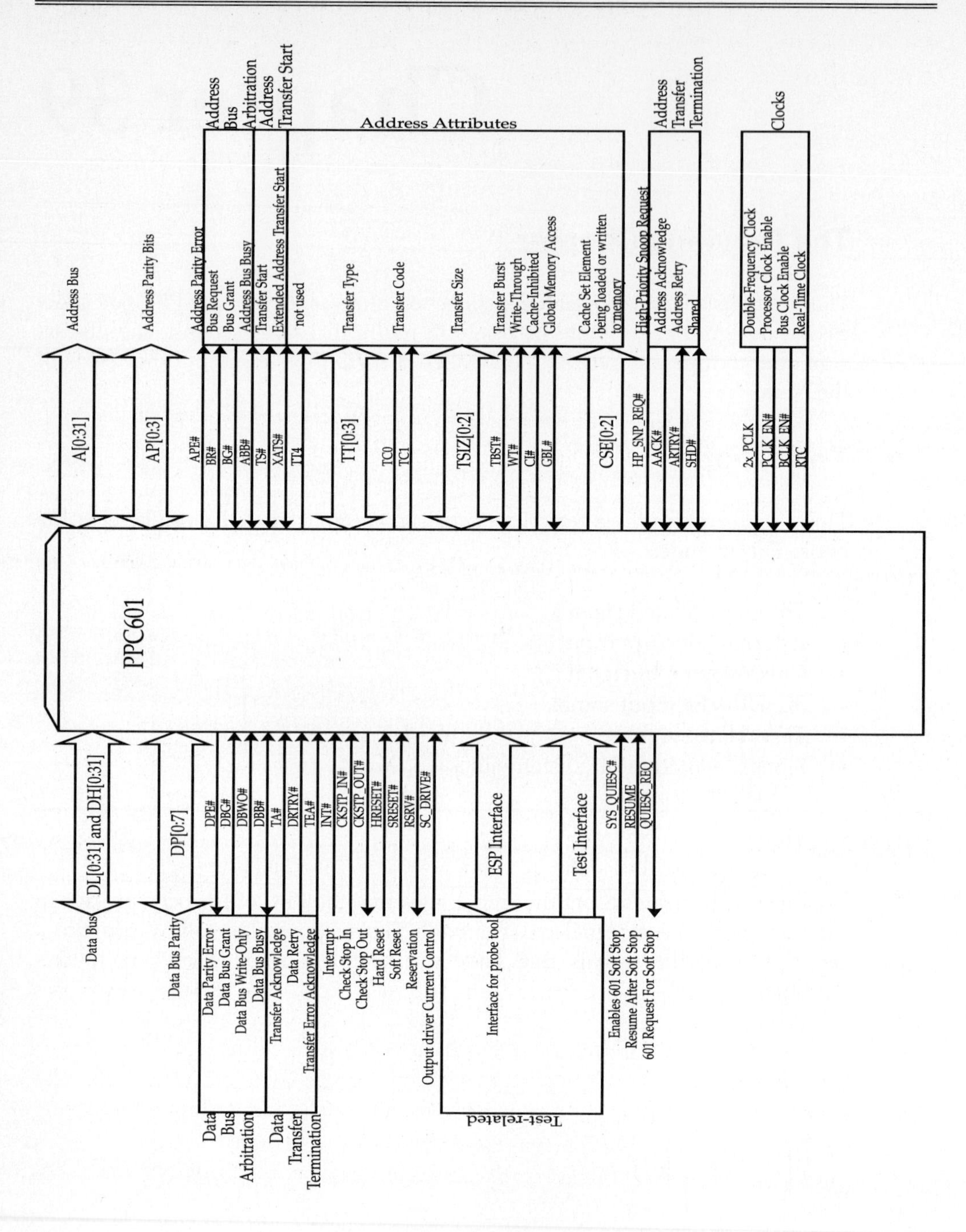

Figure 39-1. PPC 601 Signal Groups

Processor's Clock-Related Signals

The signals related to the processor clock are listed in table 39-1. Figures 39-2 and 39-3 are used during the following discussion of the clock-related signals.

2x_PCLK and PCLK_EN#

The processor requires that a double-frequency clock be supplied on the 2x_PCLK input pin. It also requires the PCLK_EN# signal to select the phase of the internal PCLK derived from the 2x clock. Internally, the processor uses the 2x_PCLK signal to clock the PCLK_EN# signal through a D flip-flop. This produces an output 1/2 the input frequency and delayed by a half-cycle of the 2x_PCLK signal. This signal is then inverted and delayed by another half-cycle of the 2x_PCLK signal. The result: the internal processor clock, or PCLK, signal is the same frequency as the PCLK_EN# signal, is inverted, and is delayed one full cycle of the 2x_PCLK signal. The PCLK_EN# input signal may be used to synchronize multiple PPC601 processors. The internal PCLK signal, also called P_CLOCK, is not available as an output.

Logical Bus Clock

It is important to note that ***there is no bus clock output signal from the processor***. Internally, however, the ***rising-edge of the processor's bus clock signal is used to drive and sample all bus-related signals***.

The rising-edge of the internal bus clock, or BCLK, signal is derived from the rising-edge of PCLK and the state of the BCLK_EN# input signal. Figure 39-2 illustrates this. When BCLK_EN# is asserted, the rising-edge of PCLK serves as the rising-edge of BCLK. In figure 39-2, the designer has tied the BCLK_EN# input asserted. As a result, the BCLK rising-edges follow the PCLK rising-edge. In other words, the bus will run at the same speed as the processor core.

In figure 39-3, however, the designer is utilizing the BCLK_EN# signal to divide the PCLK frequency by two to yield a half-speed BCLK. Using this methodology, the platform designer may select the bus speed.

Table 39-1. Clock-Related Signals

Signal	Description
2x_PCLK	Double-frequency input clock. Divided by two internally to yield the internal processor clock (also referred to as PCLK or P_CLOCK).
PCLK_EN#	Processor Clock Enable. Processor input that selects the phase of the internal PCLK.
BCLK_EN#	Processor input that regulates the frequency of the processor bus clock used during bus transactions.
P_CLOCK	Internal processor clock. Also referred to as PCLK. Supplies basic timing for internal processor operations.

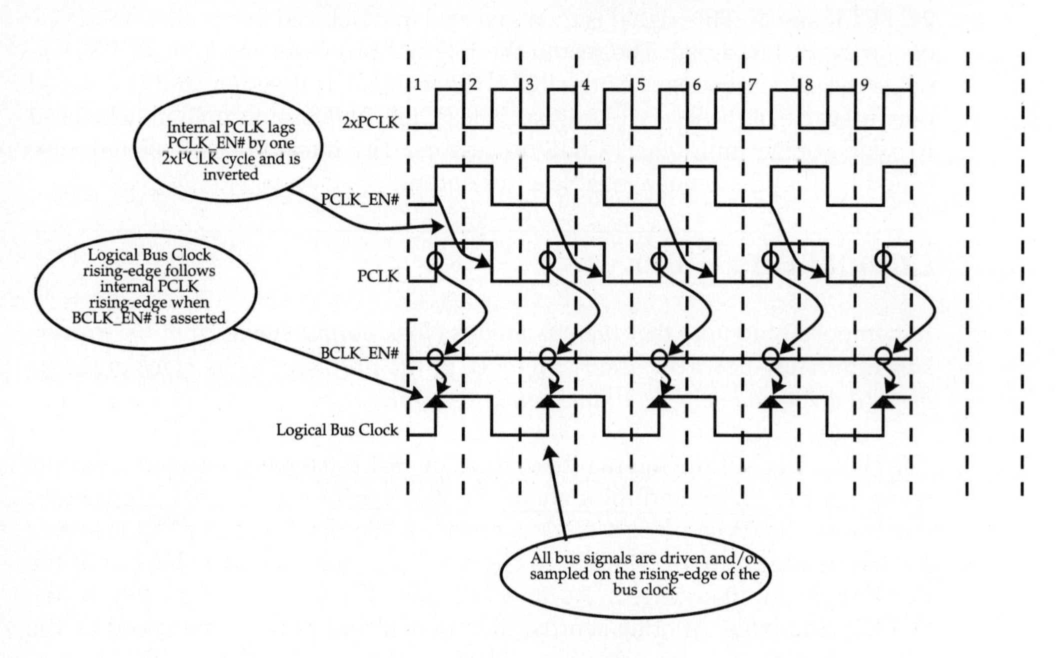
1
2
3
4
5
6
7
8
9
Internal PCLK lags PCLK_EN# by one 2xPCLK cycle and is inverted
2xPCLK
PCLK_EN#
Logical Bus Clock rising-edge follows internal PCLK rising-edge when BCLK_EN# is asserted
PCLK
BCLK_EN#
Logical Bus Clock
All bus signals are driven and/or sampled on the rising-edge of the bus clock

Figure 39-2. Clock-Related Signals Illustrating Fastest Bus Clock

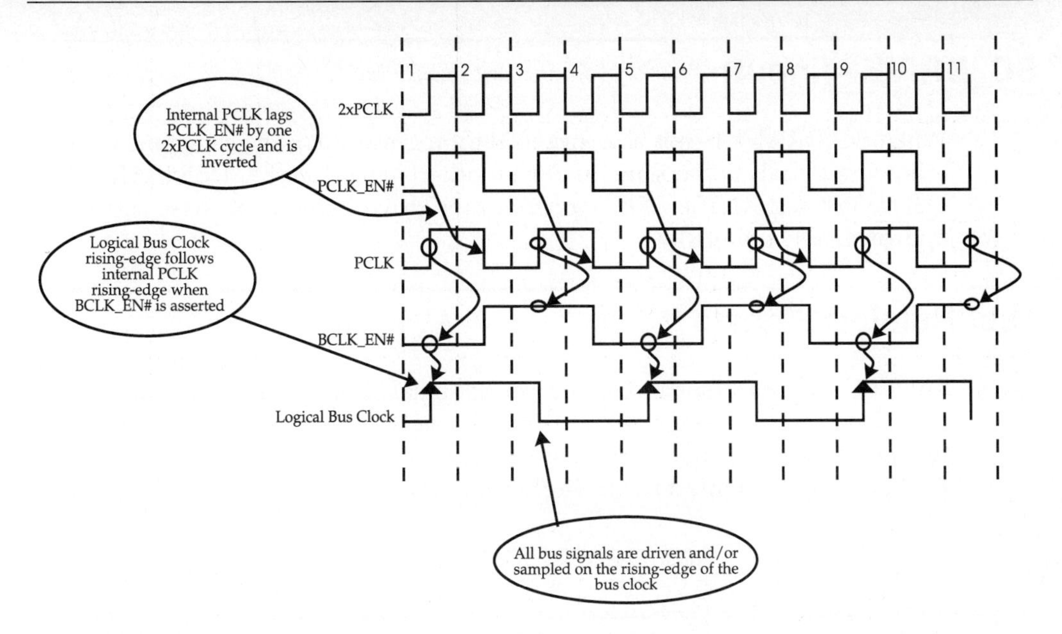
Internal PCLK lags PCLK_EN# by one 2xPCLK cycle and is inverted
Logical Bus Clock rising-edge follows internal PCLK rising-edge when BCLK_EN# is asserted
2xPCLK
PCLK_EN#
PCLK
BCLK_EN#
Logical Bus Clock
1
2
3
4
5
6
7
8
9
10
11
All bus signals are driven and/or sampled on the rising-edge of the bus clock

Figure 39-3. Clock-Related Signals Illustrating Bus Clock Regulated by BCLK_EN#

External Interrupt (INT#)

When an external interrupt controller detects one or more interrupt requests issued by I/O subsystems, it asserts INT# to the processor. If the processor is enabled to recognize external interrupts (MSR[EE] = 1), the processor will take the external interrupt on the next instruction boundary. A detailed description of interrupt handling can be found in the chapter entitled "Interrupts)."

Checkstop In (CKSTP_IN#)

When the platform logic external to the processor detects a critical failure that precludes continues safe program execution, it can assert CKSTP_IN# to the processor. This causes the processor to freeze by de-gating all internal clocks. The processor asserts CKSTP_OUT# when it has stopped. For more information regarding checkstop, refer to the discussion of the HID0 register in the chapter entitled "601 OS Register and Instruction Set."

SC_DRIVE# (input)

When SC_DRIVE# is not asserted to the processor, the drive current for the following signals is the same as for all other signals: ABB#, DBB#, ARTRY#, SHD#, TS# and XATS#. When asserted, the drive current for these signals is approximately doubled.

Test-Related Signals

The PPC 601 processor includes a set of signals that facilitate debug control and observation through a special port (the COP interface). The PPC 601 manual does not include a discussion of these signals. They are also used as the boundary scan interface during system test. They are listed in table 39-2.

Table 39-2. COP/SCAN Interface Signals

Signal	Description
SCAN_CTL	Input to the processor (the author believes that this is the boundary scan test mode select input).
SCAN_CLK	Used to clock serial data into the PPC 601 on SCAN_SIN and out of it on SCAN_OUT.
SCAN_SIN	Serial data input.
ESP_EN#	Enable Engineering Support Processor interface.
BSCAN_EN#	Enable boundary scan interface.
RUN_NSTOP (output)	Indicates whether the processor is currently running or has stopped (speculation on the author's part).
SCAN_OUT	Serial data output.

The PPC 601 also includes a set of test signals that are completely undocumented. They are listed in table 39-3.

Table 39-3. Other Test-Related Signals

Signal	Description
TST[2:3, 5, 6:10, 12, 14:18, 19:22]	Test input pins (undocumented).
JTAGEN#	Set to 0, all PPC 601 bi-directional pins are set to input mode. Set to 1, all are set to output mode.

System Quiesce

In the test environment, the tester may issue a request to the processor to enter the soft stop state. The processor enters the soft stop state by ceasing all instruction execution on the next instruction boundary, performing all bus transactions in its queue and stopping. The content of all registers are kept intact. The tester issues the request as a serial command through the boundary scan interface.

When the processor has entered the soft stop state, it asserts its QUIESC_REQ output. In a multiprocessor environment, the QUIESC_REQ output of one processor is connected to the SYS_QUIESC# input of the next processor in the chain. Assertion of SYS_QUIESC# causes the processor to enter the soft stop state.

This methodology permits the tester to force all processors to quiesce in an orderly fashion. When the tester wishes to resume normal operation, it asserts RESUME.

2x_PCLK. This is the double-frequency input clock to the PPC 601 processor. The processor divides it by two to yield its internal clock, PCLK (also referred to as P_CLOCK). The platform logic uses the PCLK_EN# input to the processor to select the phase of the internal PCLK.

A[0:31]. Processor's address bus. When the processor is the bus master, it drives the address onto the address bus. A[0:28] identifies the doubleword address, while A[29:31] identifies the start address of the target operand within the doubleword. When another bus master is performing a transaction and has asserted GBL# to command all processors to snoop the address, A[0:26] are inputs to the processor. This is the 32-byte aligned address of the target sector being addressed by the other master.

AACK#. Address Acknowledge. Sampled by the PPC 601 processor to determine when to terminate its address transaction. The PPC 601 must continue to drive the address, transaction type and transaction attributes until AACK# is sampled asserted. It may then terminate the address transaction and deassert ABB#. AACK# is asserted by the target that claims the transaction. Address-Only transactions are broadcast in nature. They do not target a particular device. In this case, a central resource asserts AACK# to permit the bus master to terminate the transaction.

ABB#. Address Bus Busy. Asserted by the PPC 601 processor when it initiates an address transaction. The processor continues to assert ABB# until it samples AACK# asserted. ABB# is then deasserted.

Access Rights. Each BAT register and page table entry contains two access rights bits, PP[0:1]. The processor uses these two bits in conjunction with the selected key bit (from the BAT register or the selected segment register) to determine if the currently-running program has read-only, read/write, or no access rights within the block or page being accessed. The processor will generate either a data storage or instruction storage interrupt if the attempted access violates the indicated rights.

Access Violation. See Access Rights.

Address Bus. The PPC 601 uses its address bus to address a target device and indicate the transaction type. The processor also has a set of signals associated with address bus acquisition and termination of the address transaction.

Address Packet 0. During an I/O transaction, the PPC 601 processor outputs the target BUC number, the processor ID and the transaction type in the first packet of address information.

Address packet 1. During an I/O transaction, the PPC 601 processor outputs the I/O port address and the byte transfer count in the second packet of address information.

Address Tenure. The period of time that a bus master owns and is using the address bus.

Address Translation Logic (MMU). Translates the logical or effective address to either a physical memory address or an I/O address.

Address Translation Logic (External). Logic typically located in the host/PCI bridge that ensures that a target is addressed correctly based on the current endian storage mode. For more information, refer to the chapter entitled, "Big vs. Little-Endian Operation and External Support Logic."

Address-Only Transaction. The address-only transactions are used for the following purposes: enforce cache consistency between processors; enforce TLB consistency between processors; force L2 cache with a posted write buffer to flush its buffer to memory.

Allocate-On-Write Policy. In a page or block with a write-back policy for handling memory writes, a store miss on the L1 cache results in a cache block fill operation. The transaction type initiated by the PPC 601 processor is a rwitm. When the cache block has been read into the cache, the processor immediately stores into it and marks it modified.

Alternate Sector Reload. This feature of the PPC 601 processor can be enabled or disabled via two bits (DRF and DRL) in the HID0 register. If enabled and the processor must read a sector from memory, the processor will automatically schedule a low-priority read to fetch the other sector of the line into the cache as well.

ALU. Arithmetic Logic Unit. Part of the Integer Unit.

AP[0:3]. Address bus parity bits. When the PPC 601 processor places an address on the bus, it uses AP[0:3] to force odd parity on the four groups of eight address outputs. During a snoop of another bus master's memory access, the processor checks the state of AP[0:3] for odd parity on the address being snooped. If there is an error, the processor asserts its APE# output.

APE#. Address Parity Error. See AP[0:3]

API. Abbreviated page index. Refer to the chapter entitled, "Virtual paging" under the section entitled, "Why the Entire Page Address Doesn't Have To Be In the PTE."

ARTRY#. Address Retry. Asserted by a snooper under two circumstances: it snooped the address in its cache and experienced a snoop hit on a modified cache block; or its snoop logic is currently busy and cannot report snoop results back to the initiator of the transaction.

ASR. Address Space Register. Only implemented in 64-bit PowerPC processors. Contains the physical start memory address of the segment table.

Atomic Access. An read or write access that can be completed in one access. If the addressed operand were mis-aligned, the processor would have to perform two accesses to transfer it.

BAT Register. Block Address Translation register. Used by the operating system programmer to define a large block of memory as having one set of operational rules.

BAT. See BAT register.

BCLK. Bus Clock. This internal, PPC 601 signal is used by the processor's system interface to pace its actions during a bus transaction. All signals are sampled and/or driven on the rising-edge of the bus clock. The rising-edge of the internal bus clock, or BCLK, signal is derived from the rising-edge of PCLK and the state of the BCLK_EN# input signal. For additional explanation, refer to the chapter entitled, "Other PPC601 Bus Signals."

BCLK_EN#. See BCLK.

BE[7:0]#. The byte able outputs of the Intel Pentium processor. used to indicate which data paths will be used during a transaction and which locations are being addressed within the currently-addressed doubleword (group of eight bytes).

BG#. Bus grant. Asserted by the bus arbiter to grant ownership of the address bus to a bus master. The bus master cannot begin using the address bus until it samples BG# asserted, ABB# deasserted, and ARTRY# deasserted.

Big-Endian Storage Mode. When the PowerPC processor is operating in its native big-endian storage mode, it stores the MSB from the specified source GPR register into the start memory address and the descending bytes from the register into the ascending memory locations immediately following the start address.

BIST. Built-In Self-Test. Prior to fetching the first instruction from memory, the PPC 601 processor performs an internal BIST to test its on-chip logic. The BIST is contained in microcode ROM within the processor.

Block. The meaning of this term depends on the context in which it is used. The cache stores information in its cache in blocks of a fixed length. These are referred to as cache blocks. The cache block length is processor design-dependent. As an example, a PPC 601 cache block is 32 bytes long. Using the BAT registers, the operating system programmer can define a large block of memory as having one set of operational rules (cacheable or not, write-through or write-back, accessed by other processors or not, etc.). The block defined by a BAT register and the cache block should not be confused. There is no connection between the two.

BLPI. Block Logical Page Index. This field in the PPC 601 processor's BAT registers defines the start effective address of the block defined by the register. The length of the block is defined in the BAT register's BSM (block size mask) field.

Boundary Scan Interface. Used in the manufacturing and depot-level test environments. Discussion of boundary scan is outside the scope of this document.

BPU. Branch Processor Unit. Handles branch instruction execution.

BR#. Bus Request signal. The PPC 601 processor asserts BR# to request ownership of the address bus to run a transaction. The arbiter will assert BG# to the processor to grant it the bus.

Branch Folding. The branch processor extracts branch instructions from the prefetch queue, thereby removing them from the instruction stream.

Branch Prediction. The method whereby the branch processor determines whether or not a conditional branch instruction will take the indicated branch (in other words, whether the specified condition will be met or not). Also refer to Static Branch Prediction.

Bridge. A bridge is basically a translator between two dissimilar bus environments. As an example, a host/PCI bridge is connected to the host processor bus on one side and to the PCI bus on the other side. When the host processor initiates a bus transaction, the bridge determines if the target device is on the PCI side. if it is, the bridge must arbitrate for ownership of the PCI bus and then perform the PCI bus equivalent of the host transaction. In the opposite direction, the PCI bridge must translate PCI transactions to host transactions when a PCI master is attempting a transfer with a target residing on the host bus.

BSCAN_EN#. Boundary scan enable. When asserted by external logic, the processor's boundary scan interface is enabled. A discussion of boundary scan is outside the scope of this document.

BSM. Block Size Mask field in the PPC 601 processor's BAT registers. Used by the operating system programmer to define the size of a block (anywhere from 128KB to 8MB in size).

BUC. Bus Unit Controller. I/O controller that controls access to a group of I/O ports (up to 4GB of I/O space per BUC). For additional information, refer to the chapter entitled, "I/O Transactions."

Burst Read or Write Transaction. Performed by the PPC 601 processor when it is reading a sector into the L1 cache or when it is writing a modified sector back to memory. The processor performs a burst write in response to a snoop hit on modified sector or when it has to cast out a modified sector to make room for a new sector being read into the cache.

Bus Clock. See BCLK.

Bus Master. Any device that is capable of initiating a bus transaction.

Bus Parking. The bus arbiter assets grant to a bus master even though it hasn't requested use of the bus. This ensures that the bus master will have fast access to the bus if it does need it.

Cache Block. The block of information that a cache copies from memory and records in the cache. The size of a cache block is cache design-dependent.

Cache Block Fill. Operation where the processor reads a cache block from memory and stores it in its cache.

Cache Sector Fill. See cache block fill.

Cast Out Operation. When a cache has to write a modified cache block back to memory to make room for a new cache block being read into the cache from memory.

CDB. Command descriptor block. A SCSI host bus adapter reads the CDB from memory to determine the type of command to perform, the target SCSI controller and target LUN, the start record number and the number of records to be transferred.

Changed Bit. One of the two page history bits found in each page table entry, or PTE. The processor sets the changed bit to one if any store is performed into the page. Also see the referenced bit.

Checkstop State. If the processor internal logic detects a failure, the associated checkstop enable and master checkstop enable bits are set to one in the HID0 register, the processor degates all internal clocks and freezes. The processor also enters the checkstop state if external logic asserts CHKSTP_IN# to the processor.

CI#. PPC 601 Cache Inhibit output. Asserted by the processor when performing a memory access in a page or block of memory designated as non-cacheable by the operating system programmer (in a PTE or BAT register). Essentially, this is the inverted form of the I bit from the WIM bits.

CIA. Current Instruction Address. This is the return address stored in SRR0 and used by the rfi instruction when an instruction caused interrupt is generated.

CKSTP_IN#. Checkstop In. When asserted to the PPC 601 processor, causes the processor to enter the checkstop state. Also see Checkstop State.

CKSTP_OUT#. Checkstop Out. Asserted by the PPC 601 processor when its enters the checkstop state. See also Checkstop State.

Clean Block. A cache block in the exclusive or the shared state. In other words, the contents of the cache block is identical to the block in memory. It has not been modified.

Clean Sector Transaction. When performed by a PPC 601 processor, instructs all other processors to snoop the supplied address in their caches. In the event of a snoop hit on a modified cache sector, the processor that experienced the hit must perform a four beat burst write to deposit the modified block into memory and then mark its copy exclusive. In other words, this transaction instructs a processor to render the target block in memory clean (up-to-date).

Clean Sector. See Clean Block.

Code Cache. Only stores copies of instruction cache blocks from memory (not data).

Command Descriptor Block. See CDB.

Context Switch. The change of operational state experienced by a processor when an interrupt occurs. The old state is copied from MSR to SRR1 and MSR is then altered to place the processor in the proper operational mode to service the interrupt.

COP/SCAN Interface. Control and Observation Port and boundary scan interface. Used for testing.

CR. Condition Register.

CR0. Condition Register Field Zero. Contains integer condition bits.

CR1. Condition Register Field One. Contains FPU condition bits.

CSE[0:2]. Cache Set Element bus. If the processor is performing a burst memory read to read a cache block into the L1 cache, it will indicate (using CSE[0:2]) which of the eight entries in the selected L1 cache set it will use to record the block. If the processor is performing a burst memory write to write a modified cache block back to memory, it will indicate which of the set of eight entries the cache block is originating from.

CTR. Count Register. Has two uses: can contain a loop count; can contain start address of a routine that can be conditionally called using the branch conditional to count register instruction.

DABR. Data Address Breakpoint Register. Also referred to as HID5. Used by a debug facility for setting load/store breakpoint.

DAR. Data Address Register. When either an alignment or data storage interrupt occurs, contains the effective address of the data operand being accessed.

Data Bus Steering Logic. When a PowerPC processor operating in one endian mode is performing a transfer with a device operating in the opposite mode, data bus steering logic external to the processor may need to steer data to the correct data paths. For more information, refer to the chapter entitled, "Big vs. Little-Endian Operation and External Support Logic."

Data Bus. Used by the processor to transfer data between itself and a target memory or I/O device.

Data Cache. Only stores copies of data cache blocks from memory (not instructions).

Data Lanes 0 – 7. Used by the PPC 601 processor to transfer bytes between the processor and locations 0 – 7 in the currently-addressed doubleword.

Data Object. In this book, data operands are sometimes referred to as data objects. An operand can be between one and eight bytes in size.

Data Paths 0 – 7. See Data Lanes 0 – 7.

Data Tenure. The period of time during which a bus master owns the PPC 601 bus and is using it to perform a data transfer.

DBAT Registers. Data Block Address Translation Registers. Used by the operating system programmer to define up to four data blocks in memory.

DBB#. Data Bus Busy. Asserted by the PPC 601 processor when it starts a data transfer. Deasserted when the final TA# is received from the target device. Also see DRTRY#.

DBG#. Data Bus Grant. When asserted by the bus arbiter, informs the PPC 601 processor that it will be the next owner of the data bus.

DBWO#. Data Bus Write-Only. For a complete description, refer to the chapter entitled, "The Split-Bus Concept" under the heading "The Data Bus Write-Only Feature."

dcbf Instruction. Data Cache Block Flush instruction. Commands all data caches to flush copies of the specified cache block from their caches. If the cache block is in the invalid state, there is no effect. If the cache block is in the exclusive or shared state, it is invalidated in the cache. If the cache block is in the modified state, it is pushed back to memory and then invalidated in the cache.

dcbi Instruction. Data Cache Block Invalidate instruction. Commands all data caches to invalidate the specified cache block if present in the cache.

dcbst Instruction. Data Cache Block Store instruction. Commands all data caches to perform a lookup in their caches. If the cache block is in the invalid state, exclusive or shared state, there is no effect. If the cache block is in the modified state, it is pushed back to memory and then marked exclusive in the cache.

dcbt Instruction. Data Cache Block Touch Instruction. A programmer uses this instruction as a performance hint to the processor. It informs the processor that a subsequent instruction may attempt to read from the location indicated. In response, the processor may schedule a low-priority cache block fill operation to prefetch the data block into the cache. In response to the dcbt instruction, the processor will determine if the memory unit has room in its queue to post the cache block fill request. If it doesn't, the request to load the cache block from memory isn't fulfilled. If a queue position exists, the system interface will post the read in the queue, but will mark it discardable if a higher priority request arrives (due to the execution of subsequent instructions) prior to the initiation of the burst memory read transaction to fulfill the dcbt request. If another higher-priority request requires action and no other queue position is available, the system interface will discard the dcbt fill request. If the request is not discarded and the bus becomes available and no other higher-priority queue entries exists, the system interface will read the requested cache block from memory and make the cache entry.

dcbtst Instruction. Data Cache Block Touch For Store instruction. Informs the processor that a subsequent instruction may attempt to write to the location indicated. If the MU has queue space to record the request and then subsequently reads the cache block from memory, it generates a flush bus transaction before reading the cache block from memory. This forces any other processor with a copy of the cache block in the modified state to write it back to memory and then invalidate its copy. Any processor with an unmodified copy of the cache block marks its copy invalid.

dcbz Instruction. Data Cache Block Zero instruction. The programmer specifies a cache block start address with the dcbz instruction. If the block is already in the data cache, it is set to zero and marked modified. If the block isn't in the data cache, an entry is created in the data cache and is marked modified.

DEC. Decrementer register. Used by the operating system to set up a time slice for an applications program in a multitasking operating system environment. The DEC decrements at the same rate that the TimeBase increments and generates a decrementer interrupt when its count is exhausted.

Demand-Mode Paging. See Paging.

DH[0:31]. High half (upper four data paths) of PPC 601 data bus. DH[0:7] is data path 0 and DH[24:31] is data path 3. DL[0:31] is the lower half of the data bus. DL[0:7] is data path 4 and DL[24:31] is data path 7.

Direct-Store Segment. Another term for an I/O segment. See I/O segment.

DL[0:31]. See DH[0:31].

DMA Controller. Direct Memory Access controller. Primitive bus master that can be programmed to transfer a block of data between an I/O device and memory or between two areas of memory.

Doubleword Address Bus. The PPC 601 processor uses A[0:28] to identify a doubleword in memory. A doubleword is a group of eight memory locations starting at an address divisible by eight. A[29:31] identify the start location of the operand within the doubleword, while TSIZ[0:2] indicates the size of the operand (in bytes).

Doubleword. In relation to addressing: in the PowerPC world, a group of eight locations starting at an address divisible by eight; in the Intel ix86 world, a group of four locations starting at an address divisible by four. In relation to a data operand, eight bytes in the PowerPC world and four bytes in the Intel ix86 world.

DP[0:7]. Data parity bits for data paths 0 – 7. When performing a write, the processor drives the byte or bytes onto the appropriate data paths and, using the parity output associated with each path, forces the parity to odd for each byte. During a read, the processor checks for odd parity received for each byte and, in the event of a data parity error, asserts its DPE# output. The action taken by the platform in response is design-dependent.

DPE#. See DP[0:7].

DRF. Data reload on fetch. Feature bit in HID0. Used by the operating system programmer to disable or enable alternate sector reload during cache sector fill caused by an instruction fetch miss on the PPC 601 cache. For more information, refer to Alternate Sector Reload.

DRL. Data reload on load or store. Feature bit in HID0. Used by the operating system programmer to disable or enable alternate sector reload during cache sector fill caused by a load or store miss on the PPC 601 cache. For more information, refer to Alternate Sector Reload.

DRTRY#. Data Retry. For more information, refer to the chapter entitled, "The Data Phase" under the heading "On a Read, Target Verifies Validity of Data Read By Master."

DSISR. Data Storage Interrupt Status Register. On entry to the data storage interrupt handler, contains status bit indicating the interrupt cause. On entry to the alignment interrupt handler, identifies the type of instruction that caused the interrupt. In both cases, DAR contains the address of the data operand being accessed.

DW. Abbreviation for doubleword.

Dynamic Branch Prediction. Branch prediction mechanism wherein the processor maintains a branch target buffer, or BTB, in which execution history is continually updated for each conditional branch instruction. The Pentium PPC 604 processors both use dynamic branch prediction, while the PPC 601 processor uses static branch prediction.

EAR. External Access Register. The operating system programmer initializes the EAR with the resource ID of a target external device. The programmer may then transfers a word at a time with this device using the ecowx and eciwx instructions. For more information, refer to the chapter entitled, "External Control Transactions."

EAX. Extended AX Register. This is a general-purpose Intel ix86 register that can contain up to four bytes of data.

eciwx Instruction. External Control Input Word Indexed instruction. Used to read a word from the resource identified in the EAR into a GPR register.

ecowx Instruction. External Control Output Word Indexed instruction. Used to write a word to the resource identified in the EAR from a GPR register.

Effective Address. The 32 or 64-bit address specified by the programmer for a load, store or an instruction fetch. This address is then submitted to the MMU for translation to either a physical memory address or an I/O address.

Effective Segment ID. All accesses fall within one of the 256MB segments of address space. The upper portion of the effective address identifies the segment being accessed. In a 32-bit processor or a 64-bit processor operating in 32-bit mode, EA[0:3] identifies which one of the 16 effective segments is being accessed. In a 64-bit processor operating in 64-bit mode, EA[0:35] identifies which one of the 2^{36} effective segments is being accessed. The target effective segment is referred to as the effective segment ID, or ESID.

Effective Segment. See Effective Segment ID.

eieio Instruction. Enforce In-Order Execution of I/O instruction. When an eieio instruction is executed, all writes posted prior to the execution of the eieio instruction are marked for performance on the bus before any writes that may be posted subsequent to the execution of the eieio instruction.

ELE Bit. Exception Little-Endian Mode. See ILE.

Elementary Load or Store. A load or store of an operand that can be accessed in one transfer. In other words, the operand is not mis-aligned.

ESID. See Effective Segment ID.

ESP_EN#. Engineering Support Processor Enable. When asserted, permits special test equipment to access the processor's internal logic for testing purposes. A discussion of the ESP interface is outside the scope of this document.

Exception. Alternative term for interrupt.

Exclusive Ownership. A cache block is said to be exclusively owned by a processor if it is in the exclusive state. This indicates two things: no other cache has a copy of the block; and the cache block is the same as memory. Having a copy of a cache block in the exclusive state does not mean that no other cache may obtain a copy from memory. It just means that, at this instant in time, no other cache has a copy of it.

Exclusive State. See Exclusive Ownership.

Extended Address Transfer Code. Also referred to as XATC and I/O opcode. This is the I/O transaction type output by the PPC 601 processor in address packet 0 at the start of an I/O address transaction. The XATC is output on the eight-signal bus created by concatenating TT[0:3], TBST# and TSIZ[0:2].

Extended Opcode. All PowerPC instructions are one word in length. The most-significant six bits of the instruction are the opcode, identifying the type of instruction. Some instructions also include an extended opcode field that further defines the instruction type.

External Control In Transaction. Generated by the PPC 601 processor in response to the execution of an eciwx instruction. Used to read one word from the resource specified in the EAR register into a GPR register.

External Control Out Transaction. Generated by the PPC 601 processor in response to the execution of an ecowx instruction. Used to write one word to the resource specified in the EAR register from a GPR register.

Feed-Forwarding. When the instruction currently being executed requires the result deposited into a register by the previous instruction, the PPC 601 processor forwards the result to the second instruction at the same time that the result of the first instruction is being stored into the specified target register.

Flush Transaction. Performed by the PPC 601 processor in response to the execution of a dcbf instruction. Any processor observing the flush transaction must snoop the specified sector address in its cache. If it misses the cache, there is no effect. If it hits on a sector in the exclusive or shared state, the sector is invalidated in the cache. If it hits on a sector in the modified state, the processor pushes the modified sector into memory and then invalidates its copy of the cache block.

Four-Beat Read or Write Transaction. See Burst Read or Write Transaction.

FPR. Floating-Point Registers FPR0 – FPR31. Used to hold and manipulate floating-point data operands.

FPSCR. Floating-Point Status and Control Register. The bits in this register serve the following purposes: reflect detected exceptions (interrupt status bits); reflect the result of the previously-executed floating-point operation (result status bits; no interrupt encountered); provide a mechanism for selectively enabling or disabling types of exceptions (interrupt enable bits); provide a mechanism for placing the Floating-Point Processor in IEEE or non-IEEE mode (the NI bit); and for controlling rounding (the RN bits).

FPU. Floating-Point Unit. Executes all floating-point instructions. In the PPC 601 processor the FPU depends on the integer unit to perform memory accesses to load or store data operands (because all addressing is performed using the integer unit's GPR registers).

Frame Buffer. Video Frame buffer resides in memory and is used to store the video image. The video graphics adapter reads the video data from the frame buffer and converts it to pixel information for the screen.

Fresh Block. A cache block that contains the latest data.

Fresh Sector. See Fresh Block.

G Bit. Guarded Memory bit. Resides in the BAT registers and in each PTE. When set to one, instructs the processor not to perform any speculative accesses (such as instruction prefetching) within this page or block. An area of memory is marked as guarded if memory is not implemented within the address range or if memory-mapped I/O ports reside within that region of memory space.

GBL#. Global memory access. Asserted by a PPC 601 processor when it is performing a memory access within a page or block with the M bit set to one. This indicates that other processors also access the same area of memory and may have cached information from it. For this reason, all processors must watch accesses performed by other entities within that memory region (in order to ensure that each processor is aware of memory accesses performed by other processors). The GBL# signal is the inverted form of the M bit from a BAT register or a PTE.

GPR. General Purpose Registers 0 – 31. Used for load and store addressing, temporary storage of data operands, and for the manipulation of data operands.

Guarded Memory. See G Bit.

H Bit. Hash Bit. Each PTE contains a hash bit that must be checked by the MMU when it is performing page address translation. For a detailed description of the hash bit's function, refer to the chapter entitled, "Virtual Paging" under the heading "The Primary Scan, or Hash."

Halfword. Two bytes of data.

Hard Reset. Asserted by external logic during initial system power-up. Initializes the processor to a known start-up state. For a detailed description of hard reset's effects on the PPC 601 processor, refer to the chapter entitled, "The Processor Start-Up State."

Hash Bit. Refer to H Bit.

HBA. Host Bus Adapter. The SCSI HBA provides the bridge between the PCI bus and the SCSI bus. The HBA associated with an IDE hard drive provides the basic address decode logic for up to IDE hard drives.

HID0. Hardware Implementation-Dependent Register 0. Also referred to as the checkstop enables/sources register. HID0 contains four groups of bits: Checkstop enable/disable bits; Checkstop status bits; Bits used to enable/disable miscellaneous features; HID0[30] is the cache initialization error bit. If no error occurred during the BIST and initialization of the L1 cache, this bit is cleared to zero. Otherwise, it is set to one.

HID1. Hardware Implementation-Dependent Register 1. Also referred to as the Debug Modes Register. Used to enable or disable the PPC 601 processor's hardware breakpoint capability. For a more detailed discussion, refer to the chapter entitled, "The Supervisor Register and Instruction Set" under the heading "Debug Modes Register, or HID1."

HID15. Hardware Implementation-Dependent Register 15. Also referred to as the Processor ID Register, or PIR. Contains the PPC 601 processor's ID. The ID is used during PPC 601 I/O transactions and can be used by the operating system in a multiprocessor environment to identify which processor a task is running on.

HID2. Hardware Implementation-Dependent Register 2. Also referred to as the Instruction Address Breakpoint Register, or IABR. Used by a debug facility for setting instruction execution breakpoint.

HID5. Hardware Implementation-Dependent Register 5. Also referred to as the Data Address Breakpoint Register, or DABR. See DABR.

High-Priority Snoop Request. For a detailed description, refer to the chapter entitled, "Cache and Memory Unit Operation" under the heading "High-Priority Snoop Request."

Hint Bit. Refer to Static Branch Prediction.

Host Bus Adapter. See HBA.

Host Bus. The bus that the host processor or array of host processors reside on.

Host Processor. The central processor that boots the operating system and controls the actions of all other system entities.

Host/PCI Bridge. See Bridge.

HP_SNP_REQ#. High-Priority Snoop Request. For a detailed description, refer to the chapter entitled, "Cache and Memory Unit Operation" under the heading "High-Priority Snoop Request."

HRESET#. Hard Reset. See Hard Reset.

HTABMASK. Hash Table Mask. This field in the SDR1 register defines the size of the page table in memory.

HTABORG. Hash Table Origin. This field in the SDR1 register defines the start physical address of the page table in memory.

I Bit. Cache Inhibit bit. Found in the BAT registers and in each PTE, the operating system programmer uses this bit to define each page or block as a cacheable or non-cacheable region of memory. When the processor performs a memory transaction on the external bus, it outputs the invert of the I bit on its CI# output.

I/O Controller. See BUC.

I/O Load Immediate Transaction. When performed by a PPC 601 processor, loads an intermediate word of an I/O load series from an I/O device into a GPR register over the upper four data paths, 0 – 3.

I/O Load Last Transaction. When performed by a PPC 601 processor, loads the final word of an I/O load series from an I/O device into a GPR register over the upper four data paths, 0 – 3.

I/O Load Reply Transaction. Generated by a BUC at the completion of the transfer of a series of one or more words from the BUC to a PPC 601 processor. Address packet 0 contains the processor ID and the completion status bit.

I/O Load Request Transaction. Generated by a PPC 601 processor to initiate the transfer of a series of words from a BUC to the processor's GPR register set. This is an address-only transaction.

I/O Opcode. See Extended Address Transfer Code.

I/O Segment. A 256MB area of effective address space that has been mapped into I/O space by the operating system programmer. This is accomplished by setting the segment type bit (the T bit) in the segment register (32-bit processor) or a STE (64-bit processor) to a one. The segment register contains the target BUC all accesses within the I/O segment will be mapped to.

I/O STE. I/O Segment Table Entry. Maps a 256MB effective segment either to a virtual memory segment or to an I/O BUC. STEs only exist in a 64-bit processor implementation (such as the PPC 620).

I/O Store Immediate Transaction. When performed by a PPC 601 processor, stores an intermediate word of an I/O store series to an I/O device from a GPR register over the upper four data paths, 0 – 3.

I/O Store Last Transaction. When performed by a PPC 601 processor, stores the final word of an I/O load series to an I/O device from a GPR register over the upper four data paths, 0 – 3.

I/O Store Reply Transaction. Generated by a BUC at the completion of the transfer of a series of one or more words to the BUC from a PPC 601 processor. Address packet 0 contains the processor ID and the completion status bit.

IABR. Instruction Address Breakpoint Register. See HID2.

IBAT Registers. Instruction Block Address Translation registers. Used by the operating system programmer to set up a large region in memory with one set of operational rules. The block contains instructions.

icbi Instruction. Instruction Cache Block Invalidate instruction. When executed, causes the processor to perform a lookup in its code cache and, in the event of a hit, to invalidate the cache block entry. Has no effect on a unified code/data cache.

ILE Bit. Interrupt Little-Endian storage mode. When an interrupt is taken, the processor automatically saves the current state of MSR[LE] into SRR1 and then copies MSR[ILE] to MSR[LE]. This automatically places the processor into the desired endian mode for interrupt servicing. ILE = 0 selects big-endian mode, while ILE = 1 selects little-endian mode.

Illegal Opcode. All PowerPC instructions are one word in length. The most-significant six bits of the instruction are the opcode, identifying the type of instruction. If a PowerPC processor decodes an instruction and determines that it is illegal (not implemented) on this processor, it generates a program interrupt.

Imprecise Interrupt. Implementation of imprecise interrupt support is optional in the PowerPC processor specification. If implemented, only the floating-point unit may generate imprecise interrupts (if it is enabled to do so). When an imprecise floating-point interrupt occurs, SRR0 will point either to the instruction that caused the interrupt or to a subsequent instruction. If it points to a subsequent instruction, that instruction has not yet been executed. The programmer would have to scan backward in memory to discover the last floating-point instruction in the instruction stream. This is the one that caused the interrupt.

Indirect Addressing. The programmer specifies one GPR register that contains the address for the load or store.

Indirect With Immediate Index Addressing. The programmer specifies an immediate value to be added to the contents of a specified GPR register to form the target address for the load or store.

Indirect With Index Addressing. The programmer specifies that the contents of two GPR registers be added together to yield the target address for the load or store.

Instruction Dispatcher. The processor logic responsible for dispatching one or instructions to the processor's execution units.

INT#. The PPC 601 processor's external interrupt input line. It is generated by the external interrupt controller whenever an external hardware subsystem generates an interrupt request. In response, if recognition of external interrupts is currently enabled (MSR[EE] = 1), the processor will jump to the external interrupt hander.

Integer Unit. Executes all non-floating-point and non-branch instruction: in other words, the bulk of the instructions are executed by the integer unit.

Intelligent Bus Master. A subsystem, typically microprocessor-based, that has the ability to perform bus transactions to communicate with other memory and/or IO devices.

Interleaved Memory. A DRAM memory architecture in which multiple memory banks are structured such that each can supply the maximum amount of data the processor can request in one access. In other words, the width of each DRAM bank matches the width of the processor's data bus. As an example, the PPC 601 data bus is eight bytes (one doubleword) wide. Two-way interleaved memory is structured so that each successive doubleword is in the opposite bank of memory. During a cache block fill operation, the processor reads a doubleword from one bank, the second doubleword from the opposite bank, the third from the original bank and the fourth from the other bank. When a DRAM bank is accessed for a read, the DRAM cells are discharged during the read and need to charge back up before the bank can be successfully accessed again. If an interleaved memory architecture is used implemented, the charge up (referred to as the precharge delay) of each DRAM bank is hidden behind the processor access to the opposite bank. This results in better performance.

Interrupt Controller. External hardware subsystem that require servicing by the host processor asserts its interrupt request line when service is required. The interrupt request signal lines are inputs to the interrupt controller. When the interrupt controller detects one or more pending requests for service, it asserts INT# to the host processor. For more information, see INT#.

Interrupt Handler. Also referred to as an interrupt service routine. The program that handles a specific type of interrupt event. An example of a hardware interrupt handler would be the SCSI HBA's interrupt handler. An example of a software interrupt handler would be the page fault handler.

Interrupt Prefix. The base address of the interrupt vector table is selected by the state of the interrupt prefix, or IP, bit in MSR. In a 32-bit processor with IP = 0, the interrupt vector table base address is 00000000h. With IP = 1, the base address is FFF00000h. In a 64-bit processor with IP = 0, the interrupt vector table base address is 0000000000000000h. With IP = 1, the base address is FFFFFFFFFFF00000h. The processor forms the address to jump to by adding the offset associated with the interrupt type to the base address. At startup time, after reset is removed, IP is set to one. Also referred to as the EP bit (exception prefix).

Interrupt Request. See Interrupt Controller.

Interrupt Table. The area of memory that contains the entry points to each of the processor's interrupt handers. Also referred to as the interrupt vector table. For more information, see Interrupt Prefix.

Interrupt Vector. The offset of an interrupt handler's entry point within the interrupt table. Each interrupt handler has a dedicated entry point in physical memory. For more information, refer to the chapter entitled, "Interrupts."

Invalid State. State of a cache entry that does not currently contain a valid copy of a cache block from memory.

ITLB. The instruction translation lookaside buffer, or ITLB, is a performance enhancement tool outside the scope of the PowerPC processor specification. It is a small, very fast lookaside cache that can hold up to four entries. Each entry can contain either: a copy of the block address translation information from a BAT register pair, or a page table entry, or PTE. When the instruction fetcher generates an effective address to request the next instruction from memory, the effective address is submitted first to the ITLB for a lookup. In the event of a hit on the ITLB, the information, BAT or PTE, from the entry is used to perform the effective to physical address translation and also supplies the access rights and caching rules (WIM bits). This leaves the BAT and page translation logic available to simultaneously service an address translation request from the integer unit. When there is a miss on the ITLB, the BAT or page logic performs the translation of the address from effective to physical address. When a match is found on a BAT register pair or a page table entry, the BAT or PTE contents are copied into the ITLB to service subsequent request. Although the ITLB is quite small, it can yield a very high hit rate for instruction accesses. This is due to the fact that most program execution is sequential in nature, so a block or page mapping in the ITLB will typically yield a high hit rate.

Key Bits. Each segment register and each BAT register contains a set of key bits referred to as Ks and Ku (Ku is sometimes referred to as Kp, but Ku is preferred). When a load, store or an instruction fetch is attempted, the MMU performs address translation using either the contents of a BAT register or through the paging logic. The processor uses the privilege level of the currently-running program to select either the Ks (supervisor mode key bit) or the Ku (user mode key bit) to be used in conjunction with the PP bits from the PTE or the BAT register. The selected key bit and the PP bits are interrogated to determine if the current task is permitted read-only, read/write or no access to the block or page. If the access is permitted, the address is translated to a physical memory address. If the access is denied, the processor generates either a data storage or an instruction storage interrupt.

Kill Transaction. Generated by the PPC 601 processor to kill copies of the specified cache block in all other caches in the system. All other caches must perform lookups in their caches and invalidate copies of the specified cache block. For more information on the causes of the kill transaction, refer to the chapter entitled, "Instructions/Conditions That Result In Bus Transactions."

Ks. See Key Bits.

Ku. See key Bits.

L1 Cache. Level One Cache. The processor's internal cache.

L2 Cache. Level Two Cache. A secondary cache external to the processor.

lbz Instruction. Load Byte and Zero instruction. The processor loads the byte from the specified location into the LSB of the specified GPR register and zero-fills the MSBs in the register.

ld Instruction. Load Doubleword instruction. The processor loads the byte from the specified location into the LSB of the specified GPR register and zero-fills the MSBs in the register.

ldarx Instruction. Load Doubleword and Reserve Indexed instruction. Used to read a doubleword semaphore from memory into the specified GPR register and establish a reservation on the cache block area containing the semaphore. Only implemented in 64-bit PowerPC processors. For more information, refer to the chapter entitled, "Acquiring Ownership of Shared Resources."

lhz Instruction. Load Halfword and Zero instruction. The processor loads the two bytes from the specified location and the next sequential location into the two LSBs of the specified GPR register and zero-fills the MSBs in the register.

li Instruction. The load immediate instruction does not actually exist. When the li instruction is specified by the programmer, the assembler encodes it as an add immediate, or addi, instruction. This mnemonic is supplied to make the programmer's code listings more readable.

Line. In general usage, means the same as a cache block. In the PPC 601 processor, a cache line is 64 bytes long and consists of two 32 byte sectors. A sector is a cache block.

lis Instruction. The load immediate and shift left instruction does not actually exist. When the lis instruction is specified by the programmer, the assembler encodes it as an add immediate and shift left, or addis, instruction. This mnemonic is supplied to make the programmer's code listings more readable.

Little-Endian Storage Mode. When the PowerPC processor is operating in little-endian storage mode, it stores the LSB from the specified source GPR register into the start memory address and the ascending bytes from the register into the ascending memory locations immediately following the start address.

lmw Instruction. Load multiple word instruction. When executed, the processor loads the specified number of words into the GPR register set starting at the specified GPR register. The number words to be loaded is implied in the start GPR number (31 minus the start GPR number). The words are read from memory or I/O staring at the specified, word-aligned start effective address.

Load Hit. The processor is performing a load from cacheable memory and the requested data is present in the L1 cache. The cache supplies the data to the integer or floating-point unit and no external bus transaction is necessary.

Load Miss. The processor is performing a load from cacheable memory and the requested data is not currently present in the L1 cache. A cache block read is posted in the MU. The system interface then performs a burst read transaction to read the block from memory and supplies the data to the cache as well as the integer or floating-point unit. The cache block is recorded in the data cache.

Load With Update. The processor loads the specified data operand into the specified GPR register. The computed effective address is loaded into the GPR register specified in the instruction's rA field.

Load. Loads a byte, halfword, word or doubleword into the specified GPR register from the specified effective address.

Load/Store Multiple. See lmw.

Local Bus. The bus structure connected directly to the processor's bus interface pins. Depending on the machine architecture this may be the host bus or it may be buffered from the host bus by a look-through L2 cache associated with the processor.

Logical Address. See Effective Address.

Logical Bus Clock. See Bus Clock.

Lookaside Cache. An L2 cache that resides on the host bus along with the host processor and the main memory array. It sits off to the side and observes all memory accesses initiated by the processor. If it experiences a hit for a processor-initiated access, it disables main memory and supplies or accepts the data much more quickly than main memory could.

Look-through Cache. A cache that resides in between the processor and main memory. It attempts to service all processor-initiated memory accesses from its cache. As long as it can do this, the main memory bus remains available for use by other (e.g., PCI) bus masters.

LR. Link Register. Used to supply the branch address of a routine for the branch to link register instructions. Also used to store a return address if a branch specifies that a link back to the caller be stored in the LR. The called routine can then return to the caller by executing a branch to link register instruction.

LRU Algorithm. Least-Recently Used Algorithm. Used by a cache to determine where to store a new cache block being read into the cache from memory.

LSB. Least-Significant Byte.

lsb. Least-Significant Bit.

lscbx Instruction. Load String and Compare Byte Indexed instruction. Refer to the PowerPC 601 processor user manual for more detail.

lswi Instruction. Load String Word Immediate instruction. Refer to the PowerPC 601 processor user manual for more detail.

lswx Instruction. Load String Word Indexed instruction. Refer to the PowerPC 601 processor user manual for more detail.

LUN. Logical Unit. A target SCSI controller can control access to multiple LUNs. As an example, a target SCSI controller hung on the SCSI bus may have an array of disk drives that it controls. They are LUNs.

lwarx Instruction. Load Word and Reserve Indexed instruction. Used to read a word semaphore from memory into the specified GPR register and establish a reservation on the cache block area containing the semaphore. Only implemented in 64-bit PowerPC processors. For more information, refer to the chapter entitled, "Acquiring Ownership of Shared Resources."

lwz Instruction. Load word and zero instruction. The processor loads the word from the specified location into the four LSBs of the specified GPR register and zero-fills the MSBs in the register. On a 32-bit processor, the word occupies the entire GPR register and there are no upper MSBs to zero. In a 64-bit processor, the GPR can hold eight bytes. The upper four bytes would be zero-filled.

M Bit. Memory coherency required. See WIMG bits.

Machine Check. If external logic asserts TEA# to the PPC 601 processor while it is performing a bus transaction, the processor aborts the transaction. If the processor is enabled to recognize machine checks (MSR[ME] = 1], assertion of TEA# causes the processor to take the machine check interrupt. If recognition is disabled, the processor enters the checkstop state (it freezes).

Main Memory. In this document, refers to the main array of DRAM memory that the processor caches from.

Memory Coherency Required Bit. See WIMG bits.

Memory Management Unit, or MMU. When enabled to do so, the MMU translates the effective addresses for loads, stores and instruction fetches to physical memory addresses. It also check for access rights violations and generates an exception when one is detected. Via the BAT registers and the PTEs, also defines the WIMG bit settings for each page and block of memory. If an access is mapped to an I/O segment by the MMU, it translates the effective address into an I/O address.

Memory Segment. An area of memory 256MB in size starting at an address divisible by 256MB. Also see Segment Register.

Memory Semaphore. A special memory operand used by a task to determine if a resource shared with other processors or other tasks running on this processor is currently available for access. For more information, refer to the chapter entitled, "Acquiring Exclusive Ownership of a Shared Resource."

Memory STE. A segment table entry that maps a 256MB effective segment to a 256MB virtual memory segment. For more information, refer to the chapter entitled, "Virtual Paging."

Memory Unit, or MU. The MU acts as a posted memory read/write buffer. This includes loads and stores in cacheable memory space and in non-cacheable memory space. Address-only transactions are also posted (in the read buffer). I/O transactions are not posted. Once a transaction has been posted in the MU, the MU issues a request to the processor's system interface. The system interface arbitrates for ownership of the external bus and then performs the transaction or transactions currently posted in the MU.

Memory-Forced I/O Segment. This feature of the PPC 601 processor is outside the scope of the PowerPC processor specification. When the integer unit initiates a memory access, the effective address is submitted to the MMU for translation. If the segment register selected by the upper digit of the effective address defines this as an I/O segment (T bit = 1) and the BUC number is 7Fh, the access is considered to be a memory access. The assumed WIM bit setting is x11b (non-cacheable and memory coherency required).

Memory-Mapped I/O Port. An I/O register that responds to memory rather than I/O accesses.

MESI Protocol. At a given instant in time, each cache block in the data cache may be one of the following states: modified (M), exclusive (E), shared, (S), or invalid (I). Each of these states is defined in the glossary.

mfdec Instruction. Move from decrementer register. Used to copy the contents of the DEC register to one of the GPRs.

mfmsr Instruction. Move from MSR instruction. Used to copy the contents of the MSR register to one of the GPRs.

mfspr Instruction. Move from SPR instruction. Used to copy the contents of one of the processor's SPRs to one of the GPRs.

mfsr Instruction. Move from segment register. Used to copy the contents of one of the processor's segment registers to one of the GPRs.

mfsrin Instruction. Move from segment register indirect instruction. The contents of the segment register selected by the upper digit in a specified GPR is copied into the memory location specified by another GPR.

mftb Instruction. Move from time base instruction. Used to copy the contents of TBL into the specified GPR.

mftbu Instruction. Move from time base upper instruction. Used to copy the contents of TBU into the specified GPR.

Microcode. The BIST in the PPC 601 processor is implemented in microcode ROM inside the processor.

MMU. See memory management unit.

Modified State. When a cache block is in the modified state, it has been modified by the processor since it was copied from memory.

mov Instruction. This is an Intel ix86 instruction. It is used to perform a register-to-register, register-to-memory, or memory-to-register move.

Move Assist Instructions. These are the load and store string instructions. Unlike the load and store multiple word instructions, the start address does not have to be word aligned.

MQ. This PPC 601 register is outside the scope of the PowerPC processor specification. It holds the product for the multiply instruction and the dividend for the divide instruction. It is also used for long rotate and shift instructions.

MSB. Most-significant byte.

msb. Most-significant bit.

MSR. Machine State Register.

MSR[BE]. Machine State Register branch trace enable bit.

MSR[DR]. Machine State Register data relocation bit. When set to one, the MMU performs effective-to-physical address translation for loads and stores. When set to zero, loads and stores are performed without translating the address. In other words, the effective address is the physical memory address that will be accessed. The DR bit is also referred to as the DT bit (data translation).

MSR[DT]. Machine State Register data translation bit. See MSR[DR].

MSR[EE]. Machine State Register external interrupt enable bit. When set to one, the processor recognizes interrupts received from the external interrupt controller on the INT# input and invokes the external interrupt handler. Recognition of the decrementer interrupt is also enabled. When cleared to zero, the processor will not recognize external or decrementer interrupts.

MSR[ELE]. Machine State Register exception little-endian bit. See MSR[ILE].

MSR[EP]. Machine State Register exception prefix bit. See MSR[IP].

MSR[FE[0:1]]. Machine State Register floating-point interrupt enable bits. These bits are used to enable the FPU to report imprecise or precise interrupts. The PPC 601 processor only supports precise interrupts.

MSR[FP]. Machine State Register FPU enable bit. When cleared to zero, the FPU is disabled (or not present). Any attempt to execute a floating-point instruction results in floating-point unavailable interrupt.

MSR[ILE]. Machine State Register interrupt little-endian mode bit. When any interrupt occurs. The processor saves the state of the MSR[LE] bit in SRR1 and then copies ILE to LE before branching to the interrupt handler. In this way, the operating system programmer forces the processor to automatically switch to the desired endian storage mode for interrupt servicing.

MSR[IP]. Machine State Register interrupt prefix bit. See Interrupt Prefix.

MSR[IR]. Machine State Register instruction relocation bit. When set to one, the MMU performs effective-to-physical address translation for instruction fetches. When set to zero, instruction fetches are performed without translating the address. In other words, the effective address is the physical memory address that will be accessed. The IR bit is also referred to as the IT bit (instruction translation).

MSR[IT]. Machine State Register. See MSR[IT].

MSR[LE]. Machine State Register little-endian bit. When set to one, processor uses the little-endian storage method. When cleared to zero, the processor uses its native big-endian storage method. The PPC 601 processor is non-compliant with the spec in this area. The LE bit is implemented in HID0 rather than the MSR register.

MSR[ME]. Machine State Register machine check enable bit. See Machine Check.

MSR[POW]. Machine State Register power management bit. When cleared to zero, the processor operates in full-power mode. When set to one, the processor's power management features are enabled. The PPC 601 processor doesn't implement this bit.

MSR[PR]. Machine State Register privilege mode bit (also referred to as the problem mode bit). When cleared to zero, the processor is operating at the supervisor privilege level. When set to one, the processor is operating at the user privilege level.

MSR[RE]. Machine State Register. See MSR[RI].

MSR[RI]. Machine State Register recoverable interrupt bit. For a detailed description, refer to the chapter entitled, "Interrupts" under the heading The Recoverable Interrupt Bit." The PPC 601 processor doesn't implement this bit.

MSR[SE]. Machine State Register single-step trace enable bit. When cleared to zero, the processor does not generate a single-step trace interrupt at the completion of each instruction. When set to one, it does. The PPC 601 processor implements this bit, but its usage deviates from the specification. For a detailed description of trace interrupt implementation in the PPC 601 processor, refer to the chapter entitled, "PPC 601 Interrupts."

MSR[SF]. Machine State Register sixty-four bit mode. Only implemented in 64-bit processors (e.g., the PPC 620 processor). When cleared to zero, the processor generates 32-bit effective addresses. When set to one, the processor generates 64-bit effective addresses.

mtdec Instruction. Move to decrementer instruction. Used to move a value from the specified GPR register to the DEC register.

mtmsr Instruction. Move to MSR instruction. Used to move a value from the specified GPR register to the MSR register.

mtspr Instruction. Move to special purpose register instruction. Used to move a value from the specified GPR register to the specified SPR.

mtsr Instruction. Move to segment register instruction. Used to move a value from the specified GPR register to the specified segment register.

mtsrin Instruction. Move to segment register indirect instruction. Used to move a value from the memory location specified by a GPR register to the specified segment register.

mttbl Instruction. Move to timebase lower instruction. Used to move a value from the specified GPR register to the TBL register.

mttbu Instruction. Move to timebase upper instruction. Used to move a value from the specified GPR register to the TBU register.

MU. Memory Unit. See Memory Unit.

NIA. Next Instruction Address. When an interrupt occurs that is not caused by the attempted execution of an instruction, the NIA is copied to SRR0 as the address to return to when the rfi is executed at the end of the interrupt handler.

Opcode. See Extended Opcode.

Operand. The data object specified for a load, a store or a logical operation. It can be a byte, a halfword, a word, or a doubleword.

ori Instruction. OR immediate instruction. The specified immediate value is ORed with the contents of one GPR register and the results is stored the a GPR register.

Page Access History Bits. The CHANGED and REFERENCED bits in the PTE keep track of the access history within the page. The REFERENCED bit is set by the MMU whenever the page is accessed for a read or a write. The CHANGED bit is set to one when the page is stored into.

Page Fault Handler. The interrupt handler that is invoked when an effective addresses cannot be mapped by either the BAT registers or the page table. In other words, the processor is attempting to access a memory location that does not reside with a memory block nor within a page that is currently resident in physical memory. This handler must verify if the currently-executing program is permitted access to the page. If it isn't, the task must be shut down. If it is permitted to access the page, the page fault handler must read the page into memory from mass storage and create a PTE that indicates where the page originated and where it was placed in physical memory. The Page fault handler then executes an rfi to re-execute the instruction that caused the page fault. The access now completes without generating an interrupt because the PTE is found.

Page Fault. Occurs when the processor is attempting to access a memory location that does not reside with a memory block nor within a page that is currently resident in physical memory. See also Page Fault Interrupt Handler.

Page Table Entry Group, or PTEG. The page table in memory is comprised of page table entries, or PTEs. It is further organized into eight PTEs per PTEG. The number of PTEGs in the page table depends on the size of the page table (as specified in the SDR1 register). The page table can be anywhere from 64KB to 32MB in size in a 32-bit processor, and up to 64TB (terrabytes) in size in a 64-bit processor.

Page Table Entry, or PTE. A PTE consists of eight bytes of information in a 32-bit processor and 16 bytes in a 64-bit processor. The layout of the PTE can be found in the chapter entitled, "Virtual Paging." Also see Page Table Entry Group. Each PTE maps a page within a virtual segment on mass storage to a physical page in memory. Each PTE also contains the page access rights bits, page access history bits, and the WIMG bits for accesses within the page.

Page Table Scan. The process wherein the MMU walks through the primary and secondary PTEGs looking for a match on the virtual segment ID and the page number.

Page Table. Contains PTEs that each map a page within a virtual segment on mass storage to a physical page in memory. Each PTE also contains the page access rights bits, page access history bits, and the WIMG bits for accesses within the page.

Page. 4KB of information starting on an address divisible by 4KB. The information on mass storage devices is divided into pages by the operating system, as is the array of physical memory in the system.

PCI Bus Master. A PCI device that has the ability to perform PCI bus transactions to communicate with other devices in the system.

PCI Bus. Peripheral Component Interconnect Bus. For a complete description of the PCI bus, refer to the MindShare publication entitled, "PCI System Architecture."

PCLK_EN#. See 2x_PCLK definition. Processor clock enable signal. The platform uses this input to the PPC 601 processor to select the phase of the PCLK signal developed internally by the processor (by dividing the 2x_PCLK signal by two. The platform can use the PCLK_EN# signal to synchronize the PCLKs in an array of processor to each other. Since each processor's internal bus clock is developed from its PCLK, this will also sync up their bus clocks.

P_CLOCK. See 2x_PCLK definition.

Physical Address. The memory addresses output onto the address bus by the processor when it performs memory-oriented bus transactions.

Physical page. The MMU's paging logic views the 4GB of physical memory space to be divided into 2^{20} pages, each 4KB in size. Via the page table, the MMU keeps track of what virtual pages are currently resident in each physical memory page.

Pipeline. Each of the processor's execution units incorporates its own set of stages that an instruction must pass through to completion. During a given PCLK cycle, an execution unit could have a separate instruction occupying each stage of this internal instruction pipeline. With each clock cycle, the instructions in the pipeline each advance to the next stage of the pipeline.

PIR. Processor ID Register. Also referred to as HID15.

Platform. The overall PC system.

Policy of Inclusion. When a processor is connected (via its local bus) to a look-through L2 cache, all information that is read into the L1 cache has to pass through the L2 cache. The L2 cache therefore has a complete copy of the information that is contained in the L1 cache at a given instant in time. This is the policy of inclusion. The L2 cache can then act as a snoop filter for the processor. Whenever another bus master is accessing main memory, the L2 cache snoops the address to determine if it has a copy of the target cache block in its cache. If it doesn't, then it needn't force the L1 cache to snoop the access. The L2 cache only has to alert the L1 cache about another bus master's memory access when it has a hit on its cache.

Posted Read Buffer. See Memory Unit.

Posted Write Buffer. See Memory Unit.

PP Bits. Page Protection bits in the PTE and BAT registers. Combined with the selected key bit, the MMU uses this three bit field to determine the access rights of the currently-running program within the page or block.

Precise Interrupt. Refer to the discussion of the floating-point interrupts in the chapter entitled, "Interrupts."

Prefetch Queue. The buffer the instruction prefetcher places instruction words into when they have been fetched from memory. They are then made available to the processor's execution units.

Prefetcher. Performs speculative reads from memory to fetch the instruction word stream. Unless told otherwise by the processor's branch prediction logic, the prefetcher fetches instruction words from sequential memory words. It always attempts to keep the instruction prefetch queue full of instruction words to be fed to the processor's execution units.

Primary Page Table Hash. The process where the MMU selects the first PTEG to search for a match on the virtual segment ID and page number. For additional information on this process, refer to the chapter entitled, "Virtual Paging."

Primary PTEG. The first PTEG searched by the MMU for a match on the virtual segment ID and page number. For additional information on this process, refer to the chapter entitled, "Virtual Paging."

Primary Segment Table Hash. The process where the MMU selects the first STEG to search for a match on the effective segment ID. For additional information on this process, refer to the chapter entitled, "Virtual Paging."

Primary STEG. The first STEG searched by the MMU for a match on the effective segment ID. For additional information on this process, refer to the chapter entitled, "Virtual Paging."

Privilege Level. The MSR[PR] bit has two possible states (set and cleared). If it is cleared to zero while the current program is running, the processor is operating at the supervisor privilege level and the programmer has access to all of the registers and instructions. If MSR[PR] is set to one, the processor is operating at the user privilege level and the programmer has access to a subset of the registers and instructions.

Privileged Instruction. Instructions that may only be executed when the processor is operating at the supervisor privilege level (MSR[PR] is cleared to zero).

PTE. See Page Table Entry.

PTEG. See Page Table Entry Group.

Push Back Operation. Performed by a snooping processor if it has a snoop hit on a modified cache block. The processor performs a burst write transaction to push the modified cache block into memory.

PVR. Processor Version Register.

Q0 – Q7. PPC 601 processor's prefetch queue entries.

Quadword (as defined by Intel). A group of eight contiguous locations starting at an address divisible by eight.

Quadword (as defined by PowerPC specification). A group of sixteen contiguous locations starting at an address divisible by sixteen.

QUIESC_REQ. Output from the PPC 601 processor. Asserted when the processor has entered the soft stop state. In a multiprocessor system, connected to the SYS_QUIESC# input of the next processor. See Soft Stop State and SYS_QUIESC#.

rA. Instruction field used to specify a GPR to be used as a source or as a destination.

rB. Instruction field used to specify a GPR to be used as a source.

rD. Instruction field used to specify a GPR to be used as a destination.

RE Bit. See RI Bit.

Read Atomic Transaction. Performed by a PPC 601 processor in response to the execution of a lwarx instruction to read a semaphore from memory.

Read With Intent To Modify, or rwitm, Transaction. Performed by a PPC 601 processor in response to a store miss within a page or block with a WIM bit setting of 00xb (write-back, cacheable). Announces the processor's intention to read the target cache block into the cache and then immediately store into it and mark it modified.

Real Address Mode. The processor's MMU is operating in real address mode if its ability to perform address translation has been disabled via the MSR registers IT and/or DT bits. The effective address specified by the programmer or the prefetcher is used to address physical memory.

Referenced Bit. See Page Access History Bits.

Replacement Algorithm. See LRU Algorithm.

Reservation. The processor establishes a reservation on a cache block of memory space when it executes a lwarx or ldarx instruction to read a memory semaphore into a GPR to perform a bit-test-and-set operation on it. The chapter entitled, "Acquiring Ownership of a Shared Resource" explains the reservation concept.

Resource ID. The field in the EAR register that identifies the external device that the processor will address when ecowx or eciwx instructions are executed.

RESUME. Assertion of this input to the PPC 601 processor instructs it to exit the soft stop state and resume normal program execution. See Soft Stop State.

Retry. Issued by a processor to the current bus master if the processor's snoop logic is busy and cannot snoop the bus master's memory access or if the snoop results in a snoop hit on a modified block. In either case, reception of a retry causes the current bus master to abort its transaction and retry it again later. On the PPC 601 processor's bus, ARTRY# is the signal used to issue a retry to the current bus master.

rfi Instruction. Return from interrupt instruction. This is always the last instruction in an interrupt handler. It causes the processor to restore the original MSR state from the SRR1 register and then to resume program execution at the instruction pointed to by the SRR0 register.

RI Bit. See MSR[RI].

RSRV#. This is the PPC 601 processor's reservation output. The chapter entitled, "Acquiring Ownership of a Shared Resource" explains the reservation concept and use of RSRV#.

RTC. Real-Time Clock. In the PPC 601 processor, the RTC supplies the time-of-day function. It tracks the passage of time in seconds and nanoseconds since the last second incremented.

RTC input signal. 7.8125MHz input clock that drives the processor's RTC and DEC registers.

RTCL. Real-Time Clock lower register. The lower half of the PPC 601 processor's RTC register.

RTCU. Real-Time Clock upper register. The upper half of the PPC 601 processor's RTC register.

RUN_NSTOP. This PPC 601 processor output is part of the test interface. It's usage is not documented in the user's manual.

rwitm Atomic Transaction. A variation on the rwitm transaction. Generated when the PPC 601 processor executes a stwcx or stdcx instruction that misses the cache within a page or block with a WIM bit setting of 00xb (write-back, cacheable). The processor performs a rwitm atomic transaction to read the sector that contains the semaphore into the cache so it can store into it and mark it modified. The chapter entitled, "Acquiring Ownership of a Shared Resource" explains the reservation concept and memory semaphore usage.

rwitm Transaction. See Read With Intent To Modify Transaction.

sc Instruction. System call instruction is used to make an unconditional call to the operating system. Execution of the sc instruction causes the processor to take the system call interrupt. In the system call interrupt handler, the operating system handles the request and then executes an rfi instruction to resume execution of the calling program at the instruction that follows the sc instruction.

SC_DRIVE#. Super-Charged Drive. When asserted to the PPC 601 processor, causes it to approximately double the drive current it uses on the following signals: ABB#, DBB#, ARTRY#, SHD#, TS# and XATS#. When deasserted, these signals use the same amount of drive current as all of the other processor signals.

SCAN_CLK. This is the boundary scan interface's clock signal. It is used to clock serial data into the processor on the SCAN_IN signal and out of the processor on the SCAN_OUT signal.

SCAN_OUT. See SCAN_CLK.

SCAN_SIN. See SCAN_CLK.

SCSI. Small Computer System Interface.

SDR1. Search Descriptor Register One. Defines the start physical address and size of the page table in memory.

Secondary Page Table Hash. The process where the MMU selects the second PTEG to search for a match on the virtual segment ID and page number. For additional information on this process, refer to the chapter entitled, "Virtual Paging."

Secondary PTEG. The second PTEG searched by the MMU for a match on the virtual segment ID and page number. For additional information on this process, refer to the chapter entitled, "Virtual Paging."

Secondary Segment Table Hash. The process where the MMU selects the second STEG to search for a match on the effective segment ID. For additional information on this process, refer to the chapter entitled, "Virtual Paging."

Secondary STEG. The second STEG searched by the MMU for a match on the effective segment ID. For additional information on this process, refer to the chapter entitled, "Virtual Paging."

Sector Fill. See Cache Block Fill.

Sector. 32 byte cache block in the PPC 601 processor. One half of a PPC 601 processor cache line.

Segment. A 256MB area of effective address space starting at an address divisible by 256MB. Each segment is divided into 64K pages, each 4KB in size.

Segment Fault Handler. The interrupt handler invoked when the primary and secondary STAB scans fail to find a match on the target effective segment ID. The data storage interrupt handler is invoked and DSISR[10] is set to one. For more information, refer to the chapter entitled, "Virtual Paging" under the heading "Paging Implementation In 64-Bit PowerPC processors."

Segment Fault. See Segment Fault Handler.

Segment Register. In a 32-bit processor, used by the operating system programmer to map an effective segment to one of 2^{24} virtual memory segments. Not implemented in a 64-bit processor. For more information, refer to the chapter entitled, "Virtual Paging."

Segment Table, or STAB. Only implemented in 64-bit processors. Contains STEs that each map one effective segment to either a virtual memory segment or to an I/O segment. Organized into 32 segment table entry groups, or STEGs, each containing eight segment table entries, or STEs. The ASR register points to the start physical address of the STAB in memory.

Segment Table Entry, or STE. See Segment Table.

Segment Table Entry Group, or STEG. See Segment Table.

Segment Type. The T bit in a segment register or STE defines whether the effective segment is mapped to a virtual memory segment or to an I/O segment. T = 0 indicates mapping to a virtual memory segment, while T = 1 indicates mapping to an I/O segment.

Semaphore. See Memory Semaphore.

Sender ID. When the PPC 601 processor is performing an I/O transaction, it embeds its processor ID (from its PIR) in address packet 0. At the end of the I/O load or store transaction series, the I/O BUC controller embeds its BUC number in address packet 0 in its reply transaction. In these cases, the processor ID and BUC number are referred to as the sender ID.

Set. The set of cache entries selected by the line being accessed. The PPC 601 processor's L1 cache is eight-way set-associative, so a set of eight entries are selected for comparison during a lookup in the cache.

Shared State. Indicates that copies of the cache block exist in at least one other cache in the system and none of the processors with copies of the block have altered their copy since reading it from memory.

SHD#. When the PPC 601 processor is bus master and is performing a memory access with GBL# asserted, all other processors must snoop the transaction and report the snoop result on SHD# and ARTRY#. If SHD# is asserted, at least one of the snooping processors has a copy of the target cache block. The state of ARTRY# indicates whether any processor has a copy of the target cache block in the modified state.

Single-Beat Read or Write. Performed by the processor to read or write from one to eight bytes. For more information, refer to the chapter entitled, "The Data Phase."

SLB. Segment Lookaside Buffer. A high-speed, lookaside cache in the MMU that caches segment table entries to improve performance for future accesses within the effective segment. Inclusion of the SLB in a PowerPC is optional.

slbia Instruction. SLB invalidate all instruction. Must be executed when the operating system programmer switches to a new segment table by loading a new segment table start address into the ASR register. Causes all entries in the SLB to be invalidated.

slbie Instruction. SLB invalidate entry instruction. When executed, causes the SLB to invalidate just the specified entry. Must be executed when a segment table entry has been changed by the operating system programmer.

Snarf. The ability of a third party in a transaction to quietly latch data from the data bus as it is being passed between the current bus master and a target device.

Snoop Filter. See Policy of Inclusion.

Snoop Hit On Clean Block. While snooping a memory transaction initiated by another bus master, a snooper discovers that is has a copy of the target cache block in the exclusive or shared state. In either case, the snooping processor has not modified the cache block since reading it from memory (hence the term "clean").

Snoop Hit On Modified Block. While snooping a memory transaction initiated by another bus master, a snooper discovers that is has a copy of the target cache block in the modified state. This means that the current bus master is about to access a stale cache block in memory. The snooper issues a retry to the current bus master to force it to terminate its transaction without transferring data. The bus master will retry the transaction at a later time. The snooper then pushes (writes) the modified cache block into memory.

Snoop Miss. While snooping a memory transaction initiated by another bus master, a snooper discovers that does not have a copy of the target cache block in its cache. No action is taken.

Snoop Push Back Operation. See Push Back Operation.

Snoop result. When a PPC 601 processor detects that another bus master has initiated a memory transaction and has asserted GBL#, it must perform a lookup (a snoop) in its cache to determine if it has a copy of the target cache block. It must then report the snoop result back to the initiator on the snoop result signals, SHD# and ARTRY#. For a detailed discussion of the snoop result, refer to the chapter entitled, "The Memory Address Phase."

Snoop. See Snoop Result.

Snooper Busy Condition. If the current bus master is commanding all PPC 601 processors to snoop the current transaction and report snoop results and a snooper's logic is busy, it indicates its busy state by asserting ARTRY# to the master. This causes the master to retry the transaction again at a later time.

Snooper. A cache that has been commanded by the current bus master to perform a lookup in its cache and report the results of the lookup to the master.

Soft Reset. When the PPC 601 processor's SRESET# input is asserted, it branches to the reset vector in the interrupt table. The location of the interrupt table is determined by the current state of the MSR[IP] bit. Soft Reset is not destructive (i.e., the interrupted program can be resumed by executing an rfi instruction at the end of the reset interrupt handler).

Soft Stop State. The PPC 601 processor may be commanded to enter the soft stop state in two ways: through its boundary scan interface or by assertion of its SYS_QUIESC# input. The processor asserts QUIESC_REQ when it has entered the soft stop state. This state is entered when all pending bus transactions have been completed. When it enters the soft stop state, the processor stops all program execution and freezes. It will resume normal operation when its RESUME input is asserted.

Special Purpose Register, or SPR. Many of the processor's registers are implemented as SPRs and are accessed using the mtspr and mfspr instructions.

Speculative Access. Access performed by a processor functional unit before it has actually been determined that the instruction should be executed (i.e., there is an unresolved conditional branch preceding the instruction in the instruction stream). An example would be instruction prefetches performed before it has been determined that the fetched instruction will be executed.

Spin Loop. A tight piece of code that loops until some condition is met.

Split Cache. Processor implements separate code and data caches.

SPR. See Special Purpose Register.

SPRG0. SPR General register 0. Stack pointer register to be used by interrupt handlers.

SPRG1. SPR General register 1. Scratch register to be used by interrupt handlers.

SPRG2. SPR General register 2. Operating system-specific usage.

SPRG3. SPR General register 3. Operating system-specific usage.

SR0 – SR15. Segment registers 0 – 15. See Segment Register.

SRESET#. See Soft Reset.

SRR0. Save and Return Register 0. When an interrupt occurs, the processor snapshots the NIA or CIA in SRR0 as the return address to resume execution at when the interrupt handler executes the rfi instruction.

SRR1. Save and Return Register 1. When an interrupt occurs, a snapshot of the processor's current operational state is taken in SRR1 by copying a number of the MSR bits to the corresponding bits in SRR1. In addition, SRR1 contains status bits that indicate why the interrupt occurred.

STAB. Segment Table. See Segment Table.

Stack. Area of memory that interrupt handers save the contents of processor registers in.

Stale Block. A block in memory that has been copied into a cache and then modified by a processor in the cache but not in memory. The block then contains stale data and the modified cache block contains the "fresh" data.

Stale Sector. See Stale Block.

Static Branch Prediction. Unless told otherwise when the instruction is coded, the assembler clears the branch prediction hint bit in the instruction. This has the following effects: backward relative conditional branch is predicted taken; forward relative conditional branch is predicted not taken; conditional branch to the address contained in LR or CTR is predicted not taken.

stb Instruction. Store byte instruction. Stores the LSB from the specified GPR into the location specified.

std Instruction. Store doubleword instruction. Stores the doubleword from the specified GPR register into the eight locations starting at the location specified.

stdcx Instruction. Store doubleword conditional indexed. Attempts to store the doubleword semaphore in the specified GPR register into the specified doubleword in memory. If the reservation previously established by the ldarx instruction paired with the stdcx is still intact, the doubleword is stored into memory. If the condition is no longer intact, the store is unsuccessful. Success or failure is indicated via the equal bit in CR0 being set or cleared.

STE. Segment table entry. Each STE in the memory-based segment table maps one effective segment to either a virtual memory segment or an I/O segment. Only used in 64-bit processors. See Segment Table.

STEG. See Segment Table.

sth Instruction. Store halfword instruction. Stores the two LSBs from the specified GPR into the two locations starting at the location specified.

stmw Instruction. Store multiple word instruction. When executed, the processor stores the specified number of words from the GPR register set (starting at the specified GPR register) into memory or I/O starting at the specified word-aligned effective address. The number words to be stored is implied in the start GPR number (31 minus the start GPR number).

Store Hit. The processor performs a store that results in a hit on the L1 cache. The specified byte, halfword, word or doubleword is updated in the cache entry. If the page or block is marked write-through, the data is also written through to external memory using a single-beat write transaction. If the page or block is marked write-back, one of three actions is taken. If the cache block is marked exclusive, it is marked modified after the store and the data is not written to memory. If the cache block is marked shared and M = 1, the processor broadcasts a kill transaction and then stores into the cache block and marks it modified. The data is not written to memory. If the cache block is marked modified, the processor stores into it and doesn't change its state. The data is not written to memory.

Store Miss. The action taken by the processor's L1 cache depends on whether the page or block is marked as write-through or write-back. If write-through, the processor performs a single-beat write transaction to write the byte, halfword, word or doubleword to memory. If write-back, the processor performs a rwitm transaction to read the cache block from memory. When the cache block has been read, it is placed into the cache, stored into and immediately marked modified.

Store With Update. The processor stores the specified data operand from the specified GPR register into memory or I/O. The computed effective address is loaded into the GPR register specified in the instruction's rA field.

Store. Stores a byte, halfword, word or doubleword into memory or I/O.

stswi Instruction. Store string word immediate instruction. Stores a string of bytes from the GPR register set into memory or I/O.

stswx Instruction. Store string word indexed instruction. Stores a string of bytes from the GPR register set into memory or I/O.

stw Instruction. Store word instruction. Stores the four LSBs from the specified GPR into the four locations starting at the location specified.

stwcx Instruction. Store word conditional indexed. Attempts to store the word semaphore in the specified GPR register into the specified word in memory. If the reservation previously established by the lwarx instruction paired with the stwcx is still intact, the word is stored into memory. If the condition is no longer intact, the store is unsuccessful. Success or failure is indicated via the equal bit in CR0 being set or cleared.

Superscalar. A processor implementation wherein multiple instructions may be executed simultaneously.

Supervisor Privilege Level. The processor operates at the supervisor privilege level when MSR[PR] = 0. The operating system programmer has full access to the register and instruction set.

sync Instruction. When executed, causes the processor core to stall on the sync instruction until the MU has performed all posted operations on the external bus. The processor then performs an address-only sync transaction to force any external posted write buffer (in the L2 cache) to flush all posted writes to memory. See the chapter entitled, "Access Ordering" for more information.

Sync Transaction. See Sync Instruction.

SYS_QUIESC#. When asserted to a PPC 601 processor, requests it to finish all posted bus accesses and then enter the soft stop state. The processor asserts QUIESC_REQ# when it has entered the soft stop state. See also Soft Stop State.

System Interface. The processor unit that performs all required bus transactions.

T Bit. The segment type bit in segment registers or STEs. T = 0 indicates the register or STE maps the effective segment to a virtual memory segment. T = 1 indicates that the effective segment is mapped to an I/O segment.

TA#. Transfer Acknowledge. During a read, this input to the PPC 601 processor is asserted by the target device when it is presenting the requested data to the processor on the data bus. When sampled asserted on a rising edge of its bus clock, the processor latches the data from the bus. It may not forward the data to the processor core for use, however, until the target verifies its validity by keeping DRTRY# deasserted on the next bus clock rising-edge. During a write, the target asserts TA# to indicate that it has latched the data being written to be the processor. The processor can therefore stop driving the data item onto the bus.

Tag Address. This term is synonymous with page address. The cache keeps a copy of the page, or tag, address that a cache block was read from in it its directory. The high-speed static RAM, or SRAM, that forms the cache directory is referred to as the tag RAM.

Tag RAM. See Tag Address.

Target Controller. In SCSI, denotes a controller that resides on the SCSI bus. The controller controls a SCSI device or an array of SCSI devices.

TBL. TimeBase Lower register.

TBST#. Transfer Burst output signal. Asserted by the PPC 601 processor when it is performing a four-beat burst memory read or write transaction to read a sector into the cache or to write a modified sector back to memory. When not asserted, the processor is performing a single-beat transaction to read or write between a byte and eight bytes.

TBU. TimeBase Upper register.

TC0. Transfer Code 0 output bus signal. During a memory read transaction, the processor clears its TC0 output (TC stands for transfer code) to zero if a data read is in progress, or sets it to one to indicate that a code read is in progress. When the processor is performing a four-beat burst write transaction to write a modified cache block back to memory, it will use TC0 to indicate to the L2 cache whether or not it will mark the cache block invalid in its L1 cache after the write-back has been completed. TC0 clear to zero indicates that the cache block will not be invalidated, but will be marked exclusive or shared. For additional information, refer to the chapter entitled, "The Memory Address Phase."

TC1. Transfer Code 1 output bus signal. If the processor is currently performing a burst read to fetch a cache sector from a line and the processor's memory unit has a read posted to fetch the opposing sector as well, it will assert TC1 = 1 to indicate this. This information can cause a look-through L2 cache to initiate a memory read to fetch the other sector before it is actually asked for.

TEA#. Transfer Error Acknowledge. When asserted to the processor while it is performing a bus transaction, causes the processor abort the transaction and to either: invoke the machine check interrupt handler (if MSR[ME] = 1) or to enter the checkstop state (if MSR[ME] = 0).

Test-and-Set Operation. The process wherein a program determines if a memory semaphore is currently locked and if it isn't, attempts to lock it. For a detailed description of memory semaphores, refer to the chapter entitled, "Acquiring Ownership of a Shared Resource."

TLB Invalidate Transaction. Performed by the processor in response to the execution of a tlbie instruction. Causes all other processors to perform a lookup in their TLBs and to invalidate the indicated set of entries.

TLB. Translation Lookaside Buffer. A high-speed, lookaside cache in the MMU that caches page table entries to improve performance for future accesses within the page. Inclusion of the TLB in a PowerPC is optional.

tlbia Instruction. TLB invalidate all instruction. Causes the MMU to invalidate all entries in the TLB. Should be executed when the operating system programmer loads the start address of a different page table into the SDR1 register.

tlbie Instruction. TLB invalidate entry instruction. Causes the MMU to perform a lookup in its TLB and to invalidate the indicated set of TLB entries. Also causes the processor to broadcast an address-only TLB invalidate transaction to kill the indicated TLB entries in the TLBs of all other processors, as well. Should be executed whenever the operating system programmer changes the contents of a PTE in the page table.

Translation Lookaside Buffer. See TLB.

TRDY#. PCI Target Ready signal. For a detailed description, refer to the MindShare publication entitled, "PCI System Architecture."

TS#. Transfer Start. Asserted by the PPC 601 processor when it initiates a memory, address-only, or an external control transaction. Indicates that the processor has placed a valid address and transaction type on the address bus and that all memory and external control targets should examine the transaction to determine which one is the target of the transaction.

TSIZ[0:2]. Transfer Size bus. During a memory-oriented transaction, the PPC 601 processor uses these output signals to indicate the number of byte to be transferred within the currently-addressed doubleword. Only has meaning during the performance of a single-beat transaction (meaningless during a burst). During the performance of an external control transaction, the four bit bus consisting of TBST# and TSIZ[0:2] identifies the external resource being addressed. During address packet 0 of an I/O transaction, the eight bit bus comprised of TT[0:3], TBST# and TSIZ[0:2] indicates the I/O transaction type. During address packet 1 of an I/O transaction, this same eight bit bus indicates the number of bytes to be transferred.

TT[0:4]. Transaction Type bus. During a memory-oriented or external control transaction, the TT[0:3] outputs of the PPC 601 processor indicate the transaction type. During address packet 0 of an I/O transaction, the eight bit bus comprised of TT[0:3], TBST# and TSIZ[0:2] indicates the I/O transaction type. During address packet 1 of an I/O transaction, this same eight bit bus indicates the number of bytes to be transferred.

UBATs. Universal BAT registers. The PPC 601 processor only implements the four IBAT registers. It does not implement the four DBAT registers defined in the specification. In addition, the usage of the IBATs differs from that described in the specification. The specification indicates that the MMU will only perform lookups in the IBAT registers for instruction fetches, not for loads or stores. In the PPC 601 processor, the MMU performs lookups in the IBATs for instruction fetches, loads and stores. In other words, although they are called instruction BAT registers, they are really universal BAT registers.

Unified Code/Data Cache. A cache implementation wherein both code and data are stored in the same cache. The alternative would be a split cache architecture.

Update. See Load With Update, and Store With Update.

User Privilege Level. The processor operates at the user privilege level when MSR[PR] = 1. The applications programmer has limited access to the register and instruction set.

Video Frame Buffer. See Frame Buffer.

Virtual Address. When address translation is enabled (MSR[IT] and/or MSR[DT] are set to one), the MMU translates the specified effective address into a virtual address and then translates the virtual address to a physical memory address. This process is described in detail in the chapter entitled, "Virtual Paging."

Virtual page. One of 64K pages within a virtual memory segment. For a detailed description of address translation, refer to the chapter entitled, "Virtual Paging."

Virtual Segment ID, or VSID. Each segment register or STE maps a 256MB effective segment to one of a large number of 256MB virtual memory segments. The VSID field in the segment register or STE identifies the virtual memory segment that the effective segment is mapped to. For a detailed description of address translation, refer to the chapter entitled, "Virtual Paging."

Virtual Segment. See Virtual Segment ID.

VL Bus. VESA Local bus. For a description of the VL bus, refer to the MindShare publication entitled, "PCI System Architecture."

Vs. Each BAT register has a Vs and Vu bit. The privilege level of the currently-running program selects one of these two valid bits. If the selected V bit is set to one, this BAT register defines a memory block for use at this privilege level. If cleared to zero, the BAT does not define a memory block for use at this privilege level.

VSID. See Virtual Segment ID.

Vu. See Vs.

W Bit. See WIMG Bits.

Wait State. During the address phase of a bus transaction, a slow target can force the PPC 601 processor to stretch the duration of the address phase by keeping AACK# deasserted. The processor is forced to continue to drive the address and transaction type information until AACK# is sampled asserted on a rising-edge of the processor's bus clock.

Way. A bank of cache SRAM memory.

WIMG bits. The operating system programmer uses the WIMG bits in each PTE and BAT register to define the rules of operation with a page or block of memory. These bits define whether the cache uses a write-through or write-back policy for stores (the W bit), whether the page or block is cacheable (the I bit), whether other processors may also access the same page or block (the M bit), and whether the processor is permitted to perform speculative accesses within the page or block (the G bit). The PPC 601 processor does not implement the G bit. When the MMU is disabled, the processor operates with an assumed WIM bit setting of 001b (write-back, cacheable, and other processors also access the area).

Word. 32-bits of information.

Write Atomic Transaction. A write transaction performed by the processor to write a memory semaphore into memory.

Write With Flush Transaction. A single-beat write transaction. Any other processor snooping the transaction that experiences a hit on a cache block in the exclusive or shared state invalidates its copy. A snooper with a hit on a modified copy issues a retry to the master and then performs a snoop push-back operation to deposit the modified cache block into memory. It then invalidates its copy of the cache block. The bus master that received the retry then re attempts the write successfully.

Write With Kill Transaction. A four-beat burst write transaction. The initiator of the transaction is writing a modified cache block back to memory. Any other processor snooping the transaction should kill its copy in the event of a hit (because the current bus master is overwriting the entire cache block in memory).

Write-Back Policy. If a page or block is designate as write-back, the processor doesn't perform writes into external memory. Rather, the data is modified in the cache. If the data to be updated is not currently resident in the cache, the processor reads the cache block that contains it into the cache and then stores into it and marks it modified. For a description of the VL bus, refer to the MindShare publication entitled, "PCI System Architecture."

Write-through Cache. If a page or block is designate as write-through, the processor performs writes into external memory on both cache hits and misses. In the event of a cache miss, the data is written to memory, but is not copied into the cache.

WT#. The PPC 601 processor's write-through output signal. This is the inverted form of the W bit from the PTE or BAT register. During a memory write bus transaction, WT# indicates to the L2 cache whether it should use a write-back (WT# deasserted) or write-through (WT# asserted) policy.

XATC. See Extended Address Transfer Code.

XATS#. Extended Address Transfer Start. Asserted by the PPC 601 processor when it initiates an I/O transaction. Memory and external control targets should ignore the transaction. I/O BUCs should decode the target BUC number in address packet 0 to determine which of them is the target BUC. The target BUC asserts AACK# to claim the transaction and permit the processor to terminate the address phase of the transaction.

XER. Integer Exception register.

PPC 601 Signal Glossary

2x_PCLK. This is the double-frequency input clock to the PPC 601 processor. The processor divides it by two to yiled its internal clock, PCLK (also referred to as P_CLOCK). The platform logic uses the PCLK_EN# input to the processor to select the phase of the internal PCLK.

A[0:31]. Processor's address bus. When the processor is the bus master, it drives the address onto the address bus. A[0:28] identifies the doubleword address, while A[29:31] identifies the start address of the target operand within the doubleword. When another bus master is performing a transaction and has asserted GBL# to command all processors to snoop the address, A[0:26] are inputs to the processor. This is the 32-byte aligned address of the target sector being addressed by the other master.

AACK#. Address Acknowledge. Sampled by the PPC 601 processor to determine when to terminate its address transaction. The PPC 601 must continue to drive the address, transaction type and transaction attributes until AACK# is sampled asserted. It may then terminate the address transaction and deassert ABB#. AACK# is asserted by the target that claims the transaction. Address-Only transactions are broadcast in nature. They do not target a particular device. In this case, a central resource asserts AACK# to permit the bus master to terminate the transaction.

ABB#. Address Bus Busy. Asserted by the PPC 601 processor when it initiates an address transaction. The processor continues to assert ABB# until it samples AACK# asserted. ABB# is then deasserted.

AP[0:3]. Address bus parity bits. When the PPC 601 processor places an address on the bus, it uses AP[0:3] to force odd parity on the four groups of eight address outputs. During a snoop of another bus master's memory access, the processor checks the state of AP[0:3] for odd parity on the address being snooped. If there is an error, the processor asserts its APE# output.

APE#. Address Parity Error. See AP[0:3].

ARTRY#. Address Retry. Asserted by a snooper under two circumstances: it snooped the address in its cache and experienced a snoop hit on a modified cache block; or its snoop logic is currently busy and cannot report snoop results back to the initiator of the transaction.

BCLK. Bus Clock. This internal, PPC 601 signal is used by the processor's system interface to pace its actions during a bus transaction. All signals are sampled and/or driven on the rising-edge of the bus clock. The rising-edge of the internal bus clock, or BCLK, signal is derived from the rising-edge of PCLK and the state of the BCLK_EN# input signal. For additional explanation, refer to the chapter entitled, "Other PPC601 Bus Signals."

BCLK_EN#. See BCLK.

BE[7:0]#. The byte able outputs of the Intel Pentium processor. used to indicate which data paths will be used during a transaction and which locations are being addressed within the currently-addressed doubleword (group of eight bytes).

BG#. Bus grant. Asserted by the bus arbiter to grant ownership of the address bus to a bus master. The bus master cannot begin using the address bus until it samples BG# asserted, ABB# deasserted, and ARTRY# deasserted.

BR#. Bus Request signal. The PPC 601 processor asserts BR# to request ownership of the address bus to run a transaction. The arbiter will assert BG# to the processor to grant it the bus.

BSCAN_EN#. Boundary scan enable. When asserted by external logic, the processor's boundary scan interface is enabled. A discussion of boundary scan is outside the scope of this document.

CI#. PPC 601 Cache Inhibit output. Asserted by the processor when performing a memory access in a page or block of memory designated as non-cacheable by the operating system programmer (in a PTE or BAT register). Essentially, this is the inverted form of the I bit from the WIM bits.

CKSTP_IN#. Checkstop In. When asserted to the PPC 601 processor, causes the processor to enter the checkstop state. Also see Checkstop State in the glossary of terms.

CKSTP_OUT#. Checkstop Out. Asserted by the PPC 601 processor when its enters the checkstop state. See also Checkstop State in the glossary of terms.

COP/SCAN Interface. Control and Observation Port and boundary scan interface. Used for testing.

CSE[0:2]. Cache Set Element bus. If the processor is performing a burst memory read to read a cache block into the L1 cache, it will indicate (using CSE[0:2]) which of the eight entries in the selected L1 cache set it will use to record the block. If the processor is performing a burst memory write to write a modified cache block back to memory, it will indicate which of the set of eight entries the cache block is originating from.

Data Lanes 0 - through - 7. Used by the PPC 601 processor to transfer bytes between the processor and locations 0 - through - 7 in the currently-addressed doubleword.

Data Paths 0 - through - 7. See Data Lanes 0 - through - 7.

DBB#. Data Bus Busy. Asserted by the PPC 601 processor when it starts a data transfer. Deasserted when the final TA# is received from the target device. Also see DRTRY#.

DBG#. Data Bus Grant. When asserted by the bus arbiter, informs the PPC 601 processor that it will be the next owner of the data bus.

DBWO#. Data Bus Write-Only. For a complete description, refer to the chapter entitled, "The Split-Bus Concept" under the heading "The Data Bus Write-Only Feature."

DH[0:31]. High half (upper four data paths) of PPC 601 data bus. DH[0:7] is data path 0 and DH[24:31] is data path 3. DL[0:31] is the lower half of the data bus. DL[0:7] is data path 4 and DL[24:31] is data path 7.

DL[0:31]. See DH[0:31].

Doubleword Address Bus. The PPC 601 processor uses A[0:28] to identify a doubleword in memory. A doubleword is a group of eight memory locations starting at an address divisible by eight. A[29:31] identify the start location of the operand within the doubleword, while TSIZ[0:2] indicates the size of the operand (in bytes).

DP[0:7]. Data parity bits for data paths 0 - through - 7. When performing a write, the processor drives the byte or bytes onto the appropriate data paths and, using the parity output associated with each path, forces the parity to odd for each byte. During a read, the processor checks for odd parity received for each byte and, in the event of a data parity error, asserts its DPE# output. The action taken by the platform in response is design-dependent.

DPE#. See DP[0:7].

DRTRY#. Data Retry. For more information, refer to the chapter entitled, "The Data Phase" under the heading "On a Read, Target Verifies Validity of Data Read By Master."

GBL#. Global memory access. Asserted by a PPC 601 processor when it is performing a memory access within a page or block with the M bit set to one. This indicates that other processors also access the same area of memory and may have cached information from it. For this reason, all processors must watch accesses performed by other entities within that memory region (in order to ensure that each processor is aware of memory accesses performed by other processors). The GBL# signal is the inverted form of the M bit from a BAT register or a PTE.

High-Priority Snoop Request. For a detailed description, refer to the chapter entitled, "Cache and Memory Unit Operation" under the heading "High-Priority Snoop Request."

HP_SNP_REQ#. High-Priority Snoop Request. For a detailed description, refer to the chapter entitled, "Cache and Memory Unit Operation" under the heading "High-Priority Snoop Request."

HRESET#. Hard Reset. See Hard Reset in the glossary of terms.

INT#. The PPC 601 processor's external interrupt input line. It is generated by the external interrupt controller whenever an external hardware subsystem generates an interrupt request. In response, if recognition of external interrupts is currently enabled (MSR[EE] = 1), the processor will jump to the external interrupt hander.

Local Bus. The bus structure connected directly to the processor's bus interface pins. Depending on the machine architecture this may be the host bus or it may be buffered from the host bus by a lookthrough L2 cache associated with the processor.

Logical Bus Clock. See Bus Clock.

PCLK_EN#. See 2x_PCLK definition. Processor clock enable signal. The platform uses this input to the PPC 601 processor to select the phase of the PCLK signal developed internally by the processor (by dividing the 2x_PCLK signal by two. The platform can use the PCLK_EN# signal to synchronize the PCLKs in an array of processor to each other. Since each processor's internal bus clock is developed from its PCLK, this will also sync up their bus clocks.

P_CLOCK. See 2x_PCLK definition.

QUIESC_REQ. Output from the PPC 601 processor. Asserted when the processor has entered the soft stop state. In a multiprocessor system, connected to the SYS_QUIESC# input of the next processor. See Soft Stop State in the glossary of terms and SYS_QUIESC#.

RESUME. Assertion of this input to the PPC 601 processor instructs it to exit the soft stop state and resume normal program execution. See Soft Stop State in the glossary of terms.

RSRV#. This is the PPC 601 processor's reservation output. The chapter entitled, "Acquiring Ownership of a Shared Resource" explains the reservation concept and use of RSRV#.

RTC input signal. 7.8125MHz input clock that drives the processor's RTC and DEC registers.

RUN_NSTOP. This PPC 601 processor output is part of the test interface. It's usage is not documented in the user's manual.

SC_DRIVE#. Super-Charged Drive. When asserted to the PPC 601 processor, causes it to approximately double the drive current it uses on the following signals: ABB#, DBB#, ARTRY#, SHD#, TS# and XATS#. When deasserted, these signals use the same amount of drive current as all of the other processor signals.

SCAN_CLK. This is the boundary scan interface's clock signal. It is used to clock serial data into the processor on the SCAN_IN signal and out of the processor on the SCAN_OUT signal.

SCAN_CTL. Boundary scan test mode select input.

SCAN_OUT. See SCAN_CLK.

SCAN_SIN. See SCAN_CLK.

SHD#. When the PPC 601 processor is bus master and is performing a memory access with GBL# asserted, all other processors must snoop the transaction and report the snoop result on SHD# and ARTRY#. If SHD# is asserted, at least one of the snooping processors has a copy of the target cache block. The state of ARTRY# indicates whether any processor has a copy of the target cache block in the modified state.

Soft Reset. When the PPC 601 processor's SRESET# input is asserted, it branches to the reset vector in the interrupt table. The location of the interrupt table is determined by the current state of the MSR[IP] bit. Soft Reset is not destructive (i.e., the interrupted program can be resumed by executing an rfi instruction at the end of the reset interrupt handler).

SRESET#. See Soft Reset in the glossary of terms.

SYS_QUIESC#. When asserted to a PPC 601 processor, requests it to finish all posted bus accesses and then enter the soft stop state. The processor asserts QUIESC_REQ# when it has entered the soft stop state. See also Soft Stop State in the glossary of terms.

TA#. Transfer Acknowledge. During a read, this input to the PPC 601 processor is asserted by the target device when it is presenting the requested data to the processor on the data bus. When sampled asserted on a rising edge of its bus clock, the processor latches the data from the bus. It may not forward the data to the processor core for use, however, until the target verifies its validity by keeping DRTRY# deasserted on the next bus clock rising-edge. During a write, the target asserts TA# to indicate that it has latched the data being written to be the processor. The processor can therefore stop driving the data item onto the bus.

TBST#. Transfer Burst output signal. Asserted by the PPC 601 processor when it is performing a four-beat burst memory read or write transaction to read a sector into the cache or to write a modified sector back to memory. When not asserted, the processor is performing a single-beat transaction to read or write between a byte and eight bytes.

TC0. Transfer Code 0 output bus signal. During a memory read transaction, the processor clears its TC0 output (TC stands for transfer code) to zero if a data read is in progress, or sets it to one to indicate that a code read is in progress. When the processor is performing a four-beat burst write transaction to write a modified cache block back to memory, it will use TC0 to indicate to the L2 cache whether or not it will mark the cache block invalid in its L1 cache after the write-back has been completed. TC0 clear to zero indicates that the cache block will not be invalidated, but will be marked exclusive or shared. For additional information, refer to the chapter entitled, "The Memory Address Phase."

TC1. Transfer Code 1 output bus signal. If the processor is currently performing a burst read to fetch a cache sector from a line and the processor's memory unit has a read posted to fetch the opposing sector as well, it will assert TC1 = 1 to indicate this. This information can cause a look-through L2 cache to initiate a memory read to fetch the other sector before it is actually asked for.

TEA#. Transfer Error Acknowledge. When asserted to the processor while it is performing a bus transaction, causes the processor abort the transaction and to either: invoke the machine check interrupt handler (if MSR[ME] = 1) or to enter the checkstop state (if MSR[ME] = 0).

TRDY#. PCI Target Ready signal. For a detailed description, refer to the MindShare publication entitled, "PCI System Architecture."

TS#. Transfer Start. Asserted by the PPC 601 processor when it initiates a memory, address-only, or an external control transaction. Indicates that the processor has placed a valid address and transaction type on the address bus and that all memory and external control targets should examine the transaction to determine which one is the target of the transaction.

TSIZ[0:2]. Transfer Size bus. During a memory-oriented transaction, the PPC 601 processor uses these output signals to indicate the number of byte to be transferred within the currently-addressed doubleword. Only has meaning during the performance of a single-beat transaction (meaningless during a burst). During the performance of an external control transaction, the four bit bus consisting of TBST# and TSIZ[0:2] identifies the external resource being addressed. During address packet 0 of an I/O transaction, the eight bit bus comprised of TT[0:3], TBST# and TSIZ[0:2] indicates the I/O transaction type. During address packet 1 of an I/O transaction, this same eight bit bus indicates the number of bytes to be transferred.

TT[0:4]. Transaction Type bus. During a memory-oriented or external control transaction, the TT[0:3] outputs of the PPC 601 processor indicate the transaction type. During address packet 0 of an I/O transaction, the eight bit bus comprised of TT[0:3], TBST# and TSIZ[0:2] indicates the I/O transaction type. During address packet 1 of an I/O transaction, this same eight bit bus indicates the number of bytes to be transferred. TT4 is reserved.

WT#. The PPC 601 processor's write-through output signal. This is the inverted form of the W bit from the PTE or BAT register. During a memory write bus transaction, WT# indicates to the L2 cache whether it should use a write-back (WT# deasserted) or write-through (WT# asserted) policy.

XATS#. Extended Address Transfer Start. Asserted by the PPC 601 processor when it initiates an I/O transaction. Memory and external control targets should ignore the transaction. I/O BUCs should decode the target BUC number in address packet 0 to determine which of them is the target BUC. The target BUC asserts AACK# to claim the transaction and permit the processor to terminate the address phase of the transaction.

- PowerPC instructions that did not exist in the POWER architecture typically use opcodes that were designated invalid in the POWER architecture. Any POWER architecture program that expects an invalid opcode exception when executing one of the new instructions will therefore not function correctly.
- Some POWER architecture privileged instructions have been made non-privileged in the PowerPC. Any POWER architecture program that expects an privilege violation exception when executing one of the new instructions will therefore not function correctly.
- Treatment of some reserved bits in instructions has changed.
- Treatment of some reserved bits in registers has changed.
- The POWER architecture alignment check bit (in MSR) is not supported in PowerPC.
- Difference in use of Condition Register usage by some instructions.
- Difference in interpretation of Link and Record bits by some instructions.
- Difference in interpretation of some BRANCH CONDITIONAL instruction bits.
- Difference in implementation of the BRANCH CONDITIONAL TO COUNT REGISTER instruction.
- Difference in implementation of the SYSTEM CALL instruction.
- Some bits in the XER (Integer Exception Register) are reserved in PowerPC, but were defined in the POWER architecture.
- PowerPC requires that RA not be equal to either RT or 0. Instructions that violate this rule are considered invalid. The POWER architecture does not flag this as an error, but instead discards the effective address.
- In the PowerPC, during multiple register loads, RA and RB may not be in the range of registers to be loaded. POWER architecture handles this by just skipping theses registers during the load.
- For load/store multiple instructions, the PowerPC requires the effective address to be word-aligned. Violation will cause an alignment interrupt or boundedly undefined results.
- There is some incompatibility in the implementation of MOVE ASSIST instructions.
- The SYNC and ISYNC instructions cause much more pervasive synchronization in PowerPC than in POWER architecture.
- There are some differences in the instructions used to move to/from the Special Purpose Registers.
- There is a difference in the handling of the FR and FI status bits in the FPSCR.
- There is a difference in the implementation of the floating-point store instruction.

- When a move from the FPSCR is performed, the POWER architecture defines the upper 32 bits as FFFFFFFFh, while the PowerPC architecture says they are undefined.
- The dclz and dcbz instructions have the same opcode, but operate differently.
- Floating-point load/store to a direct-store segment is handled differently.
- Implementation of the segment register access instructions differs.
- The tlbi/tlbie instructions have the same opcode, but operate differently.
- MSR[20] is used to control the occurrence of floating-point exceptions in both architectures, but it is one of a two-bit field in PowerPC used to control floating-point exceptions.
- The POWER architecture supplies a real-time clock function, while the PowerPC architecture uses a time base.
- The implementation of the Decrementer differs between the two architectures.

A more complete description of the POWER and PowerPC architectures may be found in appendix G of the document entitled "PowerPC Architecture."

Index

B

C

D

E

F

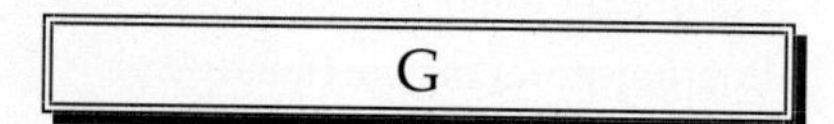

Index

J

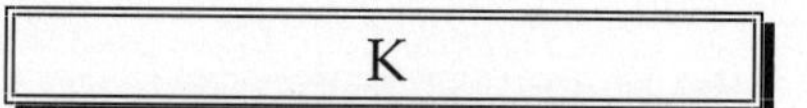

K

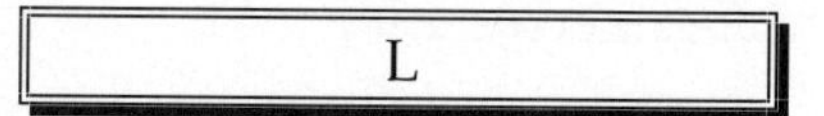

L

M

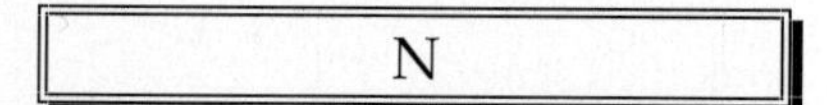

N

O

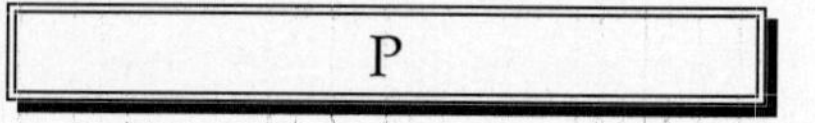

P

Q

R

T

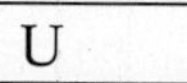

U

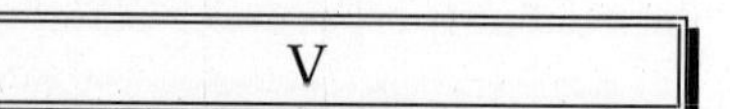

V

W

MindShare, Inc.
Technical Seminars

MindShare Courses

Public Seminars

Onsite Seminars

Contact MindShare at: